D1281341

FEEDBACK

In the series

Wide Angle Books

Edited by Erik Barnouw, Ruth Bradley, Scott MacDonald, and Patricia Zimmermann

FEEDBACK

The Video Data Bank Catalog of
Video Art and Artist Interviews

Edited by Kate Horsfield
and Lucas Hilderbrand

Temple University Press

Philadelphia

Temple University Press
1601 North Broad Street
Philadelphia PA 19122
www.temple.edu/tempress

Copyright © 2006 by Temple University
All rights reserved
Published 2006
Printed in the United States of America

The paper used in this publication meets the requirements of the American National Standard for Information Sciences–Permanence of Paper for Printed Library Materials, ANSI Z39.49-1992

Cataloging-in-Publication Data available from the Library of Congress

ISBN 1-59213-182-4

2 4 6 8 9 7 5 3 1

Table of Contents

Introduction to the Video Data Bank Collections

Kate Horsfield

This catalog includes all distributed tapes in the two main Video Data Bank collections: video art tapes and interviews with individual artists from various disciplines. The video art tapes span the entire 39-year history of video as an artistic medium and include many of the form's most original works. The video interviews, collectively called On Art and Artists, feature some of the most prominent visual artists, critics, and photographers of the past 26 years. This unique collection records developing trends in American art and culture from abstract expressionism through the late 20th century. Both collections were designed for exhibition in cultural institutions such as museums, media arts centers, and alternative art spaces or for educational use in college and university settings. Artists, curators, television programmers, educators, students, and arts audiences are the intended viewers.

The Video Art Collection

As the use of video has grown from a handful of early pioneers into a field of hundreds of artists and independent producers, the Video Data Bank has continued to build a collection of the most innovative and challenging works made during the past three decades. This catalog lists and describes these important historical and contemporary video works that outline the styles and directions taken by artists throughout the entire history of video art. Almost all the works originated in video format; a few titles, however, were shot on film and transferred to video for distribution. The collection also includes some titles generated and distributed on CD-ROM.

The video art collection is mostly experimental and can best be understood by knowing the aesthetic, technical, cultural, theoretical, and political conditions in which in which the work was made. Video emerged as an art practice amidst complex influences during the social turmoil of the late 1960s. It began in resistance to the dominant television practices with a mandate to create a new type of media and production process that was more personal, more creative, more egalitarian, and more politically engaged.

The many types of video art have been made with a wide variety of intentions, ideas, content, working styles, and structures. Some address pure aesthetic concerns, where others prioritize content in less formal but still original and more deeply personal ways. There are just a few characteristics that link all video art into a common practice. For example, the term "video art" indicates that the makers use television technology—recording and playback equipment, frames, signals, scan lines, edits, sounds, images, or all the above—to create pieces of art or cultural criticism. Artists expect spectators to respond actively to these experiences that provoke thoughts, sensations, critiques, analyses, or actions. As in other art practices, video can be realist, abstract, conceptual, and minimal; figural, landscape, or non-representational; and two-dimensional, sculptural, or interactive. In addition, almost all video has performative aspects in which artists' bodies or voices provide central components of the work. In fact, performance video constitutes one of the form's primary genres.

Three other broad genres of video—documentary, experimental, and narrative—correspond those in film but are not usually deployed as singular strategies. Instead, video artists mix modes to create complex visual strategies and imagined realities from piece to piece, sometimes even in individual works. Since video can be made exclusively from original footage shot by the artist or fused with appropriated images from movies, television, archival films, home movies, and other sources, the mix itself functions as a new type of textual and visual assimilation not seen in other art forms. Since most video art, with the exception of performance-based video, cannot be defined by pure "genre" categories, critiques based on a singular approach are often inadequate.

This complexity makes video the interesting trickster of the art world. Video comes from the same technology as television and can be screened like film but behaves in radically different ways according to the artist and the intended audience. Video art maintains an outsider perspective from which it can challenge conventional attitudes by creatively elaborating on art, politics, media, or other aspects of contemporary cultural discourse.

Video has its own history as a practice, but it is neither widely known nor firmly established within the broader histories of art or film. Because of the range of ideas, intentions, and working strategies, the history of video is open to interpretations depending on the perspectives of curators, critics, historians, and viewers. The lack of consistent critical review of video over the past three decades has contributed to its fragmented assessment and historiography. Art institutions and screening venues tend to show videos that emphasize the aesthetics of time-based image making, such as motion, performance, rhythm, duration, scale, sound, and repetition. These works are evaluated according to their innovation as well as how they align with the practices of other contemporary art forms. Alternatively, video has also been curated to prioritize content over form, addressing greater social issues and cultural discourse on politics, sociology, psychology, identity, representation, or the media.

The works represented in the Video Data Bank video art collection reflect all of these various complexities and differing approaches to video making. Some works in the collection are art works and are exhibited and collected as such; other works lean away from pure art world practices to use video as a tool for reportage. Still other works were made by non-professional makers from community-based media centers and speak directly to the interests of a particular community or network of communities. Video Data Bank seeks out the best contemporary video made by both emerging and established makers across a broad landscape of uses.

While the Video Data Bank video art collection is primarily experimental, the collection is particularly strong in certain areas, such as activist, performance, and feminist video. For this reason we have invited three noted scholars or artists to write essays to contextualize these aspects of the collection.

Video art began as an activist endeavor by responding to the freedom movements of the late 1960s by employing the newly released portable video equipment to challenge the hegemonic power of commercial television. The low cost and small-scale portable video equipment allowed artists and activists to go places and record scenes from art-based or activist perspectives that challenged the conventional notions of art, media, and society.

After nearly three decades, almost all the titles in the video art collection contain some component of political or cultural activism. These works were made by artists committed to overriding the limitations of mainstream media to seek out people, stories, alternative perspectives, and creative approaches beyond the limitations of commercial media productions. Artists mostly choose subject matters and points of view that are provocative or controversial: AIDS, race, feminism, gay and lesbian equality, anti-war sentiments, power and the people who have it, or dissections of cultural canons. They use video to enlarge and broaden the cultural discussion beyond the limitations of conventional thinking. New, often non-narrative and visually based narratives are constructed to elaborate on unpopular subjects that provoke the viewer into new ways of thinking. Each decade has produced new versions of activist media that still resist, enlarge, or create alternatives to mainstream concepts—recording anti-Vietnam marches of the late '60s, feminism in the '70s, AIDS activism and education in the late '80s, and "identity politics" in the '90s.

The Video Data Bank acquisition policy is designed to keep the collection broad-based and inclusive by selecting the best works in all genres with subject matter that appropriately addresses contemporary thought. To maintain this breadth, the Video Data Bank staff review a very wide range of unsolicited works submitted through an "open door" acquisition program. Simultaneously, the staff actively seeks out artists and works that demonstrate excellence and originality. The two criteria for acquisition are that the work must be visually and structurally innovative and must make a significant contribution to contemporary art or cultural discourse. The video art collection, seen as a whole, provides excellent examples of the accomplishments of video artists and their attempts to create a new media of substance, sometimes breathtaking originality, and extraordinary courage in a world of increasing conformity.

The On Art and Artists Collection

Over the past 27 years, the Video Data Bank has actively produced and collected interviews with artists. The On Art and Artists collection focuses on the development of each artist's body of work as told by the artist to an interviewer. The tapes are primary documents of each artist's development from first wanting to become an artist through the obstacle-ridden course of developing an established reputation as an artist. The tapes are quiet and intimate, made with only the artist, a camera operator, and an interviewer present in the room during the interview. The small-scale video productions create intimate discussions of artists' intentions, influences, and values. Video Data Bank has interviewed painters, sculptors, photographers, video artists, and performers, as well as critics, who have made important contributions to the course of art over the past several decades. In addition to producing interviews, the Video Data Bank also collaborates with the Visiting Artist Program at the School of the Art Institute of Chicago to record interviews with artists brought in to the School. We also collect interviews made by other organizations, such as the Artists TV Network, the University of Colorado Visiting Artists Program, Long Beach Museum of Art, Fellows of Contemporary Art, and MICA-TV. These tapes and the organizations and programs that produced them are described more fully on the introduction that precedes the listings in the collection.

The OAA collection was originally designed for dedicated art students and, hopefully, gives them a sense of available creative choices, methodologies, and processes in addition to the overall commitment necessary to become serious artists. Since artists create their own futures through the small decisions in their works, the subject matter of each tape varies according to the values, intentions, and types of work. Often the artists describe their work in very different ways than critics, curators, or art historians.

Averaging an hour in length, the interview tapes are edited down from the original footage to distill the content to the most important and relevant dialogue from the interview process. The focus is close-up on the artist with the interviewer out of frame but heard asking questions. This format was chosen to keep the viewer concentrating on the often dense and complex descriptions of the creative process as each artist reveals it. At times, these early interviews also have extreme close-up camera work. This is a result of creative explorations by the cameraperson in an era that encouraged great experimentation with the new technology.

Video technology has improved dramatically over the past 30 years and, for this reason, we have launched a preservation project to improve some visual aspects of the original footage in the re-editing process. For some older tapes, recently re-edited and re-mastered by Blithe Riley in 2003-04, I have chosen to change the original interviews from color to black and white. These tapes were made with very primitive color cameras released in the late '70s that often recorded with poor contrast and fading color. Re-mastering the interviews in black and white was done so that image deteriorization would not distract from the artists' comments.

All of the works listed in this catalog provide a valuable record of the rise of technology over the past three decades and its power to create new art forms and to record ideas expressed through other forms of art. The FEEDBACK catalog includes all titles in distribution as of October, 2003. Titles added to the collections after this date are accessible at http://www.vdb.org.

—Kate Horsfield, Video Data Bank, Executive Director, August, 2004

Acknowledgements

I am very grateful to Lucas Hilderbrand, my catalog co-editor, for his brilliant feedback, and very sharp eye. Without him this catalog could not have been completed. And to Carl Lorentzen for setting up the Quark files and his quick responses to all Quark emergencies as I formatted the book. And to Vanalyne Green, Gregg Bordowitz, and Peggy Phelan for contextualizing aspects of the collection in their insightful essays.

Additional thanks to the staff of the Video Data Bank – Abina Manning, Dara Greenwald, Tom Colley, Woody Sullender and Kent Lambert – for their enormous support, tireless work and patience during the two years of my absence while this catalog was in the making. Their work cannot be underestimated since 15 years of information on 1500 individual titles had to be screened for accuracy, spelling, sources of quotes, correct dates and running times. In addition, the whole collection had to be reviewed, tapes to be screened and often relabeled and recataloged and images had to be made for each title.

Special thanks to others who contributed to this process: Cynthia Chris, Jose Friere, Anna McCarthy, Allison McCracken, Blithe Riley, KJ Mohr, and Chris Straayer.

And finally thanks to Temple University Press for giving the Video Data Bank the opportunity to make this, the very first, catalog of our collection available.

ESSAYS

Busting the Tube: A Brief History of Video Art

Kate Horsfield

Setting the Stage

The 1960s was a decade of sweeping social change driven by political confrontation and creative and ideological activism inspired by the civil rights movement, the Beat poets, the Vietnam war controversy, and the rise of a rebellious youth movement stimulated by politics, drugs, and rock'n'roll. As the decade progressed, tension increased between the traditionalist mainstream and the youthful counterculture that desired a more open and egalitarian society. This emerging and very politicized generation began to emphasize critical ideas and means of production that could be used to develop a new and more inclusive society, alternative institutions and accessible types of cultural production that reflected their social values. By establishing a new and often oppositional culture based on creative, and often low-cost production methodologies, they launched new tools and a powerful critique that influences activists, artists, and documentarians to this day.

Radical theorists such as Herbert Marcuse proposed that mass media had direct relationships to social control and created a "one-dimensional man" who lived in a bland world of conformity and had become too comfortable to engage in ideas that critiqued or opposed mainstream society in any way that could lead to meaningful social change.[1] Marcuse's Marxist call for the end of social oppression and his support for all efforts of radical liberation inspired young activists to envision a new society based on alternative institutions and modes of thought that did not replicate social or economic oppression of minority or other disenfranchised groups. To drive this social change, Marcuse's concept called for a more engaged individual personally committed to political ideas that would lead to change. This individual could become a new subject by stepping out of the blandness of the 1950s to change his or her personal consciousness. A change in one's personal consciousness was seen as the starting point on the path to creating a new and better society. The concept took several other forms besides political awareness and activism during this period, including using drugs, free love, music, and mastering Eastern philosophical and disciplinary practices, such as yoga and meditation. All were efforts to create mind-altering states of consciousness to create a new, more enlightened self.

Feminist theory also focused on issues of personal consciousness. This can be seen in the famous slogan "the personal is the political," a perspective that required that one look inside through consciousness-raising to begin the feminist political process. Consciousness-raising was a process of gathering radical feminists together in small groups to study, and analyze the personal situation of each woman, discuss the new feminist literature and strategize on what actions could be taken to change the oppression of women in society. The goal was to create a mass movement for social change by helping women understand how they could alter their positions as objects (of male desire) to subjects that could determine their own future. The new subjectivity of the feminist movement demanded that its followers analyze power relations between the genders and how institutional structures enforce gender inequality or support economic or other forms of gender-biased exploitation. This critique merged with other anti-establishment ethos of the counterculture and other liberation movements that were focused on social change and working towards an expanded democracy that allowed greater equality and participation for all subjects, no matter what their color, gender, or class.

Armed with this new sense of subjectivity and political commitment, protests focused on institutions that supported unequal systems of power. Almost all centralized institutions were suspect, particularly the family, the church, the educational system, and corporations. Cultural institutions were also at the center of critique because they preserve dominant cultural canons that created closed and exclusionary systems of power based on standards and histories determined by white, male authorities. Meta-narratives that privilege certain points of view, such as those created by religion, literature, and art history, were highly critiqued. The goal was to create a new type of cultural production and alternative institutions to support more egalitarian and pluralistic notions of political and cultural interaction:

> The argument was not only about producing new form for new content, it was also about changing the nature of the relationship between reader and literary

Kate Horsfield is a co-founder and executive director of the Video Data Bank at the School of the Art Institute of Chicago. She is also an artist and has co-produced more than 200 artist interviews with Lyn Blumenthal.

text, between spectator and spectacle, and the changing of this relationship was itself premised upon new ways of thinking about the relationship between art (or more generally "representation") and reality.[2]

Television was a primary target.

Throughout the 1950s, television had gained enormous power; more than 85 percent of American households owned at least one television set by the end of the decade. While the masses were increasingly mesmerized by television's presence, others, particularly intellectuals and media theorists, saw that it reinforced the status quo while simplifying, or omitting altogether, representations that did not fit consumerist demographics. Even Newton R. Minow, Chairman of the FCC, had expressed concerns over the negative effects of formula based television programming when he described television as "a vast wasteland." The issue was how representations on television not only created a market for products but also created social acceptance and rejection through conformity. Women, in spite controlling large amounts of money designated for household spending, were seen as manipulated and controlled by images from television; people of color and others who were not seen by advertisers to be important in the marketplace were mostly excluded from any television representations at all. Protesters also criticized news coverage of the Vietnam war, arguing that the media could not be trusted because it was biased as part of the consciousness industry[3]; the news was packaged for commercial television programming and controlled by the government and corporate monopolies.

*Queen Mother Moore Speech at
Greenhaven Prison*
People's Communication Network, 1973

While television programming was heavily critiqued, Canadian media theorist Marshall McLuhan offered a new and creative interpretation of how new technologies could transform society. McLuhan outlined a new utopian vision for media that emphasized a new relationship between the medium and the human senses. This vision imagined that electronic communications were an extension of the human nervous system and operated in a binary kind of progression—as technology advances, so does the human sensory perception needed to receive it. This spoke directly to artists, media visionaries, and those in the counterculture that were already actively experimenting with altered states of consciousness:

> Rapidly, we approach the final phase of the extensions of man—the technological simulation of consciousness, when the creative process of knowing will be collectively and corporately extended to the whole of human society, much as we have already extended our senses and our nerves by the various media.[4]

Mayday Realtime
David Cort and Mary Curtis Ratcliff, 1971

McLuhan's ideas placed technology at the center of human transformation and emphasized that the emerging technology not only would transform consciousness but also provide a very powerful path to social change.

In 1965, Sony marketed the first portable video recording equipment, providing the means by which artists, activists, and other individuals launched an era of alternative media, using television-based technology to record images of their own choosing. Prior to this time the government and corporate media giants exclusively controlled all television production, programming, and broadcasting. The new Sony portable camera and recording deck, called the Portapak, was designed for small business and industrial uses but was released precisely in the midst of the political turmoil of the '60s. Video immediately captured the attention of artists who saw its potential as a creative tool and of social activists who saw it as "a weapon and a witness" to be used to create new types of representation that opposed the ubiquitous commercialism of the television industry.

In 1970, the Raindance Corporation, a collective of artists, writers, and radical media visionaries who were inspired by McLuhan, began publishing *Radical Software*, a journal for the small but rapidly growing community of videomakers. Presenting the view that power had shifted to those who control media, *Radical Software* proposed an alternative information order, outlining a visionary combination of technology, art, and the social sciences to revolutionize the world of communications. The masthead of *Radical Software #1* articulates this immense shift in power:

> Power is no longer measured in land, labor, or capital, but by access to information and the means to disseminate it. As long as the most powerful tools (not weapons) are in the hands of those who would hoard them, no alternative cultural vision can succeed. Unless we design and implement alternate information structures which transcend and reconfigure the existing ones, other alternate systems and life styles will be no more than products of the existing process.[5]

Having laid out the ideological agenda for a new, de-centralized communications system, *Radical Software* goes on to identify video as the tool to create it:

> Fortunately, however, the trend of all technology is towards greater access through decreased size and cost. Low-cost, easy-to-use, portable videotape systems, may seem like "Polaroid home movies" to the technical perfectionists who broadcast "situation" comedies and "talk" shows, but to those of us with as few preconceptions as possible they are the seeds of a responsive, useful communications system.[6]

While television was seen as the central force behind an increasingly consumerist society, concern over the commodification of culture was also affecting the art world. Artists rightfully felt the gallery system had begun to limit exhibition to only those artists and works that were highly marketable, thereby limiting art to the level of commodity. Although mostly limited to painting, the highly influential critique of Clement Greenberg also contributed to concern over the commodification of art by forbidding the acceptance of any art forms outside its formalist thesis. This thesis maintained the purity of painting by centering critical discourse on the unique properties of painting while simultaneously insisting on a complete separation between art disciplines as well as between popular culture and high art. Driven by a desire to create new types of art that defied both the modernist doctrine, as well as the commercialism of the gallery system, artists began working with materials and processes that challenged these boundaries. This shift in artistic practice began to destroy the modernist imperative of the gallery-based object and replace it with a more ephemeral version of art that emphasized process, critique, or experience over pure form.

Wall/Floor Positions
Bruce Nauman, 1968

These new, post-modernist works also blurred the boundaries between high art and the everyday world. John Cage and his emphasis on the importance of chance lead to the Happenings of the late '50s. Happenings were spontaneous art events occurring on the streets, made up of a combination of live performance and found materials. Fluxus's anti-art events used irony and humor to mock the stature of art history and art institutions. Pop art of the early '60s filled the galleries with replicas of mass-produced consumerist goods thereby challenging the concept of the "original" in art. Earthworks, made far away in the western deserts and difficult to see firsthand, used the earth itself as material and could rarely be seen except in documentary photographs. Performances, an emerging art form, were ephemeral presentations often staged only once. The shifting notions of art practice and use of materials occurred precisely at the moment in which portable video equipment was released into the consumer market.

John Cage: Artist Reading
Artists TV Network, 1978

Early Video Practice

Immediately after its release, the use of portable video equipment exploded in many directions simultaneously. It was a brand new medium with no history of its own but with tremendous potential to carry out several different cultural and political agendas. Media visionaries like those involved in *Radical Software* saw it as a tool to be used in establishing a decentralized communication system and used to produce alternative media content for communicating countercultural ideas outside the restrictions of mainstream channels. Artists embraced video because it was new, had significant undeveloped aesthetic potential, and could be used as a medium for personal expression.

For a brief period in the late '60s and early '70s, the handful of early video practitioners enthusiastically embraced all the different uses of the new medium. Since everyone in this small community, artists and activists alike, was influenced in some way by the powerful politics of the counterculture, all videomakers had a very optimistic vision of how video could be used to affect change in art and the society at large.

Women's Liberation March NYC
Peoples Video Theater, 1971

Media activists saw handheld video equipment as a tool to document a new type of direct-from-the-scene reportage that was not manipulated, biased, or reshaped in any way to distort reality. Sometimes called "guerilla television" because its practitioners used video in a war-like operation against the domination of network television, the video verité method used technology in an unassuming way, going places where cameras had never been without drawing much attention. The attraction was that video "reversed the process of television, giving people access to the tools of production and distribution, giving them control over their own images and, by implication their own lives."7 Footage was gathered from underground clubs, "live" from the midst of street confrontations, or from major events of importance to the counterculture like the Woodstock festival or the Chicago Seven trial. The low quality, grainy, and shaky footage was usually black and white and unedited, which offered a new type of straight-from-the-scene authenticity that challenged the presumed objectivity of broadcast television. One video collective, Peoples Video Theater, shot events in the streets on video and brought it back to a loft in lower Manhattan for instant playback meant to trigger discussion and "feedback" from the community. This is a micro-example of how video activists used video to increase a sense of participation in the televisual process, as well as an attempt to democratically respond to the unfolding social and political events.

In the artworld, video was initially used as a handy and low-cost tool to document live performances that had no mobility or permanence, thereby making these forms transportable and more accessible to audiences beyond the original site of presentation. These performances were solo pieces in which the artist performed with few or no props in front of a single camera. They presented a variety of conceptual or perceptual exercises investigating the body, self, place, or relationship to others and society itself. These performances were based on conceptual art that emphasized process and idea over form to analyze texts, language, and the image.

Baldessari Sings LeWitt
John Baldessari, 1972

One of the two earliest video pieces in the Video Data Bank collection, Bruce Nauman's *Stamping in the Studio* (1968) is an example of early performance work. The artist continuously moves in a circle outlining the frame of the picture on the monitor for the full 60 minutes of the performance. The mindset of the viewer changes very slowly through the duration of the piece—often from boredom to an almost reflective meditation kept in motion by the sound of feet stamping on the floor. The piece seems to be addressing the mental preparation the artist goes through upon entering the studio. Another prominent early piece, *Baldessari Sings LeWitt* (1972) is a humorous tape featuring John Baldessari singing *Sentences on Conceptual Art*, the widely read text that outlined the perimeters of conceptual art to different popular tunes, such as "Tea for Two."

Pryings
Vito Acconci, 1971

Other artists used performance to investigate social and power relations between individuals or between individuals, audiences, and larger social systems. An example is Vito Acconci's *Pryings* (1971), a tape of a live performance, in which two performers are engaged in physical conflict—she (Kathy Dillon) attempts to keep her eyes closed while he (Vito Acconci) attempts to pry them open. This represents the continuous exchange of power between two individuals, in this case, a man and a woman. No one wins, and no one loses as the tape presents the audience with an uncomfortable exercise in power relations. These early performance pieces employ straightforward aesthetic strategies without the embellishment of any video effects, which were not yet available.

Quickly artists saw that the video medium was rich with possibilities for aesthetic experimentation that included using the medium as a window to the perception of time, space, and sound or as a mirror to the self, consciousness, or cultural patterns of subjectivity. It could function as a witness in the surveillance of observer and the observed; as a conceptual tool deconstructing language, text, or cultural apparatus. Eventually the video signal itself became a site for investigation into the intrinsic properties of the medium.

Access to advanced equipment was extremely rare and most early users of video had to work with a tiny selection of electronic equipment, usually just a black and white camera and recording deck. Editing equipment was expensive and very difficult to use; an edit could only be made through a laborious process of rewinding and marking points on each of the two reels of tape, then hitting the edit button on the record and playback decks simultaneously. Since tapes were so hard to edit artists often abandoned editing altogether. The video art piece was often the same duration as the reel of tape, hence the name "reel-time" and the prevalence of 20, 30 and 60 minute pieces. Regardless of the limitations of the early video equipment, it did have specific characteristics that were used in creative ways and the limitations of the medium often became a resource for aesthetic experimentation beyond simply recording an event or performance in front of a camera. Feedback, the endless mirror effect that occurs when a camera is pointed directly at a monitor displaying its image, and instant replay are unique visual characteristics of video that were available to any artist with a camera, monitor, and recording deck.[8] These two effects were commonly used for experimentation until later in the decade when more complex visualizing equipment became available. Beyond the interesting visual quality these effects metaphorically represented aspects of a reconfigured and reciprocal interactivity between artist and audience. Instant replay, the capacity to simultaneously watch what the camera is recording provides an opportunity for immediate response to the recorded information, and feedback is the reciprocal loop of participation between the content and the audience. These two characteristics were used both to explore social issues or for purely aesthetic experimentation. Joan Jonas's *Vertical Roll* (1972) is a performance piece re-scanned from an image on a monitor on which the vertical roll control was set off kilter. The visual effect is of an image continuously rolling vertically out of the frame that deliberately interferes with the visual pleasure of watching a woman on camera, yet Jonas creates a virtual performance that interacts with the unstable televisual signal.

Stamping in the Studio
Bruce Nauman, 1968

On Screen
Lynda Benglis, 1972

Some video equipment new to the market in the early '70s allowed for more complex visualizing effects, such as keying, mixing, colorizing, layering, and input from multiple cameras, but access to this technology remained scarce. Artists who wanted to experiment with controls beyond what was commercially available needed to understand engineering. Such artists began to design or modify equipment that could utilize deeper parts of the video technology such as scan lines and signal manipulation. Influenced by the Moog Synthesizer, a modular audio synthesizer that was used in clubs by rock bands, these artists worked collaboratively with scientists grounded in electronics to design visualizing tools called video synthesizers to alter, control, and synthesize video signals to produce abstract and highly colorized images. Many different synthesizers, called "image processors" were designed and built by artists. Examples are Woody and Steina Vasulka's Digital Image Processor, Stephen Beck's Video Weaver, Dan Sandin's Sandin Image Processor, and Nam June Paik and Shuya Abe's Paik-Abe synthesizer.

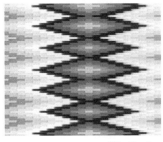

Video Weavings
Stephen Beck, 1976

Working with synthesizers was difficult and somewhat unpredictable, requiring study and practice; therefore, the emphasis was placed on the artists' process rather than making finished tapes for distribution outside the performance event. Synthesizers were used in live public performances in which elaborate installations of several video processors were linked to audio synthesizers created oscillating, abstracted, and often mandala-like images and sound that transported the audience into a radically new sphere of alternative sensory experience that paralleled McLuhan's theory of technology as a means of expanding the human senses.[9]

Expansion of the New Medium

A seminal art exhibition launched great interest in the new medium of video art, *TV as a Creative Medium*, presented at the Howard Wise Gallery in New York City in May, 1969. This exhibition leveraged interest in video while allowing those who were experimenting with the medium to take themselves seriously as artists. The exhibition brought together artists from a variety of backgrounds—music, painting, performance, kinetic and light sculpture, and electronics—and debuted several important video installations, including Nam June Paik's *Participation TV* and *TV Bra for Living Sculpture*, Ira Schneider and Frank Gillette's *Wipe Cycle*, Aldo Tambollini's *Black Spiral*, Eric Seigel's *Einstein*, and Paul Ryan's *Everyman's Mobius Strip*. The exhibition accelerated interest in video as experimental television, and this interest extended to public television stations such as WBGH in Boston, KQED in San Francisco, and WNET in New York City, all of which began workshops to support video projects made by artists on the station's state-of-the-art television equipment.

Leo Castelli, the most prominent art dealer of the time, embraced the new medium as early as the late '60s. His gallery purchased equipment for artists to experiment with video, and the gallery published the first video catalog listing works for distribution by Bruce Nauman, Richard Serra, John Baldessari, Lawrence Weiner, Lynda Benglis, Nancy Holt, Robert Morris, Vito Acconci, and others. The tapes were sold or rented to other galleries, museums, and organizations, thereby expanding the exhibition of video to locations beyond the major art centers of New York and Los Angeles.

Exchange
Robert Morris, 1973

In 1970, the New York State Council for the Arts (NYSCA) became the first state council to include video as a category in their funding guidelines. They offered funding for individuals, media arts centers, and media projects. The first funding cycle accepted all kinds of video works, including video installations and videotapes of performances, processed video art made on video synthesizers, and documentary footage from the streets. The availability of government and foundation funding had an enormous effect on the new medium of video. It allowed video artists to see themselves as legitimate artists, and the grant money allowed them to continue making new works. NYSCA also funded media centers, setting an example for other arts councils; soon many new centers sprang up across the country. This created a small but national network of exhibitors for film and video. These new non-profit media arts centers also offered low-cost access to film and video equipment for artists and individuals from local communities. These access centers reached out to youth, people of color, artists, women, Native Americans, prisoners, and activists to encourage them to make media telling their own stories, thus de-centralizing the existing communication system by establishing an alternative that focused on broadening representation in media.

Simultaneous to the development of the media arts centers, the '70s was also a period of tremendous growth in non-commercial artist-run exhibition spaces. Artists spaces were established across the country and contributed to a network of approximately 300 sites nationwide that made up the artists' space movement. Artists' spaces were also funded by state arts councils, foundations, and the National Endowment for the Arts. These non-profit galleries exhibited new and non-commercial art forms such as performance, installation, conceptual photography, and video art, forms that had not yet gained recognition in mainstream galleries but were of great interest to younger members of the art world.

Video screenings of new work expanded across all types of venues and presented many new opportunities for the exhibition of video art—from museums, galleries, alternative art spaces, and media arts centers to community-based centers. Soon colleges and universities began to add video and performance studies to the curriculum. The acceptance of video in the academy helped validate its use among scholars at a moment in which Jacques Derrida's theories of media and deconstruction were gaining influence. Derrida's interest in cultural production and interpretation of linguistic systems, signs, and the construction of meaning created a use for alternative renditions of cultural subject matter. His theories opened up a dialectical relationship between the art work and various other discourses; this, in turn, allowed video to be seen as another tool for analyzing the avant-garde, film theory, psychoanalysis, feminism, genre theory, post-modernism, and cultural studies from an alternative perspective. Since Derrida's work had also become prominent in the art world, his emphasis on hierarchies and oppositions offered a new focus for analysis and followed the agenda established in

Radical Software, which promoted a variety of uses of video as decentralized and more democratically inclusive of marginalized voices and content to reveal the biases and social inequalities of our culture. Video, standing at the edge of art, community, individual expression, and mass communications, was uniquely positioned to reveal layers of meaning as well as paradoxes and contradictions in the hierarchical constructions in art, media, and society. Video artists used the strategy of deconstruction to analyze issues of political difference in class, race, gender, and sexual orientation. A single video art piece, such as Martha Rosler's *Semiotics of the Kitchen* (1975), could be critiqued through numerous different theoretical discourses: art, performance, feminism, cultural studies, politics, gender studies, philosophy, and psychology.

Semiotics of the Kitchen
Martha Rosler, 1975

The cross-disciplinary interpretation of video art had clear advantages in terms of its use and value in academia. Although museums included video in exhibitions and often had ongoing screening programs for video and film, single channel video art was more problematic in the gallery system. For one thing, video could easily be mass-produced and was not an original object like a painting or drawing; therefore, it was hard to sell. Castelli-Sonnabend had already figured this out by 1985, when the gallery dispersed its prestigious collection to two non-profit video organizations, the Video Data Bank in Chicago and Electronic Arts Intermix in New York. And with such a large range of content and working styles, it was difficult for the critical apparatus of the art world to get a grip on a single set of standards that governed video as an aesthetic form with clear concepts that aligned with other art forms. Many video artists also had ambivalence towards the art world. Some artists preferred to be aligned with filmmakers or documentarians, others saw themselves as emerging television producers.

This complexity is described by Marita Sturken, a prominent writer and critic of video:

> What emerged from this complex set of events was not a medium with a clear set of aesthetic properties and cleanly defined theoretical concepts. Instead, one sees paradox, the paradox of video's apparent merging of (hence its negation of) certain cultural oppositions—art and technology, television and art, art and issues of social change, collectives and individual artists, the art establishment and anti-establishment strategies, profit and non-profit worlds, and formalism and content.[10]

Nevertheless, video practitioners continued to expand the medium's visual and conceptual potential. As time passed, patterns in types of work fell into relatively clear genres, and the beginnings of a historical map could be seen. Writers and critics who are interested in work examining social issues have a version of the history of video while the art world has a different version. Since critical writing on video art has been historically sporadic and fragmented according to the interests of the writer, a uniform and progressive critique does not exist. Nor does a standardized history of the medium.

The growing attention to media and technology throughout the whole culture meant that more video artists were being hired to teach college courses and more students were studying and producing video art tapes. Video had become an established practice and an artist or documentarian could achieve recognition and funding by working in video.

The Second Phase
By the 1980s many of the more visionary and revolutionary aspects of the video movement had passed. Video was still considered to be an alternative to broadcast television, but the alternative aspects shifted more to content and subject matter as artists sought to make their work as visually authoritative as possible. Video artists of the '80s had become very interested in mastering the powerful state-of-the-art technology and even showing their work on television. Since more funding was available for video, post-production equipment became more accessible to video artists. Yet, access was still very expensive, so several non-profit organizations—such as the Experimental Television Center in Owego, New York; the Standby Program in New York City; and the Bay Area Video Coalition in San Francisco, among others—offered discounted rates for

artists. The post-production studio, mostly used by advertisers and television production companies, offered a variety of dazzling visual effects. An artist typically worked with a professional editor for on-line editing to achieve broadcast-standard production values.

Kiss the Girls: Make Them Cry
Dara Birnbaum, 1979

Many of the visual strategies in video of the '80s were based on post-production technology, such as multiple camera inputs, fades and wipes, slow motion, collage effects, scrolling text, and animation. The wide availability of VHS recording equipment in the mass market also had an enormous effect on video art, allowing artists to record information directly from television to use in their work. Artists were no longer solely reliant on images made by themselves with a camera but could take images directly from television programming and advertisements, archival films, Hollywood films, or home movies. Appropriation became a new type of post-modern visual and textual critique based on uprooting images from their original contexts and proscribed new meanings determined by the artist. For example, in *Kiss the Girls: Make Them Cry* (1979) Dara Birnbaum uses clips from the game show *Hollywood Squares* to construct an analysis of the coded gestures of gender. The actors' close-up facial expressions, far from neutral and innocent, are re-positioned to exemplify the desire of television to achieve states of submission in the viewer. Joan Braderman's *Joan Does Dynasty* (1986) is a classic feminist deconstruction of the popular prime time television soap opera, *Dynasty*, in which the artist inserts herself on screen amidst appropriated images to analyze patriarchal elements of the narrative. Tony Cokes's *Black Celebration* (1988) juxtaposes footage of the riots in the black community of the 1960s with voice-over from the Situationist text *The Decline and Fall of the Spectacle-Commodity Economy* to interpret rioting as a refusal to participate in the logical apparatus of capitalism.

Black Celebration
Tony Cokes, 1988

These tapes are examples of how artists have recycled and combined existing texts to construct new and critical meanings and to shed light on how media reinforces cultural ideologies as a means of social control.

Deconstruction of media took on a darker and more urgent agenda as AIDS began to sweep through the country in the mid-'80s, infecting and killing huge numbers of people. Artists joined up with AIDS activists to fight against rising hysteria caused by ignorance, omission, and misinformation presented in mainstream media. Video affinity groups such as Damned Interfering Video Artists Television (DIVA TV) documented ACT-UP demonstrations, and this footage had a leveraging effect that maintained communication, community support, and enthusiasm in the midst of a long and strenuous battle. Activists were not just fighting unfair representations in media but also strove to obtain government funds for research, access to medication and home care, and to spread prevention information through creative productions. Tom Kalin's experimental videotape *They are lost to vision altogether* (1989) is an example of the passion, rage, and commitment often seen in AIDS tapes that eloquently argues for a compassionate and humane response to AIDS without forgoing the gay community's passion and sexuality. Ellen Spiro's documentary *DiAna's Hair Ego: AIDS Info Upfront* (1989) features a hair dresser, DiAna DiAna, who teaches safe sex from her salon in Columbia, South Carolina, in frustration over the inadequacy of information on AIDS prevention. These tapes and many others demonstrate how artists and activists used video in grassroots campaigns long before mainstream media even acknowledged that AIDS was a crisis.

They are lost to vision altogether
Tom Kalin, 1989

A natural outgrowth of AIDS activism was a unification of the gay community and the rise of a new queer cinema. Queer film and video festivals sprang up across the nation and screened all types of work by and about gay men, lesbians, and trans-gendered people. One very young videomaker, Sadie Benning, began using video in her teens and went on to produce a very important body of work made with a Pixelvision camera. Benning's intimate, diaristic pieces held a tight focus on her own face and were shot in her childhood bedroom. This work crossed out of the usual boundary lines of video art to touch audiences everywhere. Benning's work, while focusing on her emerging lesbian identity, forms a part of a larger genre of works made in the early '90s to examine political identity. Recognition and the need to establish specific historical and community identities organized around shared experience as the Other drove identity politics, and many important video works made from the perspectives of Asian, Hispanic, black, and urban youth artists.

It Wasn't Love
Sadie Benning, 1992

Shifting Patterns

The late '80s and early '90s witnessed an era of culture wars, battles against the art and gay communities lead by right-wing politicians. Both artists and non-profit arts organizations were under attack, and the effect was an overwhelming decline in funding for the arts. The funding that did exist became highly restricted and shifted away from individual artists and towards community and youth-oriented projects. Since the non-profit world had always provided the most stable home for single channel video art, the collection, exhibition, and preservation of video became more difficult to sustain. After almost three decades of growth due to government and foundation support, video artists were entering an era in which they would have to struggle to continue making and exhibiting their work. However, during the same period in which funding began to decline, other opportunities, particularly the advance of digital technology, began to energize videomakers in new ways.

Fast Trip, Long Drop
Gregg Bordowitz, 1993

The Sony Video 8 camcorder was released into the consumer market in the late '80s; because of its size, high quality picture resolution, and low cost, it was the era's equivalent of the Portapak. The Video 8 camcorder was closely followed by Hi8 camcorders that were the same size but had technically finer image quality due to more lines of resolution. The camcorder was popular in the consumer market, and so newer versions were released almost every 18 months until finally, in 1995, the first digital camcorders were marketed. Digital camcorders had superior technology and image resolution that meant that artists and other independent producers could finally make broadcast quality tapes on low-cost consumer equipment.

Equally important, digital editing software like Avid and Media 100 and later, Final Cut Pro, began to revolutionize post-production. Non-linear editing software began to replace older forms of analog on-line equipment used in post-production studios. The new digital editing software made it economically possible for artists to edit on computers rather than in very expensive post-production suites. This conveniently collapsed the cost of production/post-production during a time in which opportunities for funding were on the decline. Rapidly improving digital technology has energized and streamlined video production; it has also narrowed the distinctions between film and video and offers tremendous possibilities for the distribution of media in a variety of new digital processes and formats.

Redefining Video

As long ago as the early '60s, Nam June Paik began exhibiting his modified television sets in galleries as the first video installations. Other artists such as Dan Graham, Bruce Nauman, and Vito Acconci created notable bodies of work in video installation. Several videomakers, such as Bill Viola and Gary Hill, who began with single channel video shifted to making video installations and achieved great success in the gallery system. However, single channel video art was mostly overlooked in galleries until around 1995 when dealers introduced a concept coming from photography and print-making, limited editions. Rather than exhibit single channel video displayed on a monitor, galleries began to project the work onto the wall or other large surface. By presenting single- or multi-channel pieces as large-screen projections and calling them limited editions, video was re-invented and popularized within the gallery system. Limited editions also resolved the problem of how to sell videos; they were now bought, sold, collected and auctioned like painting, drawing, photography, and sculpture. Since artists couldn't simultaneously be single channel artists distributing their work in the more traditional film/video venues and also sell the work as limited editions, this shift called for clear distinctions in the work. Gallery artists chose to make work with strict aesthetic strategies: repetition, scale, slow-motion, extreme close-up, sound and meditative or metaphoric content that speaks from an art-based experimental narrative position. This work has been very successful in attracting larger audiences (and collectors) to video art. However, the popularity of this new type of gallery-based video art attracted new curators, critics, and audiences who were largely unfamiliar with the rich but fragmented history of single-channel video art. In an era of decline of funding for screening programs, video artists now had a choice and could pre-determine markets for their works. Non-gallery based single channel works made prior to the mid-'90s have been relegated to the sideline of the new definition of "video art." Yet older, histori-cally important works are still in circulation, and more and more artists are making sin-gle-channel pieces.

Video plays a very important cultural role as a kind of media trickster operating from the edge of several different but often overlapping systems of communication: personal expression, the art world, independent cinema, television, and academic studies. One of the strengths of video art is that it has never been absorbed by any one of these sys-tems but remains peripheral to all. Video art uses this unique position to function as the research and development wing of media production, as the test market for new ideas and working styles in the festival market, as the avant-guard provocatively speaking out from an alternative perspective on social and cultural issues, as a town meeting on the concerns of the community, and as an artistic practice encouraging audiences to engage with creative forms of media.

"Talk About the Passion"
Jem Cohen and C-Hundred Film Corp, 1988

Video art has achieved its greatest success when it parallels and articulates ideas com-ing out of contemporary cultural, art, and political movements. Whether it is AIDS activism, feminism, anti-war sentiments, racism, global trade, or other emerging issues, video is a medium engaged in questioning, stirring up, provoking, engaging, educating, inventing, informing, and articulating new ideas. While it did not achieve the visionary dreams of the '60s by creating a whole new society based on egalitarian notions of democracy, it did present new alternative models, offer support and encouragement, forge communal bonds, and dare to speak out in the fight against sameness and con-formity in the midst of a world rapidly consumed by global media enterprises and cor-porate interests. Video presented the first, small-scale and closed circuit model of how a decentralized media could participate in challenging mainstream culture and contin-ues to provide creative, alternative uses of the medium to this day.

Notes

[1] Herbert Marcuse, *One-Dimensional Man: Studies in the Ideology of the Advanced Industrial Society* (Boston: Beacon Press, 1964).

[2] Sylvia Harvey, *May '68 and Film Culture* (London: British Film Institute, 1978), p. 56.

[3] Consciousness Industry

[4] Lucinda Furlong, "Notes Toward a History of Image Processed Video" *Afterimage* 11:5 (1983). -get McLuhan quote from article

[5] Beryl Korot and Phyllis Gershuny, editors, "Masthead," *Radical Software*, 1:1, 1970, p. 1.

[6] *Radical Software*,1:1.

[7] *Radical Software* 1:1.

[8] See Rosalind Krauss, "Video: The Aesthesis of Narcissism," *October* 1 (Spring 1976).

[9] See Gene Youngblood, *Expanded Cinema* (New York: Dutton, 1970).

[10] Marita Sturken

[11] Dara Birnbaum

Grow Gills and Swim: The Evolution of Activist Video

Gregg Bordowitz

The massive body of work constituting "activist video" can be likened to an enormous lake–a lake so huge that it appears oceanic when you stand upon its shores. Activist video is like Lake Michigan, a couple of city blocks from the Video Data Bank in the School of the Art Institute of Chicago. The sea-like reservoir of activist material collected and distributed by the VDB has been fed by three primary currents: technology, politics, and art.

Television delivers people. This is both the title and the chief theoretical assertion of Richard Serra's seminal 1973 videotape. A simple tape adhering to the strictures of minimalist sculptural practices, *Television Delivers People* consists of scrolling text accompanied by a soundtrack of cloying Muzak. With lucid precision the text explains how corporations abstract audiences into demographics that are bought, sold, and traded by advertisers. TV isn't free. It's paid for by advertising, and shows are designed to give you just enough entertainment to persuade you to sit through commercials.

In the '70s, people rightly thought that there could more socially beneficial uses for such miraculous technology. The problematic of producing alternatives challenging the U.S. television networks' centrality was first articulated in the magazine *Radical Software*. Produced by the members of a media think-tank called the Raindance Corporation, *Radical Software* established the foundation for the past 30 years' activist video practices.[1] The mission statement, published in the first issue, shows the germinal ideas for a revolution:

> Power is no longer measured in land, labor, or capital, but by access to information and the means to disseminate it. As long as the most powerful tools (not weapons) are in the hands of those who would hoard them, no alternative cultural vision can succeed.[2]

Presciently using the metaphor of "software" long before the personal computer became standard equipment for daily living, *Radical Software* took its cues from theorist Marshall McLuhan, declaring that media literacy was displacing the status of the written word. Video was anointed as the new software for an electronic culture.

> Videotape can be to television what writing is to language. And television, in turn, has subsumed written language as the globe's dominant communications medium. Soon accessible VTR [videotape recorder] systems and video cassettes… will make alternate networks a reality.

> Those of us making our own television know that the medium can be much more than "a radio with a screen" as it is still being used by the networks as they reinforce product oriented and outdated notions of fixed focal point, point of view, subject matter, topic asserting their own passivity, and ours, giving us feedback of feedback of information rather than asserting the implicit immediacy of video, immunizing us to the impact of information by asking us to anticipate what already can be anticipated–the nightly Vietnam reports to serialized single format shows.[3]

Three concerns leap off the page when reading this excerpt. First is the emerging awareness of a globally integrated information economy. Second is the differentiation of television from radio. Third is the Vietnam war.

In the *Medium Is the Massage*, McLuhan famously summed up a shift of epochal proportion: "Ours is a brand-new world of allatonceness. 'Time' has ceased, 'space' has vanished. We now live in a global village… a simultaneous happening."[4] For McLuhan, television constituted the ground for a new tribalism–bands of tuned-in dissidents and pranksters of all kinds riding the waves of telecommunications, incorporating broadcast signals into an aural culture of dissent. McLuhan's "primitivism" was not fearful of technology. It embraced it as the psychedelic spiritualism of the '60s zeitgeist. He recognized that television had unintentionally enlisted a generation of young people into a participatory culture. TV intimately connected people to events occurring clear across

Television Delivers People
Richard Serra, 1973

Gregg Bordowitz is a writer, AIDS activist, and film-and videomaker. His work, including *Fast Trip, Long Drop* (1993) and *Habit* (2001), documents his personal experiences of testing positive and living with HIV within the context of a personal and global crisis. His writings are collected in *The AIDS Crisis is Ridiculous and Other Writings:1986-2003*. He is currently on faculty in the Film Video and New Media department at The School of the Art Institute of Chicago.

the globe, and the young wanted to do something to change what they saw—and more importantly, heard.

Rather than emphasize the visual nature of television transmission, McLuhan realized the aural nature of broadcast. In the American household, the TV was always on as a background to daily business. Television really was a kind of domestic furniture, and its developmental history was much closer to radio than to cinema. The remarkable features of both radio and television were their abilities to pump information directly into millions of homes. Like radio, broadcast television did not necessarily have to be centralized and controlled by state and corporate interests. Radio first and then television held out the possibilities for radically decentralized systems of communication exchanging information from many to many—a community-run service. The respective technologies could have arisen as regional systems governed by civic interests rather than the profit motives of big business. The *Radical Software* editors showed disdain for the notion of "radio with a screen." With the benefit of hindsight they knew that the democratic potential for radio suffered a tragic fatality. They wanted to resist the same end for TV, and that's why they were invested in videotape's potential as the new book. With the coming consumer availability of video players and recorders—anticipated but not yet realized when *Radical Software* put out its first issue—the potential for an ungovernable dissemination of words, sounds, and images emerged.

This electrified free speech movement was catalyzed by a counter-culture that drew its energies from the liberation movements and radical utopian aspirations of the '60s and '70s. The Vietnam war was the ground for many seemingly disparate social upheavals. The sounds and sights of the war were the backdrop to most Americans' mundane daily dramas. Anti-war activism politicized huge segments of the population, but television brought the war home. It connected radicalized youth with the plight of suffering Vietnamese. It made senseless deaths of American soldiers visible. War coverage produced a groundswell of revolutionary sentiment. You didn't have to be a communist to be sickened by the body counts and macabre scenes broadcast nightly.

McLuhan understood that electric circuitry was "an extension of the central nervous system. Media, by altering the environment, evoke in us unique ratios of sense perceptions. The extension of any one sense alters the way we think and act—the way we perceive the world. When these ratios change, men change."[5]

Video activists desperately wanted change: to end the war and to fight poverty, racism, and many other social ills. And they had portable video recording technology: the Portapak. A rather cumbersome affair compared to today's consumer camcorders, the reel-to-reel recording decks were very large, heavy boxes. A thick cord connected the recorder to a large, sensitive tube camera that was easily burned out and destroyed by pointing the lens directly into the sun. Microphones also attached to the recorder, so all together the set-up required two or three people operating the equipment in the field. Today individual video activists can run around on their own, producing far better quality material. Yet, regardless of the difficulties we now laugh about, the portapak enabled an independent electronic news media to flourish.

Young rebels added media activism to the arsenal of organizing tools used by the liberation movements of the '70s. Documenting historic public demonstrations such as the first Women's Liberation March in New York, the first Gay Pride March, and direct actions by Puerto Rican and Native American militants, Peoples Video Theater (PVT) used video technology as a feedback mechanism to inform people about political struggles and give activists a means to view and assess their actions. AIDS activists would later use these same tactics in the '80s. Another exemplary body of counter-cultural media was produced by TVTV (Top Value Television) in a series of behind-the-scenes investigations of the 1972 Republican Convention, the 1976 Super Bowl, and the 1976 Academy Awards. PVT and TVTV are just two examples of the larger history of activist video as a collective enterprise. The communal ethos of the '70s informed the way television technology could be implemented through egalitarian modes of production that challenged notions of authorship. Researching these groups leads the historian to long lists of names and groups, many overlapping within several collective efforts.

Significantly, a large number of artists were involved in early video activism. Several members of Raindance were or became video artists showing work in galleries. The San Francisco collective Ant Farm was proudly multidisciplinary, drawing from the talents of video makers, sculptors, performers, designers, and activists. Ant Farm also designed the book *Guerilla Television*, written by TVTV co-founder Michael Schamberg, who also co-founded of Raindance Corporation and edited *Radical Software*. Videofreex was another group that seemed to be involved in everything, from the short-lived CBS alternative television program *Subject to Change* to the Media Bus traveling workshop. Video activism was a vital social movement with an enormous amount of people passing through, collaborating, and forming shifting alliances.

The many collective efforts of the '70s were informed by a shared interest in the politics of "the spectacle," a word often used to describe the mystifying pageantry of modern commercial media. However, the term "spectacle" has a specific meaning derived from the Situationist theorist Guy Debord. In Debord's seminal work *The Society of the Spectacle*, we learn that the substance of the spectacle is not contained within any specific image. Rather, the concept refers to the ways that representations in general mediate our social relations. Through complex operations of mediation "the spectacle" renders invisible the domination exercised by a privileged and powerful few over the far greater number of alienated and disenfranchised people who must toil daily at meaningless jobs.[6]

Ant Farm's legendary tape *The Eternal Frame* is an excellent example of an intervention into "the spectacle" as defined by Debord. *The Eternal Frame* is an iconoclastic assault on the sacred image repertoire that traumatized a generation. In 1975 members of the collective traveled to Dallas to reenact the 1963 assassination of President John F. Kennedy with eerie precision and in gory detail. They mimicked the Zapruder footage of the President getting shot and the First Lady trying to flee the scene. Political assassinations killed the hopes and dreams of a generation–John Kennedy, Martin Luther King, Malcolm X, Bobby Kennedy. The '60s were a time of violent upheaval and the wreckage left people confused, distraught, and angry. Ant Farm's reconstruction of the Kennedy assassination, and its self-reflexive examination of the morbid fascination with images of the dead president, captured the deep alienation people felt at the time.

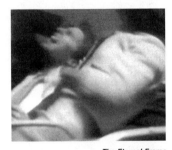

The Eternal Frame
Ant Farm and T.R. Uthco, 1976

The Eternal Frame also successfully embodies the meeting point of activism, media, and art. In the tape, one member of Ant Farm asked another if he thought what they were doing in Dallas was art. He replied, "It's not not art." This use of the double negative is an appropriate answer to the question of whether video activism in general should be construed as high art. All the examples in this short essay share the modernist avant-garde aspirations to merge art with life and to produce revolutionary change using the current technology. Consider, for example, Soviet filmmakers Dziga Vertov and Alexander Medvekin or the international Fluxus movement. In fact, pioneer video artist Nam June Paik was involved in Fluxus. His writing appears in the first issue of *Radical Software*, and VDB distributes Paik's tape *Merce by Merce by Paik* (1975), a two-part tribute choreographer Merce Cunningham and artist Marcel Duchamp, as part of *Surveying the First Decade*.

Merce by Merce by Paik
Nam June Paik, Shigeko Kubota, and
Charles Atlas, 1975

The role of technology in 20th century art was a major issue that has been extensively theorized. Anticipating the rise of fascism in Europe before World War II, the brilliant intellectual Walter Benjamin warned artists that they must use new technological innovations in their work to critically disarm the lethal myths propagated by Nazi fascism.[7] Though historical circumstances have evolved tremendously after World War II, the first video activists of 30 years ago understood the continuing relevance of Benjamin's argument. Network television and its controlling interests dominated the cultural landscape at the end of the 20th century. Practitioners who dared to represent their own versions of reality had to seize the means of production themselves. Creative people were forced to work at the margins, using tools not necessarily designed for their own use. Ironically, the same capitalist system that many tried to reform or obliterate provid-

Production Notes: Fast Food for Thought
Jason Simon, 1986

ed artists with the tools to act. Capitalist mass production made technology available and affordable, enabling the proliferation of video productions beyond the control of network television; placing gear in the hands of consumers disidentified with establishment institutions: schools, corporations, and the government.

One of the finest examples of betrayal by a disgruntled employee with a political consciousness is Jason Simon's *Production Notes: Fast Food for Thought* (1986). While working at a commercial production house, Simon appropriated the production notes and footage for seven television commercials, making a very popular and instructive video showing exactly how corporations use media to manipulate people into buying things they don't need. The term "appropriation" describes any activity that borrows or samples sources drawn from the glut of images streaming out of commercial culture. Appropriation actually emerged out of the criminal impulse to reclaim something that we, consumers of culture, are denied—access to the means of production of subjectivity. Stealing advertising images and using state-of-the-art equipment at the production company where he labored, Simon took back what his employers expropriated: his creativity.

DiAna's Hair Ego: AIDS Info Upfront
Ellen Spiro, 1989

Video activism in the '80s was infused with fresh vitality. Relatively inexpensive, easily portable equipment seemed to arrive exactly when it was needed by a new generation of progressive activists. A conservative political movement gathered force throughout the country during the '70s and landed on the political landscape in 1980 when Ronald Reagan was elected president. Corporate corruption, state-sponsored terrorism, poverty, homelessness, and most significantly the AIDS crisis marked the period. The body of work produced by AIDS activists in the late-'80s and early-'90s extended the concerns and methods of the previous generation onto new terrain. This generation was raised on television and their productions demonstrated a greater fluency with the language of the medium. Some elevated video to a level approaching poetry or literature. Tom Kalin's *They are lost to vision altogether* (1988) is an impressive lyrical work. The VDB preserved the fomentation of AIDS activism in its anthology *Video Against AIDS*[8] and distributes other signal works of the period: Ellen Spiro's tape *DiAna's Hair Ego: AIDS Info Upfront* (1989), Marlon Rigg's *Non Je Ne Regrette Rien* (1992), and my own contributions to the corpus, *Fast Trip, Long Drop* (1993) and *Habit* (2001).

The most significant feature of AIDS video activism was the way it placed people with AIDS at the center of the public discussion about the epidemic. The dominant media of the '80s perpetrated a great violence against people with AIDS through representations that refused to address the concerns of the sick. The scapegoating messages of panic fostered by the commercial media were intended for an audience of uninfected people. They played to the worst fears and prejudices of a fictional "general public." AIDS video activism successfully reversed the priorities of the public discussion on the epidemic in the '80s and '90s, insisting that the people who needed care most should determine the way the disease is pictured.

They are lost to vision altogether
Tom Kalin, 1988

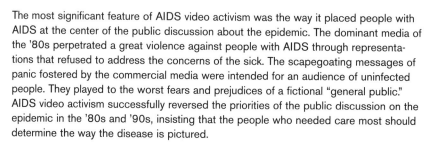

The VDB continues to provide a home for the most audacious and radical electronic culture. Technology continues to advance and the Data Bank follows right along with it. Christine Tamblyn's CD-ROMs *Mistaken Identities* (1995) and *She Loves It, She Loves It Not* (1993), though now seemingly outmoded, are some of the most interesting early explorations of hypertext and interactive media. Reginald Woolery's *World Wide Web/Million Man March* and Art Jones' *Culture vs. the Martians* are just two more examples that investigate the potential for digital activism. The subversive organization ®™ark 's tape *Bringing It All to You* (2001) deftly hijacks the form of the infomercial to advertise acts of anti-corporate sabotage. Activist video continues to be a vital endeavor with many practitioners entering new fields of production.

An enduring principle continues to inform activist video production: progressive social projects produce themselves as they represent themselves. Self-representation is inextricably linked with the agenda of self-determination. Video activists are no mere recorders of events. Their activity plays a central role in organizing dissent. Coming from within social movements themselves, video activists can be the poets of revolution. They occupy the place of conscience; they are the voice of rage. Finally, they are often the most eloquent representatives of broad constituencies, making the righteous case for justice to vastly larger audiences than any single speech or demonstration can reach.

As video activism continues to reshape history, the practice has been greatly extended by new digital technologies. We now have the benefit of 30 years' experience and work to study the practice of political video art. VDB, on the shore of Lake Michigan, is the single most comprehensive repository of several generations of activist efforts. Staring out at the surface of a huge body of water can be deceiving to the eye. The calm surface of the sea often hides the forces stirring below. And water doesn't record the traces of the many vessels that navigate through it. So we must dive. We must explore. If we don't possess the gear to breathe underwater, we must grow gills and swim. Activism requires acts of volition that defy the poverty of our resources and our own bodies' limits.

Notes

[1] *Radical Software*, along with informative historical notes, can be found online at www.radicalsoftware.org.

[2] Ibid., 1:1.

[3] Ibid.

[4] Marshall McLuhan and Quentin Fiore, *The Medium Is the Massage: An Inventory of Effects* (San Francisco: Hardwired, 1996 [1967]), 63.

[5] Ibid., 40-41.

[6] Guy Debord, *The Society of the Spectacle*, Trans. Donald Nicholson-Smith (New York: Zone Books, 1995).

[7] Walter Benjamin, "The Work of Art in the Age of Its Technological Reproducibility," *Walter Benjamin, Selected Writings 1935-1938, Volume 3* (Cambridge, Mass.: Harvard University Press, 2002), 101-133.

[8] *Video Against AIDS* was removed from distribution when Video Data Bank's original contracts with the artists expired in the late 1990s. VDB is committed to keeping AIDS activist work available and may re-release the anthology pending updated legal arrangements.

On my way to and from classes when I was a student at California Institute of the Arts in the early 1970s, I always passed the video editing rooms, and I always saw only men at the stations, and they were always making electronic paintings. This quotidian scene occurred during the seismic shifts of the civil rights movement, women's liberation, black liberation, and impassioned resistance to the war in Vietnam. I, like so many women artists then, was convinced that content as the driving force for formal invention was profoundly more relevant and original than using video as a canvas for the already-told story of abstract expressionist painting. I pitied the guys in those rooms—how backward, how vacant, how outside the story of history.

The recorders of art history, though, wanted what they already knew: the story of men, or, as renowned art historian and critic Griselda Pollock has put it, history's "patriarchal and phallocentric thought and formations."[1] Alienated from an art world that admitted virtually no recognition of their lives, women deployed media such as performance, concept art, and experimental film and video in unique ways. They contributed to—if not caused—the historic rupture between modernism's attention to form and the monoculture of a master—read male—narrative and postmodernism's investigations of identity, sexuality, and selfhood that allowed previously silenced "others" to testify.[2]

Women artists of the '70s and '80s did enter the pages of art criticism and history but not as agents in the story of video's beginnings.[3] Further, historians and curators have elided numerous interventions that feminist artists, educators, and writers made. Some of the startling works by women in the beginning years remain unrecognized, destroyed, or lost. The Video Data Bank distributes crucial tapes and feminist anthologies, such as *I Say I Am* and *e-[d]entity*, that recuperate history from the trauma of erasure and that write the unwritten. The following essay surveys this history as inscribed in the Video Data Bank's collection.

Background

The introduction of the electronic medium of video occurred as feminism, the most important philosophical movement of the 20th century, was once again entering the public consciousness of America, this time as the Second Wave.[4] Video offered new possibilities for women no longer content to be known as male artists' wives or girlfriends; there were no "founding father" mythologies because no one took video seriously as an art medium. True, men were still capable of self-mythologizing, but they had not yet been historicized in coffee table books about the 20th century. Video was as close to a "master-free zone" as one could get. The physical aspects of video included simultaneous feedback: with a $1,500 Portapak, a reasonably lightweight open-reel camera and playback deck, artists could record and view images simultaneously without going to prohibitively expensive television production facilities. It was both an electronic mirror in the privacy of one's own art studio or a means to be in the world actively rather than passively. For women taught to compartmentalize their lives as wives, mothers, mistresses, wallflowers, good or bad girls, video was a reflecting device to enact and express the limitations of their positions as listeners and watchers. Video was accessible; one didn't have to be a card-carrying famous artist to get a hold of the equipment. Often video projects required working in crews; women could use the medium itself to subvert the discourse about women as petty and competitive. And perhaps most important, in video's incarnation as television, it was the very medium used to misrepresent and underrepresent the lives of women. Video was an opportunity to re-represent, with the tools of mass culture, a critique of the way mass culture had made meaning out of women.[5]

The Video Data Bank Collection

Each woman's version of feminism is slightly proprietary. I have a similar sense when dipping into the Video Data Bank collection; it is emblematic of different or opposing philosophies, theories, and aesthetics. But such arguments exist within a larger framework about the need to challenge dominant modes of address, to define and create audience, to "speak truth to power," and to co-author the relationship between a medium and its history. The video works circle around several historical and theoretical issues: representation, the politics of everyday life ("the personal is political"), differ-

Vertical Hold:
A History
of Women's
Video Art

Vanalyne Green

Nun and Deviant
Nancy Angelo and Candace Compton, 1976

Green studied poststudio art at California Institute of the Arts where she received her BFA and was in the first historic feminist art program directed by Judy Chicago and Sheila Levrant de Bretteville. She was a founding member of No More Nice Girls, an agitprop group known for its pro-sex, pro-abortion actions and is currently a member of the Feel Tank Chicago. Green's videotapes playfully and bitterly examine the paradoxes of American citizenship within such social practices as addiction, sports, sexuality, and, most recently, prayer. She is a professor of fine arts at University of Leeds.

ence, a television of consequence, and audience (activism).

Representation

Key to the discourse about representation is a psychoanalytic interpretation of narrative. Since 1969 the British journal *Screen* has been publishing articles analyzing mass media in theoretical terms redeploying the work of Bertolt Brecht, Sigmund Freud, and Jacques Lacan, among others. In 1975 *Screen* published Laura Mulvey's pivotal essay "Visual Pleasure and Narrative Cinema." [6] Mulvey suggested that the Hollywood filmic spectacle had a rationale to it, one that soothed male spectators' unconscious psychic insecurities about their masculine identity by creating an illusionistic space in which the female body is fetishized, fragmented, and punished. The implication for women film and video makers was profound: a liberatory practice required rethinking visual strategies in particular ways. One had to ensure that viewers didn't suspend disbelief and unconsciously absorb a director's version of reality. This included a rejection of Renaissance space and editing strategies that turned audiences into "invisible guests." One also had to reconsider the representation of the female body in the frame. For artists challenging repressive stereotypes of women's sexuality, Mulvey's article was both instructive and restrictive. Some of Yvonne Rainer's works contemplate Mulvey's ideas, through which Rainer skews "the traditional axes of the gaze, power, identification." [7] I place some of my earlier videos (*A Spy in the House that Ruth Built*, 1989) in the middle of that argument, agreeing with Mulvey's goals but disputing proscriptions of women's physical presence onscreen.

Even before "Visual Pleasure and Narrative Cinema," women were examining the interface between female pleasure and the "male gaze." In Lynda Benglis's *Female Sensibility* (1972), for example, two women kiss and caress, but they're also clearly looking at a monitor. Rather than objects, they're actually agents in producing and complicating the voyeuristic gaze as the audience is fixed between looking and being caught looking at a putative lesbian scene. Suzanne Lacy's *Learn Where the Meat Comes From* (1976) and Nina Sobell's *Hey! Baby Chickey* (1978) critique sexual objectification through funny and unnerving parodies of a homemaker/cook who treats pieces of raw flesh the way women themselves often felt treated.

The Personal Is Political

Because the feminist slogan "the personal is political" has been repeated to exhaustion, it's difficult to understand how compelling its meaning was in the early '70s. The first-person voice that feminism legitimized as both political speech and the source of theoretical insight enabled young artists to speak in a language that couldn't be disputed: the language of their own life experiences. I sub-categorize practices that formed around this idea in three ways—as woman-centered, Marxist/feminist, and feminism as subtext.

Woman-Centered

In the Peoples Video Theater footage of a women's liberation march in New York (1971), a woman says, "I've marched for welfare rights…. and by god, I'm marching for women today, and I don't want to hear 'peace.' I want to hear women's liberation, now!"

Learn Where the Meat Comes From
Suzanne Lacy, 1976

Newly politicized and alienated by the lack of recognition of gender disparity in the left, peace, and civil rights movements, white middle-class women looked to communities of women for intellectual and emotional sustenance to explore an ontology of the feminine. Women artists working out of such a project made extraordinary and original work. For instance, Nancy Angelo and Candace Compton were core members of the Woman's Building in Los Angeles, a cultural center for women. [8] In *Nun and Deviant* (1976) Compton performs as a bad girl who steals for "the Revolution," while Angelo plays the good-girl nun. Each takes turn methodically smashing bottles in the background as the other talks directly to camera. But slowly their positions begin to merge. Compton's bad girl confesses that she didn't actually steal all that much; Angelo's nun admits she's fed up with the goodie-two-shoes schtick. Shot in a parking lot in front of a white industrial building on old black-and-white half-inch video, the mise-en-scène is elegant, with a beauty reminiscent of Antonioni's *L'Eclisse* (1962). The piece is paradigmatic of the sustained attempts artists made to create a language about women working together as opposed to the socially constructed scenario of competition and scarcity.

The Los Angeles Woman's Building attracted a visible component of separatist feminists—women who argued that, for a while at least, it was necessary to have as little contact with men as possible until women could reconstitute themselves as people fully independent from sexist dogma. Yet their work illustrates the porous relationship such women artists had with avant-garde artists at the time. Their use of direct address to camera, a performative rather than a theatrical style, and repetitive actions is formally akin to early video work by Richard Serra and John Baldessari, for example. In *Take Off* (1974), Susan Mogul (then studying in the Feminist Studio Workshop, the educational component of the Woman's Building) parodically reenacts Vito Acconci's well-known video *Undertone* (1972). In a genre-bending tour-de-force Mogul used her vibrator as a prop to create an homage, a critique, and a sex-education tape. Such works were sophisticated interventions into conceptual art practices of the time, revolutionizing the field through both formal invention and social substance.

Take Off
Susan Mogul, 1974

Marxist-Feminist Practices

Feminists who remained theoretically and politically identified with Marxism dialectically critiqued the social construction of everyday life, employing both feminist and class analyses of power. Martha Rosler's *Semiotics of the Kitchen* (1975) is a case in point.

Wearing an apron, Rosler stands in the middle of a kitchen, performing to the camera directly in front of her, much as a television cook might do. She displays kitchen utensils one-by-one in alphabetical order, making physical gestures upon reciting each utensil's name. Instead of using the ladle or the knife or the nutcracker in the usual manner, however, Rosler either makes stabbing gestures or pretends to pitch make-believe ingredients to one side. The gestures are hostile; the rage contained. In calling the tape *Semiotics of the Kitchen*, Rosler hoisted post-structuralist theory[9] out of its safe nook in the academy and set it down in the theoretically unprivileged sphere of the housewife.

Rosler made *Semiotics of the Kitchen*, as well as *Vital Statistics of a Citizen, Simply Obtained* (1977) and *Losing: A Conversation with the Parents* (1977) while living on the West Coast, the epicenter of the human potential movement, which had seeped into feminist practices. In looking for a method to speak to her experience as scholar, artist, and young mother, Rosler turned not only to feminism but also to social historians critical of the new age movement's utopian rhetoric. Her early videos dramatically expanded the possible histories and analyses of power then in play for women artists. And women artists took note; we can chart their trajectories in the generations that followed.

Vital Statistics of a Citizen, Simply Obtained
Martha Rosler, 1977

Employing the language and experience of everyday life, women made work critical of American foreign policy, consumer culture, and colonialism, among other issues. In *A Womb with a View* (1986), *Out of the Mouth of Babes* (1986), and *Scenes from the Micro-war* (1985) Sherry Millner mapped her experiences of pregnancy and family life onto the political scenarios of Reagan's space wars and the U.S. government's policies in South America. More recently, Tran T. Kim Trang's *Blindness Series* (1992-1997) has investigated different aspects of blindness as a metaphor; in *Operculum* (1993), Tran looks at the intersection between bletharoplasty (cosmetic eyelid surgery) and Western ideals of beauty. In *Marx: The Video* (1990) Laura Kipnis creates a dialectical work about women's bodies as the site for the state's social and political anxiety, interpreting anorexia and bulimia as symptomatic of capitalism's compulsive consumption.

Feminism as Subtext

In the history of women's art many works exist because of a feminist framework, even if they do not present explicitly feminist messages. Often these works use formal elements to examine the psychology of power, boundaries, and interiority.

Vertical Roll
Joan Jonas, 1972

In Joan Jonas's *Vertical Roll* (1972) a steady thrum of sound matches a descending, desynchronized vertical roll. Jonas performs various gestures, such as clapping and walking, trapped within the destabilized and repetitive lines of the vertical roll. But Jonas's imprisonment within the frame is repeated in the experience of the viewer, who is as caught as Jonas is by the relentless movement of the rolling frame. Jonas not only enacts the role of the captive but also the capturer. At the end of the tape, the artist appears in front of the still destabilized frame and slowly looks to the camera. Jonas invokes John Berger's often-quoted observation about the trope of the female model, always painted looking away from the viewer and thus representing objecthood and lack of consciousness. Breaking the fourth wall, Jonas rejects the traditional image of the unconscious female body. The effect is a layered meditation on object/subject, woman/frame.

Difference

In a 1983 interview cultural theorist Marita Sturken asked curator John Hanhardt, "Has your programming of women and minority artists been conscious? Do you seek out that work?" Hanhardt replied, "It's a conscious effort on my part, and I'm still not doing enough. I feel I should be showing more women, and more minorities. It's a problem. ... We should do more. ... I think we should look to what's being done around the issues of neighborhood-oriented programs and the films and videotapes that they're showing."[10]

Queen Mother Moore Speech at
Greenhaven Prison
People's Communication Network, 1973

The history of women's video art iterates similar problems: lower-income women of color did not feel welcomed in the high art world. Post-colonial theorist Gayatri Spivak has urged us to ask, "How does the other woman see me?" in every sphere. In the case of video's first 10 years, what the "other" women saw were almost exclusively white producers; in other words, women of color were being represented rather than representing themselves. As such, however, their presence is unforgettable: *Queen Mother Moore at Greenhaven Prison* (1972) by People's Communication Network, for example, is an historically important document in which Queen Mother Moore, a life-long follower of Marcus Garvey and activist who died in 1997, "re-presents" received assumptions about crime in the African-American community. To the African-American prisoners she says, "You can't steal. You can only take back." But few women of color were making videos. Shigeko Kubota was a remarkable exception. Her piece *My Father* (1975) is a moving lamentation about the death of her father that begins with the sister-ly words: "I called Shirley Clarke. She asked me how I was. I told her I was crying. She said, 'Why don't you videotape yourself crying?'"

French theorists Gilles Deleuze and Félix Guattari conceptualized a minor literature (that is, a literature by minorities) that takes the established codes of a "master language" to create a new, radical language. Deleuze and Guattari use Franz Kafka's skeletal, inward-turning writing as emblematic of such subversive practices. But in video the revolutionary aspect of a minor literature is often visual complication, which turns many mainstream visual and narrative styles against each other. Made in 1991, Rea Tajiri's *History and Memory* is an index of memories and histories, both real and imagined, related to the internment of Japanese-Americans during WWII. A work of astonishing complexity, Tajiri employs found footage of the attack on Pearl Harbor, the Spencer Tracy film *Bad Day at Black Rock* (1955), and *Come See the Paradise* (1990). She also recreates her family's experiences and stages ones she imagined as a child. The result is a piece that is part lamentation, part indictment, and part love poem to her family.

Videos that juxtapose different visual texts—appropriated and/or original—often evoke uneasy senses of place within placelessness. Leah Gilliam's *Sapphire and the Slave Girl* (1995), for example, takes scissors to film noir classics to problematize the anxious connection between identity and urban space. Mona Hatoum's *Measures of Distance* (1988) threads letters from her mother into a visual montage that speaks of her personal and cultural distance from her Palestinian origins. Meena Nanji's *Voices of the Morning* (1992), about the effects of Islamic law on women, uses different visual sources to create productive tensions between the various narrative registers.

Women challenging heteronormativity have created some of the most original and pow-erful work in video art, almost single-handedly reinvigorating the field in the late '80s and '90s. Marginal in society's terms, such artists have often traveled to the center of mainstream storytelling to make their point. Sadie Benning's career stands out as a striking example.

In Benning's early tapes she often remains in her apartment. Life outside is chaotic and painful as she recounts, for example, the serial killings of children of color in *A Place Called Lovely* (1991). Lesbians are invisible or discriminated against—unpersons (*If Every Girl Had a Diary*, 1990). Safe inside her home, though, Benning asks the hard questions, mourns, and meditates on the difference between lust and love (*It Wasn't Love*, 1992). Ironically, Benning, the consummate outsider, uses the tropes, clichés, and icons of mainstream Hollywood: James Cagney-like tough guys, Patty McCormack's *The Bad Seed* (1956), and patriotic songs. Benning takes the hype, dis-appointment, and grief that the world has to offer and transforms them into art.

If Every Girl Had a Diary
Sadie Benning, 1990

Cecilia Dougherty, on the other hand, literally inhabits the mainstream—in her case to re-invent it as a social space inclusive of sexual difference. Her approach could be likened to an invasion. In such videos as *Coal Miner's Granddaughter* (1991), Dougherty cre-ates a lesbian dialogue within the ordinary life of a working-class family. The result is a narrative in which lesbianism is matter-of-fact, as opposed to the sensationalized images of gay women in mass media. In *Gone* (2001), Dougherty re-enacts an episode of the inaugural television verité documentary series *An American Family* with a partially gender-reversed cast. Dougherty restages mother Pat Loud's visit to New York City, where her son Lance was camped out in the famous Chelsea Hotel, a refuge for bohemians, artists, gays, and lesbians. During this groundbreaking episode, Lance came out to her, and the footage was unlike any prior representation of gay life on tele-vision.

A "Television of Consequence"[11]

A *locus classicus* for women video artists is television. Dara Birnbaum, one of the first artists to appropriate mass culture images in her 1978 *Technology/Transformation: Wonder Woman*, has called her tapes "ready-mades," playing on the Duchampian notion of defining everyday objects as art. In his book *Kant After Duchamp* art historian Thierry de Duve suggests that the first ready-mades were, in fact, manufactured tubes of paint, not artist Marcel Duchamp's found urinals or pieces of a coat rack.[12] Perhaps the analogy holds when looking at Birnbaum's early pieces. Her methods of repetition and pastiche, through a roll of karaoke lyrics or the stutter-stop repetition of frames from *Wonder Woman* or *Hollywood Squares* (in *Kiss the Girls: Make Them Cry*, 1979), create a sense of wonder as one is confronted with isolated and rewritten frag-ments of television spectacle.

Technology /Transformation: Wonder Woman
Dara Birnbaum, 1978

Many artists use found footage, but few understand the power that such images have; their meanings are overdetermined by their ubiquitousness in mass media. You have to think hard to get through the familiar emotions and associations that they almost auto-matically evoke. Birnbaum may have been the first to do so. But Diane Nerwin, Yvonne Rainer, Rea Tajiri, Sherry Millner, Elizabeth Subrin, Leah Gilliam, and Joan Braderman have all also used archival and mass media footage—spanning a range from 1950s medical films about menopause to clips from *Blade Runner* (1982)—to create their own themes and messages. In Braderman's *Joan Does Dynasty* (1986), she literally and symbolically inhabits the central narrative of one of TV's most successful prime-time '80s soap operas. She electronically inserts herself into scenes, both confessing her love of the sleazy soap and analyzing its anti-woman, anti-working people message. "Life is messy," as Simone de Beauvoir acknowledged. Braderman's love of contradic-tion attests to the pleasures of complex life.

Audience, or Acts of Citizenship

The rhetoric that we subscribed to was that "the people are the information." Everybody could do it, and everybody should do it. That was the mandate—pick it up, it's there. Like the power to vote—vote, take responsibility. Make it and see it.[13]

Learn Where the Meat Comes From
Suzanne Lacy, 1976

Reflecting both the times and the urgency that women felt about working to better the conditions for other women, many decided to know themselves in the world via an activist art practice. Citizenship and feminism were activities, not identities. Naming the unnameable and creating an "escape route out of impossible situations"[14] were imperative for a female constituency. Often the strategies of address included conscious attempts to reach audiences beyond the art world. Some of the work gathered information and brought it into the art realm; other work went outward into communities to interact.

In *The Politics of Intimacy* (1974) Julie Gustafson mimed aspects of the consciousness-raising group, a feminist-created safety zone where women could talk about the things they'd never said before. The women talk so forthrightly about serving their boyfriends that the tape still causes men to squirm with discomfort. Cara DeVito's *Ama L'Uomo Tuo* (*Always Love Your Man*, 1975) presents an intimate account of her grandmother's abusive husband and an illegal and dangerous late-term abortion. The tape is riveting for the way it takes a story that's usually highly polemical and renders it as a dialectical conversation between the two women. Kathy High invoked avant-garde techniques of disjunctive narrative with aspects of traditional documentary to create a tape that could reach cross-over audiences. In *I Need Your Full Cooperation* (1989) she integrates commentaries by Barbara Ehrenreich and Carroll Smith-Rosenberg with a dramatization of Charlotte Perkins-Gillman's *The Yellow Wallpaper* and archival footage to create a scathing critique of modern medicine's disservices to women.

I have not written about work that addresses the complex dynamic between generations of women artists, in which, for one thing, younger women artists suffer from the career perils of identifying with older women artists, marginalized as feminism has been. And yet, as Mira Schor has noted, this is the first time in history that young artists can have an intellectual lineage to women in the generation before them—they can be "sired" by other women[15] The Video Data Bank offers examples of this and other histories for readers to discover on their own. The happiest moments I've had looking at the Video Data Bank collection have occurred while viewing a compilation reel, when I have happened upon an unfamiliar piece of work sandwiched between two others, or when, out of idle curiosity, I've asked to see a work about which I knew nothing. This way I've discovered videos that may be less well known, but that are equally vital pieces of women's history and equally necessary to the history of art.

Notes

[1] Griselda Pollock, "Introduction," *Vision and Difference* (New York: Routledge, 2003).

[2] Lucy Lippard, "Sweeping Exchanges: The Contribution of Feminism to the Art of the Seventies," *Art Journal* 41:1/2 (1980), 362. See also Nicole Dubreuil-Blondin, "Feminism and Modernism: Some Paradoxes," in *Modernism and Modernity: The Vancouver Conference Papers*, eds. Benjamin H.D. Buchloh, Serge Guilbaut, and David Solkin (Halifax: Nova Scotia College of Art and Design Press, 1984), 197.

[3] See Martha Gever, "Pomp and Circumstances: The Coronation of Nam June Paik," *Afterimage* (October 1982), for an analysis of the founding father mythologies.

[4] In *Griswold v. Connecticut* (1965), a state law banning the provision of contraceptives to married couples was struck down by the U.S. Supreme Court, which declared that "the right to privacy" implicit in the Bill of Rights guaranteed access to birth control for married couples. Casey Hayden and Mary King, women active in SNCC, wrote a paper on the role of women in the movement, which was attacked by male radicals. It was published as a two-part article, "Sex and Caste," in *Liberation*, (April, December issues, 1966).

[5] This description of video traverses a complex argument about whether or not video has "essential" properties. I'm taking a dialectical (or paradoxical, depending on one's point of view) approach: I'm describing the logic of the time for some—that video feedback systems offered unique and liberatory possibilities. At the same time video, as a

technology, inherits technology's legacy as a controlling and repressive force in society. See Martha Rosler, "Video: Shedding the Utopian Moment" in *Illuminating Video, An Essential Guide to Video Art,* eds. Doug Hall and Sally Jo Feiffer (New York: Aperture, 1990).

[6] Laura Mulvey, "Visual Pleasure and Narrative Cinema," *Screen* 16:3 (1975). It's important to note that Mulvey herself later revised her provocative argument.

[7] *Yvonne Rainer, A Woman Who... Essays, Interviews, Scripts* (Baltimore: Johns Hopkins University Press, 1999), 277.

[8] Artist Judy Chicago, graphic designer Sheila Levrant de Bretteville, and art historian Arlene Raven founded the first independent school for women artists, the Feminist Studio Workshop, in 1973. They believed that the arts should not be separated from other activities of the women's community and chose a site that could also be shared with other organizations and enterprises. That space was the Woman's Building in Los Angeles, which was host to women's art events, conferences, and grass-roots political action groups from 1973 to 1991.

[9] A theoretical movement originating in linguistics and the anthropology of Claude Lévi-Strauss and then redefined by, among others, Michel Foucault, post-structuralism was the *sine qua non* of university cocktail party chit-chat in the 1980s.

[10] Marita Sturken, "The Whitney Museum and the Shaping of Video Art. An Interview with John Hanhardt," *Afterimage* (May 1983), 4-7.

[11] David Ross, "Truth or Consequences: American Television and Video Art," *Video Culture: A Critical Investigation*, ed. John G. Hanhardt (Rochester: Visual Studies Workshop Press, 1986). Ross opposes a television of no consequence with artists such as Dara Birnbaum's "television of consequence," 169.

[12] Thierry de Duve, *Kant After Duchamp* (Cambridge, Mass.: MIT Press, 1996).

[13] Chris Hill, "Attention! Production! Audience!: Performing Video Art in Its First Decade," in *Rewind: Video Art and Alternative Media in the United States*, ed. Chris Hill (Chicago: Video Data Bank, 1996), 12.

[14] As Sandra M. Gilbert and Susan Gubar described one of the dominant themes in 19th century women's literature and that women found just as relevant in 1975. Gilbert and Gubar, *The Madwoman in the Attic: The Woman Writer and the Nineteenth-Century Literary Imagination*, second edition (New Haven: Yale University Press, 2000).

[15] Mira Schor, *Wet: On Painting, Feminism, and Art Culture* (Durham: Duke University Press, 1997).

Performance Art and Experimental Video: Highlights from the VDB Collection

Peggy Phelan

It would not be too much to claim that performance art forms the conceptual nucleus of experimental video. Borrowing heavily from each other, especially in the United States, the most influential work in both performance art and experimental video emerged in the 1960s and '70s. The Video Data Bank's collection does much more than provide an extensive documentary record of performance art; it also reveals the ways in which video was (and still is) a provocative agent in live art's attempt to challenge and reconcile itself to the age of mechanical reproduction.

Performance art, like other ephemeral art forms, such as dance or sand painting, has been both bedeviled and inspired by the issue of its own disappearance. On the one hand, live performance art promised a unique, once-in-a-lifetime event and on the other, it seemed to betray art's deep bid for transcendent, even immortalizing, grandeur. This paradox was both allayed and provoked by the emergence of cheap, portable, and relatively simple recording devices, especially video. Video, first and foremost, allowed performance artists the security they needed to pursue what would otherwise be an ephemeral art form. This was especially needed in the United States where funding opportunities, nevermind scholarly or international discussion, necessitated some form of documentation. The first phase of the conjoining links between performance art and experimental video is best described as "the documentary period."

In those heady days of the '60s, when video began to emerge as a new art form, the avant-garde performance art world was under the spell of the Judson Dance Theatre. The dancers and choreographers included Yvonne Rainer, Trisha Brown, Lucinda Childs, and Steve Paxton, among many others. At the heart of their work was an exploration of what they called "task-like movement." Seeking to dismantle the notion that dance required certain virtuosic movements performed by young skinny people, the Judson dancers championed what they called "the neutral doer." Concentrating on literally pedestrian movements such as walking, sitting, running, and jumping, the Judson Dancers expanded the category, both conceptual and actual, of what counted as dance and who could be a dancer. People of all physical descriptions—fat, skinny, disabled, young, old, black, brown—were now encouraged to see their everyday movements as dance.

The Judson's emphasis on "the neutral doer" also set the stage for Andy Warhol's otherwise gnomic claim, "I want to be a machine" and ushered in not only the matter-of-fact representation of Pop Art but the first phase of experimental video as well. Early on, the emphasis was on a static camera calmly and "neutrally" recording performances; often shot in black and white with little or no sound or editing, these videos were extremely important for the foundation of the field of Performance Studies, for they provided material that could be taught, studied, and shown to those who might have missed the live event.

Semiotics of the Kitchen
Martha Rosler, 1975

Among the many valuable documentary tapes in the Video Data Bank's extraordinary collection, two of the best are of Gordon Matta-Clark's *Clock Shower* (1976) and Kim Jones's *San Francisco Walk* (1979). (Both are available on the anthology *Endurance, Reel 3*). *Clock Shower* is a tour de force: Matta-Clark turns New York's Clock Tower into a stage and pursues the pedestrian movements celebrated by Ana Halperin and the Judson Dancers. He showers, shaves, and brushes his teeth while suspended above the New York streets. Jones walks in the streets of San Francisco dressed as the Mudman, a shaman-like figure who looks like a lost warrior. Covered with mud and carrying a strange assemblage of tree branches on his back, Jones's performance invokes images of Vietnam soldiers and anticipates the rise of homelessness in the United States. As gripping as Jones's calm stroll is, the friendly reactions of the other pedestrians are even more astonishing. Interested, and not at all fearful, the strollers say hello and ask to have their photographs taken with him. (His face is covered with nylon.) More than serving to record Jones's walk, this video documents a radically different cultural moment than our own.

While both *Clock Shower* and *San Francisco Walk* were shot outdoors and therefore seem full of accidental and spontaneous events, Vito Acconci's *Waterways: 4 Saliva*

Peggy Phelan is the Ann O'Day Maples Chair in the Arts at Stanford University. She is author of *Unmarked: The Politics of Performance* and *Mourning Sex: Performing Public Memories* and co-editor of *Acting Out: Feminist Performances* (with Lynda Hart) and *The Ends of Performance* (with Jill Lane).

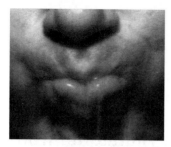

Waterways: 4 Saliva Studies
Vito Acconci, 1971

Studies (1971) illuminates a more rigorously controlled approach to documentation. Here the emphasis is strictly on documenting Acconci's investigation of saliva as expressive medium. Using only an occasional zoom, the camera exemplifies the idea of the neutral machine for recording that which disappears—saliva, skin, body. The tight close-up on Acconci's lips in the first study also makes a sly but important comment about the history of portraiture in painting, which traditionally emphasizes either the costume and social props integral to self-fashioning, or the eyes, the so-called "windows of the soul." Stripping away these features of portraiture, Acconci's video performance shows us new ways of measuring presence and of assessing bodily expressiveness. His emphasis on bodily fluids in this and other work of the '60s and '70s now seems eerily prescient of the preoccupation with these same fluids at the height of the AIDS crisis in the United States in the '80s and '90s.

It quickly became apparent, however, that video was not the same thing as live performance. Confining video strictly to a documentary role in relation to live performance was both a limitation of video as a medium and a falsification of what live performance truly was. Live performance, at its best, promised that both the performers and the spectators of the live event could be transformed by what took place during the enactment of the performance. In the initial encounter between video and performance art, video was seen primarily as a reliable witness to that promised transformation. The term "witness" is often associated with crime, ethics, justice, and history, reminding us that human witnesses are often unreliable, subject to the vagaries of memory, and attracted to narrative distortion in service of the well told tale. Video witnessing seemed to do away with these sometimes troubling aspects of human witnessing by offering us a mechanical and therefore an apparently impartial record. (This is the appeal of surveillance videotape as well.) But, of course, the video is operated, directed, and edited by a human, often an artist, and experimental video artists wanted to welcome distortion and creativity in all its rough and tumble allure. This aspect of experimental video might best be described as "documentation plus." Richard Serra, Bruce Nauman, and Joan Jonas, among others, were interested in how the particular features of video, film, and television informed the experience of watching the documentation of a live performance. In Jonas's celebrated *Vertical Roll* (1972), for twenty minutes a female figure attempts to find her footing in a space unable to overcome a problem with vertical hold. One of the first experimental videos to use the technological glitch as a way to express a psychological and political condition, *Vertical Roll* presciently indicates the ways in which the technologically mediated definition of space would soon become inseparable from our sense of ground. We tell time less and less based on the "natural" turn of the Earth and increasingly by the time and channel our favorite television shows are broadcast. When our televisions or computers have error messages, it is as if the world itself is malfunctioning. Jonas's *Vertical Roll* captures the dizzying moment when the technological glitch became psychologically and physically disorienting. Miranda July's *The Amateurist* (1998) returns to that moment 26 years on, and shows how intense the condition has become.

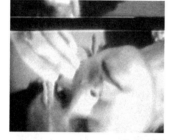

Vertical Roll
Joan Jonas, 1972

Gilbert & George: The Singing Sculpture
Gilbert & George and Philip Haas, 1992

Another important feature of videos dedicated to exploring "documentation plus" is their quite often brilliant pedagogical force. One of the best is Philip Haas's remarkable video, *Gilbert & George: The Singing Sculpture* (1992, available on the anthology *Endurance, Reel 1*). The performance *Singing Sculpture*, in which Gilbert & George stand on a table and sing to a tape of "Underneath the Arches," a 1930s English music hall standard about homelessness and hope, while slowly traversing a small circle atop a table in an art gallery, was originally performed in 1968-69. It was also performed in 1971 at the Sonnabend Gallery in New York, and on the 20 year anniversary of that performance, Gilbert & George did it again, this time for Haas's video and a small live audience. In the live performances, Gilbert & George repeated the performance of the song and dance for many hours. (Hence its inclusion in the category of Endurance Art). But in the 23-minute tape, each performance or portion of the performance of the song is offset by remarkably lucid interviews by Gilbert & George exploring the origin of the piece, their intentions for it, and their sense of its future. One of the very best (and clearest) discussions of art made about life, this tape should be shown to anyone interested in the philosophy of conceptual art and especially those interested in the ever fainter distinction between art and life.

As experimental video proceeded apace, of course it responded to the shifting political and intellectual currents of the '80s and '90s. Among the most powerful influences on experimental video and performance were feminism, and a bit later, the struggle for gay and lesbian rights. This struggle was refracted through the dismaying history of AIDS. The VDB's collection contains some of the best work done in these two fields in the past 30 years.

After a thorough investigation of the male gaze and the structure of patriarchy that pre-occupied experimental video artists such as Lynda Benglis and Suzanne Lacy (both well represented in the VDB's collection) in the '70s, feminist artists began to take up an interior mode of reflection and narration in video work of the '80s and '90s. Sadie Benning has been assembling an extended video diary of her life. At the center of that record is her discovery of sexuality and lesbian politics. Beginning in 1989 when she was only 16, Benning's work provides one of the most complete and well-told "coming of age" narratives I've seen. Vanalyne Green's work, also rooted in autobiography, examines those peculiar illnesses and symptoms given (and taken) in the name of love. From alcoholism in the family to sexually transmitted diseases without, Green mines personal history to create art about our twin desires for love and destruction.

Other notable feminist work in the VDB collection includes Martha Rosler's classic *Semiotics of the Kitchen* (1975), a witty and vivid demonstration of the ways in which domesticity cooks up violence against and within women. The Austrian-born Valie Export's *A Perfect Pair* (1987) sends up the commodification of the women's body and in a scene that updates what anthropologists call "the traffic in women" as a female prostitute and a male body builder flirt by suggesting new advertising spaces that they each can sell to new companies. Frightening and funny, Export's satire is becoming all too true.

Laurie Anderson's brilliant *What You Mean We?* (1986) takes up a Warholian trick: the busy star creates a clone, a stand-in, to handle her extensive interview requests. Witty and technologically adept at looking incompetent, Anderson also employs Walter Benjamin's elegiac text about the Angel of History to give her clone the words to a song, a song that haunts and aches some 70 years after he wrote it. Other highlights include the astonishing performances of Meredith Monk, Linda Montano, and Suzanne Lacy, all of whom advanced feminist live art in ways that are still being felt in the contemporary scene.

What You Mean We?
Laurie Anderson, 1986

Among the "younger generation" feminist artists in the VDB collection, Elisabeth Subrin and Miranda July are among the most talented. Subrin's *The Fancy* (2000) is particularly innovative. Based on the photography, life, and suicide of Francesca Woodman, a precociously talented photographer who killed herself in 1981, *The Fancy* imaginatively represents the scenes, architectural inspirations, and props central to Woodman's work. Employing a small group of women to re-perform Woodman's characteristic poses, Subrin uses video to animate the dead force of still photography, a deadness that seems particularly alive in the case of the deceased artist. As an homage and conversation across media—and across the line that divides life and death—*The Fancy* suggests that grief might be re-creative.

Grief has been central to the experimental videos that have been central to documenting and protesting the AIDS crisis. Tom Kalin, Gregg Bordowitz, Stuart Marshall, and Alisa Lebow have made especially crucial work in this area. The visual art collective Gran Fury (of which Kalin was a key member) documents the important ad campaign the collective created in *Kissing Doesn't Kill* (1990); his subsequent experimental work includes important very brief "commercials" of sorts, employing sentences from great writers such as Virginia Woolf, Jane Bowles, and James Baldwin. The English artist Marshall's *Bright Eyes* (1986) astutely deconstructs the repressions of the mass media and science central to the AIDS crisis. Created with passion, *Bright Eyes* is a call to arms, urging viewers to refuse to participate in such sanctioned repression. Lebow's

Bright Eyes
Stuart Marshall, 1986

Internal Combustion (1995) usefully addresses the issues of lesbians and AIDS. Bordowitz's work is deeply autobiographical and deeply intelligent. *Fast Trip, Long Drop* (1993) weaves together the artist's own HIV-positive diagnosis, the diagnosis of a woman friend's breast cancer, and the sudden death of his grandparents. A meditation on death and dying as an event that is both utterly personal and profoundly social, *Fast Trip, Long Drop* is an important contribution to death studies, as well as a crucial text in the brief history of art and AIDS.

The VDB distributes the best extant collection of the encounter between performance and video. Documenting the early work of artists as diverse in style and theme as Paul McCarthy and Richard Serra, and continuing on through more recent work by performers such as the French artist Orlan, who uses plastic surgery as the medium for her art, the VDB also has extensive holdings in anti-racist work as well. Guillermo Gómez-Peña's work is all here, as is the less well known but also crucial work of James Luna. Gómez-Peña's performances use the U.S.-Mexican border as a point of departure for a broader examination of borderlines in our political, erotic, linguistic, and technological imaginations. One of his virtuoso bits involves him playing both roles in a radio interview and during the "live" transmission on stage; the (imaginary) radio sporadically loses its transmission, thus allowing us to hear only bits and pieces of the interview. As we "fill in" the rest, Gómez-Peña demonstrates how it is we cope with what and who we cannot fully hear or acknowledge. Luna, a Native American artist, has done a series of brilliant and moving performances called Indian Tales. One of these is documented in *The History of the Luiseno People* (1993).

The VDB collection is full of surprises and has astonishing depth. Moreover, in many cases, the VDB has artists' entire corpuses, thus allowing scholars and commentators access to the development and trajectory of an artist's work. It's quite extraordinary, and we are lucky to have it.

VIDEO ART

®™ark

®™ark is an alternative mutual fund that pays dividends in cultural projects aimed at sabotage of corporate control. The aim of ®™ark is to bring subversion into the public marketplace. ®™ark sponsors a number of anti-corporate projects, described on their extensive web site, www.rtmark.com.

Bringing It to You!

Abate, Bobby

Bobby Abate, like Britney Spears, is a slave to ritual, commercialism, self-reflexivity, and contradiction. Not a boy, not yet a man—you might say he's painfully wedged under pop culture with his little head sticking out and screaming for help.

Acconci, Vito

A poet of the New York school in the early- and mid-1960s, Vito Acconci moved toward performance, sound, and video work by the end of the decade. Acconci changed direction in order to "define [his] body in space, find a ground for [him]self, an alternate ground for the page ground [he] had as a poet." Acconci's early performances—including *Claim* (1971) and *Seedbed* (1972)—were extremely controversial, transgressing assumed boundaries between public and private space, and between audience and performer. Positioning his own body as the simultaneous subject and object of the work, Acconci's early video tapes took advantage of the medium's self-reflexive potential in mediating his own and the viewer's attention. Consistently exploring the dynamics of intimacy, trust, and power, the focus of Acconci's projects gradually moved from his physical body

Bringing It All to You!
®™ark
2001, 53:00, U.S., color, sound
®™ark is an organization dedicated to bringing anti-corporate subversion and sabotage into the public marketplace. This updated video compilation includes a glitzy promotion for the ®™ark system (*Bringing It All to You!*); a behind-the-scenes look at some ®™ark propaganda efforts; an ®™ark PowerPoint presentation concerning "the Y2K bug"; a Danish television report about ®™ark and Hitler; a Boston news report about ®™ark; and, finally, the grand prize winner of ®™ark 1998 Corporate Poetry Contest, reading his winning entry. This updated version also includes a segment on www.gwbush.com and anti-eToys news stories. This compilation is highly recommended for anyone who wishes to get a more complete picture of how ®™ark intervenes in and disrupts corporate logic.

Bringing It to You!
®™ark
1998, 11:00, U.S., color, sound
Corporations are persons and have been for over a century. Since 1886, when the US Supreme Court gave them full constitutional rights, corporations have used their wealth and power to subvert democracy and its processes. But now, with this video, you can learn how the same inalienable rights that corporations have stolen over the years are used by ®™ark to bring anti-corporate sabotage into the public marketplace.

One Mile per Minute
Bobby Abate
2002, 10:00, U.S., color, sound
Take a joyride through comfortable suburbia—a landscape molded by seductive television and corporate America (and keep in mind: disaster is another logo for your consumption...). This is the age of the "culture jammed" consumer preened with *Friends* hair, *Survivor* courage, and CNN awareness. A generation emptying their wallets for the most important corporate product of all: lifestyle. The psychological road trip across a slightly battered America travels at *One Mile per Minute*.

Association Area
Vito Acconci
1971, 1:02:13, U.S., b&w, sound
As a document of an early performance, this tape details the process of orientating the body and self in space, providing a physical metaphor for the process of adjusting oneself in society. "Blindfolded, ears plugged: our goal is to sense each other's movement and bearing, to attempt to assume the same movement and bearing. An off-screen voice, heard only by the audience, gives directions that would help us attain our goal."
–Vito Acconci, "Concentration-Container-Assimilation," *Avalanche* 6 (Fall 1972)
This title was in the original Castelli-Sonnabend video art collection.

Centers
Vito Acconci
1971, 22:43, U.S., b&w, sound
"Pointing at my own image on the video monitor: my attempt is to keep my finger constantly in the center of the screen—I keep narrowing my focus into my finger. The result [the TV image] turns the activity around: a pointing away from myself, at an outside viewer."
–Vito Acconci, "Body as Place-Moving in on Myself, Performing Myself," *Avalanche* 6 (Fall 1972)
"By its very mise-en-scène, *Centers* typifies the structural characteristics of the video medium. For *Centers* was made by Acconci's using the video monitor as a mirror. As we look at the artist sighting along his outstretched arm

Acconci, Vito
(continued)

(*Conversions,* 1971) toward the psychology of interpersonal transactions (*Pryings,* 1971), and later, to the cultural and political implications of the performative space he set up for the camera (*The Red Tapes,* 1976). Since the late '70s, Acconci has designed architectural and installation works for public spaces.

and forefinger toward the center of the screen we are watching, what we see is a sustained tautology: a line of sight that begins at Acconci's plane of vision and ends at the eyes of his projected double."
—Rosalind Krauss, "Video: The Aesthetics of Narcissism," *October* 1 (Spring 1976)
This title was in the original Castelli-Sonnabend video art collection.

Claim Excerpts
Vito Acconci
1971, 1:00:20, U.S., b&w, sound
"In this record of a live performance, Acconci gives physical manifestation to the subterranean regions of the artist's mind and will, revealing the effort he must make as an artist to simultaneously convince himself and his audience. Perhaps no other piece from the early 1970s more thoroughly spells out the psychologized drama engendered by performance-based video…. Blindfolded, seated in a basement at the end of a long flight of stairs, armed with metal pipes and a crowbar, threatening to swing at anyone who tried to come near, Acconci simultaneously invited and prohibited every visitor to the 93 Grand Street loft to descend into the world of the unconscious."
—Kathy O'Dell, "Performance, Video, and Trouble in the Home," in *Illuminating Video: An Essential Guide to Video Art,* eds. Doug Hall and Sally Jo Fifer (New York: Aperture Books, 1991)
This title was in the original Castelli-Sonnabend video art collection.

Command Performance
Vito Acconci
1973, 57:23, U.S., b&w, sound
Torn over the pressure to perform for his audience, Acconci fantasizes about "a dancing bear" who takes his place, performing in the spotlight, doing what others want, "what I always had to do." The viewer is placed in the position of an authority or analyst, above Acconci's head, listening to his hallucination. This fantasy becomes increasingly erotic as Acconci unburdens himself psychologically and reveals his contradictory need to control and to be controlled.
This title was in the original Castelli-Sonnabend video art collection.

Face-Off
Vito Acconci
1972, 32:54, U.S., b&w, sound
Acconci listens to his own recorded monologue of sexually intimate secrets and repeatedly tries to obscure these secrets by shouting over the tape, demonstrating the paradoxical situation of the artist confounded by two desires: to reveal oneself for the sake of pleasing the audience, and the conflicting desire to protect one's own ego. As viewers, we are intrigued and tantalized by the confession we never hear. In this way, Acconci characteristically implicates the viewer in his performance; the viewer awaits and encourages the artist's sacrifice, reveling in the promise of his self-exposure.
This title was in the original Castelli-Sonnabend video art collection.

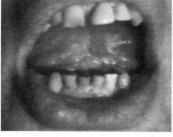
Open Book

Open Book
Vito Acconci
1974, 9:10, U.S., color, sound
Acconci's open mouth is framed by the camera in an extreme close-up, bringing the viewer uncomfortably close. A desperate sense of strained urgency comes across as Acconci gasps, "I'll accept you, I won't shut down, I won't shut you out…. I'm open to you, I'm open to everything…. This is not a trap, we can go inside, yes, come inside…." Acconci continues to plead in this way for the length of the tape, his mouth held unnaturally wide open. The pathological psychology of such enforced openness betrays a desperate struggle to accept and be accepted by others. The sustained image of Acconci's open mouth also evidences a sinister, vaguely threatening streak that is more or less evident in much of Acconci's work.
This title was in the original Castelli-Sonnabend video art collection.

Pryings

The Red Tapes

Pryings

Vito Acconci

1971, 16:16, U.S., b&w, sound

This extraordinary performance carries a wealth of associative meanings in the sexual dynamics of privacy and power—man and woman pitted against each other in a struggle for mental and physical control.

"In *Pryings*, one of his earliest and least verbal tapes, the artist is seen trying to force open and gain entry into any and all of the orifices of a woman's face. His persistence outlasts the running time of the tape, as does the persistence of the woman under attack, who manages to persevere in her attempt to guard her metaphysical privacy."

—David Ross, "A Provisional Overview of Artists' Television in the US," *Studio International* 191 (May/June 1976)

This title was in the original Castelli-Sonnabend video art collection.

The Red Tapes

Vito Acconci

1976, 2:20:00, U.S., b&w, sound

The Red Tapes is a three-part epic that features the diary musings of a committed outsider: revolutionary, prisoner, artist. The series offers a fragmented mythic narrative and a poetic reassessment of the radical social and aesthetic aspirations of the previous decade. Acconci maps a "topography of the self," constructing scenes that suggest both the intimate video space of close-up and the panoramic landscape of film space. The production of *The Red Tapes* involved painters and filmmakers Erika Beckman, Ilona Granet, Richie O'Halloran, Kathy Rusch, David Salle, and Michael Zwack.

"I'm thinking of landscape in terms of movie—I'm forced then to treat landscape as a dream, myth, history of a culture. Thinking of person, close-up, in terms of video—I'm forced then to treat person on-the-spot news, convoluted soap opera."

—Vito Acconci, 1976

Excerpt (Tape 2, 58:00) also available on the anthology *Surveying the First Decade, Program 3.*

This title was in the original Castelli-Sonnabend video art collection.

Remote Control

Vito Acconci

1971, 1:02:15, U.S., b&w, sound

Two performers, Acconci and a young woman, occupy two wooden boxes in separate rooms, connected via monitor, camera, and microphone. The situation is symbolic of a vicarious and distended power relation, a relationship built through and reliant upon technological mediation. Watching her on a monitor, Acconci coaches the woman through tying herself up, urging her to pretend he is winding the rope around her legs and neck. Acconci states, "The tying up is an occasion for me to get into wrapping you up in a more generalized way." The rope represents Acconci's will in the woman's space, binding her physically and mentally, as she stops resisting and acquiesces to his demands. As a study of consent and control, an underlying theme of the work is the manipulative potential of media technology, which reaches isolated viewers and subjects them to its organizing control.

Note: *Remote Control* was originally a two-channel installation. To recreate Acconci's intended environment, each of the 62-minute tapes should be shown simultaneously on separate monitors.

This title was in the original Castelli-Sonnabend video art collection.

Sounding Board

Vito Acconci

1971, 21:26, U.S., b&w, sound

Acconci literally feels the music in this tape as he lays down on speakers playing jazz. The sound pulses through his body while a collaborator massages his nude back in time with the music, occasionally striking Acconci like a rhythm instrument.

This title was in the original Castelli-Sonnabend video art collection.

Theme Song
Vito Acconci
1973, 33:17, U.S., b&w, sound
In a vile and ingenious way, Acconci pleads with the camera/spectator to join with him, to come to him, promising to be honest and begging, "I need it, you need it, c'mon... look how easy it is." Acconci addresses the viewer as a sexual partner, acting as if no distance existed between them. The monitor becomes an agent of intimate address, presenting a disingenuous intimacy that is one-sided and pure fantasy, much like the popular love songs in the background with which Acconci croons, "I'll be your baby, I'll be your baby tonight, yeah, yeah."
This title was in the original Castelli-Sonnabend video art collection.

Turn-On
Vito Acconci
1974, 21:56, U.S., b&w, sound
Acconci again confronts both the viewer's and his own expectations of his performance, saying, "I've waited for the perfect time, for the perfect piece, I'm tired of waiting... but no, you want me to have something ready for you, something prepared." Acconci addresses the artist's perpetual wait for both inspiration and appreciation. He pulls apart the relationship of the artist to the audience, which for Acconci constitutes a mixture of independence and co-dependence, relying on the viewer to both validate and motivate his work. Near the end of the tape, Acconci turns against his viewer, his work and himself, saying, "It's me, I can't find any reason anymore to do art.... I'm waiting for you to leave."
This title was in the original Castelli-Sonnabend video art collection.

Turn-On

Two Track
Vito Acconci
1971, 28:35, U.S., b&w, sound
Acconci sits with a man and a woman before a microphone. The man and the woman read from two different texts (novels by Mickey Spillane and Raymond Chandler), and Acconci repeats everything the man says. From time to time, an off-screen voice asks Acconci something about what the woman has been saying, and he tries to answer. The focus of the tape is the relationship between modes of attention, direct and peripheral, in a situation where simultaneous strands of information are being presented.
This title was in the original Castelli-Sonnabend video art collection.

Undertone
Vito Acconci
1972, 37:20, U.S., b&w, sound
In this now infamous tape, exemplary of his early transgressive performance style, Acconci sits and relates a masturbatory fantasy about a girl rubbing his legs under the table. Carrying on a rambling dialogue that shifts back and forth between the camera/spectator and himself, Acconci sexualizes the implicit contract between performer and viewer—the viewer serving as a voyeur who makes the performance possible by watching and completing the scene, believing the fantasy.
"In a visual style of address exactly equivalent to the presidential address, the face-to-face camera regards The Insignificant Man making the Outrageous Confession that is as likely as not to be an Incredible Lie. Who can escape the television image of Nixon?"
—David Antin, "Television: Video's Frightful Parent," *Artforum* (December 1975)
Excerpt (10:00) also available on the anthology *Surveying the First Decade, Program 1.*
This title was in the original Castelli-Sonnabend video art collection.

Waterways: 4 Saliva Studies
Vito Acconci
1971, 22:25, U.S., b&w, sound

Acconci explodes the notion of an artist's creation, his creative act being the build-up and discharge of saliva, an activity more properly belonging to the realm of necessary and autonomic bodily functions than art. Positioning himself as a hyper self-conscious artistic subject, Acconci fuses the terrains of body art and process art, formulating the body as process, and art as a natural function of the body.

Also available on the anthology *Endurance, Reel 1.*

This title was in the original Castelli-Sonnabend video art collection.

Vito Acconci: An Interview (see On Art and Artists)
Vito Acconci – Conversations (see On Art and Artists)

Ahwesh, Peggy

Peggy Ahwesh has made mesmerizing, experimental films and videos for two decades. Her eclectic works explore gender and cultural identities through deeply textured visuals and fascinating narratives. Her work explores dark themes of ritual, sexual exploration, and death through medium-precise methods, from grainy Super-8 to decayed 16mm to the virtuality of digital video. She has taught at Brown University, the San Francisco Art Institute, University of Wisconsin-Milwaukee, the School of Visual Arts, and Bard College.

73 Suspect Words & Heaven's Gate
Peggy Ahwesh
2001-02, 8:00, U.S., b&w, sound

Two text videos from a series that distills to a poetic and symbolic core, a variety of texts, source code, search results, and/or coded messages from the unruly databases that glut the net.

Only available on *Pistolary! Films and Videos by Peggy Ahwesh, Disc 3.*

The Deadman
Peggy Ahwesh in collaboration with Keith Sanborn
1990, 40:00, U.S., b&w, sound, 16mm to video

"Charting the adventures of a near-naked heroine who sets in motion a scabrous free-form orgy before returning to the house to die, this film combines elegance, raunchy defilement and barbaric splendor."
–Jonathan Rosenbaum, "Dubbed and Dubber," *Chicago Reader* (21 February 1997)

With Jennifer Montgomery, Ramon Quanta la Gusta, Scott Shat, Diane Torr, and Leslie Singer.

Only available on *Pistolary! Films and Videos by Peggy Ahwesh, Disc 2.*

Martina's Playhouse
Peggy Ahwesh
1989, 20:00, U.S., color, sound, Super-8 to video

"In *Martina's Playhouse* everything is up for grabs. The little girl of the title oscillates from narrator to reader to performer and from the role of baby to that of mother. While the roles she adopts may be learned, they are not set, and she moves easily between them. Similarly, in filmmaker Peggy Ahwesh's playhouse of encounters with friends, objects aren't merely objects but shift between layers of meaning. Men are conspicuously absent, a 'lack' reversing the Lacanian/Freudian constructions of women as Ahwesh plays with other possibilities."
–Kathy Geritz, program notes (Berkeley: Pacific Film Archive, 1990)

With Martina Torr and Jennifer Montgomery.

Only available on *Pistolary! Films and Videos by Peggy Ahwesh, Disc 1.*

Nocturne
Peggy Ahwesh
1998, 28:12, U.S., b&w, sound, 16mm to video

The woman has perhaps murdered her lover and is living in an unstable world when he returns to her at night, in her dreams and into her arms, as witness to the subversive violence of nature, corporeality, and desire.

With Anne Kugler, Bradley Eros, and Karen Sullivan. Additional cinematography by Robert Fenz.

Only available on *Pistolary! Films and Videos by Peggy Ahwesh, Disc 2.*

Pistolary! Films and Videos by Peggy Ahwesh

Total running time 3:24:42.
Contents:
Disc 1:
The Scary Movie, Peggy Ahwesh, 1993, 9:00, U.S., b&w, sound, 16mm
 to video
She Puppet, Peggy Ahwesh, 2001, 15:30, U.S., color, sound
Martina's Playhouse, Peggy Ahwesh, 1989, 20:00, U.S., color, sound,
 Super-8 to video
The Star Eaters, Peggy Ahwesh, 2003, 24:00, U.S., color, sound
Disc 2:
The Deadman, Peggy Ahwesh in collaboration with Keith Sanborn, 1990,
 37:00, U.S., b&w, sound, 16mm to video
Nocturne, Peggy Ahwesh, 1998, 30:00, U.S., b&w, sound, 16mm to video
Disc 3:
the vision machine, Peggy Ahwesh, 1997, 20:00, U.S., color and b&w,
 sound, 16mm to video.
73 Suspect Words & Heaven's Gate, Peggy Ahwesh, 2001-02, 8:00, U.S.,
 b&w, sound
Strange Weather, Peggy Ahwesh in collaboration with Margie Strosser,
1993, 50:00, U.S., color, sound

The Scary Movie

Peggy Ahwesh
1993, 10:00, U.S., b&w, sound, 16mm to video
Two girls personalize the horror genre with a plot and shot-by-shot structure
of their own design, reveling in their ability to reproduce the tropes of horror
while, at the same time, taking control of its meaning.
With Martina Torr and Sonja Mereu.
Only available on *Pistolary! Films and Videos by Peggy Ahwesh, Disc 1.*

She Puppet

Peggy Ahwesh
2001, 17:00, U.S., color, sound
Lara Croft, the virtual girl-doll of the late 20th century, is recast as a triad of
her personas: the alien, the orphan, and the clone in this work based on
appropriated footage from the game *Tomb Raider.*
Only available on *Pistolary! Films and Videos by Peggy Ahwesh, Disc 1.*

The Star Eaters

Peggy Ahwesh
2003, 24:00, U.S., color, sound
A short and inconclusive treatise on women and gambling. The allure of risk-
taking, the contradictions of excessive behavior, and a penchant for failure
combine in this fairy-tale set in the abandoned decay that was once a glamorous Atlantic City. A sentimental education at the seashore off-season.
With Jackie Smith, Alex Auder, and Ricardo Dominguez.
Only available on *Pistolary! Films and Videos by Peggy Ahwesh, Disc 1.*

Strange Weather

Peggy Ahwesh in collaboration with Margie Strosser
1993, 50:00, U.S., color, sound
A quartet of crack addicts, absorbed by their life of pure sensation, are holed
up inside while the world outside is about to explode.
"*Strange Weather* is about a moment when the roar of the elements becomes
an imperceptible din and all belief is suspended. Jan, a paranoid, upper-class
pipedreamer; Centipede, a sexually tepid rockhound; and Patty, strung-out on
fantasies of the good life, comprise a stuporous enclave, protecting themselves against elemental moral decay from without. But storm warnings on
the tube augur a fearsome change. Shot in Pixelvision, Peggy Ahwesh's taint-
ed soap opera is by visual definition a small world. Minute details—a smolder-
ing cigarette, the grout between tiles, particles of kitty litter—are rendered
large but with anemic resolution as though the characters' surroundings have

Strange Weather

prominence but no meaning. In *Strange Weather*, Florida is anything but a picture postcard."
–Steve Seid, *Ex Post-Factory: After Warhol* (Berkeley: Pacific Film Archive, 1994)
With Deirdre Lewis, Cheryl Dunye, Jennifer Kay Baker, and Franck Messin
Only available on *Pistolary! Films and Videos by Peggy Ahwesh, Disc 3.*

the vision machine

Peggy Ahwesh
1997, 20:00, U.S., color and b&w, sound, 16mm to video
The spinning disks of Duchamp and the sex jokes of Buñuel collide in this essay about the feminine speaking subject, her wit, and its relation to her unconscious.
With Lucy Smith and Diane Torr.
Only available on *Pistolary! Films and Videos by Peggy Ahwesh, Disc 3.*

Almy, Max

Max Almy has experimented with video, film, computer, and interactive media in works ranging from multi-media installations to single-channel works for exhibition and broadcast. Her early video works explore the complexity of post-modern attitudes toward technology, media, and social issues.

Leaving the 20th Century

Deadline

Max Almy
1981, 4:00, U.S., color, sound
An insert square of a man running is superimposed over a magnified mouth that speaks to him–first in nurturing encouragement, then with a no-win *Mommie Dearest* kind of criticism. Originally presented as an installation on six monitors, *Deadline* focuses on "the stress man feels in the urban environment," using a range of digital video effects to stretch, compress, flip and fracture the image. Whereas her previous video projects focused on details of behavior within interpersonal relationships, this piece shifts to focus on man's larger relationship to society.

Leaving the 20th Century

Max Almy
1982, 11:00, U.S., color, sound
Believing that we are, "dragging our feet into the 21st century," Almy made this video trilogy to celebrate technology and the future in an ironic melange of politics, sociology, sexuality, and economics. Flawlessly melding sound and image, the tape moves through three sections, "Countdown," "Departure," and "Arrival." In the end, Almy posits this paradox: technology as a human development is rapidly making humans obsolete and interpersonal contact impossible, making the future of man's presence and very existence uncertain.
Also available on the anthology *e-[d]entity, Tape 2.*

Modern Times

Max Almy
1979, 30:00, U.S., color, sound
Originally presented as a live performance piece using actors, multiple monitors, and music, *Modern Times* is a consolidation of seven short chapters in the life of a modern woman. In the first sequence, the objects in a suburban home are inventoried: "nice couch," "nice car," and so on–ending with the titles "nice concept," "nice image"–and unmasking this materialistic world as an impossible consumer fantasy. In the next scene, an attractive man sunbathes. It is only this image, accompanied by a voice, which at first describes him as an irresistible being, then, after some strange and almost imperceptible wordplay, finally declares him extremely boring.

Perfect Leader

Max Almy
1983, 4:00, U.S., color, sound
A satire of a political television spot, *Perfect Leader* shows that ideology is the product and power is the payoff. The process of political imagemaking and the marketing of a candidate is revealed as an omnipotent computer manufactures the perfect candidate, offering up three political types: Mr. Nice Guy, an evangelist, and an Orwellian Big Brother. Symbols of political promises quickly degenerate into icons of oppression and nuclear war.

The Thinker
Max Almy
1989, 7:00, U.S., color, sound
The evolution of man from ape to yuppie flashes before the viewer amid 3-D animation, paint box images, and digital compositions while a narrator provides satiric play-by-play commentary. Conceptually, verbally, and graphically, man leaps forward through the centuries to master the litany of pop clichés and consumer culture acronyms of the modern age. And yet, he's never quite free of his original grunts.

Utopia
Max Almy in collaboration with Teri Yarbrow
1994, 5:00, U.S., color, sound
Playing off the notion of "interactivity," *Utopia* poses itself as a video game plugged into the social consciousness of contemporary California. The viewer/player seemingly makes choices from the menu offering utopian or dystopian realities; however, the score is always the same: the winner loses and vice-versa. *Utopia* combines video, oil paintings, and CDI Interactive media and features Rachel Rosenthal as the host of a macabre interactive game that pushes the boundaries of performance and interactive media.

Alpert, John
(see Downtown Community Television Center)

Ammann, Hanspeter

Hanspeter Ammann has been making videos and installation works since the 1980s; his work has been shown extensively by international festivals, galleries, museums, and broadcasters. He lives in Zurich and London and has practiced as a Freudian psychoanalyst since 1992.

Couch
Hanspeter Ammann
1994, 11:00, Switzerland, b&w, sound
From the point of view of the psychoanalyst's chair, we witness images that place us implicitly within the scene. The images explore the relationship between two embracing men and suggest a complex and ambiguous web of associations. The embrace is both erotic and tender, and invites questions about power relationships. The pain of love and possible rejection is exposed through the flash of a naked leg or the vulnerability of a fleeting expression.

Couple
Hanspeter Ammann
1998, 11:00, Switzerland, color, sound
"The title implies a relationship between the two persons in the frame of the image. The woman in the foreground appears somewhat sad, the man in the background concerned. In the slowed-down motion of the video, these expressions become intensified, and heightened to levels of romantic tragedy by the accompaniment of Chet Baker's melancholy song, 'You Don't Know What Love Is.'
"As we become more involved in this narration, the slightest shift of her head or the subtlest movement of his eyes become important players in this relation.... Stories come to mind; one's own experiences; memories of friends relating situations of crises—any one of them could fit this couple...."
—Annette Schindler and Hanspeter Ammann, *Where Is Your Rupture?* (New York: Swiss Institute, 1998)

Anderson, Laurie

Laurie Anderson has been one of the most distinctive and influential artists of the past quarter century. Her high-tech performances have repeatedly redefined the avant-garde and multimedia as they pulse with electronic currents and hybridize installation, projection, music, storytelling, movement, and sound.

What You Mean We?
Laurie Anderson
1986, 20:00, U.S., color, sound
Strapped for time due to her busy schedule of personal appearances, Anderson creates a rather clumsy-looking clone to take over and keep up her artistic production. Anderson plays both parts, pitting the chain-smoking, productive male half against the laid-back female half. In the end, one highly successful clone begets another clone, a situation spoofing the rise and fall of the '80s art star.

Laurie Anderson: An Interview (see On Art and Artists)
Laurie Anderson: Conversations (see On Art and Artists)

Andrews, Lawrence

Lawrence Andrews's powerful and effective work tackles difficult social issues such as race, power, and representation. His tapes are virtual epics, addressing broad themes in an open-ended, digressive collage style of appropriated images, text, and original footage.

Angelo, Nancy and Candice Compton

Angelo and Compton were actively involved with the Los Angeles Woman's Building, an outgrowth of the Feminist Studio Workshop. They collaborated on the videotape *Nun and Deviant* (1976), and the work reflects many of the theoretical concerns and activities generated within these pioneering institutions. Angelo was also member of Sisters of Survival, a performance group, and a member of the Feminist Art Workers.

Animal Charm

Animal Charm is the collaborative project of Rich Bott and Jim Fetterley, sound and media artists. Assuming a deconstructive take on propriety, Animal Charm began creating videos as an act of Electronic Civil Disobedience. Diving the dumpsters of video production companies and scrounging through countless hours of industrial, documentary, and corporate video footage, Animal Charm often edits the tapes in live mix performances. By re-editing images derived from a wide variety of sources, they scramble media codes, creating a kind of convulsive babble that disrupts conventional forms with subversive messages.

An I for an I
Lawrence Andrews
1987, 18:00, U.S., color, sound

A formidable collage of striking images, this powerful and provocative work confronts racial violence through images of ecological mayhem, machismo, pornography, and Third World poverty—images that return to the taboo body of a black man. "Directed and produced by our culture," *An I for An I* studies how violence is internalized and psychologized as it overlaps soundtracks, printed texts, recurrent images, doctored footage, and split screens. The tape attacks racist culture and pleads for an alternative recourse to violence.

And They Came Riding into Town on Black and Silver Horses
Lawrence Andrews
1992, 30:00, U.S., color, sound

And They Came Riding into Town on Black and Silver Horses looks at how media representations shape our perception of violence and violent crime, in effect creating racist stereotypes. Andrews suggests that the evidence against young black men is gathered not at the scene of the crime but at the scene of representation. Entrained by the actual story of an individual wrongly jailed for a crime based on "eye-witness" testimony, the tape is composed as a series of verses—sometimes poetic, sometimes documentary—with segments using appropriated images and interviews with people connected to the event.

Nun and Deviant
Nancy Angelo and Candace Compton
1976, 20:00, U.S., b&w, sound

A classic example of feminist performance videos of the 1970s, which often incorporated autobiography, expansion of self through personae, and assertions of a new identity for women. In *Nun and Deviant* the performers come to happier terms with their identities both as women and as artists. As Angelo and Compton don and dismantle stereotypical guises before the camera/viewer, *Nun and Deviant* explores how repressive representations circulating in our culture are formulated as opposites such as Madonna-whore (nun-deviant)—cliches that force women to assume restrictive, paradoxical roles.

Excerpt (13:00) also available on the anthology *Surveying the First Decade, Program 4.*

Animal Charm Videoworks: Volume 1

This compilation is a fresh, witty, and compelling addition to video's rich legacy of media deconstruction. Through appropriation and reassemblage, these intriguing works upset the hypnotic spectacle of TV viewing by displacing its logic and forcing viewers to make new connections among its codes and conventions. While this disruption is playful, it also reveals the tragic underbelly of corporate message-making—the way it appropriates and suppresses nature and "unpredictability," the way it preys on human vulnerability, and the way it shamelessly celebrates mediocrity and distraction.
Total running time 19:00.
Contents:
Ashley, Animal Charm, 1997, 9:00, U.S., color, sound
Lightfoot Fever, Animal Charm, 1996, 1:30, U.S., color, sound
Slow Gin Soul Stallion, Animal Charm, 1996, 2:30, U.S., color, sound
Stuffing, Animal Charm, 1998, 4:00, U.S., color, sound
Working Together, Animal Charm, 1996, 2:00, U.S., color, sound

Animal Charm Videoworks: Volume 2, Hot Mirror Mix

A collection of videotapes from Animal Charm that reconfigure found footage, creating a compelling new world of odd juxtaposition and sinister strangeness.
Total running time 26:00.
Contents:

Family Court, Animal Charm, 1998, 4:00, U.S., color, sound
Hot Mirror, Animal Charm, 1998, 11:30, U.S., color, sound
Marbles, Animal Charm, 1998, 6:30, U.S., color, sound
Mark Roth, Animal Charm, 1998, 4:00, U.S., color, sound

Animal Charm Videoworks: Volume 3, Computer Smarts
Furthering the Animal Charm mission to undermine normality and create new stories from old, the videotapes in this collection seek to reinterpret and/or disrupt the flow of found footage narrative.
Total running time 14:15.
Contents:
Body Prep, Animal Charm, 2002, 1:30, U.S., color, sound
Brite Tip, Animal Charm, 2002, 3:00, U.S., color, sound
Camera Dance, Animal Charm, 2002, 3:45, U.S., color, sound
Computer Smarts, Animal Charm, 2002, 1:30, U.S., color, sound
Il Mouille, Animal Charm, 2002, 4:30, U.S., color, sound

Ashley

Ashley
Animal Charm
1997, 9:00, U.S., color, sound
Ashley seems to develop a conventional story about a modern mother and wife with typically modern desires. But the insertion of incongruous soap opera scenes soon ensures that the seductive images take on an absurd and oppressive charge.
"The antiseptic cleanliness of the imagery has a superficial appeal, but begins to feel claustrophobic—or toxic—after prolonged exposure."
–Fred Camper, "First Friday Film," *Chicago Reader* (26 December 1997)
"A tour de force of incongruous juxtapositions, startling dislocations and ingenious visual rhymes assembled from the banal detritus of late night TV."
–New York Video Festival (1998)

Also available on the compilation *Animal Charm Videoworks: Volume 1* and on the anthology *American Psycho(drama): Sigmund Freud vs. Henry Ford.*

Body Prep

Body Prep
Animal Charm
2002, 1:30, U.S., color, sound
Body Prep helps fortify and support the body during any level of activity—low, medium, or high intensity. It compares various alternatives to weightlifting with natural and artificial light sources. Exercise is explored through the change of seasons.

Also available on the compilation *Animal Charm Videoworks: Volume 3, Computer Smarts.*

Brite Tip
Animal Charm
2002, 3:00, U.S., color, sound
"*Brite Tip* explores the indoctrination of children and police through an assortment of cross-fades, wipes, and other stock transitions. A highly danceable essay on breastfeeding."
–Gavin Smith
Also available on the compilation *Animal Charm Videoworks: Volume 3, Computer Smarts.*

Camera Dance
Animal Charm
2002, 3:45, U.S., color, sound
The union of humankind and the camera is a long and sordid tale. This lyrical dance illustrates the inseparable nature of the two.
Also available on the compilation A*nimal Charm Videoworks: Volume 3, Computer Smarts.*

Computer Smarts
Animal Charm
2002, 1:30, U.S., color, sound
By accident, the content of a computer encyclopedia is transferred into the brain of an animated parrot resulting in the emotional breakdown of a fine peach. "I would never have known how to do anything on my computer if it wasn't for *Computer Smarts*."
—Mark Roth
Also available on the compilation *Animal Charm Videoworks: Volume 3, Computer Smarts.*

Family Court
Animal Charm
1998, 4:00, U.S., color, sound
Family Court introduces us to the world of good, clean, family fun and leisure.
Also available on the compilation *Animal Charm Videoworks: Volume 2, Hot Mirror Mix.*

Family Court

Hot Mirror
Animal Charm
1998, 11:30, U.S., color, sound
A hyper-collage endurance test of sado-masochistic proportions, mixing an anthology of corporate video music with a feng shui video.
Also available on the compilation *Animal Charm Videoworks: Volume 2, Hot Mirror Mix.*

Il Mouille
Animal Charm
2002, 4:30, U.S., color, sound
You never thought that Franco-American relations could be so fun! A French thriller in the tradition of the Marquis de Sade, getting it on with Roger Corman's from-the-hip philosophy.
Also available on the compilation *Animal Charm Videoworks: Volume 3, Computer Smarts.*

Lightfoot Fever
Animal Charm
1996, 1:30, U.S., color, sound
Fuelled by lavish doses of disjointed hyper-editing, super-talented Jim Bailey dances with wild animals in this hot and exciting performance of "Fever."
Also available on the compilation *Animal Charm Videoworks: Volume 1* and on the anthology *American Psycho(drama): Sigmund Freud vs. Henry Ford.*

Marbles
Animal Charm
1998, 6:30, U.S., color, sound
Meatballs - (Bill Murray + leading cast) = *Marbles*. A Hollywood classic re-visited and re-edited until our hero is no longer in sight.
Also available on the compilation *Animal Charm Videoworks: Volume 2, Hot Mirror Mix.*

Marbles

Mark Roth
Animal Charm
1998, 4:00, U.S., color, sound
An electronic disturbance created during a live audio meltdown by Animal Charm as part of their *Hot Mirror Mix* in the fall of 1998.
Also available on the compilation *Animal Charm Videoworks: Volume 2, Hot Mirror Mix.*

Preserve Your Estate

Animal Charm

1998, 9:30, U.S., color, sound

This single-channel tape was created from a 4-channel live mix of 4 VCRs, an A/V mixer, and a sampler. Hypnotic music, idiosyncratic singing, and soft yet insistent voice-overs accompany television images portraying notions of happiness, the work ethic, and social success in a subtly alienating video collage. "Repeat with me: I now feel confident about opening to others and projecting charisma."

Slow Gin Soul Stallion

Animal Charm

1996, 2:30, U.S., color, sound

The unusual combination of a sound like a singing saw accompanies sweet images of frolicking lambs in the meadow, galloping horses, and a strange boy, is eerily beautiful and pure.

Also available on the compilation *Animal Charm Videoworks: Volume 1*.

Stuffing

Animal Charm

1998, 4:00, U.S., color, sound

In this masterful example of video montage, a monkey is mesmerized as he watches two dolphins toss a woman from snout to snout. Go cross-eyed with cross-cutting. Sometimes, in order to prevent the insidious absorption of mass media, it is necessary to apply Vaseline to your eyes and ears. Other times, you only need to watch *Stuffing*—it's inside of everything.

Also available on the compilation *Animal Charm Videoworks: Volume 1* and on the anthology *American Psycho(drama): Sigmund Freud vs. Henry Ford*.

Target

Animal Charm

1999, 8:30, U.S., color, sound

Why is this injured man driving around and around a shopping center parking lot? Just what is his *Target*? An atmospheric mystery tale that hints at a sad story.

Working Together

Animal Charm

1996, 2:00, U.S., color, sound

What are all of these photographers trying to capture, and just who is collaborating with whom? This short piece could be a take on fame and the cult of the personality—or a tourist portrait with the audience as subject.

Also available on the compilation *Animal Charm Videoworks: Volume 1*.

Animal Charm: An Interview (see On Art and Artists).

Stuffing

Ant Farm

A San Francisco-based collective of artists and architects working from 1968 to 1978, Ant Farm's activity was distinctly interdisciplinary—combining architecture, performance, media, happenings, sculpture, and graphic design. With works that functioned as art, social critique, and pop anthropology, Ant Farm tore into the cultural fabric of post-World War II, Vietnam-era America and became one of the first groups to address television's pervasive presence in everyday life.

As graphic artists, Ant Farm contributed to numerous underground publications, including

Cadillac Ranch/Media Burn

Ant Farm

1975, 37:00, U.S., color, sound

"We buried ten Cadillacs in a row alongside Interstate 40 (the old Route 66), just west of Amarillo, Texas; each car represented a model change in the evolution of the tail fin. This was clearly a sculptural act, but with a minimal amount of formal manipulation.

Media Burn, created a year later in San Francisco, was a live performance. It was a spectacle staged for the camera culminating in the 4000 pound *Phantom Dream Car* crashing through a pyramid of TV sets to the cheers of the audience of 400. This image and the videotape have become classics of the first decade of video art."

—Chip Lord, 1988

Ant Farm
(continued)

Radical Software, and designed Michael Shamberg's *Guerrilla Television* (1971). Ant Farm members included Chip Lord, Doug Michels, Hudson Marquez, and Curtis Schreier. T.R. Uthco was a multi-media performance art collective that engaged in satirical critiques of mass media images and cultural myths, using irony, theatricality, and spectacle as its primary strategies. Founded by Doug Hall, Diane Andrews Hall, and Jody Procter in 1970.

Antin, Eleanor

Eleanor Antin has been a leading performance artist since the 1970s, using fictive personas to explore the idea of the self and female identity as developed in feminist writings. Her performances feature a recurring set of "historical" characters—past lives invented and acted out by Antin, including Russian ballerina Eleanora Antinova and Nurse Eleanor of the Crimean War.

Antioch College Free Library
(see People's Communication Network)

Arnold, Skip

Los Angeles-based artist Skip Arnold follows in the tradition of Chris Burden, Paul McCarthy, and Bob Flanagan, using his body as his medium for work that evokes forms of power and aggression. Arnold's slight build heightens his physical provocation: there is a brutal simplicity to Arnold's projects as he courts physical risk and evinces a punk sensibility. Many of Arnold's performances take place outside the boundaries of the art world, finding audiences in nightclubs and on cable television.

Artenstein, Isaac
(see Gómez-Peña, Guillermo)

Artists TV Network
(see On Art and Artists)

Atlas, Charles
(see Paik, Nam June and Rainer, Yvonne)

Austin Community TV
(see Stoney, George)

Avalos, David

David Avalos works make confrontational and philosophical works that engage in the Chicano art movement. His work focuses on issues of local communities, mixed-race identity, and public/private divisions. Avalos is an artist, activist, and educator at University of California-San Marcos.

The Eternal Frame
Ant Farm and T.R. Uthco
1976, 23:00, U.S., color, sound
Irreverent yet poignant, *The Eternal Frame* is a re-enactment of the assassination of John F. Kennedy as seen in the famous Zapruder film. This home movie was immediately confiscated by the FBI yet found its way into the visual subconscious of the nation. *The Eternal Frame* concentrates on this event as a crucial site of fascination and repression in the American mindset. "The intent of this work was to examine and demystify the notion of the presidency, particularly Kennedy, as image archetype...."
–Doug Hall, 1984

Also available on the anthology *Surveying the First Decade, Program 7.*

The Adventures of a Nurse
Eleanor Antin
1976, 15:00 excerpt (of 1:04:00), U.S., color, sound
Playing with cliched feminine personae, Eleanor Antin in *The Adventures of a Nurse* manipulates cut-out paper dolls to tell the story of innocent Nurse Eleanor who meets one gorgeous, intriguing, and available man after another. Nurse Eleanor is the fantasy creation of Antin, who is costumed as a nurse. Staged on a bedspread and acted by a cast of one, *The Adventures of a Nurse* moves through successive layers of irony to unravel a childlike, self-enclosed fantasy of a young woman's life.
Only available on the anthology *I Say I Am, Program 2.*

Eleanor Antin: An Interview (see On Art and Artists)

Marks
Skip Arnold
1984, 13:23, U.S., color, sound
Skip Arnold conceived of *Marks* as a live performance broadcast on television for MP/TV-Los Angeles on January 23, 1984.
"Intent: to use my body to make marks on the walls of an 8' x 8' x 8' white room while an audience watched on closed circuit TV. The piece ended when I lost consciousness."
Only available on the anthology *Endurance, Reel 3.*

Punch
Skip Arnold
1992, 00:10, U.S., color, sound
Arnold's slight build heightens his physical provocation, as in *Punch* from 1992, where the artist asked an athletic man to punch him in the stomach.
Only available on the anthology *Endurance, Reel 3.*

Ramona: Birth of a Mis-ce-ge-nation
David Avalos
1991, 20:00, U.S., color, sound
California has been multicultural for a least 100 years, home to Indians, Spaniards, and Anglos. An 1884 romance novel, in fact, paired a half-European/half-Indian woman with the son of a Luiseño Indian chief. This experimental video essay examines the conventional wisdom on mixing of the races and includes popular movie images from Elvis Presley's film *Flaming Star*, *The Last of the Mohicans*, and *West Side Story*.

Baby Maniac
(see Cheang, Shu Lea)

Baldessari, John

Influenced by dadaist and surrealist literary and visual ideas, John Baldessari began incorporating found materials into his canvases, playing off of chance relationships among otherwise discreet elements. Allowing pop-cultural artifacts to function as "information"— as opposed to "form"—Baldessari's works represented a radical departure from and often a direct critique of the modernist sensibility that dominated painting for decades. From his photo-text canvases in the 1960s to his video works in the 1970s to his installations in the 1980s, John Baldessari's varied work has been seminal in the field of conceptual art. Baldessari's videotapes, like his phototext canvases, point to the gap between perception and cognition by employing strategies of disjunction (*Some Words I Mispronounce*, 1971), recontextualization (*Baldessari Sings Lewitt*, 1972), and allegory (*The Way We Do Art Now and Other Sacred Tales*, 1973).

I Will Not Make Any More Boring Art

Baldessari Sings LeWitt

John Baldessari
1972, 12:35, U.S., b&w, sound

"One of Baldessari's most ambitious and risky efforts. Seated and holding a sheaf of papers, he proceeds to sing each of Sol LeWitt's 35 conceptual statements to a different pop tune, after the model of *Ella Fitzgerald Sings Cole Porter*. What initially presents itself as humorous gradually becomes a struggle to convey Lewitt's statements through this arbitrary means".
—Helene Winer, "Scenarios/Documents/Images," *Art in America* 61 (March 1973)

Excerpt (4:00) also available on the anthology *Surveying the First Decade, Program 1*.

This title was in the original Castelli-Sonnabend video art collection.

Ed Henderson Reconstructs Movie Scenarios

John Baldessari
1973, 24:04, U.S., b&w, sound

Baldessari has Ed Henderson examine obscure movie stills and attempt to reconstruct the films' narratives. By removing the image from its ordinary context–in this instance the chronological flow of film time–the process of interpretation itself and the contextual meaning carried by images is examined. During these interpretative exercises, Ed Henderson urges the viewer to question where the meaning of an image lies: within the image itself or within the spectators' reading of the image.

This title was in the original Castelli-Sonnabend video art collection.

I Am Making Art

John Baldessari
1971, 18:46, U.S., b&w, sound

"A good example of Baldessari's deadpan irreverence is the 1971 black-and-white videotape entitled *I Am Making Art*, in which he moves different parts of his body slightly while saying, after each move, 'I am making art.' The statement, he says, 'hovers between assertion and belief.' On one level, the piece spoofs the work of artists who, in the late 1960s and early 1970s, explored the use of their own bodies and gestures as an art medium. The endless repetition, awkwardness of the movements made by the artist, and the reiteration of the statement 'I am making art,' create a synthesis of gestural and linguistic modes which is both innovative (in the same way that the more serious work of his peers is innovative) and absurdly self-evident."
—Marcia Tucker, "John Baldessari: Pursuing the Unpredictable," *John Baldessari* (New York: New Museum, 1981)

This title was in the original Castelli-Sonnabend video art collection.

I Will Not Make Any More Boring Art

John Baldessari
1971, 32:21, U.S., b&w, sound

"'I will not make any more boring art,' John Baldessari wrote over and over again in a work done in 1971. The impulse for the piece, he says, came from dissatisfaction with the 'fallout of minimalism,' but its implications are far greater. It is typical of Baldessari's work, for not only is it extremely funny, but it is also a strategy, a set of conditions, a directive, a paradoxical statement, and a commentary on the art world with which it is involved. Like all his work to date, it addresses, on many complex levels, issues about art, language, games and the world at large."
—Marcia Tucker, "John Baldessari: Pursuing the Unpredictable," *John Baldessari* (New York: New Museum, 1981)

This title was in the original Castelli-Sonnabend video art collection.

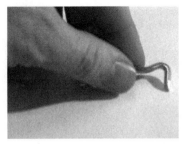

Inventory

The Meaning of Various Photographs
to Ed Henderson

Teaching a Plant the Alphabet

Inventory
John Baldessari
1972, 23:34, U.S., b&w, sound
"In Baldessari's wonderful *Inventory,* the artist presents to the camera for thirty minutes an accumulation of indiscriminate and not easily legible objects arranged in order of increasing size and accompanied by a deadpan description—only to have the sense of their relative size destroyed by the continual readjustment of the camera [in order to] keep them within the frame. Who can forget Adlai Stevenson's solemn television demonstration of the 'conclusive photographic evidence' of the Cuban missile sites, discernible over the TV screen as only gray blurs?"
—David Antin, "Video: The Distinctive Features of the Medium," *Video Art: An Anthology*, eds. Ira Schneider and Beryl Korot (New York: Harcourt Brace Jovanovich: 1974)
This title was in the original Castelli-Sonnabend video art collection.

The Meaning of Various News Photos to Ed Henderson
John Baldessari
1973, 13:20, U.S., b&w, sound
Baldessari asks Ed Henderson to discuss the meaning of selected news photos. Henderson invents the conditions of the where, when, and why each was taken—and decides whether the photo was altered in any way. This exercise complicates the reception of news media images and encourages a more analytical attitude towards the implicit meaning, and potentially faked reality, of such images.
This title was in the original *Castelli-Sonnabend* video art collection.

The Meaning of Various Photographs to Ed Henderson
John Baldessari
1973, 14:08, U.S., b&w, sound
Baldessari presents photographs to his friend Ed Henderson and asks him to reconstruct the meaning of the images. In each case, Baldessari's strategy is to appropriate an existing image and remove it from its context in order to deconstruct the process of interpretation and call the supposed objectivity of interpretation into question. The tape implicates the viewer in Henderson's groundless exegesis, as he hypothesizes about the meaning of several photographs, speculating on their actual or staged reality.
This title was in the original Castelli-Sonnabend video art collection.

Teaching a Plant the Alphabet
John Baldessari
1972, 18:08, U.S., b&w, sound
"[A] rather perverse exercise in futility," this tape documents Baldessari's response to Joseph Beuys's influential performance, *How to Explain Pictures to a Dead Hare.* Baldessari's approach here is characteristically subtle and ironic, involving ordinary objects and a seemingly banal task. The philosophical underpinnings of Baldessari's exercise are structuralist theories about the opaque and artificial nature of language as a system of signs. Using a common houseplant to represent nature and instructional flashcards to represent the alphabet, Baldessari ironically illustrates this theorem. That language is the structuring element of the tape—the length of the tape was determined by the number of letters in the alphabet—enforces the connection between language and art, a recurrent theme in Baldessari's work.
This title was in the original Castelli-Sonnabend video art collection.

The Way We Do Art Now and Other Sacred Tales
John Baldessari
1973, 29:00, U.S., b&w, sound
"A spoof on current art attitudes [that] stretches the definition of what can be considered art. Because the late 1960s and early 1970s were periods of innovation, using the human body as art, making process equivalent to product... [etc.], Baldessari questions that very sense of originality and exploration

by taking it to its (rather mundane) limits. By taping a stick at one end, then picking it up at the other, he is both questioning and spoofing what constitutes art."
—Marcia Tucker, "John Baldessari: Pursuing the Unpredictable," *John Baldessari* (New York: New Museum, 1981)
This title was in the original Castelli-Sonnabend video art collection.

Xylophone
John Baldessari
1972, 25:15, U.S., b&w, sound
Presenting a series of flashcards to the camera, Baldessari continues his exploration of visual semantics, defining the intersection of language and image. In this instance, each flashcard bears a picture that represents a letter of the alphabet. Like *Teaching a Plant the Alphabet*, a secondary theme of *Xylophone* is a critique of learning as memorization, with the length of the tape producing—not surprisingly—an effect of boredom rather than insight. This title was in the original Castelli-Sonnabend video art collection.

John Baldessari: An Interview (see On Art and Artists)
John Baldessari: Some Stories (see On Art and Artists)

Xylophone

Banker, Lisel
(see Umen, Alix)

Barbie Liberation Organization

The Barbie Liberation Organization (BLO) is a cultural activist organization that challenges gender stereotyping in the toy industry through intervention tactics and gendered voice reassignment surgeries.

BLO Nightly News
Barbie Liberation Organization
1994, 30:00, U.S., color, sound
In a form of subversive media terrorism, BLO operatives purchased talking Barbie and G.I. Joe dolls, both of which were programmed to speak crude cultural clichés. The dolls were then taken to the BLO headquarters where "corrective surgery" was performed: switching the dolls' voice boxes. The dolls were then placed back on the store shelves in a process of reverse shoplifting—"shopgiving." In the format of a nightly news program, this witty and satiric video documents the activities of the Barbie Liberation Organization, including the "corrective surgery" procedure and the "shopgiving" actions. The tape functions as witness and instruction manual on culture jamming—an interference strategy used by guerrilla art and media activists to expose and undermine the logic and domination of corporate-controlled media and capitalist culture.

Barbier, Annette

Annette Barbier began working in video in Chicago in the 1970s during an era of inventing abstract and colorized images on the Sandin Image Processor. Barbier went on to create feminist narratives through serial thematic groupings of images of personal content. Barbier is a professor in Radio, Television and Film at Northwestern University.

Women's Movements
Annette Barbier
1989, 28:00, U.S., color, sound
In Barbier's meditative journey through India, she deconstructs the myth of the objective documentary by using textual commentary and off-camera remarks to address the problematic relationship of observer to observed. Framing the images through the artist's subjective and distinctly female point of view, she explores images of women working, sweeping, cooking, and tending children in direct juxtaposition to men who sit, relax, and observe the spectacle. As this imagery unfolds, the frequent interruptions of a three-year-old daughter demanding attention interrogate the relationships of camera to subject, and that of the woman working behind the camera to those working in front of it.

Barbour, Maida

Maida Barbour made the tape *Linda M. Montano's Seven Years of Living Art* while working on her MFA in film at the University of Texas-Austin. She later installed Richard Linklater's *Countdown/Tailout Mural #2* (1998) in the lobby of the American Museum of the Moving Image (Astoria, NY).

Linda M. Montano's Seven Years of Living Art
Maida Barbour
1994, 13:13, U.S., color, sound
A video collage that chronicles the issues and events that arose in Montano's life while she devoted a year to each of the seven chakras. Beginning as a piece devoted to themes of commitment and limitation, the work becomes a fascinating hybrid of art and life as Montano experiences the onset of menopause, her mother's death, her choice to enter and then leave a convent, the suffering of a stroke, and thoughts of her own death—all within the

structural confines of an intense work of art.

Contributors to the work include Ellen Fullman, Gisela Gamper, and Annie Sprinkle.

Also available on the anthology *Endurance, Reel 4.*

Barret, Elizabeth

Elizabeth Barret is a community-based media maker whose films and videos focus on the history, culture, and social issues of the Appalachian region. A native of Kentucky, Barret has been creating work with Appalshop since 1973. Her films include *Fixin' to Tell about Jack* (1975), *Quilting Women* (1976), *Coalmining Women* (1982), *Long Journey Home* (1987), and *Stranger with a Camera* (2000).

Béar, Liza

From the late 1970s to the mid-'80s, Liza Béar created an intriguing body of work that consistently focused attention on communications issues—specifically the use of technology by the press and the disempowered role of the public in communications policy. Central to Béar's work is a desire to tie the means of production (technology) to the reasons for production (capitalist, national ideology, etc.). While Béar's concerns are global, her approach is always personal and experimental—collapsing the norms of narrative and documentary, subjective authorship and objective document.

Satellite TV: Birth of an Industry (Parts 1 & 2)

Stranger with a Camera
Elizabeth Barret
2000, 1:01:00, U.S., color, sound
Elizabeth Barret's *Stranger with a Camera,* a fascinating study of the politics of representation, returns to the Johnson-era War on Poverty to reexamine the killing of a documentary filmmaker by an Appalachian landowner.

Spanish subtitled version available.

Only available on the anthology *Frames of Reference: Reflections on Media, Volume 5, Program 2.*

Earthglow
Liza Béar
1983, 8:00, U.S., color, sound
Earthglow is a poem written for the character generator and switcher that conveys a writer's internal dialogue through both subtle and dramatic color changes and through movement, size, and placement of words. The ambient soundtrack evokes the confluence of past and present perceptions.

Lost Oasis
Liza Béar
1982, 10:00, U.S., color, sound
A loosely structured and evocative drama that centers on the search for a lost oasis. Shot in a bizarre Californian landscape, the piece is a contemporary desert fantasy.

Polisario: Liberation of the Western Sahara
Liza Béar
1981, 29:00, U.S., color, sound
A historical analysis of the ongoing war in the Western Sahara. Liza Béar interviews Abdullah Majid, the Polisario Front's United Nations representative. The tape addresses Morocco's U.S.-backed military effort to subjugate the indigenous Sahrawi population and annex one of the world's largest phosphate deposits, as well as the Sahrawis' conditions for a referendum.

Satellite TV: Birth of an Industry (Parts 1 & 2)
Liza Béar
1980, 56:00, U.S., color, sound
Part of a cable TV series called *Communications Update* that aired on public access in New York City in 1980, these tapes provide an early example of television made by artists. The series centered on the democratization of the media. *Birth of an Industry* covers a Miami satellite TV convention attended by thousands of backyard satellite TV enthusiasts, inventors, and entrepreneurs. Many of the attendees joined forces to track the orbital arc of foreign satellite signals, in particular the Russian "bird." Footage of this activity is inter-cut with interviews of some of the industry's pioneers, including inventors Bob Coleman, Taylor Howard, and Bob Cooper, one of the industry's chief promoters. The availability of this technology opened tremendous possibilities to rural America and to countries seeking to diversify and expand the programming available to them.

Send/Receive I and Send/Receive II
Liza Béar and Keith Sonnier
1977, 50:00, U.S., color, sound
A primer in satellite system operation, *Send/Receive* extends the critique of the media as commodities by asking questions concerning the people's right to access satellites. Part I presents an in-depth study of the politics and pos-

sibilities of using satellite networks to establish a two-way communication system for public use, as opposed to the industry-driven, militaristic, and mass media uses to which satellites are restricted. Part 2 excerpts a live satellite feed between New York City and San Francisco.

Towards a New World Information Order
Liza Béar
1979, 1:00:00, U.S., color, sound
Addressing the imbalance of information flow between the wealthy and the destitute nations of the world, *Towards a New World Information Order* suggests means by which this imbalance might be rectified, including ways to control the press. A survey of several *Communications Update* programs investigating "hardcore" communications policy issues, from communications satellites to cable franchising, produced by Béar and carried on NYC cable. *Towards a New World Information Order* includes dialogues between media specialists and communications lawyers from Zimbabwe, Costa Rica, Nigeria, the U.K., and the U.S., statistical graphics from the Non-Aligned Movement, and film footage from North Africa. Dialogue demystifies the rhetoric and jargon surrounding this controversy, allowing viewers to examine tacit assumptions behind the discourse.

Towards a New World Information Order

Beatty, Maria
(see On Art and Artists)

Beck, Stephen

Arriving at video through music, Stephen Beck moved from jazz to electronic music to electronic instrument building. He is best known for creating the Direct Video Synthesizer, a computer built in 1970 during his residency with the National Center for Experiments in Television. Like many of the early video tool designers, Beck was interested in exploring the relationship between synthesized images and human perception.

Beckman, Ericka

Ericka Beckman's experimental films include *We Intimate* (1978), *We Break-Up* (1978), *The Broken Rule* (1979), *Out of Hand* (1981), *You the Better* (1983), *Cinderella* (1986), and *Switch Center* (2001). *Blind Country* (1989), a collaborative video project made with Mike Kelley, has games and role playing at its core. *Hiatus* (1999), a videotape, is a game construct combining animation and in-camera effects with a contemporary "strung out on the 'net'" story. She has shown extensively in museums and festivals worldwide.

Video Weavings
Stephen Beck
1976, 4:00 excerpt (of 28:00), U.S., color, sound
Inspired by the analogy between weaving (vertical warp threads traversed by horizontal weft threads) and the construction of the television image (vertical and horizontal scans of an electron gun), Stephen Beck built the Video Weaver in 1974 and produced *Video Weavings* in 1976. The patterns in this tape are based on sequences of colors in dynamic mathematical progressions, inspired by non-representational Islamic art.

Only available as an excerpt on the anthology *Surveying the First Decade, Program 5.*

Blind Country
Ericka Beckman and Mike Kelley
1989, 20:00, U.S., color, sound
This collaborative video project is based on a short story by H.G. Wells called "The Country of the Blind" about a man who travels to a country of blind people and attempts to dominate their sensual, feminine culture with his male, sight-derived power. Following this theme, *Blind Country* begins with animated fruit dancing over Kelley's body and the admonition of "Northerners" to "refill the quickly emptying sack." In the male-dominated land of the North, candy-spurting piñatas stand as phallic symbols. Presumably castrated and stripped of his authority, Kelley acts the buffoon as he is led through the murky land of the South, a "female," earthy, "realm of the senses" opposing the phallocentric world of the North.

Hiatus
Ericka Beckman
1999, 30:00, U.S., color, sound
Madi plays an interactive online computer game in the privacy of her apartment. Wearing a computer corset that stores her programs in a "Garden Interface," she propels her go-go cowgirl construct WANDA through the game world, encountering an assortment of logged-on players and game identities who trick and confuse her. An aggressive male character WANG logs on and inserts his cold architecture into her coordinates, draining the power in her corset. His expanding architecture threatens to overtake her Garden Reservoir. To confront this powerful takeover artist, she must rely on her organic memory and is forced to establish some psychological boundaries to protect her identity and preserve her freedom.

Only available on the anthology *e-[d]entity, Tape 1.*

Benglis, Lynda

Sculptor Lynda Benglis executed a number of videos in the mid-1970s, continuing her exploration of female sexuality and identity. Benglis aggressively uses the properties of the video medium to expose the process and limitations of the form—for example, re-shooting footage on the monitor and technically manipulating the image on screen. In this way Benglis negotiates a personal space for herself, maintaining a deliberate distance from the medium even as she uses her own image. Benglis's work consistently critiques video's inherent properties: the sense of "real" time, its supposedly immediate and truthful relationship to the world, and its privileged viewpoint in relation to events.

The Amazing Bow-Wow
Lynda Benglis
1976, 30:20, U.S., color, sound

The only Benglis video with a discernable plot, *The Amazing Bow-Wow* follows the adventures of a talking, hermaphroditic dog given to Rexina and Babu by a carnival barker. Rexina and Babu soon decide to make the dog a sideshow act, hoping to earn their fortune. Babu eventually becomes jealous of Rexina's devotion to the dog and one night attempts to castrate it, accidentally cutting off its tongue. The dog's head becomes hideous and skeletal, ruining its sideshow career and the profits. A farce of the Oedipal complex, *Bow-Wow* comments on the moral position of artists in society—the way in which artists are exploited by the media as oddities on the level of sideshow attractions.

This title was in the original Castelli-Sonnabend video art collection.

Collage
Lynda Benglis
1973, 9:30, U.S., color, sound

Three basic compositions are played and recombined in *Collage:* a hockey game; arms swinging across the screen; and a hand holding one, two, then three oranges. As in her other work, Benglis plays with several generations of each shot, rescanning the screen, and placing objects in front of the monitor. Organized around color and rhythm, each segment uses bright colors, rapid movements, and complex layers of images to present a mesmerizing compendium of information that frustrates any sense of narrative. The accompanying soundtrack is an independent collage of noises, feedback, and static that create a gritty aural texture.

This title was in the original Castelli-Sonnabend video art collection.

Discrepncy
Lynda Benglis
1973, 13:03, U.S., b&w, sound

This structurally simple tape, shot through Benglis's apartment window, contains a "distinct disjuncture between the visual and aural components of the tape. The chatter of a radio frequently distracts the viewer, initially presented with a contemplative view of nature. As the camera zooms in and out, it establishes a dichotomy: indoors and outdoors, the man-made and the natural. The window frame echoes the limited view framed by the camera, while the wide expanse of the outdoors and the reflections in the window panes suggest the infinite possibilities of the world just beyond view."
—Carrie Przybilla, "Synopses of Videotapes," *Lynda Benglis: Dual Natures* (Atlanta: High Museum of Art, 1991)

This title was in the original Castelli-Sonnabend video art collection.

Document

Document
Lynda Benglis
1972, 6:08, U.S., b&w, sound

With Benglis standing in front of a photograph of herself, which is then affixed to a monitor bearing her image, the notion of "original" is complicated—making the viewer acutely aware of the layers of self-images and layers of "self" that are simultaneously presented. Like Martha Rosler's *Vital Statistics of a Citizen, Simply Obtained*, Benglis presents the viewer with a "document" of questionable veracity. It is a document attesting not to the "real" Benglis but to the impossibility of discerning one real identity. Through this exercise, Benglis draws attention to the nature of video as a medium based on mechanical reproduction, putting it at odds with the whole notion of the "authentic" in art.

This title was in the original Castelli-Sonnabend video art collection.

Enclosure

Female Sensibility

Enclosure

Lynda Benglis

1973, 7:23, U.S., b&w, sound

Benglis uses the video format as a metaphor for other types of limiting conditions or limited realities. "The constant motion of Benglis's hand-held camera (scanning her studio and two television sets) calls attention to the limits of the camera's field of vision: the walls of the studio are the ultimate 'enclosure' of the camera's eye. The open window and the sound of children (from the street) seem to suggest release; yet the confines of the studio are never truly broken."

—Carrie Przybilla, "Synopses of Videotapes," *Lynda Benglis: Dual Natures* (Atlanta: High Museum of Art, 1991)

This title was in the original Castelli-Sonnabend video art collection.

Exchange (see Morris, Robert)

Female Sensibility

Lynda Benglis

1973, 14:00, U.S., color, sound

As two heavily made-up women take turns directing each other and submitting to each other's kisses and caresses, it becomes increasingly obvious that the camera is their main point of focus. Read against feminist film theory of the male gaze, the action becomes a highly charged statement of the sexual politics of viewing and role-playing; and, as such, is a crucial text in the development of early feminist video.

"This video is Benglis's emphatic response to the notion of a distinctly feminine artistic sensibility and to the belief in a necessary lesbian phase in the women's movement—ideas that were often debated in the early 1970s."

—Susan Krane, "Introduction," *Lynda Benglis: Dual Natures* (Atlanta: High Museum of Art, 1991)

Also available on the anthology *Surveying the First Decade, Program 4.*

This title was in the original Castelli-Sonnabend video art collection.

The Grunions Are Running

Lynda Benglis

1973, 5:41, U.S., b&w, sound

Using imagery from a Japanese "creature feature" and a chewing gum commercial, Benglis's camera focuses on different parts of the screen to emphasize different messages. With dialogue and sound replaced by the sound of frogs croaking outside Benglis's studio, the absurdly comic visuals of the movie and commercial oddly begin to echo each other, raising questions about the nature of the absurdity beamed into our homes and uncritically accepted as entertainment.

This title was in the original Castelli-Sonnabend video art collection.

Home Tape Revised

Lynda Benglis

1972, 28:00, U.S., b&w, sound

"In *Home Tape,* Benglis took a portable video tape recorder with her when she visited her family in Louisiana. She saw most of the experience through the video camera, thus giving her a distance from an emotionally involving situation. The tapes were replayed and reshot off a monitor and commented about by Benglis.... It is a deeply personal tape about an emotionally involving situation, but it is precisely controlled. It makes use of the intimacy of video, of the one to one relationship between the viewer and the monitor which distinguishes video so much from film, resulting in the feeling of a shared experience though the experience is not in the least dramatized. ...

"Besides using the intimacy of television and the instant replay capability of video in *Home Tape,* Benglis uses the fluidity of time with instant replay and the capability of carrying on a dialogue with oneself due to a combination of the characteristics of instant replay and intimacy."

—Bruce Kurtz, "Video Is Being Invented," *Arts Magazine* (December 1973)

This title was in the original Castelli-Sonnabend video art collection.

How's Tricks

How's Tricks
Lynda Benglis
1976, 34:00, U.S., color, sound
"There is a crudeness to *How's Tricks*, Benglis's first venture into narrative fiction. No attempt is made to hide the mechanics of making the tape. At one point, while Benglis and [Stanton] Kaye argue about the tape they are making of [Bobby] Reynolds (a real carny who also appears in *The Amazing Bow-Wow*), Kaye is seen reaching over to turn off the video recorder—and thus the scene ends. ...
"The Nixon footage exposes the media structure that props up public person-ae, thus revealing the disjuncture between the media's presentation and the behind-the-scenes reality. *How's Tricks* points out how easily television's 'magic box' is able to distort and deceive. The glee and transparency with which the magic tricks are presented also points to the willingness by which a captive audience is misled."
–Carrie Przybilla, "Synopses of Videotapes," *Lynda Benglis: Dual Natures* (Atlanta: High Museum of Art, 1991)
This title was in the original Castelli-Sonnabend video art collection.

Monitor
Lynda Benglis
1999, 00:20, U.S., color, sound
Cyclops/"monitor"/minotaur.
Note: a 20-second video loop self-portrait.

Mumble
Lynda Benglis
1972, 20:00, U.S., b&w, sound
Part of an ongoing video correspondence with sculptor Robert Morris, *Mumble* brings together repeated scenes and gestures, featuring Morris and Jim Benglis (the artist's brother), and a narrative of irrelevant, confusing, and often purposefully untrue, statements. Although the viewer is inclined to accept Benglis's narrative as true, such trust is called into question by her statements about actions taking place off camera—actions that cannot be ver-ified. As Benglis's narration degenerates into a meaningless, repetitive pulse, *Mumble* disrupts the convenient fiction that the image presented on screen is complete unto itself.
This title was in the original Castelli-Sonnabend video art collection.

Noise
Lynda Benglis
1972, 7:15, U.S., b&w, sound
The earliest of Benglis's videoworks, *Noise* calls attention to the assemblage element of video by allowing the image to disintegrate into static between edits. Benglis also plays back several generations of image and soundtrack to introduce increasing amounts of distortion. Conversation is reduced to unin-telligible noise, resulting in the disassociation of sound and image that to some extent characterizes her later work.
This title was in the original Castelli-Sonnabend video art collection.

Now

Now
Lynda Benglis
1973, 10:00, U.S., color, sound
Throughout the video, Benglis asks "Now?" and "Do you wish to direct me?" and repeats commands such as "Start the camera" and "I said start record-ing." As in *On Screen*, she makes faces and sounds in reply to the images on a monitor; at one point she appears to kiss herself. The word "now," used as both question and command, focuses attention on the deceptive "real" time of video, and reveals the structure underlying her presence in the video. Her first color tape, Benglis experiments with the effect of unnatural color, turning up the levels until the colors are high and artificial, which diffuses the idea of video as an impartial or "direct" medium.

Also available on the anthology *I Say I Am: Program 2.*
This title was in the original Castelli-Sonnabend video art collection.

On Screen
Lynda Benglis
1972, 7:25, U.S., b&w, sound
"Benglis manipulates generations of video footage to confound our sense of time; she implies an infinite regression of time and space—Benglis making faces in front of a monitor of her making faces in front of a monitor of her... ad infinitum. The viewer retains a sense of the images sequentially, although the sequence of creation is not revealed in a logical, orderly fashion, and is heavily obscured by the random layering and continual repetition of aural and visual components."
—Carrie Przybilla, "Synopses of Videotapes," *Lynda Benglis: Dual Natures* (Atlanta: High Museum of Art, 1991)
This title was in the original Castelli-Sonnabend video art collection.

Lynda Benglis: Dual Natures (see On Art and Artists)

"Aerobicide" (Julie Ruin)
Sadie Benning
1998, 4:00, U.S., color, sound
This music video for the band Julie Ruin, fronted by Kathleen Hanna, formerly of Bikini Kill, critiques the cynical music marketeers of corporate America. Criticism particularly targets campaigns aimed at women, which Benning and Hanna refer to here as the "Girls Rule (kind of) Strategy."

Flat is Beautiful
Sadie Benning
1998, 50:00, U.S., b&w, sound
Flat is Beautiful is an experimental live-action cartoon using masks, animation, subtitles, drawings, and dramatic scenes to investigate the psychic life of an androgynous eleven-year-old girl. Growing up in a working class neighborhood with her single mother and gay roommate, Taylor confronts the loneliness of living between masculine and feminine in a culture obsessed with defining gender difference. Shifting between black-and-white film and grainy Pixelvision video, *Flat is Beautiful* explores the internal and external worlds of sad people.
Also available on the compilation *Sadie Benning Videoworks: Volume 3.*

German Song
Sadie Benning
1995, 5:00, U.S., b&w, sound, Super-8 to video
Shot in black-and-white Super-8, this lyrical short follows a wandering, disengaged youth through gray afternoons. Features the hard-edged music of Come, an alternative band from Boston.
Also available on the compilation *Sadie Benning Videoworks: Volume 3.*

Girl Power
Sadie Benning
1992, 15:00, U.S., b&w, sound
Set to music by Bikini Kill (an all-girl band from Washington), *Girl Power* is a raucous vision of what it means to be a radical girl in the 1990s. Benning relates her personal rebellion against school, family, and female stereotypes as a story of personal freedom, telling how she used to model like Matt Dillon and skip school to have adventures alone. Informed by the underground riot grrrl movement, this tape transforms the image politics of female youth, rejecting traditional passivity and polite compliance in favor of radical independence and a self-determined sexual identity.
Spanish subtitled version available.
Also available on the compilation *Sadie Benning Videoworks: Volume 2* and

Benning, Sadie

Sadie Benning is a lesbian videomaker who began making videos when she was 15 years old. Benning's early works were made in the privacy of her childhood bedroom with scrawled text from diary entries to recorded thoughts and images that reveal the longings and complexities of a developing identity– trapped and uneasy. Evoking in-turn playful seduction and painful honesty, Benning's floating, close-up Fisher Price Pixelvision toy camera, functions as a witness to her intimate revelations and as an accomplice in defining her evocative experimental form. Her later work moves into animation and film.

German Song

on the anthology *Frames of Reference: Reflections on Media, Volume 1, Program 1.*

If Every Girl Had a Diary

Sadie Benning
1990, 6:00, U.S., b&w, sound

Setting her Pixelvision camera on herself and her room, Benning searches for a sense of identity and respect as a woman and a lesbian. Acting alternately as confessor and accuser, the camera captures Benning's anger and frustration at feeling trapped by social prejudices.

Also available on the compilation *Sadie Benning Videoworks: Volume 1.*

It Wasn't Love

It Wasn't Love

Sadie Benning
1992, 20:00, U.S., b&w, sound

Benning illustrates a lustful encounter with a "bad girl" through the gender posturing and genre interplay of Hollywood stereotypes: posing for the camera as the rebel, the platinum blonde, the gangster, the '50s crooner, and the heavy-lidded vamp. Cigarette poses, romantic slow dancing, and fast-action heavy metal street shots propel the viewer through the story of the love affair. Benning's video goes farther than romantic fantasy, describing other facets of physical attraction including fear, violence, lust, guilt, and total excitement. As she puts it, "It wasn't love, but it was something...." It was a chance to feel glamorous, sexy, and famous all at the same time.

Also available on the compilation *Sadie Benning Videoworks: Volume 2.*

Jollies

Jollies

Sadie Benning
1990, 11:00, U.S., b&w, sound

Benning gives a chronology of her crushes and kisses, tracing the development of her nascent sexuality. Addressing the camera with an air of seduction and romance, giving the viewer a sense of her anxiety and special delight as she came to realize her lesbian identity.

Also available on the compilation *Sadie Benning Videoworks: Volume 1.*

The Judy Spots

Sadie Benning
1995, 15:00, U.S., b&w, sound

These five short videos introduce Judy, a paper maché puppet who ruminates on her position in society. Like Judy of the famous Punch and Judy puppet duo, Benning's Judy seems to experience the world from the outside, letting things happen to her rather than making things happen around herself.

Also available on the compilation *Sadie Benning Videoworks: Volume 3.*

Living Inside

Sadie Benning
1989, 6:00, U.S., b&w, sound

When she was 16, Benning stopped going to high school for three weeks and stayed inside with her camera, her TV set, and a pile of dirty laundry. This tape mirrors her psyche during this time. With the image breaking up between edits, the rough quality of this early tape captures Benning's sense of isolation and sadness, her retreat from the world. As such, *Living Inside* is the confession of a chronic outsider.

Also available on the compilation *Sadie Benning Videoworks: Volume 1.*

Me and Rubyfruit

Sadie Benning
1990, 6:00, U.S., b&w, sound

Based on a novel by Rita Mae Brown, *Me and Rubyfruit* chronicles the enchantment of teenage lesbian love against a backdrop of pornographic images and phone sex ads. Benning portrays the innocence of female romance and the taboo prospect of female marriage.

Also available on the compilation *Sadie Benning Videoworks: Volume 1.*

A New Year
Sadie Benning
1989, 6:00, U.S., b&w, sound
In a version of the teenage diary, Benning places her feelings of confusion and depression alongside grisly tales from tabloid headlines and brutal events in her neighborhood. The difficulty of finding a positive identity for one-self in a world filled with violence is starkly revealed by Benning's youthful but already despairing voice.

Also available on the compilation *Sadie Benning Videoworks: Volume 1.*

A Place Called Lovely
Sadie Benning
1991, 14:00, U.S., b&w, sound
"Nicky is seven. His parents are older and meaner." *A Place Called Lovely* references the types of violence individuals find in life–from actual beatings, accidents, and murders to the more insidious violence of lies, social expecta-tions, and betrayed faith. Benning collects images of this socially pervasive violence from a variety of sources, tracing events from childhood: movies, tabloids, children's games, personal experiences, and those of others. Throughout, Benning uses small toys as props and examples by handling and controlling them the way we are, in turn, controlled by larger violent forces.

Also available on the compilation *Sadie Benning Videoworks: Volume 2.*

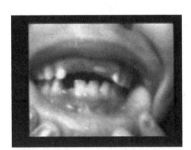

A Place Called Lovely

Sadie Benning Videoworks: Volume 1
A compilation of five of Sadie Benning's early works.
Total running time 35:00.
Contents:
If Every Girl Had a Diary, Sadie Benning, 1990, 6:00, U.S., b&w, sound
Jollies, Sadie Benning, 1990, 11:00, U.S., b&w, sound
Living Inside, Sadie Benning, 1989, 6:00, U.S., b&w, sound
Me and Rubyfruit, Sadie Benning, 1990, 6:00, U.S., b&w, sound
A New Year, Sadie Benning, 1989, 6:00, U.S., b&w, sound

Sadie Benning Videoworks: Volume 2
Volume 2 includes three Pixelvision works made in 1991-92.
Total running time 49:00.
Contents:
Girl Power, Sadie Benning, 1992, 15:00, U.S., b&w, sound
It Wasn't Love, Sadie Benning, 1992, 20:00, U.S., b&w, sound
A Place Called Lovely, Sadie Benning, 1991, 14:00, U.S., b&w, sound

Sadie Benning Videoworks: Volume 3
A collection of three remarkable works by Sadie Benning, produced between 1995 and 1998.
Total running time 1:10:00.
Contents:
Flat Is Beautiful, Sadie Benning, 1998, 50:00, U.S., b&w, sound
German Song, Sadie Benning, 1995, 5:00, U.S., b&w, sound, Super-8 to
  video

The Judy Spots, Sadie Benning, 1995, 15:00, U.S., b&w, sound

Girl Power

Berliner, Alan
Alan Berliner creates intensely personal documentaries—focusing on his family and his namesake—that are not only accessible but engaging as they portray the director's search for his own identity and his negotiation of treacherous family relationships. Berliner's work combines photos, home movies, found footage, interviews, and narratives of his own search for understanding.

Nobody's Business
Alan Berliner
1996, 1:00:00, U.S., color, sound
Berliner punctuates montages of archival documents, photographs, and home movies with newsreel footage of boxing matches to metaphorically suggest the contentious yet comedic battle the filmmaker wages with his father over the Berliner family history.

Spanish subtitled version available.

Only available on the anthology *Frames of Reference: Reflections on Media, Volume 6, Program 2.*

Berliner, Roberto

Roberto Berliner directs documentaries, advertisements, and music videos for popular bands in Brazil. In 1978 he began working in film and video, and later became the director of Anteve, a production company documenting musical events within the Rio performance space Circo Voador. Berliner is well known for his 1988 documentary *Angola* and is a founding partner of the non-profit organization TV Zero. *You Are What You Are Born For* (1999) forms part of a series of work documenting street musicians.

Billingham, Richard

One of the most celebrated Young British Artists, Richard Billingham shot a moving series of photographs of his family and their lives in a housing project outside Birmingham, England. These pictures were studies for paintings but were also published as photo portraits in *Ray's a Laugh* (1996); the images stand as powerful testaments to the impact of his father's alcoholism and unemployment. In 1998, Artangel and BBC television commissioned *Fishtank*.

Birnbaum, Dara

An architect and urban planner by training, Dara Birnbaum began using video in 1978 while teaching at the Nova Scotia College of Art and Design, where she worked with Dan Graham. Recognized as one of the first video artists to employ the appropriation of television images as a subversive strategy, Birnbaum recontextualizes pop cultural icons (*Technology/Transformation: Wonder Woman*, 1978-79) and TV genres (*Kiss the Girls and Make them Cry*, 1979) to reveal their subtexts. Birnbaum describes her tapes as new "readymades" for the late 20th century—works that "manipulate a medium which is itself highly manipulative."

A pessoa é para o que nasce (You Are What You Are Born For)
Roberto Berliner
1999, 6:00, Brazil, color, sound, in Portuguese with English subtitles
You Are What You Are Born For features three blind sisters who sing for their survival on the streets of Campina Grande, Brazil. By providing personal testimony about the intimate details of their everyday experiences, these women bring into question the act of seeing and perceiving. The piece opens with a collage of abstract images, a sequence of rotated landscapes. As viewers, we are subject to what Berliner describes as "vertigo provoked by vision," an alternative vision that invites us to consider how perception affects our identity.

Only available on the anthology *Betraying Amnesia, Portraying Ourselves: Video Portraits by Latin American and Latino Artists.*

Fishtank
Richard Billingham
1998, 46:40, U.K., color, sound
An alcoholic, emaciated father; a grossly obese, tattooed mother; a goofy, hormone-addled brother—all together in a claustrophobic council flat. Welcome to the Billinghams's. Richard Billingham wowed the art scene with his book *Ray's a Laugh. Fishtank,* his first film, charts the emotional territory of the flat and the family members who play out their lives within its confines. Billingham draws on 50 hours of video footage, shot over two years, to provide a mesmerizing yet dull home movie of life in his parents' British Midlands tower block flat, laying bare their intense relationship for the camera. Sometimes they talk; sometimes they argue; mostly, they drive each other mad. The verité style leaves no room for technical niceties. The camera lingers on Ray's neck, his cavernous nostrils, knotty veins, and sagging skin and follows the path of Liz's eyeliner as it traces the rim of her eye, thickly applying a path of blue.

Canon: Taking to the Streets
Dara Birnbaum
1990, 14:00, U.S., color, sound
Starting with student-recorded VHS footage of two successive Take Back the Night marches at Princeton University, Birnbaum develops a saga of political awareness through personalized experiences. This localized student activity then progresses to and is contrasted with the 1988 National Student Convention at Rutgers University. Through this dynamic portrait, Birnbaum posits a series of compelling questions: How can the voice of the individual make itself seen and heard in our technocratic society? What forms of demonstration support this expression? How is a voice of dissent made possible? Breaking with traditional documentary format and using tools from the low and high ends of video technology, Birnbaum here replays events of student activism in the United States.

Damnation of Faust: Charming Landscape
Dara Birnbaum
1987, 7:00, U.S., color, sound
The final work in the *Damnation of Faust Trilogy,* ironically titled *Charming Landscape*, investigates the way in which the urban landscape is a place "where you lose your identity." Two female residents of the inner city tell their stories in casual, on-the-street interviews. Building upon the theme of submerged violence, Birnbaum presents the fiery culmination of the legend in eerie slow-motion collage scenes of political unrest—from the lunchroom protests of Greensboro, NC, to the student revolts in Tiananmen Square. Also available on the compilation *Dara Birnbaum: Damnation of Faust.*

Damnation of Faust: Evocation
Dara Birnbaum
1983, 10:00, U.S., color, sound
Using "found" imagery shot in a SoHo playground, the first part of the

Damnation of Faust trilogy explores the possible relations between childhood play and a woman looking on from outside. Without dialogue, the gestures of the characters become their primary mode of communication. Visual motifs of pillars and fans, achieved through video wipes, plunge the viewer into the image while building parallels of movement and feeling.

Also available on the compilation *Dara Birnbaum: Damnation of Faust.*

*Damnation of Faust: Will-o'-the-Wisp
(A Deceitful Goal)*

Damnation of Faust: Will-o'-the-Wisp (A Deceitful Goal)
Dara Birnbaum
1985, 10:00, U.S., color, sound

The second part of the *Faust* project centers on the development of Marguerite, the female character in the *Faust* legend. Masterfully composing fragmentary "memory" images in elegant 19th-century Japanese compositions, Birnbaum traces the process of deception and abandonment through the heroine's mournful description of her state of mind. Passing images are suffused with light, obscured in a blinding brightness, to suggest forgetting.

Also available on the compilation *Dara Birnbaum: Damnation of Faust.*

Dara Birnbaum: Damnation of Faust Trilogy

Using Wagner's *Faust* as a touchstone, *Damnation of Faust* is a trilogy of highly structured and composed video works evoking a free-floating, non-linear dream or memory. The broad themes of the work are conflicting forms of societal restraint and the struggles to define and express personal identity. Total running time 27:00.

Contents:

Damnation of Faust: Evocation, Dara Birnbaum, 1983, 10:00, U.S., color, sound
Damnation of Faust: Will-o'-the-Wisp (A Deceitful Goal), Dara Birnbaum, 1985, 10:00, U.S., color, sound
Damnation of Faust: Charming Landscape, Dara Birnbaum, 1987, 7:00, U.S., color, sound

Kiss the Girls: Make Them Cry

Kiss the Girls: Make Them Cry
Dara Birnbaum
1979, 7:00, U.S., color, sound

Using selected details of TV's *Hollywood Squares*, Birnbaum constructs an analysis of the coded gestures and "looks" of the actors, including Eileen Brennen and Melissa Gilbert. Birnbaum exposes television as an agent of cultural mimicry and instruction. The actors' expressions are far from valueless; they are the ideological content of such programming.

"As a result of the precision with which Birnbaum employs these allegorical procedures we discover with unprecedented clarity to what degree the theater of professional close-ups on the television screen has become the new historical site of the domination of human behavior by ideology. Physiognomic detail and its meaning speak off … in the tape *Kiss the Girls: Make Them Cry.*"
−Benjamin H.B. Buchloh, "Allegorical Procedures: Appropriation and Montage in Contemporary Art," *Artforum* 21:1 (September 1982)

New Music Shorts
Dara Birnbaum
1981, 6:00 U.S., color, sound

This tape includes two short music videos profiling the work of New York alternative or new music musicians. The first piece is entitled *Radio Fire Flight*, in which Jules Baptiste and Lefferts Brown sample and re-record Jimi Hendrix rifts, while the second piece is Glen Branca's *Symphony No.1*, an arrangement for guitars, synthesizers, sticks, bottles, and trash cans. Using footage of the musicians on stage, Birnbaum employs inset boxes and screen graphics to provide visual counterpoints to the structure of the music, building a complex assemblage of references to past musicians and natural phenomena.

PM Magazine/Acid Rock

Dara Birnbaum

1982, 3:00, U.S., color, sound

Appropriating material from the introduction to the nightly television show *PM Magazine* and a commercial for Wang Computers, Birnbaum uses enlarged still frames from both of the sources to compound a new image of the indelible American Dream. To the soundtrack of an acid rock version of the Doors's "L.A. Woman," repetitive images of an ice skater, baton twirler, cheerleader, and young girls licking ice cream exemplify dominant cultural images of women—images that emphasize their performative natures: the idea that women are spectacles arranged for the (male) viewers' pleasure. The culmination of a series of works from 1978-82 dealing directly with television imagery and ideology, this tape is one of four channels shown simultaneously in Birnbaum's installation at *Documenta 9* in 1982.

Pop-Pop Video: General Hospital/Olympic Women Speed Skate

Dara Birnbaum

1980, 6:00, U.S., color, sound

"Dara Birnbaum's *Pop-Pop Video*... [has] been hailed as [a] classic of the new wave. [The tape] juxtaposes fragments from a soap opera with sequences of ice skating races. The graceful movements of the skaters punctuate repeated excerpts from a dreadfully intense discussion between a doctor and his patient: 'He doesn't do anything, doesn't say anything.... It's just the way he looks at me.... That sound crazy?' The narrative builds up slowly as a few more words of the deadly dialogue are released. Extended in this way, the pathos is bare, the narrative content becomes meaningless and the result is particularly moving."
–Katherine Elwes, *Performance* (July/August 1981)

Pop-Pop Video: Kojak/Wang

Dara Birnbaum

1980, 4:00, U.S., color, sound

Pop-Pop Video: Kojak/Wang takes a shootout from *Kojak* and extends the shot and counter-shot into a potentially endless battle. In the original TV fragment, images, gestures and actions rebound off one another like the echoes of repeated bursts of gunfire. Birnbaum compares gunfire with the beams of laser light from a computer in a Wang commercial, connecting destruction and violence with the products of advancing technology.

Pop-Pop Video: Kojak/Wang

Remy Martin/Grand Central Trains and Boats and Planes

Dara Birnbaum

1980, 4:00, U.S., color, sound

In a piece commissioned by Remy Martin, Birnbaum adopts the language of commercial advertising, using the body, gestures, and glances of a heavily made-up woman to create a scene of glamour and romance—while slipping in a disparaging narrative that touches on the actual use and abuse of Remy Martin's product. Birnbaum sets up a typical commercial, then allows the fictive narrative to intrude, upsetting the advertised fantasy with a dose of unpleasant reality. Burt Bacharach's peppy song intones, "Trains and boats and planes took you away from me/I pray they bring you back," while the beautiful model stands at a railroad crossing, the bottle lifted to her lips, guzzling cognac.

Technology/Transformation: Wonder Woman

Dara Birnbaum

1978, 7:00, U.S., color, sound

A stutter-step progression of "extended moments" unmasks the technological "miracle" of Wonder Woman's transformation, playing psychological transformation off of television product. Birnbaum considers this tape an "altered state [that] renders the viewer capable of re-examining those looks which, on the surface, seem so banal that even the supernatural transformation of a secretary into a 'Wonder Woman' is reduced to a burst of blinding light and a turn of the body—a child's play of rhythmical devices inserted within the morose belligerence of the fodder that is our average television diet."

Also available on the anthology *Surveying the First Decade, Program 7.*

Bitomsky, Harmut

Hartmut Bitomsky is a writer, filmmaker, and producer who has made more than 40 films, predominantly documentaries. He studied at the Free University and the Film Academy in Berlin.

Blau, Dick
(see Condit, Cecilia)

Blumberg, Skip

Skip Blumberg is one of the original camcorder-for-broadcast TV producers, and among the first wave of video artists in the 1970s. His early work reflects the era's emphasis on guerilla tactics and medium-specific graphics, but his more recent work takes on more global issues. His work has screened widely on television and at museums. His video *Pick Up Your Feet: The Double Dutch Show* (1981) is considered a classic documentary video and was included in the Museum of Television and Radio's exhibition *TV Critics' All-time Favorite Shows.*

Blumenthal, Lyn

Lyn Blumenthal forged new directions and objectives for the field of independent video—not only creating important video pieces but also envisioning alternative video as a critical voice within the culture, capable of exposing the numerous foibles and blind spots of mainstream media. Committed to the application of feminist theory to video practice, Blumenthal's early '80s art tapes investigate issues of women's identity and sexuality as a crisis of representation. Her tapes weave together stunning visuals and theoretical analysis, most with an incisive humor that tears away the veil from cultural institutions such as television and the family. Blumenthal was also a founding co-director of the Video Data Bank at the School of the Art Institute of Chicago.

B-52—Excerpts from a Work in Progress
Hartmut Bitomsky
2002, 22:00, U.S., color, sound
Utilizing the grand cinematographic style of a John Ford Western, Harmut Bitomsky's *B-52* documents the demolition of a fleet of World War II-era planes in a barren Arizona airfield.
Only available on the anthology *Frames of Reference: Reflections on Media, Volume 3, Program 1.*

Abscam (Framed) (see Lord, Chip)

Weekend in Moscow (unofficial art)
Skip Blumberg
2002, 35:40, U.S., color, sound
It was 1990 and, although the iron curtain was falling, Soviet official control was still iron-fisted. Camcorder reporter Skip Blumberg went along with a group of art aficionados on a tour of the Moscow studios of the unofficial artists, an underground community of talented, courageous, and often wacky conceptual artists. His report reveals an insider's view of the art world and, at the same time, is a video about making a video.

Arcade
Lyn Blumenthal and Carole Ann Klonarides
1984, 11:00, U.S., color, sound
"The syntactic structure and lateral movement of *Arcade* match its fairground equivalent. The work includes a series of images recycled from television and film, interspersed with location footage of Chicago El stations and punctuated with paintings created by Ed Paschke on a computerized paint box. Flashing insights and lights, the ready-made imagery presents a sideshow of current concerns playing on the slippage between the televised and the real."
—Judith Russi Kirshner, "The Science of Fiction/The Fiction of Science, Video Data Bank," *Artforum International* 23 (December 1984)

Doublecross
Lyn Blumenthal
1985, 8:00, U.S., color, sound
Daughter: "What do you and Daddy talk about when I'm not around?"
Mother: "Oh, I don't know—everything."
Daughter: "You do a lot of laughing. ... I hear you sometimes."
Mother: "You shouldn't be listening."
Blumenthal constructs a loose narrative around the sexual evolution of a woman (played by Yvonne Rainer) through a stunning collage of images appropriated from TV and film. Certain images come to dominate this effusive stream—tall buildings, sex scenes, an Elvis movie, the courtroom, fireworks. *Doublecross* pits the indeterminate, disruptive power of the erotic against the rigid, normalizing structures of family, law, marriage, popular culture, movies, and music—societal institutions that codify sexual relations. The "doublecross" is that in a society that equates sex with pleasure, the definitions of what is permissible and what pleasures are off limits catching individuals in a double-bind of sanctioned pleasures.

Lyn Blumenthal Videoworks: Volume 1
The two *Social Studies* tapes call into question fundamental assumptions about the cross-purposes of entertainment: to entertain, to present cultural values, to mediate public policies, and to define social relationships.
Total running time 38:00.

Contents:
Social Studies, Part I: Horizontes, Lyn Blumenthal, 1983, 20:00, U.S., color, sound, in Spanish with English subtitles.
Social Studies, Part II: The Academy, Lyn Blumenthal, 1983, 18:00, U.S., color, sound

Social Studies, Part I: Horizontes
Lyn Blumenthal
1983, 20:00, U.S., color, sound, in Spanish with English subtitles
Horizontes incorporates scenes from a popular Cuban soap opera with running commentary in the form of a propagandistic advertising text. Blumenthal examines media programming as presenting, through the filter of a generalized moralism, a reconstructed history that mirrors the values of the dominant class. The media both "collects and corrects public memory."
Also available on the compilation *Lyn Blumenthal Videoworks: Volume 1.*

Social Studies, Part II: The Academy
Lyn Blumenthal
1983, 18:00, U.S., color, sound
The "dazzling, delightful, and delicious" messages of broadcast television get scrutinized in *Social Studies, Part II: The Academy.* Stripped of its glitzy animation and played out against the frozen backdrop of a single spectacular image, the standard Academy Awards ceremony fare of introductions, applause, film clips, commentary, self-promotion, and professional banter shifts the banal mise-en-scène into proto-fascist theater.

Also available on the compilation *Lyn Blumenthal Videoworks: Volume 1.*

Social Studies, Part I: Horizontes

Bobe, German

Chilean artist German Bobe has lived and studied in Argentina, the United States, France, Italy, and Libya. The cosmopolitan artist remains concerned with the dilemma of "how to be happy in Chile." He explores the question in experimental videos by evoking the nation's social and political conflicts without narrative or commentary. He mingles classic images with the baroque and kitsch, arriving at a glorious confusion of postmodern aesthetics and social consciousness. In addition to video, Bobe works in photography, painting, performance, and film.

Hombres Muertos de Amor y la Jauria de Mujeres
German Bobe
1991, 7:45, Chile, color, sound
This dreamlike, poetic video provokes the viewer to question the nature of the most human of experiences. The collage aesthetic exposes how human relationships—between men and women, men and men, women and women—are mediated by dominant ideologies as represented in the mass media and religion. Bobe posits no theories and draws no conclusions, leaving the viewer with a truly postmodern conundrum about life, love, art, men, women, and death.
Also available on the anthology *Betraying Amnesia, Portraying Ourselves: Video Portraits by Latin American and Latino Artists.*

Matsushima Ondo
German Bobe
1991, 4:00, Chile, color, sound
Combining collage and animation with an Asian-influenced soundtrack, images of women dancing sensually, and devotional imagery, *Matsushima Ondo* compares religious devotion with sexual representation. The viewer is invited to make connections and recognize the irony in some of the similarities.

Portrait of Christophe in Mind
German Bobe
1988, 8:00, Chile, color, sound
This lyrical piece celebrates the male body simply and elegantly. Its subject, Christophe, is exquisitely portrayed by the sepia-toned balletic video. Three men dressed in overcoats dance in and out of the frame in front of a mostly stationary camera. Occasionally they open or partially remove the overcoats to display beautifully sculpted male bodies.

La Profesora (The Professor)
German Bobe
1993, 7:13, Chile, color, sound, in Spanish and English
In this caricature of a professor teaching English to non-native speakers, her

La Profesora (The Professor)

mannerisms, her accent, and the content of her speech are all absurd in the tradition of an Ionesco character. Images of the professor alternate with collages, many taken from Bobe's other works. Through its ironic humor, *La Profesora* foregrounds the absurdity of teaching English in a country where many cannot read their native language. The prevalence of the English language in post- and neo-colonial societies is thus called into question, both politically and socially.

Resume
German Bobe
1994, 9:00, Chile, color, sound, in Spanish
This short piece introduces the visual artist German Bobe. A narrator explains Bobe's background in various media, stressing that his work—the media he chooses and the themes he revisits—presents a synthesis of the concerns of his generation.

Bode, Peer

Working in film until the early 1970s, Peer Bode was first exposed to electronics by his father, Harold Bode (a developer of the first modular audio synthesizer). He worked for the Experimental Television Center, in Owego, New York, as program coordinator, collaborating with resident artist/engineers in constructing prototype imaging tools, thus continuing his commitment to "tool expansion" and "personal studio making." Recognizing the limits imposed by designers of industrial and consumer technology, Bode sought to externalize the "hidden coding and control structures" of the video signal. His videotapes investigate the semiotics and phenomenology of the medium, specifically through the synthesis of audio and video signals.

Music on Triggering Surfaces
Peer Bode
1978, 3:00, U.S., b&w, sound
In *Music on Triggering Surfaces,* Bode constructs an interface between audio and video systems. The luminance information (voltage) from the visual images traversed by the black dot is routed to an oscillator to produce the audio signal, which varies according to the changing luminance. The video image itself then triggers the audio. The shifting gray-scale of the image becomes a two-dimensional sound map or audio score. This tape was produced at the Experimental Television Center.
Only available on the anthology *Surveying the First Decade, Program 5.*

Video Locomotion
Peer Bode
1978, 5:00, U.S., b&w, silent
In this homage to photographer Eadweard Muybridge, a photo grid of a walking man is resituated in video space. Movement is created by detuning the video synchronization (time base) signal, producing horizontal and vertical drifts that expose the electronic space between the video frames, which is visually identifiable as black horizontal and vertical bars. A second image is luminance-keyed into this area, giving the appearance of two discrete image layers. These image planes are manipulated to apparently "drift" at different speeds in different directions. Borrowing images from Muybridge's serial photographic studies in the perception of motion, Bode produces a crude persistence of vision system, creating his own type of "para-cinematic shutter." Produced at the Experimental Television Center.
Only available on the anthology *Surveying the First Decade, Program 5.*

Bollinger, Rebeca

Bollinger reformats existing data and images, synthesizing and utilizing the leftovers of the information age in new forms, from video installations to cookies.

Alphabetically Sorted
Rebeca Bollinger
1994, 5:18, U.S., b&w, sound
Alphabetically Sorted is a scrolling list of 644 keywords downloaded from CompuServe and spoken by "Victoria: High Quality," a speech synthesis program.
Only available on the anthology *e-[d]entity, Tape 2.*

Bordowitz, Gregg

Gregg Bordowitz is a writer, AIDS activist, and film-and videomaker. His work, including *Fast Trip, Long Drop* (1993) and *Habit* (2001), documents his personal experiences of testing positive and living with HIV within the context of a personal and global crisis. His writings are collected in *The AIDS Crisis is Ridiculous and*

Fast Trip, Long Drop
Gregg Bordowitz
1993, 53:58, U.S., color, sound
In the spring of 1988, video-maker/activist Gregg Bordowitz tested HIV-antibody positive. He then quit drinking and taking drugs and came out to his parents as a gay man. This imaginative autobiographical documentary began as an inquiry into these events and the cultural climate surrounding them. While writing the film, a close friend was diagnosed with breast cancer and his grandparents were killed in a car accident. The cumulative impact of

Bordowitz, Gregg
(continued)

Other Writings:1986-2003. He is currently on faculty in the Film Video and New Media department at The School of the Art Institute of Chicago.

these events challenged his sense of identity, the way he understood his own diagnosis, and his relationships between illness and history.

Habit
Gregg Bordowitz
2001, 52:23, U.S., color, sound
Habit is an autobiographical documentary that follows the current history of the AIDS epidemic along dual trajectories: the efforts of South Africa's leading AIDS activist group, the Treatment Action Campaign, struggling to gain access to AIDS drugs and the daily routine of the videomaker, a veteran AIDS activist in the U.S. who has been living with AIDS for more than ten years. The videomaker moves through his day, attending to mundane errands, eating, taking pills, having conversations with friends (some of whom have diseases such as AIDS and Breast Cancer, and others of whom are healthy), as recurring memories of a recent trip to South Africa interrupt the routine. *Habit* presents a rigorous working-through of ideas concerning privilege, ethics, responsibility, futility, solidarity, hope, and struggle.

some aspect of a shared lifestyle
Gregg Bordowitz
1986, 22:00, U.S., color, sound
Focusing on early media reportage of the AIDS epidemic and the struggle for gay rights, *some aspect of a shared lifestyle* begins with the outraged response of the gay community to the 1982 Supreme Court ruling upholding a Georgia sodomy law, effectively banning gay sex. Reframing the debate from one of moral calumny to a matter of the Constitutional right to privacy, Bordowitz portrays the complexity of issues surrounding the AIDS epidemic as it emerged in the early 1980s in this country, forcefully arguing for the need to confront AIDS as an equal-opportunity threat to all members of society.

Bott, Rich
(see Animal Charm)

Boyce, Bryan

San Francisco native Bryan Boyce is a film and video artist whose work skewers American culture through appropriation and perversion of found footage. His work has screened at film festivals internationally

State of the Union

Pixelhead
Bryan Boyce
1998, 3:00, U.S., color, sound
"A stark and simple drama of man versus TV, *Pixelhead* is an exploration of my love-hate relationship with the television medium in the form of an exaggerated, tragi-comic, semi-autobiography."
—Bryan Boyce

State of the Union
Bryan Boyce
2001, 1:43, U.S., color, sound
Baby Bush meets Tubbyland. Completed in August 2001, this project was initially just a simple comic skewering of George W. Bush and his defense policies—but after September 11th, it took on a whole new meaning. *State of the Union* now has a surreal documentary quality that is genuinely disturbing. "George W. Bush is reimagined as *Teletubbies*' giant baby-in-the-sky for Bryan Boyce's uproarious short *State of the Union*; Daddy's boy makes the same gurgling sounds, though his eyes launch smart bombs at the small, defenseless bunnies who hop around the countryside (one hauntingly devoid of Teletubbies)."
—Jessica Winter, "The Targets Shoot First," *Village Voice* (12 March 2002)

World's Fair World
Bryan Boyce
2002, 9:40, U.S., color, sound
In 1939, Westinghouse made a film about a small-town family visiting the New York World's Fair. Trapped inside that film was a completely different film that shows a mysterious alternate universe, revealed by Bryan Boyce's own patented brand of narrative deconstruction and evisceration. The outcome is a chilling family drama with hints of communism and pedophilia.

Braderman, Joan

With a reputation in both academic and media circles for producing "stand-up" theory, Joan Braderman is a noted video artist and writer. Throughout the 1970s Braderman wrote and spoke widely on imagemaking and the politics of representation, co-founding the influential feminist journal *Heresies*. Displaying a unique sense of dark humor, Braderman's critical tapes on soap opera and celebrity are simultaneously highly articulate, politically compelling, and scandalously humorous. Braderman is also Professor of Video, Film and Media Studies at Hampshire College.

Bratton, Chris
(see Goldson, Annie)

Breder, Hans

Hans Breder studied painting in his native Germany before coming to the U.S. in the mid-1960s. He was a Professor Emeritus of art at the University of Iowa, where he founded the Intermedia and Video Art Program in 1968 and served as its Director until his retirement in December 2000. His work has been exhibited in the Whitney Biennial, the Museum of Modern Art, and numerous international festivals.

Breer, Emily

For more than 15 years, New York-based artist Emily Breer has made films and videos that fuse live-action and playful animation. She frequently collaborates with performer and video artist Joe Gibbons (*The Phony Trilogy*, 1997, and *Classics Exposed*, 1999) to create loony portraits of megalomania and misinformation. Her work has screened at festivals and festivals internationally and been broadcast on PBS. In addition, her music videos and spots have screened in the more pop-oriented forums MTV and Comedy Central.

Joan Does Dynasty
Joan Braderman
1986, 35:00, U.S., color, sound
In *Joan Does Dynasty*–a hilarious classic of feminist media deconstruction–critic Braderman literally projects herself onto the set of the favorite series of 100 million people in 78 countries. Her do-it-yourself deconstruction of TV's most successful nighttime soap opera is at once a succinct critical analysis of the disturbing cultural assumptions inherent in the narrative and an unabashed appreciation of the show's seductive power.

Joan Sees Stars
Joan Braderman
1993, 1:00:00, U.S., color, sound
A tape in two parts ("Starstruck" and "MGM: Movie Goddess Machine") focusing on celebrity culture, identity, and the body. "What is Liz Taylor doing in my bed, in the bed of my friend Leland, as he dies of AIDS?" These and related questions are enacted in a series of encounters between the artist/performer/spectator and a host of famous people from Liz to Anita Hill. In *Joan Sees Stars*, Braderman addresses the subversive potential of masquerade in a parade of video-assisted star sightings.

The Nazi-Loop
Hans Breder
1996, U.S., color, sound, CD-ROM
The Nazi-Loop ponders the horror of the Holocaust and the social diseases that characterized it: ethnocentrism, xenophobia, and anti-Semitism. Images and text from Weimar and Nazi Germany are woven into a complex montage, which includes representations of contemporary neo-Nazism and those who oppose it. Also woven in are essays by social thinkers that reflect upon the meaning of the historical horror of the Holocaust. *The Nazi-Loop* suggests that the obsessive ethnocentrism, xenophobia, and anti-Semitism of past times and places are cyclical and present, here and now.
Note: only available on CD-ROM.

Caddy
Emily Breer
1997, 1:00, U.S., color, sound
Against a background of live action and animation, the caddy's golf club turns into a guitar as he reminisces about playing golf with Iggy Pop: "Hell of a guy, hell of a golfer."
Only available on the anthology *American Psycho(drama): Sigmund Freud vs. Henry Ford* or on the compilation *The Phony Trilogy*.

Classics Exposed
Like a couple of kids pawing through a costume trunk, filmmaker Emily Breer and performance artist Joe Gibbons delight in trying on the attitudes and artifacts of culture. High culture and low–everything is fair game as far as these witty creatures of surreal collision are concerned. Breer's breezy, off-hand declaration, "I'm a postmodern superhero–watch me deconstruct!" perfectly captures the playful spoofing of academia and the anarchic spontaneity found in both artists' work.... These comic pieces seem like off-the-cuff improvisations, but their humor is built on a critique of celebrity and machismo. The pathos of those nerds who fantasize about their unsung influence carries through into *Moby Richard*, which pokes fun at such icons of authority as the museum and the university. Gibbons's rants may be funniest to those who've mastered the pseudo-art of lit-crit, but his loony passion will win over even those who made it through English 101 on *Cliff's Notes* alone.
Total running time 11:00.
Contents:
Kafka's Bugaboo, Emily Breer, 1999, 5:00, U.S., color, sound
Moby Richard, Emily Breer, 1999, 6:00, U.S., color, sound

The Horror
Emily Breer
1997, 2:00, U.S., color, sound
Joe Gibbons sits and sweats on a family beach while telling the story of how he was the inspiration for Francis Ford Coppola's *Heart of Darkness*. The mix of live-action and animation bring to life his hilarious fantasy.
Only available on the anthology *American Psycho(drama): Sigmund Freud vs. Henry Ford* or on the compilation *The Phony Trilogy*.

Kafka's Bugaboo
Emily Breer
1999, 5:00, U.S., color, sound
A neurotic scholar (Joe Gibbons) leads a "buggy" ride tour through historic Charleston where, according to the professor, Franz Kafka wrote *The Metamorphosis* after taking a wrong turn on his way to Hollywood. Live-action with six-legged animation.
Also available on the compilation *Classics Exposed*.

Kafka's Bugaboo

Moby Richard
Emily Breer
1999, 6:00, U.S., color, sound
Psychologically disturbed Professor Herville (Joe Gibbons) analyzes the literary classic *Moby Dick*. He gives a tour of the Herman Melville Museum and makes much ado about the book's Oedipial themes. Breer mixes in footage of the Hollywood adaptation starring Gregory Peck and her own irrepressible animation.
Also available on the compilation *Classics Exposed*.

The Phony Trilogy
A real-time video-meets-digital animation trilogy of shorts featuring the highly excited (and mildly delusional) Joe Gibbons. Brilliant computer animation by collaborator Emily Breer provides an additional layer of biting commentary. Total running time 4:00.
Contents:
Caddy, Emily Breer, 1997, 1:00, U.S., color, sound
The Horror, Emily Breer, 1997, 2:00, U.S., color, sound
Pool Boy, Emily Breer, 1997, 1:00, U.S., color, sound

Pool Boy
Emily Breer
1997, 1:00, U.S., color, sound
In an exuberant mix of animation and live action, Joe Gibbons' springboard becomes a surfboard as he fantasizes about his days as a lifeguard in 1963 when the young Brian Wilson would sit and jot down the songs he would sing while saving lives.

Only available on the anthology *American Psycho(drama): Sigmund Freud vs. Henry Ford* or on the compilation *The Phony Trilogy*.

Broadside TV

Active from 1973 to 1978, Broadside TV was a unique experiment in community-based cable production. Founded by Ted Carpenter as a video training and production center in Johnson City, Tennessee, Broadside TV produced tapes for local programming. Drawing on the oral tradition of the mountains, the tapes featured local history and issues of regional importance, such as the history of union struggles, resistance to strip mining, music, and midwifery.

Jonesboro Storytelling Festival: Kathryn Windham Telling Ghost Stories (The Jumbo Light)
Broadside TV
1974, 6:00, U.S., b&w, sound
This tape features Kathryn Windham, a noted children's author and librarian from Selma, Alabama, relating a ghost story about "The Jumbo Light" at the 1974 Jonesboro Storytelling Festival. This front porch gathering is typical of the casual nature of several of the Broadside tapes.

Only available on the anthology *Surveying the First Decade, Program 6*.

Brown, Tom E.

Tom E. Brown is a self-taught filmmaker based in San Francisco. His shorts include *Don't Run, Johnny*, *Rubber Gloves*, and *Das Clown* and have screened at festivals and museums nationwide and broadcast on television internationally.

Don't Run, Johnny
Tom E. Brown
1996, 7:10, U.S., b&w, sound, 16mm to video
Shot in a schlock-horror mode reminiscent of Ed Wood, Tom E. Brown's film *Don't Run, Johnny* is a witty and poignant AIDS parable that was a major hit on the festival circuit. After testing HIV-positive, the protagonist experiences a panic attack that sends him sprinting through deserted urban streets shot in menacing, high-contrast black and white. Finally, he stops running, saying to himself, "Maybe I am a freak, but in a way... aren't we all?"
Spanish subtitled version available.

Only available on the anthology *Frames of Reference: Reflections on Media, Volume 4, Program 1*.

Bucher, François

François Bucher is an artist from Cali, Columbia, who lives and works in New York City. He combines a variety of media and sources to consider power, violence, and geography. His work has been exhibited internationally in group and solo shows as installations and single-channel pieces. He also co-founded and co-edits *Valdez* magazine.

White Balance (to think is to forget differences)
François Bucher
2002, 32:00, U.S., color, sound
White Balance (to think is to forget differences) is an effort to uncover the geographies of power, the frontiers of privilege. It revisits this problem from different angles, creating short circuits of meaning which are hosted by improbable audiovisual matches. Media and Internet footage is intermixed with images shot in downtown Manhattan before and after the September 11th attacks. The video presents a question that needs to be visited over and over, a question that is always and necessarily larger than ourselves. Yvonne Rainer asked this question in her film *Privilege*: "...is 'permanent recovering racists' the most we can ever be?" In this sense, offering a meta-narrative that would pretend to describe the issues at stake is a failure to understand the layers of unspeakability that are hidden in the question of whiteness. The piece opts for a poetic language, an address that seeks to arouse thought by concentrating on the openings of the audiovisual experience, in the short-lived moment of the in-between.

Buckner, Barbara

Barbara Buckner began working with video and computers in 1972 while studying with engineer and electronic tool designer Bill Etra. In 1976 Buckner moved to Rhinebeck, New York, where she and fellow media artists Gary Hill, David Jones, and Stephen Kolpan lived collectively under the auspices of Woodstock Community Video. Buckner later worked at the Experimental Television Center, where she experimented with a complex array of electronic imaging tools and systems.

Pictures of the Lost
Barbara Buckner
1978, 8:00 excerpt (of 23:00), U.S., color, silent
Composed in 22 movements that introduce a series of silent, haunting, other-worldly landscapes, Pictures of the Lost hovers between figuration and abstraction, and reveals Buckner's sustained interest in spirituality. Produced at the Experimental Television Center in Owego, New York.
"I began with a desire to create a kind of electronic poetics, where the video image expressed a metaphoric identity emerging from its organic structure, yet had a universal quality drawing on the traditions of poetry, painting, and music. There were always two central concerns—exploring the medium with the tools that were available and expressing inner states of beingness and becoming."
—Barbara Buckner

Only available as an excerpt on the anthology *Surveying the First Decade, Program 5*.

Buil, José
(see Sistach, Maryse)

Bull, Peter and Alex Gibney

While students at the University of California-San Diego, Peter Bull and Alex Gibney produced experimental films and worked as assistant producers in commercial television before collaborating on *The Ruling Classroom* (1979). They spent a semester documenting an experiment conducted in a Mill Valley seventh grade classroom in which students invented and enacted the political, social, and economic aspects of an imaginary country.

The Ruling Classroom
Peter Bull and Alex Gibney
1979-80, 58:25, U.S., color, sound
The Ruling Classroom documents a social studies experiment played out by seventh graders in Mill Valley, California. The students reorganized their classroom as an imaginary country until the principal staged a coup and brought the classroom republic to a halt. The educational experiment was the brainchild of teacher George Muldoon, who suspended the normal social studies curriculum in order to let his students learn about government by constructing it for themselves. Bull and Gibney videotaped the proceedings using a verité approach coupled with after-school interviews with students. Over the course of the semester the make-believe society, like the one they would soon inher-

it, develops serious problems such as freedom of the press, white collar crime, economic monopolies, and unemployment. The tape was aired nationally on PBS and stirred up local controversy when the school's principal called off the experiment after the video team uncovered a story about a teacher slapping a student. He then unsuccessfully tried to prevent the tape's further release.

Only available on the anthology *Surveying the First Decade, Program 8.*

Bureau of Inverse Technology

Formed in 1992, Bureau of Inverse Technology (BIT) is an organization that exists in geographic dispersion (Melbourne, San Francisco, and Berlin). BIT questions the safety of the corporate imagination and its design upon our technological futures as a self-described "information agency for the information age."

BIT Plane
Bureau of Inverse Technology
1999, 13:00, U.S., b&w, sound
A Bureau-guided miniature spy plane mission into the glittering heart of the Silicon Valley to investigate the progress of the Information Age.

Suicide Box
Bureau of Inverse Technology
1996, 13:00, U.S., color, sound
"A documentary video about the BIT Suicide Box—a motion-triggered camera developed by the Bureau of Inverse Technology (a private information agency), and installed within range of the Golden Gate Bridge to capture a video record of anything that falls from the bridge, and provide an accurate measure of the suicide rate. The tape points to confusing roles for technology within contemporary culture."
—Whitney Biennial (New York: Whitney Museum of American Art, 1996)
Spanish subtitled version available.

Also available on the anthologies *The New McLennium, Program 1* and *Frames of Reference: Reflections on Media, Volume 5, Program 1.*

Burns, Torsten Z.
(see HalfLifers)

Bush, Paul

Paul Bush's films challenge the boundaries that separate fiction, documentary, and animation. He taught himself how to make films while a member of the London Film Makers Co-op and Chapter Film Workshop in Cardiff. He has lectured, run workshops, and tutored at numerous art and film courses around the world.

Dr. Jekyll and Mr. Hyde
Paul Bush
2001, 5:15, U.K., color, sound
Imagine that the camera is possessed with a psychosis similar to human schizophrenia; suppose that this disease subtly changes every single frame of film while leaving the narrative superficially intact. Then imagine that these symptoms came on as a result of the trauma of recording bizarre or horrific events, for instance those of the 1941 horror film *Dr. Jekyll and Mr. Hyde.* Adapted from the novel by Robert Louis Stevenson.

Furniture Poetry
Paul Bush
1999, 5:15, U.K., color, sound
"What prevents me from supposing that this table either vanishes or alters its shape when no one is observing it and then when someone looks at it again changes back? But one feels like saying—who is going to suppose such a thing?"
—Ludwig Wittgenstein, *On Certainty* (Oxford: Blackwell, 1969)
The filmmaker accepts the challenge of the philosopher and changes not only a table but also chairs, shoes, jugs, teapots, and almost everything else lying around his house.

PAS DE DEUX DE DEUX
Paul Bush
2001, 5:30, U.K., color, sound
The orchestra begins, and male and female dancers move from opposite sides of the stage. The dancers embrace and begin the *White Swan pas de deux*; however, the choreography has been re-staged so that in every single frame the two original dancers have been replaced by the bodies of four new ones. The movement remains continuous and the characteristics of the dancers' movements and gestures the same, but in each frame a different person occupies the dancers' body spaces. A parasitic population has completely taken over the body of its host while allowing its movements and mannerisms to remain intact. This is an exploration in which science is tempered

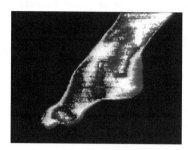

Rumour of True Things

C-Hundred Film Corp.

The C-Hundred Film Corp was founded in 1987 by Jim McKay and Michael J. Stipe. In the early 1990s the organization produced an award-winning series of 21 public service announcements, collectively titled *Direct Effect.* Since then the company has developed numerous independent features, including *Girls Town* (Jim McKay, 1996), *Benjamin Smoke* (Jem Cohen and Peter Sillen, 2000), *Our Song* (Jim McKay, 2000), *The Sleepy Time Gal* (Christopher Munch, 2001), and *Stranger Inside* (Cheryl Dunye, 2001).

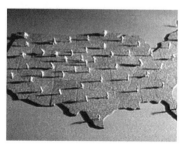

Step out of the Shadows

with humor, and one that is led by an instinctive and experimental approach to the techniques and equipment of filmmaking rather than any prescriptive ideas either about the psychology of perception, Freudian analysis, film, or ballet.

Rumour of True Things
Paul Bush
1996, 26:00, U.K., color, sound
Most of the moving images produced for science, industry, commerce, and medicine are seen only by specialized audiences and are then discarded soon after they are made. *Rumour of True Things* is constructed entirely from such moving image ephemera, including computer games, weapons testing, production lines, monitoring, and marriage agency tapes. *Rumour of True Things* is a remarkable anthropological portrait of a technologically-based society obsessed with imaging itself.

Also available on the anthology *The New McLennium, Program 1.*

Direct Effect PSAs, Volume 1
C-Hundred Film Corp.
1990, 9:00, U.S., color, sound
Contents:
What Does Away Mean? by Jem Cohen advertises the need to recycle through reconsideration of landfills and garbage disposal.
Pro-Choice is Pro-Life by Jane Pratt makes its point with the simple logic that every child should be cared for and wanted.
Historic Preservation by Jim McKay counsels for the preservation of historic buildings endangered by urban decay.
Love Knows No Color by Tom Gilroy spreads the message that love is more than skin deep through a series of images of interracial couples.
Be Caring, Be Careful by James Herbert advertises safe sex practices and the use of condoms to spread love, not AIDS.
Chemical Farming by Michael J. Stipe urges serious re-consideration of the use of the pesticides that are contaminating our food supply.
World Peace by Susan Robeson and KRS-One brings the message that the only peace is world peace.

Direct Effect PSAs, Volume 2
C-Hundred Film Corp.
1991, 9:00, U.S., color, sound
This tape collects public service announcements created by a number of independent producers, including Jem Cohen and Michael J. Stipe of R.E.M. Powerful and provocative, these PSAs address issues such as organic farming, abortion rights, street harassment, and the environment.
Contents:
They Have Dreams by Natalie Merchant and Abigail Simon focuses on the plight of homeless children.
Monuments by Adam Cohen considers which monuments we leave for the future in the wake of military build-ups and ever-expanding landfills.
Family by Yalonda Busbee and Dorothy Owusu confronts the negative assumptions about single black mothers with the positive, life-affirming truths.
Right to Know by Jason Kliot announces the federal ruling granting all citizens access to information on toxic waste locations.
Sexual Harassment by Jane Pratt and Patti Hunter reframes the issue of sexual harassment as a matter of respect for a woman's privacy on the street and elsewhere.
Step out of the Shadows by Joana Vincente emphasizes that the right to vote is a responsibility and a privilege that leads to empowerment.
This Is a Condom by Jim McKay provides basic information about condoms, providing slang terms, in the service of safe sex education.

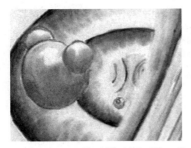

Direct Effect PSAs, Volume 3

Direct Effect PSAs, Volume 3
C-Hundred Film Corp.
1992, 11:00, U.S., color, sound
The third compilation in a series of progressive, creative public service announcements for under-reported issues. Featuring various styles and formats, from street photography to optical printing, from edgy black-and-white film to hand-drawn animation.
Contents:
The Breathing Tree by Eric Darnell and Doug Loveid is an animated, easy-to-understand explanation of how forests contribute to life by producing oxygen.
Put Crime in Perspective by Dorothy Owusu, Rob Grobenbieser, and Brendan Dolan comments on the media's overemphasis on inner-city crime, as compared to government corruption which is just as, if not more, serious.
More Than Luck by Stephanie Black with a poem by Mutabaruka shows that rather than lotteries and get-rich-quick schemes, we need equal economic opportunity.
America the Beautiful by Marce Sterner and Jim McQuillan is an appeal to recycle; the emblematic American eagle is replaced with the '90s version—a sea gull sitting on a pile of landfill trash.
Listen to Your Heart by Barry Ellsworth asks you to decide for yourself whether or not to circumcise your son, rather than listening to social or religious pressures.
Warning... (Patriarchal Values May Be Hazardous to Your Health) by Donna Olson shows the many phrases still commonly used that can erode a woman's self-esteem.
Change by Jason Kliot and Jacob Ribicoff plays on the title to point out that to combat homelessness, poverty, and other problems, you can give away change (coins) or you can create real change by voting for housing and education.

"Talk about the Passion" (R.E.M.)
Jem Cohen and C-Hundred Film Corp.
1988, 4:00, U.S., color, sound
An alternative music video featuring R.E.M. and directed by Jem Cohen. A poetic and passionate indictment of a world where out-of-control military budgets are paid for at the expense of the impoverished.

Also available on the Jem Cohen compilations *Just Hold Still* and *Jem Cohen: Early Works.*

Campus, Peter

Peter Campus's early tapes explore the anatomy of the video signal in relation to human psychology and perception. In the mid-1970s Campus produced work in the Experimental TV Labs at WGBH-Boston and WNET-New York. In addition to numerous single-channel works, he has investigated the characteristics of live video through closed-circuit video installations and elaborate sculptural works with components including video cameras, projectors, and monitors.

Canner, Elizabeth
(see Julia Meltzer)

Double Vision
Peter Campus
1971, 15:00, U.S., b&w, sound
Campus investigates the metaphoric overlap between properties of the video camera and processes of human perception, an area of great interest to many early videomakers. *Double Vision* inventories strategies for comparing simultaneous images of a loft space produced by two video cameras whose signals are fed through a mixer, thus producing an electronic version of what in film would be called a "double exposure." The cameras are set up to perform variations of binocular vision; for example, in the section entitled "Copilia," the two cameras are set at different focal lengths and search independently around an empty room, attached to the same moving body. In "Convergence," the cameras are stationary and separated but focused on the same distant wall; their images gradually merge as the artist repeatedly returns to the cameras and moves them closer together. *Double Vision* is an elegant and systematic exploration of vision using basic video technology.

Only available on the anthology *Surveying the First Decade, Program 2.*

Cardoso, Maria Fernando and Ross Rudesch Harley

Maria Fernanda Cardoso is a Colombian artist whose works incorporate unconventional natural materials. She made her own circus, the Cardoso Flea Circus, and she's ringmaster, flea-trainer, costume designer and friend to a bunch of highly-educated fleas. Ross Rudesch Harley is an interdisciplinary artist and writer.

Carelli, Vincent
(see Video in the Villages)

Castle, Jane
(see Cheang, Shu Lea)

Centro Trabalho Ingenista
(see Video in the Villages)

Chan, Paul

Paul Chan is an artist based in New York City.

RE:THE_OPERATION

Cardoso Flea Circus
Maria Fernanda Cardoso and Ross Rudesch Harley
1997, 8:00, Australia, color, sound
No one believed it would be possible to train fleas, but Maria Fernanda Cardoso has proven everyone wrong. After five years of intensive research, the Cardoso Flea Circus is presented here in this sensational video. Produced by Philadelphia's Fabric Workshop and Museum on the occasion of Cardoso's residency, this video will convince even the most hardened skeptics that it's all true! Thanks to sophisticated video equipment and high-tech lenses, Ross Rudesch Harley has captured the feats of these prodigious insects in the world's smallest spectacle: the Cardoso Flea Circus!

Also available on the anthology *American Psycho(drama): Sigmund Freud vs. Henry Ford.*

BAGHDAD IN NO PARTICULAR ORDER
Paul Chan
2003, 51:00, U.S., color, sound, in Arabic, Chinese, English, French, German, Italian, and Spanish with English subtitles
Notes, gifts, promises, paintings, trash, and other ephemera from the city, which is now hardly a city. What if Walter Benjamin didn't kill himself, learned html, bought a camera, and thought himself useful enough to work in an impending war zone? *BAGHDAD IN NO PARTICULAR ORDER* is an ambient video essay of life in Baghdad before the U.S. invasion and occupation. Men dance, women draw, and sufis sing as they await the coming of another war.
Note: This is Part I, a single-channel video; Part II is a website that can be viewed online at www.nationalphilistine.com/baghdad.

Now Let Us Praise American Leftists
Paul Chan
2000, 2:30, U.S., b&w, sound
Now Let Us Praise American Leftists is an experimental video animation that seeks to eulogize and ridicule the American leftist movement of the past century. Foregrounding the exclusionary nature of American leftist politics and its persistent refusal to allow more diversity in terms of race, ethnicity, and sexual orientation to enter into the larger political dialogue, the video presents representations of American leftists as they are: men with mustaches. More than 60 leftist groups in the history of American leftist politics are represented with different types of mustaches, created using FACES™, a computer application used by North American law enforcement agencies to create composite pictures of criminals and suspects for wanted posters.

RE:THE_OPERATION
Paul Chan
2002, 27:30, U.S., color, sound
Based on a set of drawings that depict George W. Bush's administration as wounded soldiers in the war against terrorism, *RE:THE_OPERATION* explores the sexual and philosophical dynamics of war through the lives of the cabinet members as they physically engage each other and the "enemy." Letters, notes, and digital snapshots "produced" by the members on their tour of duty become the basis of video portraits that articulate the neuroses and obsessions compelling them toward an infinite war. Produced out of rage at the military actions against Afghanistan, Chan endows the Bush cabinet and military leaders with the qualities—philosophical depth, moral doubts, and human lust—that he wishes they had. Part *M*A*S*H* and part *Three's Company*, part philosophical meditation and part character assassination, *RE:THE_OPERATION* exists as a single channel video and a set of desktop replacement icons for MAC and PC computers.

Cheang, Shu Lea

Shu Lea Cheang tackles conceptions of racial assimilation in American culture, examining the political underbelly of everyday situations that affect the relationship between individuals and society. Using video in formally innovative installations, her works include the *Airwaves Project* (1991), which focuses on the one-way flow of global information and industrial waste, and *Those Fluttering Objects of Desire* (1992), an installation presenting the work of women artists negotiating interracial sexual politics. Cheang's single-channel tapes, made independently and in collaboration as E.T. Baby Maniac, explore ethnic identity and lesbian erotics. E.T. Baby Maniac includes Ela Troyano, a Cuban-born director and producer, and Jane Castle, a noted camerawoman.

Coming Home
Shu Lea Cheang
1995, 5:00, U.S., color, sound, in Japanese with English subtitles
This humorous video begins with two women—one white, the other Asian—attempting to fit into a Japanese bathtub. The awkward fitting of bodies into a small space is just one of the allegorical scenarios dramatized in a pressing appeal for lesbian rights. In a game of hanafuda (flower cards), the terms of lesbian domesticity are cleverly played out according to such legalities as joint property, social security, and pensions.
With script and performance by Izumo Marou and Claire Maree, Superdyke, Inc., Japan; music by Chu.
Also available on the compilation *Shu Lea Cheang: Lesbian Shorts.*

Fingers and Kisses
Shu Lea Cheang
1995, 4:00, U.S., color, sound, in Japanese with English subtitles
Cheang has taken her camera to the streets for a candid glimpse of lesbian public sexuality. If Asian women and lesbians share a certain amount of invisibility in the culture, *Fingers and Kisses* offers not only a bold representation of both but also a challenge to the question "What do lesbians do?" Tokyo's own out-and-loud music by Chu punctuates the narrative as what begins in the streets continues under the sheets.
With script and performance by Izumo Marou and Claire Maree, Superdyke Inc., Japan.
Also available on the compilation *Shu Lea Cheang: Lesbian Shorts.*

Fresh Kill
Shu Lea Cheang
1994, 1:18:41, U.S., color, sound
Shu Lea Cheang's witty narrative *Fresh Kill* envisions a post-apocalyptic landscape strewn with electronic detritus and suffering the toxic repercussions of mass marketing in a high-tech commodity culture.
Spanish subtitled version available.
Only available on the anthology *Frames of Reference: Reflections on Media, Volume 5, Program 1.*

Sex Bowl
Baby Maniac (Shu Lea Cheang and Jane Castle)
1994, 7:00, U.S., b&w, sound
All forms of human sport become sites for sexual play and celebratory eroticism. "The tape's images are quick, suggestive, and sexy: fingers moving into bowling balls, shoe-smelling and toe-sucking, a dog wearing chain jewelry, fish being wrapped at the market, young naked couples having sex.... Edited like a music video, the image track is a constant flow of fetishes that lure us into the promiscuous pace of girls who keep lists of their sexual encounters."
—Chris Straayer, *Deviant Eyes, Deviant Bodies: Sexual Re-orientations in Film and Video* (New York: Columbia University Press, 1996)
Also available on the compilation *Shu Lea Cheang: Lesbian Shorts.*

Sex Fish
E.T. Baby Maniac (Shu Lea Cheang, Jane Castle, and Ela Troyano)
1993, 6:00, U.S., b&w, sound
An erotic lesbian video involving swimming upstream, female power, and fish love. Made as a collaboration under the name E.T. (Ela Troyano) Baby (Jane Castle) Maniac (Cheang).
"In *Sex Fish* water provides the common denominator for nature imagery and explicit sex. Unlike 1970s feminist imagery, however, nature is sexualized rather than sex naturalized. Dripping from the faucet, spraying against a shower curtain, swirling down a toilet, water leads viewers from one sex scene to another, private to public and back again. Swimming through the video are various fish, seemingly unaware of the derogatory pun they enact, and all gulping enviously as cunnilingus surrounds them."

Sex Fish

—Chris Straayer, *Deviant Eyes, Deviant Bodies: Sexual Re-orientations in Film and Video* (New York: Columbia University Press, 1996)
Also available on the compilation *Shu Lea Cheang: Lesbian Shorts.*

Shu Lea Cheang: Lesbian Shorts

Cheang's work from the early-to-mid 1990s demonstrated an exciting fusion of identity politics and erotic exploration, making her one of the period's most prominent queer media artists. This collection presents two of her solo works, along with two collaborations.
Total running time 22:00.
Contents:
Coming Home, Shu Lea Cheang, 1995, 5:00, U.S., color, sound
Fingers and Kisses, Shu Lea Cheang, 1995, 4:00, U.S., color, sound
Sex Bowl, Baby Maniac,1994, 7:00, U.S., b&w, sound
Sex Fish, E.T. Baby Maniac, 1993, 6:00, U.S., b&w, sound

Those Fluttering Objects of Desire

Shu Lea Cheang
1992, 1:00:00, U.S., b&w, sound
This tape was originally an installation at the Whitney Museum of American Art, part of which included the video collaboration *Channels of Desire.* Recreating coin-operated porno booths, *Channels* aired one photo image on seven TVs, interrupted only by the viewer inserting a coin and choosing a segment. The concept behind it was the construction of desire in categorical ways, the form of the piece speaking to sexual desire as something that is constantly evading the viewer. The images present women's experiences with interracial, lesbian, and heterosexual encounters. *Those Fluttering Objects of Desire* also investigates the different construction of sexuality among white and black women, as well as multicultural readings.

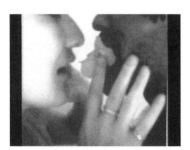
Those Fluttering Objects of Desire

Those Fluttering Objects of Desire (Excerpt)

Shu Lea Cheang
1992, 19:00, U.S., b&w, sound
Condensed from the full-length version, this excerpt of *Those Fluttering Objects of Desire* focuses on the lesbian tapes from the installation, including *I've Never* by Pamela Jennings, *Vanilla Sex* by Cheryl Dunye, *What's the Difference Between a Yam and a Sweet Potato?* by Adriene Jenik and J. Evans, and *Brown Sugar Licks Snow White* by Robin Vachal and Suzie Silbar.

Shu Lea Cheang: An Interview (see On Art and Artists)
The Trial of Tilted Arc (see Serra, Richard in On Art and Artists)

Child, Abigail

Abigail Child's work investigates pop cultural constructions of gender identity, sexuality, and voyeurism, while employing soundtracks layered with canned music, suggestive noises, and dialogue. Through rapid collages of image fragments from industrial, rare, and early films and newsreels, Child constructs experimental narratives while drawing attention to conventional devices such as costumes, looks, poses, and gestures used to build narrative continuity and excitement.

Both

Abigail Child
1989, 3:00, U.S., b&w, sound
A beautifully ambiguous study of the nude in light and movement, this short silent film focuses on the dimly lit bodies of two women shot from Child's distinctly non-male perspective.

Covert Action

Abigail Child
1984, 10:00, U.S., b&w, sound
Covert Action is a stunning melange of rapid-fire retro imagery accomplishing Child's proclaimed goal to "disarm my movies." "I wanted to examine the erotic behind the social and remake those gestures into a dance that would confront their conditioning and, as well, relay the multiple fictions the footage suggests (the 'facts' forever obscured in the fragments left us). The result is a narrative developed by its periphery, a story like rumor: impossible to trace, disturbing, explosive."

Mayhem
Abigail Child
1987, 20:00, U.S., b&w, sound
Through a catalogue of looks, movements, and gestures, *Mayhem* presents a social order run amok in a libidinous retracing of film noir conventions. Sexuality flows in an atmosphere of sexual tension, danger, violence, and glamour; antagonism between the sexes is symbolized in the costuming of women in polka dots and men in stripes. Censored in Tokyo for its use of Japanese lesbian erotica, this tape creates an image bank of what signifies the sexual and the seductive in the history of imagemaking, pointing to the way we learn about our bodies, and how to use them from images.

Mercy
Abigail Child
1989, 10:00, U.S., b&w, sound
Child masterfully composes a rhythmic collage of symmetries and asymmetries in a fluid essay that foregrounds the treatment of the body as a mechanized instrument—placing the body in relation to the man-made landscape of factories, amusement parks, and urban office complexes. Vocals performed by Shelley Hirsch.

Mutiny

Mutiny
Abigail Child
1982, 11:00, U.S., b&w, sound
Mutiny employs panoply of expression, gesture, and repeated movement. Its central images are of women: at home, on the street, at the workplace, at school, talking, singing, jumping on trampolines, playing the violin. The syntax of the film reflects the possibilities and limitations of speech, while "politically, physically, and realistically" flirting with the language of opposition.

Perils
Abigail Child
1985, 5:00, U.S., b&w, sound
Perils is a homage to silent film—the clash of ambiguous innocence and unsophisticated villainy—dramatizing the theatrical postures of melodrama to confront and examine our ideas of romance, action, and drama. Child says, "I had long conceived of a film composed only of reaction shots in which all causality was erased. What would be left would be the resonant voluptuous suggestions of history and the human face." Charles Noyes and Christian Marclay constructed the sound montage from Warner Brothers cartoons and improvisations.

Prefaces
Abigail Child
1981, 10:00, U.S., b&w, sound
Prefaces is composed of wild sounds constructed along entropic lines, placed tensely beside bebop rhythms, and a resurfacing narrative cut from a dialogue with poet Hannah Weiner. Child tells us, "The tracks are placed in precise and asynchronous relation to images of workers, the gestures of the marketplace, colonial Africa, and abstractions, to pose questions of social force, gender relations and subordination." This tape serves as a pre-conscious preface to the parts that follow, whose scope and image bank are more narrowly defined.

Swamp
Abigail Child
1990, 35:00, U.S., b&w, sound
Child uses the soap opera format to play with the structure and expectations of the family melodrama. Following the melodramatic formula that "if it can happen, it will happen," coincidence and unlikely events abound in *Swamp*'s gleeful send-up of lurid intrigue, threatened morality, and endless double-crosses. With looped and repeated edits, fast-paced action, and aggressively

funky video effects, Child layers on artifice and excess in an overdone remake of the TV serial.
With Carla Harryman, Steve Benson, Susie Bright, Tede Matthews, Marga Gomez, and George Kuchar.

Cohen, Jem

Jem Cohen is a New York-based film- and videomaker. Often shooting in hundreds of locations with little or no additional crew, Cohen collects street footage, portraits, and sounds. Some of the projects are personal/political city portraits while others reflect upon daily life and ephemeral moments: things seen out of the corner of the eye and pulled into the center. Cohen has made two feature-length documentaries, *Instrument* (with and about *Fugazi*, 1999) and *Benjamin Smoke* (co-directed by Peter Sillen, 2000), as well as the feature project *Chain* (2004). Cohen has also worked with numerous musicians including R.E.M., Sparklehorse, Elliott Smith, Jonathan Richman, Patti Smith, Vic Chesnutt, Stephen Vitiello, and Gil Shaham with the Orpheus Orchestra.

Buried in Light (Central and Eastern Europe in Passing)

Amber City
Jem Cohen
1999, 48:00, U.S., color, sound, 16mm to video
A portrait of an unnamed city in Italy. Sidestepping the tourist attractions that make the city famous, the film/video posits an almost-imaginary place that draws closer to the reality of its inhabitants. Using a voice-over narration that collages direct observation, literary texts, historical fact, local folklore, and a bit of sheer fabrication, the film/video melds documentary and narrative, past and present. Visuals range from verité street footage, to formal portraits of residents, to an unusual type of time lapse cinematography that allows filming in the low-intensity light of night landscapes and museum interiors. Made in collaboration with local residents and institutions, *Amber City* reflects on the "in-betweeness" of places whose historical and geographical location renders their reality strangely invisible.

Black Hole Radio
Jem Cohen
1992, 8:00, U.S., b&w and color, sound, Super-8 to video
"In the late 1980s I saw ads in New York for a telephone 'Confession Line.' To call in and 'confess' was free; listening in incurred a by-the-minute charge. The soundtrack was built from a collection of these actual, anonymous calls. Adultery, theft, and regret; ghosts spun through phone wires and televisions."
—Jem Cohen

An installation version was created for the 1992 Worldwide Video Festival (Amsterdam).
Soundtrack by Jem Cohen with Ian MacKaye.
Also available on the compilation *Jem Cohen: Early Works*.

Blood Orange Sky
Jem Cohen
1999, 26:00, U.S., color, sound, 16mm to video
A portrait of Catania, Sicily. Includes the ocean at 5 a.m., the fish market, the distributor of pornographic films, the woodworker, the elephant statue, housing projects, and a young girl in an orange sweater. Catania is a large and remarkable city without many tourists or tourist attractions. Its people live in the shadow of Mt. Aetna, an active volcano. Mark Linkous of the band Sparklehorse composed original soundtrack for the project, which also contains music by local Catania musicians.
Note: this film/video was made at the invitation of the Sicilian arts group Officine.

Buried in Light (Central and Eastern Europe in Passing)
Jem Cohen
1994, 1:00:00, U.S., b&w and color, sound, Super-8 to video
"A meditation on history, memory, and change in Central and Eastern Europe, *Buried in Light* is a non-narrative journey, a cinematic collage. Cohen's 'search for images' began at a time of extraordinary flux, as the Berlin Wall was dismantled—opening borders yet ushering in a nascent wave of consumer capitalism. What he saw struck him as a profound paradox: the moment Eastern Europe was revealed was simultaneously the moment it was hidden by the blinding light of commercialism. Cohen's images are neither the tourist's roster of picturesque vistas and monuments, nor the mass media's definitive catalog of dramatic moments. Instead, he focuses on details, ordinary objects, and forgotten places—filming daily life as seen on the street."
—Linda Dubler, *Art at the Edge* (Atlanta: High Museum of Art)

Drink Deep

Drink Deep
Jem Cohen
1991, 10:00, U.S., b&w and color, sound, Super-8
Drink Deep is a lyrical vision of friendship, hidden secrets, and desires.
Cohen uses several types of film image to add texture to the layered composition. Beautiful shades of gray, silver, black and blue echo the water, reminiscent of early photography and silverprints. Cohen says, "The piece was constructed primarily from footage I'd shot of skinny-dippers at swimming holes in Georgia and rural Pennsylvania. It's about water and memory and stories just submerged. It is also, in part, a response to thinking about censorship. I would say that *Drink Deep* is both unabashedly and deceptively romantic. Surface, flow, and undertow. What looks like paradise is always paradise lost."
With music composed by Stephen Vitiello and performed with Gabriel Cohen and Mary Wooten.
Also available on the compilation *Jem Cohen: Early Works*.

Instrument
Jem Cohen
1999, 1:55:00, U.S., color, sound, Super-8/16mm/video
A collaboration between Jem Cohen and the band Fugazi, this project covers the ten-year period following the band's inception in 1987. Far from a traditional documentary, the project is a musical document: a portrait of musicians at work.
"With no desire on my part or the band's to create a factual career survey or any kind of promotional vehicle, the project presented an opportunity to cut things loose. Mixing sync-sound 16mm, Super-8, video, and a wide range of archival formats, the piece includes concert footage, studio sessions, practice, touring, interviews, and portraits of audience members from around the country. Piecing it together over the course of 5 years, I thought of bringing 'dub' to documentary—of a project where unadulterated real-time performances, abstract, rough-hewn Super-8 collages and archival artifacts would collide and conjoin in a way that honestly represented musical experience. The project was edited with band members and extensively uses soundtrack elements provided by Fugazi specifically for the film."
—Jem Cohen

Jem Cohen: Early Works
This compilation features several of Cohen's pieces from the late 1980s and early 1990s: a paean to both the physical and mental aspects of the New York City landscape, an exploration of cinematic genres from narrative to music video, a sensual and romantic portrait of swimmers at a water hole, and a sound and image piece inspired by a telephone confession line.
Total running time 1:15:00.
Contents:
Black Hole Radio, Jem Cohen, 1992, 8:00, U.S., b&w and color, sound,
Super-8 to video
Drink Deep, Jem Cohen, 1991, 10:00, U.S., b&w and color, sound, Super-8
Just Hold Still, Jem Cohen, 1989, 35:00, U.S., b&w and color, sound,
Super-8
This Is a History of New York, Jem Cohen, 1987, 23:00, U.S., b&w, sound,
Super-8 to video

Black Hole Radio

Just Hold Still
Jem Cohen
1989, 35:00, U.S., b&w and color, sound, Super-8
In his New York City landscape, Cohen finds inspiration in disturbance.
Looking to life for rhythm and to architecture for state of mind, he locates simple mysteries. *Just Hold Still* is comprised of an interconnected series of short works and collaborations that explore the gray area between documentary, narrative, and experimental genres. The first part concerns a personal, poetic approach to narrative and includes *4:44 (From Her House Home)*,

Never Change (with Blake Nelson), *Love Teller* (with Ben Katchor), and *Light Years*. The second part involves hybridized use of verité footage and the confrontation of documentary concerns with the music video format and includes *Selected City Films*, *Glue Man* (with Ian MacKaye), and *Talk about the Passion* (with R.E.M). The work can be considered as a whole, or each piece in the project can be viewed (and rented) as a separate entity.

Also available on the compilation *Jem Cohen: Early Works.*

Little Flags
Jem Cohen
2000, 6:30, U.S., b&w, sound, Super-8 to video
Cohen shot *Little Flags* in black and white on the streets of lower Manhattan during an early-'90s military ticker-tape parade and edited the footage years later. The crowd noises fade and Cohen shows the litter flooding the streets as the urban location looks progressively more ghostly and distant from the present. Everyone loves a parade—except for the dead.

Lost Book Found
Jem Cohen
1996, 37:00, U.S., b&w and color, sound, Super-8 and 16mm to video
The result of more than five years of Super-8 and 16mm filming on New York City streets, *Lost Book Found* melds documentary and narrative into a complex meditation on city life. The piece revolves around a mysterious notebook filled with obsessive listings of places, objects, and incidents. These listings serve as the key to a hidden city: a city of unconsidered geographies and layered artifacts—the relics of low-level capitalism and the debris of countless forgotten narratives. The project stems from the filmmaker's first job in New York—working as a pushcart vendor on Canal Street. As usual, Cohen shot in hundreds of locations using unobtrusive equipment and generally without any crew. Influenced by the work of Walter Benjamin, Cohen created "an archive of undirected shots and sounds, then set out to explore the boundary" between genres. During the process, Cohen said, "I found connections between the street vendor, Benjamin's 'flaneur,' and my own work as an observer and collector of ephemeral street life."

Lost Book Found

This Is a History of New York
Jem Cohen
1987, 23:00, U.S., b&w, sound, Super-8 to video
A history of New York City from Prehistoric times through the Space Age, composed entirely from documentary street footage.

"The richness of Cohen's vision is found in his haunting imagery and the perception that the thriving city of New York is really the accumulation of humanity's failures, as well as its triumphs."
—Steve Seid, *Seduced and Abandoned: The Homeless Video by Sachiko Hamada & Scott Sinkler and Jem Cohen* (Berkeley: Pacific Film Archive, 1989)

Also available on the compilation *Jem Cohen: Early Works.*

This Is a History of New York

Jem Cohen: An Interview (see On Art and Artists)

Cokes, Tony

Juxtaposing re-edited broadcast and archival footage with quotations in the form of on-screen text and voiceovers, Cokes's experimental documentaries explore the ideological implications of media representation and rhetoric. His work foregrounds theoretical questions of racial and sexual difference, enunciation, and history.

2@
Tony Cokes
2000, 6:00, U.S., color, sound
The first in a five-part series called *Pop Manifestos,* a video project realized by Tony Cokes in collaboration with two former students and originally conceived as part of a series for the conceptual band SWIPE. In addition to *2@,* the series also includes *3#, 6^,* and *Ad Vice.*

"*2@* rehearses a subjective, skeptically positioned history of rock to a generic song by the noise-pop band SWIPE. My approach was inspired by Dan Graham's videotape *Rock My Religion,* which deploys a punk-influenced documentary technique to construct a consumer discourse about rock history. I borrow Graham's desire to put rock music's history of production and recep-

tion in a critical context."
—Tony Cokes

3#

3#
Tony Cokes
2001, 4:38, U.S., color, sound
3# uses a track composed by media artist Seth Price, its music is based on the forms of 1980s electronic pop songs. Price uses music production software to copy the structure of popular music from the recent past. By editing out one element (in this case, the singer), he comments on the genre through an imperfect copy. The video uses text and graphic transitions to outline an argument about how and why pop music functions, pointing to its promise of unique, infamous, and sublime experiences through repetition and mass distribution. *3#* borrows lyrics from British "mope pop" icon Morrissey.

5%
Tony Cokes and Scott Pagano
2003, 10:00, U.S., color, sound
"*5%* is a ten-minute work that questions the cult of pop stardom, deconstructs music industry practices, considers the problematics of live performance, and suggests other, more anonymous working strategies. For this work I decided to collaborate closely with musician, media artist, and designer Scott Pagano who, along with Marc Pierson, currently forms the core of SWIPE. Our idea of generic music came out of a belief that pop music was more about life under post-industrial commodity capital than it was about 'love,' 'emotion,' or 'personal expression.' Narratives of superstardom were the grease that kept the idiotic grind looped, moving in place. The soundtrack is two recent SWIPE tracks: 'mm_2' (2000) and '1cc_v2+' (2001)."
—Tony Cokes

6^
Tony Cokes
2001, 4:33, U.S., color, sound
*6^*, based on a music track by Damian Kulash, blends essayistic text and quoted song lyrics to self-reflexivity question the desires of both performers and audience in pop music forms. Kulash's song "init: A Song for Cynical Art #4" invokes the desire to write songs, rehearses the possible subject matters, then questions the subjective authenticity of such a gesture. The video literalizes the song's implicit criticism in theoretical (essay) and practical (quoted song lyrics) registers, underlining "individual" desire as a mere shell for mass marketing. The consumer's desire for a representation of her own personal "emotion" is sold repeatedly in atomized niches globally.

Ad Vice
Tony Cokes
1999, 6:36, U.S., color, sound
"*Ad Vice* consists of a succession of colored projection surfaces with segments of text from the worlds of advertising, sport, and popular culture.... The comfort of fast changing images and catchy slogans is undermined by probing questions that appear on the projection surface: Do you feel good? Why do you feel so lonely? Am I a stranger in my own world? ... And in this way, Cokes seems to question the essence of our individual existence. Who or what are you? Are you a product of present-day consumer society? So are you happy with that? Are you really happy?"
—Anita de Groot, World Wide Video Festival (Amsterdam, 2000)

Black Celebration
Tony Cokes
1988, 17:00, U.S., color, sound
Subtitled *A Rebellion against the Commodity*, this engaged reading of the urban black riots of the 1960s references Guy Debord's Situationist text, "The Decline and Fall of the Spectacle-Commodity Economy," *Internationale*

Situationniste #10 (March 1966). Along with additional commentary adapted from Barbara Kruger and musicians Morrissey and Skinny Puppy, the text posits rioting as a refusal to participate in the logic of capital and an attempt to de-fetishize the commodity through theft and gift. Cokes asks, "How do people make history under conditions pre-established to dissuade them from intervening in it?"

Also available on the compilation *Tony Cokes Videoworks: Volume 1*.

Fade to Black
Tony Cokes
1990, 32:00, U.S., color, sound
In this meditation on contemporary race relations, two black men discuss in voice-over certain "casual" events in life and cinema that are unnoticed or discounted by whites—gestures, hesitations, stares, off-the-cuff remarks, jokes—details of an ideology of repressed racism.

Also available on the compilation *Tony Cokes Videoworks: Volume 1*.

No Sell Out...
Tony Cokes and X-Prez (Doug Anderson, Kenseth Armstead, and Mark Pierson)
1995, 5:37, U.S., color, sound
Using a pulsing rock soundtrack and music video-style editing, Tony Cokes combines archival footage of Malcolm X, advertisements, and corporate logos in *No Sell Out* to provide a scathing commentary on commodity culture.

Spanish subtitled version available.

Also available on the anthology *Frames of Reference: Reflections on Media, Volume 1, Program 1*.

Tony Cokes Videoworks: Volume 1
In this agit-pop double feature, Cokes celebrates civil disobedience and deconstructs race relations. Cokes inter-cuts political slogans and social facts with an array of footage and juxtaposes the images with pop, rock, and rap soundtracks.
Total running time 49:00.
Contents:
Black Celebration, Tony Cokes, 1988, 17:00, U.S., color, sound
Fade to Black, Tony Cokes, 1990, 32:00, U.S., color, sound

Fade to Black

Compton, Candace
(see Angelo, Nancy)

Condit, Cecelia

Since the early 1980s Cecelia Condit's narrative tapes have explored the not-so-average experiences of the "average woman" in a social climate of sublimated violence, fear, and misogynist aggression. Her dark-humored tapes conflate fairy tale morals with the grisly sensationalism of tabloid headlines, incorporating live action, appropriated television images, and original music into frequently operatic narratives. Condit is also Professor of Film and Video at the University of Wisconsin-Milwaukee. Dick Blau works in photography and film and is Professor and co-founder of the Department of Film at the University of Wisconsin-Milwaukee. His film work is distributed by Canyon Cinema, and his photographs have been published widely, most recently in Jane Gallop's *Living with His Camera* (2003).

Beneath the Skin
Cecelia Condit
1981, 12:00, U.S., color, sound
"Relating a tale told by a girl on a swing, *Beneath the Skin* explores the contrast between the impersonal horror of a news story heard on television and the involvement of the storyteller in a nightmare, which gradually becomes more familiar and commonplace as the tale unfolds. The straightforward approach of the teller is humorously or frighteningly contrasted by a bombardment of visual images which mock or intensify the macabre flavor of the work."
—Cecelia Condit

Also available on the compilation *Cecelia Condit Videoworks: Volume 1*.

Cecelia Condit Videoworks: Volume 1
Though the use of fairytales and dark fantasies, these works combine the commonplace with the macabre to construct a new world of the subconscious.
Total running time 1:10:00.
Contents:
Beneath the Skin, Cecelia Condit, 1981, 12:00, U.S., color, sound
Not a Jealous Bone, Cecelia Condit, 1987, 11:00, U.S., color, sound
Oh, Rapunzel, Cecelia Condit and Dick Blau, 1996, 35:00, U.S., color, sound
Possibly in Michigan, Cecelia Condit, 1983, 12:00, U.S., color, sound

Not a Jealous Bone
Cecelia Condit
1987, 11:00, U.S., color, sound
Invoking a Biblical story of life coming from dry bones, Condit constructs an experimental narrative about an older woman's confrontation with her own mortality after the death of her mother. The bone represents the promise of youth and hope—a promise jealously coveted by the young but needed more by those grown old. Inverting cultural values, Condit represents feminine youth as a mannequin and seeks humanity in the form of the older woman, who is reborn by overcoming her fear of death.
Also available on the compilation *Cecelia Condit Videoworks: Volume 1.*

Oh, Rapunzel
Cecelia Condit and Dick Blau
1996, 35:00, U.S., color, sound
This fairy tale wrapped around documentary shows the life of 80-year-old Annie Lloyd Condit—a descendant of what was once one of the great families of Pennsylvania and the artist's mother. Ms. Condit was for some years a virtual prisoner in her own home (now a decaying estate), where she lived with a daughter, son-in-law, and their children. Her story is told through contemporary video and scenes from the Rapunzel story. By revising the classic tale and dumping the prince, Condit restages the old woman's life, giving it a happy ending that comes true.
Also available on the compilation *Cecelia Condit Videoworks: Volume 1.*

Possibly in Michigan

Possibly in Michigan
Cecelia Condit
1983, 12:00, U.S., color, sound
Possibly in Michigan is an operatic fairytale about cannibalism in Middle America. A masked man stalks a woman through a shopping mall and follows her home. In the end, their roles are reversed when the heroine deposits a mysterious Hefty bag at the curb. Like Condit's other video narratives, *Possibly in Michigan* shows bizarre events disrupting mundane lives. Combining the commonplace with the macabre, humor with the absurd, she constructs a world of divided reality.
"Putting on femininity with a visual and narrative vengeance Condit's disconcerting irony and sweetly gruesome stories also 'put-on' and undo societal prescriptions and taboos regarding women's options to subjugation by violence or the gaze, letting us see and hear what often remains hidden, behaving with impropriety."
—Patricia Mellencamp, "Uncanny Feminism: The Exquisite Corpses of Cecelia Condit," *Afterimage* 14 (September 1986)
Also available on the compilation *Cecelia Condit Videoworks: Volume 1.*

Why Not a Sparrow
Cecelia Condit
2003, 12:50, U.S., color, sound
In *Why Not a Sparrow* a girl enters a fairy tale land where the distinction between human and other animal species is blurred. In this kingdom, survival and extinction are on the tip of every bird's tongue.

Conrad, Tony

Tony Conrad was active in performance and music composition during the 1960s and was associated with the founding of minimalist music and underground film in New York City. Conrad's work in film ranged from experiments transforming the celluloid's surface to theatrical productions. He observed that his early 1970s tapes "deal with the construction of the viewer in the authorizing context of the art environment or within a broader sociopolitical context."

Cycles of 3s and 7s
Tony Conrad
1976, 3:00 excerpt (of 30:54), U.S., b&w, sound
Cycles of 3s and 7s is a performance in which the harmonic intervals that would ordinarily be performed by a musical instrument are represented through the computation of their arithmetic relationships or frequency ratios. Conrad and the other members of the Theater of Eternal Music—LaMonte Young, Marian Zazeela, John Cale, and Angus MacLise—composed and performed "dream music" in the early '60s. This seminal group was a major influence on what became known as minimalist music. Conrad's tape points to an important intersection of conceptual and performative experimentation in

which the theoretical basis of sound and visual imagine tools were explored by musicians, filmmakers, videomakers, and electronic instrument designers.

Only available as an excerpt on the anthology *Surveying the First Decade, Program 2.*

Coonley, Ben

Boston-bred and Brooklyn-based artist Ben Coonley makes films, videos, installations and performances. He has created two series of playful Pony pieces (2002), including *One Trick Pony, 3D Trick Pony,* and *Trick or Treat Pony.* Coonley's other work further explores unexpected formats, gastronomic history, and animal subjectivity: *Titanic* (Super-8, 1998), *Pie Eating 101: 101 Years of Pie* (video, 1998), *Installations for Domestic Cats* (video installation, 2001), and *Wavelength 3D* (video, 2003).

3D Trick Pony
Ben Coonley
2002, 5:30, U.S., color, sound
An audience-interactive demonstration of Lev Kuleshov's famous editing experiment, and a 3D review of loosely related principles of subject/spectator empathy.
Note: should be viewed through 3D glasses.
Also available on the compilation *The Pony Collection: Trick Pony Trilogy.*

The Pony Collection: Post Pony Trilogy
The ponies are sometimes absent and sometimes present for this, the second trilogy of *The Pony Collection*. Without the ponies, the world is a darker place as we are witness to an explanation of global currency markets. Things lighten up as the ponies return to take us through a game of Mad Libs and invite the audience to a dance party.
Total running time 22:50
Contents:
Pony Changes Everything, Ben Coonley, 2003, 9:15, U.S., color, sound
Every Pony Plays the Fool, Ben Coonley, 2003, 7:50, U.S., color, sound
The Last Pony, Ben Coonley, 2003, 5:45, U.S., color, sound

The Pony Collection: Trick Pony Trilogy
The Pony Collection is made up of *Trick Pony Trilogy* and *Post Pony Trilogy*. The pieces were originally created for an ongoing series of *Movies with Live Soundtracks* screenings held in Providence. The six videos were presented serially over the course of 2002-2003, with a new episode released every few months. In keeping with the rules of the event for which they were produced, the soundtracks to these pieces are intended to be narrated live by the director and pony while the videos are projected. The soundtracks on the videos in this collection are simulations of these live soundtracks and may be used in the director's absence.
Total running time 18:40
Contents:
One Trick Pony, Ben Coonley, 2002, 4:50, U.S., color, sound
3D Trick Pony, Ben Coonley, 2002, 5:30, U.S., color, sound
Trick or Treat Pony, Ben Coonley, 2002, 8:20, U.S., color, sound

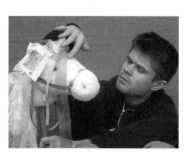

Every Pony Plays the Fool

Every Pony Plays the Fool
Ben Coonley
2003, 7:50, U.S., color, sound
An audience-interactive game of *Mad Libs*, with support from a linguistically challenged newcomer. We replace various parts of speech in newspaper articles to create new, customized meanings.
Also available on the compilation *The Pony Collection: Post Pony Trilogy.*

The Last Pony
Ben Coonley
2003, 5:45, U.S., color, sound
Ponies discover an equine Shangri-La. The audience is introduced to a classic dance step. Chubby Checker provides the musical accompaniment.
Also available on the compilation *The Pony Collection: Post Pony Trilogy.*

One Trick Pony
Ben Coonley
2002, 4:50, U.S., color, sound
Introduces the audience to the rockin' talkin' pony, who provides musical accompaniment for a series of Texas country-dance lessons.
Also available on the compilation *The Pony Collection: Post Pony Trilogy.*

Pony Changes Everything

Cort, David

Cort was a member of the Videofreex, a pioneering collective of 10 video activists and technicians formed in 1969 with Mary Curtis Ratcliff, Parry Teasdale, and several others. CBS invited the group to produce a pilot magazine show, *Subject to Change,* on the American scene. With the money provided by CBS for the project, the Videofreex acquired a sophisticated editing system, which they used in subsequent projects and made available to other independents. The program never went on the air, but the Videofreex continued to produce tapes and incorporated the Media Bus, traveling around the state with a mobile workshop program. In 1972 they moved to Maple Tree Farm in Lanesville, New York, where members lived and worked collectively.

Cowie, Norman

Norman Cowie's work interrogates the relations of power and domination in contemporary society and seeks to expose the ways in which meaning and consent are constructed through the media.

Cuevas, Ximena

Ximena Cuevas was born in Mexico City and educated in Paris and New York City. Cuevas is obsessed with the micro movements of daily life, with the border between truth and fiction, and with the "impossibility" of reality. Her prolific work relentlessly seeks out the layers of lies obscuring the everyday representations of reality and systematically explores the fictions of national identity and gender, redefining documentary in the process.

Pony Changes Everything
Ben Coonley
2003, 9:15, U.S., color, sound
A man explains global currency markets without the help of his formerly trusty rockin' talkin' pony, who is missing. Without the pony, the world is as disorientating as it is depressing. The audience is invited to help make order of the chaos.
Also available on the compilation *The Pony Collection: Post Pony Trilogy.*

Trick or Treat Pony
Ben Coonley
2002, 8:20, U.S., color, sound
A rockin' talkin' pony and its human companion examine the evolution of Halloween games from the ancient rite of bobbing for apples to the contemporary spectacle of American football. Confronting liminality on 3rd down and long, the pony BRINGS IT TO THE HOUSE.
Also available on the compilation *The Pony Collection: Post Pony Trilogy.*

Mayday Realtime
David Cort and Mary Curtis Ratcliff
1971, 10:00 excerpt (of 1:00:00), U.S., b&w, sound
As a verité documentation of the May 1, 1971 demonstration against the Vietnam war staged in Washington, D.C., *Mayday Realtime* presents a largely unedited flow of events from the point of view of participants on the street. Cort's camera captures the random, disorienting incidents that marked the day—demonstrators holding up traffic in the Capitol, skirmishes with police, on-the-scene interviews with onlookers. The camera impulsively responds to shouting and movement on the street. Voice-over narration is absent, and the real-time images are left to convey the urgency and confusion of unpredictable events. The Portapak was promoted as a tool of the counterculture, recording video images that challenged its representation by the mainstream media. As social history, the tape provides a window into the ideological divisions that rocked society during these years, capturing demonstrators fleeing tear gas and helicopters air-lifting troops, not to a battlefield in Vietnam but to a trimmed lawn in the nation's Capitol.
Only available as an excerpt on the anthology *Surveying the First Decade, Program 6.*

Scenes from an Endless War (2001-2002)
Norman Cowie
2002, 32:00, U.S., color, sound
Scenes from an Endless War is an experimental documentary on militarism, globalization, and the "war against terrorism." Part meditation, part commentary, *Scenes* employs recontextualized commercial images, rewritten news crawls, and original footage and interviews to question received wisdom and common sense assumptions about current American policies.

A la Manera de Disney
Ximena Cuevas
1992, 3:00, Mexico, color, sound
Colorful lines follow the gestures of a conductor leading the orchestra until he disappears just at the point of crescendo. As the music slows, he starts to reappear. A sketch as a tribute to Walt Disney.
Also available on the compilation *El Mundo del Silencio (The Silent World).*

Alma Gemela (Soulmate)
Ximena Cuevas
1999, 2:00, Mexico, color, sound, in Spanish with English subtitles
The innocence of creating a mirror, only to repeatedly crush it underfoot.
Also available on the compilations *El Mundo del Silencio (The Silent World)* and *Dormimundo (Sleepworld Volume 1: Discomfort).*

Baba de Perico (Parrot's Saliva)
Ximena Cuevas
1999, 2:00, Mexico, color, sound
A soft-focus close-up of mouth and lips is set to the sounds of lovemaking. Simulated pornography.
Only available on the compilation *El Mundo del Silencio (The Silent World)*.

Calzada de Kansas (Kansas Avenue)
Ximena Cuevas
1999, 2:00, Mexico, color, sound, in Spanish
Dorothy doesn't reach her dream of the Emerald City. Rather, she already will have been over the rainbow by the time she arrives at the worst corner in Kansas.
Also available on the compilations *El Mundo del Silencio (The Silent World)* and *Dormimundo (Sleepworld Volume 1: Discomfort)*.

Cama (Bed)

Cama (Bed)
Ximena Cuevas
1998, 2:00, Mexico, color, sound, in Spanish with English subtitles
"The life of objects intrigues me. Apparently inanimate, they adopt the souls, actions and lifestyles of their keepers. Here, a bed testifies to what goes on behind the closed door of a decent family's bedroom."
–Ximena Cuevas
Also available on the compilations *El Mundo del Silencio (The Silent World)* and *Dormimundo (Sleepworld Volume 1: Discomfort)*.

Colchones Individuales (Single Beds) Volume 1: Desolación (Desolation)
Ximena Cuevas
2002, 18:00, Mexico, b&w and color, sound
"Emptiness: I just watched your latest video, *Colchones Individuales (Single Beds), Volume 1: Desolación*, and I wanted to write you about it. Oddly, *Single Beds* sums up much of what I have been thinking lately. In these times of speed, where everything is propelled forward at an incredibly spiraling rate, it is only in moments of pause, of inertia, that we examine what is occurring to us. Your piece, *Single Beds*, performs an arrested time, a succinct suspension of time. (It is in many ways a companion piece to an earlier video of yours, *Staying Alive*.) These dreams of decay–like looking at the mildew in the trash can, the slow dance in the pool between the woman and the golden retriever dog, a woman unraveling hospital tape with the words isolation from round her head while in a bedroom, alone at night, with a single bed–these images are loaded, and point to certain anxieties that exist within our lives. With their slow motion, these segments in *Single Beds* represent the moments of hesitation, the doubts, the questions asked, and are authentic means to examining our current reality."
–Kathy High, letter to Ximena Cuevas

Contemporary Artist
Ximena Cuevas
1999, 5:00, Mexico, b&w, sound, in Spanish with English subtitles
After working in solitude at the studio, the artist leaves, uncomfortable with the idea of having to put on a face for the art world, where they expect you to say something articulate in order to grab the curator's attention.
Also available on the compilations *El Mundo del Silencio (The Silent World)* and *Dormimundo (Sleepworld Volume 1: Discomfort)*.

Corazón Sangrante (Bleeding Heart)
Ximena Cuevas
1993, 5:00, Mexico, color, sound, in Spanish with English subtitles
In this humorous short, Astrid Hadad, dressed in traditional folkloric costumes and religious garments, sings and performs a Chilean love ballad before a painterly background of fantastic landscapes. Her hyperbolic posturings enact the song's tale of a woman's heartbreak. This satirical presentation of

femininity references pathos and the role of the victim. Cuevas's use of animation and video montage adds a playful tone to the heartfelt melodrama of love songs, familiar touchstones in all cultures.

Cuerpos de Papel (Paper Bodies)
Ximena Cuevas
1997, 4:00, Mexico, color, sound, in Spanish with English subtitles
Cuerpos de Papel is a dense visual meditation on sexuality, loss, jealousy, and intimacy. It uses rich sensual images to weave a digital portrait of an intimate, erotic, and emotional past. As the images transform, we are left with a slippery sense of intangibility and delicacy.

Destino (Fate)
Ximena Cuevas
1999, 2:00, Mexico, color, sound, in Spanish with English subtitles
Erase the 1940s. The desire to better appearances. To try to record a love story. It's in this way that a facial can become the biggest remaining pleasure. Also available on the compilations *El Mundo del Silencio (The Silent World)* and *Dormimundo (Sleepworld Volume 1: Discomfort)*.

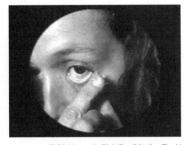

El Diablo en la Piel (Devil in the Flesh)

El Diablo en la Piel (Devil in the Flesh)
Ximena Cuevas
1998, 5:00, Mexico, color, sound
"The palms of Lana Turner's hands were full of scars; the technique she used in order to achieve melodrama was to tighten her fists, digging her fingernails into them until she began to cry. Day after day, soap opera actresses smear Vick's VapoRub into their eyes in order to cry. The effects of these false tears are the tears of the public. In *Devil in the Flesh* we see the camera's tricks, and even so the action seems dramatic. This piece once again exemplifies my fascination with the artificial: the fabricated emotions, the Christian looking for pain in order to live out Passion, the discomfort of the everyday melodrama, the emptiness that defeats everything. So, as in all my work, I am obsessed with lying's various disguises. It doesn't interest me to watch that which is not hidden."
–Ximena Cuevas, 1999
Also available on the compilations *El Mundo del Silencio (The Silent World)* and *Dormimundo (Sleepworld Volume 1: Discomfort)*.

Dormimundo (Sleepworld Volume 1: Discomfort)
"If there's something big, big that you want to reach for, you begin by dreaming."
–Ivonne and Ivette
"The discomfort in *Sleepworld Volume 1* is that of being oneself. The videos included here look at who we are and what we imagine we are. They are experiments in appearances, about the use of artifice to improve life or hide it. It is a reflection on moral displacement, hypocrisy, self-contained dreams, self-loathing, self-destruction in order to repeatedly kill our dreams. Formally, this is an exercise in automatism. My camera reveals reality developing over real time. Seven of the nine videos included in this series were completed in less than a month as chance operations. They are pure documents that use life as a laboratory. In addition, I created a self-imposed assignment to complete things the same night that I began."
– Ximena Cuevas, 1999
Total running time 26:00
Contents:
Alma Gemela (Soulmate), Ximena Cuevas, 1999, 2:00, Mexico, color, sound, in Spanish with English subtitles
Calzada de Kansas (Kansas Avenue), Ximena Cuevas, 1999, 2:00, Mexico, color, sound, in Spanish
Cama (Bed), Ximena Cuevas, 1998, 2:00, Mexico, color, sound, in Spanish with English subtitles
Contemporary Artist, Ximena Cuevas, 1999, 5:00, Mexico, b&w, sound, in Spanish with English subtitles

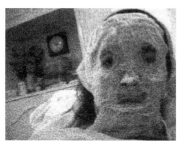

Destino (Fate)

Destino (Fate), Ximena Cuevas, 1999, 2:00, Mexico, color, sound, in
    Spanish with English subtitles
El Diablo en la Piel (Devil in the Flesh), Ximena Cuevas, 1998, 5:00,
    Mexico, color, sound
Exito (Success), Ximena Cuevas, 2002, 1:00, Mexico, b&w, sound
Hawaii, Ximena Cuevas, 1999, 2:00, Mexico, color, sound
Natural Instincts, Ximena Cuevas, 1999, 3:00, Mexico, color, sound
Estamos Para Servirle (We're Here to Serve You), Ximena Cuevas, 1999,
    3:00, Mexico, color, sound

Estamos Para Servirle (We're Here to Serve You)
Ximena Cuevas
1999, 3:00, Mexico, color, sound
"I made this video after assisting at a conference where the artists acted like
flies in a barnyard. They gathered tropical fruits to make it less disagreeable
for themselves."
—Ximena Cuevas
Also available on the compilations *El Mundo del Silencio (The Silent World)*
and *Dormimundo (Sleepworld Volume 1: Discomfort)*.

Exito (Success)
Ximena Cuevas
2002, 1:00, Mexico, b&w, sound
A fireworks display heralds the appearance of our heroine. She walks a hotel
corridor with balloons held aloft and champagne on call. But then she stumbles. The perils of success.
Also available on the compilation *El Mundo del Silencio (The Silent World)*.

Hawaii
Ximena Cuevas
1999, 2:00, Mexico, color, sound
"You don't have to go to Hawaii to be in Hawaii. Nor do you have to be sensual to feel sensual. You look the way you are supposed to look. The sensuali-
ty of Hawaii completely fascinates me in this video."
—Ximena Cuevas
Also available on the compilations *El Mundo del Silencio (The Silent World)*
and *Dormimundo (Sleepworld Volume 1: Discomfort)*.

Help!
Ximena Cuevas
1999, 2:00, Mexico, color, sound
On a television screen the people sing "Eleanor Rigby." The camera closes in
on one woman's face and the sad words take on new significance.
Also available on the compilation *El Mundo del Silencio (The Silent World)*.

Medias Mentiras (Half-Lies)

Medias Mentiras (Half-Lies)
Ximena Cuevas
1995, 37:00, Mexico, color, sound, in Spanish with English subtitles
A video poem about the nature of social relations and mass media, *Half-Lies*
exposes the seemingly innocuous ways we distort truth. Harmonious families,
trade treaties, and current events are among the mediated realities that
Cuevas interrogates. *Half-Lies* makes the viewer question the half-truths we
encounter daily. The video walks the haunting gray area between documentary and drama, creating a world that is both shockingly grotesque and star-
tlingly authentic. Using mass-mediated images, animation, image
manipulation, and fantasy, *Medias Mentiras* interprets the chaotic landscape
of politics, urban chaos, and everyday existence.
Also available on the anthology *Frames of Reference: Reflections on Media,
Volume 3, Program 3*.

El Mundo del Silencio (The Silent World)
Cuevas is obsessed with the micro movements of daily life, with the border

Hawaii

between truth and fiction, with the "impossibility" of reality. Her work relentlessly seeks out the layers of lies covering the everyday representations of reality and systematically explores the fictions of national identity and gender. Total running time 1:02:00.

Contents:

Turistas (Tourists), Ximena Cuevas, 2002, 5:00, Mexico, color, sound

Estamos Para Servirle (We're Here to Serve You), Ximena Cuevas, 1999, 3:00, Mexico, color, sound

Natural Instincts, Ximena Cuevas, 1999, 3:00, Mexico, color, sound, in Spanish with English subtitles

Hawaii, Ximena Cuevas, 1999, 2:00, Mexico, color, sound

Help!, Ximena Cuevas, 1999, 2:00, Mexico, color, sound

La Tombola (Raffle), Ximena Cuevas, 2001, 7:00, Mexico, color, sound, in Spanish with English subtitles

Televisión, Ximena Cuevas, 1999, 3:00, Mexico, b&w, sound

Colchones Individuales (Single Beds), Ximena Cuevas, 2002, 5:00, Mexico, b&w and color, sound

La Puerta (The Door), Ximena Cuevas, 2000, 5:00, Mexico, color, sound

Cama (Bed), Ximena Cuevas, 1998, 2:00, Mexico, color, sound, in Spanish with English subtitles

Baba de Perico (Parrot's Saliva), Ximena Cuevas, 1999, 2:00, Mexico, color, sound

Destino (Fate), Ximena Cuevas, 1999, 2:00, Mexico, color, sound, in Spanish with English subtitles

Alma Gemela (Soulmate), Ximena Cuevas, 1999, 2:00, Mexico, color, sound

Staying Alive, Ximena Cuevas, 2001, 3:00, Mexico, color, sound

El Diablo en la Piel (Devil in the Flesh), Ximena Cuevas, 1998, 5:00, Mexico, color, sound

A la Manera de Disney, Ximena Cuevas, 1992, 3:00, Mexico, color, sound

Contemporary Artist, Ximena Cuevas, 1999, 5:00, Mexico, b&w, sound, in Spanish with English subtitles

Exito (Success), Ximena Cuevas, 2002, 1:00, Mexico, b&w, sound

Calzada de Kansas (Kansas Avenue), Ximena Cuevas, 1999, 2:00, Mexico, color, sound, in Spanish

Natural Instincts
Ximena Cuevas
1999, 3:00, Mexico, color, sound, in Spanish with English subtitles
"This is a video of musical terror where I superficially–this is the beginning of a larger project–look at one of the Mexican phenomena that horrifies me the most: internalized racism and being ashamed of one's own roots. The fantasy of waking up white."
–Ximena Cuevas
Also available on the compilations *El Mundo del Silencio (The Silent World)* and *Dormimundo (Sleepworld Volume 1: Discomfort).*

La Puerta (The Door)
Ximena Cuevas
2000, 5:00, Mexico, color, sound
"Hell is oneself. There's nothing to escape from and nothing to escape to."
–T.S. Eliot
"*La Puerta* makes us spin out of control in the long and cruel corridors of an institutional nightmare."
–inSite 2000 program, San Diego Museum of Art
Also available on the compilation *El Mundo del Silencio (The Silent World).*

Staying Alive
Ximena Cuevas
2001, 3:00, Mexico, color, sound
Blind man: "It is bad to be alone."
The Creature: "Alone, bad."
–*The Bride of Frankenstein*

Televisión

It can be so bad to be alone that even artificial heat is better than none.
Also available on the compilation *El Mundo del Silencio (The Silent World)*.

Televisión
Ximena Cuevas
1999, 3:00, Mexico, b&w, sound
"The vacuum cleaner becomes the device of the feminist 'liberation,' or the monster that devours us."
—inSite 2000 program, San Diego Museum of Art
Also available on the compilation *El Mundo del Silencio (The Silent World)*.

La Tombola (Raffle)
Ximena Cuevas
2001, 7:00, Mexico, color, sound, in Spanish with English subtitles
"Take back the airwaves: Mexico's video art doyenne Ximena Cuevas books herself onto the tabloid talk show *Tombola (Raffle)*, toying at first with whimsical deconstruction until she turns the whole affair on its head by seizing the televisual flow itself."
—MIX: The New York Lesbian and Gay Experiemental Film/Video Festival (2002)
Also available on the compilation *El Mundo del Silencio (The Silent World)*.

Turistas (Tourists)
Ximena Cuevas
2002, 5:00, Mexico, color, sound
"*Turistas (Tourists)* deals with the letdown of a world that is pre-mediated and post-digested—a video travelling guide that updates the 19th century artist's Grand Tour and downgrades it to 21st century not-so-Grand status."
—Maria-Christina Villaseñor, Associate Curator of Film and Media Arts, Guggenheim Museum

Only available on the compilation *El Mundo del Silencio (The Silent World)*.

Cumming, Donigan

Donigan Cumming uses video, photography, and multi-media installation to challenge the taboos of representation. His treatment of society's abject heroes began with a three-part cycle of photographs, *Reality and Motive in Documentary Photography* (1986), which created a fictional community whose struggles and existence he has continued to explore on tape. Cumming's portraits of others are unforgettable; his self-portraits are equally unsparing.

After Brenda
Donigan Cumming
1997, 39:59, Canada, color, sound
Donigan Cumming's improvisational style traverses the boundaries of tragedy and comedy, drama and documentation. In *After Brenda*, Cumming redefines the genre of popular romance. His abject hero is Pierre, a 50-something male who has lost everything in the name of love. He is homeless and adrift, an unwanted guest with nothing to offer but a tale. *After Brenda* searches the hearts and rooms of his audience, seizing the evidence of sex, love, and survival.
Also available on the compilation *Donigan Cumming Videoworks: Volume 2*.

Cold Harbor
Donigan Cumming
2003, 3:00, Canada, color, sound
"With *Cold Harbor*, Donigan Cumming uses a minimum of elements to create a powerful anti-war message. Initially, the video seems enigmatic, almost abstract. An amateur Handycam moves tentatively around a hospital room, panning and zooming from the view out the window to the dark-skinned old man lying on the bed. The image is shaky, blurred, often out of focus. Off-screen, a radio or television blares the news. On the soundtrack we also hear Cumming's own voice quoting from a general's memoirs: 'I've always regretted that the last assault at Cold Harbor was ever made.'"
—Visions du Réel (Nyon, Switzerland, 2003)

Culture
Donigan Cumming
2002, 17:04, Canada, color, sound
In his signature photographic style, Donigan Cumming eulogizes a dying friend through his exploration of "culture" in all its manifestations:

1. culture: a particular civilization at a particular stage
2. culture: the tastes in art and manners that are favored by a social group
3. culture: all the knowledge and values shared by a society
4. culture: the growing of micro-organisms in a nutrient medium
5. culture: the raising of plants or animals

Cut the Parrot

Donigan Cumming
1996, 40:16, Canada, color, sound
The police phoned. They left a message on the machine. They said he was dead. The tape unwinds through stories of sex for rent, unclaimed bodies, cigarette burns, and other monuments of life's long run from wall to wall. *Cut the Parrot* is three grotesque comedies in one: the stories of Gerry, Susan, and Albert. Songs of hope and heartbreak spill from the mouths of the performers. The order of impersonation rules.
Also available on the compilation *Donigan Cumming Videoworks: Volume 1.*

Docu-Duster

Donigan Cumming
2001, 3:30, Canada, color, sound
To be a man, to be a hero, to be a wife: these conflicting voices inhabit the body of a documentary filmmaker as he re-enacts the climax of a Western morality play, *3:10 to Yuma.*
Also available on the compilation *Donigan Cumming Videoworks: Volume 3.*

Docu-Duster

Donigan Cumming: Four Short Pieces

Four short pieces: three featuring anecdotes and conversations, the fourth an icy landscape.
Total running time 10:39.
Contents:
Four Storeys, Donigan Cumming, 1999, 2:04, Canada, color, sound
Petit Jesus, Donigan Cumming, 1999, 3:02, Canada, color, sound, in French
Shelter, Donigan Cumming, 1999, 3:22, Canada, color, sound
Trip, Donigan Cumming, 1999, 2:11, Canada, b&w, sound

Donigan Cumming Videoworks: Volume 1

Utilizing a mix of documentary and improvisational styles, the portraits featured in these three videos highlight the often forgotten, the marginal, those on the edge of society. The portraits are equally grotesque, comic and tender, and Cumming's photography is characteristically unblinking and relentless.
Total running time 1:16:16.
Contents:
Cut the Parrot, Donigan Cumming, 1996, 40:16, Canada, color, sound
Karaoke, Donigan Cumming, 1998, 3:00, Canada, color, sound, in Inuktitut
A Prayer for Nettie, Donigan Cumming, 1995, 33:00, Canada, color, sound

Donigan Cumming Videoworks: Volume 2

In these two videos, Cumming investigates the worlds of a pair of abject heroes, Colin and Pierre, one a recovering alcoholic, the other an addict. One talks angrily about his former addiction and of the sacrifices he made for the "romance" of a life on the street. The other has lost everything in the name of love, and now tells the tale in a manner both tragic and comedic.
Total running time 1:29:59.
Contents:
After Brenda, Donigan Cumming, 1997, 39:59, Canada, color, sound
Erratic Angel, Donigan Cumming, 1998, 50:00, Canada, color, sound

Donigan Cumming Videoworks: Volume 3

Three short pieces highlighting how difficult it is to create images that make sense in a world where everything is flawed and everything has already been said.
Total running time 7:30.
Contents:

Docu-Duster, Donigan Cumming, 2001, 3:30, Canada, color, sound
A Short Lesson, Donigan Cumming, 2001, 1:00, Canada, color, sound
Wrap, Donigan Cumming, 2001, 3:00, Canada, color, sound

Erratic Angel
Donigan Cumming
1998, 50:00, Canada, color, sound
"I'm not finished. I don't know how long it's going to take. As far as I'm concerned I'm officially dead." In his 50th year, Colin looks back on a life of drug and alcohol abuse. Four years into recovery, he is angry and articulate about addiction, treatment, and the romance of the street. In the chaos and claustrophobia of an ice storm, Colin waits to be reborn. His erratic angel is late.
Also available on the compilation *Donigan Cumming Videoworks: Volume 2.*

Four Storeys
Donigan Cumming
1999, 2:04, Canada, color, sound
The confession of a woman who took flight.
Also available on the compilation *Donigan Cumming: Four Short Pieces.*

if only I
Donigan Cumming
2000, 35:00, Canada, color, sound
What if… Colleen's life, in her own words, has been "wretched." She was sexually abused by her father, betrayed by her husband, separated from her children, driven by her love for a heroin addict to attempted suicide. Colleen has survived by taking responsibility for her decisions and dreaming of a safer place, sometimes relying on the kindness of strangers. *if only I* marks another hot summer in crisis. Colleen presents herself, broken and whole, to the camera.
"*if only I* is a moving portrait of a troubled soul, a failed suicide caught in the grip of the medical bureaucracy, and her helpmeet and champion, a recovering schizophrenic who has only recently dragged himself up from the streets."
—New York Video Festival (2000)

if only I

Karaoke
Donigan Cumming
1998, 3:00, Canada, color, sound, in Inuktitut
An ailing, elderly man listens to a private performance in his room. The singing is a halting mix cross-cultural—Inuktitut and country & western. Transgressive and mesmerizing, *Karaoke* distorts the landscapes of sound and body.
Also available on the compilation *Donigan Cumming Videoworks: Volume 1.*

Locke's Way
Donigan Cumming
2003, 21:00, Canada, color, sound
Locke's Way is the photographic path to knowledge, full of twists and turns, treacherously steep. "One of the central questions of philosophy has always been: what can be known? *Locke's Way* provides a vivid illustration of this perennial philosophical dilemma. In this short video, Donigan Cumming is preoccupied with the story of his older brother, who seems to have been brain-damaged and spent much of his life in institutions. Cumming sifts through old family photos and medical documents, commenting on what they do—or do not—reveal.... Cumming has said that his main references for this work are the English philosopher John Locke and the French novelist Marcel Proust. Locke argued for an empirical approach to knowledge, while Proust relied on remembered experience. *Locke's Way* pits these two approaches against each other, but the outcome—like the question of Jerry's life—remains unresolved."
—Visions du Réel (Nyon, Switzerland, 2003)

My Dinner with Weegee

My Dinner with Weegee
Donigan Cumming
2001, 36:26, Canada, color, sound
In *My Dinner with Weegee* Donigan Cumming weaves together two life stories. The central figure, a man in his 70s named Marty, remembers his experiences in New York as a young Catholic labor organizer and peace activist
and his friendships with David Dellinger, the Berrigan brothers, Bayard
Rustin, Weegee, and James Agee. This mixture of first-hand knowledge and
gossip brightens Marty's dark passage—he is old, sick, depressed, and alcoholic. The other story is Cumming's in his 54th year, as he examines his own
radicalism in light of the "wheezing dirty beacon" up ahead.

Petit Jesus (Little Jesus)
Donigan Cumming
1999, 3:02, Canada, color, sound, in French
It's Christmas Eve. A man alone finds someone he can talk to.
Also available on the compilation *Donigan Cumming: Four Short Pieces.*

A Prayer for Nettie
Donigan Cumming
1995, 33:00, Canada, color, sound
A Prayer For Nettie dramatizes the death of an elderly woman who was
Cumming's photographic model from 1982 to 1993, presenting an improvised series of prayers and memorials for Nettie Harris by people who knew
her and some who did not. In its ambiguous mix of tenderness and aggression, *A Prayer for Nettie* extends the traditions of the grotesque and the
absurd. Indifference, forgetfulness, and the presence of the camera undermine the fervent prayers of the actors. In the end, comedy turns the tables on
piety and remembrance as Nettie looks up from the grave.
Also available on the compilation *Donigan Cumming Videoworks: Volume 1.*

Shelter
Donigan Cumming
1999, 3:22, Canada, color, sound
A conversation about marriage and horses between two unseen men.
Also available on the compilation *Donigan Cumming: Four Short Pieces.*

A Short Lesson
Donigan Cumming
2001, 1:00, Canada, color, sound
One minute, two mysteries: The shelf life of genius and why we try to make
pictures when, as Robert Lowell put it, "No voice outsings the serpent's
flawed, euphoric hiss."
Also available on the compilation *Donigan Cumming Videoworks: Volume 3.*

Trip
Donigan Cumming
1999, 2:11, Canada, b&w, sound
A camera on thin ice.
Only available on the compilation *Donigan Cumming: Four Short Pieces.*

Voice: off
Donigan Cumming
2003, 39:00, Canada, color, sound
Voice: off is the autobiography of a forgotten man. Brain damaged, body violated, emotions crushed, Gerry—who rarely spoke—has now lost the power of
speech. The video camera is his prosthesis, and he borrows the memories of
people who no longer need them. How can this be a comedy? It is.
"Donigan Cumming looks at the violence of time that damages the body and
exhausts memories. For the main character in *Voice: off*, Gerald, the illness is
incurable. Two cancers are at work, one of which is attacking his throat. The
first images are the irrefutable ones of a naked man who has reached old age

and whose voice is failing. The capturing in real time of death at work is one of the terms of this dense and complex film. But Cumming also likes to go back in time in search of a state of innocence. In his studio he spreads out the photographs of Gerald's life.... With obsession he seeks for legitimacy in his approach in-between fascination with hints of morbidity and reflections of a metaphysical bent. Iconoclastic and brutal in its hurried search, *Voice: off* is strangely fraternal. One scene in particular reflects this. Gerald and a friend are standing in a small room. Time stands still. Nothing happens, they appear to be waiting aimlessly. Like characters out of Beckett's works they are left to the absurd fate of humanity."
—Visions du Réel (Nyon, Switzerland, 2003)

Wrap
Donigan Cumming
2001, 3:00, Canada, color, sound
System failure: A man repeats the story of a prison stabbing as something goes wrong with the tape.

Also available on the compilation *Donigan Cumming Videoworks: Volume 3.*

De Fanti, Tom
(see Sandin, Dan)

DeVito, Cara

Cara DeVito began producing videotapes in 1972 and went on to work on the independent documentary series *Changing Channels*, produced by University Community Video for KTCA-St. Paul. Her documentary work—focusing primarily on social and cultural issues—has received a number of awards, including an Emmy. She is best known for her pioneering feminist portrait of her grandmother, *Ama L'uomo Tuo* (*Always Love Your Man*, 1975), produced at a time when the high incidence of rape and violence against women was first being widely recognized.

Ama L'Uomo Tuo (Always Love Your Man)
Cara DeVito
1975, 19:00, U.S., b&w, sound
This carefully structured documentary is both a character study of DeVito's grandmother, Adeline LeJudas, and an incisive social critique of patriarchal society. In contrast to the domestic comforts of her Brooklyn home, Adeline recounts the violence she suffered at her abusive husband's hands and how she survived a dangerously late, illegal abortion. The intimacy of the video camera (requiring only a one-person crew) plays an intrinsic role in the type of exchange created between granddaughter and grandmother. *Ama L'Uomo Tuo* is based on the sharing of personal histories, a common practice of the early women's movement and consciousness-raising groups. Growing numbers of feminist health projects in the early '70s advocated for health information networks, the development of clinics for safe, legal abortions, and intensified public scrutiny of rape and violence against women. *Ama L'Uomo Tuo* is, admittedly, an example of a very sympathetic documentary; DeVito's presence and relationship with her grandmother is obvious and informs much of the oral history that she manages to record.

Only available on the anthology *Surveying the First Decade, Program 4.*

DiStefano, John

John DiStefano is a writer, teacher, curator, and artist who works across various media, including video, photography, and installation. His recent projects examine identity and displacement through the concepts and perceptions of memory, space, and time that shape the articulation of subjectivity. He is Senior Lecturer at Victoria University of Wellington (New Zealand).

Hub
John DiStefano
2001, 22:00, U.S., sound, color
Hub proposes that the idea of home is today perhaps better expressed as a sense of being between places. Within the dialectical interplay between global processes and local environments, *Hub* suggests that displacement and mobility itself might be thought of as a new way of belonging. *Hub* uses the transitory space of the airport—defined by its arrivals and departures—to introduce the notion of disappearance to articulate new ideas on belonging and identity. *Hub* proposes that we think of the airport as both a type of home and a place of disappearance—not in the sense of vanishing, but rather in the sense of transformation, dis-appearing. Rather than being an "empty" space, *Hub* proposes that the airport becomes a rich and complex repository of interlacing personal and political histories—a new space of belonging.

Dibble, Teddy

Exploring the elastic possibility of his face, Kansas City-based Teddy Dibble creates brief, parodic vignettes about television.

Born Yesterday
Teddy Dibble
1991, 12:00, U.S., color, sound
As with his predecessor Ernie Kovacs, everything is fair game for ridicule in Dibble's gentle and eccentric humor. Skillfully manipulating the video image in these brief sketches, Dibble gives us his view on subjects ranging from the practical application of Newton's Law to the prospect of video dating. *Born*

Yesterday includes *Newton's Law, Mr. Dibble, 3 Things, Video Dating, Cantankerous Television,* and *Fine Tuning/Credits.*
Also available on the compilation *Teddy Dibble: Complete Works.*

Lover of Life/TV

Teddy Dibble
1990, 1:00:00, U.S., color, sound
If television is truly the opiate of the masses, then Teddy Dibble is a living room crack dealer. This newly compiled series of television art comedy includes *The Cough, Secrets I'll Never Tell, The Shot Heard 'Round the World, Rabbit Rabid Raw Bit, The Man Who Made Faces, What a Difference a Day Makes, The Sound of Music, The Sound of Defiance, A Scary Story, The Nose Knows,* and *Q&A.*
Also available on the compilation *Teddy Dibble: Complete Works.*

Teddy Dibble: Complete Works

This compilation contains many of Teddy Dibble's best comic vignettes. Everything is up for grabs in these visual and linguistic puns, including video dating, telephone operators, New Years Eve celebrations, fruit, and the theory of evolution.
Total running time 1:12:00.
Contents:
Born Yesterday, Teddy Dibble, 1991, 12:00, U.S., color, sound
Lover of Life/TV, Teddy Dibble, 1990, 1:00:00, U.S., color, sound

Anthony Discenza Videoworks: Volume 1

"The ideas in much of my recent work orbit elliptically around the attempt to generate new forms out of the destruction or decay of appropriated material; trying to capture the traces of things as they dissipate, and finding ways of rendering those traces visible. Paired with this is a morbid fascination with the endless stream of mediated images that surrounds and informs our daily lives. The video signal compacted, compressed, imploded–methodologies to reduce disparate visual events into a discrete form. A destruction of any hierarchies of content through the formation of a schizophrenic space in which all information is equivalent and non-orderable, generated through an alchemical shift whereby the many are unified through a kind of annihilation. Through the compression/decay of the electronic signal that transmits them, images are drained of all meaning save that of sensory data, of information… A densely scrambled, post-space of visual detritus."
–Anthony Discenza
Total running time 34:42.
Contents:
December 3rd, 1998–12.03-1:17 A.M., Anthony Discenza, 1999, 7:12,
U.S., color, sound
Phosphorescence, Anthony Discenza, 1999, 13:50, U.S., color, sound
Suspension, Anthony Discenza, 1997, 8:40, U.S., color, sound
The Vision Engine, Anthony Discenza, 1999, 5:00, U.S., color, sound

December 3rd, 1998–12.03-1:17 A.M.

Anthony Discenza
1999, 7:12, U.S., color, sound
A specific period of late-night TV channel surfing is dissected and manipulated through fast forward and freeze frame. Cultural icons (*Roseanne, Mary Tyler Moore, The Golden Girls*) can occasionally be glimpsed amongst the detritus, while the echoing and ghostly soundtrack pays homage to the cultural isolation of solitary viewing.
Also available on the compilation *Anthony Discenza Videoworks: Volume 1.*

Object 8242600

Anthony Discenza
2001, 8:30, U.S., color, sound
"A trance is a state of detachment with aspects of the ecstatic. Paradoxically, a trance can be induced by a surfeit of input or by its deprivation… In

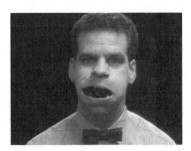

Lover of Life/TV

Dick, Kirby
(see Flanagan, Bob)

Discenza, Anthony
(see also HalfLifers)

Anthony Discenza appropriates and reworks television footage to "literalize and accelerate the decay of media-based imagery, whose effectivity is always contingent upon rapid consumption and obsolescence." In addition to various individual projects, he participates in *HalfLifers*—an ongoing collaboration with longtime friend and fellow video artist, Torsten Z. Burns. Discenza's solo and collaborative work has been shown at numerous national and international venues.

Anthony Discenza's *Object 8242600*, television imagery is reduced to a flood of unanchored signifiers reorganized as a motive mosaic."
—Steve Seid, Pacific Film Archive

Phosphorescence
Anthony Discenza
1999, 13:50, U.S., color, sound
Broken up into "chapters," *Phosphorescence* features an array of abstractions created by manipulating television images. At times almost painterly, the resulting images are set to an ambient electronic soundtrack.
Also available on the compilation *Anthony Discenza Videoworks: Volume 1*.

Suspension
Anthony Discenza
1997, 8:40, U.S., color, sound
Constructed from a destroyed rescan of fashion magazine ads and a video self-portrait, *Suspension* is a meditation on the implicitly narcissistic nature of desire within a commodified context.
Also available on the compilation *Anthony Discenza Videoworks: Volume 1*.

The Vision Engine
Anthony Discenza
1999, 5:00, U.S., color, sound
Blurred images, glowing like a foggy moon and reminiscent of early television broadcasts, are rhythmically set to a relentless, pulsing soundtrack.
Also available on the compilation *Anthony Discenza Videoworks: Volume 1*.

Suspension

Dougherty, Cecilia

Cecilia Dougherty's videotapes explore family interactions, outsider psychology, role-playing, lesbian sexuality, and popular culture. Her tapes *Grapefruit* (1989) and *Coal Miner's Granddaughter* (1991) work from within mass culture norms to create a lesbian dialogue within the "normal"—what Dougherty calls "the life of the ordinary lesbian and her working-class family." Her more recent tapes explore lesbian identity within a separate social sphere.

Cecilia Dougherty Videoworks: Volume 1
A compilation of two videos that wittily explore counter-cultural identity through lesbian portrayals of iconic personalities: in this case, The Beatles' John Lennon and British playwright Joe Orton.
Total running time 1:32:00.
Contents:
Grapefruit, Cecilia Dougherty, 1989, 40:00, U.S., color, sound
Joe-Joe, Cecilia Dougherty, 1993, 52:00, U.S., b&w, sound

Cecilia Dougherty Videoworks: Volume 2
These three videos from Cecilia Dougherty deal with particular states of mind: that of a participant in a symbiotic relationship, the melancholy felt at the end of a romantic union, and the solitary non-space created by a regular commute.
Total running time 41:00.
Contents:
The Drama of the Gifted Child, Cecilia Dougherty, 1992, 6:00, U.S., color, sound
The dream and the waking, Cecilia Dougherty, 1997, 15:00, U.S., color, sound
My Failure to Assimilate, Cecilia Dougherty, 1995, 20:00, U.S., color, sound

Coal Miner's Granddaughter
Cecilia Dougherty
1991, 1:20:00, U.S., b&w, sound
Shot primarily in Fisher Price Pixelvision, for the "murky look of memory," *Coal Miner's Granddaughter* is a profoundly moving family portrait focusing on the youngest daughter Jane, as she leaves her Pennsylvania home and finds sexual independence in San Francisco. This semi-autobiographical narrative is remarkable for Dougherty's unconventional approach: working with non-professional, plain-looking actors and improvised dialogue to recreate the life of the "average" family, and women who are "Plain Janes with big desires."

The Drama of the Gifted Child
Cecilia Dougherty
1992, 6:00, U.S., color, sound

This tape is about the idea of narcissistic transference, sexual dependency, and the failure to distinguish between the self and the loved one. It is also about using love to create a border between oneself and political and psychological oppression.

Also available on the compilation *Cecilia Dougherty Videoworks: Volume 2.*

The dream and the waking
Cecilia Dougherty
1997, 15:00, U.S., color, sound

The dream and the waking is a documentation of my commute between New York and Boston, which I make every week for my job. I wanted to document not only the fact of the commute—where I go and how I get there, what I am leaving behind and what I am going to—but also the stream of thought that runs through my mind on this commute. The trip was not something I would normally do unless I absolutely had to, and for almost a year it was the one part of my life that never changed. The space of the commute is like a non-space, like a recurring dream. It combines the public space of the road with a deeply solitary mental space. There is nothing in-between.

Also available on the compilation *Cecilia Dougherty Videoworks: Volume 2.*

Gone

Gone
Cecilia Dougherty
2001, 36:42, U.S., color, sound

Gone is a two-channel installation based on the second episode of *An American Family*—the landmark PBS verité documentary about the Loud Family of Santa Barbara, California. Dougherty has created a free-form variation on the theme of parental visits to wayward queer children by mapping the dialogue and plot onto a contemporary community of artists and writers in New York today, paying homage to the art underground and the city itself. "Dougherty tests new limits of digital video technologies in her latest work. Partially a re-staging of one episode from '70s proto-reality-TV series *An American Family, Gone* presents elaborate and intricate new possibilities for narrative through the use of double-screen projection, evoking complex themes of nostalgia, history, memory and loss. Pixelated, popping with lush colors, and elaborate sound design, *Gone* recombines low fidelity with high concept to create a unique vision of inner and outer life on the margins of culture."

—New York Underground Film Festival (2001)

With Laurie Weeks, Amy Sillman, and Frances Sorensen and music by Le Tigre and Mike Iveson.

Grapefruit
Cecilia Dougherty
1989, 40:00, U.S., color, sound

With an all-female cast, featuring Susie Bright as John Lennon, *Grapefruit* plays with the romanticized history of the iconic Fab Four, gently mocking John and Yoko's banal squabbles and obsessive rituals of self-display. Based obliquely on Yoko Ono's book, the tape works on many levels to reposition this mythic tale of Beatles boy's life by casting '80s women in mod drag—effectively mapping the lesbian subculture onto heterosexual mass culture. Discounting the importance of reproducing facts and historical accuracy, Dougherty gives an incisive reading of the creation of pop culture icons: it doesn't matter who plays John Lennon because ultimately John Lennon is not a person anymore. As a star, he is a projection of our society's collective needs and desires.

Also available on the compilation *Cecilia Dougherty Videoworks: Volume 1.*

Joe-Joe
Cecilia Dougherty
1993, 52:00, U.S., b&w and color, sound

Taking queer artistic license, Dougherty and Leslie Singer together portray a gay male playwright who took 1960s London by storm. The result is a witty play on narcissism and split personality that captures the banality of stardom while paying tribute to promiscuity and transgression. Filmed in black and white Pixelvision and color video, this tape continues Dougherty's exploration of counter-culture identity through lesbian portrayal, the same ingenious bait-and-switch device seen at work in the lesbian portrayal of The Beatles in her earlier tape *Grapefruit.*

Also available on the compilation *Cecilia Dougherty Videoworks: Volume 1.*

My Failure to Assimilate
Cecilia Dougherty
1995, 20:00, U.S., color, sound

"*My Failure to Assimilate* muses on the profound sense of melancholy that sets in after the end of a relationship. The tape uses poetry, songs, collage, interviews, and narrative elements to construct a complex picture of the resulting loss of direction and loss of identity. The tape is organized into three sections: Part I: 'Schizophrenia,' Part II: 'Alienation,' and Part III: 'True Self.' Central to the question of identity is the interplay between imaginary and symbolic identification."
–Maria Troy and Thompson Owen

Also available on the compilation *Cecilia Dougherty Videoworks: Volume 2.*

Cecilia Dougherty: An Interview (see On Art and Artists)

Downey Brad, Tim Hansberry, and Quenell Jones

Brad Downey, has immersed himself in the world of illegal installation art as both documentarian and participant. Tim Hansberry works as an on-line editor. Quenell Jones is passionate about the art of cinematography, both fiction and non-fiction.

Public Discourse
Brad Downey, Tim Hansberry, and Quenell Jones
2003, 46:00, U.S., color, sound

Public Discourse is an in-depth study of illegal installation art: the painting of street signs, advertising manipulation, metal welding, postering, and guerrilla art. These passionate illegal artists want their work to be seen by a wide range of people rather than be confined to the systemic structures of galleries and museums. This non-fiction film presents an in-depth study of the use of subversive messages, mimicking of advertising methods, and the presentation of three-dimensional sculptures to the public. Shot in the classic cinema verité style using compact mini-DV and video 8 cameras, *Public Discourse* follows art-making from initial idea through to exhibition, capturing the artists' private and personal moments of exuberance and regret.

Downey, Juan

Born in Santiago, Chile, Juan Downey studied in Paris and New York City. He was already experimenting with audio delays and instant playback when he heard about video in 1966. In early work, he created electronic environments and multi-channel installations. Beginning in 1971, Downey took a portable 1/2-inch camera and embarked on what he termed "cultural expeditions" through Mexico and Central and South America; in the process he created tapes that combine autobiography and anthropology. His later work (*Las Meninas*, 1975, and *The Looking Glass,* 1981) meditates on architecture and psychology.

The Laughing Alligator
Juan Downey
1979, 27:00, U.S., color, sound

The personal odyssey recorded in *The Laughing Alligator* combines methods of anthropological research with diaristic essay, mixing objective and subjective vision. Recorded while Downey and his family were living among the Yanomami people of Venezuela, this compelling series of anecdotes tracks his search for an indigenous cultural identity. This tape was made after the 1973-75 *Video Trans America* series. Downey, trained as an architect, was interested in the funerary architecture of the Yanomami, who ritually consume the pulverized bones of their dead in a banana soup, giving rise to outsiders' claim that they are cannibals. A curious incident occurs while hiking through the jungle. Downey looks through the viewfinder of his camera and turns to see his Yanomami guides pointing their weapons at him, acknowledging–seriously or playfully?–his camera as a weapon. Downey participates in the theater by continuing to shoot video. In his documentation of the tribe's use of natural psychedelic drugs for healing, Downey mixes in image processed allusions to the North American urban psychedelic and underground scenes.

Only available on the anthology *Surveying the First Decade, Program 6.*

Downtown Community Television Center

Healthcare: Your Money or Your Life
Downtown Community Television Center
1978, 1:00:00, U.S., color, sound

A classic exposé on the disparity of health care services for the rich and poor

Downtown Community Television Center

(continued)

Founded in 1972 by Jon Alpert, Keiko Tsuno, and Yoko Maruyama in New York's Chinatown, Downtown Community Television Center (DCTV) is one of the oldest community video access centers to offer video training, equipment access, and social-issue programming.

Drew, Jesse

Jesse Drew is a multimedia artist, writer, and educator who seeks to challenge the complacent relationship between the public and new media technologies. His work fosters a critical perspective and Do-It-Yourself ethic as it incorporates satellite technology, mini-FM radio transmitters, digital video, internet and website projects, and multimedia kiosks. His writings have appeared in numerous publications, including *Resisting the Virtual Life* (1995) and *Reclaiming San Francisco: History, Politics, Culture* (1998).

in America, this incisive investigative report exemplifies the advocacy journalism of the Downtown Community Television Center (DCTV). The tape was produced by Jon Alpert and Keiko Tsuno, DCTV's founders. With the viewer as direct witness to the unfolding life-and-death dramas, *Healthcare: Your Money or Your Life* contrasts two Brooklyn hospitals: Kings County Hospital, an overcrowded, understaffed, and under-funded city-run institution, and the Downstate Medical Center, a well-financed private hospital across the street. A strong indictment of the economics of the medical system is articulated by victimized patients and beleaguered hospital personnel. It is noteworthy that the hospitals cooperated in this tape's production.

Only available on the anthology *Surveying the First Decade, Program 8*.

Manifestoon
Jesse Drew
1995, 8:20, U.S., color, sound
Displaying a broad range of Golden Age Hollywood animation, *Manifestoon* is a homage to the latent subversiveness of cartoons. Though U.S. cartoons are usually thought of as conveyors of capitalist ideologies of consumerism and individualism, Drew observes: "Somehow as an avid childhood fan of cartoons, these ideas were secondary to a more important lesson—that of the 'trickster' nature of many characters as they mocked, outwitted, and defeated their more powerful adversaries. In the classic cartoon, brute strength and heavy artillery are no match for wit and humor, and justice always prevails. For me, it was natural to link my own childhood concept of subversion with an established, more articulate version [of] Marx and Engels's *Communist Manifesto*. Mickey running over the globe has new meaning in today's mediascape, in which Disney controls one of the largest concentrations of media ownership in the world."
Also available on the anthology *The New McLennium, Program 2*.

Newe Segobia Is Not for Sale: The Struggle for Western Shoshone
Jesse Drew
1993, 29:00, U.S., color, sound
Newe Segobia Is Not for Sale documents land activists Mary and Carrie Dann confronting Federal Bureau of Land Management officers determined to impound the women's livestock until they pay grazing fees on land the Shoshone have never sold or otherwise legally transferred to the U.S. government. Part of an ongoing conflict over who will control ancestral lands in Nevada, this videotape depicts a standoff between the two groups, as activists speak about their ties to the land and their determination to keep it at any cost. At the heart of the confrontation is a disagreement about what the land means. Using the argument (dating to the first land seizures) that they know how to best develop and use the land, the Nevada BLM claims to be acting in the best environmental interests. This is the same bureau that encourages nuclear waste disposal, open-pit gold mining with cyanide leech ponds, and military weapons testing on the same land.

Short Circuit
Jesse Drew
2001, 10:20, U.S., color, sound
Short Circuit is an experimental documentary—a semi-autobiographical rant that challenges the obsolescence of human labor at the vortex of the machine and digital ages. Through a flow of images, text, and sound, the mechanical and the electronic clash in the thought processes of our protagonist. Is the global revolt of the machines at hand?

Dubois, Doug
(see Finley, Jeanne C.)

DuBowski, Sandi

Sandi DuBowski's first videowork, *Tomboychik*, portrays playful conversations with his grandmother. His 2001 feature documentary, *Trembling Before G-d*, focuses on gay Orthodox Jews who negotiate their sexuality and identity in religious communities—often having to abandon their intertwined worlds of family and faith. The film screened internationally at film festivals, where it won numerous awards, before a theatrical release.

Tomboychik
Sandi DuBowski
1993, 15:00, U.S., color, sound

A series of intimate video-8 vignettes depicting the fierce love between Malverna and Sandi, 88 and 22, grandmother and grandson. The two play-mates dress up drag-esque for this moving portrait of a woman's lifetime struggle with gender and sexuality. Since Malverna's death, *Tomboychik* has become a living memorial to the intensity of her spirit.

"You can't get more low-budget than this, but you can't get much more emotionally powerful either. Here rare and intimate moments of pure love, regret, admiration, and naivete are shared between grandmother and grandson/film-maker. Sometimes quite hilarious (grandma trying to figure out a video cam-era) and sometimes intensely touching, its loose, low-tech approach makes *Tomboychik* a remarkable personal document."
—Melbourne International Film Festival (1994)

Duesing, James

James Duesing is an animator and video artist. His visually complex work uses sophisticated computer graphics and animation programs, combined with hand-drawn imagery and draws references from a variety of sources, including underground comics, contemporary art, literature, and Warner Bros. cartoons.

East Tennessee State University
(see Broadside TV)

E.T. Baby Maniac
(see Cheang, Shu Lea)

Law of Averages
James Duesing
1996, 15:00, U.S., color, sound

In this futuristic computer-animated landscape, confused relationships between objects and people play out before the backdrop of a lush garden and interactive theatre known as the Big Ghost. The commodity of this the-atre is Vynola, an exotic creature who obsesses the minds of all who come to visit her and represents an escape from the daily grind. *Law of Averages* is a wonderfully dense, witty, and visually stunning work about obsession, death, real estate, technology, and America.

Eisenberg, Daniel

Daniel Eisenberg's work has been shown throughout Europe and North America. Eisenberg has also edited numerous television documentaries, including *Eyes on the Prize: America's Civil Rights Years* and *Vietnam: A Television History*. Eisenberg is Chair of Film, Video and New Media at the School of the Art Institute of Chicago.

Electric Eye
(see Ginsburg, Arthur)

Persistence
Daniel Eisenberg
1997, 1:16:00, U.S./Germany, color, sound

"Eisenberg uses the temporal and spatial plasticity of cinema to produce a way of rethinking the narrative possibilities of historical representation. In the context of Berlin as a physical site in transition, the film calls into question lin-ear and causal narratives of historical time to suggest a history of superimpo-sition and simultaneity, raising the possibility that, in the filmmaker's words, 'What is present now may also have been present before, and what is absent now may be present tomorrow?'"
—Jeffrey Skoller, "Reconstructing Berlin", *Afterimage* 26:1 (July/August 1998)

Emshwiller, Ed

In the late '60s Ed Emshwiller worked as a science fiction illustrator and established his place in the American avant-garde cinema with such works as *Relativity* (1966) and *Image, Flesh and Voice* (1969). His early films featured collaborations with dancers and choreo-graphers, a theme he carried over into his videoworks. His pioneering experiments with synthesizers and computers included the electronic rendering of three-dimensional space, the interplay of illusion and reality, and manipulations of time, movement, and scale that explore the relationship between "external reality and subjective feelings." Emshwiller passed away in 1990. An extensive collection of his work is housed by Anthology Film Archives.

Crossings and Meetings
Ed Emshwiller
1974, 4:00 excerpt (of 27:33), U.S., color, sound

Crossings and Meetings explores the image and sound of a walking man, expanding a simple image into increasingly complex permutations and arriving at what Emshwiller calls a "visual fugue" in time and space. Emshwiller uses various techniques to develop his images: fast-forward, rewind, multiple key-ing, and audio modulations. With its rhythmic repetition of images and con-catenation of sound, this tape represents the fusion of audio, video, and dance explored by many artists during the period. According to Emshwiller, this tape was an attempt to use video techniques in an essentially musical structure. Produced at the TV Lab at WNET, New York.

Only available as an excerpt on the anthology *Surveying the First Decade, Program 5*.

Experimental TV Center
(see Hocking, Ralph)

Exit Art
(see anthologies, Endurance)

Export, Valie

Austrian-born Valie Export is an artist, independent filmmaker, and theoretician who has created works in a variety of media, including documentary and narrative film, video, performance, photography, installation, sculpture, and drawing. Regarded as one of Europe's most influential feminist filmmakers and a central figure in the Austrian conceptual and avant-garde film movements since the 1960s, Export is renowned for her early risqué guerrilla performances.

Faber, Mindy

Grounded in biting humor, a surreal sensibility, and personal narrative, Mindy Faber's tapes are informed by political and feminist thought, exploring the construction of female identity as a result of social expectations and limitations. Blending intimate stories with an investigation of broad social forces, Faber's tapes chart the complexities of female psychology in mother/daughter and interpersonal relationships.

Suburban Queen

A Perfect Pair
Valie Export
1987, 14:00, U.S., color, sound
A Perfect Pair posits the idea that individual consumers are walking billboards for the products they use, product slogans and brand names peeking out from every crevice and cranny of the actors' bodies. Export demonstrates how the body of the consumer, especially that of the female consumer, is co-opted by commercialism. In tongue-in-cheek fashion, *A Perfect Pair* celebrates the modern-day co-mingling of fetish objects, as a body builder seduces a prostitute at a bar saying, "Your eyes are the most beautiful blue ad space. Your cheek could promote a Mercedes. Your neck could be a slogan for styled technology." *A Perfect Pair* illustrates the inescapability of advertising's "regime of signs," the signifying network of personal and product values that is effectively encoded on the space of women's bodies.

Delirium
Mindy Faber
1993, 23:00, U.S., b&w and color, sound
Defiantly humorous in its tone, *Delirium* reflects Faber's mother's personal experience with what has been classified as "female hysteria." While never reducing her mother's condition to a single explanation, *Delirium* firmly and convincingly links her illness to the historically embattled position women hold in a patriarchal culture. The tape layers haunting imagery and humorous iconoclasm, referencing everything from television episodes of *I Love Lucy* to Charcot's 19th-century photos of female hysterics. *Delirium* contends that female mental illness must be understood within the political/social arena, and that in many instances women's reactions of violence, anger, and depression are indeed sane reactions to abhorrent situations.

Identity Crisis
Mindy Faber
1990, 3:00, U.S., color, sound
With wit and humor, seven-year-old Kendra portrays ten female stereotypes, including an ingratiating Southern belle, a motorcycle-riding tough chick, and a simpering housewife. Under the rubric of playing dress-up, the tape illustrates the pervasive, prescribed personalities available to women and the early age at which girls recognize these choices. But, as outtakes reveal, spirited Kendra is infinitely more complex than the cardboard cutouts she depicts.

Suburban Queen
Mindy Faber
1985, 3:00, U.S., color, sound
This classic feminist tape deviates from David Byrne's and Jonathan Demme's popular 1980s versions of suburban life, *True Stories*. Rather than poking sarcastic fun at the woman locked in the split-level, *Suburban Queen* poignantly evokes a daughter's longings. Portraying the relationship of a mother and daughter inextricably bound yet puzzled by each other's lives, Faber recounts her frustration with her mother's depression and passivity, and her fantasy of how her mother might transcend these conditions.

Farocki, Harun

Harun Farocki has made almost 90 films, including features, essay films, and documentaries; he has also worked in collaboration with other filmmakers as a scriptwriter, actor, and producer. Since 1966 he has written for numerous publications and from 1974 to 1984 he was editor and author of the Munich-based journal *Filmkritik*. His work has shown in many national and international exhibitions and installations, and he has taught in Berlin, Düsseldorf, Hamburg, Manila, Munich, Stuttgart, and Berkeley.

An Image

Between Two Wars
Harun Farocki
1978, 1:23:00, Germany, b&w, sound, in German with English subtitles
"A film about the time of the blast furnaces—1917-1933—about the development of an industry, about a perfect machinery which had to run itself to the point of its own destruction. This essay ... on heavy industry and the gas of the blast furnace, convinces through the author's cool abstraction and manic obsession and through the utilization of a single example of the self-destructive character of capitalistic production: 'The image of the blast furnace gas is real and metaphoric; an energy blows away uselessly into the air. Guided through a system of pipes, the pressure increases. Hence, a valve is needed. That valve is the production of war material.' *Between Two Wars* is also a film about the strains of filmmaking and a reflection on craft and creation. Farocki distances himself radically from the thoughtless sloppiness of average television work. The clarity and the precise ordering of his black and white images, which do not illustrate thoughts but are themselves thoughts, are reminiscent of late Godard. The poverty of this film—its production took six years—is at the same time its strength."
—Hans C. Blumenberg, *Die Zeit* (2 February 1979)

The Creators of Shoppings Worlds
Harun Farocki
2001, 1:12:00, Germany/U.S., color, sound
Brave new shopping worlds are being created. What have mall owners, architects, surveillance technicians, and supermarket workers done to turn human subjects into pure streams of consumers, into the perfect inhabitants of shopping mall paradise?

I Thought I Was Seeing Convicts
Harun Farocki
2000, 25:00, Germany/U.S., color, sound
"Images from the maximum-security prison in Corcoran, California. A surveillance camera shows a pie-shaped segment of the concrete yard where the prisoners, dressed in shorts and mostly shirtless, are allowed to spend half an hour a day. When one convict attacks another, those not involved lay flat on the ground, arms over their heads. They know that when a fight breaks out, the guard calls out a warning and then fires rubber bullets. If the fight continues, the guard shoots real bullets. The pictures are silent, the trail of gun smoke drifts across the picture. The camera and the gun are right next to each other."
—*Human Rights Projects* (Bard College, 2001)

An Image
Harun Farocki
1983, 25:00, Germany/U.S., color, sound, in German with English subtitles
"Four days spent in a studio working on a centerfold photo for *Playboy* magazine provided the subject matter for my film. The magazine itself deals with culture, cars, a certain lifestyle. Maybe all those trappings are only there to cover up the naked woman. Maybe it's like with a paper-doll. The naked woman in the middle is a sun around which a system revolves: of culture, of business, of living! (It's impossible to either look or film into the sun.) One can well imagine that the people creating such a picture, the gravity of which is supposed to hold all that, perform their task with as much care, seriousness, and responsibility as if they were splitting uranium."
—Harun Farocki

Inextinghishable Fire
Harun Farocki
1969, 25:00, Germany, b&w, sound, in German with English subtitles
"When we show you pictures of napalm victims, you'll shut your eyes. You'll close your eyes to the pictures. Then you'll close them to the memory. And then you'll close your eyes to the facts." These words are spoken at the

beginning of this agitprop film that can be viewed as a unique and remarkable development. Farocki refrains from making any sort of emotional appeal. His point of departure is the following: "When napalm is burning, it is too late to extinguish it. You have to fight napalm where it is produced: in the factories." Resolutely, Farocki names names: the manufacturer is Dow Chemical.

Interface (Schnittstelle)
Harun Farocki
1995, 23:00, Germany, color, sound
"Harun Farocki was commissioned by the Lille Museum of Modern Art to produce a video about his work. His creation was an installation for two screens that was presented within the scope of the 1995 exhibition *The World of Photography*. The film *Interface (Schnittstelle)* developed out of that installation. Reflecting on Farocki's own documentary work, it examines the question of what it means to work with existing images rather than producing one's own, new images. The German title plays on the double meaning of 'Schnitt', referring both to Farocki's workplace, the editing table, as well as the 'human-machine interface', where a person operates a computer using a keyboard and a mouse."
—3sat television guide, September, 1995

Jean-Marie Straub and Daniele Huillet at Work on Franz Kafka's Amerika
Harun Farocki
1983, 26:00, Germany, color, sound, in German with English subtitles
"This film is at once a self-portrait and an homage to Jean-Marie Straub, Farocki's role model and former teacher. Farocki's admiration for Straub was so great that he said of *Between Two Wars*, 'Perhaps I only made this film to earn Straub's recognition.' In this observation-driven film, Farocki documents the fulfillment of his wish. The film shows Farocki, under Straub's direction, rehearsing for his role as Delamarche in the film *Klassenverhältnisse* (1983). … Farocki filmed a work of resistance against traditional cinema, against which his own films rebel."
—Tilman Baumgärtel

Still Life
Harun Farocki
1997, 56:00, Germany/U.S., color, sound
According to Harun Farocki, today's photographers working in advertising are, in a way, continuing the tradition of 17th century Flemish painters in that they depict objects from everyday life: the still life. The filmmaker illustrates this intriguing hypothesis with three documentary sequences that show the photographers at work creating a contemporary still life: a cheese-board, beer glasses, and an expensive watch.

War at a Distance

War at a Distance
Harun Farocki
2003, 54:00, Germany/U.S., color, sound
"Farocki's *War at a Distance* brilliantly navigates and explores the connections between machine-vision, violence, and capitalist production practices in the context of the Gulf War and the global economy. Farocki demonstrates that our naive anthropocentric notions of vision and the visible are obsolete in today's world."
—San Francisco Cinemateque (2004)

Workers Leaving the Factory
Harun Farocki
1995, 36:00, Germany, b&w, sound
"*Workers Leaving the Factory*—such was the title of the first cinema film ever shown in public. For 45 seconds, this still-existent sequence depicts workers at the photographic products factory in Lyon, owned by the brothers Louis and Auguste Lumière, hurrying, closely packed, out of the shadows of the factory gates and into the afternoon sun. … In his documentary essay of the

Fetterley, Jim
(see Animal Charm)

Finley, Jeanne C.

Jeanne C. Finley is a California-based independent video producer. Through the use of true stories set in an experimental documentary form, her videoworks explore the tension between individual identity and the cultural and social institutions that both shape and affront that identity. Finley is currently a Professor and Chair of Film/Video/Performance at the California College of Arts and Crafts. Since 1988, John H. Muse has worked collaboratively with Jeanne Finley on numerous experimental documentaries and multi-channel video installations. Finley and Muse published an essay detailing their experience in *Art and Innovation: The Xerox PARC Artist-in-Residence Program*, ed. Craig Harris (1999). Muse is currently a Ph.D. candidate in Rhetoric at the University of California-Berkeley. Gretchen Stoeltje creates documentaries that feature confronting issues of female power and identity.

same title, Harun Farocki explores this scene right through the history of film. The result of this effort is a fascinating cinematographic analysis in the medium of cinematography itself, ranging in scope from Chaplin's *Modern Times* to Fritz Lang's *Metropolis* to Pier Paolo Pasolini's *Accattone*. Farocki's film shows that the Lumière brothers' sequence already carries within itself the germ of a foreseeable social development: the eventual disappearance of this form of industrial labor."
–Klaus Gronenborn, *Hildesheimer Allgemeine Zeitung* (21 November 1995)

A.R.M. around Moscow
Jeanne C. Finley and Gretchen Stoeltje
1994, 59:07, U.S., color, sound
A.R.M. around Moscow documents participants in A.R.M. (American-Russian Matchmaking) to explore the relationship of personal power to domestic identity and economic and political structure. Finley and Stoeltje followed 21 American men as they traveled to Russia to meet 500 local women. Each man was provided with a car, driver, translator, apartment, and meals for a "14-day tour of Russia's most beautiful and highly educated women" at the cost of about $4,700. From the moment of their anxious arrival at the Moscow airport, and throughout their dances, dates, and tearful departures from their newly acquired fiancées, these American men repeatedly disparaged American women as "too feminist," "demanding," and most importantly, "lacking in traditional family values." The Russian women, exhausted from balancing their careers and domestic responsibilities, look to these men as a possible hope for a better life and mutual love. "At its heart, *A.R.M. Around Moscow* is about a new U.S. export, the feminist backlash. Whereas the Russian women yearn for liberation from an uncertain future, the American men look to a past where they were armed for domination."
–Steve Seid, *American Cultures* (Berkeley: Pacific Film Archives, 1994)

Accidental Confessions
Jeanne C. Finley
1987, 5:00, U.S., color, sound
Accidental Confessions combines scenes from a demolition derby with statements taken from automobile insurance claims. In these claims, drivers were instructed to summarize the details of their accidents in the fewest words possible, resulting in absurd and contradictory statements.

The Adventures of Blacky
Jeanne C. Finley and John H. Muse
1997, 6:00, U.S., color, sound
Using a psychoanalytic tool from the 1950s, a series of black and white drawings illustrate the adventures of a family of dogs, dramatizing a young girl's appointment with her psychiatrist.

At the Museum: A Pilgrimage of Vanquished Objects
Jeanne C. Finley
1989, 23:00, U.S., color, sound
Commissioned by the Oakland Museum, this tape provides an artist's interpretation of the museum's displays and collections. The voice of a friendly narrator enlarges the image-objects with historical and social information, while a written text provides ironic commentary. "The term curator is derived from the Latin 'curatus'–one responsible for the care of souls." The daughter represented in the famous Dorothea Lange photograph *Migrant Mother* recounts the circumstance surrounding the now-celebrated photograph and how it impacted her life. Ultimately, the definition of "museum" is questioned for both what it is (cemetery) and what it is not (critique).

Based on a Story
Jeanne C. Finley and John H. Muse
1998, 44:00, U.S., color, sound
Based on a Story explores the widely publicized encounter between a Jewish

Cantor, Michael Weisser, and Nebraska's former Ku Klux Klan Grand Dragon, Larry Trapp. After months of harassment from Trapp by mail, phone, and cable TV, the Weisser family befriended Trapp, who then renounced the Klan, moved into the Weisser family's home, and converted to Judaism. Trapp, who was a double amputee and blind from childhood diabetes, died in the Weisser's home six months after he moved in. The Weisser/Trapp story, which was sold by the Weissers to Disney, is presented as an intimate tale of family and childhood that evolves into a media event, built around the fear and shifting terrain of public and private life. The unique visual construction of the video concludes with the narrator appearing on camera, suggesting that the piece's narrative shares the constructive nature of the interview footage.

Common Mistakes
Jeanne C. Finley
1986, 13:00, U.S., color, sound
Common Mistakes uses four synonyms for the word "mistake" (fallacy, error, accident, and blunder) to present a sample of widely held "truths" that later proved to be misconceptions. The mistakes are illustrated with documentary, before-and-after photographs, diagrams, and video footage, and are prefaced with a clip from a children's educational film on how to prevent accidents.

Conversations Across the Bosphorous
Jeanne C. Finley in collaboration with Ternar Mine
1995, 41:45, U.S., color, sound

Conversations Across the Bosphorous

Conversations Across the Bosphorous intertwines the narratives of two Muslim women from Istanbul, Mine and Gokcen, who demonstrate through poetic voices how their relationship to faith has shaped and determined their personal lives. Set on the banks of the Bosphorous, the narrow waterway that divides the Asian and European continents, *Conversations* suggests that the relationship of personal faith to cultural and political struggles is one of the most critical issues in both the Islamic and Christian worlds. In conjunction with evocative visual imagery, sound, and lively debate, these narratives evaluate the possibility of continued peaceful co-existence between groups of opposing ideologies in a relentless urban landscape.

Deaf Dogs Can Hear
Jeanne C. Finley
1983, 5:00, U.S., color, sound
Deaf Dogs Can Hear is an autobiographical work that traces the tragic yet humorous episodes of the artist as a young girl and her pet chihuahua. Her love for this deformed and unattractive pet only grows deeper as one tragedy after another befalls the dog and the creature becomes repulsive to all eyes but its owner's.

I Saw Jesus in a Tortilla
Jeanne C. Finley
1982, 3:00, U.S., color, sound

I Saw Jesus in a Tortilla

Taken almost verbatim from a report in *The Arizona Daily Star*, this tape recounts the story of Ramona Barrara, a New Mexico woman who saw the face of Jesus in a tortilla when she was rolling her husband's burrito. Although she attempted to manipulate the media to her advantage, the media ultimately exploited the most important event of this woman's life for its sensational value.

Involuntary Conversion
Jeanne C. Finley
1991, 9:00, U.S., color, sound
A chilling and revealing look at bureaucratic techno-speak, Finley provides a course in "official" media rhetoric, presenting terms and decoding for the audience (i.e. "soft target = city," "involuntary conversion = crash") against a slow-motion collage of military imagery. This intensely visual tape illustrates how the urban environment has become the site of tactical language, render-

ing our daily lives in a science-fiction state of constant fear. The visual elements create a rhythm of threat that is punctuated by high altitude shots of military jets. The tape concludes with quotes from Dan Quayle as he unsuccessfully attempts to manipulate the complicated language developed by his own political "fraternity."

Language Lessons
Jeanne C. Finley and John H. Muse
2002, 9:00, U.S., color, sound
Language Lessons entwines the search for the fountain of youth with the dream of a common language. The fountain both promises and frustrates eternity, while this dream offers hope for common ground. The lessons, made vivid by watery, elemental images and multiple voices, suggest that communication remains at the limits of our imagination.
Music by Pamela Z.

Loss Prevention
Jeanne C. Finley, Doug Dubois and John H. Muse
2000, 17:00, U.S., color, sound
Loss Prevention combines documentary and fiction to tell the story of Irene, arrested at the age of 79 for stealing a bottle of aspirin from a Miami Wal-Mart and sentenced to ten weeks of Senior Citizen Shoplifting Prevention School. Narrated through the voice of her daughter, this film explores the alienation of aging and the evolving relationship between a daughter and an elderly mother. The visual material combines the lush Florida landscape with intimate Super-8 footage to create a subtle meditation on the conflicts of parent and child, boredom and pleasure, accident and intention, authority and subterfuge.
Originally recorded for broadcast on the radio program *This American Life* in July 1999, the interviews are audio-only to protect the identities of the subjects.

Loss Prevention

NOMADS at the 25 DOOR
Jeanne C. Finley
1991, 43:00, U.S., color, sound
NOMADS at the 25 DOOR is presented in three chapters and based around a series of interviews between Finley and Mickey Yates, a 22-year-old woman serving a double life sentence in the Nevada Women's Correctional Institution for the murder of her mother. Interweaving interview excerpts with footage of the upheaval in Eastern Europe, the tape explores the memory's construction of an ephemeral homeland when a concrete one is lost, stolen, or left behind. The evocative visual imagery of *Nomads* creates an elusive document of the shifting balance of power between the individual and the family, the government and its people, and the documented and the betrayed.

NOMADS at the 25 DOOR

So, You Want to be Popular?
Jeanne C. Finley
1988, 18:00, U.S., color, sound
Through the memory of a high school classmate, footage from a film for teenagers called *Be Popular,* a video dating tape, and performances by political and entertainment figures, *So, You Want to be Popular?* examines how cultural stereotypes determine the individual's sense of acceptance and self-worth.

Time Bomb
Jeanne C. Finley and John H. Muse
1998, 7:12, U.S., color, sound
Time Bomb tells the story of a young girl's experience at a Baptist retreat, where she is called upon to accept Jesus into her life after a coercive game of terror. This piece explores memory, the power of crowds, rituals of conversion, and the isolation of a child lost in the world of adults. Fear and family values motivate action and create an empty arena for escape. Visually, *Time*

Bomb proceeds through a sequence of images that figure the "light" of memory as simultaneously revelatory and obscuring, constructive and destructive. *Time Bomb* was created during an artist residency at Xerox's Palo Alto Research Center designed to give artists and scientists working with new technologies the opportunity to collaborate.

Finn, Jim

Jim Finn lives in Chicago and makes videos about small animals, communism, love, and the disease-like spread of world capitalism. His house is a kind of MGM lot for experimental animal videos. He makes his videos with 16mm film, mini-DV, and appropriated footage. He studied poetry writing at the University of Arizona and uses poetic constructs in his work. When the units of sense in a passage of poetry don't coincide with the verses, and the sense runs on from one verse to another, the lines are said to be enjambed. He treats the text in his videos as lines of poetry and the image as the verse. Though the audio and video sources of his work do not always coincide, there is another kind of sense being made in the work.

el güero

comunista!
Jim Finn
2001, 3:30, U.S., color, sound
"You are invited to Jim's party! Snake optional."
—Cinematexas Festival (Austin, 2001)
"Three more sing-alongs, this time with swans, a snake, and the Red Army Chorus."
—L.A. Freewaves festival
Also available on *Jim Finn Videoworks: Volume 1.*

Decision 80
Jim Finn
2003, 10:00, U.S., color, sound
Appropriated network-TV footage of Jimmy Carter's "I see risk" speech from the 1980 Democratic Convention meets Ronald Reagan's gloomy inaugural ride through D.C.: "If you succumb to a dream world, you'll wake up to a nightmare."

el güero
Jim Finn
2001, 3:00, U.S., color, sound, in Spanish with English subtitles
"A refreshing look at karaoke, psychedic dance moves, and donuts all mashed together into a small and swinging film about a man who considers his private thoughts and private jokes worth sharing with a large audience. And it's unlikely that many would disagree."
—Impakt Festival (Utrecht, the Netherlands, 2001)
Also available on *Jim Finn Videoworks: Volume 1.*

Jim Finn Videoworks: Volume 1
Jim Finn's short works encompass a world of communism, dancing, karaoke, and small animals.
Total running time 12:30.
Contents:
comunista!, Jim Finn, 2001, 3:30, U.S., color, sound
el güero, Jim Finn, 2001, 3:00, U.S., color, sound, in Spanish with English subtitles
sharambaba, Jim Finn, 1999, 3:00, U.S., color, sound
wüstenspringmaus, Jim Finn, 2002, 3:00, U.S., color, sound

sharambaba
Jim Finn
1999, 3:00, U.S., color, sound
A young communist girl named *Sharambaba* resists her suitor in a carriage. She speaks of what he calls her "fantasy world." All of the dialogue is played backwards with accommodating subtitles.
Also available on *Jim Finn Videoworks: Volume 1.*

super-max
Jim Finn
2003, 13:00, U.S., color, sound
"Finn's chilling *super-max* is a tour of maximum security prisons shot from a moving car, their hulking forms framed by telephone poles and power lines that divide landscape and sky. The concluding voice-over, making reference to Lewis and Clark, implicitly equates the European occupation of this continent with imprisonment."
—Fred Camper, *Chicago Reader* (28 March 2003)

Flanagan, Bob

Working in collaboration with Sheree Rose, Bob Flanagan's performance career began in the late 1970s in Los Angeles nightclubs; later Flanagan performed S/M scenes that drew metaphoric and literal connections between his illness and his masochism. His life and work have been documented in the book *Bob Flanagan: Supermasochist* (1993) and the documentary *Sick: The Life and Death of Bob Flanagan, Supermasochist* (1997).

Fleming, Sherman

Washington D.C.-based artist Sherman Fleming has explored the relationship between psychical endurance and social structures as well as the intersection of race and gender. In subjecting his body to a series of "tests"—not unlike the repetitious contests in Acconci's early work— Fleming reveals the absurdity and chaos in the attempt to control the inevitable.

Fletcher, Harrell

Since the early 1990s Harrell Fletcher has worked collaboratively and individually on interdisciplinary, site-specific projects exploring the dynamics of social spaces and communities. Along with this work he has developed a series of more personal and idiosyncratic pieces that take various forms: drawings, prints, writings, events, videos, and sculptural objects.

wüstenspringmaus
Jim Finn
2002, 3:00, U.S., color, sound
"'The gerbil has long been associated with New World capitalism because of its incessant energy.' The Golden Age of Hollywood takes on the history and evolution of this delightful household pet."
—International Film Festival Rotterdam (2003)

Also available on *Jim Finn Videoworks: Volume 1*.

Autopsy
Bob Flanagan, Sheree Rose, and Kirby Dick
1994, 15:40, U.S., color, sound
Autopsy is the first production of an ongoing video and film collaboration between the artists Bob Flanagan and Sheree Rose and filmmaker Kirby Dick. The objective of this collaboration is to produce a series of videos and installations that focus on Flanagan and Rose's themes of masochism, dominance and submission, illness, and death. Dick ultimately developed this footage into the full-length documentary film *Sick: The Life and Death of Bob Flanagan, Supermasochist* (1997).

Only available on the anthology *Endurance, Reel 4*.

AxVapor
Sherman Fleming
1989, 10:00, U.S., color, sound
AxVapor is from a series of performances Fleming undertook under the name *RODFORCE*. In it, he wore shoes bolted to halves of bowling balls, round side down, and spun and fell repeatedly on an Oriental rug.
"My performance work employs childhood games, ritual dance actions derived from voodoo religion and African and pre-Columbia cultures. ... This bodily behavior, which I have defined as 'psycho-physical behavior,' operates through the act of repetition; its duration is determined by my body's stamina. My objective is to maintain the quality of stability through the behavioral constructions of rotation, suspension, inversion, and inertia."
—Sherman Fleming

Only available on the anthology *Endurance, Reel 4*.

Blot Out the Sun
Harrell Fletcher
2002, 22:45, U.S., color, sound
A garage in central Portland, Oregon is the setting for this conceptual re-working of James Joyce's *Ulysses*. The garage owner Jay, mechanics, and neighborhood denizens serve as narrators, reading lines from the novel that focus on death, love, social inequality, and the relationship between individuals and the universe.
"With only three weeks to work, Fletcher scrambled to find the right filmic form to mesh Leopold Bloom's Dublin with Jay's Portland. He tried a documentary approach, but the employees were too busy, and it didn't seem the right fit. So, by now well into his reading of *Ulysses*, he decided instead to gather choice passages from the book, write them out on cue-cards, and ask people to read them aloud on camera. The result is an unbelievably Joycean mix of mundane details and moments of epiphany, the carnal and spiritual, as a thickly-mustached mechanic reads his way through one of Joyce's lustiest passages, his lips moving from reluctant to jubilant as he reads on, swept up into the current of words."
—Chris Thompson, "On the Fly: A Day in the Life with Fletcher Harrell," *The Portland Phoenix* (15 August 2002)

Problem of Possible Redemption
Harrell Fletcher
2003, 13:00, U.S., color, sound
A video adaptation of James Joyce's *Ulysses* shot at the Parkville Senior

Center in Connecticut, with the seniors reading the lines from cue cards. The piece addresses society, war, and personal mortality.

"For over ten years Fletcher has worked collaboratively and individually on interdisciplinary, site-specific projects exploring dynamics of social spaces and communities. Fletcher describes his artistic approach as 'the hanging out method,' as he starts each of his projects by observing and talking to people in order to respond to a specific place. ... Fletcher initiates mini-theaters for stories, fantasies and memories to be shared in new ways."
–Robert Beck Memorial Cinema (New York City, 17 July 2003)

Foreman, Richard

Richard Foreman founded the Ontological-Hysteric Theater in 1968. Since then he has written, directed, and designed more than 20 major productions characterized by complex interplay between spoken language and visual tableaux. Foreman reconceived theater as a video experience and employed disruptive devices that puncture theatrical illusions and audience assumptions. Foreman's plays and essays have been collected in the publications *Plays and Manifestos* (1976) and *Reverberation Machines, the Later Plays and Essays* (1985).

Out of Body Travel
Richard Foreman
1976, 24:00 excerpt (of 42:00), U.S., b&w, sound
A "young woman who finds herself surrounded by the relics of Western culture" is the subject of Richard Foreman's formal tableaux. The narration centers on a young woman's struggle to find a relation between her body and her self as mediated by language. The text is a poetry of formal relations that carries personal and historical implications, including the desires of the woman paradoxically voiced by a male narrator. The title suggests the vivid virtuality of dreaming; scenes repeatedly refer to both reading and sleeping. Richard Foreman, founder and director of the Ontological-Hysteric Theater in New York, produced this first videotape project with students from the American Dance Festival and cinematographer Babette Mangolte.

Only available as an excerpt on the anthology *Surveying the First Decade, Program 3.*

Forti, Simone

Simone Forti gained recognition as a dancer and performance artist in the early '70s; reacting against the studied formalism of many modern dance practitioners, Forti composed movements "designed to give people the feel of their own bodies and put them in touch with the physicality of movement without any effort to dazzle with technical virtuosity." Although many of her early performances escaped video documentation, *Three Grizzlies* (1974) and *Solo No. 1* (1975) provide insight into Forti's creative process.

Solo No. 1
Simone Forti
1975, 8:00, U.S., color, sound
Adopting the movements of various animals, Forti begins her performance by walking hypnotically in circles. She falls to the floor and begins a cycle of walking and crawling that becomes an open metaphor for evolution and aging. Through the course of the performance, the camera follows Forti's circling motion at increasingly close range, creating an interactive dance between camera and performer. While "rustic" in respect to the quality of the video image and sound, *Solo No. 1* serves as an engaging document of Forti's dedicated study of natural movement.

Three Grizzlies
Simone Forti
1974, 17:00, U.S., color, sound
Forti uses the camera as a research tool to record the movements of three grizzly bears pacing anxiously behind the bars of their cage in the Brooklyn Zoo. The collected visual information becomes part of the basis for Forti's movements in *Solo No. 1.*

Fox, Terry

A central participant in the west coast performance, video, and conceptual art movements of the late '60s and early '70s, Terry Fox became well-known for his political, site-specific performances that explored ritual and symbolic content in the objects, places, and natural phenomena of everyday life. Describing *Children's Tapes* (1974), Fox says, "The medium of video was chosen largely because the subjects were too intimate for performance, and because of the special appearance and attention-holding power of TV for children."

Children's Tapes
Terry Fox
1974, 30:00, U.S., b&w, sound
Phenomenological dramas involving household objects like candles, spoons, and matches unfold with an extreme economy of gesture. Fox balances a spoon and a piece of ice on top of a bent fork. We watch as the ice melts and the spoon is thrown off balance and falls. Inventing new situations with the same objects, Fox posits these works as an alternative to commercial children's television—a critique of the pace of television, which never affords the time to see the processes develop. The play of objects in delicate flux with each other serves as a meditative exercise on the symmetry of physical forces. A wide-angle camera lens delivers this intimate tabletop performance world to a larger audience. The sublime beauty of these elemental observations recalls the aesthetic of Fox's one-time mentor, Joseph Beuys.

Only available on the anthology *Surveying the First Decade, Program 2.*

Freed, Hermine

During the late '60s Freed began using video to produce a series of contemporary artist portraits, beginning with painter James Rosenquist. Although the program did not meet WNYC's broadcast standards, Freed continued to produce the series, showing the tapes to her students and at other venues. Freed continued to produce both documentaries and artworks exploring female perception and self-image, including *Art Herstory* (1974). She died in 1998.

Art Herstory

360°
Hermine Freed
1972, 8:00, U.S., color, sound

The frame is filled with two concentric magnifying lenses, one larger than the other is. Behind them is a mirror. The mirror turns and reflects the landscape around it. Distortions of the moving images appear in the lenses while the space behind remains stationary. A voice-over reports what is being seen in each of the layers of space. There are at least three simultaneous sound-tracks. One scene is a country house and garden, another is a city apartment. A short video that is deeply concerned with the psychology of perception, especially in relation to female identity, the video image, and the role of spectator.

Art Herstory
Hermine Freed
1974, 22:00, U.S., color, sound

"In her brilliant video *Art Herstory*, [Freed] has restaged art history, putting herself in the model's role in numerous paintings. ... Time dissolves under her humorous assault—one moment in the painting, then out of the canvas and into that period, then back in the studio.
—Jonathan Price, "Video Art: a Medium Discovering Itself," *Art News* 76 (January 1977)
Excerpt (15:00) available on the anthology *Surveying the First Decade, Program 4.*

Family Album
Hermine Freed
1973, 10:00, U.S., b&w, sound

Over a montage of family photographs, Freed's narration questions the consistency of memory and self over time, with Freed displaying a quizzical and sometimes hostile relation to her past. In a manner that recalls philosopher Roland Barthes's poetic unraveling of photography—in particular photography's power to bind memory and desire within a still image—Freed attempts to uncover the "stranger" that is her childhood self and discover how her past has shaped her present. "As *Art Herstory* was about time in history, *Family Album* deals with time in memory. Using photos and film footage from my past, I mix past and present and superimpose my then-present face over a photo of my childhood self. Time is arranged non-sequentially in the mind. Memories of relatives are brought in to contrast with my own."
—Hermine Freed.

New Reel
Hermine Freed
1976, 12:00, U.S., color, sound

In a tape that stands out as one of the earliest examples of the use of appropriated television footage, Freed assembles a collage of images representing American media icons, from Mickey Mouse to Richard Nixon to *The Wizard of Oz*. Placing cartoon images next to images of the war in Vietnam, Freed creates an appropriately surreal vision of American culture and begs the question whether an anthropologist of the future would be able to decipher the truth of the age from such a confused mix of representations. Continuing a theme brought up in several of her earlier videos, Freed asks, "If history is made of memories, whose memories is it made of?"

Show and Tell
Hermine Freed
1974, 11:00, U.S., b&w, sound

"There are three scenes in this work, all reflecting a changing sense of time. Each has a voiceover soundtrack with a similar structure but with different information. Some of the comments presume that the viewer is privy to information which is never given…" Freed's voiceover provides a stream of information about the images, their source, and the method of presentation she is employing. What is disquieting is the fact that her analysis is resolutely similar in each case–a combination of exegesis and confession, with Freed providing information about the images along with her personal misgivings about the process of videotaping. In this way, Freed establishes a dichotomous voice on the tape, an insecure "authority" that reveals the artist's uncertain attitude toward creation.

Two Faces
Hermine Freed
1972, 8:00, U.S., b&w, sound
In her oft-cited essay "Video: The Aesthetics of Narcissism," Rosalind Krauss says, "self-encapsulation–taking the body or psyche as its own surround–is everywhere to be found in the corpus of video art" (*October* 1, Spring 1976). This certainly applies to this early work of Hermine Freed. Utilizing a split and reversed screen, Freed faces herself, caressing and kissing her doubled image. Without narration, the tape shows Freed suspended between two images, existing as a doubled person. In light of feminist discourse on women's alienation from themselves in a male-dominated culture and the co-option of women's images by advertising and the media, this tape reads as Freed's attempt to contact her self-image directly–to, in effect, claim her image.
Also available on the anthology *I Say I Am: Program 2*.

Two Faces

Water Glasses
Hermine Freed
1972, 5:00, U.S., b&w, sound
An experiment in "video cubism." Two rows of three cylindrical water glasses are lined up to fit the frame of the monitor. The glasses disappear, then reappear; the action of placing them on the table is never seen. The glasses are filled with water with the image parallel to the picture plane; then again, with two cameras–one above and one straight on. *Water Glasses* investigates the psychology of perception–especially in relation to female identity, the video image, and the role of spectator.

Fulbeck, Kip
Kip Fulbeck is a performance and video artist based in southern California. From a Cantonese, English, Irish, and Welsh background, he explores the Asian male experience through humorous and angry autobiographical stories. Fulbeck confronts media imagery of Asian men, interracial dating, and icons of race and sex in the United States, continually questioning where Hapas (people of mixed race with Asian or Pacific Islander ancestry) belong in a country that ignores multiraciality.

Asian Studs Nightmare
Kip Fulbeck
1994, 6:00, U.S., color, sound
Asian Studs Nightmare examines the racial politics behind the hit U.S. television dating show *STUDS*. Fulbeck frantically recalls somewhat fictional nightmares of Asian male identity. Over a multi-layered visual of the actual *STUDS* show and Asian male stereotypes, *Asian Studs* reveals the pervasive racial hierarchies and taboos depicted in mass media and probes their relation to interracial dating patterns and minority status in the United States.
Also available on the compilation *Kip Fulbeck Videoworks: Volume 1*.

Banana Split
Kip Fulbeck
1991, 37:30, U.S., color, sound
Kip Fulbeck's landmark video *Banana Split* defined the genre of multiracial exploration in contemporary video and established him as one of the premiere artists exploring Hapa and multracial identity. Completed while Fulbeck was still in graduate school, *Banana Split* screened throughout the U.S. and abroad, and is still used in classes today. Fulbeck's brilliant storytelling takes the viewer from childhood fights to adult dilemmas, questions interracial dating patterns and media depictions of Asian men, and explores the idea of ethnic identity in a country that ignores multiraciality.
"Touches the raw nerves of Amerasian sensibility–the desire to embrace, yet question every cultural icon."
–Chiori Santiago, "Don't worry, be happa: Asian-American International Film Showcase examines hardships of Amerasians," *Oakland Tribune* (8 March 1992)

Game of Death

Game of Death
Kip Fulbeck
1991, 6:30, U.S., color, sound

"[A] hilarious look at the beautification of Bruce Lee. Footage of the title sequence from the eponymous film–a success even though Lee died halfway through the filming–is overlaid with crude video-generated titles. Chuck Norris is tagged 'bad hairy white guy,' while Kareem Abdul-Jabbar (!) is ID'd as 'very very bad black guy.' It's a subversion of two martial arts movie cliches at once: stupid subtitles and one-dimensional characters. Along the way, Fulbeck notes that the film was completed by a stand-in called 'Bruce Li,' identified here as 'FAKE.' 'Somebody wake me up: Can people really not notice?' Fullbeck asks. *Game* shows how Asian America's desperation for a hero has led to Lee's devolution into an inhuman, and ultimately replaceable, chopsocky icon."
–Jeff Yang, "Shooting Back," *The Village Voice* 37:20 (19 May 1992)
Also available on the compilation *Kip Fulbeck Videoworks: Volume 1.*

Kip Fulbeck Videoworks: Volume 1
These three videos utilize images gathered from television, film, and print media to explore society's hidden hierarchies and taboos in relation to Asian male identity, interracial dating, and the race and gender wars.
Total running time 21:00.
Contents:
Asian Studs Nightmare, Kip Fulbeck, 1994, 6:00, U.S., color, sound
Game of Death, Kip Fulbeck, 1991, 6:30, U.S., color, sound
Some Questions for 28 Kisses, Kip Fulbeck, 1994, 8:30, U.S., color, sound

Lilo & Me
Kip Fulbeck
2003, 9:35, U.S., color, sound

Which celebrity do you most resemble? For artist Kip Fulbeck, this question starts a rollicking ride that is part autobiography, part family portrait, part pop-culture survey, and all Disney all the time. Watch as Fulbeck documents his uncanny resemblance to Pochahontas, Mulan, Aladdin, and other "ethnically ambiguous" animated characters. Both hilarious and touching, this educating video examines the muting of race in mainstream media and its effects on multiracial Americans.

Nine Fish
Kip Fulbeck
1996, 23:45, U.S., color, sound

From childhood memories to recurring nightmares, *Nine Fish* attacks and illuminates the indecision and confusion surrounding euthanasia and care of the elderly in the United States. In this deeply spiritual and personal video, Fulbeck chronicles his Cantonese grandmother's physical decline and its continuing impact on his family. The shifting complexities of personal identity, family communication, and cultural assimilation are explored through nine semi-fictional stories.

Sex, Love & Kung Fu
Kip Fulbeck
2000, 7:00, U.S., color, sound

Two crazed Kung Fu film fanatics argue over Asian-American masculinity (yes!), Asian-American media representation (no!), the homoerotic subtexts of martial arts movies (what?), and the ultimate question: what channel to watch. Fulbeck brings his blistering pace, comedic skill, and critical eye to bear on the Hapa and Asian-American male experience–parodying the relationships between sex, love, and martial arts movies. Hilarious and fast-paced, *Sex, Love & Kung Fu* entertains as it explores the mysteries of David Carradine, Brandon Lee, and the size of Dolph Lundgren's penis.

Lilo & Me

Some Questions for 28 Kisses

Kip Fulbeck

1994, 8:30, U.S., color, sound

Fulbeck force-feeds the viewer scores of all-too-familiar Asian female/Caucasian male pairings in Hollywood films and combines them with contemporary excerpts from best-selling novels, magazines, and dating services. *Some Questions for 28 Kisses* delves into the causes and purposes of these created images and their relation to interracial dating, ethnic fetishes, race and gender wars, and Hapa identity.

Also available on the compilation *Kip Fulbeck Videoworks: Volume 1.*

Sweet or Spicy?

Kip Fulbeck

2000, 7:10, U.S., color, sound

Ever listen to *Loveline*? Well, here's an episode with a 24-year-old Korean-American guy who's never been kissed. They're offering free concert tickets to any girl who'll come in and take a chance. The girls get their tickets, and "David" gets to pick one of them for his first smack. Trouble is … no volunteers. Combining personal dating stories and the hypnotic imagery of multi-colored koi, *Sweet or Spicy?* explores Hapa and Asian-American male sexuality in popular culture.

Fung, Richard

Richard Fung is a Trinidad-born, Toronto-based video artist and cultural critic whose work deals with the intersection of race and queer sexuality, and with issues of post-colonialism, diaspora, and family. He has published many essays in journals and anthologies, including his famous "Looking for My Penis: The Eroticized Asian in Gay Video Porn," in *How Do I Look?*, ed. *Bad Object-Choices* (1991).

Chinese Characters

Richard Fung

1986, 21:00, Canada, color, sound

Quoting Confucius, that "food and sex are human nature," *Chinese Characters* builds a parallel between the Chinese legend about the search for the source of the Yellow river and contemporary Asian-American gay men's search for pleasure via their relationship to gay pornography. Advancing the positive value of pornography as a way to help fantasize and experience greater sexual pleasure and ingenuity, personal techniques are demonstrated and deployed in a *High Noon* dream of sexual adventure.

Dirty Laundry

Richard Fung

1996, 30:30, Canada, color, sound

Dirty Laundry speculates upon the buried narratives of gender and sexuality in Chinese-Canadian history of the 19th century, when Chinese communities were almost exclusively male. A story about a chance late-night encounter between a steward and a passenger on a train interweaves with documentary interviews with historians and writers and historical documents brought to life. The tape poses nagging questions about the personal and political stakes in the writing of history and in our interpretations of the past.

Fighting Chance

Richard Fung

1991, 30:00, Canada, color, sound

Fighting Chance is a continuation of Richard Fung's previous documentary *Orientations*, which told of the personal challenges and struggles of Asian-Canadian gays and lesbians to express their sexual identities. When Fung produced *Orientations* in 1984, AIDS had not yet fully manifested itself (particularly among Asians), but by 1991, as we see in *Fighting Chance*, the epidemic has become threateningly widespread. Individuals and couples candidly discuss the various hurdles and challenges that AIDS has presented. Those affected must confront families, friends, the community, and most important, their inner selves.

Islands

Richard Fung

2002, 8:45, Canada, color, sound

In *Islands* Fung deconstructs the 1956 John Huston film *Heaven Knows Mr. Allison* to comment on the Caribbean's relationship to the cinematic image. A

Fighting Chance

story of the unrequited love of a shipwrecked American marine (Robert Mitchum) for an Irish nun (Deborah Kerr), *Heaven Knows Mr. Allison* is set in 1944 in the Pacific, but was shot in 1956 in Tobago using Trinidadian-Chinese extras to portray Japanese soldiers. The artist's Uncle Clive was one such extra, and Fung searches the film for traces of his presence.

My Mother's Place

My Mother's Place
Richard Fung
1990, 49:50, Canada, color, sound
My Mother's Place is an experimental documentary focusing on the artist's mother, a third-generation Chinese-Trinidadian who at 80 still has vivid memories of a history lost or quickly disappearing. She conveys these with a story-telling style and a frankness that is distinctly West Indian. A tape about memory, oral history, and autobiography, *My Mother's Place* interweaves interviews, personal narrative, home movies, and verité footage of the Caribbean to explore the formation of race, class, and gender under colonialism.

Orientations: Lesbian and Gay Asians
Richard Fung
1984, 56:00, Canada, color, sound
In response to the dominant impression that gay people are white people, *Orientations* aims to set the record straight on homosexual identity. More than a dozen men and women of different Asian backgrounds speak frankly, humorously, and often poignantly about their lives as members of a minority within a minority. They speak about coming out, homophobia, racism, cultural identity, sex, and the ways that being gay and Asian have shaped who they are.

School Fag
Richard Fung
1998, 16:35, Canada, color, sound
A fast-talking and fabulous teen recounts his experiences as an out and loud Toronto queer. With catty wit, he recalls his confrontations with straight students at school and his gay prom at a Toronto gay youth community center, told with a flair for drama and punctuated with enactments of his Wonder Woman fantasies. Fung keeps the format simple, giving voice to his subject.

Sea in the Blood

Sea in the Blood
Richard Fung
2000, 26:00, Canada, color, sound
Sea in the Blood is a personal documentary about living with illness, tracing the relationship of the artist to thalassemia in his sister Nan, and AIDS in his partner Tim. At the core of the piece are two trips. The first is in 1962, when Richard went from Trinidad to England with Nan to see a famous hematologist interested in her unusual case. The second is in 1977 when Richard and Tim made the counterculture pilgrimage from Europe to Asia. The relationship with Tim blossomed, but Nan died before their return. The narrative of love and loss is set against a background of colonialism in the Caribbean and the reverberations of migration and political change.
"*Sea in the Blood* was to be a meditation on race, sexuality, and disease, but after working with the material for three years, it was the emotional story that came through. It's hard to work with such personal material, but in the end the work takes on a life of its own. 'Richard' is a character. Because of the subject matter—disease and death—I wanted to avoid sentimentality. I'd like the audience to think as well as feel."
—Richard Fung

Steam Clean
Richard Fung
1991, 4:00, Canada, color, sound
A Gay Men's Health Crisis sex re-education PSA in which an interracial gay male couple hooks up at a bath house, having steamy sex safely.

The Way to My Father's Village
Richard Fung
1988, 38:00, Canada, color, sound
In the fall of 1986, Richard Fung made his first visit to his father's birthplace, a village in southern Guangdong, China. This experimental documentary examines the way children of immigrants relate to the land of their parents and focuses on the ongoing subjective construction of history and memory. *The Way to My Father's Village* juxtaposes the son's search for his own historical roots and his father's avoidance of his cultural heritage.

Fusco, Coco

Coco Fusco is an interdisciplinary artist and writer. Working with Guillermo Gómez-Peña, she created the *Year of the White Bear* (1992), a multi-faceted project that included a touring exhibition, audio art, performances, video, and a book. Their experimental radio pieces have been aired on National Public Radio and performed throughout the United States, Spain, Britain, Australia, Canada, Puerto Rico, and Mexico.

The Couple in the Cage: Guatianaui Odyssey
Coco Fusco, co-produced with Paula Heredia
1993, 31:00, U.S., b&w and color, sound
In a series of 1992 performances, Coco Fusco and Guillermo Gómez-Peña decked themselves out in primitive costumes and appeared before the public as "undiscovered AmerIndians" locked in a golden cage—an exercise in faux anthropology based on racist images of natives. Presented eight times in four different countries, these simple performances evoked various responses, the most startling being the huge numbers of people who didn't find the idea of "natives" locked in a cage objectionable. This provocative tape suggests that the "primitive" is nothing more than a construction of the West and uses comic fiction to address historical truths and tragedies.

Pochonovela: A Chicano Soap Opera
Coco Fusco
1996, 27:00, U.S., color, sound
Pochonovela is a bilingual, bicultural blend of Latin America's and the United States' most popular television genres—the telenovela and the sitcom, respectively. Members of the Los Angeles-based comedy troupe Chicano Secret Service and other U.S. Latino actors capture the humor and madness of life in East L.A. This provocative comedy touches on political, social, cultural, linguistic, and family issues attendant to the cross cultural life of Mexican-Americans living near or on the border—both psychologically and geographically. Music composed by the band Cholita.

Gallois, Dominique
(see Carelli, Vincent)

Garcia-Ferraz, Nereida
(see Horsfield, Kate)

Garrin, Paul

Paul Garrin started working for Nam June Paik on the day that Reagan was shot in March 1981 and spent the day recording TV news broadcasts of the event. Since then he has become a master of image processing techniques, using layered digital imagery to achieve dense, atmospheric effects while addressing issues of public and private space.

By Any Means Necessary
Paul Garrin
1990, 30:00, U.S., color, sound
Spanning two years of protest and resistance, this tape chronicles the politically motivated police harassment of the homeless population in Manhattan's Lower East Side, including suspected arson, illegal eviction, and the demolition of buildings that forced families onto the street. Taking its title from a quote by Malcolm X, *By Any Means Necessary* is an indictment of government systems that violate the law willfully and at random in the service of wealthy real estate developers.

Free Society
Paul Garrin
1988, 4:00, U.S., color, sound
Free Society is a short experimental music video that juxtaposes images of police harassment in the U.S. with images of the military quelling revolutionary opposition. Includes comments from televangelist Jerry Falwell.
Also available on the compilation *Paul Garrin Videoworks: Volume 1*.

Home(less) Is Where the Revolution Is
Paul Garrin
1990, 2:00, U.S., color, sound
With animated collages of street conflicts and high-tension video effects, this

short advertises what has been called the "next World War": the war of the poor, disenfranchised, and homeless against a government controlled by and serving only the wealthy. The intriguing image of the White House lawn occupied by thousands of homeless people calls attention to the prevailing injustice of a system that leaves citizens to live on the streets, civil and human rights unacknowledged.
With music by Elliott Sharp.

Man with a Video Camera
Paul Garrin
1988, 7:00, U.S., color, sound
After an all-night session of editing *Free Society,* Garrin headed home with video-8 camera in hand, only to happen upon the Tompkins Square riots. As police tried to enforce a curfew aimed at removing homeless people from the park, Garrin began gathering footage of cops beating up protesters. Police also then attacked him as the camera continued to roll. The footage was subsequently incorporated into *Free Society,* in which the military myth of "protect and serve" is dismantled by first-hand experience.
Also available on the compilation *Paul Garrin Videoworks: Volume 1.*

Paul Garrin Videoworks: Volume 1
Garrin advocates the use of video as an activist and community tool and a means for people to represent themselves. These three pieces examine the Tompkins Square riots, police harassment, and the use of home video equipment to record a truly democratic local news.
"Once 'Big Brother' was the state watching the people, now the people can begin watching the state."
—Paul Garrin
Total running time 12:00.
Contents:
Free Society, Paul Garrin, 1988, 4:00, U.S., color, sound
Man with a Video Camera, Paul Garrin, 1988, 7:00, U.S., color, sound
Reverse Big Brother, Paul Garrin, 1990, 1:00, U.S., color, sound

Reverse Big Brother
Paul Garrin
1990, 1:00, U.S., color, sound
This alternative commercial promotes the aggressive democratic use of home video equipment to record local news of community activism and other events that don't make the headlines for political reasons.
With music by Elliot Sharp.

Also available on the compilation *Paul Garrin Videoworks: Volume 1.*

Man with a Video Camera

Gibbons, Joe

Joe Gibbons conveys his dry humor through obsessive monologues that suggest a monomaniacal mind spilling forth with fantasies of power, destruction, and death. In his tapes, the hand-held camera allows Gibbons's alter ego to surface as he gives vent to tyrannical rants that comically invert social values.

Barbie's Audition
Joe Gibbons
1995, 13:00, U.S., b&w, sound
Gibbons plays the sleazy director and lampoons the movie audition and its legendary corollary, the casting couch. Barbie is recast, not as the impossible-to-attain ideal beauty, but as the victim of sexual harassment and exploitation.
Also available on the compilation *Joe Gibbons Videoworks: Volume 1.*

Elegy
Joe Gibbons
1991, 11:00, U.S., b&w, sound
It's the first day of autumn, and Gibbons can already smell death in the air. Leading us and his dog Woody on a walk through a cemetery, Gibbons voices his obsessive thoughts of death and destruction saying, "I want to be a leaf; I want to fall from a great height and crush whatever I land on." Waxing weirdly philosophical, Gibbons satirically tries to impress the concept of mortality on his dog; the video, shot in Pixelvision, approximate's his dog's black-and-white vision.
Also available on the compilation *Joe Gibbons Videoworks: Volume 1.*

Final Exit
Joe Gibbons
2001, 5:00, U.S., b&w, sound

In *Final Exit*, an aged one is confronted with his options in blunt terms. Does he want to drag out his existence, increasingly infirm and a burden to his caretakers or go quietly before resentment overwhelms sentiment? Does he wish to go on living, the quality of his life increasingly diminishing or be euthanized? Would he prefer cremation or burial? This tape confronts the issues of morality and advancing decrepitude that face even the friskiest.

Halloweened (see Oursler, Tony)

His Master's Voice
Joe Gibbons
1994, 6:00, U.S., b&w, sound

Gibbons presents a Son of Sam-like relationship between a man and his dog in which the man takes the dog to task for the terrible things he has made him do. Shot in Pixelvision.
Also available on the compilation *Joe Gibbons Videoworks: Volume 1*.

Joe Gibbons Videoworks: Volume 1

In his grainy, black-and-white tapes, Gibbons presents obsessive monologues on the human condition and one-sided dialogues of contentious inter-personal relationships by interacting with non-humans: his dog and dolls.
Total running time 43:00.
Contents:
Elegy, Joe Gibbons, 1991, 11:00, U.S., b&w, sound
Sabotaging Spring, Joe Gibbons, 1991, 10:00, U.S., b&w, sound
His Master's Voice, Joe Gibbons, 1994, 6:00, U.S., b&w, sound
Pretty Boy, Joe Gibbons, 1994, 3:00, U.S., b&w, sound
Barbie's Audition, Joe Gibbons, 1995, 13:00, U.S., b&w, sound

Multiple Barbie

Multiple Barbie
Joe Gibbons
1998, 9:00, U.S., b&w, sound

Shot in Pixelvision, *Multiple Barbie* features the artist as a smooth-talking psychoanalyst imploring the silent doll to explore her multiple personalities in order to purge their power from her psyche.
Also available on the anthology *American Psycho(drama): Sigmund Freud vs. Henry Ford*.

ONOUROWN (see Oursler, Tony)

Pretty Boy
Joe Gibbons
1994, 3:00, U.S., b&w, sound

Tension between a man and his handsome young rival (a Ken doll) erupts into violence. Their interaction devolves from a series of tussles to a spanking.
Also available on the compilation *Joe Gibbons Videoworks: Volume 1*.

Sabotaging Spring
Joe Gibbons
1991, 10:00, U.S., b&w, sound

"It's spring, it's spring, and I feel I'm giving birth myself, to something monstrous, something ugly." Gibbons enters the woods to begin his destructive campaign against spring, snapping the buds off trees while babbling maniacally. *Sabotaging Spring* is an impressionistic peek at Gibbons's paranoid fancy; he explains the facts of life, evolution, and whistling to his dog Woody.
Also available on the compilation *Joe Gibbons Videoworks: Volume 1*.

Joe Gibbons: An Interview (see On Art and Artists)

Gibney, Alex
(see Bull, Peter)

Gilbert & George

Gilbert & George have collaborated for more than 25 years. The collaborators' initial notoriety came in 1968 when they performed *The Singing Sculpture*, dressed in suits and painted gold as they moved in sync to a Flanagan and Allen song. Philip Haas produced several films about artists, including his *Magicians of the Earth* series (1989-90) and *The Singing Sculpture* (1992), before turning to narrative features such as *The Music of Chance* (1993), *Angels and Insects* (1995), and *Up at the Villa* (1999).

Gillette, Frank

In the late '60s and early '70s, Frank Gillette built video matrixes that integrated the viewer's mage with pre-recorded information. In 1969 he and Ira Schneider produced the interactive video installation *Wipe Cycle*, a seminal work that expanded the relation of the audience to the artwork, from passive receptors to actual participants. He experimented further with incorporating the viewer's image in delayed feedback loops, thereby questioning the apparent passivity of transmitted information while exposing the changes that technological interaction causes in the audience. Gillette was also a member of Raindance Corporation.

Gilliam, Leah

Leah Gilliam's complex video work destabilizes categories of identity, temporality, and genre. In addition to producing single-channel work, she has curated several exhibition programs, produced the CD-ROM *Split* and artist's flipbook, and has been awarded several grants and awards. Gilliam is a professor of film at Bard College.

Gilbert & George: The Singing Sculpture
Gilbert & George and Philip Haas
1992, 23:00, U.S., color, sound
Moving with slow, robotic gestures to "Underneath the Arches," a depression-era song about homelessness, Gilbert & George alternate roles as gilded men in business suits. *Singing Sculpture* harkens back to the pathos and desperation of marathon dancing of the 1930s while also reflecting the alienation of our post-industrial society. "This presentation of 'The Singing Sculpture,' and the film documenting it, mark the 20th anniversary of the opening of the Sonnabend Gallery in New York. … Through their stylized performance, Gilbert & George deliberately blur the lines between life and art, reality and contrivance. This ambiguity does not rely on a transformation from living to sculptural form. On the contrary, they have merged the two in order to obliterate, rather than emphasize, the distinctions between life and art."
—Walker Art Center (Minneapolis)

Only available on the anthology *Endurance, Reel 1.*

Muse
Frank Gillette
1973, 26:00, U.S., b&w, sound
Characteristic of much of Gillette's work—which treats video as a field of light, movement, and reflection—*Muse* extends beyond optical sensation to engage the viewer in metaphysical contemplation. The narrator states the dilemma of human rationality in the face of nature's unswerving course: "This is senseless. Shall I make sense or tell the truth? Choose either—I cannot do both… To be at all is to be wrong." Over quiet landscape images, the narrative builds to a claustrophobic, Beckett-like atmosphere of suspended struggle, while a dense collage of visual and auditory textures conveys the intricacy of all natural systems—including consciousness.

This title was in the original Castelli-Sonnabend video art collection.

Tetragramaton
Frank Gillette
1973, 23:00, U.S., b&w, sound
Taking its title from the four consonants of the ancient Hebrew name for God, *Tetragramaton* contemplates the relationship between man, technology, and ecological systems. The sweeping camera movements, sudden changes of scale, and layers of natural and man-made sound result in a visceral, turbulent, and hypnotic dialogue between the artist's camera and the environment.

This title was in the original Castelli-Sonnabend video art collection.

Apeshit
Leah Gilliam
1999, 6:30, U.S., color, sound, Super-8 to video
Employing footage from an obscure 8mm film trailer for *Battle for the Planet of the Apes* to highlight the unstable relationship between the real, historical past and the distant, imaginary future, this project revolves around a central question: Is alien-ness indeed the metaphor for the 20th century as power relationships have been embodied within our subconscious? Is there a relationship between these forgotten formats and the discontinued political ideologies that they depict? Transferred from Super-8 and then processed using a combination of high-end digital and vintage analog processing techniques, *Apeshit* emphasizes the contradictory references found in both the original text and its adaptation. Serving up *Battle for the Planet of the Apes* as proof, *Apeshit* puts forth tolerance as an outmoded technology.

Sapphire and the Slave Girl
Leah Gilliam
1995, 17:30, U.S., b&w, sound
Loosely based on the 1950s British detective film *Sapphire,* in which two Scotland Yard detectives investigate the murder of a young woman who is passing for white, *Sapphire and the Slave Girl* examines the determinants of

Sapphire's murder investigation through its cinematic representation. Referencing detectives from Marlowe to Shaft, *Sapphire and the Slave Girl* enacts its analysis in the persona of the hard-boiled detective in order to highlight transgressions of identity and location. Featuring a multifarious cast of identity-shifting Sapphires, this fast-paced genre bash visualizes and problematizes the way that identity is negotiated and performed within urban spaces.

Ginsberg, Arthur

In 1969 Arthur Ginsberg joined the Bay Area media arts center and communications nexus Electronic Eye; the group then changed its name to Video Free America. The center offered regular screenings of video installations, including *The Continuing Story of Carel and Ferd* (1970-75), and sponsored a visiting artist series with the Vasulkas and Stephen Beck, among others. In the mid-'70s, Ginsberg used his theater training and connections to collaborate with the Chelsea Theater Center on three plays (*Kaspar*, 1974, and *AC/DC* and *Kaddish*, 1977) that incorporated video into the staging.

The Continuing Story of Carel and Ferd
Arthur Ginsberg and Video Free America
1972, 33:00 excerpt (of 1:00:00), U.S., b&w, sound
From 1970 to 1972, Arthur Ginsberg and Video Free America (formerly Electric Eye) recorded the private life of a not-so-average American couple—Carel Rowe and Ferd Eggan. She is a porn actress and filmmaker; he is a bisexual junkie. The video verité camera captures the desires and frustrations of their evolving relationship and their responses to the ongoing videotaping exercise. The tape, a study in "the effect of living too close to an electronic medium," reveals attitudes and discussions that also render it a fascinating social document of the West Coast counterculture. Produced before the landmark PBS documentary *An American Family*, this project foregrounds the roll played by media in contemporary life by positioning a video crew within the living space of a couple.
Note: Like a number of documentary projects at the time, *The Continuing Story of Carel and Ferd* was originally shown as a 3-channel video installation on 8 monitors, with a live camera feed of the audience, and often with Carel and Ferd present. This excerpt from the one-hour tape, which was broadcast on WNET's series *Video and Television Review* in 1975, features an interview with Carel, Ferd, and Ginsberg five years later.

Only available as an excerpt on the anthology *Surveying the First Decade, Program 3*.

Glass, Elliot
(see Peoples Video Theater

Godmilow, Jill

In the last the decades Jill Godmilow has earned a substantial reputation as a film director whose work varies in form from experimental documentary to speculative historical fictions. Her work includes *Antonia: a Portrait of the Woman* (1974), *Far from Poland,* (1984), *Waiting for the Moon* (1987), *Roy Cohn/Jack Smith* (1995), *What Farocki Taught* (1998), and *Lear '87 Archive (Condensed)* (2002). Godmilow teaches filmmaking and critical courses at the University of Notre Dame.

What Farocki Taught
Jill Godmilow
1998, 30:00, U.S., color, sound
What Farocki Taught is literally and stubbornly a remake—that is, a perfect replica in color and in English of Harun Farocki's black-and-white 1969 German-language film *Inextinguishable Fire*. Taking as its subject the political and formal strategies of Farocki's film about the development of Napalm B by Dow Chemical during the Vietnam War, Godmilow's unabashedly perfect copy reopens Walter Benjamin's discussion of art in the age of mechanical reproduction. *What Farocki Taught* thus becomes an agit-prop challenge to the cinema verité documentary's representation of information, history, politics, and "real" human experience. In an epilogue to her remake, Godmilow prods contemporary filmmakers towards the original film's political stance and strategies, emphasizing its direct audience address and refusal to produce the "compassionate voyeurism" of the classic documentary cinema.

Goldson, Annie

Annie Goldson was a founding member of XChange TV, a network that distributed television broadcasts from Central America. A prolific video producer, Goldson has created numerous works documenting social injustice and the efforts of people around the world to throw off political oppression, from Northern Ireland and Nicaragua to the Black Panther Movement in the U.S. Goldson lives and works in New Zealand. Chris Bratton was an independent video producer and professor. Bratton is currently President of the San Francisco Art Institute.

Counterterror: North of Ireland
Annie Goldson and Chris Bratton
1990, 29:00, U.S., color, sound
This program takes its departure from the BBC's coverage of the killing of three IRA volunteers by British Security Forces in Strabane, a small town on the border between Northern Ireland and the Irish Republic. Interrogating television discourse, the video examines what is referred to as the British "shoot to kill" policy of planned assassination in the North. In the words of resident Eammon McCann, "Even if the notion of objectivity and balance had meaning, they still wouldn't produce a fair account of what is happening here for the very simple reason that what is happening here is not itself fair."

Deathrow Notebooks
Annie Goldson
1992, 12:00, U.S., color, sound
Deathrow Notebooks is structured around an interview with Mumia Abu-Jamal, a political prisoner on death row in Pennsylvania. Former president of the Association of Black Journalists, Abu-Jamal is a writer and creator of widely broadcast radio programs who continues to write from prison. He was accused of killing a police officer and was convicted in a trial that contained many irregularities. To date, all of his appeals have failed. Abu-Jamal has been placed in highly punitive conditions; he is denied reading material and visitors because, for religious reasons, he refuses to cut his hair. Abu-Jamal describes his early history in Philadelphia, his work as an information officer with the Black Panthers, his interest and later affiliation with MOVE, and his arrest and imprisonment.
Note: Co-produced with Chris Bratton and Lamar Williams

Framing the Panthers in Black and White
Annie Goldson and Chris Bratton
1990, 28:00, U.S., b&w and color, sound
In the words of activist Dhoruba Bin Wahad, "Historical and social events are subject to almost instant censorship by those who have better access and control over the medium of communication. It is important that there exist people skilled in the use of the technological instruments of communication who will seek out the real truth behind the headlines and tell it for all to see, know, and hear." *Framing the Panthers* charts the FBI's covert campaign against the Black Panther Party, focusing on the story of one of its targets, Dhoruba Bin Wahad. A former Panther leader, Bin Wahad spent 19 years in prison as a result of COINTELPRO, the FBI's Counterintelligence Program, which was designed to destroy political activism in the 1960s and '70s. On evidence of government misconduct, his conviction was overturned in March 1990, and he was released from prison on bail. In December of 1991, however, the New York State Appeals Court reinstated his conviction. Dhoruba Bin Wahad now faces further imprisonment. Part two of the *Counterterror* series.

Framing the Panthers in Black and White

Gómez-Peña, Guillermo

Guillermo Gómez-Peña's artistic production has centered around his life mission: to make experimental yet accessible art; to work in politically and emotionally charged sites for diverse audiences; and to collaborate across racial, gender, and age boundaries as a gesture of citizen-diplomacy. His work, which includes performance art, video, audio, installations, poetry, journalism, critical writings, and cultural theory, explores cross-cultural issues and border relations in the era of globalization. Utilizing his body, language and wit as primary tools, Gómez-Peña's work challenges conventions of race, culture and class. Born and raised in Mexico, Gómez-Peña came to the United States in 1978 and he currently lives and works in San Francisco. Isaac Artenstein is a writer, director, and producer whose credits include *Break of Dawn* (1988), a biography of Pedro J. Gonzalez, a pioneer of Los Angeles' Spanish-language radio in the 1930s. Gustavo Vazquez is a film- and videomaker originally from Tijuana and now living in San Francisco. He is a founding member of Cine Acción and the 1996 film festival director of Festival Cine Latino.

Border Brujo
Guillermo Gómez-Peña and Isaac Artenstein
1990, 52:00, U.S., color, sound
Sitting at an altar decorated with a kitsch collection of cultural fetish items and wearing a border patrolman's jacket decorated with buttons, bananas, beads, and shells, Gómez-Peña delivers a sly and bitter indictment of U.S. colonial attitudes toward Mexican culture and history. Whirling through various Mexican-American stereotypes and pulling on costumes as easily as accents, Gómez-Peña emphasizes the collision of Mexican and American cultures and their mixture and misunderstanding of each other—each appearing as a dream/nightmare reflection of the "Other." In turns powerful and playful, *Border Brujo* poignantly illustrates the double edge of forced cultural occupation.

Borderstasis
Guillermo Gómez-Peña
1998, 22:00, U.S., color, sound
This strange, lyrical performance video diary is a millennial reflection on the impossibility to "reveal" one's self in stormy times such as ours. The piece is also about the intricate connections between performance and everyday life; about language, identity, love, nostalgia, and activism amidst the California apocalypse. Through a series of poetic tableaux vivants, performance actions, and found footage, *Borderstasis* articulates the fluid boundaries between public and private, mythical and real as they exist in the life of a "migrant performance artist" living in a fully globalized world.

The Great Mojado Invasion (The Second U.S.-Mexico War)
Guillermo Gómez-Peña and Gustavo Vazquez
2001, 30:00, U.S., b&w and color, sound

In *The Great Mojado Invasion (The Second U.S.-Mexico War)*, writer/performer Guillermo Gómez-Peña and filmmaker Gustavo Vazquez combine Chicano wit and political vision to create an ironic, post-millennial and post-modern look at the future of US/Mexican relations. Both artist and director generate a complex commentary on history, society, pop culture, the politics of language, and the repercussions of ethnic dominance. Like a ghost from the future, Gómez-Peña (also known as the Border Brujo and El Webback) narrates this mockumentary, which envisions a queue of mojados (wetbacks) who reconquer lost Mexican territory to establish the new "U.S. of Aztlan." Through the juxtaposition of clips from campy Mexican genre films (sci-fi, wrestler, soft porn, historiographical, and other exoticized kitsch) against stereotypes long popular in Hollywood, Gómez-Peña, along with his accomplice Vazquez, fabricates "a videographic hall of mirrors." The result is a multi-faceted reflection shifting between fiction and the realities that expose the depth of internalized racism in this country. Gómez-Peña and Vazquez attack hard reality with large doses of irony and black humor.

El Naftazteca: Cyber-Aztec TV for 2000 A.D.
Guillermo Gómez-Peña and Adriene Jenik
1994, 58:00, U.S., color, sound

Interrupting the nightly news in an act of guerrilla television, Gómez-Peña returns to the persona of a Chicano-Aztec veejay—"The Mexican who talks back, the illegal Mexican performance artist with state of the art technology"—to elaborate the complications of American identity. This post-NAFTA Cyber Aztec pirate commandeers the television signal from his underground "Vato bunker," where virtual reality meets Aztec ritual. Gómez-Peña embodies the doubly radical Chicano performance artist, delivering radical ideas through a radical form of entertainment.

With guest performances by Roberto Sifuentes and Ruben Martinez.

El Naftazteca: Cyber-Aztec TV for 2000 A.D.

Son of Border Crisis
Guillermo Gómez-Peña and Isaac Artenstein
1990, 16:00, U.S., color, sound, in Spanish and English

In these seven short video performances, Gómez-Peña confronts Mexican-American culture clashes, stereotypes, and the Fourth World (immigrants). Speaking through a bullhorn or on the airwaves of mock-station Radio Latino FM, he broadcasts a message that will not be silenced. He delivers such comic comparisons as between "tacos without salsa" and "art without ideas" and such pointed statements as "thanks to marketing and not to civil rights, we are the new generation." The taped monologues include *Son of Border Crisis, El Post-Mojado, The Mexican Fly, Dear Californian, Employer Sanctions, The Year of the Yellow Spider*, and *The Year of the Hispanic*.

Goss, Jacqueline

Jacqueline Goss is a videomaker and new media artist whose work explores muted personal and historical narratives and negotiates the slides and snags one encounters while moving between written and spoken communication. She currently teaches in the Film and Electronic Arts Department at Bard College.

So to Speak
Jacqueline Goss
2000, 20:00, U.S., color, sound

"Employing the 'case studies' of Helen Keller, Genie the 'wild child' and *An Angel at My Table* author Janet Frame, Goss's extraordinary video contemplates the struggle to be heard, to break free from the prison of the incommunicable self. '[A] Tour of the house and grounds of language,' constructed with beguiling visual spaces and surfaces, startling edits, and insinuatingly layered sound design."
—New York Video Festival (2000)

There There Square
Jacqueline Goss
2002, 14:00, U.S., color, silent

The desire to own and name land and the pleasures of seeing from a distance color this personal survey of the history of mapmaking in the New

World. *There There Square* takes a close look at the gestures of travelers, mapmakers, and saboteurs that determine how we read—and live within—the lines that define the United States.

Graham, Dan

Dan Graham's work includes critical writing about art, architecture, and television culture; performances exploring self awareness, architectural space, and group behavior; and conceptual works designed for popular and art magazines. Incorporating mirrors, windows, surveillance cameras, and video projectors, Graham's installations address the social function of architecture and television in mediating public and private life. His single-channel works include documentation of performances and, later, documentary essays exploring suburbia and punk music. Graham has published numerous critical essays, as well as *Video-Architecture-Television* (1979) and *Rock My Religion: Writings and Art Projects* 1965-1990 (1993).

Performer/Audience/Mirror
Dan Graham
1975, 23:00, U.S., b&w, sound
In *Performer/Audience/Mirror*, Graham uses video to document an investigation into perception and real time informational "feedback." The performance is doubly reflected back to the audience by the artist's lecturing and the architectural device of a mirrored wall. Graham has written extensively on how video, which can deliver information in real-time, functions semiotically as a mirror. Using the mirror at the back of the stage as a monitor, Graham voices his unrehearsed observations, activating the various feedback cycles taking place within himself as performer, between the performer and audience, and among audience members. Issues of duration and attention are critical for both performer and audience.

Only available on the anthology *Surveying the First Decade, Program 1.*

Gran Fury

Gran Fury was formed in 1987 as a subgroup of ACT-UP/NY (AIDS Coalition to Unleash Power) that opposed the government and institutional efforts to render people with AIDS invisible. Named after the Plymouth vehicle that was the predominant model of police cars nationwide, the collective produced video work and print ads to raise AIDS awareness and to protest governmental apathy.

Kissing Doesn't Kill
Gran Fury
1990, 4:00, U.S., color, sound
Part of a campaign initiated in 1989, this videotape is a component of Gran Fury's plan to raise consciousness and advance medical and federal reform on AIDS policy. These ads ran on TV as a counterpart to controversial bus posters, which generated some intensely negative reactions. Using Benetton's "United Colors" ad campaign to a decidedly different end, simple but powerful images and modern text deliver an enlighteningly direct message.

Green, Vanalyne

Vanalyne Green's videotapes playfully and bitterly examine the paradoxes of American citizenship within such social practices as addiction, sports, sexuality, and, most recently, prayer. Green is a professor of fine arts at the University of Leeds. Publications by and about–her can be found in *Performance Artists Talking in the Eighties* and *Women of Vision*, in addition to *M/E/A/N/I/N/G: An Anthology of Artists' Writings, Theory, and Criticism.*

Saddle Sores: A Blue Western
Vanalyne Green
1999, 20:00, U.S., color, sound
Video artist meets a handsome and enigmatic "Marlboro Man"; video artist gets a sexually transmitted disease. In a wry and pointed work that's part Ibsen and part Danielle Steele, Vanalyne Green reworks the sex-education film to take a critical look at cherished stereotypes about romance, the American West, and cowboys. Expanding on a body of work that investigates the idea that public spaces are gendered, Green revisits the myth of the rugged outdoors, and the West will never be the same. By combining elements of silent movies and classic Westerns, the director weaves a hysterically sad tale of purity and contamination in a hysterically funny way.

A Spy in the House that Ruth Built
Vanalyne Green
1989, 30:00, U.S., color, sound
Green appropriates the all-male forum of baseball to create a visual essay about family, loss, and sexuality. Thinking of herself as a spy assigned by the female sex, Green reinterprets baseball's symbolism—its womb-like landscape, its cycles and rituals—and constructs an iconography that pays homage to the female. In one magnificent montage, numerous phallic symbols pass by as Green sees the real purpose of the game: baseball is the only sport about returning home. And where is home? In a mother's belly. With humor and irony, Green creates a tape that is both a personal revelation and a heretical portrait.

Trick or Drink

Grzinic, Marina and Aina Smid

Marina Grzinic and Aina Smid have collaborated on more than 30 video art projects and media installations since 1982. Independently they have directed several video documentaries and television productions. Both artists live and work in Ljubljana, Slovenia—Grzinic as a researcher at the Institute of Philosophy at the Slovenian Academy of Science and Art; Smid as an art historian at the Faculty of Philosophy.

Gusella, Ernest

Ernest Gusella produced a series of abstract videotapes generated by the signal from an audio synthesizer between 1971 and 1974. In 1974 he began a series of dadaist rituals in front of the camera that utilized electronic manipulation of sound and image.

Video-Taping

Gustafson, Julie

Julie Gustafson began producing documentaries on women's issues in the early '70s. She was co-director with John Reilly of Global Village, a major center for video documentary production

Trick or Drink
Vanalyne Green
1984, 20:00, U.S., color, sound
Adapted from a performance by the same name, this courageous video fuses autobiographical material with information about how an alcoholic family perpetuates addictive behavior. Elements of Alcoholics Anonymous meetings, such as the "Hi, my name is…" introduction are used along with photomontage and a disjointed narrative. In addition to being shown at venues such as the Museum of Modern Art and the New Museum, *Trick or Drink* has been used regularly by hospitals and alcohol treatment centers throughout the United States.

On the Flies of the Market Place
Marina Grzinic and Aina Smid
1999, 7:00, Slovenia, color, sound
On the Flies of the Market Place deals with the idea of the European space, divided and sacrificed. In a visually surreal world of facts and emotions—using documents from books and magazines—the video suggests a re-reading of the European space, i.e. Eastern and Western Europe. Referencing history, philosophy (Kant), and art, the video elaborates on the idea of Eastern Europe as the indivisible residue of all European atrocities. Eastern Europe is a piece of shit and the bloody symptom of the political, cultural, and epistemological failures of the 20th century.

Only available on the anthology *e-[d]entity, Tape 1.*

Exquisite Corpse
Ernest Gusella
1978, 3:00, U.S., color, silent
The "exquisite corpse" named in the title of this piece refers to a favorite game of the Surrealists, played by passing a folded sheet of paper among a group; each person draws one section of a body on the folded segment without looking at the other sides. What was done with pen and paper Gusella accomplishes electronically using the VideoLab. Utilizing quick, voltage-controlled live switching between two cameras, Gusella approximates composite images. For examples, his torso appears to combine with a close-up of his face. The perceptual effect is mesmerizing and disorienting.

Only available on the anthology *Surveying the First Decade, Program 5.*

Video-Taping
Ernest Gusella
1974, 8:00, U.S., b&w, silent
Gusella's title creates a pun on the term video "tape" by using a split screen in which one half is the electronic negative of the other. Gusella set up a glass sheet and suspended it from light poles. The glass was covered with black or white tape. As he slowly removes the obscuring tape from one half of the screen, his ghostly negative image emerges, further confusing the viewer. Electronically constructed using a VideoLab—a voltage controller, multi-channel switcher, keyer, and colorizer built by Bill Hearn—the tape relies on the use of a luminance keyer to "cut out" specific brightness levels (determined by voltage) from one video signal and replace them with a video signal from a second camera. Keying is a video effect seen commonly on television weather reports, in which the images of the map displayed behind the announcer are electronically matted into the image.

Only available on the anthology *Surveying the First Decade, Program 5.*

The Politics of Intimacy
Julie Gustafson
1974, 10:00 excerpt (of 52:20), U.S., b&w, sound
The setting for *The Politics of Intimacy* recalls the widespread consciousness-raising (CR) groups in the late '60s and early '70s inspired by the emerging feminist movement. CR groups provided a forum to openly and col-

Gustafson, Julie

(continued)

in New York. Gustafson collaborated with Reilly on award-winning video documentaries that scrutinized American society.

Ha, Joon Soo

Joon Soo Ha is a video artist, filmmaker, and graphic designer whose work combines abstract concepts of time and space within a cultural context, creating an intuitive metaphoric language. Ha's works decipher the sociocultural context by representing personal vision and symbolic images. Originally from Korea, he studied filmmaking in U.S. with the support of a Fulbright scholarship.

Haas, Philip
(see Gilbert & George)

HalfLifers

HalfLifers is an ongoing collaborative project created by longtime friends Torsten Zenas Burns and Anthony Discenza. HalfLifers creates videotapes and installations incorporating improvised performance, low-fi processing, and absurd humor. From ritualized "crisis re-enactments" to zombie seminars and space explorations inside old barns, HalfLifers embraces speculative fiction and slapstick to chart our anxious relationship to a complex world. HalfLifers's installation projects and single channel tapes have shown at numerous venues internationally.

Control Corridor

lectively validate women's otherwise private experiences. In the tape Dr. Sherfy, one of the first doctors to write about female sexuality, and nine women of different ages, sexual preferences, and economic and social situations, discuss their sexual experiences.

Only available as an excerpt on the anthology *Surveying the First Decade, Program 6.*

Just
Joon Soo Ha
2002, 6:00, U.S., color and b&w, sound
Through a process of degeneration of both sound and image, *Just* endows the iconic American flag with new context and implication. The image is repeated by generations, using different processes such as digital video, computer printout and photocopying, and then combined with degenerated sound. Single frames of original digital images are exported and evolve through the repetition of process before being metamorphosed back to digital image by scanning and rendering. This working process explores how differently an image can be read when put in a specific context, which separates it from its universal meaning. In *Just* the process not only conveys the idea but also creates the concept; the form acts as a clue to decipher the content. *Just* plays with image, sound, and language but breaks down their karma and builds up new combinations of meaning.

Actions in Action
HalfLifers
1997, 10:30, U.S., color, sound
The first work in the *Action* series plunges into a world of frantic heroes trapped in a continual crisis of dissolution and reification. An ordinary domestic setting is recast as a psychoactive landscape in which the concept of function becomes situational and fluid. Only through the strategic application of organic and inorganic "devices" can this zone be successfully navigated and the mission be saved.

Also available on the compilation *HalfLifers: Action Series* and on the anthology *American Psycho(drama): Sigmund Freud vs. Henry Ford.*

Aquatics
HalfLifers
1997, 6:30, U.S., color, sound
Actions speed up, slow down, and run at regular speed. The usual props are there, as is a wet dog. Subtle nuances are revealed as the behavior of the anxiety-laden protagonists is rendered, for once, in real-time.

Also available on the compilation *HalfLifers: Rescue Series.*

Control Corridor
HalfLifers
1997, 11:00, U.S., color, sound
In a fictional conduit space, language and function are recontextualized as two navigators struggle to re-assess the nature of their mission while engaged in an eternal cycle of maintenance and communication routines. "Slipping freely in tone between editing session and Hollywood story conference, they wreak havoc on the conventions of shot-countershot as their jargon-laced exchanges turn oddly self-reflexive, a comic subterfuge that's the linguistic equivalent of biceps-flexing before the mirror."
—Jim Supanick, "Quest for What?" *Film Comment* (September/October 1999)

Also available on the compilation *HalfLifers: Action Series* and the anthology *American Psycho(drama): Sigmund Freud vs. Henry Ford.*

Fear of Rescue
HalfLifers
1997, 10:00, U.S., color, sound

In this attempt to resolve the ongoing crisis, Burns and Discenza find themselves located in, variously, a children's adventure playground, a garage, and a yard. They utilize a mechanical digger to till the soil, they skip and pogo, they vacuum each other. Eventually a type of surgery is performed.

Also available on the compilation *HalfLifers: Rescue Series*.

HalfLifers: Action Series

The *Action* Series finds our alienated heroes in desperate attempts to communicate and find a way out of their endless crisis scenarios. The two pieces share a domestic setting, though this is no comfortable home away from home. Rather, the ephemera of daily life becomes the conduit for possible salvation, as food is applied to the body and domestic rituals are repeated in a quest for closure.

Total running time 21:30.
Contents:
Actions in Action, HalfLifers, 1997, 10:30, U.S., color, sound
Control Corridor, HalfLifers, 1997, 11:00, U.S., color, sound

HalfLifers: Rescue Series

Fear of Rescue

Rescue Series is a HalfLifers project that attempts to articulate deep-seated anxieties about the loss of functionality or purpose through a series of spontaneous "crisis re-enactments." As these fears overwhelm the psyche, the simplest and most mundane activities become potentially hazardous. The inhabitants of *Rescue Series* (Burns and Discenza) exist in an obsessive psychic space, where emergencies, mishaps, and training sessions are continually catalogued and explosively re-staged in a desperate and absurd attempt to restore a sense of security.

"These frenzied, fast-motion videos turn ordinary places (a children's pool, a four-door sedan, a suburban garage) into potential harried 'crisis re-enactments.' Hilarious and ominous, the *Rescue [Series]* uses video as something between a children's toy, a surveillance camera in hyperspeed, and a disaster record."
—Anthony Kaufman, "The Two-Faced Format: Documents and Experiments at NY's Video Fest," *indieWIRE* (17 July 1998)

Total running time 28:30.
Contents:
Aquatics, HalfLifers, 1997, 6:30, U.S., color, sound
Fear of Rescue, HalfLifers, 1997, 10:00, U.S., color, sound
Rescue Parables, HalfLifers, 1994, 4:30, U.S., b&w, sound
Return to Rescueworld, HalfLifers, 1996, 7:30, U.S., color, sound

Harvest

HalfLifers
1999, 12:00, U.S., color, sound
An alternative earth music video. An epic last stand. A portrait of two utilitarian workers engaging in a collaboration with Karen, manifesting improvisational geographic friendships....

Homesteaders

Homesteaders

HalfLifers
1999, 16:00, U.S., color, sound
A HalfLifers journey to a lush interior landscape where some domestic chores and an unexpected encounter provoke a crisis at Mission Control, paving the way for a seasonal reflection upon the meaning of "home."

I.S.L.A.N.D.S. Series

HalfLifers
1998, 23:15, U.S., color, sound
I.S.L.A.N.D.S. #1: In Residence
Dual trajectories through lush innerscapes propel us into color-saturated action-scenarios where the mission to re-establish identity and sustain communication linkage is never-ending.

I.S.L.A.N.D.S. #2: Operation Big Yellow
A useful inanimate object, burdened with excessive psychic residue, is funneled through the HalfLifers for a complete wipe-down and a few healthy exercises.

I.S.L.A.N.D.S. #3: Belief in a Watery Country
Frantic re-application of a fluid medium within pre-sensitized areas transports us to the edge of a churning sea of potential activity. Pitted against the pounding energy currents, the HalfLifers find they can barely hold their own. And when the tap runs dry it's time to move on.

Mess Hall
HalfLifers
1999, 10:00, U.S., color, sound
The third installment in the *Action Series.* Two characters engage Ann Hamilton's *Headlands* kitchen-space and create temporal resonances. To survive they must break the fast (a midnight snack) and service the meal.

Rescue Parables
HalfLifers
1994, 4:30, U.S., b&w, sound
Various scenarios are envisaged where a rescue might be possible. Props include a hoist, a trolley, various doors and windows, ladders, and a length of hose. It is unclear whether our two heroes help or hinder one another. What is sure is that no rescue is in sight.
Also available on the compilation *HalfLifers: Rescue Series.*

Return to Rescueworld
HalfLifers
1996, 7:30, U.S., color, sound
One of four short tapes that make up the *Rescue Series,* a HalfLifers project that attempts to articulate deep-seated anxieties about the loss of functionality or purpose through a series of spontaneous "crisis re-enactments."
Also available on the compilation *HalfLifers: Rescue Series.*

The Amarillo News Tapes
Doug Hall, Chip Lord, and Jody Procter
1980, 25:00, U.S., color, sound
"This videotape reflects my interest in examining cultural institutions. In *The Amarillo News Tapes*, we were interested in observing and dissecting what makes news in a small, Midwestern television market. The tape shows the three of us in our respective roles as anchor, weatherman, and sportscaster, interacting with the real Pro News Team on the set. In such episodes as: 'Opening Routine,' 'Liberal Fire,' and 'Two Stories', we attempted to draw attention to the oddities of language and theater that are a part of television news. Although these sections are humorous, our purpose was not to parody the news for its own sake but to examine its style and ritual, which is as much about fiction as it is about fact."
–Doug Hall

Songs of the 80s
Doug Hall
1983, 17:00, U.S., color, sound
This collection of five shorts includes "These Are the Rules," a frightening incantation of "dos and don'ts" delivered by a red-faced fascist figure played by Hall. Each unique video "song" conveys and elicits a psychological space that is at times beautiful and often disturbing.
"This tape is quite different from my earlier work in video. In the sense that my earlier tapes deal with the media, its language and the way that affects us, this tape deals with a more internal space and as a result is more sensuous, painterly, and certainly more ambiguous than most of my earlier single-channel tapes."
–Doug Hall

Mess Hall

Hall, Doug

(see also Ant Farm)

Doug Hall's work centers upon the idea of media presentation as anthropological rite—a social spectacle heavily encoded with cultural values and contradictions. In addition to his well-known solo projects, during the 1970s Hall was a member of the media collective T.R. Uthco (with Diane Andrews Hall and Jody Procter) and a collaborator with Ant Farm. From the late 1980s to the present, Hall has produced a significant body of work in still photography, in addition to his work in video and video installation. He also co-edited (with Sally Jo Fifer) *Illuminating Video: An Essential Guide to Video Art* (1990).

The Speech

Doug Hall

1982, 4:00, U.S., color, sound

"This tape grew out of my fascination with Ronald Reagan and his uncanny ability to demonstrate what I called the 'Signifiers of Americanism.' Through gesture and intonation, he seemed to suggest many of the virtues that Americans hold dear. Although not directly about Reagan, *The Speech* suggests some of these issues, while remaining purposely ambiguous. The tape is really a speech about speeches."

–Doug Hall

Storm and Stress

Doug Hall

1986, 48:00, U.S., color, sound

Displays of violent weather conditions, electrical storms, tornadoes, floods, fires, and other eruptions are contrasted and equated with equally awe-inspiring images of technology that harnesses or mimics nature. Pitting the specter of nature against technology in time-lapsed images, this thoughtful and stirring tape paints a portrait of the encounter between the man-made and the natural—between man's controlling power and that which eludes man's control.

This Is the Truth

Doug Hall

1982, 4:00, U.S., color, sound

"Similar in structure to *The Speech,* this tape suggests the gesture and language of the television proselytizer as opposed to the politician."

–Doug Hall

"*This Is The Truth* is a recitation of the rules and social codes that makes evident the results of strategic posturing and facial expression on television. Through emblems and selected phrases, Hall dissects those components that produce the image of authority."

–Bob Riley, *The CAT Fund Presents: Doug Hall* (Boston: Institute of Contemporary Art, 1986-87)

This Is the Truth

Halleck, DeeDee

DeeDee Halleck is a media activist, was one of the founders of Paper Tiger Television and the Deep Dish Satellite Network, and was a professor in the Department of Communication at the University of California-San Diego. Her first film, *Children Make Movies* (1961), was about a filmmaking project at the Lillian Wald Settlement in Lower Manhattan. She has led media workshops with elementary school children, reform school youth, and migrant farmers.

The Gringo in Mañanaland

DeeDee Halleck

1995, 1:01:00, U.S., color, sound

Since the turn of the century, popular media in the U.S. have promoted a stereotyped image of Latin America in order to justify the concept of U.S. dominance in the hemisphere. *The Gringo in Mañanaland* uses travelogues, dramatic films, industrial films, newsreels, military footage, geographical textbook illustrations, and political cartoons to take a detailed look at United States media representations of Latin America. This tape is not dry documentation or didactic lesson: it is a look at history and the telling of history. It is a look at how myths are created and passions aroused. It is a comedy, a melodrama, an adventure story, and, as today's headlines attest, a tragic farce.

DeeDee Halleck and Bob Hercules: An Interview (see On Art and Artists)

Hansberry, Tim
(see Downey, Brad)

Harley, Ross Rudesch
(see Cardoso, Maria Fernanda)

Harris, Thomas Allen

Working in a variety of styles including autobiographical narrative and documentary, independent videomaker Thomas Allen Harris explores issues of gender, identity, racial prejudice, and homosexual desire in starkly poignant and visually beautiful works.

Black Body

Thomas Allen Harris

1992, 5:00, U.S., color, sound

Black Body is a harsh and compelling meditation on the contradictory values assigned to black bodies in American culture: they exist as both desired and feared, abject and powerful. The "black body" is a body whose surface reflects projected fears and repressed desires; as such, it exists as a site of ideological struggle, a surface that is simultaneously eroticized and denigrated. With nightmarish narratives and loaded terms hovering over an image of a naked torso bound with wire, Harris shows how these contradictory values continue to cripple and contort the self-image of blacks. The video conveys a powerful sense of confusion and trauma, the problem of inhabiting a body that is a cultural taboo.

Heaven, Earth and Hell
Thomas Allen Harris
1993, 26:00, U.S., color, sound
Reflecting upon the figure of "Trickster" in African and Native American culture while recounting the story of his first love, Harris creates a graceful, deeply moving lament for the loss of innocence in a world without magic. "[I]n his beautifully rendered *Heaven, Earth and Hell*, [Harris searches] among the deceptions of race, history, and love. Harris describes a transformative journey, recounting his yearning for acceptance and the choices made to construct himself out of blackness."
—PopcornQ.com

Splash
Thomas Allen Harris
1991, 7:00, U.S., color, sound
A fable-like tale, *Splash* explores the interplay between identity, fantasy, and homosexual desire in pre-adolescence within the narrow confines of black masculinity. The tape is an exploration of the filmmaker's psychosocial and sexual development within a society that encourages the consumption of whiteness and heterosexuality. *Splash* reveals how the family becomes the agency through which sexual repression and gender conformity are carried out.

Splash

Vintage: Families of Value
Thomas Allen Harris
1995, 1:12:00, U.S., color, sound, Super-8 to video
Vintage: Families of Value is a documentary film that explores three African-American families through the eyes of lesbian and gay siblings, including the filmmaker and his younger brother. *Vintage: Families of Value* places the camera into the hands of seven different family members to construct a collective and autobiographical portrait of modern American families. Shot in Super-8 and Hi-8, this film takes five years of footage and presents it in a cohesive package that tackles some difficult issues. All three African-American families have sets of gay siblings, and it is from this viewpoint that the story unfolds. "Mommy gonna talk to you soon," says one sibling to another, "…About your homosexuality. Did you know that? She don't wanna know the details." But as the subjects gradually get used to filming each other, the details do emerge. From innocent sibling rivalry to one family member contracting the HIV virus, it is a fascinating and very real journey that reveals a simple message: we are all in this together.

Hatoum, Mona
Mona Hatoum's work centers around issues of fear, fascination, and the body. She works in performance, video, installation, and photography. Hatoum was born in Lebanon and attended Beirut University College. Her graduate education in London was followed by a residency at Western Front in Vancouver.

Measures of Distance
Mona Hatoum
1988, 15:00, U.S., sound, color
Reading aloud from letters sent by her mother in Beirut, Hatoum creates a visual montage reflecting her feelings of separation and isolation from her Palestinian family. The personal and political are inextricably bound in a narrative that explores individual and family identity against a backdrop of traumatic social rupture, exile, and displacement.

Hendricks, Geoffrey
During the past 30 years Geoffrey Hendricks, an American artist associated with Fluxus, has made work that investigates the body. Hendricks's performances adhere to a notion of ritual, based in the actualities of everyday life. Hendricks's better-known performance pieces

Body/Hair
Geoffrey Hendricks
1971, 10:00 excerpt (of 8:00:00), U.S., color, sound
In an interview with Lars Movin, Hendricks reflected on *Body/Hair* and explained, "Shaving was a private way of saying 'I'm Different, I'm shedding skin, shedding one aspect of myself to become sort of reborn.' I wrote … 'A

Hendricks, Geoffrey

(continued)

explore personal experiences, including his 48-hour public sleeping and journaling project *Dream Event* and 12-hour divorce performance *Ring Piece* (both 1971).

Henricks, Nelson

A musician, writer, curator, and artist, Nelson Henricks is best known for his videotapes, which have been exhibited worldwide. His writings have been published in *Fuse*, *Public* and *Coil* magazines, and in the anthologies *So, To Speak* (1999) and *Lux* (2000). Henricks also co-edited an anthology of artists' video scripts entitled *By the Skin of Their Tongues* (1997) with Steve Reinke. He lives and works in Montréal.

Conspiracy of Lies

snake sheds its outgrown skin. The skin is left in the landscape. What do we remember of the past? Fragments. What do we know of the past? Fragments. A relic is like a dream." Although the artist shaves off his body hair, he does not shave off his beard, an omission Hendricks explored next in *Unfinished Business–The Education of a Boy Child*. Hendricks explained, "In a way the growing of the beard was a declaration of independence, but then the removal of the beard was saying through this skin shedding, I'm accepting myself as a gay male, making that change manifest."

Only available as an excerpt on the anthology *Endurance, Reel 1*.

Comédie

Nelson Henricks

1994, 7:00, Canada, b&w, sound, in English with French subtitles

"This video in two parts is a newcomer's portrait of Montréal and focuses on two of my architectural obsessions: the Hydro Québec building and the Métro. I spent my first winter in Montréal in a cold, dark, first-floor apartment. I sat in the kitchen beside the electric heater, drinking coffee and watching the disk on the electric meter spin faster and faster, all the while wondering how I would manage to pay the bills. At night, I lay in bed and looked at the enormous illuminated 'Q' on the Hydro Québec building and wondered how much it cost to keep it lit every night. A quote from a physics text brought this first section into focus. The second section is less autobiographically based. In it, a man searches for the meaning of life in the tile patterns of Champ-de-Mars metro station. Though I did spend a great deal of time at that particular station asking some of the same questions he does, I took his search to an end much more absurd than anything I could hope to enact. The moral of these two tales is 'Don't lose your sense of humor.' It's from this cliché that the piece derives its title."

—Nelson Henricks

Also available on the compilation *Nelson Henricks Videoworks: Volume 1*.

Conspiracy of Lies

Nelson Henricks

1992, 12:00, Canada, b&w and color, sound

"*Conspiracy of Lies* speaks of the alienation of minorities, of consumer culture, urban isolation, and the fine balance between mental order and chaos. The tape begins with a voice (my own) recounting the story of the discovery of a series of diary entries and lists written by an anonymous author. When I found the texts, I assumed the author to be a white, gay man, like myself. Through the use of 12 narrators of different race, gender, religion, and sexual orientation, I attempted to destabilize my own subjectivity and challenge my pre-existing assumptions regarding difference. The tape begins and ends with two texts written by myself. This, I hope, helps to render the boundary between myself and the anonymous author more fluid, thereby questioning the 'authority' of authorship."

—Nelson Henricks

Also available on the compilation *Nelson Henricks Videoworks: Volume 1*.

Crush

Nelson Henricks

1997, 12:00, Canada, b&w and color, sound

Crush is the story of a man who wants to turn into an animal as told by the man himself and one or two observers. He employs a variety of techniques to transform himself into a beast, including cutting off parts of his body, exercising, swimming; he wants to return to the water, to speed up evolution a little. Has he gone mad, or is he just tired of being human? As the narrator descends into private obsessions, we begin to perceive the distorted outlines of reason, which guide his descent. The trajectory he defines allows us to reflect upon the correlation between the body and identity, our culture's obsession with the body beautiful, and what it means to be human.

Also available on the compilation *Nelson Henricks Videoworks: Volume 2*.

Emission

Emission

Nelson Henricks

1994, 12:00, Canada, b&w and color, sound

"The videotape *Emission* found its origin in three performances which I wrote between 1988 and 1991. In their original form, the performances dealt with sex, romance, and communication technologies. The videotape elaborates upon these themes to speak of how human beings exist in a margin between nature and technology, and works towards confounding any simplified analysis of this worn-out duality. Structurally speaking, *Emission* comprises eight episodes that are grouped into three 'acts.' The first of these deals with technology and language; the second implies a breakdown of language and a movement towards 'being animal'; the third envisions a confrontation with our animal nature, yet with an ultimate resignation to 'keep talking' and remain human."

–Nelson Henricks

Also available on the compilation *Nelson Henricks Videoworks: Volume 1*.

Handy Man

Handy Man

Nelson Henricks

1999, 10:30, Canada, b&w and color, sound

Handy Man examines the window as a site of voyeurism and surveillance. With his Hi-8 camera, Henricks documents two workers in his interior courtyard. The camerawork has a secretive and furtive feel, treating the male body as an erotic object. This footage forms the basis of a video that attempts to implicate the viewer in processes of exhibitionism and image fetishization. *Handy Man* is part of a trilogy of works exploring one of the principle metaphors of video: the window.

Also available on the compilation *Nelson Henricks Videoworks: Volume 2*.

Nelson Henricks Videoworks: Volume 1

"The videowork of Nelson Henricks, though quite varied in treatment and theme, has worked toward the articulation of a single concern: How can love fly through the air and be received by me?"

–Steve Reinke

Total running time 38:00.

Contents:

Comédie, Nelson Henricks, 1994, 7:00, Canada, b&w, sound

Conspiracy of Lies, Nelson Henricks, 1992, 12:00, Canada, b&w and color, sound

Emission, Nelson Henricks, 1994, 12:00, Canada, b&w and color, sound

Shimmer, Nelson Henricks, 1995, 7:00, Canada, b&w and color, sound

Nelson Henricks Videoworks: Volume 2

Three of these four works form a trilogy that explores one of the principle metaphors of video: the window. The window is used to examine notions of knowledge, voyeurism, surveillance, and time. The fourth piece, *Crush*, is a reflection on identity and what it means to be human.

Total running time 38:00.

Contents:

Crush, Nelson Henricks, 1997, 12:00, Canada, b&w and color, sound

Handy Man, Nelson Henricks, 1999, 10:30, Canada, b&w and color, sound

Time Passes, Nelson Henricks, 1998, 6:30, Canada, b&w and color, sound

Window/Fenêtre, Nelson Henricks, 1997, 3:00, Canada, color, sound

Planetarium

Nelson Henricks

2001, 21:00, Canada, b&w and color, sound

A whimsical science fiction comedy with a soundtrack of pop music and experimental electronica. File under experimental. Play at maximum volume.

"When modern urban life brought light into the night, starry skies were moved to the planetarium. *Planetarium* is a science fiction comedy concerned with the cosmos that surrounds us and the universe that exists inside our heads. It

is also a whimsical post-*fin de siècle* ode to the death of utopia as embodied by the American space exploration program of the 1960s. *Planetarium* explores current cultural obsessions with UFOs, extra-terrestrials, technology, and outer space. Henricks contemplates the infinite, ever-expanding darkness with tiny flashlights, glow-in-the-dark astronauts, spirals, eyeballs, disco balls, and spinning tops."
—YYZ Artists' Outlet (Toronto, 2001)

Shimmer
Nelson Henricks
1995, 7:00, Canada, b&w and color, sound
"Look at a landscape and imagine a different one there. Touch the body and let it slip from memory. Imagine a desert when what you see is winter. The filmmaker evokes a territory where fragile shifts—the links between things, emotions, and places—materialize and dematerialize."
—Nicole Gingras

Also available on the compilation *Nelson Henricks Videoworks: Volume 1.*

Time Passes
Nelson Henricks
1998, 6:30, Canada, b&w and color, sound, Super-8 to video
Using a Super-8 camera, Henricks employs time-lapse photography to document the interior and exterior of his apartment. Inspired by the work of Virginia Woolf, *Time Passes* uses writing as a metaphor for notions of temporality and impermanence.

Also available on the compilation *Nelson Henricks Videoworks: Volume 2.*

Window/Fenêtre
Nelson Henricks
1997, 3:00, Canada, color, sound
"Over the course of one year, I periodically shot footage from the front window of my third floor apartment. This material became the basis of *Window*, a video about knowing. How do we come to know a place or a person? Through repetition and variations; our knowledge comes from more than one unique experience. It is the sum of many things. 'The sum of all sight and sound. The sum of all motion.' *Window* attempts to show how a whole can be more than merely the sum of the parts."
—Nelson Henricks

Also available on the compilation *Nelson Henricks Videoworks: Volume 2.*

Time Passes

Hercules, Bob

Bob Hercules is an independent documentarian whose work has been seen nationally at film festivals and through numerous PBS broadcasts. Hercules was a frequent contributor to the PBS series *The '90s* during its three-year run, as well as a co-founder and past producer for the award-winning cable series *Labor Beat*. He has also long been involved with the Deep Dish Television Network.

Stoney Does Houston
Bob Hercules
1992, 15:00, U.S., color, sound
In this irreverent and hilarious videotape, renowned street performer Stoney Burke leads us on a subversive tour of the 1992 Republican National Convention in Houston's Astrodome. Burke disregards the traditional terms of "political debate" offered by the network news establishment and zeroes in on the questions that never get asked, confronting such Republican luminaries as Oliver North, Neil Bush, Pat Robertson, Jack Kemp, Alfonse D'Amato, and Rush Limbaugh (among others), on issues that are glossed over during the convention. Hercules's and Burke's unobtrusive recording allowed them to take advantage of the on-stage/off-stage character switches of successful politicians, illuminating the murky space between public servant and celebrity.

Produced by Tom Weinberg and Joel Cohen for the PBS series *The '90s*, the tape's more controversial face-offs were censored by Chicago PBS affiliate WTTW before feeding it to the satellite for national broadcast.

Hershman Leeson, Lynn

Lynn Hershman Leeson has made 50-plus videotapes and seven interactive installations that have garnered many international awards, and she has produced two feature films considering the intersections of technology and desire, *Conceiving Ada* (1998) and *Teknolust* (2002), both starring Tilda Swinton.

High, Kathy

Kathy High's single-channel videotapes include documentary and experimental forms and touch upon topics including body politics, science fiction, and the paranormal. Her work frequently incorporates archival footage, interviews and fictional footage, and a sense of irony. Her work has been shown in festivals, galleries, and museums internationally, and she has curated numerous video exhibitions. In 1991 she founded the critical journal *FELIX: A Journal of Media Arts and Communication* and currently teaches at Rensellaer Polytechnic Institute.

Icky and Kathy Trilogy

Seduction of a Cyborg
Lynn Hershman Leeson
1994, 6:00, U.S., color, sound
A poetic allegory about technology's invasion of the body and the destruction of the immune system, witnessing the pollution of history that drowns us. Sponsored by the CICV-Belfort, France.

Only available on the anthology *e-[d]entity, Tape 2.*

Animal Attraction
Kathy High
2001, 59:04, U.S., color, sound
Animal Attraction is a documentary about the relationship between people and animals that questions the way we project our hopes and desires onto our pets and ascribe human qualities and attributes to their gestures. The tape was inspired by the plight of the filmmaker who was frustrated by the obnoxious behavior of her cat, Ernie. As a last resort, she gave in to a friend's suggestion to contact an animal communicator. This is her journey with inter-species telepathic communicator Dawn Hayman from Spring Farm CARES, an animal sanctuary in upstate New York. Both the filmmaker and the viewer become involved in a complex examination of our relationship to "nature."

Spanish subtitled version available.

Also available on the anthology *Frames of Reference: Reflections on Media, Volume 5, Program 2.*

I Need Your Full Cooperation
Kathy High
1989, 28:00, U.S., color, sound
Juxtaposing feminist readings of medical tracts, narratives of patient treatment, and archival footage, *I Need Your Full Cooperation* reveals the evolution of women's relationship to modern medicine. The tape dramatizes Charlotte Perkins Gilman's "rest cure," adapting her 1892 story "The Yellow Wallpaper," and includes critical commentary by activist/writer Barbara Ehrenreich and historian Carroll Smith-Rosenberg.

Icky and Kathy Trilogy
Kathy High
1999, 9:00, U.S., b&w, sound
Shot in black and white, this rough-and-ready trilogy is about twin sisters who "act out" and act up in their own best interests. At the age when young girls might discover their own sexuality, they explore themselves (and each other) in "games" and playtime together. In the three sections—"Icky and Kathy Find Liberty," "The Babysitter," and "Learning To Suck"—the girls engage in slightly illicit acts together. Being naughty can be fun!

Shifting Positions
Kathy High
1999, 27:40, U.S., color, sound
"*Shifting Positions* is a semi-autobiographical/fictional trilogy exploring becoming queer later in life, my father's dementia, and our mid- and end-of-life crises. The selling of our family home of 40 years prompted the making of the first section, entitled 'Last Home,' which investigates the ways memories and spirits inhabit a house. In the remaining two sections—'Napping' and 'Behavior of Fascination'—the relationship between father and daughter is looked at through 'home movies' and documented intimate moments of private life."
—Kathy High

Underexposed: The Temple of the Fetus
Kathy High
1993, 58:00, U.S., color, sound
This feature-length experimental narrative about women's relationships to new

reproduction technologies and genetic engineering combines documentary interviews with field experts and a science fiction segment depicting stories of in-vitro fertilization and other methods. *Underexposed: The Temple of the Fetus* examines ways the news media shapes perceptions and social attitudes towards medical topics. The fictional part follows the political awakening of a TV journalist who unearths the possible dangers of these new technologies as she investigates them for her medical news series. High exposes the medical establishment's attitude towards women, reflected in society's view of women in general.

Hill, Gary

Gary Hill was a Santa Monica surfer who studied sculpture and painting in Woodstock. He first explored video in 1973, when he borrowed a video portapak from Woodstock Community Video. He later worked as a TV lab coordinator for WCV and then had a residency at the Experimental Television Center. Hill's early works investigated synthesized imagery, ecological subjects, and post-minimalist political statements (*Hole in the Wall*, 1974). Hill's works from the late '70s and early '80s, including *Soundings* (1979) and *Around and About* (1980), explore the intertextuality of image, sound, speech, and language. Hill has gained an international reputation for his video art tapes and installations.

Hock, Louis

Louis Hock is an artist who began using video casually as a way to interact with his Mexican neighbors. The resulting videos testify to the complexity of these people's ambivalent status in the U.S., tracing their stories of frequent border crossings and daily fear of Immigration and Naturalization Service raids. Hock has also worked with Elizabeth Sisco and David Avalos to produce several public art events on border topics, including *Arte Reembolso (Art Rebate)* in 1993.

Soundings
Gary Hill
1979, 18:00, U.S., color, sound
Soundings is a meditation on the phenomenology of sound, the translation of image into sound and sound into image through a series of experiments on an audio speaker. The speaker delivers sound both audibly and visibly, with the camera revealing the minute vibrations of the speaker's cone. Referring to the cloth covering of the speaker as a "skin," Hill intones, "This is the skin of space where I voice from." The materialized voice is clearly an extension of the artist's intention. Hill proceeds to bury, puncture, burn, and drown the audio speaker in an effort to physically alter or overwhelm the sound coming out of it, the sound of his own voice. Each carefully constructed experiment explores the confluence of sound, image, and text, suggesting a kind of concretized poetry or "electronic linguistics."
–Lucinda Furlong, "A Manner of Speaking: An Interview with Gary Hill," *Afterimage* 10:8 (March 1983)

Only available on the anthology *Surveying the First Decade, Program 2*.

El Gringo: The Mexican Tapes, Episode 1
Louis Hock
1986, 53:00, U.S., color, sound, in English and Spanish with English subtitles
The first installment of *The Mexican Tapes: A Chronicle of Life Outside the Law* focuses on Hock's status in the community. At first Hock is "el gringo" (the outsider)–the tourist who doesn't understand his neighbors' jokes. It's only months later that he becomes a close friend, travelling back to visit Mexican homes and families and beginning to empathize with their struggles.
Also available on the compilation *The Mexican Tapes: A Chronicle of Life Outside the Law.*

La Lucha: The Mexican Tapes, Episode 4
Louis Hock
1986, 55:00, U.S., color, sound
In *La Lucha* (the fight), families struggle to cope with frequent deportations and the constant threat of INS sweeps that, in the end, completely dismantle the community. Following up two years later, Hock reports their triumphs and setbacks. The tape ends with hope–but no real promise–of a brighter future for those living on the unrecognized margin of society.
Also available on the compilation *The Mexican Tapes: A Chronicle of Life Outside the Law.*

The Mexican Tapes: A Chronicle of Life Outside the Law
This series of four videos explores Hock's growing friendship and empathy with his Mexican neighbors, his acceptance into their community, and an examination of their day-to-day struggles.
Total running time 3:41:00.
Contents:
El Gringo, Louis Hock, 1986, 53:00, U.S., color, sound
El Rancho Grande, Louis Hock, 1986, 1:00:00, U.S., color, sound, in English and Spanish with English subtitles
The Winner's Circle and la Migra, Louis Hock, 1986, 53:00, U.S., color, sound
La Lucha, Louis Hock, 1986, 55:00, U.S., color, sound

El Rancho Grande: The Mexican Tapes, Episode 2

Hocking, Ralph

Ralph Hocking has been a leader in the field of
electronic media art since 1968, when he
founded one of the first campus-based media
access programs. In 1970 he established the
independent non-profit Experimental Television
Center, which offered training programs,
equipment access, and exhibition programs.

Holt, Nancy

In the mid-'60s, Nancy Holt, along with her
husband, Robert Smithson, helped introduce a
post-minimalist sensibility to the field of
sculpture. Holt's early tapes, like her site-
specific sculptures, explore the recorded
experience of a particular time and place and
the function of memory in perception. Holt's
tapes twist the technical limits of video, calling
attention to the medium's artificial nature and
maintaining a critical distance between public
presentation and private reality.

El Rancho Grande: The Mexican Tapes, Episode 2
Louis Hock
1986, 1:00:00, U.S., color, sound, in English and Spanish with English subti-
tles
In the second installment of *The Mexican Tapes*, Hock begins to participate
more in the family life of La Colonia, attending baptisms and helping shop for
new cars. Hock interviews the white residents of the complex who resist the
Mexican community and rumor that it will soon be torn down.
Also available on the compilation *The Mexican Tapes: A Chronicle of Life
Outside the Law.*

The Winner's Circle and la Migra: The Mexican Tapes, Episode 3
Louis Hock
1986, 53:00, U.S., color, sound
As documented in *The Winner's Circle and la Migra* (the emigrant), the move
north brings many changes to family life, specifically mothers going to work
and children learning English in school. Hock explores the fact that women
often adapt more easily than the men to American life, learning English more
rapidly. This becomes a source of conflict between the men and women as
they compete for better-paying jobs.

Also available on the compilation *The Mexican Tapes: A Chronicle of Life
Outside the Law.*

Complex Wave Forms
Ralph Hocking
1977, 4:00 excerpt (of 5:00), U.S., color, sound
Produced without camera input, this intense electronic landscape transports
the viewer into a world that is an abstract study in machine-generated
imagery. Produced at the Experimental Television Center. "*Complex Wave
Forms* is one in a series of short tapes which explored oscillators. In the
series oscillators had multiple uses: to create images and sounds directly and
to control voltages, which interfaced with additional image processing instrumentation. Signals were generated, mixed and controlled in amplitude and
frequency by using a machine that was designed and built by David Jones
and Richard Brewster. The audio and visual were controlled by the same voltages, resulting in an interconnection between the two. The video output was
fed into a Paik/Abe colorizer and recorded, along with the sound audio signal
in real time."
–Ralph Hocking

Only available as an excerpt on the anthology *Surveying the First Decade,
Program 5.*

Boomerang (see Serra, Richard)

East Coast, West Coast
Nancy Holt
1969, 22:00, U.S., b&w, sound
In this rare and humorous record of the art dialogue of the late 1960s, Holt
and "guest" Robert Smithson assume opposing artistic viewpoints: the
uptight, intellectual New Yorker versus the laid-back Californian. Their play-
acting lays bare the clichés and stereotypes of a "bi-coastal" art world. While
Holt stresses analytic, systematic thinking, Smithson represents the polar
opposite, privileging visceral experience and instinct, saying, "I never read
books. I just go out and look at the clouds" and "Why don't you stop thinking
and start feeling?"
This title was originally in the Castelli-Sonnabend video art collection.

Going Around in Circles
Nancy Holt
1973, 15:15, U.S., b&w, sound
Holt establishes an optical system, pointing the camera through a prop with
five regularly spaced apertures, at a grooup of five actors executing choreo-

graphed movements on a hillside outside the window. In a self-referential dialog of excruciating detail, Holt and the performers discuss the discrepancies between what is seen of the performance and what the conditions of the actual performance were. As in *Locating #2*, Holt's discourse examines how video limits vision and disturbs the viewer's perception of scale, distance and motion. As an early conceptual piece, this tape touches upon many of the dominant ideas of '70s art practice, namely the operation of chance, order, and creation of a self-referential dialog around an artwork.

Points of View: Clocktower

Points of View: Clocktower
Nancy Holt
1974, 44:04:21, U.S., b&w, sound
A circular image moves across a black background while two people attempt to describe what they are seeing. A prime example of Nancy Holt's examination into the way we interpret what we see, *Points of View* features four couples (Lucy Lippard and Richard Serra, Liza Béar and Klaus Kertess, Carl Andre and Ruth Kligman, and Bruce Boice and Tina Girouard) talking to each other while watching the moving ellipse. Each of the four sections takes in the "view" from a different direction, north, south, east and west. The participants take part in an optical experiment as they try to interpret what they might be looking at, discuss the process itself, talk about the role of fantasy in interpretation of the unknown, the cultural impact of television, architecture, and the culture of watching

Locating No. 2
Nancy Holt
1972, 14:00, U.S., b&w, sound
Shot through a tube pressed against the camera lens, this tape abstracts space and depth through an effect of tunnel vision. Holt and Jerry Clapendale discuss what they see, speculating about the shapes and grey values of a fragmented urban space. The tape effectively defamiliarizes a mundane lanscape, so that windows, car wheels, and landscaping stones become the objects of inquiry and doubt. When the tape concludes, the image is unmasked to reveal a space in full view that does not, perhaps, look as one might expect after seeing it in pieces.

Revolve
Nancy Holt
1977, 1:17:00, U.S., b&w, sound
"Nancy Holt's *Revolve*, a videotape where the artist, off-camera, interviews her friend Dennis Wheeler who is dying of leukemia, uses his illness and mental reflection as a metaphysical site. Her interview is recorded from the perspective of three video cameras that each capture Wheeler from a different point of view. The three-point perspective was designed to give the illusion of infinity. Holt's three-camera perspective grips the observer with the reality of the finiteness of death. ... The editing process is pendulous, dialectical—like Wheeler living on the borrowed time of chemotherapy, swinging from remission to illness."
—Carrie Rickey, "Nancy Holt: Whitney Museum of American Art, New York," *Arts Magazine* 52 (November 1977)

Underscan

Underscan
Nancy Holt
1974, 20:07, U.S., b&w, sound
Holt's terrain is her Aunt Ethel's home in New Bedford, Massachusetts presented in still images and excerpts from letters to the artist from her aunt. Holt pays particular attention to her aunt's poignant story of aging, altering the images by "underscanning" them—a technical process that compresses the edges of the video image—building an intrinsic limitation into the tape: the compression of time and personal history represented by the images and narrative. This process echoes Holt's reading, slightly distorting and compressing the information in the letters as she presents them.

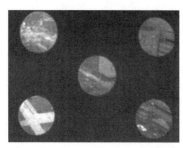

Zeroing In

Holzer, Jenny

Jenny Holzer verbalizes ideas, expressed in the form of signs. The power of language to distort and manipulate is the basis of Holzer's art, which is intellectual rather than visual. She is internationally renowned for her linguistic interventions in every inch of the social arena, from parking meters to T-shirts to billboards to electronic sign boards.

Hoolboom, Mike

Mike Hoolboom has made 25 fringe films and videos in both short and feature forms. His work combines original material with appropriated footage as his first-person narration helps create mesmerizing and intimate accounts of contemporary, mass-mediated subjectivity and mortality. He wrote the tongue-in-cheek autobiography *Plague Years* (1998) and has also published *Inside the Pleasure Dome: Fringe Film in Canada* (2001) and co-edited *Landscape with Shipwreck* (2001).

Zeroing In
Nancy Holt
1973, 31:15, U.S., b&w, sound
"Perceptual concerns predominate in my videoworks. In *Locating #2*, *Zeroing In*, and *Points of View*, large outdoor spaces—as much as five miles in depth and one mile in width from 15 floors up—are spanned on the video screen. Space is flattened and contracted. By placing a prop (a movable tube or a piece of cardboard with holes that open and close) in front of the camera, I block off most of the static camera view, leaving one or more circular images to come and go. Background and foreground merge in the circular segments; ordinary objects become difficult to discern as they come into view. What is seen is immediately put into works in the audio system by two persons, chosen initially because of their interpretations of what is seen."
—Nancy Holt

Sign on a Truck
Jenny Holzer
1984, 35:00, U.S., color, sound
On the eve of the 1984 Presidential election, Jenny Holzer used a truck equipped with a sound system and an 18-foot Diamond Vision electronic board to displayed images, statements, and man-on-the-street interviews. This tape presents a tightly edited version of the art, texts, and interviews that occurred throughout the day. Artists/activists who participated in the event include Ida Applebroog, Jonathon Borofsky, Vito Acconci, Susan Silas, Madre, Leon Golub, Dan Hurley, Jeff Turtletaub, Mike Smith, Jolie Stahl, Claes Oldenburg, Keith Haring, Ben Chase, Jenny Holzer, Coosje van Bruggen, Randy Twaddle, Mark Stahl, Barbara Kruger, Mike Glier, Kim Jones, Justin Ladda, Shelly Silver, Kim Higgins, Maartje Higgins, Jacquie Leader, Patricia Blair, Craig Stockwell, Knight Landesman, Charles Guarino, John Fekner, Double Trouble, and Richard Admiral.

Televised Texts
Jenny Holzer
1990, 13:00, U.S., color, sound
Holzer adopts the form and language of commercial messages to disrupt communication, presenting kamikaze texts that are designed to stimulate thought with humor and inspire a critical attitude in an often passive audience. As in all of Holzer's work these television spots present deceptively simple sequences of text that mix provocative social commentary with resonant poetic reflection.

Imitations of Life
Mike Hoolboom
2003, 1:15:00, Canada, b&w and color, sound
"Mike Hoolboom's latest work is an extraordinary palimpsest in action. It is packed with cinema images that follow one another, interpenetrate, fertilize and repel one another. Taken from Hollywood fiction films but also from newsreels and documentary and scientific works, all these images patiently collected against the background of a salutary hold-up (the scenes are excised without any particular precaution from the gigantic body of cinema films and by extension from the myths that it conveys) have something of the construction of a metafilm. ... This time that passes is essential, modeled by the images of the world in which Mike Hoolboom's archaic fears and dreams reside. The end of *Imitations* is rainy and slow-moving, but it ends with a gag—the filmmaker's elegant way of not giving in to melancholy."
—Jean Perret
Contents:
In the Future, 3:00; Jack, 15:00; *Last Thoughts*, 7:00; *Portrait*, 4:00; *Secret*, 2:00; *In My Car*, 5:00; *The Game*, 5:30; *Scaling*, 5:00; *Imitation of Life*, 21:00; and *Rain*, 03:30.

In the Dark
Mike Hoolboom
2003, 8:00, Canada, color, sound
A meditation on birth, silence, and American cinema, sealed with a kiss.

Tom
Mike Hoolboom
2002, 1:15:00, Canada, color, sound
A cinematic firestorm of found footage and pilfered Hollywood images, Mike Hoolboom's hallucinatory *Tom*—described by the filmmaker as "cinema as déjà vu or déjà voodoo"—pays mesmerizing experimental tribute to the life and work of friend and fellow avant-gardist Tom Chomont.

Hope, Melanie Printup

Melanie Printup Hope's work explores her Tuscadora/Native American identity and ancestry, conveying her personal experiences of cultural and spiritual growth through the use of drawing, traditional beadwork, sculpture, computer-generated images, animation, digitized sound, video, and installation.

I Turn My Head
Melanie Printup Hope
1993, 3:00, U.S., color, sound
A performance-based video, *I Turn My Head* examines the duality in Native American identity. Shot in close-up, Hope's face is made-up to make her resemble a "redskin" on on half of her face and to pass as white on the other; she turns her head back and forth as she shares conflicting experiences that have shaped her identity. At the end, she faces forward, speaking of the duality that allows her to understand both Native American and white cultures.
Spanish subtitled version available.

Only available on the anthology *Frames of Reference: Reflections on Media, Volume 2, Program 2*.

Horsfield, Kate, Nereida Garcia-Ferraz, and Branda Miller

Kate Horsfield is an artist and a co-founder and executive director of the Video Data Bank at the School of the Art Institute of Chicago. She co-produced more than 200 interviews with contemporary artists with Lyn Blumenthal. Cuban painter and photographer Nereida Garcia-Ferraz is a Cuban-American painter and photographer. Branda Miller is a noted educator and videomaker.

Ana Mendieta: Fuego de Tierra
Kate Horsfield, Nereida Garcia-Ferraz, and Branda Miller
1987, 49:00, U.S., color, sound, in English and Spanish
Performance artist/sculptor Ana Mendieta used the raw materials of nature: water, mud, fire, rock, and grass. The consciousness of her politics and the poetics of her expression fill her work with an emotionally charged vision that is powerfully conveyed in this posthumous video profile. Drawing upon the raw spiritual power of Afro-Cuban religion, Mendieta used her art as a ritualistic and symbolic activity to celebrate the forces of life and the continuum of change. A silhouette of her own body inserted in the land emphasizes the universal/primal relations between the two bodies: female and Earth.

English or Spanish subtitled versions available.

Intermedia Arts
(see University Community Video)

Jenik, Adriene

Committed to using and abusing new technologies, Adriene Jenik is an award-winning media artist, filmmaker, and educator, currently teaching in visual arts at University of California-San Diego. She has been an active member of the Paper Tiger TV collective and Deep Dish TV. Her previous directorial credits include *What's the Difference Between a Yam and A Sweet Potato?* (1992) and *El Naftazteca: Cyber-Aztec TV for 2000 A.D.* (1994).

El Naftazteca: Cyber-Aztec TV for 2000 A.D. (see Gómez-Peña, Guillermo)

Mauve Desert: A CD-ROM Translation
Adriene Jenik
1997, U.S., color, sound, CD-ROM
Based upon the novel *Le Desert Mauve* by Quebeçoise author Nicole Brossard, *Mauve Desert*, a CD-ROM road movie, was five years in the making. Shot on film and video, framed by original graphics and creative programming structures, and performed in three languages, *Mauve Desert* finds its voice in the driver's seat (of a computer). Mélanie is a 15-year-old girl who steals her mother's Meteor every chance she gets and drives away from her mother's lover Lorna and toward the dawn. Maude Laures is the middle-aged academic who stumbles upon Mélanie's life in a second-hand bookshop and translates her into another tongue.

Note: only available on CD-ROM.

Jeremijenko, Natalie
(see Bureau of Inverse Technology)

Jonas, Joan

Widely know for her performances from the mid-'60s, Joan Jonas first incorporated a live video camera and monitor into her work with *Organic Honey's Visual Telepathy* (1972). In the same year, she began producing single-channel tapes, among them *Vertical Roll,* which are recognized as landmark investigations into the structural and performative nature of the medium. Jonas's tapes draw on the essential connection between performance art and the video monitor, as time-based media especially suited to materializing the artist's psyche. Exploring the dislocation of physical space and mythical female archetypes, Jonas's work occupies an important position in the development of both early formalist and early feminist video.

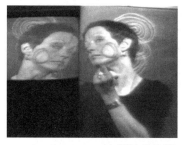

Left Side Right Side

Disturbances
Joan Jonas
1974, 15:00, U.S., b&w, sound
Jonas uses reflections on a lake as a mirror to displace reality, creating a disruption and the illusion of presence. "Disturbances begins with a Symbolist-like image of two women, dressed in white, seen only as reflections in water. … Throughout the tape the water fills the monitor, creating layers of images. The reflections on the surface of the water are superimposed on the activities that take place underneath the surface."
—David Ross, "Joan Jonas's Videotapes" in J*oan Jonas: Scripts and Descriptions, 1968-1982,* ed. Douglas Crimp (Berkeley: University of California Press, 1983)

Double Lunar Dogs
Joan Jonas
1984, 25:00, U.S., color, sound
Based on Robert Heinlein's 1941 story "Universe," *Double Lunar Dogs* presents a vision of post-apocalyptic survival aboard a "spacecraft," travelling aimlessly through the universe, whose passengers have forgotten the purpose of their mission. As a metaphor for the nature and purpose of memory, the two main characters (portrayed by Jonas and Spalding Gray) play games with images of their past; but their efforts to restore their collective memories are futile, and they are reprimanded by the "Authority" for their attempts to recapture their past on a now-destroyed planet Earth.

I Want to Live in the Country (And Other Romances)
Joan Jonas
1974, 25:00, U.S., color, sound
Jonas inter-cuts scenes of the Nova Scotia countryside with images of a studio set-up reminiscent of a di Chirico painting. The soundtrack includes both music and spoken excerpts from a journal Jonas kept while travelling in Nova Scotia. *I Want to Live in the Country* ultimately deals with observation and fantasy, living in the country, and the stifling aspects of the city and one's art. This title was in the original Castelli-Sonnabend video art collection.

Left Side Right Side
Joan Jonas
1972, 3:00, U.S., b&w, sound
"In *Left Side Right Side,* Jonas explores the ambiguities caused by her attempt to identify correctly the spatial orientation of images simultaneously played back by a monitor and reflected in a mirror. This is confusing because, contrary to what one might expect, the monitor image gives back a 'true' reading of the space while the mirror reverses it. …
"Throughout the course of the tape, the image switches back and forth between the double image of monitor and mirror to the simple 'real' image of Jonas's face."
—David Ross, "Joan Jonas's Videotapes" in J*oan Jonas: Scripts and Descriptions, 1968-1982,* ed. Douglas Crimp (Berkeley: University of California Press, 1983)
This title was in the original Castelli-Sonnabend video art collection.

Upside Down and Backwards
Joan Jonas
1980, 29:00, U.S., color, sound
"[This tape] gives a clear picture of the consistency of Jonas's concerns. The performance was based upon the merging of two fairy tales—*The Frog Prince* told backward and *The Boy Who Went Out To Learn Fear* told forward. These two tales become intertwined into a single text whose transformations are effected through fragmentation, demonstrating a process "unhitched" from time, as free from the laws of physics as are the fairy-tale sources. "
—David Ross, "Joan Jonas's Videotapes" in J*oan Jonas: Scripts and Descriptions, 1968-1982,* ed. Douglas Crimp (Berkeley: University of California Press, 1983)

Vertical Roll

Joan Jonas

1972, 19:30, U.S., b&w, sound

In this well-known early tape, Jonas manipulates the grammar of the camera to create the sense of a grossly disturbed physical space. The space functions as a metaphor for the unstable identity of the costumed and masked female figure roaming the screen, negotiating the rolling barrier of the screen's bottom edge.

"[Making] use of a jarring rhythmic technique to develop a sense of fragmentation, *Vertical Roll* uses a common television set malfunction of the same name to establish a constantly shifting stage for the actions that relate both to the nature of the image and to the artist's projected psychological state."
–David Ross, "Joan Jonas's Videotapes" in *Joan Jonas: Scripts and Descriptions, 1968-1982*, ed. Douglas Crimp (Berkeley: University of California Press, 1983)

Also available on the anthology *Surveying the First Decade, Program 1*.

This title was in the original Castelli-Sonnabend video art collection.

Jones, Art

Art Jones is an image/sound manipulator and VJ working with film, digital video, and hybrid media. His films/videos, CD-ROMs, live audio/video mixes, and installations often concern the inter-relationships between popular music, visual culture, history, and power.

#FFFFFF

Art Jones

2001, U.S., color, sound, CD-ROM

The third in a series of interactive CD-ROMs, *#FFFFFF* is a collage/essay, in several parts, about the reception aesthetics of pixels and some other things, including a photo essay on the male body as used in advertising, an instructional guide on how to gain success as an artist, computer karaoke, and a video interview with DJ Spooky.

Contents: *Insert, Subvertising, Blow, Copkilla, Stitch, Visual politics of pimps and ho's, part 2, fflx#2, How to Get Over, Brooklyn Zoo mix#1,* and *aka that Subliminal Kid.*

Note: only available on CD-ROM.

Culture vs. the Martians

Art Jones

1998, U.S., color, sound, CD-ROM

A CD-ROM collection of videos, sounds, screensavers, and interactive work. Playful, thought provoking, and sexy, *Culture vs. the Martians* is a series of digital explorations of our media-saturated cultural landscape.

Note: only available on CD-ROM.

Know Your Enemy

Know Your Enemy

Art Jones

1991, 27:00, U.S., color, sound

Through distorted audio and visual representations of interviews with music journalists, this tape critiques the mass media's treatment of the rap group Public Enemy and accusations that their lyrics are anti-Semitic. This experimental documentary includes scenes from Public Enemy performances and music videos, as well as archival footage of the black power movement and Malcolm X. *Know Your Enemy* details the war being waged by black artists on the battleground of representation, a struggle against forms of expression which are already co-opted. As observed by Malcolm X and quoted in the tape, "They hold you in check through this science of imagery."

Love Songs #1

Art Jones

2001, 12:00, U.S., color, sound

Love Songs #1 is composed of three pieces that pose questions about urban culture, race, and politics. Found footage images are manipulated and juxtaposed with popular music; the effects are unsettling, ironic, and sometimes humorous. *Blow #2* is a description of digitized female forms juxtaposed with text and set to a Delfonics classic. The pixilated visual environment eventually crystallizes into an image of potential violence/beauty. *Nurture* is a meditation on the anthropomorphic trends in "hardcore" hip-hop.

In the video, rappers become animals, animals become rappers, all in a context of mediated nihilism and the environmental trend toward self-destruction. Ol' Dirty Bastard's classic 1996 song "Brooklyn Zoo" is the engine for our discovery channel nightmare. Riotously ironic and self consciously deployed, the director poses the question: "Where my dogs at?" *Over Above* is about the physical and social distances through which everyday horror is seen. Airplanes, buses, and helicopters: these provide the windows that filter our perceptions of early 21st century America, where not quite seeing has become the dominant mode of vision. The visual "effect" is two fold: the first, composited through a helicopter window, is the beating of Thomas Jones by the Philadelphia police on July 12, 2000. The second is a view of a scene from a bus window.

With music by Cibo Matto.

Media Assassin
Art Jones
1990, 5:00, U.S., color, sound
An experimental documentary that asks, "What is Hip Hop?," *Media Assassin* deals with popular magazine coverage of the black music scene and efforts to define the new musical forms emerging since the late '80s. The tape focuses on the story of Harry Allen, a former music journalist for *The Village Voice*, who handled public relations for the rap group Public Enemy.

Art Jones: An Interview (see On Art and Artists)

Jones, Kim

Since the mid-1970s, artist Kim Jones has developed the performance/action/ritual called *Mudman*, a symbol of ritual pairs: man-woman, human-divine, fetus-skeleton, and life-death. Jones also explores these issues through drawing and sculpture.

San Francisco Walk
Kim Jones
1979, 6:00, U.S., color, sound
"The Mudman's mudcaked, nearly nude body is reminiscent of the Australian shamanic practice of covering the body with mud or feces to signify a return from the netherworld. A mud/dirt/feces covered body is a vegetable symbol suggestive of continual generation and regeneration. While the Mudman's body is covered with and represents the 'made-up,' unborn, and mythical part of the earth—almost to the point of non-differentiation from the earth—the stick structure on his back is by comparison stiff and rigid. It restricts movement, inflicts pain, and has a visual and structural dominance over Jones.
"The Mudman is a figure who carries his own destruction upon his back while at the same time promising rebirth by his direct connection to the earth and the undifferentiated. ... This two-part image makes Jones the Mudman into a true 'threshold figure,' symbol of ritual pairs: man-woman, human-divine, fetus-skeleton, and life-death."
—Angelika Festa

Only available on the anthology *Endurance, Reel 3*.

Jones, Quenell
(see Downey, Brad)

July, Miranda

Portland-based artist Miranda July makes performances, movies, and recordings—often in combination. Her videos *(The Amateurist, Nest of Tens, Getting Stronger Every Day)* present complicated parallel narratives with characters who experience loneliness, exploitation, unexpected phobias, and often inexplicable relationships. July has also recorded several performance albums released by Kill Rock Stars and K Records. In 1995 she founded Joanie 4 Jackie, an on-going movie distribution network for independent women moviemakers.

The Amateurist
Miranda July
1998, 14:00, U.S., b&w, sound
A captivating video about surveillance, identity, watching, and being watched, *The Amateurist* slides along the edges of horror and satire to create an unsettling portrait of a woman on the brink of a technologically driven madness. "*The Amateurist* alternately adores and rejects three familiar tropes: the sick and examined woman, the starlet/stripper, and the genius/talentless woman. As a performer living with a chronic illness who has been both a child actress and a stripper, I choose not to speak with an autobiographical voice, which would, in itself be yet another cliché (the confessional). Instead, I create women who are predictable amalgamations of single types. ... What I choose to say with these figurines is much less articulable, though no less familiar. The prescribed lines dismantle themselves with mutual interrogation and this process releases fumes of true loneliness, relentless strength, insatiable desire."
—Miranda July

Atlanta

Atlanta
Miranda July
1996, 10:00, U.S., color, sound
A 12-year-old Olympic swimmer and her mother (both played by July) speak to the public about going for the gold.
"As the film progresses through subtle editing-in-reverse, July reveals the world around the televised facade. ... [T]he 23-year-old performer convincingly plays both Dawn Schnavel and her mom, or rather, vanishes into them. What's noticeable isn't so much the ease with which July transforms herself into a pre-teen girl and an older woman but the similarities and differences between the daughter and the mother July becomes."
–Derk Richardson, "The Marvelous World of Miranda July," *San Francisco Bay Guardian* (3 June 1998)

Getting Stronger Every Day
Miranda July
2001, 6:30, U.S., color, sound
"There are two movies I saw on TV about boys who were taken from their families and then returned to them years later. One boy was on a fun spaceship for years, and the other boy was kidnapped and molested. These boys were never the same again, and they just couldn't re-integrate into the family. I saw these movies when I was little. I've often described them to people, always paired together. They are sort of the comedy and tragedy version of the same story, and it is a mundanely spiritual story. *Getting Stronger Every Day* includes these boys' tales, but they are like mystical objects placed on the living reality of the man storyteller. In other parts of the movie actual mystical objects hover in people's lives without a myth or story attached. I like to think about how these dimensions interact simply and can be enacted: real life/story/worldly/spirit/video/flat drawing."
–Miranda July

Nest of Tens
Miranda July
1999, 26:36, U.S., color, sound
Nest of Tens is comprised of four alternating stories that reveal mundane yet personal methods of control. These systems are derived from intuitive sources. Children and a retarded adult operate control panels made out of paper, lists, monsters, and their own bodies.
"A young boy, home alone, performing a bizarre ritual with a baby; an uneasy, aborted sexual flirtation between a teenage babysitter and an older man; an airport lounge encounter between a businesswoman (played by July) and a young girl. Linked by a lecturer enumerating phobias in a quasi-academic seminar, these three perverse, unnerving scenarios involving children and adults provide authentic glimpses into the queasy strangeness that lies behind the everyday."
–New York Video Festival (2000)

Nest of Tens

Miranda July: An Interview (see On Art and Artists)

Kalin, Tom
(see also Gran Fury)

Tom Kalin's work focuses on the portrayal of gay sexuality both in the age of AIDS and historically, as in his acclaimed New Queer Cinema feature *Swoon* (1992). Informed by his work with two AIDS activist collectives, ACT UP and Gran Fury, Kalin's video work is characterized by beautifully murky appropriated images and

Confirmed Bachelor
Tom Kalin
1994, 2:45, U.S., color, sound
"Criminality may present itself as a kind of saintly self-mastery, an absolute rejection of hypocrisy."
–Angela Carter, *The Sadeian Woman and the Ideology of Pornography* (New York: Pantheon Books, 1978)
Confirmed Bachelor shakes up a mix of written and spoken text. Angela Carter's quote counterpoints fundamentalist voices; shots of hothouse flowers play over a born-again doctor's commentary on the ins and outs of gay male carnality. This humorless spew of a turgid imagination was lifted from *The Gay Agenda*, an agit-prop tape circulated in the Senate by Christian conservatives. A collision of disco hooks, floating quotes, and fertile nature,

Kalin, Tom
(continued)

vibrant original portraits and performances. Kalin co-produced the feature films *Go Fish* (Rose Troché, 1994) and *I Shot Andy Warhol* (Mary Harron, 1996) and is on the film faculty at Columbia University.

Darling Child

Confirmed Bachelor lovingly smothers their moralistic posturing under a blanket of blooms.

Also available on the compilations *Tom Kalin Videoworks: Volume 2* and *Third Known Nest*.

Dark Cave
Tom Kalin
1998, 4:15, U.S., b&w and color, sound, Super-8 to video
"His heart was a dark cave filled with sharp toothed, fierce clawed beasts that ran snapping and tearing through his blood. In pain he left the work table and prowled around the room, singing to himself, 'Who can I be tonight? Who will I be tonight?'"
—Alfred Chester, *Exquisite Corpse* (New York: Simon and Schuster, 1967)
An intimate tone poem in two parts, the first passage of *Dark Cave* consists of black-and-white footage of the flora and fauna of my backyard garden with a montage of nature sounds. Alfred Chester's quote bridges the opening section and yields to a second, contrasting movement. Sun-drenched color Super-8 images of the historic fortress, cemetery, and beaches of Old San Juan combine with Victoria William's laconic song "Happy" to evoke the ambivalence of memory.
Also available on the compilation *Third Known Nest*.

Darling Child
Tom Kalin
1993, 2:00, U.S., color, sound
"But we are alone, darling child, terribly, isolated each from the other; so fierce is the world's ridicule we cannot speak or show our tenderness; for us death is stronger than life, it pulls like a wind through the dark, all our cries burlesqued in joyless laughter; and with the garbage of loneliness stuffed down us until our guts burst bleeding green, we go screaming round the world, dying in our rented rooms, nightmare hotels, eternal homes of the transient heart."
—Truman Capote, *Other Voices, Other Rooms* (New York: Random House, 1948)
Dramatizing a quote by Truman Capote, this tape presents a virtuoso treatment of urban isolation and modern loneliness. Through a collage of views from high-rise apartments and hotel rooms, Kalin illuminates the inhumanity of urban architecture, which reads as a metaphor for the social structures of fear and prejudice that divide individuals from one another.
Also available on the compilations *Tom Kalin Videoworks: Volume 2* and *Third Known Nest*.

Eight (Roland Barthes)
Tom Kalin
2000, 00:30, U.S., color, sound
"But I—already an object, I do not struggle."
—Roland Barthes, *Camera Lucida: Reflections on Photography*, trans. Richard Howard (New York: Hill and Wang, 1981)
Only available on the compilation *Third Known Nest*.

Every Evening Freedom
Tom Kalin
2002, 2:45, U.S., color, sound
"Like any other great city, this one offered its populace more than merely every evening freedom. It offered a variety of slaveries to which the freedom might be put. This was necessary, Goliath knew, because he who has given away his soul between nine and five cannot usually bear to face it (or does not know where to find it) between five and nine. The city offered distractions, glorious dreams."
—Alfred Chester, *Behold Goliath: A Collection of Stories* (New York: Random House, 1965)
Also available on the compilation *Tom Kalin: Behold Goliath – or The Boy with the Filthy Laugh*.

finally destroy us

finally destroy us
Tom Kalin
1991, 4:00, U.S., color, sound
"But these meetings, these partings, finally destroy us."
–Virginia Woolf, *The Waves* (New York: Harcourt, 1978)
"Since the release of his celebrated feature *Swoon,* Kalin has produced a number of fascinating short videos. While all have a strong relation to music video, *finally destroy us* is perhaps the most personal and reminiscent of his earlier project… Defiantly romantic, *finally destroy us* is a video torch song to the sound of Annie Lennox singing Cole Porter. His subject is the end of a relationship, and his offering is a scrapbook of lush recollections of love."
–Jason Simon, *Downsizing the Image Factory* (travelling video exhibition)
Also available on the compilations *Tom Kalin Videoworks: Volume 2* and *Third Known Nest.*

FIVE (Alfred Chester)
Tom Kalin
2000, 00:55, U.S., color, sound
"Where the robots can eat food, they eat chemicals instead–as one would expect. Where they can live and act, they sit in dark rooms and watch others do it for them. Where they can have faith, they mistrust the honest. Where they can have suspicions, they believe the treacherous. Where they can suffer, they prefer to be tranquil. Where they can laugh, they snicker. Where they can praise, they scorn. Where they can scorn, they worship. Where they can do almost anything but love, they do nearly nothing but hate. And where they can hate, they imagine that they love."
–Alfred Chester, "In Praise of Vespasian" in *Head of a Sad Angel: Stories, 1953-1966,* ed. Edward Field (Santa Rosa: Black Sparrow Press, 1990)
Only available on the compilation *Third Known Nest.*

FOUR (Oscar Wilde)
Tom Kalin
2000, 00:15, U.S., color, sound
"Ah! It is so easy to convert others. It is so difficult to convert oneself."
–Oscar Wilde, "The Critic as Artist" in *The Complete Works of Oscar Wilde* (New York: HarperCollins, 1989)
Only available on the compilation *Third Known Nest.*

Give Me Your Future

Give Me Your Future
Tom Kalin
1999, 7:00, U.S., color, sound
"Turn the lights down / Way down low / Turn up the music / Hi as fi can go / All the gang's here / Everyone you know / It's a crazy scene / Hey there, just look over your shoulder / Hoo hoo / Get the picture? / No no no no / Yeah / Walk a tight rope / Your life-sign line / Such a bright hope / Right place, right time / What's your number? / Never you mind / Take a powder / But hang on a minute, what's coming round the corner? Wooooo woo woo / Have you a future? / No no no no / Yeah."
–Roxy Music, "Mother of Pearl"
Also available on the compilation *Third Known Nest.*

I hung back, held fire, danced and lied
Tom Kalin
1997, 5:00, U.S., color, sound
"I hung back, held fire, danced and lied. I was not going to come crawling out of my ruined house, all bloody, no, baby, sing no sad songs for me."
–James Baldwin, "The Black Boy Looks at the White Boy," *Esquire* (May 1961)
Only available on the compilation *Third Known Nest.*

Information Gladly Given But Safety Requires Avoiding Unnecessary Conversation

Tom Kalin

1995, 1:05, U.S., color, sound

"I borrowed this absurd phrase from a sign posted on the conductor's booth in the Washington, D.C. subway. The language of civil service here borders on unintentional parody, with its blankly polite tone and bureaucratic single-mindedness. *IGGBSRAUC* revisits my 1992 tape, *Nation*, and features a dense chorus of faces and voices. These strangers ask us to consider the question, 'Who is the public?'"

—Tom Kalin

Only available on the compilation *Third Known Nest.*

Nation

Nation

Tom Kalin

1992, 1:00, U.S., color, sound

Commissioned by the Whitney Museum of American Art and The American Center in Paris as part of their international *Trans Voices* project, *Nation* flashes contradictory formulations of language, politics, and medicine across a sharp and close screen. Blurring geography with the body's landscape, *Nation* reminds us that our bodies, like land, have been shaped by history into zones to be charted, conquered, divided, or made whole. "Think globally act locally," in one dense minute.

Only available on the compilation *Third Known Nest.*

NINE (James Baldwin)

Tom Kalin

2000, 00:30, U.S., color, sound

"The roles that we construct are constructed because we feel that they will help us to survive and also, of course, because they fulfill something in our personalities; and one does not, therefore, cease playing a role simply because one has begun to understand it. All roles are dangerous. The world tends to trap and immobilize you in the role you play; and it is not always easy—in fact, it is always extremely hard—to maintain a kind of watchful, mocking distance between oneself as one appears to be and oneself as one actually is."

—James Baldwin, "The Black Boy Looks at the White Boy," *Esquire* (May 1961)

Only available on the compilation *Third Known Nest.*

Nomads

Tom Kalin

1993, 4:50, U.S., color, sound

"I fear nomads. I am afraid of them and afraid for them too."

—Jane Bowles, "Camp Cataract" in *My Sister's Hand in Mine* (New York: Ecco Press, 1978)

"Tom Kalin's recent videos draw from literary quotations to instigate video corollaries. Inspiring this travelogue is a line from Jane Bowles. The figure of the nomad has recently been invoked to describe a number of modern phenomena, including the urban homeless, the artist, and the computer hacker—none of whom necessarily share a connection to the North African societies visited by Jane Bowles. But video is unique in its global scope, and Kalin employs the medium's ability to transform our sense of time and space in this compelling depiction of the point of view of the traveler. Set to speed-metal, *Nomads* is not so much an invocation of itinerant tribes as a passing glance at the world as an image."

—Jason Simon, *Downsizing the Image Factory* (travelling video exhibition)

Also available on the compilations *Tom Kalin Videoworks: Volume 2* and *Third Known Nest.*

ONE (Jane Bowles)

Tom Kalin

2000, 00:30, U.S., color, sound

"We each have only one single life which is our real life, starting at the cradle and ending at the grave. I warn Dorothy every time I see her that if she doesn't watch out, her life is going to be left aching and starving on the side of the road and she's going to get to her grave without it. The farther a man follows the rainbow, the harder it is for him to get back to the life which he left starving like an old dog."

–Jane Bowles, "Plain Pleasures" in *My Sister's Hand in Mine* (New York: Ecco Press, 1978)

Only available on the compilation *Third Known Nest.*

Robots of Sodom

Tom Kalin

2002, 2:45, U.S., color, sound

"Sodom–for those of you who haven't been there–is an island about ten miles in length by about two miles in width. There is no depth to it at all. It was built by men as a memorial to God, much the same reasons that I am writing this … to praise and fulfill Him because they had heard He was dead and because His work had apparently come to nothing.

"The great buildings of Sodom are shaped like tombstones, and the island is populated almost entirely by robots. Man created the robots in his own image, and he created the island in the image of a cemetery. Like Man and God, the robots are omnipotent and omniscient–except in four ways. They cannot be anything but robots. They cannot love. They cannot know they are robots, and they cannot know they cannot love."

–Alfred Chester, "In Praise of Vespasian"

Also available on the compilation *Tom Kalin: Behold Goliath – or The Boy with the Filthy Laugh.*

Robots of Sodom

SEVEN (Virginia Wolf)

Tom Kalin

2000, 00:30, U.S., color, sound

"And the poem, I think, is only your voice speaking."

–Virginia Woolf, *The Waves* (New York: Harcourt, 1978)

Only available on the compilation *Third Known Nest.*

SIX (Virginia Woolf)

Tom Kalin

2000, 00:30, U.S., color, sound

"Look how the willow shoots its fine sprays into the air! Look how through them a boat passes, filled with indolent, with unconscious, with powerful young men. They are listening to the gramophone; they are eating fruit out of paper bags. They are tossing the skins of bananas, which then sink, eel-like, into the river."

–Virginia Woolf, *The Waves* (New York: Harcourt, 1978)

Only available on the compilation *Third Known Nest.*

Some Desperate Crime on My Head

Tom Kalin

2003, 3:00, U.S., color, sound

"I was fourteen when I put on my first wig. It was, I believe, my sister's idea. So she and my mother and I went – I forget where … Simmons and Co.? – some elegantish salon with gold lamé drapes where they did not do such splendid work. I sat and accepted the wig. It was like having an ax driven straight down the middle of my body. Beginning at the head. Whack! Hacked in two with one blow like a dry little tree. Like a sad little New York tree. … Hat people and wig people. Wig people at school. Hat people at home. This went on for years, decades. The terror of encountering one side in the camp of the other. I could bear no reference to the wig. If I had to wear it, all right. But I wasn't going to talk about it. It was like some obscenity, some desper-

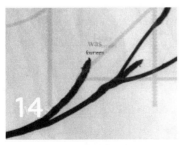

Some Desperate Crime on My Head

ate crime on my head. It was hot coals in my mouth, steel claws gripping my heart, etc. I didn't want to recognize the wig, the wig people, the hat, the hat people, or even my baldness. It just wasn't there. Nothing was there. It was just something that didn't exist, like a third arm, so how could you talk about it? But it hurt, it hurt. Now I think I look quite glamorous."
—Alfred Chester, "The Fool"
Also available on the compilation *Tom Kalin: Behold Goliath − or The Boy with the Filthy Laugh*.

They are lost to vision altogether
Tom Kalin
1989, 14:00, U.S., color, sound
Made in 1989, *They are lost to vision altogether* is an erotic counterstrike to the Helms Amendment, the U.S. government's refusal to fund AIDS prevention information explicitly for gay men, lesbians, and IV drug users. Kalin paints a portrait of the national fear and hysteria that has usurped compassion and care for people with AIDS. With Kalin's usual visual finesse, the tape eloquently conveys the need for a sane and human response to the crisis that still acknowledges passion and sexuality.

Third Known Nest
"*Third Known Nest* is a collection of nine short works completed approximately one each year from 1991 to 1999. Interwoven by nine quotations from some of my favorite writers, the 18 short entries in *Third Known Nest* function as an intimate visual diary—fractured pictures from my day-to-day life. … Partially provoked by music video, each entry in the cycle of tapes pairs a literary touchstone with a song. They're somewhere in between formal 'experimental film' montage and the bombardments of our noisy pop culture. Though individual works are distinct in tone, the overwhelming impact of the program is emotional, nostalgic. Above all else, *Third Known Nest* works as a gallery of portraits in flux—myself and the people I love: some living, some dead."
—Tom Kalin
Total running time 37:10.
Contents:
ONE (Jane Bowles), Tom Kalin, 2000, 00:30, U.S., color, sound
finally destroy us, Tom Kalin, 1991, 4:00, U.S., color, sound
Nation, Tom Kalin, 1992, 1:00, U.S., color, sound
TWO (Patricia Highsmith), Tom Kalin, 2000, 00:55, U.S., color, sound
Nomads, Tom Kalin, 1993, 4:50, U.S., color, sound
Darling Child, Tom Kalin, 1993, 2:00, U.S., color, sound
THREE (Derek Jarman), Tom Kalin, 2000, 00:40, U.S., color, sound
Confirmed Bachelor, Tom Kalin, 1994, 2:45, U.S., color, sound
FOUR (Oscar Wilde), Tom Kalin, 2000, 00:15, U.S., color, sound
Information Gladly Given But Safety Requires Avoiding Unnecessary Conversation, Tom Kalin, 1995, 1:05, U.S., color, sound
FIVE (Alfred Chester), Tom Kalin, 2000, 00:55, U.S., color, sound
I hung back, held fire, danced and lied, Tom Kalin, 1997, 5:00, U.S., color, sound
SIX (Virginia Woolf), Tom Kalin, 2000, 00:30, U.S., color, sound
Dark Cave, Tom Kalin, 1998, 4:15, U.S., b&w and color, sound
SEVEN (Virginia Wolf), Tom Kalin, 2000, 00:30, U.S., color, sound
EIGHT (Roland Barthes), Tom Kalin, 2000, 00:30, U.S., color, sound
Give Me Your Future, Tom Kalin, 1999, 7:00, U.S., color, sound
NINE (James Baldwin), Tom Kalin, 2000, 00:30, U.S., color, sound

THREE (Derek Jarman)
Tom Kalin
2000, 00:40, U.S., color, sound
"I am a mannish / Muff-diving / Size queen / With bad attitude / An arse-licking / Psychofag / Molesting the flies of privacy / Balling lesbian boys / A perverted heterodemon / Crossing purpose with death / I am a cock-sucking /

They are lost to vision altogether

Straight-acting / Lesbian man / With ball-crushing bad manners / Laddish nymphomaniac politics / Spunky sexist desires / Of incestuous inversion and / Incorrect terminology / I am a Not Gay"
–Derek Jarman, *Blue: Text of a Film* (Woodstock, N.Y.: Overlook Press, 1994)
Only available on the compilation *Third Known Nest.*

Tom Kalin: Behold Goliath – or The Boy with the Filthy Laugh
A work-in-progress inspired by the life and work of American writer Alfred Chester.
Total running time 8:30.
Contents:
Every Evening Freedom, Tom Kalin, 2002, 2:45, U.S., color, sound
Robots of Sodom, Tom Kalin, 2002, 2:45, U.S., color, sound
Some Desperate Crime on My Head, Tom Kalin, 2003, 3:00, U.S., color, sound

Tom Kalin Videoworks: Volume 2
One of the most prominent artists of the early-'90s New Queer Cinema, Kalin's feature film *Swoon* (1992) brought him international acclaim and attention. His videoworks from the period are similarly innovate but use a video-specific form in their combinations of appropriated images and music, text, and original footage. Like many of Kalin's videoworks, most of these tapes take inspiration from literary sources to address contemporary experiences and issues, including the AIDS epidemic, urban isolation, homophobia, and displacement.
Total running time 14:00.
Contents:
Confirmed Bachelor, Tom Kalin, 1994, 2:45, U.S., color, sound
Darling Child, Tom Kalin, 1993, 2:00, U.S., color, sound
finally destroy us, Tom Kalin, 1991, 4:00, U.S., color, sound
Nomads, Tom Kalin, 1993, 4:50, U.S., color, sound

TWO (Patricia Highsmith)
Tom Kalin
2000, 00:55, U.S., color, sound
"It is curious that in the most important periods of one's life, one never keeps a diary. There are some things that even a habitual diary-keeper shrinks from putting down in words—at the time, at least. And what a loss, if one intends to keep an honest history at all. The main value of diaries is their recording of difficult periods, and that is just the time when one is too cowardly to put down the weaknesses, the vagaries, the shameful hatreds, the little lies, the selfish intentions, carried out or not, which form one's true character."
–Patricia Highsmith, *The Blunderer* (New York: Coward-McCann, 1954)

Only available on the compilation *Third Known Nest.*

Kelley, Mike
(see Beckman, Ericka)

Kim-Trang,Tran T.
Tran T. Kim-Trang holds a BFA from the University of Iowa and an MFA from Cal Arts. She teaches at the University of California-Irvine and the California Institute of the Arts and makes experimental video and mixed media pieces. She also assembled *Under Construction: Shifting Identities in California Video* for the Long Beach Museum of Art.

Aletheia
Tran T. Kim-Trang
1992, 16:00, U.S., color, sound
The introductory tape to the *Blindness Series, Aletheia* presents an indexing of categories investigating different aspects of blindness as metaphor. Stylistic preference for the techniques and conventions of MTV and American Television in general provides the means to create connections among the categories of cosmetic surgery, sexuality, technology, language, hysterical blindness, and actual blindness.
Also available on the compilation *Blindness Series.*

alexia: Metaphor and Word-Blindness
Tran T. Kim-Trang
2000, 10:00, U.S., b&w and color, sound
alexia is an experimental video about word-blindness and metaphor. Word-

blindness is a condition that usually afflicts people who have suffered a stroke, causing them to lose the visual recognition of individual letters but perceive the entire word or vice versa. Metaphor is here discussed in its function to reveal and obscure perception. Divided into five short sections, the tape draws a pattern with the motif of the finger and the moon to ruminate on language and blindness. *alexia* opens with a quote from a well-known Buddhist passage: "Do not mistake the finger for the moon." It goes on to present Giambattista Vico's theory on the origin of language and Ludwig Wittgenstein's theory on aspect-blindness, and ends with an (fictive) account of Kussmaul's (who coined the term alexia) wife as she experiences word-blindness, or alexia.

amaurosis: a portrait of Nguyen Duc Dat

Tran T. Kim-Trang
2002, 28:00, U.S., color, sound

amaurosis: a portrait of Nguyen Duc Dat

amaurosis is an experimental documentary about Dat Nguyen, a blind guitarist living in Little Saigon, Orange County, California. Dat Nguyen was a "triple outcast": blind, Amerasian, and an impoverished orphan. *amaurosis* is a media work about an individual in a community seldom represented. Beyond their disabilities, this community of Vietnamese Americans is oppressed on many levels: language and cultural differences, immigrant and lower income status, and societal misunderstanding and alienation. From a typical Vietnamese perspective, which still holds many superstitions to be true, people with disabilities are seen as symbols of bad karma and ill omens, causes for shame and fright. Saddest of all is the wholesale dismissal of the disabled person as incapable of anything productive in life. From a Western perspective, many of these prejudices have been exposed, and although blatant displays occur less often, more insidious and subtle forms of discrimination still take place on a daily basis. The tape strives to present the life of one member from this unique community and promote his rich contributions.

Blindess Series

Kim-Trang's fascinating four-part series considers the socio-cultural meanings and actions of vision and ocular physiognomy, from eyelid shape to AIDS-related vision loss to mechanical surveillance.
Total running time 1:07:00.
Contents:
Aletheia, Tran T. Kim-Trang, 1992, 16:00, U.S., color, sound
Kore, Tran T. Kim-Trang, 1994, 17:00, U.S., color, sound
Ocularis: Eye Surrogates, Tran T. Kim-Trang, 1997, 20:00, U.S., color, sound
Operculum, Tran T. Kim-Trang, 1993, 14:00, U.S., color, sound

Ekleipsis

Tran T. Kim-Trang
1998, 22:00, U.S., b&w and color, sound

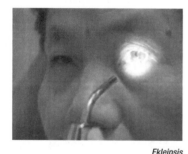

Ekleipsis

In 1992, Tran came across a *New York Times* article about a group of hysterically blind Cambodian women in Long Beach, California, known as the largest group of such people in the world. Hysterical blindness is sight loss brought about by traumatic stress and has few or no physical causes. *Ekleipsis* delves into two histories: the history of hysteria and the Cambodian civil war. Weaving together texts of these histories along with a composite case study of some of the hysterically blind Cambodian women and the artist's mother, *Ekleipsis* speaks about the somatization of pain and loss. The video also expresses the inspiration found in these ascendant personalities—those who develop the incredible will to survive traumatic events and utilize their experiences to reflect and live life in positive ways.

Kore

Tran T. Kim-Trang
1994, 17:00, U.S., color, sound
By focusing on the blindfold, *Kore* explores the eye as purveyor of desire, sexual fear, and the fantasy of blindness. An alternative sexuality is founded in

touch-based (feminine?) pleasure as opposed to a vision-based (masculine?) pleasure. This examination of institutional blind spots towards women and people of color concerning AIDS expands on the issue of vision, visibility, and the disease.

Also available on the compilation *Blindness Series.*

Ocularis: Eye Surrogates

Ocularis: Eye Surrogates

Tran T. Kim-Trang

1997, 21:00, U.S., color, sound

This video highlights several narratives concerning video surveillance—not to reiterate the conventional privacy argument but rather to engage the desire to watch surveillance materials and society's insatiable voyeurism. A variety of subjects recount their interactions with surveillance—getting caught in the act of stealing or watching pornography, being discouraged from making an illegal ATM withdrawal—and question technological determinism, asking whether we choose to develop technology or technology shapes our choices.

Also available on the compilation *Blindness Series* and on the anthology *The New McLennium, Program 1.*

Operculum

Tran T. Kim-Trang

1993, 14:00, U.S., color, sound

Kim-Trang visits with seven cosmetic surgeons specializing in blepharoplasty (cosmetic eyelid creasing surgery) in the West Hollywood/Beverly Hills area for initial consultation sessions. The doctors demonstrate different reshaping options and comment upon the prevalence and success rates for different Asian nationalities while Kim-Trang presents statistics and facts in text that frame the consultations.

Also available on the compilation *Blindness Series.*

Kipnis, Laura

Chicago-based videomaker and cultural critic Laura Kipnis's work is richly informed by her post-Marxist, post-structuralist, post-feminist, post-everything sense of humor. Her often irreverent tapes form piercing analyses of contemporary debates with an unpretentious feminist slant. Her books include *Bound and Gagged: The Politics of Fantasy in America* (1996) and *Against Love: A Polemic* (2003). Kipnis is on faculty in Radio/Television/Film at Northwestern University.

A Man's Woman

Laura Kipnis

1988, 54:00, U.S., color, sound

This fictional docudrama—based in part on the careers of Anita Bryant, Phyllis Schlafly, and Marabel Morgan—covers the fictitious assassination of Clovis Kingsley, a powerful, pro-family anti-feminist ideologue and fictional author of *The Power of Total Submission.* Those who knew her best and liked her least reconstruct the narrative in fractured and contradictory flashbacks. The tape travels beyond the faux biography to suggest that the logic of anti-feminism is a strategy of the disempowered. Ostensibly treating the rise of '80s anti-feminism, the main issue of *A Man's Woman* is the difficulty of constructing feminism as a mass political movement.

Marx: The Video

Laura Kipnis

1990, 35:00, U.S., color, sound

Kipnis describes this tape as "an appropriation of the aesthetics of both late capitalism and early Soviet cinema—MTV meets Eisenstein, reconstructing Karl Marx for the video age." She presents a postmodern lecture delivered by a chorus of drag queens on the unexpected correlations between Marx's theories and the carbuncles that plagued the body of the rotund thinker for more than 30 years. Marx's erupting, diseased body is juxtaposed with the "body politic" and posited as a symbol of contemporary society proceeding the failed revolutions of the late 1960s. Seeking a parallel between the body of the state and women's bodies, Kipnis brings to light the manner in which women's bodies have been used as the site of displacement for social and political anxiety, with the state of the nation currently reflected in a female body plagued by anorexia and bulimia, traversed by pornography, manners, and regulations on abortion.

Klonarides, Carole Ann
(see Blumenthal, Lyn and MICA TV)

Kobland, Ken

Ken Kobland has been involved in film and video since 1971, including numerous collaborative works with the Wooster Group, the New York-based experimental theater. His work explores a variety of themes, often embracing a photographic aesthetic within the context of video. Beautifully edited, his work merges diaristic and documentary categories, emphasizing the fine art of video.

Buildings and Grounds/The Angst Archive

ARISE! Walk Dog Eat Donut
Ken Kobland
1999, 29:45, U.S., color, sound
Film- and videomaker Ken Kobland returns to the urban landscapes he filmed 20 years previously, such as the New York subway and the S-Bahn in Berlin. We leave, we travel, but it's always the same images that we are drawn to. A moving road movie about eternal departure and arrival.
"A melancholy, semi-abstract video poem made up largely of blurred images shot from moving subway and elevated cars in New York City and Berlin. Woven into the film are fragments of a diary (despairing epigrams like 'all meaning evaporates') and a Russian ballad. Repetitive without becoming monotonous, the video evokes an urban sadness that is so insistent it becomes a whole philosophy of loss and resignation."
—Stephen Holden, "A Thematic Feast of Avant-Garde Videos," *The New York Times* (16 July 1999),

Berlin: Tourist Journal
Ken Kobland
1988, 19:00, U.S., color, sound
This tape is a response to Kobland's experiences as a DAAD (Deutscher Akademischer Austauschdienst) fellow in West Berlin. A journalistic collection of impressions of a haunted place, the tape evokes the landscape of past and present Germany through still images and archival film clips. Inter-cutting these images with footage shot on the plane (whether Kobland is leaving Germany or just arriving is impossible to say), *Berlin: Tourist Journal* constructs a portrait of this divided city through the eyes of an outsider.

Buildings and Grounds/The Angst Archive
Ken Kobland
2003, 45:00, U.S., color, sound
"...a rumination, a series of borrowed 'dialogues' out of an ongoing argument with myself. It meanders, mentally and physically, reflecting on the conditions of being human, on transience, consciousness, and desire. It uses landscapes as provocations, as sites of contemplation. And between the landscape and the thought, i.e. between the radical presence of the physical world and the idea, there is, more often than not, a distance, disbelief or irony."
—Ken Kobland

Flaubert Dreams of Travel But the Illness of His Mother Prevents It
Ken Kobland
1986, 20:00, U.S., color, sound
Drawing from Flaubert's *The Temptation of Saint Anthony,* his letters, travel journals, and biography, this tape layers fantasy, sexual obsession, morbidity, Romanticism, and boredom alongside the ghostliness of empty hotel rooms, aural atmosphere, and an homage to surrealist and horror films.
Co-produced by the Wooster Group and featuring Ron Vawter.

Foto Roman
Ken Kobland
1990, 28:00, U.S., color, sound
"Think of it as a prologue to a sleazy thriller. A sort of shaggy-dog plot of voyeuristic atmospheres." This tape is about the voyeuristic license of the camera: exposing, uncovering, glimpsing things obscured and revealed. A series of still images that fade to black, this piece challenges the viewer to construct the identity of the person behind the camera. Who is the subject and who is the object? Though a man's voice outlines the tape, it becomes clear that a woman is photographing—we "spy" through her eyes.

Moscow X
Ken Kobland
1993, 57:00, U.S., color, sound
A camcorder diary and chronicle of public opinion in Moscow during a time

of huge political, economic, and hence cultural, changes in the former Soviet Union. The tape reveals Kobland's own fascination with the diversity and complexity of Russians' reactions to such changes. It also represents a type of cultural exchange made newly possible by glasnost—Americans and Russians learning about each other on a popular, unofficial, direct level through video.

Shanghaied Text
Ken Kobland
1996, 20:00, U.S., color, sound
A self-described "collage piece" of "stolen images," *Shanghaied Text* starts with quiet Montana landscapes, among which are views of a powerful dam. When the dam breaks loose the viewer is "shanghaied" in places unknown, where Kobland presents a provocative mix of historical, lyrical, sexual, and political references. Using quotes and pieces from movies by Vertov, Dovjenko, and Buñuel, along with archival images of social protests from the liberation of Paris, the piece builds to an operatic culmination with Turandot's final choir. *Shanghaied Text* is a remarkable, dense, and gripping work that leaves the viewer pondering our political and cultural heritage, as well as the role and place of technology in our future.
Also available on the anthology *The New McLennium, Program 2.*

Stupa
Ken Kobland
1992, 1:00:00, U.S., b&w, sound
A one-hour helicopter flight over the suburban sprawl of Long Island to Fresh Kills, the New York City Landfill on Staten Island, accompanied by an operatic audio-mix of bad-mouth talk radio mayhem and historic nostalgia.

Shanghaied Text

Kos, Paul and Marlene

Paul and Marlene Kos produced numerous videotapes throughout the '70s that explored the hypnotic and illusory aspects of the televised image. Their installation works treat the video monitor as an essentially sculptural element with its own inherent structural language. In several cases, the monitor functions as a window offering a view of events occurring simultaneously in another location; they likewise reassess the role of the audience, actively structuring viewers into the performance of the work (*St. Elmo's Fire*, 1977).

Lightning
Paul and Marlene Kos
1976, 1:17, U.S., b&w, sound
"When I look for the lightning, it never strikes. When I look away, it does." Filmed inside a car, this tape focuses on observation of natural phenomena, presenting the obverse of the "If a tree falls in the woods..." conundrum. Does observation change the course of events? Can you believe in things you don't see? In this experiment, the camera occupies a privileged position—showing the woman and what she sees, as well as what she cannot see.
Also available on the anthology *Surveying the First Decade, Program 2.*
This title was originally part of the Castelli-Sonnabend video art collection.

Riley Roily River
Paul and Marlene Kos
1975, 1:00, U.S., b&w, sound
The seemingly groundless debate as to whether a river is "riley" or "roily" can be interpreted as an example of language's descriptive failure. A shouting match over how to describe the river has no effect; the face of nature continues unchanged. *Riley Roily River* graphically illustrates the gap of meaning that exists between the natural, empirical world and the language we use to describe it.

Search Olga Gold
Paul and Marlene Kos
1973, 19:00, U.S., b&w, sound
Originally part of a larger sculptural installation using prospector's tools, this tape reenacts the search for "Olga," a miner's wife who disappeared on her honeymoon in 1936. As Paul and Marlene Kos call out, "Olga ... Olga ...," the camera scans the Wyoming wilderness, and their search becomes ritualistic, the repetitive calls building in intensity and breaking down into chanted moans. The camera's movement follows the growing frenzy and sexual suggestiveness of the soundtrack, reinforcing the erotic subtext of the tape, and building a parallel between the prospector's desperate search for his bride

and for gold.
This title was in the original Castelli-Sonnabend video art collection.

Sirens
Paul and Marlene Kos
1977, 6:00, U.S., b&w, sound
Taking its title from the sea nymphs in Homer's *Odyssey*—the treacherous spirits whose sweet voices lured sailors to their death upon the rocks—*Sirens* presents four hallucinatory scenes, visual puns authored by a mischievous agent. Mocking laughter that shatters the illusion and causes viewers to doubt the assumptions implicit in their viewing disrupts stills of what seem to be unpopulated landscapes.

Merce by Merce by Paik (see Paik, Nam June)

Kubota, Shigeko

Originally from Japan, Shigeko Kubota moved to New York in the mid-'60s to study and discovered video through her involvement with the Fluxus Movement. In 1972 she produced the first of her video diaries (*Europe on 1/2 Inch a Day*) while also exploring the image processing equipment at WNET's TV Lab. The fusion of spontaneous autobiography and electronic processing characterized her subsequent work, which ranged in focus from everyday events to meditations on the work of Marcel Duchamp. Kubota helped coordinate the first annual Women's Video Festival at the Kitchen in 1972.

My Father
Shigeko Kubota
1975, 15:00, U.S., b&w, sound
In this classic personal elegy, Kubota mourns her father's death and recounts the last days of his life. Reflecting on Kubota's use of the video medium, the television emerges as the link between Kubota and her father, with the melodramatic crooning of Japanese pop singers providing a backdrop for Kubota's real-life tragedy.
Also available on the anthology *Surveying the First Decade, Program 1.*

Video Girls and Video Songs for Navajo Skies
Shigeko Kubota
1974, 26:00, U.S., b&w and color, sound
Documenting her stay with the Sandovar family at their home on a Navajo reservation in Arizona and paralleling her experience on the reservation with her life back in New York, Kubota experiences culture shock, becoming aware of the co-existence of two radically disparate cultures within the United States. Inter-cutting scenes of the family's daily activities with sounds and images of Navajo celebration and ritual, Kubota faithfully presents reservation life in its stark reality and uses processed images to allude to the spiritual foundations of the Navajo community.

Shigeko Kubota: An Interview (see On Art and Artists)

Kuchar, George

George Kuchar ranks among the most exciting and prolific independent videomakers working today. With his homemade Super-8 and 16mm potboilers and melodramas of the 1950s, '60s, and '70s, he became legendary as one of the most distinctive and outrageous American underground filmmakers. After his 1980s transition to the video medium, he remained a master of genre manipulation and subversion, creating dozens of brilliantly edited, hilarious, observant, often diaristic tapes with an 8mm camcorder, dime-store props, not-so-special effects, and using friends as actors and the "pageant that is life" as his studio. He teaches at the San Francisco Art Institute, where he makes many of his tapes in collaboration with his students.

500 Millibars to Ecstasy
George Kuchar
1989, 16:00, U.S., color, sound
The dark and sloppy side of touring college towns with your work. Internal exposes of external secretions that unfortunately make it to the boob tube in full color.

1980 Seven
George Kuchar
1987, 28:00, U.S., color, sound
This piece is sort of a prologue to *East by Southwest.* I prepare for that trip while visiting local artists here in San Francisco. You get to see unique sculpture by Mike Rudnick and meet the offspring and pets of the culturally inclined. There is also a gallery encounter with the late filmmaker, Curt McDowell, who attends an opening of his photomontages.

The Acrylliac
George Kuchar
1998, 10:30, U.S., color, sound
A brief visit with a graduate student in the painting department of the art college where Kuchar teaches and the discussion that follows the unveiling of his work. Stroll through a gallery of acrylic-rendered innocence gone awry and the yo-yo generation in heat.

Andy's House of Gary

George Kuchar

1993, 14:00, U.S., color, sound

A young painter and his somewhat slower roommate talk of paranormal occurrences in a room of charcoal canvases and ephemeral renderings. Eavesdrop on the improbable and the impossible (BUT TRUE!).

Ann Arbor

George Kuchar

1992, 19:00, U.S., color, sound

It stands as a mecca for 16mm film and weathers the withering breath of a shifting climate. Bundled up in opulence and optimism, the film festival goes onward and upward while I succumb to a glacial deposit that proves unflushable.

Anniversary Schmaltz

George Kuchar

1996, 13:00, U.S., color, sound

The San Francisco Art Institute's 100th anniversary is absorbed into this portrait of alumni in the heat of creation and pasta softening.

Aquatica

George Kuchar

2000, 12:00, U.S., color, sound

A reflection on the deep and the creatures that attempt to fathom its resources (such as baked salmon and rubbery crocodile meat). A visual journey into the far reaches of waterlogged consciousness, where the yearnings of the tummy meet the revulsion of the cranium—a cranium mostly made up of water in the first place, like a head of cabbage. Besides, the video is more of a head-trip to the nether reaches of Neptune's haunts where tourists glide through guts of glass to ooh and aah at the mysteries of the deep end. Taped in Frisco, Baltimore, and Pacifica, let the salt air of this far-flung journey corrode the landlubber blubber that beaches you upon the sands of sanity and render your sails impotent to the blows of the tradewind. Cast ahoy that anchor of dead meat between your thighs and let it plunge into the deep wetness from which we all ascended.

Aquatica

Arizona Byways

George Kuchar

2001, 23:00, U.S., color, sound

A cactus-strewn desert becomes the backdrop for this series of filmic stopovers that focuses on the living quarters assigned the assignee of this adventurous arrangement. Great natural beauty clashes with manufactured outdoorsmanship as a tired body and sluggish mind seek the oblivion of hotel hospitality in an arid region of artistic aspirations. The viewer is introduced to a world of prickly plants and satin-skinned succubae who prowl the alleys of western decay to staple their fig leaflets on the vertical shafts that poke unsheathed at the virgin skies of southern Arizona. The sheaths are administered, and the population prepares for cinematic coupling in a city park earmarked for culture. Enter the masculine caves that spilled forth their glittering guts onto a surface world as desperate for gems as it was for water and share in the claustrophobic terror intrinsic to the rape of rock and the pillaging of pebbles. Witness this natural spectacle—all packaged and delivered in the form of a vacation video—and marvel at the mavens of movie-making as they bombard the public with a cacophony of celluloid under the moonlit desert sky.

Art Asylum

George Kuchar

1999, 15:00, U.S., color, sound

A cold stone structure stands in frigid defiance to the moral decay that shrivels the leaves of erect extensions to the human lust for creative expression.

This video portrait of art in the making and cats on the prowl will let out of the bag a Pandora's mix of cat chow and chitchat befitting upright blokes.

Artists in Residence
George Kuchar
1991, 13:00, U.S., color, sound
The artists of the future and the past converge and converse as the funding dries up and extrapolation envisions extinction.

Attack of the Giant Garuda
George Kuchar
1998, 19:00, U.S., color, sound
A video I made with students at the California College of Arts and Crafts. It brings to life the terror and romance of cryptozoology as the hero and heroine (both played by young women) go south to bumpkin land on a search for the notorious and monstrous MOTHMAN. A fun journey in video-making desperation (the whole thing had to be shot and edited in 5 days).

Attack of the Giant Garuda

Award
George Kuchar
1992, 20:00, U.S., color, sound
A behind-the-scenes look at the man behind the trophy and the poisons that taint an otherwise jubilant jamboree.

Baldies of Burgermeister Bungalow
George Kuchar
1994, 16:00, U.S., color, sound
A Fourth of July celebration ignites the Id and unleashes a digital demon hungry for imagery of the young and the restless to appease the contraption it sees through: the cannibal camcorder in a state of carnivorous conniptions!

Bargain Basement Bumpkin
George Kuchar
1996, 12:00, U.S., color, sound
The five-and-dime store pulsates with the stench of she who shops. Follow this rag doll apparition as she haunts the futuristic landscape of our buried past and rejoice in the resurrection of the cellar celebrity.

Bay City Detours
George Kuchar
2004, 19:00, U.S., color, sound
The city of San Francisco is awash with talent and some fine eating places, too. In this seaport escapade the viewer is detoured by the smell of lamb chops and the sound of loose tongues vibrating with vitality. The heart and guts of the city spill out in a medley of munching membranes and tinkling ivories all keyed up for maximum vocalizing. The talking heads spout melodic tunes amid the barbecued splendor of tenderized meat made succulent with a Crock-Pot mentality. The not-so-young and the too old for comfort get cozy under a full moon and a full tummy as time marches on to the beat of syncopated sensualists starving for all that heaven allows in its ovens of ostracized organs.

Bay City Detours

Bayou of the Blue Behemoth
George Kuchar
1993, 5:15, U.S., color, sound
The waters run deep as massive jaws chomp and bubbles burst in a world gone mad with technological delusion and prehistoric puppetry.

Big Ones Hurt
George Kuchar
1992, 30:00, U.S., color, sound
The unstable earth becomes the epicenter of this videotape document, which

explores—in a fractured way—the relationships between the people, places, and furniture that sit atop the San Andreas Fault.

Burnout

Burnout
George Kuchar
2003, 20:00, U.S., color, sound
A metropolis awash in electrical overdrive crashes in the heat of summer and sends a Bronxite into the clutches of a waterworld further north. It is there that we witness the cooling fogs and diving mammals of maritime yore and sail free in winds of a nautical nature. A nature that fills the summer sky with twinkling tidbits and the tummy with protein rich denizens of Neptune's soup. A tour of the towering turrets of tomorrowland and the spatial splendor of yesterday's yearnings captured on both chemical and electrical media.

Butter Balls
George Kuchar
2003, 25:00, U.S., color, silent
"To counteract the talkie I had done with graduate students the day before, this undergrad project has no dialogue but just a steady stream of images we dreamed up on the spot. A psychodrama that's heavy on the beefcake, our picture deals with the sexual dementia of a sex addict undergoing hypnotherapy. It's a mixture of fantasy and desire with some animals thrown in and lots of strange angles of the leading actor's attributes."
—George Kuchar

The Cage of Nicolas
George Kuchar
1994, 10:00, U.S., color, sound
A short, atmospheric tour of a movie star's mansion and a glimpse of the living things within the chambers: things that cook, feed the sharks, and gnaw on bones.

Caged Culture
George Kuchar
1987, 15:00, U.S., color, sound
Two women, miles apart in spatial terms, chat about their art and motivational meanderings amid images of Chinese potstickers and fresh pasta. A man sits with them and chews the fat, revealing the ups and downs of social intercourse and parental secretions (secrets).

Calling Dr. Petrov
George Kuchar
1987, 20:00, U.S., color, sound
This tape focuses on the troubles at a large hospital beset with calamity and vice. We meet the doctors and nurses and get a glimpse of their personal traumas.

Celestial Cravings

Celestial Cravings
George Kuchar
2000, 20:00, U.S., color, sound
A rising moon and lowering standards in secular shenanigans highlight this documentary on the making of a sci-fi epic for mini-adults. The stakes are high and the pork chops well done as cast and crew blast off to kiddy dimensions only dreamed of by reformed perverts who revert back to more primitive states of fetishistic attire to usher in the new millennium.

Cellar Sinema
George Kuchar
1994, 12:00, U.S., color, sound
A descent into the blackness of the projected image and the curators who flick the switches and grease up all moveable parts for hot action when the lights go out.

The Celluloids
George Kuchar
1988, 27:00, U.S., color, sound
George stays in San Francisco for this tape about local filmmakers and their future projects.

The Celtic Crevasse
George Kuchar
2002, 32:00, U.S., color, sound
Taped during the summer months in New York City and Provincetown. This vacation video explores the restrictions imposed by dietary fears and the need to appease fresh and rotten appetites. Encompassing both the splendors of a maritime nature and the landlocked decadence of the delicacy dependent, the viewer is catapulted from a big city environment to a resort town mentality of mellowness and salt-encrusted habits. On the journey to more sublime table manners we skirt the buttocks of repressed fermentation to get a whiff of more floral degeneracy inherent in the oceanic wonderland beyond the green cloud of a metropolitan melting pot. Come fry in the sun and splash in the fluff of summer's most sensual treats which are sugar free yet satisfying to those who relish aging meat with their cheesecake (which is in short abundance in this weight-conscious concoction). There's some beef-cake in need of tenderizing, but the less said about that dish the better!

Chariots of Fear
George Kuchar
2001, 30:00, U.S., color, sound
This wonderful and wide-ranging saga of New Age sensibilities in conflict with down-and-dirty urges takes the viewer on a rollercoaster ride into the freak show world of actors and actresses in need of adequate direction. The cast is flamboyant and floundering in this tale of sickness and motherly love competing for the souls of the sexually ambiguous as they mature into mammals of desire and despair. Witness the majesty of digital wizardry as it attempts to zest up the zombie zeitgeist inherent in these fast-paced productions of desperate means. Acted by students at the San Francisco Art Institute and pieced together by a derelict man decades older than the talent who flaunt their floppies in the computer age. *Chariots of Fear* dares to expose the soft underpinnings of the nubile to reveal the best they have to offer for a cheap picture that aims high in the chakra department.

Chariots of Fear

Chat'n'Chew
George Kuchar
1992, 14:59, U.S., color, sound
Cats nibble, people ingest holiday toxins, and barbecues emit clouds of disembodied fat as a woman in need of caloric consumption displays the objects of her obsession.

Chigger Country
George Kuchar
1999, 24:00, U.S., color, sound
Pastures filled with the bounty of a meat-eater's fantasy fill the screen with bellows of bovine origin as testosterone-driven madness runs rampant on 20,000 acres of Oklahoma soil. A lone female turkey stuffer prepares the goodies that will nourish the sunburned as they rocket skyward on the scales of numerical poundage to come crashing earthward in time for marinated hamburgers. A trip to the Garden of Eden and its sanctuary for snakes with an appetite for dog meat.

Chili Line Stops Here
George Kuchar
1989, 21:00, U.S., color, sound
A journey that begins in a Kansas City hotel and ends up in New Mexico. The bumpy ride is fuelled with libidinous juices as it lurches through college dor-

mitories and sun-baked ghost towns. Rocks are lifted and things crawl out for all to see.

Chow Down on Cheney Street

Chow Down on Cheney Street
George Kuchar
1994, 10:00, U.S., color, sound
Ned the dog eats, growls, and passes gas as we, the viewers, pass the time with him and his keepers as they share the stolen hours with us all. It's all here: the pizza, the memories, the good times, and the bad.

City Sluckers
George Kuchar
1998, 35:00, U.S., color, sound
Summer and smoke (from pork chops) filters into every rip in my tee shirt as legs and souls are bared for the infra-red-hot digital camera that's ON THE PROWL!

Cocktail Crooners

Cocktail Crooners
George Kuchar
1997, 15:00, U.S., color, sound
Legendary filmmaker George Kuchar, in-between trips to the bathroom, visits three Bay-area friends: an eccentric filmmaking couple who produces zombie movies and performer Billy Nayer.

Come Forth, Julyowa
George Kuchar
1991, 11:49, U.S., color, sound
A stay in Fairfield, Iowa reveals the American dream being riddled with that which dwells on distant planes and the need for our nation's people to express the forces of good and evil via videography and pyrotechnical vomit.

The Confessions of Nina Noir
George Kuchar
1995, 58:00, U.S., color, sound
A bloated rendering of fear and loathing in the Bible Belt—a belt unable to circumscribe the girth of garbage that threatens to tear asunder the very fabric of Southern society. *Confessions of Nina Noir* was shot on location in South Carolina with students from the South Eastern Media Center. Some of it had to be shot at their headquarters because the local PBS affiliate hated our grit-filled guts. The feeling was mutual.

Creeping Crimson
George Kuchar
1987, 15:00, U.S., color, sound
George visits his mother in the hospital on Halloween and contemplates the autumn colors.

Cretins of the Crate
George Kuchar
1998, 11:50, U.S., color, sound
A party of past students illuminates this diary of boxed dreams, as those enclosed face the real world and nurture into existence the future people of the next millennium.

The Crimes of Armand Tessler
George Kuchar
1996, 50:00, U.S., color, sound
The daughter of a famous detective infiltrates a vice ring of white slavery, only to become ensnared in a sordid world of Burlesque houses and subterranean urges best left buried under law-enforcement paperwork. A large and exuberant cast brings this San Francisco Art Institute production into full bloom as the evil fruits are plucked into view in full color and big sound! Many guest performers from the outside world graced our soundstage for this one!

Culinary Linkage
George Kuchar
1999, 15:00, U.S., color, sound
Sausages simmer and so do the manicured remains of manly torsos as they struggle to ventilate in a manufactured world of soap opera bubbles and globular goo that bead the brows of summer folk. A bi-coastal spree of talking heads and meowing malcontents in need of ointment.

Cult of the Cubicles
George Kuchar
1987, 45:00, U.S., color, sound
In this classic example of the Kuchar style, George travels to the Bronx to visit his mother and to see old classmates from art school. "We see what they have become or are becoming or already became."

Curmudgeon of the Campus
George Kuchar
1997, 20:40, U.S., color, sound
Tippi the she-devil gets a little playmate of the feline persuasion while I dangle about the puppet-populated premises with a head full of scholastic memories that delineate several teaching gigs featuring the fruits of our intercourse.

Curse of the Kurva
George Kuchar
1990, 16:30, U.S., color, sound
Something primitive projects into the present to upset the lives of a group of people delving into past-life regression techniques. The hairy intrusion is both attractive and repellent as he strips bare a suburban carcass composed of Christian pretensions and pagan proclivities.

Cyclone Alley Ceramics
George Kuchar
2000, 12:00, U.S., color, sound
Alone in my room at the El Reno Inn, way out west from Oklahoma City, I face a big picture window that overlooks the refuse of Route 66 to ponder the fate of trailer trash in Twisterville. The skies darken and rumble to the sounds of Mother Nature in heat while Big Brother TV suffers an anxiety attack. Lightning flares up while rain pounds down on the terminal tourists of a raging planet. Only the ice-cold veneer of a sculpted ceramic gives comfort to the terrorized tenant who sweats in sequestered silence while the sky falls down.

Cyclone Alley Ceramics

The Deafening Goo
George Kuchar
1989, 15:00, U.S., color, sound
A prop-filled encounter with a young fantasy filmmaker eventually becomes muffled by an earwax problem I develop, but not before the viewer is dragged through Studio 8, where my class and I are concocting a sordid, high school melodrama.

Demon of the Tropics
George Kuchar
1998, 45:00, U.S., color, sound
A big, colorful rendering of the monster now terrorizing Puerto Rico and the hot-blooded people who have to deal with its deeper mysteries. Made with my students at the San Francisco Art Institute, the video takes the viewer to our never-never land of constructed fantasy, loaded with visiting personnel who dropped by the class and got sucked into the venture. Lots of torrid, tropical mayhem and monsters.

Demonatrix of Kebrina Castle
George Kuchar
1992, 1:05:00, U.S., color, sound
A high-pitched melodrama featuring the noise-saturated spiritual journey of a vegetarian youth embroiled in big city shenanigans and occult extravaganzas. Along the way we meet a crippled and lovely conservationist, fiery Latin lovers, a Loch Ness monster and a wide assortment of characters from the gutter and the galaxy. There is a seance and a seduction at Castle Kebrina along with a glimpse of Armageddon and a repetitive message from the future that booms new age nuances into the snap, crackle, and pop stew.

The Desert Within
George Kuchar
1987, 19:00, U.S., color, sound
This is a journey to El Paso, Texas, where the Super-8 filmmaker Willie Varella and I have a dialogue amid domestic routines, motel accommodations, and emotional baggage indicative of life on the road.

Dial a Kvetch

Dial a Kvetch
George Kuchar
1993, 19:10, U.S., color, sound
The genius and mystique of Edward D. Wood, filmmaker, actor, and author, permeates this excursion into the exposed underbelly of cookie-contaminated corruption and moral bankruptcy. Come along for the ride and experience the black-and-white world of bagged confectionery and bruised libidos as the 1940s meet the 1990s in a head-on collision of balding Bozos and blubbery bimbos. Fasten your girdles and seatbelts for the gut-expanding excursion to excitement.

Dingleberry Jingles
George Kuchar
1994, 20:55, U.S., color, sound
Christmas is here again in this diary of glittering gifts, furry friends, underground movie making, and grotesque greetings. A veneer of good cheer coats the surface like thin ice, so proceed with caution!

Diorama
George Kuchar
1998, 45:00, U.S., color, sound
A sprawling look at chunks of our country as I travel back East to present some programs and a peek at the venues that screen underground movies to the youth of today. The video also opens up big vistas of the West as I daydream about recent trips to mountainous terrain while admiring a plaster diorama of the Pacific Northwest, which I purchased at an all-you-can-eat restaurant in Pennsylvania.

Diorama

Domain of the Pixel Pixies
George Kuchar
1998, 34:00, U.S., color, sound
Sort of a portrait of the videomaker Anne McGuire, who surfaces midway from this waterlogged landscape of El Niño disasters to dispense charm and chocolate within the confines of her concrete office. There is also a flood of imagery that flows in and out of art museums, viewing facilities, and eateries that are perpetually haunted by yours truly, along with the spirit of hoboism that feeds on apple pie America.

East by Southwest
George Kuchar
1987, 38:00, U.S., color, sound
A trip to Boston to visit a local filmmaker in his studio is followed by a journey to the cinematic facilities of SUNY-Purchase and then to the kitchen and living quarters of my mother in the Bronx. My mother is in her most candid mode as we relate and debate. My brother Mike suffers dental woes, too.

Edible Atrocities

Edible Atrocities
George Kuchar
1990, 10:00, U.S., color, sound
We are what we eat, and we talk about what we are; so, naturally, we get hungry all the time. Join my friends as we not only hear but also see what they are and taste the essence of each one without the fear of emotional attachment. A leisurely, if somewhat "lazy Susan" of chewable tidbits that can be spit out if so desired (or undesired). A session of chowing down and chewing the fat with an assortment of gobblers that break bread, but no wind, with me.

Evangelust
George Kuchar
1988, 35:00, U.S., color, sound
A deliberately tasteless drama about televangelist scandals.

The Exiled Files of Eddie Gray
George Kuchar
1997, 45:40, U.S., color, sound
An 8mm video that reunites cast members of a film Kuchar made in the '60s. They stage another shoot, and the camera is left on to record old friends getting older and more childlike as time and champagne trickle away. The second part features a down-home and personal meeting with an author and investigator of the unknown, John Keel. They discuss the REAL men-in-black and muse on their possible origins. A must for all UFO buffs.

The Fall of the House of Yasmin
George Kuchar
1991, 52:00, U.S., color, sound
A pileup of human refuse and super-human powers permeates this hour-long canvas of bits and pieces documenting the smash-up of a house of healing, as the physicians in charge short circuit amid the electronic wizardry beyond the Panasonic barrier. Made with my students.

Fashion Vixen
George Kuchar
2002, 50:00, U.S., color, sound
This sprawling drama about a group of country folk sucked into the fashion world of magazine layouts and romantic intrigue features a cast of glamorously garbed gals and good-natured bumpkins. Produced in collaboration with his students at the San Francisco Art Institute, the picture delivers high-octane antics fueled by the $800 budget and creative desperation typically inherent in these types of endeavors. The cast is large and labors valiantly with the high speed shooting schedule and color-saturated subplots. The scope is big in visual excess and garbage bag set design, but the general flavor is one of syrupy sumptuousness and soapy sudsmanship with a dash of geriatric spice. Bound to be appreciated by those with a penchant for eye candy and naughty tarts.

Fashion Vixen

Felines of Castle Frauline
George Kuchar
1994, 10:00, U.S., color, sound
Cats meow and claw at exits beyond the reach of those who suffer within the walls of their own litter boxes.

Fill Thy Crack with Whiteness
George Kuchar
1989, 11:00, U.S., color, sound
A music-filled tour of Christmas good cheer overtakes this gastronomically oriented excursion through the winter season of discontent and yuletime yearnings craving ignition.

The Flakes of Winter
George Kuchar
1998, 35:00, U.S., color, sound
Snow falls gently in the background as kielbasa is cut and Walter Kapsuta mans the accordion in this Christmas special. Also on board is filmmaker Sharon Greytak as she and I discuss matters of the flesh and joints. The snowscapes of Connecticut and the Bronx are viewed through the filter of domestic hellishness. Full of ominous Christmas cheer.

Forbidden Fruits
George Kuchar
2002, 15:00, U.S., color, sound
The foliage and sprouting of urban greenery becomes the subject of this celebration to all things pollinated. The video explores hidden gardens that lie sequestered amid an array of dwellings inhabited by the not so rich and famous. Felines creep amid the blossoms as human entities enrich the soil with their leaking desires.

Foto Spread
George Kuchar
1991, 5:00, U.S., color, sound
A photographer comes to my home to take pictures and gets a lensful. His mouth and his shutter snap away as I aim my finest attributes at his cold and hard equipment.

Fur Ball Blues
George Kuchar
1996, 26:00, U.S., color, sound
Storms threaten to tarnish the Golden State as I wander through the rooms of my apartment, seeking a high in the lowering barometric pressure. Many mementos create a series of flashbacks to warm the cockles in our most secret places—some of those places being blatantly revealed in this cockle-warming picture.

Fur Ball Blues

Gastronomic Getaway
George Kuchar
1991, 15:00, U.S., color, sound
Mono Lake and Yosemite Valley, in California, highlight this excursion into the constipated crevices of once highly active fumaroles that splattered magma and chunks of hot rock onto the Western landscape. Now the vents are blocked by eating disorders that rob our nation of its free-flowing and fertilizing heritage. We follow a woman as she sinks into a dark, inland sea of great natural beauty, unable to deposit her own organic pile into the rich mineral build-up that reaches skyward toward the creator who dreamt up this exquisite landscape.

The Gates of Gomorrah
George Kuchar
2002, 20:00, U.S., color, sound
Shutters click in this clothes-dropping exhibition of photographic exposures sure to quicken the pulse of those in need of extremity expansion. The voice of artistic reason rises above orgiastic visuals that splash across the pages of glue-bound volumes oozing with sticky subjects of a carnal persuasion. Come and rejoice in the mayhem and frivolity that only Eros unchained can deliver. The soiled and the damned live again on the glossy pages of glue-bound tabloids ticketed for hell and beyond. Witness the innocent and the fun loving as they become documented fodder for light-sensitive materials too hot to handle. Get down and dirty with a deluge of messy mischief destined to flood your libido with a backwash of coffee table books that will titillate and terrify. Meet the man behind the mayhem and marvel at the clarity of it all. It's also a cake-bashing birthday celebration.

George Kuchar Goes to Work with Today's Youth
George Kuchar
1992, 45:00, U.S., color, sound
Students shoot themselves and me in action, as we grind out one schlock movie after another at the San Francisco Art Institute.

The Gifted Goon
George Kuchar
1994, 18:00, U.S., color, sound
The pages of books that deal with nostalgia and the vanishing vistas of America's past are infiltrated by the appreciative presence of two hulks from today who go their own ways through the by-ways and highways of an illustrated yesteryear. One salutes the creator of this painted paradise while the other delves within himself to vomit up columnous verbiage amidst the detailed backdrops.

The Gifted Goon

Glacier Park Video Views
George Kuchar
1993, 17:30, U.S., color, sound
Craggy, ice-encrusted peaks soar skyward as blue lagoons lap incessantly to the drumbeats of big city behemoths hell-bent on halibut and hash browns! The magic and grandeur of glacier-masked real estate is here for all to see and digest in this bountiful serving of natural delights.

The GODmother
George Kuchar
2003, 28:00, U.S., color, sound
This crime drama made with my students at the San Francisco Art Institute is a mixed bag of colorful misadventures featuring a wayward member of the clergy and a corrupting femme fatale with bangs. The couple opens a casino of ill repute with money acquired during their murderous rampage upon the population of a small community of churchgoers. The action is fast and cheap because of the $400 budget, and the cast attractive because youth itself is always beautiful.

Going Hollywood
George Kuchar
1994, 13:00, U.S., color, sound
Greasepaint flows freely as talents of Tinseltown strut their stuff amid the run-down dreams of days gone by.

Going Nowhere
George Kuchar
1992, 10:00, U.S., color, sound
Frozen in time and place yet celebrating birthdays left and right, I ponder the technology that sends me out into the world via magnetism—a magnetism that not only attracts images and sounds but also the particles of nothing that become something when activated by a dust mop. A meditation on white spots and black holes that suck and purr when plugged in or turned on.

Graffiti Junction
George Kuchar
1993, 28:00, U.S., color, sound
Surrounded by the scribbling of the indecipherable, the denizens of the dark and the cheap reach out for light and for the pearls of wisdom that lie enmeshed in a maze of grooved and spray-painted enigmas. A trip through New Age horizons and the madness just around the corner and above our heads. Come with an open mind and sit with a sealed orifice.

Greetings from Boulder

George Kuchar

1986, 50:00, U.S., color, sound

One of the earlier video diaries, in which George vacations in Colorado, reflects on scenery and animal life, and visits people.

Grotto of the Gorgons

George Kuchar

1995, 50:00, U.S., color, sound

An electronic variety show featuring poetry, theatrics, dance, songs, and a plot concerning the cultivation of literary innocence and the preservation of Rondo Hatton's memory (a horror actor in 1940s B movies). A dense work made even denser by staged incompetence. Taped with my students at the San Francisco Art Institute.

Grotto of the Gorgons

The Guzzler of Grizzly Manor

George Kuchar

2002, 12:00, U.S., color, sound

Film festivals are in progress as this video takes the viewer from the autumn-rich colors of a Washington state movie event to the Virginia countryside of flaming October foliage. In between bouts of waterlogged imagery we hear the peeps and exhortations of those in front of and behind the screens that plaster this geography with tribal dreams. Water sloshes and spurts freely in the chilly air unfrozen by stage fright, while wineglasses clink to the coming winter. Featuring festivalgoers Nicolas Cage and Guillermo Gómez-Peña.

Hefner's Heifers

George Kuchar

1989, 13:00, U.S., color, sound

A fast-paced peek at a local cable television show and the glitzy tragedies that make it to the airwaves unannounced.

Holiday Harbor

George Kuchar

2003, 14:00, U.S., color, sound

There's lots cooking in the city by the bay, and the waters smell good, too, as the viewer sails off to Sausalito for homemade bread and gets an ocular whiff of oriental cuisine. The eyeball is treated to many tasty items as the Pacific itself churns like an overtaxed tummy in preparation for a blowout. There are Christmas lights and holiday fireworks and furry playmates being squeezed by the overstuffed. It's all in good cheer and definitely good taste as the spinach pies flaunt their iron-packed punch to the gut and a bittersweet, hot, and sour merriment stalks the salivating.

Holiday Harbor

The Holiday Xmas Video of 1991

George Kuchar

1991, 20:42, U.S., color, sound

Amid the greenery of what should be a White Christmas, there sits the blackness close to my heart, and beyond that there bellows a legion of behemoths who know neither shame nor guilt. A homeless herd of heaven on earth that smell of fish and exotic ports of call. A call I fail to heed.

Holidaze, 1994

George Kuchar

1994, 15:30, U.S., color, sound

The season sweeps through in a blur of glitches, gulps, and sweetened goo as chimes wring out the old and ring in the new.

Homes for the Holiday

George Kuchar

1996, 20:00, U.S., color, sound

Visit a ghetto for the gifted in this Christmas tape that features painting, cooking, and a private tour of cubicles dedicated to culture. Revel in the un-white-ness of a Los Angeles holiday and bask in the heat of noshing newlyweds. Happy New Year!

Honey Bunnies on Ice
George Kuchar
2001, 7:00, U.S., color, sound
A winter chill sets in, making the furry residents of various dwelling places the centers of affection and reflection. The images conjured up are steeped in a twilight worthy of polar pinpoints in the grip of glaciated gloom. The crushing weight of frigid fragments of time threatens to bury the animated remains of sentient stiffs as they flex their muscles in a vain attempt to ward off encroaching crustiness. Only the lure of mammalian fur promises a few pre-cious moments of centigrade comfort in this zone of zero zoology.

Honey Bunnies on Ice

The Hurt That Fades
George Kuchar
1988, 25:00, U.S., color, sound
A three-day teleplay done at CalArts takes a sordid behind-the-scenes look at an art school professor's life.

Hush, Hush, Sweet Harlot
George Kuchar
1999, 26:00, U.S., color, sound
"The plot of this colorful and episodic video drama concerns the gifted pro-tégé of a war-torn world who is granted a glimpse into the future by reading the imprinted impressions of human buttocks. At least, that is what I think it is about. There are many loud sequences of inner and outer turmoil with pretty cast members being faithful to the weaving plot line as it spins its convoluted tale of exposed rear ends and dangling subplots. The pace is fast and pain-less as a parade of young people bring to life a story ripped from the pages of our most lurid celebrity tabloids."
–George Kuchar

ID Came from Inner Space
George Kuchar
1993, 56:00, U.S., color, sound
A colorful and sinister tale of hypno-therapists delving into the quagmire of UFO abductions and wallowing in the subconscious muck of their own primal urges. A sprawling saga of consuming passion performed by enrollees of the San Francisco Art Institute under the direction of Professor George Kuchar in Studio 8.

ID Came from Inner Space

Impaction of the Igneous
George Kuchar
1992, 44:38, U.S., color, sound
First there is a stop at Salt Lake City and a massive dose of theological imagery that prepares the viewer for the hellish landscape to come—a land of igneous outcroppings and noxious emissions peopled by mammals of exqui-site bulk. Countryside plundered of its potatoes by behemoths that head for the hills with their bounty of starch and iron. Follow them to the heights of Yellowstone National Park and the depths of Pocatello, Idaho. Follow them if you dare!

Indian Summer
George Kuchar
1991, 10:00, U.S., color, sound
The colors of fall are muted by the fog of a lingering summer and the memory of that which is dark and naked among the dappled crimson.

Indigo Blues

Indigo Blues

George Kuchar
1992, 32:45, U.S., color, sound
A volcano self-destructs ages ago, leaving in its wake a great emptiness, which is filled with all that is cold and blue. Into that blueness there gazes a horde of cellulite-laden damsels pursued by balding bullies with light meters unzipped, ready to specify F-stops and G-spots. A great and mythical beast lurks within and without, and below there spreads out, for all to see, the blue gaze of mount Mayama; once a vengeful bitch … now a magnificent ditch: a crater of unapproachable serenity and scorn: a crater lake.

The Inmate

George Kuchar
1997, 15:45, U.S., color, sound
The splendor of a mountain lake is clouded by the musings of a brain in memory mode. The head relives the heartbreak of suburbia and the vacancies that fill every motel on the edge of nowhere. The body moves through a rainbow palette of indelible stains that color the journey with the hues of heaven and hell.

Interior Vacuum

George Kuchar
1992, 18:00, U.S., color, sound
Trudging from here to there and beyond, the traveler, weary from the weight of his own body, finds replenishment in boxes both large and small, as the vast wetness of all outdoors offers water, water everywhere and not a drop to drink.

Isle of Heavenly Fury

George Kuchar
2003 17:00, U.S., color, sound
It's summertime in New York City, and the relatives are coming out of the woodwork. Cats live and die amid the high humidity, and more exotic species of God's goodness parade distressingly on the hot asphalt of a shopping mall. Scantily clad sun worshippers lounge about the greenery of saturated soils while the skies await the annual assault of holiday rocketry. An explosive climax brightens a darkening world of shady species.

Isle of Heavenly Fury

Isleton

George Kuchar
1993, 3:20, U.S., color, sound
This tape is part of the *Video Wallpaper Series* where George uses an audio/video digital mixer to create portraits of people. *Isleton* is "a bubbling, beeping abstract impression of a town in California."
Also available on the compilation *Video Wallpaper Series*.

Jungle Jezebel

George Kuchar
1994, 49:35, U.S., color, sound
Produced at the San Francisco Art Institute and featuring a few musical numbers, this jungle drama deals with a commercial corporation infiltrating the Amazon to sell beauty aids to the indigenous peoples. Witch doctor magic and political intrigue runs rampant in this hot house environment, and men and women deal with the beasts within and without.

The Kingdom by the Sea

George Kuchar
2002, 20:00, U.S., color, sound
The spirit of poets permeates the space/time occupied by an assortment of dinner engagements that occasionally erupt into physical or verbal assaults on the taste buds. Flowers of evil are absent from this foray into the spoken word, as the message is one of courage in the face of carnivorous tenden-

cies. An archivist shares his dream with us while the dreamers dabble in their own brand of munchies meant to nourish rather than negate. Mortality hovers over the hovels of the hungry as poetry becomes as concrete as the pastry offered we mortals on planet Earth.

Kiss of FRANKENSTEIN

Kiss of FRANKENSTEIN
George Kuchar
2003, 38:00, U.S., color, sound
Performed by my graduate students at the San Francisco Art Institute, this one-act play that I had written gets the best production values that $500 can afford. Shot in a large can company, we actually pre-recorded the dialogue in the "can" as the only quiet room in the facility was the toilet. The actors then went onstage to mouth the dialogue, which was piped into the P.A. system. Nobody could really memorize all that verbiage for the three-hour shooting schedule we were assigned every Thursday afternoon, so it worked out pretty well, and the thing should be viewed as a sort of puppet show as their jaws do drop now and then to the words. This was also planned as a major star vehicle for Linda Martinez, an Iowa pie-maker with aspirations toward more dubious delights.

Kiss of the Veggie Vixen
George Kuchar
1990, 16:00, U.S., color, sound
A portrait of Marion Eaton, film and stage actress, etched with a green thumb and a brown nose.

Kitchenetiquette
George Kuchar
1993, 5:03, U.S., color, sound
Part of a trilogy known as the *Video Wallpaper Series* in which George uses his new audio/video digital mixer to create a range of impressions of people and places. He calls the piece "a beeping and bubbling impression of an abstraction in a skirt."
Also available on the compilation *Video Wallpaper Series*.

Kitty Porn
George Kuchar
1996, 13:00, U.S., color, sound
My new pussy from HELL.

LA Screening Workshop
George Kuchar
1988, 30:00, U.S., color, sound
George spends a week in Los Angeles on business and at eating engagements. "I eat in Beverly Hills and do my business behind closed doors for a change...."

Last Hello
George Kuchar
1986, 20:00, U.S., color, sound
A friend visits from Canada, and we relive the past as the future becomes more and more obscured by a cloud of burning vegetation wrapped in cigarette paper and exhaled by a pair of lungs unable to supply a brain with the necessary oxygen (mercifully) to remember the past.

Letter from New York
George Kuchar
1990, 15:00, U.S., color, sound
A mother sews; a son yearns for meat; a friend relives the past via glamour shots of a forgotten slab of cheesecake that ferments off-camera. A slice of life with the bowl of cherries missing. A brief visit to a corner of the world that locks itself away with crunchy carbohydrates and six-inch protein protuberances.

The Litter Box

George Kuchar

1997, 21:20, U.S., color, sound

A tour of literary scraps that litter the highway of lost souls in search of publications to be publicized. The crush of printed pulp as it smears its way through the various media that feed off its symbols and excesses. The lust of writers made pure by the whiteness of the sheets they imprint with the shadow markings of their Smith Corona contraption as it keeps pounding late into the night.

Love Me True

George Kuchar

1989, 37:00, U.S., color, sound

Love is in the air as newlyweds chomp on cake, brides marry werewolves, and hatchets fall on adulterous heads. Amid the real-life romance is mixed the real-life business of directing my film students in a tale of runaway passions for the silver screen.

Low Light Life

George Kuchar

1988, 15:00, U.S., color, sound

Shot in low-light style, Kuchar documents his experiences with various underground filmmakers such as James Broughton and Ken Jacobs, then moves on to the other side of Hollywood lifestyle to visit Nicolas Cage. Images of crowds and facial close-ups comprise this haunting tape.

Low Light Life

Lumps of Joy

George Kuchar

2004, 14:00, U.S., color, sound

A holiday video of good cheer and feline ferocity, this annual tradition of videotaped festivities centers on the oriental and occidental tidbits that make the season worthy for bipeds on wheels as they pedal from one calorie-laden event to another. Along the way we meet many champs and chumps as they chomp away at the remaining moments of 2003. Ahead lie the lumpy treats of a New Year in need of NutraSweet.

Matinee Idylls

George Kuchar

2001, 12:00, U.S., color, sound

At the San Francisco Art Institute, a studio awaits the onslaught of creative concoctions perpetrated by a bearded atrocity that now hovers over past malpractice that cast a Technicolor pall over the whitewashed walls. The viewer becomes privy to a cesspool of cinematic venues that rage in the underworld of nice homes in need of spiritual fumigation. See the agents of these misdemeanors commit their crimes of celluloid crassness under the supervision of vision-impaired deviltry that besets lax Christians in need of baptismal bathing. Come for a visit to Studio 8 and meet the damned that craves the silver screen as the last chance for confessional salvation in this academic environment of corporate cadavers and creeping curriculums.

Matinee Idylls

Mecca of the Frigid

George Kuchar

1988, 14:00, U.S., color, sound

George visits underground filmmaker Robert Nelson in Milwaukee, and they brave the cold on Lake Michigan.

Melody for Marla

George Kuchar

1993, 11:30, U.S., color, sound

Colors swirl and shift amid pulsating blobs of light as a voice from the past takes us on an antiquated journey to the future and beyond. Revel in the mysteries of gizmo-channeled visuals and gibberish as the geometric unknown gyrates before thine own eyes.

Metropolitan Monologues

George Kuchar
2000, 45:00, U.S., color, sound
The New York City summer is fueled by the sultry emanations of hot air that tumble off the tongues of potential thespians as they attempt to decipher the gastric guesswork embedded in the prose of the pre-production process. The video camera flits across the boroughs of NYC in a splash-dash sojourn of sumptuous banquets and bohemian bombast, while the down–to-earth wisdom of the seeing impaired helps guide the protagonist into detours of wisdom befitting his putrid project. A theatrical play incubates in the balding head of the videomaker, and as its presence makes itself felt among the various victims of his vision, we share with them the horror of advancing age and the descriptive diatribes toward the destiny of the decrepit damned.

Migration of the Blubberoids

George Kuchar
1989, 11:00, U.S., color, sound
A chance to view the upper Bronx as a mantle of whiteness cloaks its natural splendor like icing on a cake and things all blubbery bob to the surface for air and a sniff of the "good life."

Motivation of the Carcasoids

George Kuchar
1988, 28:00, U.S., color, sound
A month-long video workshop at the University of Wisconsin-Milwaukee results in a loud and action-packed drama. Layers of subplots revolve around the central theme of the violent and emotional body climax in redemption.

Muffled Darkness

George Kuchar
1987, 20:00, U.S., color, sound
George is invited to the AFI Video Festival to see the screening of his tape, Video Album 5: The Thursday People but detours into a melodrama about the fear of internal spaces in buildings.

Munchkins of Melody Manor

George Kuchar
1990, 35:00, U.S., color, sound
From the fall colors of the Bronx, we travel up the Hudson River to Bard College and chew the fat with some notable faculty in the film department, who live in the shadow of the Catskill Mountains. Then it's down to Sarasota, Florida, where we prowl the manicured jungles and opulent estates on Tampa Bay. All of the above is punctuated by a symphonic squad of melodic mannequins and cranked-up antiques that spew forth jingles that jangle in jubilation at the bounty deposited in their slots.

Munchkins of Melody Manor

Murmurs of the Hearth

George Kuchar
2001, 12:00, U.S., color, sound
Another holiday season rolls into the Northern California coast along with the breakers that roil and foam in mimicry of a "white Christmas." Men, women, and felines frolic and fret amid the tinkle of holiday revelers as the short days fade into a melancholy medley of digestive sounds and crackling firewood. Music to the ears and candy to the eyes makes this annual holiday tape a tradition to treasure in this world of terror and tarnish. Come splash in the buoyant pleasures of pacific vistas and sample the crummy crust of California fruitcakes. And by the way, HAPPY NEW YEAR, too!

Nectar of the Neophytes
George Kuchar
2001, 14:00, U.S., color, sound
Two gardens of plenty sprout with the seeds of bitter fruit made sweeter by the touch of summer, which rushes in with the scent of floral flatulence. Made heady by the gorgeous gas, the subjects of this video open both heart and mouth to nature's bounty that is served in microwaveable platters of convenient disposability to protect the environment from caustic suds. A touch of poison does escape the purity of these proceedings, but the general mood is one of gregarious grimness amid the plentitudes of paradise.

Nirvana of the Nebbishites
George Kuchar
1994, 10:30, U.S., color, sound
A black cat and a polka-dotted string puppet frolic amid the painted backdrops of a happy universe, while outside in the real world the reality washes away amid the onslaught of H2O and granulated granite. A merging of the plastic and the profane.

Nirvana of the Nebbishites

Oasis of the Pharaohs
George Kuchar
1997, 17:30, U.S., color, sound
Kuchar makes it to the Isis Oasis resort just in time to catch the marriage vows of his friends Rebecca and Steve. Transposing the myth of Isis onto their union, Kuchar tries to make sense of this recreated paradise, this gathering of God's creatures, and the fates of Rebecca Von Hettman and Charlie Sheen—in this humid, steamy, stained story of the transmigration of souls.

Omewenne
George Kuchar
1995, 20:00, U.S., color, sound
Enter the classic world of a haunted creature destined for stardom in the astrological realm beyond our heads. Visit a haunted soul in her house of horrors and heavenly delights. Sip tea with a sorceress of song and sorrows, earthly eloquence and ephemeral effusions. Taste her ghoulish goulash and smack thy lips with a forked tongue, for Lucifer and Lilith reside within us all.

Orbits of Fear
George Kuchar
1988, 13:00, U.S., color, sound
A military installation is beset by unidentified flying objects while the personnel try to come to grips with their own mysterious yearnings and the cumbersome protuberances that protrude from their own species.

The Pagan Angel
George Kuchar
1998, 20:30, U.S., color, sound
A bird of paradise is pruned for the lens of a Bolex camera as my Sony camcorder documents the film and video scene out here in fog-bound Frisco. A look behind the haze that blocks from view new and old faces as they frame within the medium of choice the tidbits we eventually devour with our eyes.

Paganville Flats
George Kuchar
1996, 28:00, U.S., color, sound
Pagan and Christian souls clash in this student-collaborated mix of the defrocked and the deflowered.

Passage to Wetness
George Kuchar
1990, 14:53, U.S., color, sound
An island. A mountain. A City of Angels who scoop up the pellets dropped by other winged creatures.

The Passion Pot
George Kuchar
2003, 20:00, U.S., color, sound
This chaotic fantasy involves an underground empire of Halloween-type entities that bedevil the surface people of earth with yellow rays that cause civilians to go on murderous rampages. The picture is crammed full of schlock-like sequences and non-stop visual assaults that drop like bombs yet raise a cloud of colorful opulence into the meager stratosphere of low budget movie making. Performed by real young people and somewhat chipped mannequins, *The Passion Pot* lives up to its name and is a stew of unbridled unmentionables.

Passionate Visions
George Kuchar
2001, 15:00, U.S., color, sound
The Rudnick family runs amok with unleashed talent in San Francisco and displays a wide girth of creative curvature for all to admire over a hot cup of java. The fluidity of artistic endeavor spills over the borders of the Pacific Rim to highlight not only aquatic animals but also desert-bound creatures etched in the thirst-quenching magnificence of kitchenware crystal. The whirlwinds of painted and sculpted objects of art, in combination with eyeball-searing displays of expression, dazzle the viewer into a violent reverie of fist-swinging appreciation that adds a kinetic momentum to the unfettered madness. As if to catch our breath, we are swooped away to the wave-battered coves of Pacifica to sniff the sea-encrusted statuary of Jerry Barrish. Amid the turbulent setting of sea and sand, we meet a man and his mate awash with a tide of discarded junk transformed into museum-quality dimensionality. Come join this expedition into the sun-drenched parlors of Northern California and smell what's cooking on the Hibachi.

Passionate Visions

Phantom of the Pine Barrens
George Kuchar
1998, 49:00, U.S., color, sound
The Jersey Devil lives again in this work the students and I mounted (or disrobed) for skeptical scrutiny.

Pictures at an Exhibitionist's
George Kuchar
1989, 45:00, U.S., color, sound
A wide-ranging look at pictures I collect on my walls and in my head. A look at pictures I concoct with my students at the San Francisco Art Institute, and objets d'art collected by those whose picture is taken by my picture-taking machine.

Pilgrimage
George Kuchar
1992, 29:00, U.S., color, sound
A voyage through a California Christmas that begins in the turd-smeared streets of San Francisco and ends in a botanical wonder of ethnic endurance and faith. A journey that incorporates pelicans, palaces, and platters of plenty. A season of joy bloated with the ephemeral gasses of religious fermentation and the iconography of a movie-land Madonna.

Planet of the Vamps
George Kuchar
2000, 25:00, U.S., color, sound

This science fiction adventure centers on the interaction between a crew of Earthmen and their seduction by the love-hungry Amazons of the red planet, Mars. The tale is brought to life with all the opulence that an $800 budget can produce, and the young cast of non-actors live up to their fullest foibles as the plot thickens with a mix of romance and wartime action intertwined with a musical number or two. The ambitions were high and the necklines low in this effects-laden tribute to pulp fiction fantasy and intergalactic intercourse.

Point 'n' Shoot
George Kuchar
1989, 6:00, U.S., color, sound
A lavish home is visited, shutters click, bottoms are exposed, water splashes, and a welcome wetness stains an area unquenched for so long. A jacuzzi bubbles to life in a bedroom community that floats to sleep on aqua-filled rubber.

Portraiture in Black
George Kuchar
1995, 24:21, U.S., color, sound
A series of vignettes, anemic in color, as the absence of light threatens the vibrancy of those depicted: A Bostonian painter and her bloated model. A brunette guitarist and her assault weapon on the eardrums, and a lady from London in makeup and mourning. A canvas of black dahlias and white noise intent on smothering life, limb, and vocal chords.

Precious Products

Precious Products
George Kuchar
1989, 15:00, U.S., color, sound
"In *Precious Products* we are subtly reminded of this country's obsession with consumerism and narcissism. George, with his ever-present video-8 camera, attends an opening of *Precious Products*–an exhibition of artworks satirizing art as commodity. He leaves the art world of San Francisco to spend a Christmas holiday with friends in their opulent home. Ironically, this is the home of a celebrity (another kind of commodity), Russian defector/ballerina Natalia Makarova. Surrounded by all the luxuries of life and Makarova's image, George muses about death. Panning over a dressing table laden with products, he focuses on a *People* magazine and comments, 'We are precious products, all of us.'"
–Carole Ann Klonarides

Princess
George Kuchar
1995, 15:00, U.S., color, sound
An ex-model struts her stuff amid the dolls of desire that drive the demented to deeds of depravity and decapitation. A glitzy portrait of the vulnerable and the vulgar on the brink of disaster and a glimpse of the gaseous God who mocks their morality.

Rainy Season
George Kuchar
1987, 28:00, U.S., color, sound
Thanksgiving in California is the setting for this tape in which the viewer experiences "the depression inherent during festive periods. There were many things bothering me at this time, or maybe it was one thing that broke into many pieces."

Rainy Season

Rancho Roulette
George Kuchar
1994, 58:00, U.S., color, sound
A massive video drama made with my students at the San Francisco Art Institute that chronicles a man and wife parting ways amid the clatter of dice

in a gambling resort on a painted desert of painted women and panting men. A large cast of digitized divas and international inepts march across this colorful canvas of romanticized rubbish and low-budget lushness.

The Redhead from Riverside Terrace
George Kuchar
1991, 26:30, U.S., color, sound
An urban and suburban blend of nerd, nebbish, and nympho, united in the urge to create a cosmetic cosmology.

The Redhead from Riverside Terrace

Return to the House of Pain
George Kuchar
1988, 27:00, U.S., color, sound
"… It documents my walking through the turf and sludge of the Big Apple and many wormholes … I chomp my way back west and gnaw on all that sinks stomachward and beyond in vertiginous aching."
—George Kuchar

Rocky Interlude
George Kuchar
1990, 10:00, U.S., color, sound
A trip to a barren landscape of jagged peaks and deep crevasses becomes a playground for an over-dressed hiker and his beefcake buddy as they secrete and imbibe fluids from various containers.

Route 666
George Kuchar
1994, 7:30, U.S., color, sound
The strings of fate manipulate the living and the dead against a landscape of water vapor and watercolors that make more palatable the unacceptable and the indigestible.

Saga of Magda
George Kuchar
1990, 18:00, U.S., color, sound
A drama, enacted on the cornfields of Iowa, of a woman haunted by the legacy of her mother and the acts that lead to mom's downfall on the banks of a river. Unable to follow a different path to drier terrain, the heroine over-lubricates both inside and out and gets stuck in the muck.

Say Yes to No
George Kuchar
1989, 15:00, U.S., color, sound
A short production I concocted with the students from the School of the Art Institute of Chicago and a tour through the old Playboy Mansion in Chicago where I bedded down for several days, alone and confused.

Scarlet Droppings
George Kuchar
1991, 15:00, U.S., color, sound
Taped in Normal, Illinois during the height of autumn, a snapshot of a young girl triggers a meditation on dying innocence and sizzling sausages as a low winter sun ignites the smoke of greasy longings and meat-eating hunger.

Scarlet Droppings

Season of Sorrow
George Kuchar
1996, 13:00, U.S., color, sound
Ice falls from the sky as tears plip-plop onto wall-to-wall carpeting. No degree of renovation can enliven the dead that we mourn in our hearts as the storm of the centuries assails our heads with memories of the passing parade that got rained on. A weather diary of May-time misery.

Secrets of the Shadow World

Secrets of the Shadow World

George Kuchar

1999, 2:20:00, U.S., color, sound

This three-part mini-series explores the mysterious and the mundane in a splash of digital dioramas that wipe across the screen in a cascade of electronic barfs. Zeroing in on the paranormal theories of UFO author John A. Keel, this leisurely exposition, which was funded by the Rockefeller Foundation, sweeps the viewer into a candy-colored world of scintillating mysteries made all the more intriguing by culinary digressions. Sit back and let the aromas of kitchen coziness clash with the stench of marauding monstrosities as the shadow world engulfs the many that probe its delectable appetizers. Here, in this kaleidoscopic videotape, you will meet and marvel at the talking heads and chewing mouths that fill the soundtrack with the jingles of juju-land—jingles that sing of songs we, as a people of earth, have forgotten in our mad rush to fill the void with various vapors of vacuous virtue. Taste the treats of our ancestors and the hearty heritage of our heretics as we probe the black holes that litter the plane of cosmic luminescence above our heads. Feast upon the food of the Gods and regurgitate with scriptural elegance the message that takes shape in the shimmering sludge.

Sherman Acres

George Kuchar

1992, 1:25:00, U.S., color, sound

A drama in six episodes involving psychological breakdowns, marital showdowns, and messy obsessions. The characters include a wayward priest, a promiscuous schoolteacher and her proctologist husband, teenage thrill killers, and an obsession-driven psychotherapist with an enema bag. Lots of special effects as it moves quickly from one major crisis to another.

Showtoons

George Kuchar

2001, 29:00, U.S., color, sound

This flashy drama about theater life was made with my students at the San Francisco Art Institute and follows the various personalities that make up the show-biz milieu of a fictitious city on a fog-bound coast. The fog is thick and so is the plot as it plunges into a series of dramatic interludes which include musical numbers, war scenes, ballets, and erotic shenanigans involving the living and the animated dead. The young and the not-so-young parade through this homage to stagecraft with all the gusto that their libidos could harness and the $1000 budget filled in the blanks when they pooped out. It's a non-stop barrage of sights and sounds too dense to capsulize here.

Shutter Buggies

George Kuchar

1996, 12:00, U.S., color, sound

Cameras aim and click in this breezy short that blows hot and cold kisses to the "Big Apple" below and the maple leaf above and beyond the northern border of this great nation. Harmonize with the hairy (bleached or flea-powdered) as they smoke or yelp in unabashed abandon to the tune of time zones we all share.

Sins of Bunny Luv

George Kuchar

1994, 15:20, U.S., color, sound

A college girl runs rampant through young lives at Sarah Lawrence College and leaves behind the rubble of shattered souls and deflated desires that litter the halls of learning—by-hard-knocks.

Slippage in the Garden of Udon

George Kuchar

1995, 15:00, U.S., color, sound

The threat of disaster heightens the shallow into prominence, making their eventual fall all the more poignant as we see through their protective garments to view an eager beaver on the prowl. But beavers build and rebuild, damming back the catastrophes that threaten us all with their sinister seepage.

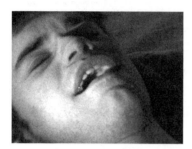

The Smutty Professor

The Smutty Professor
George Kuchar
2003, 40:00, U.S., color, sound
My teaching assistant during the spring semester (Marc Rokoff) at the San Francisco Art Institute began shooting a documentary of me and the students making our sci-fi drama, *The Planet of the Vamps*. Three years later it remained unfinished as he felt inadequate as a documentarian, and so I was offered the box of tapes to edit. I took on the task, and the result is a lively record of the production class in action as it tackles the teleplay with a minuscule budget and scanty costuming. It's a behind-the-scenes exposé of creative desperation and unbridled youth tackling the passions of dramatic exposition and erotic excess with kindergarten kinship.

Snake Goddess
George Kuchar
1991, 5:00, U.S., color, sound
A combination birthday/going away party proceeds at its own shallow pace, while revelers reminisce inwardly amid a paralyzing atmosphere of mixed drinks and emotions that choke all but the young at heart and body.

Snap 'n' Snatch
George Kuchar
1990, 6:00, U.S., color, sound
A sort-of music video that focuses on and under young women and men engaged in focusing video and movie cameras on other young men and women.

Society Slut

Society Slut
George Kuchar
1995, 58:00, U.S., color, sound
The story of a matron and a midget in the heat of an unbridled passion. The colors run thick and heavy for paint and prurient pleasures as the electronic canvas unscrolls to reveal a bevy of beasties and beauties of nature and the unnatural. A non-stop melodrama of a patron of the arts shot by real art students in a real art school! A collaborative project I worked on with my class at the San Francisco Art Institute.

Spawn of the Pagan
George Kuchar
2000, 20:00, U.S., color, sound
The voice of Mr. V. Vale resonates over the hundreds of books and record albums that line the walls of his apartment in the North Beach section of San Francisco—an apartment that he shares with his body—and soul-mate, Ms. Marian Wallace. Together they put out the series of soft-cover volumes known as *REsearch books*. Familiar titles in the series include *Incredibly Strange Films* and *Incredibly Strange Music*. See the face and force behind these literary works and hear the pagan pronouncements of a powerful presence in the world of literature and ideas. A world of the bizarre and the shocking that is our sphere of externalized and unexpurgated ecstasy.

The Stench of Satan
George Kuchar
2001, 40:00, U.S., color, sound
An All-American boy and girl are swept into an international intrigue of demonic content as items cursed with the stench of Satan make their way to a museum dedicated to the spiritual overthrow of family values. Loaded with romance, thrills, and exotic adventures, this electronic teleplay, with its color-

ful moments of scenic horror, leads the viewer on a fast-paced voyage that speeds through the ruins of Egypt, the jungles of equatorial erotica, and the puritanical Wonderland of Middle America. All this was done on the premises of the school, utilizing the dynamic impact of imported props, invited guests, and registered students. Come join this motley crew as they explore the libido-loaded excesses that fill the above-mentioned museum of horrors.

Storm Surge
George Kuchar
2004, 15:00, U.S., color, sound
A sculptor dabbles in the wetness of his craft while the skies threaten a soaking to the winterized wonderland of a Western shoreline. Words of wisdom issue from the mind of a maligned artist as his calendar of kitsch and comfort flap their pages amid a tempest of sea foam and pigeon wings. Shrimp is gnawed upon in dwellings of nutritional notoriety while the hunger of more carnal need feeds the mind with fantasies best left as fodder for a more potent farter.

Story of Ruthy
George Kuchar
1993, 35:00, U.S., color, sound
Made with my students at the San Francisco Art Institute, this video drama explores the thrills and terrors of the Big Top as a travelling circus comes to town bringing with it the promise of cotton candy, eternal youth, and high-flying beefcake. A mother and son become enmeshed in a web of sin and sawdust, licorice and lust as a town confronts its own hideous image in a maze of mirrors at a carnival of lost and found souls.

Studio 8
George Kuchar
1985, 22:07, U.S., color, sound
The place where my students and I confront each other and glimpse into a world infiltrated by beloved infidels.

Suji's House of Shame
George Kuchar
1996, U.S., color, sound
Male escorts and crytozoologists battle behemoths and bulimics in this student-teacher collaboration about undying evil and those that escape it via the Love Canal.

Summer Sketch Marks
George Kuchar
2001, 20:00, U.S., color, sound
The sun pretty much shines throughout this romp back East as waves crash against a land of plenty while the residents bathe in its nutritional offshoots. The artist Mimi Gross is seen sketching away while pets are pampered and the hefty get even bulkier on the vitamin-drenched shores of cranberry-bushed opulence. Even the cityfolk dabble in the colorful gaiety of multi-textured menus that create a montage of sea, sand, and crab dishes fit for a kingly queen. Relish in the splendors of a New England seascape and escape to New York with a tummy hungry for culture cramming.

Sunbelt Serenade, Part 1: Oklahoma
George Kuchar
1993, 17:10, U.S., color, sound
The rivers are in flood stage during a scenic tour of Tulsa, while in El Reno, Oklahoma it's as dry as a two-week-old peach cobbler. The locals puff up on breaded catfish, while an influx of British visitors seek in vain a vegetarian platter amid the thunder boom and hail clatter.

Summer Sketch Marks

Sunbelt Serenade, Part 2: Los Angeles
George Kuchar
1993, 9:20, U.S., color, sound
Flies buzz among the congestion of combustible contraptions as Western civilization gasps for air amid Oriental orifices that emits the stench of sugar and spice and everything nice.

Sunbelt Serenade, Part 3: Arizona
George Kuchar
1993, 21:00, U.S., color, sound
The rocks are red, the mood is blue, the sky is big, and the scars on the earth run deep as a man and woman shop incessantly for nature's bounty and the trinkets of a vanishing culture.

Tales of the Twilight Typist
George Kuchar
1994, 50:40, U.S., color, sound
The summer comes to an end as the viewer tours the loft and lofty art of Mimi Gross, the swinging dummies of Doug Skinner, and the mysterious real estate of famed author Whitley Strieber. Hear his story of terror and beauty under the trees and roof of his country home. See for yourself the man behind the mystery and the people who love him. Also, as an added attraction: rare shots of UFO author and investigator John Keel. An informal look at the incredible.

Tempest in a Tea Room
George Kuchar
1990, 20:00, U.S., color, sound
The artist Bruce Conner is featured in this videotape, which bounces East and West, depicting the fragility of holistic hooligans in a world of hit-and-run encounters, Prozac, and pizzas. A meditation on faulty plumbing and paradise lost … but not forgotten!

Terror by Twilight
George Kuchar
1988, 6:00, U.S., color, sound
George is in Tampa, Florida to do a one-day video workshop, so they make a fast-moving trailer for a non-existent UFO abduction movie.

Thespian Tendencies
George Kuchar
1997, 42:00, U.S., color, sound
Tours of acting gigs that come my way and the people behind the cameras that aim at my expanding torso. A bloated ham in action on the West Coast and the thespians that rub shoulders with his hind quarters. Shot in San Francisco and Hollywood, USA.

Tinseltown
George Kuchar
1999, 45:00, U.S., color, sound
A big splashy rendering of Hollywood in hot action. The babes, the boobs, the boo-boos, and the inner triumphs are all brought to the screen by the uncorked youth and uncouth old bats of the San Francisco Art Institute.

The Tower of the Astro-Cyclops
George Kuchar
1993, 18:00, U.S., color, sound
In Northern California, land of mystery, there stands an edifice of stone that probes the heavens above and the subterranean secrets below the threshold of credibility. Its occupant, Dr. Jacques Vallee, scientist and author, peers into the darkness of inner and outer space to document the elusive interactions of mortals and Magonians (folks and folklore) that inspire our dreams and evolution.

Tales of the Twilight Typist

Tinseltown

The Towering Icon

The Towering Icon
George Kuchar
1998, 35:00, U.S., color, sound
A chaotic assortment of artists tumbles forth in the first half of this video diary, and the pieces of flotsam and jetsam coalesce into the junk statuary of Jerry Barrish, sculptor. Then the piece drifts down to Baltimore where my brother, Mike, and I are invited to the premiere of *Divine Trash,* a documentary on John Waters that is being screened in an old and historic theater prowled by the media and folks in evening attire (evening-out attire). From there we join Divine's mom as she views a construction in honor of her famous son that is going up for display in a visionary art museum. A record of a gala event in full swing, plus the heartbreak and heartburn of those attending!

Trilogy of the Titans
George Kuchar
1999, 15:00, U.S., color, sound
Three ladies of the shadows come forth to illuminate themselves in the glare of a spotlight that is usually aimed at figures groomed for cinematic celebrity. Here we celebrate the force behind the funding, publicity, and exposition of our tribal dreams as we rip the mask off formality to reveal the jolly and the jubilant behind all that jazz.

Trinity
George Kuchar
1993, 5:28, U.S., color, sound
Part of a trilogy of works known as the *Video Wallpaper Series* in which George tests out his new audio/video digital mixer and creates a range of impressions of people and places. "A collage of serpent-infested gruel from Haitian hybrids."
–George Kuchar
Also available on the compilation *Video Wallpaper Series.*

Uncle Evil
George Kuchar
1996, 7:00, U.S., color, sound
The young and the innocent at the mercy of a palpable presence oozing menace and scarlet-stained goodness as a strawberry sundae melts under the glare of future hell–firestorms in search of kindling.

The Unclean
George Kuchar
1995, 24:00, U.S., color, sound
A carload of trouble embarks on a journey few will survive in this horror tale of ancient evil permeating some acreage in upstate New York. Shot on location at Bard College, on the Hudson River, this student-acted drama reeks of spiritual impurities.

Urban Doodles
George Kuchar
1996, 15:00, U.S., color, sound
Cartoonist Ben Katchor is profiled in his old diamond district studio. A Big Apple pumpkin patch that's 100% kosher.

Urchins of Ungawa
George Kuchar
1994, 15:00, U.S., color, sound
In a garden of roses and memorabilia from darkest Africa, a man and woman ponder the joy of cooking and the companionship of cats. Goodies for the guts abound in this visual essay on feline friendship and far away places. An electronic voyage beyond the stench of house and garden that transports the viewer–and cat–to the promised land.

Vermin of the Vortex
George Kuchar
1996, 30:00, U.S., color, sound
Alienation in academia beneath the chandeliered opulence of a political correctional facility that caters to clashing cultures with chicken fajitas and carefully worded alphabet soup.

Video Album 1
George Kuchar
1985, 50:35, U.S., color, sound
A very chatty array of people along with still photos and a loose-tongued cab driver make this a leisurely stroll through my social life of several years ago.

Video Album 2
George Kuchar
1986, 54:15, U.S., color, sound
The viewer meets a grab bag of gabby folks from here and abroad as I drop by to see them or they come to my apartment for tea and sympathy. You also get to visit endangered film showcases and see people who are now either deceased or divorced.

Video Album 2

Video Album 3
George Kuchar
1986, 50:00, U.S., color, sound
Curt McDowell, the director, on his feet and weaving in and out of this televised tapestry with gracious grossness and Hoosier-based hospitality.

Video Album 4
George Kuchar
1986, 50:00, U.S., color, sound
"I shuffle through this one bloated with blab and flab as we visit filmmakers, underground comic artists, and an animal or two."
—George Kuchar

Video Album 5: The Thursday People
George Kuchar
1987, 1:00:00, U.S., color, sound
The comings and goings of the late underground filmmaker, Curt McDowell—and the people and activities that came and went along with him—are the themes that run through this existential diary of daily life. McDowell was dying from AIDS-related illnesses during the production of the diary.
"An elegy for McDowell, the videowork captures Kuchar's mournful remembrances of his long-lasting friendship with the young filmmaker. But it also has the inquisitive charm, perverse humor, and quirky candor that places Kuchar's visual expressions in a gritty niche all their own."
—Steve Seid, *George Kuchar in Person* (Berkeley: Pacific Film Archives, 1988)

Video Album 5: The Thursday People

Video Wallpaper Series
"In this series I composed a series of portraits on my audio/video digital mixer, ranging from impressions of places and people to renditions of feelings their work inspired and domestic-type gossip from the kitchen and bedroom. The gallery of images and sounds were fed into my gizmo and ground up into gourmet gruel."
—George Kuchar
Total running time 19:00.
Contents:
Isleton, George Kuchar, 1993, 3:20, U.S., color, sound
Trinity, George Kuchar, 1993, 5:28, U.S., color, sound
Kitchenetiquette, George Kuchar, 1993, 5:03, U.S., color, sound

Vile Cargo
George Kuchar
1989, 36:00, U.S., b&w, sound
A black-and-white drama that lays bare the earth-shattering events surrounding the rise and fall of certain members of the communal body in a California town ravaged by subterranean forces.

Visitation Rites
George Kuchar
2003, 18:00, U.S., color, sound
Alone in an Oklahoma motel room with a mute companion, the talkative one speaks the language of memory as pussycats feast from a canned cornucopia. Murals plaster the vacancy intrinsic to American angst as horse tails whip from annoyance the nagging gnats of tomorrow's dung: a heap of uncertainty made impotent by the swashes of chipped paint that depict a netherworld of faded dreams and nostalgic neurosis for the future impaired.

The Warming of the Hell House
George Kuchar
1987, 12:00, U.S., color, sound
A trip across the bay to Concord yields a harvest of non-fruit-like beings who celebrate a housewarming that simmers with macho machinations and family discord. The mood is upbeat while the company is low brow and coming out of the bushes rather than the woodwork.

We, the Normal
George Kuchar
1987, 11:00, U.S., color, sound
On a back-to-nature trip to Boulder, Colorado George goes to the mountains but goes on the rocks emotionally.

Weather Diary 1

Weather Diary 1
George Kuchar
1986, 1:21:00, U.S., color, sound
This feature-length tape documents one month in a trailer park/motel in Oklahoma following passing weather systems and the parade of people passing by.
"The tape ultimately addresses all the big questions—death, origin and family, religion—as well as the small discomforts of the body, only to reverse their order of importance."
—Margaret Morse, *Framework* (Los Angeles Contemporary Exhibitions)

Weather Diary 2
George Kuchar
1987, 1:10:00, U.S., color, sound
In a motel in El Reno, Oklahoma, George observes the weather and copes with leaking air conditioning, food shopping, loneliness, television, and eating, among other things.

Weather Diary 3
George Kuchar
1988, 25:00, U.S., color, sound
George goes to Oklahoma, but there's a lull in storm activity. It's spring, and though there's romance in the air, the lightning just doesn't strike; so George makes his own rain—of sorts. Despite the drought, the videos must go on.

Weather Diary 3

Weather Diary 4
George Kuchar
1988, 48:00, U.S., color, sound
Attempting to apologize for the lack of good weather in *Weather Diary 3*, George arrives in Milwaukee only to find the drought back in full swing. Since there's not enough good weather, the tape becomes a social diary against the backdrop of the *Motivation of the Carcasoids* project.

Weather Diary 5
George Kuchar
1989, 38:00, U.S., color, sound
A more socially active addition to the *Weather Diary* series, we meet the natives and participate in the rituals of business and schooling and high hopes on the flatlands.

Weather Diary 6
George Kuchar
1990, 30:00, U.S., color, sound
Scenes from a vacation. Music comes on loud and clear and washes over a series of visual impressions of the land and the sky and the faulty plumbing that submerges porcelain bottoms in a sea of unmentionable froth.

Weather Watch
George Kuchar
1992, 15:00, U.S., color, sound
A window or two on the outside world is not enough, especially when you have such a lousy view of things as I had in this Oklahoma residential care home. The majesty of the console-model TV gave new dimension to the concept of time and space and shrank it all down to a 21-inch lump of nature—a 21-incher that didn't smell and permeate the atmosphere with discomfiture. A meditation on the elsewhere and wanting to be there.

The Web of Dr. Satan
George Kuchar
1989, 40:00, U.S., color, sound
A non-stop psychedelic action serial depicting the gnawing bitterness of a UFO debunker as he sinks in a sea of new age imagery and nubile neophytes.

Wet Dreams
George Kuchar
1989, 36:38, U.S., color, sound
Two young women confront careers in a world of violence, lust, and show business. This student/teacher co-production I made at the San Francisco Art Institute is a colorful collage of digital dementia.

Winter Hostilities
George Kuchar
1991, 15:00, U.S., color, sound
The ground is frozen and the whiteness hides the carcass of a thing that once was happy ... but now maybe had gotten gassed by things undigested. The bones of once-mighty and blubbery beings stand erect among midgets or dangle around the necks of dormant cannibals destined for a likewise extinction, and yet there is hope. As long as there is still a little meat on those bones our appetite for living goes on.

Woman of the '90s

Woman of the '90s
George Kuchar
1995, 17:52, U.S., color, sound
Storms batter California as 1995 ushers in a world of computerized characters and unplugged souls in search of electrified juice. The images of a naked past haunt the denizens of today as a wet tomorrow threatens to sweep them into oblivion on a tide of technology. Already water-bogged and bloated, the occupants seek the sun and the worshippers who strip in defiance of Divine dehydration.

Xmas 1987 New Years
George Kuchar
1989, 15:00, U.S., color, sound
In this sequel to *Rainy Season*, George recovers from his depression and

experiences a "little joy" during a New Year's Eve of champagne cork-popping. A tree, a carrot cake, a fire in the hearth, and a spin at *The Wheel of Fortune*—it's all here for the viewing.

Yuletide Surfers
George Kuchar
2001, 15:00, U.S., color, sound
From the crashing waves of a wintry Pacific to the haunted vestibules of a Bay Area mansion, allow entry to this motley crew of ravished revelers who bring their choppers down on an assortment of improvised bon-bons. The acting talents of those in search of holiday happiness find release in this smorgasbord of seasonal shenanigans that feasts on the bounty of the sea and the booty of the breadbasket to bake a nutty fruitcake of feisty spirits and smoked ham. The ocean rushes in as the characterizations run amok on the sands of time that shift unpredictably in this homespun yarn of tangled relationships and beached Bozos. Rejoice in the ethnic essence of forgotten ancestors as they chip away at the ancient varnish of antiquated angst to expose the grain of truth in a gingerbread house of spice and spaghetti. View the turkey and sample its stuffed innards and then awash thyself in the salty brew of a Western waterworld.

Kybartas, Stashu

In describing his work, Stashu Kybartas has said, "I have chosen to work in video and performance because these are storytelling media. I want to tell my stories and the stories of others because I believe that through telling one's story, one can be healed."

Danny
Stashu Kybartas
1987, 20:00, U.S., color, sound
This tape is a moving personal documentary about Danny, a friend of Kybartas who died of an AIDS-related illness in 1986. This powerful work explores the reason for Danny's return home and his attempts to reconcile his relationship with his family members who had difficulty facing his homosexuality and his imminent death. Retracing Danny's memory of his once-high lifestyle in the clubs and gyms of Miami, *Danny* avoids sentimentalizing its subject as it juxtaposes images, text, and voice-over to build a sense of the psychological struggle brought on by Danny's impending, premature death.

Lacy, Suzanne

Although art is often conceived and realized as a private act, in Suzanne Lacy's work the performance becomes a frame in which many people create personal expressions in relationship to a common issue. A pioneer in socially interactive, feminist public art, Lacy's large-scale performances since the mid-'70s have engaged mass audiences through media and complicated community organizing.

Crystal Quilt – Trailer
Suzanne Lacy
1992, 8:31, U.S., color, sound
"The idea was to address the cultural invisibility of older women through art and through action," the voice-over explains as this tape begins. This short tape offers an introduction to the Whisper Minnesota Project, which organized *The Crystal Quilt* performance, an event that brought together hundreds of women over 60 on a Mother's Day in Minneapolis. As the tape explains, "*The Crystal Quilt* is a case study in reframing notions of older women's beauty, power, and relevance. Through it we catch glimpses of life patterns and values lost to our generation."

Learn Where the Meat Comes From
Suzanne Lacy
1976, 14:00, U.S., b&w, sound
A classic feminist video, *Learn Where the Meat Comes From* depicts how "gourmet carnivore tastes take on a cannibalistic edge. This parody of a Julia Child cooking lesson collapses the roles of consumer and consumed: Lacy instructs us in the proper butcher's terms for cuts of meat by pointing them out on her body. As the lesson progresses she becomes more and more animal-like, growling and baring over-sized incisors. Perhaps, in her role as a gourmet cook, she is herself as much consumed as consumer."
–Micki McGee, *Unacceptable Appetites*, exhibition catalog (New York: Artists Space, 1988)
Also available on the anthology *I Say I Am: Program 1*.

Underground

Underground
Suzanne Lacy
1994, 12:00, U.S., color, sound

Each year more women undergo treatment at hospital emergency surgical centers as the result of family violence than rapes, muggings, and car wrecks combined. This startling statistic is the basis for a series of site-specific installations on domestic violence, *On the Edge of Time. Underground*, the first installation for the Pittsburgh Three Rivers Art Festival, used three wrecked cars strewn along a 180-foot section of railroad track to reference the history of abolition and the Underground Railroad and as metaphors for different aspects of abuse. After visitors experienced the installation, a phone booth awaited, where responses could be recorded in privacy on an answering machine. These comments form the voiceover, as it were, of the piece. *Underground* is a remarkable document of Lacy's temporary installation and its 500,000 visitors, and a moving testament to the power of art to effect individual and social change.

Whisper, the Waves, the Wind
Suzanne Lacy
1986, 29:00, U.S., color, sound

In today's youth-oriented society the experience and knowledge of older women is typically unheralded and neglected. Countering these ideas is Suzanne Lacy's *Whisper, the Waves, the Wind*–a performance evoking and reinforcing the strong spiritual and physical beauty of older women. Lacy says, "They reminded me of the place where the ocean meets shoreline. Their bodies were growing older, wrinkled. But what I saw was the rock in them; solid, with the presence of the years washing over them." This tape is a document of that performance.

Larsen, Ernest
(see Millner, Sherry)

Landry, Richard

Richard Landry came to video through his abiding interest in music, recognizing the medium as a new way to fuse audio recording and live performance. Constructing his music through improvisation—with equal emphasis on chance, emotional influences, and experimentation—Landry's compositions move through various harmonies toward dissonance and back again. In his performances of the 1970s, Landry pioneered the use of a quadraphonic delay system that allowed him to perform as a live quintet from his solo performance, combining his voice with four time-delayed repeats. As a founding member of the Philip Glass Ensemble, he was central to the experimental music movement of the '70s and early '80s.

1,2,3,4
Richard Landry
1972, 8:00, U.S., b&w, sound

Starting with an activity as basic as four hands clapping, Landry composes an arresting visual documentation of the fundamentals of music through a play of visual and sonic rhythms. Landry considers these movements "imaginary hand exercises for beginning drummers." As disembodied hands swim through shallow space a strobe light freezes them in the process of clapping, creating a mesmerizing play of eye-ear coordination.
This title was part of the original Castelli-Sonnabend video art collection.

Divided Alto
Richard Landry
1974, 15:00, U.S., color, sound

Utilizing a four-way split screen, *Divided Alto* documents Landry's improvised flute performance, focusing on the harmonics of the instrument as he plays double and triple chords. The camera centers on the elements that make music—the mouth and fingers of the musician—as the music moves from counterpoint to synchronization, establishing rhythms that ebb and resurface. The tape is double-tracked in sound, video, and audio.

Quad Suite (Six Vibrations for Agnes Martin, Hebe's Grande Bois, 4th Register)
Richard Landry
1972, 35:00, U.S., b&w, sound

Capitalizing on the visual aspect of musical performance, *Quad Suite* explores the essential link between the image of music and its sound. In *Six Vibrations* the camera is riveted to a close-up of the four upper frets of Landry's guitar, maintaining an image of the sound easily identified with the gridded field paintings of Agnes Martin. In *Hebe's Grande Bois* Landry improvises on a bamboo flute as the camera frames his mouth, again in extreme close-up, in the center of the screen. There is something sensual, almost obscene, about Landry's lips. *4th Register* is a sonorous piece for tenor saxophone in which Landry deliberately sets out to test the limits of the instrument.

Latham, Barbara

During the late '70s and early '80s, Barbara Latham produced a substantial body of work that innovatively meshed the formal concerns of video with autobiographical, narrative, and political content. Her belief in the active construction of identity is conveyed in her use of fragmented and manipulated images as a metaphor for lived experience. She was dedicated to furthering video art and challenging its reputation as an inaccessible, esoteric field and its hierarchical production structure. Latham was head of the video department at the School of the Art Institute of Chicago from 1978 until her untimely death in 1984.

AlienNATION (see Rankus, Edward)

Arbitrary Fragments
Barbara Latham
1978, 13:00, U.S., color, sound
Using highly manipulated and over-processed images, Latham investigates the process of video as inherently fragmented. Weaving together various people's impressions of the artist and her work, the tape demonstrates important parallels between video, storytelling, and the formation of identity—all processes of active fabrication that blend "lies" and truth in the construction of a certain reality, history, or past. Labeling an image of her talking as "her most recent explanation," Latham addresses "the construction of her video personality" as an identity outside of herself.
Also available on the compilation *Barbara Latham Videoworks: Volume 1.*

Barbara Latham Videoworks: Volume 1
The five videos featured here investigate video as a tool for storytelling and the construction of alternate identities. Ultimately Latham concludes that video is an unsatisfactory and cumbersome tool useful only for the creation of dislocated narratives.
Total running time 1:05:00.
Contents:
Arbitrary Fragments, Barbara Latham, 1978, 13:00, U.S., color, sound
Chained Reactions, Barbara Latham, 1982, 10:00, U.S., b&w, sound
Consuming Passions, Barbara Latham, 1983, 10:00, U.S., color, sound
Curtain: Untold Story, Barbara Latham, 1979, 4:00, U.S., color, sound
Feathers: An Introduction, Barbara Latham, 1978, 28:00, U.S., b&w, sound

Chained Reactions
Barbara Latham
1982, 10:00, U.S., b&w, sound
Unhinging the narrative conventions and stereotypical elements of the whodunit occult thriller, *Chained Reactions* is an update of film noir style. Calling on the cliches of gothic romance novels and television soap operas, *Chained Reactions* presents an increasingly dense collage of symbolic, absurd, and everyday images and gestures, challenging the viewer to find the associative meanings that link them. The soundtrack, composed of whispers, music, and sound effects, sets a suspenseful, unresolved tone.
Also available on the compilation *Barbara Latham Videoworks: Volume 1.*

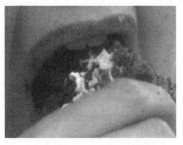

Consuming Passions

Consuming Passions
Barbara Latham
1983, 10:00, U.S., color, sound
Illustrating the modern woman's mantra "I shop, therefore I am," Barbara Latham's *Consuming Passions* examines the passion for sweets as a replacement for a sense of security and a source of erotic satisfaction. Two women speak of their obsessive and sensual relation to sweets, while a third reflects on Jung's theory of individuation, the creation of a unified identity through consumption, saying, "The acquisition of goods is what separates us from the animals." These women reveal their emotional dependency on delicacies—chocolate bon-bons and French pastries—as one character states, "It gives a kind of satisfaction I just can't get anywhere else."
Also available on the compilation *Barbara Latham Videoworks: Volume 1.*

Curtain: Untold Story
Barbara Latham
1979, 4:00, U.S., color, sound

In this tape, the unseen narrator describes her inability to communicate to the camera what she wants to say and to whom she wants to say it. The curtain is the central metaphor for the tape, representing how Latham hides behind the video medium, as well as how the medium presents an obstacle to the artist, functioning as a cumbersome intermediary to expression.

Also available on the compilation *Barbara Latham Videoworks: Volume 1*.

Feathers: An Introduction
Barbara Latham
1978, 28:00, U.S., b&w, sound

Feathers: An Introduction is a self-portrait centered on the story of Latham's grandmother's comforter, which, old and worn, scatters feathers everywhere. Displaying an arresting stage presence, Latham addresses the viewer as a potential friend or lover, speaking in a soft-spoken near-whisper, and gingerly touching and kissing the camera lens and monitor. Then, almost mocking the tape's intimacy, Latham gives us close-ups of herself chewing a sandwich and shaving her armpits, heightening the sense that she has been playing cat and mouse with the viewer all along. Despite the tape's casual and playful tone, and the use of familiar domestic props and settings, *Feathers* is carefully structured to keep the audience at a distance.

Also available on the compilation *Barbara Latham Videoworks: Volume 1* and on the anthology *I Say I Am: Program 1*.

Feathers: An Introduction

Lebow, Alisa and Cynthia Madansky

Alisa Lebow is an independent mediamaker and scholar. Cynthia Madansky is a visual artist, graphic designer, and filmmaker. They collaborated on *Internal Combustion* and *Treyf* (1998), a feature portraying two Jewish lesbians who fall in love at a Passover seder.

Internal Combustion
Alisa Lebow and Cynthia Madansky
1995, 7:30, U.S., color, sound

This experimental video breaks many the silences surrounding lesbians and AIDS. Interweaving the voices of two friends—an HIV+ Latina lesbian and an HIV- Jewish lesbian—the video juxtaposes two very different yet overlapping experiences. The tape points to the often unspoken tensions occurring within this epidemic—survival and power, mourning and loss.

Lerner, Jesse

Jesse Lerner is a documentarian, critic, curator, and professor whose work focuses on issues of Mexican-American cultural exchange and clash: the experiences of "natives" on the border, the complicated identities of mixed-race and heritage mestizaje, and the display of tribal Mexican artifacts in U.S. and European museums. Lerner curated *Mexperimental Cinema*, a traveling retrospective of 60 years of avant-garde Mexican film and video, and is a professor of media studies at Pitzer College.

Ruins
Jesse Lerner
1999, 87:31, U.S., b&w, sound, in Spanish and English with English and Spanish subtitles

Jesse Lerner's *Ruins*, a hybrid film that blurs the line between fiction and documentary, melds culturally skewed anthropological films, staged scenes, and documentation about a Mexican antiquities forger to question not only the traditional reception and understanding of Pre-Columbian culture but also our very assumptions of historical truth as mediated through the camera lens.

Only available on the anthology *Frames of Reference: Reflections on Media, Volume 4, Program 2*.

LeVeque, Les

Les LeVeque is an artist living in New York City. During the last decade, he has produced a number of videos and video installations exploring the cultural implications of technological change. Recently he has been making short projects that transform Hollywood movies into visual psychedelia. He has also collaborated with Diane Nerwen on six experimental videotapes addressing the 1991 Gulf War, the drug-prevention education program D.A.R.E., and other issues.

2 Spellbound
Les LeVeque
1999, 7:30, U.S., b&w, sound

2 Spellbound is a frame-by-frame re-editing of Alfred Hitchcock's 111-minute psychoanalytic thriller (1945) into a seven-and-a-half-minute dance video. Converting narrative suspense into visual velocity and exploiting the symmetry of Hitchcock's camera by reversing every other frame, *2 Spellbound* generates a hallucination of transference—an ecstatic dance where bodies and identities intermingle and shift.

"Normal forgetting takes place by way of condensation. In this way, it becomes the formation of concepts. What is isolated is perceived clearly."
— Sigmund Freud, *The Psychology of Everyday Life* (*The Standard Edition of*

the Complete Psychological Works of Sigmund Freud, vol. VI), 1903
Also available on the compilation *Les LeVeque Videoworks: Volume 2.*

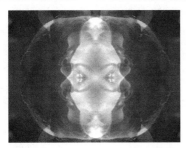

4 Vertigo

4 Vertigo
Les LeVeque
2000, 9:00, U.S, b&w, sound
In this work, Alfred Hitchcock's 128-minute film *Vertigo* (1958) has been condensed down to one frame every two seconds. The condensed film was then
duplicated four times, shifting the horizontal or vertical orientation of the
frame with each duplication. The four films were then reassembled frame-by-
frame, generating a stuttering kaleidoscopic montage where Oedipal narratives of desire and obsession are shifted and displaced.
Also available on the compilation *Les LeVeque Videoworks: Volume 2.*

Backwards Birth of a Nation
Les LeVeque
2000, 13:00, U.S., b&w, sound
Backwards Birth of a Nation is a re-editing of D.W. Griffith's 187-minute film
Birth of a Nation (1915) into a pulsating 13-minute black-and-white phantasm. By means of structural strategies of condensation, the frame-by-frame
inversion of black and white, and playing the resulting work from end to
beginning, an apparition is brought forth where images of racism float to the
surface and are contextualized as a part of the flow of United States history.
Also available on the compilations *The Reconstruction Trilogy* and *Les
LeVeque Videoworks: Volume 2.*

Dissing D.A.R.E.: Education as Spectacle
Les LeVeque and Diane Nerwen
1997, 6:00, U.S., color, sound
D.A.R.E. (Drug Abuse Resistance Education) is a hyper-war waged on over
20 million children in the United States. Despite overwhelming evidence of its
educational ineffectiveness, D.A.R.E. has gained a religious following among
educators and parents and is the only federally funded drug education program. D.A.R.E.'s imagistic and psychological assault is based on the presence of uniformed gun-toting police officers in the classroom. While
grounded in the specificity of D.A.R.E., *Dissing D.A.R.E.: Education as
Spectacle* is an allegorical rant about the cultural dominance of image over
substance, hysteria over reason.

Encoded Facial Gesture #1
Les LeVeque
1997, 2:00, U.S., color, sound
Encoded Facial Gesture #1 is a frame-by-frame animation of two mouth ges-
tures that have been encoded into ASCII (American Standard Code for
Information Interchanges) to spell out a brief text by Sigmund Freud on para-
noia.
Also available on the compilation *Les LeVeque Videoworks: Volume 1.*

Encoded Facial Gesture #1

flight
Les LeVeque
1998, 7:00, U.S., color, sound
flight is a frame-by-frame re-editing of an astronaut walking on the moon into
a seven-minute long meditation on technological transcendence. The unstable, stuttering image depicts the astronaut's struggle to separate from his
body. Comically majestic, the astronaut enacts a late 20th century ballet. A
performance of anti-heroic stumbling, falling down, and disappearance into
white light.
Also available on the compilation *Les LeVeque Videoworks: Volume 1.*

the free space of the commodity

the free space of the commodity
Les LeVeque
1995, 2:52, U.S., color, sound
"In *the free space of the commodity*, I digitally took apart moving image sequences and re-animated them into an encoded montage to create a metaphor of experience where the viewer feels like a fiber optic cable has been hard-wired into their consciousness—a look where the image is simultaneously visible and invisible. My hope was to create a work that re-presented information as a kind of subliminal narrative that critiqued the currently popular technotopian rhetoric."
—Les LeVeque
Also available on the compilation *Les LeVeque Videoworks: Volume 1.*

Les LeVeque Videoworks: Volume 1
Les LeVeque's early works, featured on this compilation, demonstrate his fascination with slowing things down in order to see them better. Found footage, often of key historical moments, are digitally re-edited, slowed down, or encoded into ASCII to highlight underlying meanings and metaphors.
Total running time 16:52.
Contents:
Encoded Facial Gesture #1, Les LeVeque, 1997, 2:00, U.S., color, sound
flight, Les LeVeque, 1998, 7:00, U.S., color, sound
the free space of the commodity, Les LeVeque, 1995, 2:52, U.S., color, sound
A Song from the Cultural Revolution, Les LeVeque, 1998, 5:00, U.S., color, sound

Les LeVeque Videoworks: Volume 2
Utilizing strategies of condensation and re-assemblage, these three pieces take Hollywood classics as their starting point. The re-editing process shifts and displaces old meanings until new ones are made.
Total running time 29:30.
Contents:
2 Spellbound, Les LeVeque, 1999, 7:30, U.S., b&w, sound
4 Vertigo, Les LeVeque, 2000, 9:00, U.S, b&w, sound
Backwards Birth of a Nation, Les LeVeque, 2000, 13:00, U.S., b&w, sound

Notes from the Underground

Notes from the Underground
Les LeVeque
2003, 4:44, U.S., color, sound
Notes from the Underground is a fragmented music video made from the 151 eye blinks George Bush made during his televised speech declaring war with Iraq. Bush's eye blinks have been encoded into Morse Code to spell out a statement from 1969 by the Weather Underground.

pulse pharma phantasm
Les LeVeque
2002, 6:17, U.S., color, sound
pulse pharma phantasm is a frame-by-frame weaving of nine different pharmaceutical television commercials into a pulsating hallucination of worry and relief.

The Reconstruction Trilogy
Through the deployment of various structural strategies, the narrative logic of three problematic and influential films is transformed into a sensuous hallucinatory unveiling of repressed representations in historical dramas of the U.S.'s critical period of nation-building.
Total running time 37:00.
Contents:
Backwards Birth of a Nation, Les LeVeque, 2000, 13:00, U.S., b&w, sound
Red Green Blue Gone with the Wind, Les LeVeque, 2001, 11:45, U.S., color, sound
Stutter the Searchers, Les LeVeque, 2001, 12:15, U.S., color, sound

Red Green Blue Gone with the Wind

Red Green Blue Gone with the Wind
Les LeVeque
2001, 11:45, U.S., color, sound
Red Green Blue Gone with the Wind is a phosphorescent deconstruction of David O. Selznick's Technicolor classic *Gone with the Wind* (1939). Through the structural devices of condensation, the frame-by-frame separation of the red, green, and blue Tehnicolor layers, and the de-interlacing of the video field, LeVeque presents a destabilized illumination of the relentless romantic nostalgia for the antebellum past.
Also available on the compilation *The Reconstruction Trilogy.*

A Song from the Cultural Revolution
Les LeVeque
1998, 5:00, U.S., color, sound
A Song from the Cultural Revolution is a stuttering music video composed of appropriated footage of Bill Gates's testimony before the U.S. Senate. Gates's hand gestures have been re-edited, frame-by-frame, into ASCII (American Standard Code for Information Interchange) signs for a text from "Methods of Thinking, Methods of Work," *Quotations from Chairman Mao Tse-tung* (New York: Bantam, 1967).
Also available on the compilation *Les LeVeque Videoworks: Volume 1*

Strained Andromeda Strain
Les Leveque
2002, 6:54, U.S., color, sound
Strained Andromeda Strain is a frame-by-frame re-edit of Robert Wise's 131-minute sci-fi biological thriller into a seven-minute anxious oscillation.

Stutter the Searchers
Les LeVeque
2001, 12:15, U.S., color, sound
Stutter the Searchers is an undulating re-edit of John Ford's frontier saga *The Searchers* (1956). Ford's violent narrative is restructured through the use of condensation, repetition, and the oscillating de-location of the image's place within the frame. This work pursues a spiraling, percussive search where flashing images endanger assumptions about home and wilderness.
Also available on the compilation *The Reconstruction Trilogy.*

Logue, Joan
Originally trained as a painter and photographer, Joan Logue is a video portrait artist who took up video soon after Sony introduced the first portable video camera in the late '60s. Logue's first video portraits were silent examinations of the faces of family and friends. Since 1980, she has perhaps become best known for her series of "TV commercials for artists." Logue also established the first video program at American Film Institute.

30-second Spots
Joan Logue
1982, 15:00, U.S., color, sound
Joan Logue considerably cuts down Andy Warhol's projection of 15 minutes of fame with this compilation of *30-second Spots*. Produced to be broadcast as individual mini-documentaries on artists and their work, Logue's short interpretive video pieces feature a prime-time selection of more than 20 New York performance artists, composers, dancers, and writers, including Arnie Zane and Bill T. Jones, Maryanne Amacher, Laurie Anderson, Robert Ashley, David Behrman, John Cage, Lucinda Childs, Douglas Ewart, Simone Forti, Philip Glass, Spalding Gray, Joan Jonas, George Lewis, Alvin Lucier, Meredith Monk, Max Neuhaus, Nam June Paik, Charlemagne Palestine, Liz Philips, Anthony Ramos, Steve Reich, Carlos Santos, Richard Teitelbaum, and Yoshi Wada.

Lord, Chip
Chip Lord has worked with video since 1971, first as a partner in the alternative media collective Ant Farm and since 1978 as an independent artist/producer. His early work draws on documentary conventions, but during the '80s he moved toward experimental narrative. His more recent works return to non-fiction: the video essay *The Aroma of*

Abscam (Framed)
Chip Lord and Skip Blumberg
1981, 11:00, U.S., b&w and color, sound
Abscam frames the FBI sting operation known as "Abscam" by mixing FBI surveillance footage of Congressman Michael "Ozzie" Myers with footage shot by Lord at the motel where the original sting occurred—in the process inserting the artist into this moment in history.
Also available on the compilations *Chip Lord Videoworks: Volume 1* and *Selected Works: Chip Lord.*

Lord, Chip

(continued)

Enchantment (1992) and *Awakening from the 20th Century* (1999). He produces video installations as well as single-channel tapes and is a Professor of Film and Digital Media at the University of California-Santa Cruz.

Awakening from the 20th Century

Aroma of Enchantment
Chip Lord
1992, 55:00, U.S., color, sound
The Aroma of Enchantment is a video essay investigating the fascination Japanese teenagers have for the America of the 1950s and '60s, sporting bobby socks and hair soaked with Brylcreem. Weaving together historical anecdotes about General Douglas MacArthur and his own feelings of alienation in the midst of Japanese culture, Lord focuses on stories told by collectors of American memorabilia in Japan and advocates of Americanization. The tape is at turns funny and wistful as it attempts to come to terms with issues of cultural displacement and Western cultural influence in the 1990s.

AUTO FIRE LIFE
Chip Lord
1984, 8:00, U.S., color, sound
Auto Fire Life is a montage of TV news footage loosely categorized by the three traditional arenas of insurance. Music by The Residents helps to distance the viewer from the traditionally "cool" stream of images, creating a disturbing anomaly.
Also available on the compilations *Chip Lord Videoworks: Volume 1* and *Selected Works: Chip Lord*.

Awakening from the 20th Century
Chip Lord
1999, 35:00, U.S., color, sound
San Francisco is a city where the virtual and the real co-exist. It is both a center of multi-media and Internet activity and a city with a vibrant street life and commitment to public space. *Awakening from the 20th Century* explores these issues by asking the questions: Is life becoming virtual? Are we witnessing the end of the city? Will the computer replace the automobile?
Also available on the compilation *Chip Lord Videoworks: Volume 2*.

Ballplayer
Chip Lord
1986, 13:00, U.S., color, sound
Actor Richard Marcus speaks directly and intimately to the viewer, relating a tale of personal loss and then changing the subject to baseball. The tape is about amateur vs. professional, personal vs. public space, and loyalty and self-confidence.
Also available on the compilation *Chip Lord Videoworks: Volume 1*.

Bi-Coastal
Chip Lord
1983, 00:40, color, sound
Standing in front of New York City's World Trade Center and San Francisco's Transamerica pyramid, Lord explains the necessities of living in the Gotham contemporary art milieu and the lure of the Bay Area's relaxed pace and affordability. The two buildings present iconic landmarks of contemporary commerce while Lord enacts a glamorous fantasy of being a jet-setting artist.
Only available on the compilations *Chip Lord Videoworks: Volume 1* and *Selected Works: Chip Lord*.

The Celebrity Author: The Willie Walker Show
Chip Lord
1977, 1:50, U.S., color, sound
The Willie Walker Show deals with the construction of identity by adopting genre conventions of television to create a self-portrait of the artist. The talk show guest attempts to name the makes of his four cars but cracks up laughing, unable to perform the masquerade.
Also available on the compilations *Chip Lord Videoworks: Volume 1* and *Selected Works: Chip Lord*.

Chip Lord Videoworks: Volume 1

A collection of the early video works of Chip Lord dealing with the deconstruction of television and the construction of identity.
Total running time 59:39.
Contents:
Ballplayer, Chip Lord, 1986, 13:00, U.S., color, sound
Easy Living, Chip Lord, 1984, 19:00, U.S., color, sound
The Celebrity Author: The Willie Walker Show, Chip Lord, 1977, 1:50, U.S., color, sound
Bi-Coastal, Chip Lord, 1983, 00:40, color, sound
The Executive Air Traveler, Chip Lord, 1979, 2:43, color, sound
Get Ready to March, Chip Lord, 1981, 1:21, color, sound
Abscam (Framed), Chip Lord and Skip Blumberg, 1981, 11:00, U.S., b&w and color, sound
Three Drugs, Chip Lord, 1983, 2:20, color, sound
AUTO FIRE LIFE, Chip Lord, 1984, 8:00, U.S., color, sound

Chip Lord Videoworks: Volume 2

Volume 2 combines two late-1990s works by Lord considering pre-millenial urban life—virtural and spatial.
Total running time 44:30.
Contents:
Awakening from the 20th Century, Chip Lord, Chip, 1999, 35:00, U.S., color, sound
Mapping a City of Fragments, Chip Lord, 1997, 9:30, U.S., color, sound

Easy Living

Chip Lord
1984, 19:00, U.S., color, sound
Easy Living ingeniously depicts leisure life in suburban America with a cast of little plastic dolls and miniature model cars—the toys that shape American children's ideas about success and adult life—focusing on a typical day in the life of an "all-American" west coast town, where recreational activity and car culture prevail.
A project of the Contemporary Art Television Fund produced by artists Chip Lord and Mickey McGowan with Jules Backus.
Also available on the compilation *Chip Lord Videoworks: Volume 1*.

Easy Living

El Livahpla: Waking Dream

Chip Lord
2000, 11:45, U.S., b&w and color, sound
El Livahpla (*Alphaville* spelled backwards) is about the ways in which we "normals" are encapsulated in architecture and technology. Through the lens of *Alphaville*, we see into a past that exists in the present, while showing a future that looks old. It is a waking dream in which the objects of design that surround us fail to provide the answers or the escape that we seek.

The Executive Art Traveler

Chip Lord
1979, 2:43, color, sound
Lord contemplates whether commercial flights can be considered performance, corporate plaques sculpture, and business travel art. This tape portrays the dreary solitude—or is it minimalist art?—of airports, airplanes, and rental cars.
Only available on the compilations *Chip Lord Videoworks: Volume 1* and *Selected Works: Chip Lord*.

Get Ready to March

Chip Lord
1981, 1:21, color, sound
Lord made this tape in response to President Reagan's National Endowment for the Arts budget cut of $86 million annually and military budget increase of

$88 million. Comprised of footage showing Ronald and Nancy Reagan mani-acally waving from a car and later from a platform during a parade, Lord juxta-poses the images with a clumsy trumpet rendition of "My Country 'Tis of Thee" on the soundtrack.

Only available on the compilations *Chip Lord Videoworks: Volume 1* and *Selected Works: Chip Lord.*

Mapping a City of Fragments

Mapping a City of Fragments
Chip Lord
1997, 9:30, U.S., color, sound
Using the opening of Godard's film *Alphaville* as a foundation, Lord constructs a vision of the evolving global city during the last years of the 20th century. Structured as a series of repetitions, the montage of the changing city is offset by shots of corporate Silicon Valley facades. The result is a dialectical contrast between urban and suburban space, body and mind, chaos and order, and the postmodern and the modern. Shot in Hi-8 video in Tokyo, Fukuoka City, Mexico City, Rome, San Francisco, Naples, and Los Angeles.

Also available on the compilation *Chip Lord Videoworks: Volume 2.*

Motorist
Chip Lord
1989, 1:09:00, U.S., color, sound
Since his early days in Ant Farm, Lord's evocation of the automobile has been the car as avatar, as the spirit of America—that consummate combina-tion of superior organized corporate technology and the pioneering triumph of the willful individual driver. *Motorist* is a 69-minute road picture in which the camera rides shotgun with TV actor Richard Marcus as he plays a drifting driver. Inter-cutting scenes of Marcus with clips of industrial films and com-mercials of the 1940s, '50s, and '60s, *Motorist* pinpoints the patriotic heroics and futuristic fantasies of Ford and General Motors, unleashing the pure romanticism of American automophilia at its most ecstatic heights.

NOT TOP GUN
Chip Lord
1987, 26:00, U.S., color, sound
This tape is a critique of the blockbuster film *Top Gun* and the attitudes of macho militarism that it embodies. The tape uses the unpopulated space of a fast food chain parking lot and the runway at Miramar Naval Air Station to present facts about the vast wasteland of American military spending. These segments are contrasted with promotional clips from *Top Gun* that condense the ideas of the film into 30-second spots.

Selected Works: Chip Lord
This tape collects seven short works made between 1977 and 1984. *The Willie Walker Show*, *Bi-Coastal*, and *The Executive Air Traveler* deal with the construction of identity by adapting genre conventions of television to create a self-portrait of the artist. *Get Ready to March* is a PSA that critiques Reagan's NEA cuts. *Abscam (Framed)*, made with Skip Blumberg, presents the FBI sting operation known as "Abscam," mixing FBI surveillance footage of Congressman Michael "Ozzie" Myers with footage shot by Lord at the motel where the original sting occurred. *Three Drugs*, subtitled "Abused by Americans," offers parodic commentary on American obsessions with caf-feine, nicotine, and gasoline. *AUTO FIRE LIFE* is a TV News collage arranged by insurance categories and set to music by The Residents.
Total running time 27:39.
Contents:
The Celebrity Author: The Willie Walker Show, Chip Lord, 1977, 1:50, U.S., color, sound
Bi-Coastal, Chip Lord, 1983, 00:40, color, sound
The Executive Air Traveler, Chip Lord, 1979, 2:43, color, sound
Get Ready to March, Chip Lord, 1981, 1:21, color, sound

Abscam (Framed), Chip Lord and Skip Blumberg, 1981, 11:00, U.S., b&w
and color, sound
Three Drugs, Chip Lord, 1983, 2:20, color, sound
AUTO FIRE LIFE, Chip Lord, 1984, 8:00, U.S., color, sound

Three Drugs
Chip Lord
1983, 2:20, color, sound
Three Drugs, subtitled "Abused by Americans," offers parodic commentary on
American obsessions with caffeine, nicotine, and gasoline. Without any dia-
logue or voice-over, Lord shows coffee drinking, cigarette smoking, and car
fuelling in close-ups that expose our excessive indulgences.
Also available on the compilations *Chip Lord Videoworks: Volume 1* and
Selected Works: Chip Lord.

El Zócalo
Chip Lord and Gustavo Vazquez
2002, 28:25, U.S., color, sound
El Zócalo is an observational portrait of Mexico City's central Plaza de la
Constitución during one day in August. Soldiers, Aztec dancers, clowns, food
vendors, protestors, rain, dogs, tourists, kites, balloons, and dignitaries all
meet in the public space of the Zócalo. This documentary presents daily life
in one of the largest and most vibrant urban centers in the world, but it
begins with a dream of history and ends with a dream of the space full of
people for a Zapitista rally.

El Zócalo

Lucas, Kristin

Kristin Lucas uses her camera as a diaristic
device, into which she unloads her anecdotal,
performative mini-dramas. Her work resonates
with a sense of social isolation and alienation
from the computer/television/electronic media
that she posits as a surrogate for personal
interaction. The backdrop to Lucas's work is the
empty world of daytime television, cable
shopping channels, and shopping.

Watch Out for Invisible Ghosts
Kristin Lucas
1996, 5:00, U.S., b&w, sound
Kristin Lucas is one of the most exciting of a new generation of young artists
working in video, installation, and performance. Lucas uses her camera as a
diaristic device, into which she unloads her anecdotal, performative mini-dramas. Her work resonates with a sense of social isolation and alienation from
the computer/television/electronic media that she posits as a surrogate for
personal interaction. The backdrop to Lucas's work is the empty world of daytime television, cable shopping channels, and shopping malls.

Only available on the anthology *e-[d]entity, Tape 1.*

Luna, James

James Luna is an artist, performer, and educator
who lives on the La Jolla Indian Reservation in
California. His performances and one-man
shows have been exhibited widely across the
United States.

The History of the Luiseno People
James Luna
1993, 27:00, U.S., color, sound
Based on his ever-changing performance *Indian Tails*, this video features
Luna sitting alone in his darkened room in front of the TV on Christmas Eve.
As he sits, he calls friends, family, and ex-lovers, excusing himself from all
their celebrations. Luna tells us, "In the work there is a thin line between what
is fictional and what is non-fiction, and what is real emotion and what is art.
… There is a cultural element where I let (or seem to let) people in on
American Indian cultures. There are also elements in the work about
American culture that everyone can identify with, and that makes for an
understanding that we are all more alike than different."

Madansky, Cynthia
(see Lebow, Alisa)

Majano, Veronica

Veronica Majano is a filmmaker born and raised
in the Mission District of San Francisco. She
received a Rockefeller Foundation grant to
create her first 16mm film, *Calle Chula*. Majano
has been developing her second project, *Prince
Saves*, about two queer Latina teenagers.

Calle Chula
Veronica Majano
1998, 12:00, U.S., color, sound, 16mm to video
Veronica Majano depicts the character of a street in the Mission District of
San Francisco. This street is personified as a 15 -year-old Salvadoran/Ohlone
girl on a search to understand the changes brought on by colonization, dislocation, and more recently, gentrification. Tracing the history of the Mission
from its first residents, the Ohlone Indians, *Calle Chula* explores the effects
of re-colonization on memory and memory loss. For Chula, memory loss is a
birthmark that was passed down to her from her ancestors. *Calle Chula* is

Majano's way of addressing the causes and consequences of cultural amnesia.

Also available on the anthology *Betraying Amnesia, Portraying Ourselves: Video Portraits by Latin American and Latino Artists*.

Manning, John
(see Rankus, Ed)

Marsh, Ken
(see Peoples Video Theater)

Marshall, Stuart

Stuart Marshall was an educator, writer, and independent film- and videomaker. His work focuses on the historical and political construction of homosexual identity as a deviant, outsider category. His documentary *Bright Eyes* (1986) presents a complex study of the fear and manipulation surrounding the AIDS crisis. Ideologically and formally, Marshall's approach to documentary comes from the alternative media tradition of offering multiple viewpoints and including interview subjects in his creative process. Marshall died of an AIDS-related illness in 1993.

Bright Eyes
Stuart Marshall
1986, 1:25:00, U.K., color, sound
Produced for Britain's Channel 4, *Bright Eyes* is an impressive and complex essay detailing the various factors that have colluded to misrepresent the true nature of the threat posed by AIDS. Exposing the relationship between the mass media, scientific systems of classification, and definitions of pathology, Marshall pinpoints the construction of sexual politics based on a reactionary morality. The tape places the AIDS crisis in the context of the historical persecution of homosexuals and focuses on the efforts of gay activist groups to combat social and medical prejudice.

Pedagogue
Stuart Marshall
1988, 10:00, U.K., color, sound
Performing artist Neil Bartlett plays a gay lecturer whose attempt to go back into the closet is betrayed by the contents of his briefcase. In reaction to Section 28, the law that forbids the "promotion" of homosexuality in schools, *Pedagogue* satirizes the upstanding instructor's dramatic influence on his students. A series of exaggerated testimonials by students parodies hysterical homophobia by proclaiming that Bartlett's arrival at Newcastle has positively disrupted their steady relationships, lives, and identities of all friends and relatives within a 12-mile radius. Burlesquing the interview/inquisition process, a roaming camera lustfully reads between the lines of Bartlett's jeans and black leather jacket.

Martínez Suarez, Carlos

Carlos Martínez Suarez has made more than 50 television reports, videos, documentaries, and training programs about indigenous communities, refugees, and popular arts. His work has screened internationally.

Tierra Sagrada en Zona de Conflicto (Sacred Land in a Conflict Zone)
Carlos Martínez Suarez
1999, 49:00, Mexico, color, sound, in Spanish with English subtitles.
In the documentary *Tierra Sagrada en Zona de Conflicto (Sacred Land in a Conflict Zone)*, Martínez Suarez works with an indigenous community in Chiapas to give testament to the destruction and dissention that the ongoing presence of the Mexican government's military troops in the region have caused.

Only available on the anthology *Frames of Reference: Reflections on Media, Volume 3, Program 3*.

Matheson, Steve

Steven Matheson is a videomaker and installation artist working at the borders of both documentary and fictional narrative forms, exploring the ways that the "everyday" can be re-framed and opened up as terrain for fictional re-invention, aesthetic experimentation, and social criticism. He teaches at Mills College.

Apple Grown in Wind Tunnel
Steven Matheson
2000, 26:00, U.S., b&w, sound
This absurdist, microscopic film noir follows the activities of an underground network of ill people, desperate to create alternative methods of self-care in a world where natural resources are disappearing. While examining the meaning of health, disease, and well-being in the post-industrial world, *Apple Grown in Wind Tunnel* imagines the development of a culture at the margins, linked by illicit radio broadcasts, toxic waste sites, the highway, and ultimately by the overwhelming desire to find a cure.
"To the immune system in the 21st century, here's a sublime video elegy: a tale of illness and grassroots conjuring against the contemporary malaise. This riveting toxic road-movie seeps and slouches forward in search of a cure."
—Craig Baldwin

Matta-Clark, Gordon

Gordon Matta-Clark (1943-78) was a New York-based artist whose work crossed such disciplines as architecture, performance, and photography. Matta-Clark is best known for his cross-section photographs of buildings with their facades sliced away. Much of his work was undocumented, but the film-to-video transfer of *Clock Shower* preserves his 1976 action.

McCarthy, Paul

Paul McCarthy gained recognition for his intense performance and video-based work on taboo subjects such as the body, sexuality, and initiation rituals. His photography and installations explore themes of family, childhood, violence, and dysfunction while using bodily fluids, paint, and food to create elaborate and grotesque critiques of cultural icons. These disturbing and compelling works have shown widely at galleries and major museums around the world.

McGuire, Anne

Anne McGuire has been lost at sea, stalked Joe DiMaggio, fallen off a cliff, had dinner with George Kuchar and Francis Ford Coppola (at the same time), and presented Robert Wise with her version of his movie *The Andromeda Strain*. Her videoworks touch on some—but not all—of this. She has taught at the San Francisco Art Institute and University of California-Santa Cruz and also worked at San Francisco's famed Castro Theater.

Stanley
Steven Matheson
1995, 15:00, U.S., color, sound
The tale of a fanatical tool collector who recreates the world according to logic dictated by his cross-wrench. An examination of the abstract technology of sanity, *Stanley* inverts the documentary portrait–incorporating interviews, found footage, weapons catalogs, and alligator wrestling. An exploration of masculinity and instrumental power as wielded both in the tool shop and in the corridors of the Pentagon, *Stanley* underscores the larger significance of daily gesture in the production of meaning.

Clock Shower
Gordon Matta-Clark
1976, 13:50, U.S., color, silent, 16mm to video
Clock Shower, originally a film, presents one of Matta-Clark's most daring performances: the artist climbed to the top of the Clocktower in downtown New York City and washed, shaved, and brushed his teeth in front of the clock. As the art world's answer to Harold Lloyd, Matta-Clark transforms the architectural facade into a theater.

Only available on the anthology *Endurance, Reel 3*.

Black and White Tapes
Paul McCarthy
1975, 33:00, U.S., b&w, sound
Black and White Tapes derive from a series of performances Paul McCarthy undertook in his Los Angeles studio from 1970 to 1975. Conceived for the camera and performed alone or with only a few people present, these short performances use video to articulate both monitor and studio space. In the first excerpt, McCarthy paints a white line on the floor with his face, dragging his body from one end of the studio to the other. In doing so, McCarthy performs a recognizable formal gesture–drawing a white line. Radically inserting his body into the painting process may have been intended as a parody of prevailing minimalist sensibilities. McCarthy confounds viewers' notions of physical space by seeming to hang from the upper frame of the picture as he spits into an unseen microphone. Body art and the physicality of artists such as filmmaker and performer Carolee Schneemann influenced McCarthy's autoerotic art. He has stated that using the body as part of the ground of the painting was a compelling issue at the time. Related impulses can be seen in happenings of the early and mid-'60s, which often fused audience and performers into the setting and action of the extended painting.

Only available on the anthology *Endurance, Reel 2* or as an excerpt (7:00) on the anthology *Surveying the First Decade, Program 2*.

After Wegman
Anne McGuire
2003, 3:30, U.S., b&w, sound
"The droll conceptualism of William Wegman gets the choke chain in Anne McGuire's ode to pedigree, *After Wegman*. The trim weimaraners of *Two Dogs Watching* are replaced with equally trim boys, better trained than their canine counterparts. Where Man Ray and pal lavished obedience on man's best artist, McGuire's attentive post-puberty pets track the scent of their own desire. Slyly, we realize that the instincts differ–the ingrained servitude of dogs being perhaps more noble than the libido's leash on guys. As epilogue, McGuire enacts another Wegman piece, the slurping of a glass of milk, grown monumental in the foreground. With the impediment of a less tactile tongue, our young lapping lad struggles toward satiation, the cloudy liquid splashing and slopping often just out of reach. There is sustenance here: at the trough of desire, yes, but also in a lineage of artists that hasn't gone to the dogs."
–Steve Seid, Pacific Film Archive

All Smiles and Sadness

All Smiles and Sadness
Anne McGuire
1999, 7:00, U.S., b&w, sound
McGuire constructs a murky black-and-white soap-opera world of endless, timeless, and placeless limbo, where the characters talk to each other entirely in clichés, bad poetry, and other contrite forms of speech—a short TV show in which nothing is resolved. The tape culminates in an absolutely stunning monologue performance by legendary underground film- and videomaker George Kuchar.

Anne McGuire Videoworks: Volume 1
"Funny and unsettling, McGuire's videos are participatory works that leave an indelible impression. … McGuire's videos give the impression that sound and image are often working against each other, that the editing conspires to obscure the content. But their unpolished quality has the impact of a guttural noise, a shocking question, potentially unanswerable, coming from a difficult, honest place."
—Nicole Armour, "Alternate States," *Film Comment* (July/August 2000)
Total running time 38:30.
Contents:
I Am Crazy and You're Not Wrong, Anne McGuire, 1997, 11:00, U.S., b&w, sound
Joe Dimaggio 1, 2, 3, Anne McGuire, 1993, 11:00, U.S., color, sound
The Telling, Anne McGuire, 1998, 3:30, U.S., color, sound
The Waltons, Anne McGuire, 1996, 7:00, U.S., color, sound
When I Was a Monster, Anne McGuire, 1996, 6:00, U.S., color, sound

I Am Crazy and You're Not Wrong
Anne McGuire
1997, 11:00, U.S., b&w, sound
A wonderfully witty work about nostalgia and desperation. Anne McGuire portrays a Kennedy-era singer performing in the space where theatre meets television. McGuire's Garland-esque gestures provide both a sense of tragedy and humor. *I Am Crazy and You're Not Wrong* weaves narrative, performance, memory, and history into an ironic and haunting work of singular proportions.
Also available on the compilation *Anne McGuire Videoworks: Volume 1* and on the anthology *American Psycho(drama): Sigmund Freud vs. Henry Ford.*

I Like Men
Anne McGuire
2000, 00:40, U.S., color, sound
Does she ever! A tiny gem that utilizes paper animation and a snippet of sound to humorous, kitsch effect.

Joe Dimaggio 1, 2, 3

Joe Dimaggio 1, 2, 3
Anne McGuire
1993, 11:00, U.S., color, sound
The artist stalks and serenades Joe Dimaggio in her car as he strolls the docks, unaware that McGuire is secretly videotaping his every step.
"McGuire's use of her camera as a conduit for shared experience [is] at the heart of the piece that first brought her to a wider audience, *Joe DiMaggio 1,2,3*, a video in three parts about a chance encounter. Sitting in her parked car in San Francisco's Marina, McGuire's camera was running when elderly baseball legend Joe DiMaggio unexpectedly walked into the shot. In the tape, she follows him, continuing to shoot, and begins making up songs about her feelings for him as she drives."
—Nicole Armour, "Alternate States," *Film Comment* (July/August 2000
Also available on the compilation *Anne McGuire Videoworks: Volume 1.*

Strain Andromeda, The
Anne McGuire
1992, 2:06:00, U.S., color, sound
"With *Strain Andromeda, The*, the video artist Anne McGuire has created an awesome and spellbinding film that throws everything from story structure to character motivation into question. Put simply, McGuire has taken Robert Wise's entire 1971 virus from outer space classic *The Andromeda Strain* and re-edited it shot-by-shot precisely in reverse, so that the last shot appears first and the first last, though nothing is actually running backwards. As the film unfolds (or reverts?), more and more information about how the characters and their surroundings came about is revealed to us. While initially confusing, the film quickly takes on an ominous and mesmerizing quality that defies description. The original film plot is one filled with tension in a 'race against time' which only adds to this effect."
—Michael Sippings, Brighton Cinematheque

The Telling
Anne McGuire
1998, 3:30, U.S., color, sound
The Telling (1994-98) shows McGuire telling two acquaintances a secret from her past using a three-camera set-up in the Desi Arnez style. The commodification of intimacy is not the strangest thing about this work. The fractured editing, silences, and lapses in continuity suggest vast narratives far more evocative than anything revealed on screen. McGuire uses television vernacular ambiguously to provoke discomfort, two things that television strives to avoid at all costs.

The Telling

Also available on the compilation *Anne McGuire Videoworks: Volume 1* and on the anthology *American Psycho(drama): Sigmund Freud vs. Henry Ford.*

The Waltons
Anne McGuire
1996, 7:00, U.S., color, sound
A deft and cunning re-examination of John Boy's near-death experience at the sawmill. A homespun midnight deconstruction of an entire era of television mannerisms.
"One of the strengths of *The Waltons*, a video that records a session of TV viewing using a handheld camera, is its ability to convey how our surroundings inform our experience. The video doesn't stray far from the images on the TV screen, but our attention is divided between the show's action and the off-camera activity in the apartment."
—Nicole Armour, "Alternate States," *Film Comment* (July/August 2000)
Also available on the compilation *Anne McGuire Videoworks: Volume 1.*

When I Was a Monster
Anne McGuire
1996, 6:00, U.S., color, sound
A performance about the artist's experience in the aftermath of an accident.
"While *When I Was a Monster* conveys McGuire's feelings about her own body after falling off a cliff, it also articulates the universal lack of satisfaction women feel when contemplating their physical selves, and encapsulates another part of McGuire's project: the demonstration of the performative, grotesque aspects of femininity. ... Though she appears to be in pain, our sympathy hasn't been solicited, and the fact that we can observe such a private examination feels like an intrusion ... McGuire confronts the audience with her weakened, disfigured body and reminds us of our own fragility."
—Nicole Armour, "Alternate States," *Film Comment* (July/August 2000)

When I Was a Monster

Also available on the compilation *Anne McGuire Videoworks: Volume* and on the anthology *American Psycho(drama): Sigmund Freud vs. Henry Ford.*

Melhus, Bjorn

Bjorn Melhus is a filmmaker and video artist who creates short, cyclic fairy-tales about movie myths, new media, eternal childhood, cloning, and split personalities. Coming from the first "TV generation" in Germany, Melhus makes uses of different phenomena related to TELE-VISION: the apparatus of identification, the mirror of doubles, and effects of an electronic virtual life.

Meltzer, Julia

Julia Meltzer's works are realized in video, installation, and performance presentations. Frequently working with collaborators, including Elizabeth Canner, Amanda Ramos, and David Thorne (as the Speculative Archive), Meltzer examines problematic institutional policies, communication, and information management.

She has taught video and digital media at Hampshire College and University of California-Irvine and is also executive director of Clockshop, a non-profit production company based in Los Angeles. David Thorne lives and works in Los Angeles. His recent work addresses the conditions of so-called globalization, notions of justice shot through with revenge, and memory practices in a moment of excessive rememorations. His current projects include the ongoing series of photo-works, *Men in the News* (1991-present), and the URL project Boom! with Oliver Ressler.

Mendiola, Jimmy

Jimmy Mendiola is a curator, critic, and filmmaker. He was the first Media Arts Curator at San Francisco's Yerba Buena Center for the Arts and worked as Director of the San Antonio CineFestival. His articles have been published in

No Sunshine
Bjorn Melhus
1998, 6:15, Germany, color, sound
A short story about new bodies, the power of denial, and a state of no sunshine. Two infantile bodies float in a cyberspace ball, connected by two subconscious bodies in the background. The attempt at unification and metamorphosis is interrupted by one part as the other is liberated. The soundtrack is made from early Michael Jackson and Stevie Wonder songs.

Performed by Bjorn and Roald Melhus.

<chatlandia>
Julia Meltzer and Amanda Ramos, 2000, 3:00, U.S., color, sound
<chatlandia> uses the public bathroom stall as format and metaphor for Internet relay chat lines (IRCs). The tape's soundtrack is composed from transcripts of actual IRC sessions; the conversations emerging from this institutional facade speak of lust, intimacy, spunky women, and "what Desirée wants," calling into question the division between humans and machines. The larger theme of how the 'net functions as social space is explored, encouraging the viewer to ask: Is the Information Age actually bringing us closer together or pushing us farther apart? Is the way we interact physically being transformed by our virtual interactions? Can we be intimate through the plastic interface of the computer, and how does the Internet feed this need? Only available on the anthology e-[d]entity, Tape 2.

It's not my memory of it: three recollected documents
The Speculative Archive (Julia Meltzer and David Thorne)
2003, 25:00, U.S., b&w and color, sound
It's not my memory of it is a documentary about secrecy, memory, and documents. Mobilizing specific historical records as memories that flash up in moments of danger, the tape addresses the expansion and intensification of secrecy practices in the current climate of heightened security. A former CIA source recounts his disappearance through shredded classified documents that were painstakingly reassembled by radical fundamentalist students in Iran in 1979. A CIA film—recorded in 1974 but unacknowledged until 1992—documents the burial at sea of six Soviet sailors during a ceremony that collapses Cold War antagonisms in a moment of death and honor. Images pertaining to a publicly acknowledged but top secret U.S. missile strike in Yemen in 2002 are the source of a concluding reflection on the role of documents in the constitution of the dynamic of knowing and not knowing. These records are punctuated by fragments of interviews with information management officials from various federal agencies who distinguish between "real" and "protocol" secrets, explain what it means to "neither confirm nor deny" the existence of records on a given subject, and clarify the process of separating classified from unclassified information.

State of Emergency: Inside the L.A.P.D.
Julia Meltzer and Elizabeth Canner
1993, 28:00, U.S., color, sound
An investigative documentary on police brutality that uses the Rodney King incident as a springboard to analyze the inner workings of the LAPD under the leadership of former police chief Daryl Gates. Containing hard-hitting footage of police violence, the tape also depicts communities working against the daily occupation of their neighborhoods. Through interviews with LAPD officers and supervisors, the tape reveals what life is like behind the "thin blue line" and documents a national crisis of violence.

Pretty Vacant
Jimmy Mendiola
1996, 33:00, U.S., b&w, sound
Jimmy Mendiola's *Pretty Vacant* takes the teen coming-of-age movie and infuses it with a spirited and wry punk mestizaje, as a young Chicana melds inspirations from the Sex Pistols to Mexican iconography to create her own

Mendiola, Jimmy

(continued)

the *San Francisco Bay Guardian, San Antonio Current, Politico,* and *Frontera Magazine.*

MICA-TV

MICA-TV was the collaborative effort between Carole Ann Klonarides and Michael Owen, who began making video portraits of contemporary artists in 1980. Unlike most film or video programs about art and artists, MICA-TV develops a unique video equivalent of the artist's work—an approach stemming from the belief that a viewer can learn more about the artist's work by seeing his ideas directly visualized in another medium. Klonarides is also an artist and curator; Owen owns and operates a film and television production company in New York City.

riot grrrl 'zine (with an emphasis on the rolling "r").

Spanish subtitled version available.

Only available on the anthology *Frames of Reference: Reflections on Media, Volume 4, Program 1.*

Cascade (Vertical Landscapes)
MICA-TV
1988, 7:00, U.S., color, sound
MICA-TV creates a video format to express the idea of verticality and optimism common to the work of artists Dike Blair, Dan Graham, and Christian Marclay. Using a 360-degree camera rig to create a seamless revolving background of vertical camera moves, the tape integrates the work of these artists who deconstruct and then reassemble elements of our culture to create their work.

"Crossover Series" (Sherman, Prince, Simmons) (see On Art and Artists)

The In-between
MICA-TV
1990, 12:00, U.S., color, sound
In this tape, MICA-TV interprets the dark spaces of architect Peter Eisenman's Wexner Center for the Visual Arts at Ohio State University through a fractured narrative of psychological perspectives. Eisenman's pastiche of historical and contemporary architectural motifs, characteristic of the postmodern style he pioneered, finds a parallel in this tale of haunted castles and a disappearing golem told through a correspondence back through time.

John Torreano's Art World Wizard (see Torreano, John in On Art and Artists)
New Urban Landscapes Exhibition (see On Art and Artists)
R.M. Fischer: An Industrial (see On Art and Artists)
Summer of Love PSA (see Rubnitz, Tom)

Miller, Branda

Branda Miller is an artist, educator, and activist who has been working with independent media since the 1970s. Her experimentation with media arts is integrally linked with community organizing. In her collaborative work with groups, Miller involves participants in varied aspects of production so they can take control of their own representation. Miller is currently a professor at Rennselear Polytechnic Institute in Troy, NY.

Ana Mendieta: Fuego de Tierra (see Horsfield, Kate)

Birth of a Candy Bar
Branda Miller
1988, 30:00, U.S., color, sound
In *Birth of a Candy Bar*, the young people who worked on the tape participate in a pregnancy prevention and parenting program at Henry Street Settlement in New York City. The title of the video comes from a poem that comments on sex and birth by way of names of candy bars ("…nine months later she had a Baby Ruth"). Poetry, fast-action music, dancing, interviews, statistics, street scenes, and docudramas are combined in segments written, taped, and produced by each participant–personalizing the problems of teenage pregnancy and assessing its causes.

talkin' 'bout droppin' out
Branda Miller, 1989, 56:00, U.S., color, sound
talkin' 'bout droppin' out examines the multiple reasons why 40% of students in New York, Boston, and Chicago drop out of high school. Students wrote, directed, shot, and edited segments of the video with Miller's technical and creative guidance. Jail, work, vocational school, problems with teachers, motherhood, easy money, drug or alcohol addiction, and boredom are just some of the reasons given for dropping out. Leverock Hazell (a Madison High School Graduate) composed original music for the piece, incorporating 15 hours of the students' taped conversations.

U & I dOt cOm

U & I dOt cOm
Branda Miller
1999, 18:42, U.S., color, sound
U & I dOt cOm is an experimental narrative/documentary hybrid about Zoey, a teenage girl who negotiates her identity in cyberspace. Dreaming about the perfect true love, she secretly navigates 3-D worlds to find romance. A web contest sweeps her into a dreamscape of desire and deception as hidden mechanisms of e-commerce, online data-mining, and real-time consumer profiling monitor her every move. When Zoey finally rebels, her sense of self, her home, and her relationship with her mother are forever transformed in the new cyber-cultural domain. A co-production of the Banff Centre for the Arts. Also available on the anthology *e-[d]entity, Tape 1.*

We Have the Force
Branda Miller
1988, 33:00, U.S., color, sound
We Have the Force opens with the letters of the alphabet appearing sequentially as the youths link each letter with activities surrounding drug use: A is for AIDS, B is for Body Bags, C is for Crack, etc. A story animated with paper dolls shows the way drug dealing is a fact of life in some neighborhoods, and too often the only employment available. The offers of television advertising promoting alcohol, sex, and "just say no" are rebuked by the kids who name a list of things they want to "say yes" to, including jobs, food, good teachers and schools, health care, drug treatment programs, and a media that treats all people equally.

What's Up?
Branda Miller
1987, 33:00, U.S., color, sound
This moving video portrait follows a group of teenage boys who attend the Masada School, a school for juvenile delinquents and social misfits. The boys worked on every phase of the video and present a picture of themselves that challenges society and their own typecasting. The humor, philosophy, and honest retelling of the students' stories details the Catch-22 of living on the street, how parents' problems are passed on to the boys through abuse and neglect, and the struggle each feels to keep hope for a better life.

Witness to the Future
Branda Miller
1995, 58:00, U.S., color, sound
An experimental documentary video project about individuals who have been transformed from so-called "ordinary" citizens into activists, *Witness to the Future* seeks connections that unite people of all cultures, communities, races, and economic classes as they struggle for environmental and social change. Represented are people from three regions of the U.S.: the "downwinders" of Hanford, WA, including Native Americans, "whistleblowers," and white-collar workers from the nuclear reservation; rural African-American, poor, and working-class communities in "Cancer Alley," LA; and Latino and Hmong farm workers and mothers in the San Joaquin Valley, CA.

Miller, Graeme
(see Smith, John)

Millner, Sherry and Ernest Larsen

Sherry Millner has been producing films, videotapes, and photomontages since the mid-1970s. Her tapes are remarkable for their mixture of humor, analysis, and personal insight. Embracing a wide range of issues in her work, from the mundane to the political, Millner portrays an acute sense of the sublime and the ridiculous—an essential virtue when tackling U.S. foreign policy. In addition to his video

41 Shots
Sherry Millner and Ernest Larsen
2000, 14:00, U.S., color, sound
Nineteen out of the 41 shots fired in ten seconds by four members of the NYPD Street Crimes Unit hit the defenseless body of one Amadou Diallo as he stood in the vestibule of the building where he lived in the Bronx. This video essay seizes on the grotesquely bald, factual precision of this numerical data, proceeding remorselessly from number one on up to number 41, rubber-banding ten seconds into 14 minutes, and then snapping it tight, in an intense, formal contemplation of how police violence is produced and then addressed by other forces on the city streets. Superimposed upon the unstable text of the city streets is the electronic pulsing of bits of computer text,

Millner, Sherry and Ernest Larsen

(continued)

collaborations with Millner, Ernest Larsen is a fiction writer, media critic, scriptwriter, and contributing producer for several PBS series and for the National Geographic Channel. His novel, *Not a Through Street* (1981), was nominated for an Edgar award, and he wrote the BFI Modern Classics monograph on *The Usual Suspects* (2001). His criticism has been published in *The Nation, Art in America, The Village Voice, The Independent, Jump Cut,* and *Transition.*

Scenes from the Micro-War

the horizontal instability of the virtual information stream—while a graphic of the scene of the police crime is retraced obsessively, decomposing into fragmented close-ups.

The Art of Protective Coloration

Sherry Millner and Ernest Larsen
1992, 16:00, U.S., color, sound

Q: What was the Cubists' greatest contribution to modernity? A: The invention of camouflage. *The Art of Protective Coloration* asks us to consider the less-than-innocent connections between the making of art and the making of war. Such questions are the first few steps into the deceptively shifting terrain of this videotape, which leaps into a lurid meditation on aggressive male fantasies, linking the domains of art, war, and sex. It looks at binocular voyeurism, the regressive illusion of the perfected body (whether female or male), the phallic gun-toting pin-up, and camouflage. Sex between rigidly impassive mannequins may take you further than your super-ego wants you to go.

Out of the Mouths of Babes

Sherry Millner and Ernest Larsen
1986, 24:00, U.S., color, sound

This video proposes an ironic metaphor to grasp the follies of U.S. government action and inaction in Central America. The process of learning U.S. policy is similar to the process of a young child acquiring the principles of language. These dual senses of literacy operate on several levels. Situating a child's consciousness within the contradictions of history comments on the illusory innocence of childhood and the unexamined but real guilt of the U.S. government, its supporters, and clients.

Scenes from the Micro-War

Sherry Millner and Ernest Larsen
1985, 24:00, U.S., color, sound

*Scenes from the Micro-Wa*r explains, "The worst of times, riots, famine, war could be just around the next corner, and in the battle to survive, this family is going to be battle-ready from here on in." This fractured narrative follows the misadventures of a family hypnotized by Reagan's Star Wars, state terrorism, and Rambo/commando fashions in a time when the family has shifted from consumerist unit to military training force.

Unruly Fan/Unruly Star

Sherry Millner and Ernest Larsen
1996, 16:10, U.S., color, sound

TV's invasion of viewers' domiciles gets turned upside down in the video as a fan's (Millner) domestic life is superimposed onto the set of *Roseanne*, driving home unexpected reverberations as the nuclear family teeters on the edge of dysfunction. A schmooze-fest between Millner and Roseanne ends by detonating the uncommon desire that both fan and star articulate, to GO TOO FAR.

Note: This tape is a director's cut of the version originally telecast as part of the PBS mini-series, *Signal to Noise*, about the videomaker's obsession with Roseanne.

Womb with a View

Sherry Millner and Ernest Larsen
1986, 40:00, U.S., color, sound

In creating this record of her pregnancy and the changes and special insight it brought, Millner borrows freely from anthropology, art history, soap operas, physical fitness scams, sex education manuals, and psychoanalysis. Through the Sunrise of Conception and the Pillar of Saltines, combating morning sickness all the way to the big finish, *Womb with a View* details one woman's odyssey into motherhood.

Mirra, Helen

Helen Mirra works in a range of media including video, sound, text, and sculpture. Her work focuses on the natural world and how people participate in it, with recent interests in deforestation, railroad building, and militarization. Her interest in the history of cinema, film structure, and documents from childhood influence her single-channel video works. The alchemic results deal with interpretation, translation, and loneliness.

Excerpts from Songs

I, Bear

The Ballad of Myra Furrow
Helen Mirra
1994, 5:00, U.S., b&w, sound
"The image comes up suddenly and then continues unwavering: a young person (Mirra) dressed in a black watch cap and pea coat stands at the edge of a large body of water and sings a sea shanty, occasionally flinching to emphasize certain lyrics or fend off the steady drizzle of rain. ... Mirra's ballad maintains the same implicit social critique [as Cindy Sherman's or Yasumasa Morimura's]: that respecting conventional gender codes means a safe but always repressed social role, devoid of any overt expressions of sexuality. The larger irony of Mirra's piece, however, questions such compliant behavior, since mixing up roles and gender codes reveals that none is more viable or mythical than any other."
–Joe Scanlan
Also available on the compilation *Helen Mirra Videoworks: Volume 1.*

Excerpts from Songs
Helen Mirra
1998, 6:00, U.S., b&w, sound
Made from silent black-and-white tube camera footage of the artist taken by her father in the early '70s, this series of loops–through the examination of particular moments and gestures–is evocative for what it reveals and conceals about their relationship.
Also available on the compilation *Helen Mirra Videoworks: Volume 1.*

Helen Mirra Videoworks: Volume 1
In the four videos on this compilation, Helen Mirra utilizes performance, repetition, and the recitation of song to evoke the natural world, the sea, and landscape. Social conventions are questioned, along with our closest relationships and the development of the self.
Total running time 30:30.
Contents:
The Ballad of Myra Furrow, Helen Mirra, 1994, 5:00, U.S., b&w, sound
Excerpts from Songs, Helen Mirra, 1998, 6:00, U.S., b&w, sound
I, Bear, Helen Mirra, 1995, 5:00, U.S., b&w and color, sound
Schlafbau (Sleeping Den), Helen Mirra, 1995, 14:30, U.S., b&w, sound, in French, German, Russian, Italian, and Swedish with English subtitles

I, Bear
Helen Mirra
1995, 5:00, U.S., b&w and color, sound
"'I am nice. I ... am nice. I am ... nice,' repeats the narrator in this personal and highly poetic exploration of the construction of self. Mirra favors repetition as the device for reconstructing the stage of development when a child learns its name. Like a bedtime story, the narrator unfolds the tale of a child who identifies herself as a bear. The story becomes increasingly complex as it moves from one voice to two, in which bear and child gradually become distinct entities and the haiku poetry of the child's identification, 'I, Bear,' is ultimately forsaken for the name Helen. *I, Bear* is filled with longing for a moment when, as undifferentiated child subjects, we could have identified ourselves as anything, including the most misunderstood of animals."
–Hamza Walker, *Persona* (Chicago: The Renaissance Society, 1996)
Also available on the compilation *Helen Mirra Videoworks: Volume 1.*

Schlafbau (Sleeping Den)
Helen Mirra
1995, 14:30, U.S., b&w, sound, in French, German, Russian, Italian, and Swedish with English subtitles
Taking its title from a poem by Paul Celan, this montage is the result of a script that reconfigures of more than 200 lines of English subtitles, lifted from films ranging from *Battleship Potempkin* to *Persona* to *The Bitter Tears of Petra Von Kant*. The disconcerting soliloquy on love and insomnolence is

deliberately attempted in the original French, German, Russian, Italian, and Swedish.

Also available on the compilation *Helen Mirra Videoworks: Volume 1*.

Mogul, Susan

Since 1973 artist/filmmaker Susan Mogul has developed a body of work that is autobiographical, diaristic, and ethnographic. Her work addresses the human dilemma of self in relationship to family, community and the culture at large. Mogul's videos of the early 1970s, as well as her recent documentaries, are often featured in exhibitions, publications, and college courses that examine the histories of video art, feminist art, and contemporary documentary.

Take Off
Susan Mogul
1974, 10:00, U.S., b&w, sound
"As a member of the Feminist Studio Workshop, I was writing an essay at the time comparing male artists' representations of their sexuality with female artists'. Vito Acconci was my model for a male perspective. I had been capti- vated by his videotapes, particularly *Undertone*, where he was supposed to be masturbating while seated at a table. The videotape was my ultimate response and commentary on Acconci as well as an expression of my own sexuality."
–Susan Mogul
"With a good deal of ironic humor, she transforms the 'girl' into a woman and an artist, who positions herself not under the table (as in Acconci's *Undertone*) but directly across from the viewer; alternately discussing the 'history' of her vibrator and occasionally using it."
–Joseph Di Mattia

Also available on the anthology *I Say I Am: Program 2*.

Monk, Meredith

Meredith Monk has been composing, choreographing, and performing since the mid- 1960s. Her voice has a unique timbre, which she explores through a cappella singing and speech. As a dancer and choreographer, she creates hybrid, theatrical productions that incorporate ritualistic movements, lighting effects, and small props. In the slender genre of dance video, Monk been cited for her skill and understanding of both mediums, and her tape *Ellis Island*, made with filmmaker Bob Rosen, has been praised as "one of the most stunning dance videos to date."

Ellis Island
Meredith Monk and Bob Rosen
1982, 28:00, U.S., b&w, sound
Between 1892 and 1927, almost 16 million people came to Ellis Island attempting to immigrate to the United States. For the 280,000 who were turned back, Ellis Island become the "Isle of Tears." Meredith Monk and Bob Rosen chose this site as the setting for a historical/psychological ghost story about our ancestors. *Ellis Island* blends documentary, experimental fiction, and dance modes in what Monk describes as "a mosaic of sounds and images woven together into formal musical design." Tableaux vivants and a photo-documentary stillness collapse the passing of time in haunting scenes of immigrants and their families moving through the clinics, classrooms, and waiting rooms that make up this landscape of memory, pain, and hope.

Meredith Monk: An Interview (see On Art and Artists)

Montano, Linda M.

Originally trained as a sculptor, Linda M. Montano began using video in the '70s. Attempting to obliterate the distinction between art and life, Montano's artwork is starkly autobiographical and often concerned with spiritual discipline. Her avowed interest lies in "learning how to live better through life-like artworks," with personal growth evolving out of shared experience, role adoption, altered consciousness, and ritual.

Anorexia Nervosa
Linda M. Montano
1981, 1:00:00, U.S., color, sound
Through the testimonies of five women, this tape lays out the complex prob- lem of anorexia, detailing how the disease develops as a response to both personal and societal pressures. The common thread in these accounts is how the disease clusters around a need to control one's body and how not eating becomes a way to gain that control, with anxieties and frustrations being displaced onto a negative obsession with food. Perhaps the most dis- turbing issue raised by the tape is the pleasure these women take in their self-starvation, the way in which the disease circulates back into itself in a cycle of self-destruction, bringing these women near death, breaking them both physically and mentally. The last woman to speak is Montano herself, who describes her own bout with an eating disorder and how she became addicted to the "high" that comes from not eating.

CHAKRAPHONICS with Jackie Gleason
Linda M. Montano
1997, 21:00, U.S., color, sound
On December 8, 1984, Linda Montano began a 7-year performance titled *7 Years of Living Art,* based on the seven Hindu chakras, and performed public and private vows and tests of personal endurance. Upon completing the proj- ect, Montano began again and titled the new work *Fourteen Years of Living*

Art. During that time she composed and performed *CHAKRAPHONICS*, a sonic experience for the chakras. This tape can be used as a guide to meditation on the chakras.

Characters Learning to Talk

Characters Learning to Talk
Linda M. Montano
1978, 45:00, U.S., color, sound
This videotape is related to *Seven Years of Living Art* (a seven-year performance of personal endurance Montano began in December of 1984) and adopts the Hindu Chakra system of seven invisible energy centers in the body as a structuring device. The adoption of the Chakra system arises from Montano's commitment to the study of eastern culture and religion. Assuming seven different personae corresponding to the Chakra system—Frenchwoman (sexuality), nun (security), jazz singer (courage), country and western songwriter (love), neurosurgeon (will), Russian choreographer (intuition), and karate black belt (bliss)—Montano questions the concept of wisdom in the Western world. Coupling serious meditation with country western music, Montano shows how to internalize wisdom while surviving in a culture of comical stereotypes.

Linda M. Montano's Seven Years of Living Art (see Barbour, Maida)

Mitchell's Death
Linda M. Montano
1978, 22:00, U.S., b&w, sound
Using performance as a means of personal transformation and catharsis, *Mitchell's Death* mourns the death of Montano's ex-husband. Every detail of her story, from the telephone call announcing the tragedy to visiting the body, is chanted by Montano as her face, pierced by acupuncture needles, slowly comes into focus and then goes out again. The chanting is reminiscent of Buddhist texts, while the needles signify the pain that is necessary for healing and understanding.
Also available on the anthologies *Endurance, Reel 3* and *I Say I Am: Program 2*.

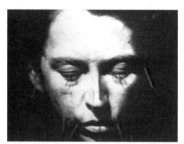
Mitchell's Death

On Death and Dying
Linda M. Montano
1982, 22:00, U.S., b&w, sound
Three nuns in dark sunglasses sit at table playing cards while a nurse is interviewed about "what death looks like" on the soundtrack. As the nurse speaks in medical detail of death as a natural process, the nuns sit with party hats on their heads and lit birthday candles stuck in bananas. *On Death and Dying* is a mocking and macabre look at the institutions of death—how hospitals and religions "manage" death. The tape resolves that "death is a job that you do by yourself."

Primal Scenes
Linda M. Montano
1980, 11:00, U.S., b&w, sound
Over grainy, black-and-white images of a woman giving birth, Montano reads the story of a nun's sexual self-discovery—recounting Sister Joan's growing awareness of her body's sensuousness and sexuality. *Primal Scenes* is an excellent example of women's erotica, focusing on a woman's experience of her body as both sexually powerful and deeply mysterious. Montano uses stirring images of women acting in the rather traditional roles of nun and mother, yet she recasts these roles and demonstrates, from a woman's point of view, the possibility of claiming a fully realized sexual intensity for women.
Also available on the anthology *Surveying the First Decade, Program 4*.

Seven Spiritual Lives of Linda M. Montano
Linda M. Montano
1996, 12:49, U.S., color, sound

"This tape addresses spiritual closure. Video gave me a chance to examine, see, and celebrate the seven spiritual venues, paths, and journeys that I have made: 1) Catholic life, 2) nun's life, 3) yoga life, 4) Buddhist life, 5) feminist life, 6) natural life, 7) life. Publicly, I am admitting that I am a spiritual materialist—been there, done that—but I am also saying that all of my spiritual experiences have worked together to prepare me for even deeper journeys combining all of the sacred technologies I have learned so that I can re-invent my own way. Using a fairytale format lightens the task of looking at my past."
—Linda Montano

The Seven Stages of Intoxication

The Seven Stages of Intoxication
Linda M. Montano
1995, 34:00, U.S., b&w and color, sound
This tape functions on two levels. Montano addresses menopause and acts out her worst nightmares around that issue—playing the out-of-control, alcoholic crone. By doing this publicly on tape, she felt that she could look at, share, and make friends with her concerns with aging. The experience of viewing this video moves from an autobiographical look at Montano's process to an interactive game for the viewer.
"Menopause was a challenging rite of passage for me. Never having had children, I had to mourn my barrenness. Never having given infinite amounts of time and attention to my body, I had to begin doing that as I aged. Never having appreciated my toned thighs and butt, I had to learn how to get along with cellulite and gravity-pulled flesh as I aged. Never having physical ailments, I had to figure out why I had a stroke at 47 years old."
—Linda Montano

Sharada, Wife of Ramakrishna
Linda M. Montano
1995, 23:00, U.S., color, sound
In 1991 Montano met a Hindu couple at Ananda Ashram, the meditation center she attends in upstate New York. Since then, the three have become friends. Mr. and Mrs. Mehta are Ayruvedic doctors; both physically resemble another Indian couple—saints Sharada and Ramakrishna, who lived in Calcutta in the 1800s—and are both known for their incredible devotion to the mystical life. Montano made this postmodern documentary to honor the Mehtas, to present an idealized model for a spiritual relationship and to hold out the possibility for spiritual ecstasy in everyday life.

Linda M. Montano: An Interview (see On Art and Artists)

Montgomery, Jennifer
Jennifer Montgomery's early film and video titles include *Troika* (1998), *Art for Teachers of Children* (1995), *Age 12: Love With a Little L* (1990), and *Home Avenue* (1989). Her work has been screened internationally and has had theatrical distribution in American and European repertory theaters. Emanating from the East Coast, she now lives in Milwaukee and teaches at the University of Illinois-Chicago.

Threads of Belonging
Jennifer Montgomery
2003, 1:33:00, U.S., color, sound
"*Threads of Belonging* depicts the daily life of Layton House, a fictional therapeutic community, where doctors live with their schizophrenic patients. The characters and events of Layton House were drawn from writings of the antipsychiatry movement, whose most famous proponent was R.D. Laing. In this film we see experimental therapies, power struggles, and the individual arcs of mental illness converge, as a community struggles to understand itself and determine its destiny. *Threads of Belonging* was made out of an interest in the alternatives to institutionalization offered by the therapeutic community."
—Jennifer Montgomery

Transitional Objects
Jennifer Montgomery
2000, 19:00, U.S., color, sound
"Begun as a consideration of the upgrading from manual to digital film editing techniques, *Transitional Objects* explores the anxiety and loss inevitable in such a transition while also suggesting the consequences of other life transitions. The video takes its title from D.W. Winnicott's theory of children's use of transitional objects to negotiate the gaps between internal reality and the

shared reality of people and things. Remarkably layered, *Transitional Objects* weaves together considerations of splicing, Winnicott, sewing, motherhood, new technology and loss of mastery."
—Carl Bogner, University of Wisconsin-Milwaukee

Morris, Robert

In 1968, Morris, well-known for his minimalist sculpture, organized *Nine at Castelli*, one of the first exhibitions of post-minimalist, anti-formalist art, which featured the work of Eva Hesse, Richard Serra, Keith Sonnier, and Bruce Nauman. Through the *E.A.T.* (*Experiments in Art and Technology*) project, Morris worked briefly in film and video in the late '60s and early '70s; he employed structural devices such as layering, framing, and mirroring to examine the medium's distinct features.

Exchange
Robert Morris
1973, 36:00, U.S., b&w, sound
In 1972, Robert Morris and Lynda Benglis agreed to exchange videos in order to develop a dialogue between each other's work. Morris's tape, *Exchange*, is a part of that process—a response to Benglis's *Mumble*. At the beginning of the tape, Morris comments on the nature of the collaboration, their interaction, and what they represent to each other. Morris's speculations about work, travel, and relationships are juxtaposed with frozen images of racecars, Benglis herself, images from Benglis's tape, and Manet's *Olympia*. An asymmetry of elements forms as the tape moves from the professional towards the personal—a shift that gives the work humanity and, concerning the development of early conceptual video, its unique historical importance.

Also available on the anthology *Surveying the First Decade, Program 1*.

This title was in the original Castelli-Sonnabend video art collection.

Morton, Phil

Phil Morton began teaching at the School of the Art Institute of Chicago in 1969, and within a year he established the country's first department to offer both BA and MFA degrees in video production. In 1972 Morton expanded the school's media resources by establishing the Video Data Bank as a small collection of student tapes and visiting artist interviews. He also collaborated with Dan Sandin in distributing plans for the Image Processor (IP), a modular video synthesizer. Morton passed away in 2003.

General Motors
Phil Morton
1976, 10:00 excerpt (of 1:00:00), U.S., color, sound
A response to the inability of his local General Motors dealer to fix Morton's 1974 Chevy van to his satisfaction, this tape blends experimental image-processing techniques with documentation of the faulty vehicle. Morton states that he is upset primarily because General Motors "can't get their tech together," and as a video producer involved with using and maintaining high-tech equipment, this strikes Morton as especially bothersome. The tape reads like a consumer's manifesto and addresses the popular notion that video could be used to reconfigure power relations, for example, between manufacturers and consumers. Morton delivers his psychedelically inflected performance with humor and the conviction of an embattled consumer.

Only available as an excerpt on the anthology *Surveying the First Decade, Program 5*.

Movin, Lars
(see Fluxus in On Art and Artists)

Muntadas, Antonio

Examining the media as an instrument of socialization and normalization, Antonio Muntadas's internationally recognized videotapes and media installations investigate the contradictory messages projected by print and broadcast media, architecture, and language. Throughout his work, Muntadas re-contextualizes available imagery in order to provoke the viewer into rethinking the meaning of the messages, creating a breach in the uniformly constructed media flow. Since 1984 Muntadas has also collaborated with Marshall Reese on *Political Advertisement*, a historical survey of presidential television campaign spots from the 1950s to the present, which they update every four years. For two decades Reese has also collaborated with Nora Ligorano on videos, video installations, and sculpture.

Between the Frames (see On Art and Artists)

Between the Lines
Antonio Muntadas
1979, 25:00, U.S., color, sound
"*Between the Lines* is an exploration of what Muntadas terms the 'informational limits' of television—the selections, programs, decisions, edits, time schedules, image fabrications and so on—specifically addressing the means by which 'facts' in the network news are transmitted on television. Muntadas slows and examines the process, observing a newscaster's exercise in assembling events, locating images, and constructing the news."
—Bob Riley, *Currents: Mediated Narratives* (Boston: Institute of Contemporary Art, 1984)

Credits
Antonio Muntadas
1984, 26:00, U.S., color, sound
"*Credits* is about re-reading information. Recycling. Image-making. Wallpaper TV. Zen. Money. Labor. And of course, credits. Through all their aspects and characteristics, credits reflect the way that programs, productions and institutions select to present themselves. ... Muntadas is again dealing with the

"invisible" information that lies behind mass media production and transmission."
–Kathy Rae Huffman, *Video: A Retrospective* (Los Angeles: Los Angeles Institute of Contemporary Arts, 1984)

Liege (12.9.77)

Liege (12.9.77)
Antonio Muntadas
1979, 18:00, Belgium/U.S., color, sound, in French and German
Produced in Liege for Belgium TV, this tape considers how broadcast television functions in a multi-lingual area. A televised Tower of Babble, Muntadas shows the rigid conformity of style and content enforced through the medium, drawing attention to the similar format of the programs broadcast in different languages. Muntadas suggests that the universal language of television is a camouflaged steamroller of meaning and relationships that flattens out reality, creating a homogeneous "TV land"–a worldwide institution that is only superficially related to the individual realities of its viewers.

Media Ecology Ads: Fuse, Timer, Slow Down
Antonio Muntadas
1982, 14:00, U.S., color, sound
A series of three videotape fragments (*Fuse, Timer, Slow Down*) presented as visual commentaries on television ads, these pieces are critical responses to the visual speed, narrative style, and format used in the making and delivering of the moving images. People producing images have been forced (for personal and public reasons) to speed up timing–time is money. This is how society builds its own schemes, structures, and culture, and how it represents them; we are consuming images as we consume food, gas, and ideas.

On Subjectivity (About TV)
Antonio Muntadas
1978, 50:00, U.S., color, sound
On Subjectivity examines how information is disseminated; how people read, screen, and interpret images. How are we affected by what the networks choose to give us, and how do we choose to interpret what we see? Considering diverse interpretations influenced by cultural difference, levels of perception, and the manipulation of the image, Muntadas provokes inquiry into the potential of television and consideration of the intentional and unintentional influence of television on our daily lives.

Political Advertisement
Antonio Muntadas and Marshall Reese
1997, 1:00:00, U.S., color, sound
Presidential candidates are sold like commercial products and naturally television is the ideal medium. *Political Advertisement* depicts the evolution of political ads over the last 44 years, beginning with Eisenhower in 1952 (which was an unqualified success) and continuing up to the ad campaigns for Ross Perot, Bob Dole, and Bill Clinton in 1996.

Political Advertisement 2000

Political Advertisement 2000
Antonio Muntadas and Marshall Reese
2000, 1:05:00, U.S., color, sound
Antonio Muntadas and Marshall Reese have been documenting the selling of the American presidency since 1984 and have expanded and updated the series with every election. *Political Advertisement 2000* features ads from the 1950s through the 2000 campaign. "Sometime in the early 1950s Madison Avenue's hucksters realized that they could sell political candidates like any other product, a throat lozenge or facial tissue. Guided by the cooing come-ons of the thirty-second TV spot, campaigns were soon reduced to photo ops, televised debates, and sound bites. Out were the whistle-stop tour and the scrappy convention; in were the instant poll and the attack ad. Artists Antonio Muntadas and Marshall Reese have created an anthology of presidential campaign spots spanning almost fifty years. Including spots from the

present campaign, *Political Advertisement 2000* is a compendium of the ideological, tactical, and stylistic transformations that have unerringly altered the electoral process. Eleven presidential elections are unfurled: from Eisenhower's minimalism equals sincerity, through Kennedy's up-tempo youthful image, to Reagan's cynical *Morning in America*, and beyond. The artists avoid commentary, allowing the prodigious stream of TV spots to reveal their own truths. You'll see revealed the utter sophistication of media campaigns, the ever-evolving techniques of marketing, and, occasionally, something about the candidates themselves."
–Steve Seid, *Fifty Years of Campaign Spots* (Berkeley: Pacific Film Archive, 2000)

Slogans
Antonio Muntadas
1991, 9:00, U.S., color, sound
Slogans is a visual deconstruction of advertising slogans, a literal and metaphorical illustration of the disintegration and loss of meaning in the contemporary media landscape. Appropriating text from a series of familiar print advertisements–*Choose Your Weapon, Play To Win, Talk is Cheap*–Muntadas enlarges, digitizes, and overlays words until they devolve into abstract mosaics. Accompanied by a banal muzak soundtrack, this display of text as image demonstrates advertising's insidious transformation of language into empty signifiers.

Slogans

Transfer
Antonio Muntadas
1975, 18:00, U.S., color, sound
"This tape is, in effect, a ready-made. Produced by the Pepsi Cola Company for its own use, it was accidentally substituted for one of my tapes in 1974. The mistake in the transfer was a communications mishap that involved a series of people and corporations. ... I wonder what accidents of this sort might reveal about secret channels of information. I see the material on this tape, innocuous as it may be, as a phenomenon that affects us without our being aware of its existence."
–Antonio Muntadas

Video Is Television?
Antonio Muntadas
1989, 4:00, U.S., color, sound
Playing back "visual quotations" of everything from *Poltergeist* to *Blade Runner*, Muntadas rescans the surface of the monitor, questioning the "nature" of media—film, television, video, and image. Television emerges as the medium to eat all mediums, raising the question: Is it possible, within the context of television, to tell art from life or fact from fiction? An endless row of generic TV monitors visually evokes a hall of mirrors as the expression of the cultural homogeneity and bland abundance achieved through the dominant medium of the late 20th century.
Music composed by Glenn Branca.

Video Is Television?

Watching the Press, Reading the Media
Antonio Muntadas
1981, 10:00, U.S., color, sound
"Reading various popular magazines through the camera, the dominance of advertising over content becomes apparent as the same cigarette ads are consistently legible, while the various articles become a blur. A quick scan with no pause for reflection is the only reading possible of the rapidly turning pages. Muntadas asks whether magazines might be manufactured to be read as passively as television, questioning the consequences of active, or critical, viewing."
–Mark Mendel, *Muntadas: Media Landscapes* (Andover, MA: Addison Gallery of American Art, 1982)

Antonio Muntadas: Video Portrait (see On Art and Artists)

Muse, John H.
(see Finley, Jeanne C.)

Muskins, Helena
(see Racké, Quirine)

Nader, Carlos

Multimedia artist, writer, and editor Carlos Nader lives in São Paulo, Brazil. His humorous and playful work addresses issues of national culture and personal identity.

Carlos Nader

Beijoqueiro (Serial Kisser)
Carlos Nader
1993, 29:00, Brazil, color, sound, in Portuguese with English subtitles
An upbeat and engaging documentary with a dynamic, experimental style. *Beijoqueiro* introduces viewers to a Brazilian man who strives for world peace by kissing all the rich and famous people he can reach. Upon hearing that Frank Sinatra was afraid to come and perform in Brazil, he felt compelled to go and kiss Sinatra to prove Brazil was a friendly place. He has suffered many injuries and broken bones as a result of his mission, which curiously enough embodies basic notions of "Christian" behavior yet scares many away. He is now a folk hero in Brazil, his place in history cemented by his successful kissing of Pelé.

Carlos Nader
Carlos Nader
1998, 15:30, Brazil, color, sound, in Portuguese with English subtitles
The question, "Who am I?" has been asked over the centuries in many different ways. Videomaker Carlos Nader adds another approach in his investigation into the nature of the individual by taking the work beyond self-examination and asking it of others. What is revealed is the impossibility of rational thinking to understand the essentialism of human identity. Nader describes this tape as a "non-autobiography-video" about its author; a video about nothing." Exploring notions of the irreducibility of identity to one's color, nationality, or politics, the tape "wants to be anyone's biography. It wants to speak about our oneness—or is it our zeroness?"

Also available on the anthology *Betraying Amnesia, Portraying Ourselves: Video Portraits by Latin American and Latino Artists.*

Nanji, Meena

Born in Kenya but of South Asian descent, Meena Nanji moved to England when she was nine and to Los Angeles when she was 17. Her work concerns the global diaspora of post-colonial peoples and the disruption and replacement of cultural values, traditions, and ideologies that result from these migrations.

It Is a Crime
Meena Nanji
1996, 5:30, U.S., color, sound
Using footage from mainstream British and Hollywood films and excerpts from a poem by Shani Mootoo, this video explores the impact of cultural imperialism and the erasure of language—residual tools of oppression on members of post-colonial societies.
Also available on the anthology *The New McLennium, Program 2.*

Voices of the Morning
Meena Nanji
1992, 13:00, U.S., b&w, sound
A multiple award winner, this experimental tape explores the psychological ramifications of a woman growing up under orthodox Islamic law. Resisting traditional definitions of a woman's role in society as first and foremost a dutiful daughter or wife, Nanji struggles to find a space amidst the web of restrictive familial and societal conventions.

Nauman, Bruce

By the late '60s Bruce Nauman had earned a prominent reputation as a pioneer in conceptual sculpture, and his works were included in the groundbreaking exhibitions *Nine at Castelli* (1968) and *Anti-Illusion* (1969). He began working in film with Robert Nelson and William Allen while teaching at the San Francisco Art Institute and later produced his first videotapes in 1968. Using his body to explore duration and

Bouncing in the Corner, No. 1
Bruce Nauman
1968, 59:48, U.S., b&w, sound
Nauman is seen standing and leaning back in a corner of his studio. Just as he bounces back to a standing position, his body falls again, momentarily collapsing, only to spring forward once more. This action places his body in an intermittent space, occupying a position halfway between standing and leaning, halfway between the wall and the room.
This title was in the original Castelli-Sonnabend video art collection.

Nauman, Bruce

(continued)

repetition, Nauman used video as a theatrical
stage and a surveillance device within an
installation context. While also working on other
mediums, Nauman is well-known for his
extraordinary video installations.

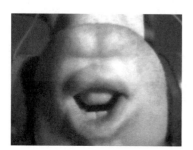

Lip Sync

Stamping in the Studio

Bouncing in the Corner, No. 2
Bruce Nauman
1969, 59:58, U.S., b&w, sound
Repeating the same activity—leaning back and bouncing forward from corner—this time the camera is positioned just above Nauman's head. This gives
his body the sense of constantly rising and falling, his chin just crossing the
bottom edge of the screen before sinking back.
This title was in the original Castelli-Sonnabend video art collection.

Flesh to White to Black to Flesh
Bruce Nauman
1968, 50:58, U.S., b&w, sound
Presenting his bare torso to the camera, Nauman meticulously applies and
removes layers of white and black pigment to his face, arms, and chest.
Beyond the link to body art and the idea of treating the human body as artistic subject matter and material, Nauman enacts a process of self-transforma-
tion—a masque applied and removed—as the tape ends where it began.
This title was in the original Castelli-Sonnabend video art collection.

Lip Sync
Bruce Nauman
1969, 1:00:32, U.S., b&w, sound
An upside-down close-up of the artist's mouth. Nauman repeats the words
"lip sync" as the audio track shifts in and out of sync with the video. The disjunction between what is seen and heard keeps the viewer on edge, struggling to attach the sound of the words with the off-kilter movements of
Nauman's mouth.
This title was in the original Castelli-Sonnabend video art collection.

Revolving Upside Down
Bruce Nauman
1968, 1:00:00, U.S., b&w, sound
The inverted camera catches Nauman standing at the end of the room, slowly
spinning around on one foot, first head down in one direction, then head up
in the other direction. The tape seems to be as much a trial of Nauman's
endurance as an exercise in becoming a human machine, some type of cog
or mechanized weather vane.
"I wanted the tension of waiting for something to happen, and then you
should just get drawn into the rhythm of the thing. There's a passage in
Beckett's *Molloy* about transferring stones from one place to another, in the
pockets of an overcoat, without getting them mixed up. It's elaborate without
any point."
—Bruce Nauman
Excerpt (10:00) also available on the anthology *Endurance, Reel 1*.
This title was in the original Castelli-Sonnabend video art collection.

Stamping in the Studio
Bruce Nauman
1968, 1:01:35, U.S., b&w, sound
From an inverted position high above the floor, the camera records Nauman's
trek back and forth and across the studio; his stamping creates a generative
rhythm reminiscent of native drum beats or primitive dance rituals. However,
Nauman is not participating in a social rite or communal ritual; he is com-
pletely individualized. Isolated in his studio, his actions have no apparent rea-
son or cause beyond his aesthetic practice.
Excerpt (5:00) also available on the anthology *Surveying the First Decade,
Program 2*.
This title was in the original Castelli-Sonnabend video art collection.

Violin Tuned D.E.A.D.
Bruce Nauman
1968, 55:34, U.S., b&w, sound

Nauman stands with his back to the camera, repeatedly drawing the bow across the strings of a violin tuned D, E, A, D. Perhaps more than any other exercise, this tape demonstrates the sense of anticipation built up in the viewer, as we wait for Nauman to walk, to turn around, to play music … to do something.

This title was in the original Castelli-Sonnabend video art collection.

Wall/Floor Positions
Bruce Nauman
1968, 58:31, U.S., b&w, sound
Making himself into a "minimalist" sculpture in the manner of Richard Serra, Nauman moves through various poses in relation to the floor and wall. While other sculptors were using wood planks, pieces of lead, or sheets of steel, Nauman uses his body to explore the space of the room, turning it into a sort of yardstick to investigate and measure the dimensions of the space.

This title was in the original Castelli-Sonnabend video art collection.

Nerwen, Diane

Diane Nerwen is a media artist and teacher living in New York City. Her experimental videotapes use collage and appropriation to explore the intersection of media, politics, everyday life, and, more recently, the intersections between German culture and Jewish identity. She has also collaborated with Les LeVeque on numerous tapes.

Dissing D.A.R.E.: Education as Spectacle (see LeVeque, Les)

In the Blood
Diane Nerwen
2000, 30:35, U.S., color, sound
In the Blood is an experimental documentary about American-Jewish attitudes towards Germans and the role the Holocaust plays in shaping Jewish identity. This layered collage combines appropriated images, original footage, sampled sounds, and fragments of audio conversations to examine representations of Germany, cultural identity, collective memory, and history.

Spank
Diane Nerwen
1999, 7:30, U.S., b&w, sound
In *Spank* an eight-second film clip has been re-edited, frame-by-frame, into a 7 1/2-minute video, which transforms discreet gestures into suggestive, pulsating sequences. This deconstruction of narrative Hollywood cinema exposes and intensifies the authoritative relationship between a man and a young girl.

Novaro, María

María Novaro has been a pioneer woman filmmaker in the male-dominated Mexican film industry. Her features include *Lola* (1989), *Danzón* (1991), and *Que no quede huella* (*Without a Trace*, 2000), which have screened internationally to acclaim for their feminist narratives and expressionist use of color.

El Jardín del Edén (The Garden of Eden)
María Novaro
1994, 1:44:00, Mexico, color, sound, in English and Spanish with English subtitles, 35mm film to video
María Novaro's narrative feature *El Jardín del Edén* chronicles the lives of numerous individuals adjusting to life in Tijuana, including a young Mexican boy who turns to photography as a means to grasp his new environment and a Chicana video curator who struggles to find her Mexican roots.

Only available on the anthology *Frames of Reference: Reflections on Media, Volume 2, Program 1.*

O'Reilly, Michael

Philadelphia-based filmmaker, composer, and writer Michael O'Reilly uses readily available consumer equipment in creating visions of life, death, and the in-between. His work is a hybrid of experimental, documentary, and narrative forms with tightly fused aural, verbal, and visual elements. Delving into installation, he created *United States vs. O'Reilly*, an exploration of the personal and the political of the American justice system.

Glass Jaw
Michael O'Reilly
1992, 17:00, U.S., b&w, sound
In this impressionistic piece, O'Reilly provides a gripping portrait of personal trauma, while detailing the severe mental and physical confusion following two incidents. In April of 1991, O'Reilly broke his jaw in a biking accident, and in July of that same year he was assaulted and had to undergo brain surgery as a result. The tape is breathtaking, as O'Reilly narrates the painful story of his recovery, his problems with Public Aid, and his daily adjustment to pain. *Glass Jaw* is a powerful contemporary comment on the nature of death and dying and touches on the politics of the American health care system.

Orion Climbs

Oppenheim, Dennis

In the early 1970s, Dennis Oppenheim used film and video as a site to challenge the self: he explored boundaries of personal risk, transformation, and communication through ritualistic performance actions and interactions.

Optic Nerve

Optic Nerve, a San Francisco collective, embraced portable video in 1972 and produced *Psychological Bullrider* (1973), a documentary on rodeo cowboys, and *Fifty Wonderful Years* (1973), a behind-the-scenes look at the Miss California Beauty Pageant. These early works established Optic Nerve's aesthetic: free-style narrative, little or no voice-over, and a strong commitment to personal contact. Founding members included Lynn Adler, Jules Backus, Mya Shore, Sherry Rabinowitz, Bill Bradbury, John Rogers, and Jim Mayer.

Orlan

French performance artist Orlan uses her body as a sculptural medium. Since 1990, she has worked on *La Reincarnation de Sainte-Orlan*, a process of plastic surgeries that she "performs," making elaborate spectacles with surgeons dressed in sci-fi costumes and broadcasting the operations live via satellite to galleries worldwide. By exploring a total transformation of self, Orlan delves into issues of identity and the malleability of the flesh.

Orion Climbs
Michael O'Reilly
1994, 30:00, U.S., color, sound
This meditation on family and friends uses, as a point of departure, the relationship between the maker and his grandparents. The piece combines colorized Pixelvision and standard Pixelvision interviews, video beamed from the space shuttle *Discovery*, and English language records from the 1940s to explore this often strained but humorous relationship. O'Reilly creates a child's world, full of curiosity, in which all questions ultimately boil down to the question of identity. In a number of short interviews spread throughout the video, various people tell their most important memories of youth. With marvelous candor, these anecdotes reveal the sense of myth and magic that belongs to children, the sense of acceptance of things as they are, alongside the wonder of discovery.

Nail Sharpening and Material Interchange
Dennis Oppenheim
1970, 6:00, U.S., color, silent
Nail Sharpening and Material Interchange is an excerpt from the compilation entitled *Aspen Projects*. The brevity of these selections give way to the intensity of the action, resonating long after the piece is over.
Only available on the anthology *Endurance, Reel 1.*

Dennis Oppenheim (see On Art and Artists)

Fifty Wonderful Years
Optic Nerve
1973, 28:00, U.S., b&w, sound
Fifty Wonderful Years provides a behind-the-scenes look at the 1973 Miss California Pageant. In the early '70s beauty pageants across the country came under fire from feminists who targeted them as spectacles that exploited women. Avoiding an overtly pejorative position, *Fifty Wonderful Years* lets the pageant organizers and contestants hang themselves.
Note: This tape was one of the first documentaries shot on 1/2-inch open reel equipment to be broadcast on television. KQED-San Francisco "image-buffed" (rescanned it off of a monitor) the tape to maximize its signal stability.

Only available on the anthology *Surveying the First Decade, Program 7.*

Opération Réussie (Successful Operation)
Orlan
1994, 8:00, France, color, sound, in French and English
Orlan denounces standards of beauty, seeing the body as a site of public debate that poses critical questions for our time. Her surgeries are a sign of protest of cosmetic surgery. For her surgery in New York she wanted important changes; for example: the bumps she now has on her temples. This performance was broadcast live with the help of the interactive telecommunication equipment at 14 sites around the world, including the Sandra Gering Gallery (New York), the Centre Georges Pompidou (Paris), and The McLuhan Center (Toronto). As usual, Orlan stayed awake during the surgery-performance while explaining her project, answering questions and comments from the public. The operating room becomes completely transformed as her artist studio. In this project, Orlan asks questions about the status of the body in our society and for future generations via genetic manipulations.
Only available on the anthology *Endurance, Reel 4.*

Orlan: An Interview (see On Art and Artists)

Oursler, Tony

Tony Oursler's expressionistic reveries incorporate phantasmagoric sets and rambling stream-of-diseased-consciousness narrative that serve to illustrate the depths of a psyche becoming unhinged. Oursler's early tapes of personal investigation and social reflection earned him a cult following among New York audiences; his more recent installation work has used projected images on sculptural forms. Oursler has collaborated with a number of other artists, including Constance DeJong, Joe Gibbons, and the band Sonic Youth.

Halloweened

The Loner

EVOL

Tony Oursler
1985, 28:00, U.S., color, sound

In *EVOL* (love spelled backwards), the audience is voyeur, peering into the delirious and erotic dreams of a young man (Oursler). We drift with him through anecdotes that poke fun at the disparity between the culturally accepted stereotypes of sex and love we are taught as children and the realities we discover in adult life.

"A dense linguistic framework of puns and multiple associations to complement his usual pictorial references to adolescent psychosexual neuroses. Low resolution heightens the most cherished myths of male sexual desire and performance."

–Christine Tamblyn, "Whose Life Is it, Anyway?" *Afterimage* 15:1 (Summer 1987)

Grand Mal

Tony Oursler
1981, 23:00, U.S., color, sound

Oursler's thematic concerns betray classic Freudian anxieties about sex and death. In *Grand Mal*, the hero takes a convoluted odyssey through a landscape of disturbing experiences. The tape's free association includes "digressions about the difference between salt and sugar and a version of the creation myth that is both banal and terrifying."

–Christine Tamblyn, "Art Notes," *Scan* (November-December 1981)

Halloweened

Tony Oursler and Joe Gibbons
1990, 6:00, U.S., color, sound

An excerpt from an episode of *ONOUROWN,* this video features the roommates preparing to "get crazy, cut loose, and celebrate the day." The incessantly ringing doorbell incites Joe to poison the "punks" outside by injecting kitchen chemicals into their Halloween candy. Kids, don't try this at home.

Kepone

Tony Oursler
1991, 11:00, U.S., color, sound

Against images of an inventor-chemist juggling brightly colored molecules, psychedelic arms passing out pesticides, and nightmarish landscapes that include trapped live subjects, Oursler presents Hopewell, Virginia, a turn-of-the-century boomtown gone bust and home to a Kepone pesticide manufacturing plant. Although the chemical Kepone's extreme toxicity was well established by 1964, production grew and employees continued to be exposed to the carcinogen—eventually poisoning the surrounding area and the James River. Locals were reluctant to criticize industry policy because Kepone manufacturing was one of the primary sources of jobs in the town. "When they told us it wouldn't hurt us, I went back to work." The tension between the factual statements about Kepone and the expressive video illustrations and soundtrack gives viewers insight into the trauma inflicted on this "sacrifice zone."

The Loner

Tony Oursler
1980, 23:00, U.S., color, sound

Tripping out on loneliness, *The Loner* drifts through one daydream about "her" after another. Oursler nightmarishly fantasizes about the dismal prospect of looking for love in a sleazy singles bar. Painfully aware of his lack, the hero is moved by his constant misrecognition of the object of his desire in an adolescent melodrama of sexual obsession and failure. As one of Oursler's earliest tapes, *The Loner* is especially crude in its details, with many of the hand-painted sets dissolving under a stream of water.

ONOUROWN

ONOUROWN

Tony Oursler and Joe Gibbons
1990, 47:00, U.S., color, sound
As state cutbacks force many mental patients out into the real world, Tony Oursler and Joe Gibbons team up to address psychiatric deinstitutionalization from a comic angle. After years of being cared for, Tony, Joe, and their dog Woody leave the cuckoo's nest and reluctantly face the prospect of finding jobs and cooking their own meals. Their darkly comic adventures include a comatose Tony tuning in to daytime TV and Joe fantasizing about death while strolling in the park.

Son of Oil

Tony Oursler
1982, 18:00, U.S., color, sound
Calling for oil like the Tin Man in the *Wizard of Oz, Son of Oil* is a tale of the well-greased machine of the mind breaking down. Nuts fall off; thoughts turn bad; things don't work. Balancing panic and hopelessness, Oursler argues with phantom voices that taunt the hero with the consequences of his action and inaction. On this starkly social stage, Oursler confronts an individual's sense of responsibility in a society filled with violence, industrial decay, and alienation.

The Weak Bullet

Tony Oursler
1983, 14:00, U.S., color, sound
A bullet fired by two children randomly intervenes in a series of scenes in Oursler's quirky, dismal puppets' land. The bullet kills a suicidal man, re-aligns an antenna, strikes a prize stud bull, and ultimately impregnates a woman by passing through her neighbor's left testicle, then lodging in her ovary. In this metaphor for the spread of violence in society, the bullet represents destructive forces of accidental death and the sexual forces that create new life.

Pagano, Scott
(see Cokes, Tony)

Paik, Nam June

Nam June Paik was born in Korea and educated in aesthetics and music in Japan and Germany. After meeting John Cage and George Maciunas, Paik participated in numerous European Fluxus events. He moved to New York in 1963 and continued to participate in the Fluxus scene. He may be best known for his sculptural "altered" TV sets and installations, but he also made single-channel pieces that explored intersections of music, dance, and video technology. These include *Global Groove* (1973) and *Merce by Merce by Paik* (1973). Paik also worked with electronics engineer Shuya Abe to build the Paik/Abe Synthesizer. Many consider Paik to be the "father" of video art.

Merce by Merce by Paik

Nam June Paik, Shigeko Kubota, and Charles Atlas
1975, 28:00, U.S., color, sound
Merce by Merce by Paik is a two-part tribute to choreographer Merce Cunningham and artist Marcel Duchamp. The first section, "Blue Studio: Five Segments," is an innovative work of video-dance produced by Merce Cunningham and videomaker Charles Atlas. Cunningham choreographed the dance specifically for the two-dimensional video monitor screen. Atlas uses a variety of video imaging effects, including chromakey, to electronically transport Cunningham's studio performance into a series of outdoor landscapes. The audio track includes the voices of John Cage and Jasper Johns. The second part, produced by Paik and Shigeko Kubota, further queries the relationship between everyday gestures and formal notions of dance. The tape includes snapshots of the New York art world, a rare interview with Marcel Duchamp by Russell Connor, and a meeting between Jasper Johns and Leo Castelli.

Only available on the anthology *Surveying the First Decade, Program 5.*

Palestine, Charlemagne

Charlemagne Palestine's work as a composer and performer in the late '60s and early '70s explored sound filtered through performers, instruments, space, and audiences in an effort to bring inner dramas to the surface. His musical interest in externalizing intense psychological and emotional states underlies his subsequent work in video. In a series of tapes and installations produced throughout the '70s, Palestine's use of sound, motion, and ritual set up a primal confrontation with the audience.

Island Song

Charlemagne Palestine
1976, 16:29, U.S., b&w, sound
Strapping a video camera to himself as he drives a motorcycle around an island, Palestine harmonizes with the engine, maniacally repeating the phrase, "Gotta get outta here… gotta get outta here…" His chanting voice merges with the vibrations of the motor, forming an incessant soundtrack that echoes the jarring motion of the camera. Palestine creates a kind of composite instrument in motion as well as an "articulated personal drama." His stated desire for escape is contained by the boundaries of the island. Palestine was trained

as a cantor, and he often used his moving body and sustained vocalizing to generate a physical and aural intensity in his musical/video performances of this period.

Only available on the anthology *Surveying the First Decade, Program 2*.

Panov, Mitko

Mitko Panov was born in Macedonia and educated in Poland and at New York University. His work has received numerous awards, and he has taught film production in New York and Munich. He is currently Assistant Professor of Radio/Film/Television at University of Texas-Austin.

Comrades

Mitko Panov
2000, 1:46:00, Macedonia/U.S., color, sound

In *Comrades*, filmmaker Mitko Panov returns to his native homeland to track down a group of friends—captured in a 1981 photograph—who served together in the Yugoslavian Army; what he finds are elusive trails to these former friends now split apart by the war and ethnic and territorial divides they rarely considered 20 years ago.

Spanish subtitled version available.

Only available on the anthology *Frames of Reference: Reflections on Media, Volume 1, Program 2*

Paouri, Arghyro

Arghyro Paouri works at the multimedia department of INRIA, the French institute for research in computer science.

Etant donné le bleu (Given the Blue)

Arghyro Paouri
1992, 2:00, France, color, sound

Etant donné le bleu is visual narrative—images breaking in a parallel universe, the realm of science fiction, and the fantastic. The repetition, multiplication, and mechanization are intended to form a radically artificial world. The dubious figures playing the roles of witnesses are of only one color. The screen divides into two, three, and four independent compartments that enlarge, in turn, to expose, analyze, and multiply the drama that is played out over and over again, without end. Tragedy rather than drama, without psychological or sociological range; the irreversible fate of blue women, the chorus which accompanies the action—enormous or minute through technology.

Only available on the anthology *e-[d]entity, Tape 1*.

Paper Tiger Television
(see Rosler, Martha)

Parnes, Laura

Laura Parnes is a multi-media installation artist and experimental videomaker who has screened, performed, and created installations at more than 30 different venues nationally and internationally. Parnes uses cinematic strategies in video forms as she fuses high art and low culture, theory and spectacle.

Hollywood Inferno (Episode One)

Laura Parnes
2002, 39:00, U.S., color, sound

Parnes moves further into her interrogation of horror genres and the art world with their sometimes overlapping cults of personality. Grappling with the danger of beauty without criticality, *Hollywood Inferno* takes the viewer through the alienating world of a teenager named Sandy, a modern-day Dante, and follows where her aspirations toward stardom lead her. "Parnes' video advances the other, much darker view—that sex and self-expression are the ultimate commodities, and things don't always work out so nicely for the youthquake in our alienated, violent land. ... Parnes' anger rivals Dante's—or at the very least, Todd Solondz's—in her description of affectless youth selling itself down the river, with only Satan (in various guises) serving as an adult role model."
—Tom Moody, *Digital Media Tree*, http://www.digitalmediatree.com/tommoody/?20467 (20 January 2003)

Note: *Hollywood Inferno (Episode One)* is also available as a two-channel installation.

No Is Yes

Laura Parnes
1998, 40:00, U.S., color, sound

Through a combination of experimental and narrative approaches, Parnes explores the commodification of rebellion as it is marketed to youth culture through the eyes of two drug-dealing teenage girls from Brooklyn who "accidentally" kill and mutilate their favorite alternative rock star. Their obsession with murders and makeovers and their confusion between fashion and transgression lead these girls into a world where nihilism is bought and sold and where rebellion is impossible.

Patten, Mary

Mary Patten is an interdisciplinary visual artist and video-maker whose work crosses and combines many media: video installation, digital media, photography, artist's books, small sculptures, ephemera, found materials, and sound. She is also an educator, writer, occasional curator, and political activist and has led and participated in public, collaborative projects for more than 25 years. Her early formal training was in painting and drawing, but for the past 15 years, she has been working primarily as an installation artist, mainly with video and video-based installation. Patten is a member of the faculty in the Film/Video/New Media Department of the School of the Art Institute of Chicago.

Letter to a missing woman
Mary Patten
1999, 5:27, U.S., color, sound
Letter to a missing woman, based partly on memories of someone who has been a political fugitive since 1983, combines documentary "evidence" and fiction in an imaginative reconstruction of public documents and private history. This is a quiet, obsessive piece addressing the human costs and repercussions of re-inventing oneself—one's body, memories, and future—as a living piece of propaganda. The writer/narrator of this "crazy letter" is an unreliable one, a composite of half-truths, paranoid digressions, and feelings of loss.

Letters, conversations: New York-Chicago, fall 2001
Mary Patten
2002, 11:05, U.S., color, sound
Letters, conversations: New York-Chicago, fall 2001 begins with short excerpts from e-mails, phone conversations, and letters between friends, family, ex-lovers, and acquaintances in the days and weeks following September 11, 2001. As the voice-over unfolds, synapses sometimes misfire, disconnect. The everyday vernacular of concern and helplessness is overtaken by musings about Oklahoma City and Timothy McVeigh, an epidemic of birds, the mortality of elderly parents, the allure of codes and secret languages. Childhood recollections of *The Arabian Nights* evoke an image of Scheherazade that maps onto the faces and bodies of burka-clad women. For the most part, the only faces visible in *Letters, conversations: New York-Chicago, fall, 2001* are slow pans of men, women, and children from Afghanistan, Pakistan, and Saudi Arabia. But these are not "real people," only extreme close-ups of photos published in magazines and newspapers during the past year—images that have come to substitute for peoples whose lives and realities were barely acknowledged in the U.S. before the fall of 2001. The tape negotiates feelings of belonging and rootlessness, normalcy and fear, the struggle between political knowledge and despair, numbness and empathy.

Pelon, Fred

During the '80s and early '90s Fred Pelon made films about political issues in Central America. Since 1998 he has worked full-time as a filmmaker/artist at Filmatelier Eyediom, a 16mm and Super-8 film studio in Amsterdam.

The Dutch Act
Fred Pelon
2001, 24:00, The Netherlands, color, sound, Super-8 to video
During 1998 and 1999, Pelon participated in various Internet newsgroups and lists where suicide was the main subject. Stories unfolded as the film was made; some reached the point of no return. The subject of suicide is very candid on the Internet, due to its anonymity and the freedom it allows from the usual taboos around the subject. The newsgroups and lists have become a relatively safe place for the many people that find themselves isolated because of their interest in the idea of suicide. During research for the film, Pelon also discovered how these meeting places are taken over by anti-suicide interventionists.
Made in co-operation with Roos Geevers, Martijn Gerfin, and Edward von Tetterode. With Ben Duivenvoorden.

People's Communication Network

People's Communication Network was a community video group founded by Bill Stephens that produced tapes for public access.

Queen Mother Moore Speech at Greenhaven Prison
People's Communication Network
1973, 17:00, U.S., b&w, sound
Two years after the riots and deaths at Attica, New York, a community day was organized at Greenhaven, a federal prison in Connecticut. Think Tank, a prisoners' group, coordinated efforts with African-American community members outside the prison walls to fight racism and poverty. The event was documented by People's Communication Network for cablecast in New York City, marking the first time an alternative video collective was allowed to document an event inside prison walls. Seventy-five-year-old Queen Mother Moore delivers powerful lessons in black history, first-person accounts of resistance in the South, and an a cappella performance of "This country 'tis to me, a land of misery…".
This tape was found in the Antioch College Free Library (Yellow Springs,

Ohio), a media access resource project organized in late 1966 by students interested in networking with social movements and media activists around the country.

Only available on the anthology *Surveying the First Decade, Program 6.*

Peoples Video Theater

Peoples Video Theater sought to bring video to the streets and vice versa. Their unique brand of journalism involved gathering man-on-the-street interviews and then inviting participants to watch their tapes at a local "hardware station" or loft space creating feedback and response to important political and cultural events.

Women's Liberation March NYC, Gay Pride March NYC, Young Lords Occupy Manhattan Church, Native American Action at Plymouth Rock

Peoples Video Theater (Elliot Glass and Ken Marsh)
1971-72, 28:00, U.S., b&w, sound

Ken Marsh of Peoples Video Theater (PVT) wrote, "the people are the information; media processes can reach out to their needs." PVT's use of video as social feedback typically involved carrying portapaks in the streets of New York City where they conducted video polls and documented public actions. People participating in street tapings would be invited to their video "theater" to watch and discuss the tapes, taking advantage of a kind of immediacy impossible with film. PVT documented historic public demonstrations by liberation movements in 1970-71. Sampled here are the first Women's Liberation March in New York, the first Gay Pride March, the Puerto Rican liberation group Young Lords' protest occupation of a Manhattan church, and an action taken by Native Americans at Plymouth Rock on the 350th anniversary of the pilgrims' landing.

Only available on the anthology *Surveying the First Decade, Program 6.*

Plokker

Plokker is a French multimedia production and publishing company established in 1998 by Emmanuel Raillard and Frederic Mastellari. Their work features interactive image manipulation, genre mixing, and original music.

Borderland

Plokker
1998, France, color, sound, CD-ROM

This French CD-ROM is an absurd lampoon of arcade games like *Mortal Kombat. Borderland* is an interactive fighting game that assaults our expectations and challenges us to choose who to fight and in what context. *Borderland* is a multimedia project that speaks about video games and the influence of computers on people's lives.

Note: only available on CD-ROM.

Ponce, Magaly

Chilean artist Magaly Ponce's passion for poetry and experimentation led to her interest in working with time-based media. Since returning to Chile from the U.S., where she studied and taught video and new media, she has worked with video, the web, and an installation piece about the cultures of Easter Island and Northern and Southern Chile to engage in a dialogue about Chilean women of the 21st century.

Magnetic Balance

Magaly Ponce
1998, 7:20, U.S., color, sound, in English and Spanish

Incorporating appropriated television footage as artistic experimentation and social critique, Chilean artist Magaly Ponce retells a history of violence and repression from her point of view. *Magnetic Balance* is a self-portrait of the artist as a member of a generation she terms the "children of Pinochet." Recalling the circumstances surrounding the execution of a family friend in 1973 at the onset of the Pinochet dictatorship, Ponce reexamines her relationship to Chilean society. The opening image, the disassembly of an audio tape, opens up a poetic space where Ponce explores the reconstruction of memory and relative truth.

Only available on the anthology *Betraying Amnesia, Portraying Ourselves: Video Portraits by Latin American and Latino Artists.*

Portable Channel

Portable Channel was founded in Rochester, New York in 1972 as a community media and documentary center. The center's activities included providing portable video equipment access and training workshops, producing for broadcast and cable TV, and publishing a quarterly newsletter, *Feedback/Feedforward*. Portable Channel was one of the first small-format video centers to have an ongoing relationship with a local PBS affiliate, WXXI-Rochester. This collaboration resulted in the regular broadcast of *Homemade TV*, a series featuring videotapes by staff, interns, workshop

Attica Interviews

Portable Channel
1971, 8:00 excerpt (of 30:00), U.S., b&w, sound

Portable Channel, a community documentary group in Rochester, New York was one of the first small-format video centers to have an ongoing relationship with a PBS affiliate (WXXI). Portapakers interviewed Sinclair Scott, a member of the negotiating team that went into Attica when the inmates rebelled at the federal prison in September 1971. Thirty-eight guards were taken hostage after prisoners' demands to improve their conditions were ignored. After a three-day standoff between inmates and authorities, Governor Nelson Rockefeller called in the National Guard. During that action, 39 prisoners and hostages were killed. The events at Attica brought national attention to conditions in and policies regarding American prisons. Portable

Portable Channel

(continued)

members, and guest artists. After 15 years, Portable Channel closed due to economic factors; the center's archives are presently housed at the Visual Studies Workshop in Rochester.

Portillo, Lourdes

Lourdes Portillo has been working as a filmmaker and writer for more than 20 years. Her work often deals with cultural and political events in Mexico, Central and South America. Previous films include *Después del Terremoto* (*After the Earthquake*, 1979), about the Nicaraguan revolution; *Las Madres de la Playa de Mayo* (*Mothers of the Playa de Mayo*, 1985), chronicling the struggle of Argentine mothers to bring the government to account for family members who have disappeared; and *La Ofrenda* (*Days of the Dead*, 1989), a portrait of the Mexican holiday that celebrates and honors the dead.

von Praunheim, Rosa

Rosa von Praunheim was born in Riga, Latvia. He chose the name Rosa to remind people of the pink triangle (rosa winkel) that homosexuals had to wear in the Nazi concentration camps. Von Praunheim has been a vital contributor to the history of Queer Cinema since the early '70s.

Proctor, Jody
(see Hall, Doug)

Raad, Walid

Walid Raad grew up in Lebanon and now lives and works in the U.S. His works include textual analysis, video, photography and documentary theory and practice, all which are used on aspects of the Lebanese civil wars and Arab-Israeli conflict. His work includes

Channel conducted interviews with lawyers, negotiators, and community members over a four-month period following the rebellion.

Note: This excerpt was taken from one of the unedited interviews housed in a regional archive.

Only available as an excerpt on the anthology *Surveying the First Decade, Program 6.*

Columbus on Trial
Lourdes Portillo
1992, 18:00, U.S., color, sound
In this political satire featuring the comedy trio Culture Clash, sharp dialogue, physical comedy, and state-of-the-art video techniques are used to dramatize a mock trial of Columbus in a present-day courtroom. With a "Spanish-by-way-of-Mexico" judge presiding, *Columbus on Trial* hits on the complexities of Latino identity in America while slicing into the kitsch consumer icons and buzzwords that stand for racial and ethnic identity in contemporary society. Claiming among his achievements bringing the horse, the wheel, and Julio Iglesias to the New World, Columbus fights for his symbolic life as the "discoverer" of America.

Corpus (A Home Movie for Selena)
Lourdes Portillo
1998, 47:00, U.S., color, sound, in English and Spanish with English subtitles
A documentary about the phenomenon of mass adulation and posthumous recognition following the murder of Selena Quintilla, a Tex-Mex pop singer. "Filmmaker Lourdes Portillo gazes beyond the tabloids and points a sensitive lens on the cultural sensation that emerged around Selena's life and death. A compassionate collage that features starry-eyed teenaged fans, poignant interviews with Selena's family, and lively exchanges with Latina intellectuals who debate her value as a role model. The film offers a fresh look at how this unique Mexican American voice still echoes in the hearts of her fans." —*POV* (PBS, 1999)

Only available on the anthology *Frames of Reference: Reflections on Media, Volume 1, Program 1.*

Transsexual Menace
Rosa von Praunheim
1996, 1:15:00, Germany/U.S., color, sound
Transsexual Menace takes its title from the name of "the most exciting political action group in the USA"—transgendered people who are defining themselves, demanding their legal rights, and fighting for medical care and against job discrimination. Considered by von Praunheim to be the "most fascinating [project] in my long life as a filmmaker," *Transsexual Menace* is a sensitive and carefully crafted portrait that deals with issues openly and honestly. "I was able to earn the trust of many who are often reluctant to be interviewed. Courageous people talked to me, who transitioned in such problematic professions as law enforcement and fire fighting." *Transsexual Menace* gives viewers remarkable insight into the home and work lives of transsexuals from many cultures and countries, including female-to-male transsexuals and those with families and children.

The Dead Weight of a Quarrel Hangs
Walid Raad
1999, 16:54, U.S./Lebanon, color, sound
This piece investigates the possibilities and limits of writing a history of the Lebanese civil wars (1975-91). The tapes offer accounts of the fantastic situations that beset a number of individuals, though they do not document what happened. Rather, the tapes explore what can be imagined, what can be said, what can be taken for granted, what can appear as rational, sayable, and thinkable about the wars.

Raad, Walid

(continued)

The Beirut Archive, an ongoing documentary photography project of post-civil war Beirut. Raad is also a member of the Arab Image Foundation, started in 1996 to promote historical research and to promote experimental video production.

Racké, Quirine and Helena Muskens

Helena Muskens and Quirine Racké have collaborated since 1997, both living and working in Amsterdam. Their work uses video and photography to explore concepts and issues such as identity, human relationships, and utopian communities. They expand documentary narratives by adopting the techniques of digital editing and animation.

Raindance Corporation
(see Ryan, Paul)

Rainer, Yvonne

Yvonne Rainer trained as a modern dancer in New York and began to choreograph her own work in 1960. She was one of the founders of the Judson Dance Theater in 1962, a movement that proved to be a vital force in modern dance in the following decades. Since 1972, Rainer has directed seven feature-length films, including *Film about a Woman Who* (1974), *Journeys from Berlin /1971* (1980), *The Man Who Envied Women* (1985), and *MURDER and murder* (1996). Collections of her writings include *Yvonne Rainer: Work 1961-73* (1974), *The Films of Yvonne Rainer* (1989), and *A Woman Who...: Essays, Interviews, Scripts* (1999).

Charles Atlas, film director and video artist, has directed more than 80 films and videotapes, many made in collaboration with choreographer/dancers (including Merce Cunningham, Douglas Dunn, Karole Armitage, Michael Clark, and Yvonne Rainer) and performers (including John Kelly,

Hostage: The Bachar Tapes (English Version)
Walid Raad
2001, 16:54, U.S./Lebanon, color, sound
Hostage: The Bachar Tapes (English Version) is an experimental documentary about "The Western Hostage Crisis." The crisis refers to the abduction and detention of Westerners in Lebanon in the '80s and early '90s by "Islamic militants" and is examined through the testimony of Souheil Bachar, who was held hostage in Lebanon between 1983 and 1993. What is remarkable about Bachar's captivity is that he was the only Arab to have been detained with the Western hostages kidnapped in Beirut in the 1980s. In 1999, Bachar collaborated with The Atlas Group (a non-profit cultural research foundation based in Lebanon) to produce 53 videotapes about his captivity. Tapes *#17* and *#31* are the only two tapes Bachar makes available outside of Lebanon. In the tapes, Bachar addresses the cultural, textual, and sexual aspects of his detention with the Americans.

Talaeen a Junuub (Up to the South) (see Salloum, Jayce)

The Tower
Quirine Racké and Helena Muskens
2001, 15:34, The Netherlands, color, sound
Back in the days of hippy bliss, Ulrike and her husband used to believe that the world would be revolutionized by their activities, consisting mainly of smoking pot and having sex. Thanks to a large family fortune, none of them has ever had to work for a living. But the "three generation millions"—one generation makes it, the second maintains it, and the third generation blows it— are slowly disappearing. So now the burden of maintaining the tower falls on the children. With the Flatzes, reality and fantasy tend to become pretty mixed up as they talk openly and with a keen sense of drama about their lives, money, art, love, misunderstandings, and dreams.
"*The Tower* is an eerie split-screen visitation with three generations of bohemians who live in a grand, crumbling stone ruin. Their stories of dysfunction, related with matter-of-fact irony, feel as gothically spooky as any page in the vampire virgin's diary."
—A.O. Scott, "New Videos Resonate Darkly," *The New York Times* (19 July 2002)

After Many a Summer Dies the Swan: Hybrid
Yvonne Rainer
2002, 31:00, U.S., color, sound
Yvonne Rainer combines a dance performance she choreographed for Mikhail Barryshnikov's *White Oak Dance Project* in 2000 with texts by Oscar Kokoschka, Adolf Loos, Arnold Schoenberg, and Ludwig Wittgenstein—four of the most radical innovators in painting, architecture, music, and philosophy to emerge from *fin-de-siècle* Vienna. The dance contains, along with a variety of movement configurations, spoken lines derived from famous and unknown people's deathbed utterances. Charles Atlas and Natsuko Inue videotaped the rehearsals of the dance. The idea for integrating some of this footage with the Vienna material came partly from the title, which both elegaically and ironically invokes a passage through time and the end of a way of life, or, more to the point, aristocratic life. Thus the passage of Baryshnikov himself is also implicated—from *danseur noble* roles in classical ballet to his current interests in postmodern dance.
"Beyond the resonance of the title, however, the 21st century dance footage (itself containing 40-year-old instances of my 20th century choreography) can be read multifariously—and paradoxically—as both the beneficiary of a cultural and economic elite and as an extension of an avant-garde tradition that revels in attacking that elite and its illusions of order and permanency. Or, finally, each dance image can be taken simply as a graphic or mimetic correlation with its simultaneous text.
"Some may say the avant-garde has long been over. Be that as it may, the idea of it continues to inspire and motivate many of us with its inducement—in

Rainer, Yvonne

(continued)

DANCENOISE, Marina Abramovic, Karen Finley, Diamanda Galas, and Leigh Bowery). Throughout his career, Atlas has also been involved as collaborator in live performance work as director and also as designer of sets, costumes, lighting, and mixed media presentations.

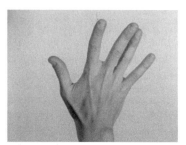

Hand Movie

the words of playwright/director Richard Foreman—to 'resist the present.'"
—Yvonne Rainer

Also available on the DVD compilation *A Woman Who...: Selected Works of Yvonne Rainer*, Disc 1.

Five Easy Pieces: Early Films

Yvonne Rainer

A compilation of five early short films made between 1966 to 1969.
Total running time 48:00.
Contents:
Hand Movie, Yvonne Rainer, 1966, 5:00, U.S., b&w, silent, 8mm
Volleyball (Foot Film), Yvonne Rainer, 1967, 10:00, U.S., b&w, silent, 16mm
Rhode Island Red, Yvonne Rainer, 1968, 10:00, U.S., b&w, silent, 16mm
Trio Film, Yvonne Rainer, 1968, 13:00, U.S., b&w, silent, 16mm
Line, Yvonne Rainer, 1969, 10:00, U.S., b&w, silent,16mm
Also available on the DVD compilation *A Woman Who...: Selected Works of Yvonne Rainer*, Disc 2.

Hand Movie

Yvonne Rainer
1966, 5:00, U.S., b&w, silent, 8mm
Close-up of a hand, the fingers of which enact a sensuous dance.
With camerawork by William Davis.
Available on the compilation *Five Easy Pieces: Early Films* and on the DVD compilation *A Woman Who...: Selected Works of Yvonne Rainer*, Disc 2.

Line

Yvonne Rainer
1969, 10:00, U.S., b&w, silent, 16mm
A blonde woman (Susan Marshall) in white pants and shirt interacts with a moving round object and the camera.
With camerawork by Phill Niblock.
Available on the compilation *Five Easy Pieces: Early Films* and on the DVD compilation *A Woman Who...: Selected Works of Yvonne Rainer*, Disc 2.

Rainer Variations

Charles Atlas
2002, 41:30, U.S., b&w and color, sound
"In the spring of 2002 I handed over to Charles Atlas a collection of films and videotapes in various formats that I had been accumulating with an eye to his editing them into what I call a 'faux Rainer portrait' (though he may well call the final product something else). The mix contained everything from interviews, rehearsals, films, and performance fragments to 'impersonations,' or actual Rainer interviews and rehearsals directed by me and re-enacted by others, in this case, the Martha Graham impersonator Richard Move and noted actor Kathleen Chalfant. Such a ploy is in keeping with my long-standing fascination with the phenomenon of performance and its potential for dodgy dissembling. Also at play here is a skepticism about the conventions of the documentary form that purports to reveal the 'real' artist who ultimately remains a persona or crafty impersonator of her own idealized self-image. ... The liberties that Atlas takes with those hallowed filmic and literary traditions of continuity and coherence appeal to my sense of mischief and play."
—Yvonne Rainer

"For me *Rainer Variations* is a hybrid: a weave of impressionistic portrait, found footage construction, and video sampler. Aside from formal issues, Yvonne Rainer's knotty process of thinking, her unique brand of humor, and her engaging presence are the things that were foremost in my mind as I worked on the tape. What I hope will emerge from this process is an interrogative portrait of an artist for whom I have great respect and affection."
—Charles Atlas

Only available on the DVD compilation *A Woman Who...: Selected Works of Yvonne Rainer*, Disc 1.

Rhode Island Red
Yvonne Rainer
1968, 10:00, U.S., b&w, silent, 16mm
Ten minutes in an enormous chicken coop.
With camerawork by Roy Levin.
Available on the compilation *Five Easy Pieces: Early Films* and on the DVD compilation *A Woman Who...: Selected Works of Yvonne Rainer, Disc 2.*

Trio A
Yvonne Rainer
1978, 10:30, U.S., b&w, silent
This tape documents a solo performance of Yvonne Rainer's seminal modern dance piece, *Trio A*, which was originally performed in 1966 at Judson Memorial Church in New York City. It has subsequently been performed in many incarnations by Rainer and dancers she has trained.
"The indivual sequences last from 4 1/2 to 5 minutes, depending on each performer's physical inclination. Two primary characteristics of the dance are its unmodulated continuity and its imperative involving the gaze. The eyes are always averted from direct confrontation with the audience via independent movement of the head or closure of the eyes or simple casting down of the gaze. ... In 1978, five years after I had stopped performing, I performed it in Merce Cunningham's studio for a 16mm film shoot (produced by Sally Banes)."
–Yvonne Rainer
With camera work by Robert Alexander.
Available on the DVD compilation *A Woman Who...: Selected Works of Yvonne Rainer, Disc 2.*

Trio A

Trio Film
Yvonne Rainer
1968, 13:00, U.S., b&w, silent,16mm
Two nudes, a man and a woman, interact with each other and a large balloon in a white living room.
Performed by Steve Paxton and Becky Arnold, with camerawork by Phill Niblock.
Available on the compilation *Five Easy Pieces: Early Films* and on the DVD compilation *A Woman Who...: Selected Works of Yvonne Rainer, Disc 2.*

Volleyball (Foot Film)
Yvonne Rainer
1967, 10:00, U.S., b&w, silent,16mm
A volleyball is rolled into the frame and comes to rest. Two legs in sneakers, seen from the knees down, enter the frame and stand beside it. Cut to new angle, same characters and actions.
With camerawork by Bud Wirtschafter.
Available on the compilation *Five Easy Pieces: Early Films* and on the DVD compilation *A Woman Who...: Selected Works of Yvonne Rainer, Disc 2.*

Volleyball (Foot Film)

A Woman Who...: Selected Works of Yvonne Rainer, Disc 1
A special edition DVD compilation of two recent works by or about media artist and choreographer Yvonne Rainer.
Total running time 1:12:30.
Contents:
After Many a Summer Dies the Swan: Hybrid, Yvonne Rainer, 2002, 31:00, U.S., color, sound
Rainer Variations, Charles Atlas, 2002, 41:30, U.S., b&w and color, sound

A Woman Who...: Selected Works of Yvonne Rainer, Disc 2
A special edition DVD compilation of one historically important dance piece and five short early films by Yvonne Rainer.
Total running time 1:08:30.
Contents:
Trio A, Yvonne Rainer, 1978, 10:30, U.S., b&w, silent, 16mm

Hand Movie, Yvonne Rainer, 1966, 5:00, U.S., b&w, silent, 8mm
Volleyball (Foot Film), Yvonne Rainer, 1967, 10:00, U.S., b&w, silent, 16mm
Rhode Island Red, Yvonne Rainer, 1968, 10:00, U.S., b&w, silent, 16mm
Trio Film, Yvonne Rainer, 1968, 13:00, U.S., b&w, silent, 16mm
Line, Yvonne Rainer, 1969, 10:00, U.S., b&w, silent, 16mm

Yvonne Rainer: An Interview (see On Art and Artists)

Ramos, Anthony

Anthony Ramos began working in video in the early '70s when, in addition to producing his own tapes, he served as a video consultant to the United Nations and the National Council of Churches. Ramos used video as a tool for breaking down mass mediated "truth" and as a means of cultural documentation. Having served an 18-month prison sentence for draft evasion, Ramos produced *About Media* (1977), juxtaposing network news stories with his own unedited footage. Ramos has documented the end of Portugal's African colonialism in Cape Verde and Guinea-Bissau, as well as the 1980 Iran hostage crisis.

About Media
Anthony Ramos
1977, 17:00 excerpt (of 26:00), U.S., color, sound
Anthony Ramos's astute deconstruction of television news focuses on his part in the media coverage of President Jimmy Carter's 1977 declaration of amnesty for Vietnam draft evaders. News reporter Gabe Pressman, whose film crew meets Ramos's video crew in a confrontation between technologies and sensibilities, interviewed Ramos, who had served an 18-month prison sentence for draft evasion. At the time, some broadcast television news crews still used 16mm film, although the expensive transition to ENG (electronic newsgathering) systems had begun in 1974. Ramos contrasts the unedited interview footage—and patronizing comments of the news crew—with Pressman's final televised news report. In his ironic manipulation of the material, Ramos exposes the illusion of "objective" news and the point of view found in any work of journalism. Ramos' tape also presents an important chapter of social history; accounts of Ramos' prison term and his friend's experience in the trenches of Vietnam underscore the extent to which the Vietnam War informed the political and cultural activity of this era.

Only available on the anthology *Surveying the First Decade, Program 7.*

Rankin, Scott

Scott Rankin's work is about personal, social, cognitive, and linguistic relationships—their structure and how they influence the way we think and view the world. Reflecting Rankin's interest in what could be called a phenomenology of linguistics, his work tracks the movement of time and people to investigate the ways in which experience is categorized and transfused into metaphor, memory, and culture.

The Pure
Scott Rankin
1993, 1:00:00, U.S., color, sound
Using footage from a trip to the Orient—images of objects, products, the city, and nature—Rankin investigates society's reverence for the "exotic" and the "pure" as manifested in tourism, Communism, Coca-Cola, Las Vegas, the Civil War, Hollywood, and photography. Examining the common idealization of things distant in time or space, *The Pure* didactically reflects upon our societal penchant for categorization that begins with childhood games and is reflected in the way our culture organizes itself and the world around it. Taking the disciplining structures of natural history, art, zoology, and law, Rankin leads the viewer through an enlightened tour of cultural analysis while providing insight into the nature of language and observation.

Rankus, Edward

Edward Rankus is an independent video artist whose work references the symbolic systems of science-fiction films, behavioral psychology experiments, and hypnosis. Concerned with the hazy borderline between inner and outer worlds, his work recalls a surrealist aesthetic. Rankus's work is masterfully edited and deeply ironic, and he is able to wring drama from mundane subjects. As a student of Dan Sandin and Phil Morton, Rankus is part of the second generation of Chicago video artists whose approach to video differed from their more process-oriented teachers. Since the mid-'70s, John Manning has been designing installations and tapes that rely

AlienNATION
Edward Rankus, John Manning, and Barbara Latham
1980, 29:00, U.S., color, sound
"Mining an ironic vein by turning technology against itself, *AlienNATION* undercuts the sociological ramifications of modern living. It is an astounding compendium of sci-fi images, textbook diagrams, special effects, and studio props, which together build multiple readings of the alien, the mysterious, and the obscure in American culture. From spaceships to tinker toys, porno pin-ups to modern office furniture, *AlienNATION* uses expert editing and a wonderfully kitsch soundtrack to examine the dizzying effect of 'the future' on mankind, including the pressure toward corporate conformity placed upon the average worker adrift in the workplace of tomorrow. Rats and laboratory mice figure throughout the tape, walking on monitors and spinning on turntables, perhaps functioning as stand-ins for humans caught in the Space/rat race. What characterizes this particular video process (or 'experimental' total flow) is a ceaseless rotation of elements that change at every moment, with the result that no single element can occupy the position of 'interpretant' (or that of primary sign) for any length of time, but must be dislodged in the following instant, where it will be 'interpreted' or narrativized by a radically different kind

Rankus, Edward
(continued)

on microcomputer-based audio and video systems for fine arts applications. Manning's sense of humor and mild disdain for science and technology are apparent in the technological dystopia of *AlienNATION* (1980).

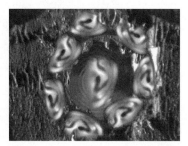

Go Fall Apart

Naked Doom

of logo or image altogether."
—Fredric Jameson, "Surrealism Without the Unconscious" in *Postmodernism, or the Cultural Logic of Late Capitalism* (Durham, N.C.: Duke University Press, 1991)
Also available on the compilation *Ed Rankus Videoworks: Volume 1.*

Edward Rankus Videoworks: Volume 1
Total running time 56:00.
Contents:
AlienNATION, Edward Rankus, John Manning, and Barbara Latham, 1980, 29:00, U.S., color, sound
Naked Doom, Edward Rankus, 1983, 17:00, U.S., b&w, sound
She Heard Voices, Edward Rankus, 1986, 10:00, U.S., b&w and color, silent

Go Fall Apart
Edward Rankus
2003, 18:25, U.S., color, sound
An erotic/mystical misadventure in which the allure of the religious path is strewn with earthly temptations. Struggling with a bogus Zen koan involving flowers in keyholes and jumping through windows, the protagonist will end up entering, by the conclusion, the realm of subatomic particles, thereby achieving transcendence-of-a-sort. On the soundtrack, operatic quotations comment ironically (and sometimes sincerely) on the visual proceedings.
"Rankus embraces the vagaries of video, pro and con, to present a multi-layered visual onslaught. Borrowing freely from the surrealists, Rankus explores the nature of destruction from various angles."
—John Petrakis, "Onion City's Art Films Have Layers," *Chicago Tribune* (12 September 2003)

Naked Doom
Edward Rankus
1983, 17:00, U.S., b&w, sound
Rankus's elegant black-and-white video takes us into an intensely dark inner world. The visual elements remind us of clues in a mystery story: dark corridors, half-revealed bodies, a man with a gun, a throw of the dice. But Rankus complicates the mystery by adding scientific symbols: a flickering brain, see-through bodies, and diagrams of the head, a skeletal hand. Rankus uses quirky props, lights, actors, and computer imaging to create a labyrinthine space reminiscent of di Chirico's paintings—one that reads as an open metaphor for the subterranean desires of the human mind.
Also available on the compilation *Edward Rankus Videoworks: Volume 1.*

Nerve Language
Edward Rankus
1995, 10:07, U.S., b&w, sound
Forming a loose trilogy with Rankus's two previous works (*Naked Doom* and *She Heard Voices*), *Nerve Language* furthers his visual investigation into the ambiguous mingling of inner and outer worlds. In strikingly composed images employing *tableaux vivant,* assemblage, and collage, Rankus fabricates a universe where the human body does not possess a discrete boundary but is imagined into objects, causing the living subject to contemplate its own objectness. The soundtrack, composed by Bob Snyder, provides a wry commentary on Rankus's vision.

She Heard Voices
Edward Rankus
1986, 10:00, U.S., b&w and color, silent
Inspired by Max Ernst's picture book *The Hundred Headless Women,* Rankus presents a collage of Surrealist motifs in this "fractured fairy tale" about a heroine threatened by a psychic usurper. The predator is the telephone, empowering disembodied voices and authorizing their faceless demands.

Rasmussen, Steen Møller
(see Weiner, Lawrence and Johnson, Ray in
On Art and Artists)

Ratcliff, Mary Curtis
(see Cort, David)

Reese, Marshall
(see Muntadas, Antonio)

Reeves, Daniel

Dan Reeves has worked in sculpture, film, video, and installation since 1970. His videos focus on personal, political, and spiritual themes, from socially condoned violence to the divine nature of existence. Since 1982 Reeves's work has concentrated on developing a video poetics and exploring personal transformation and responsibility, shaped by his Buddhist convictions.

Obsessive Becoming

"The ultimate irony of the tape lies in its silence. The viewer becomes a participant in the tele-predation, as the voice without a voice turns out to be the viewer's subverbalized reading of the captions."
—Michael Nash, "Video Poetics," *High Performance* 10:1 (1987)

Also available on the compilation *Edward Rankus Videoworks: Volume 1.*

Amida
Daniel Reeves
1983, 9:00, U.S., color, sound
Reeves approaches the issues of life and death through a meditation on light and dark, a minute observation of movement and stillness. The force of life and the inevitability of change, even violent change and decay, emerge from Reeves's glittering collage of slow-motion natural images. A glass shattering on a table and a statue of Buddha falling into swirling water suggest the Buddhist doctrine of the impermanence of life, that it cannot be contained but is forever moving on.

Ganapati/A Spirit in the Bush
Daniel Reeves
1986, 45:00, U.S., color, sound
A song of mourning, praise, and compassion for the sentient creatures with whom we share this planet. Focusing on the myth, history, and natural life of the elephant, the tape explores the gulf we have created between animals and ourselves. Powered by the poetry of Lorca, Kipling, and Reeves, this impassioned lament for subjugated and slaughtered elephants earns its polemical stance—a broader relation to inhumanity—by force of its compelling subject matter. Combining location shoots in India, Kenya, and Thailand with disturbing archival footage of an elephant electrocution, Reeves's procession of charged images involves and implicates the viewer through its silently scrolling text: the viewer becomes the narrator, assuming the voices of protagonist, poet, and predator.

Obsessive Becoming
Daniel Reeves
1995, 58:00, U.S., color, sound
This surreal, free-form autobiography is concerned with childhood and adult rituals and the longing for meaning and connection during the often wildly absurd events of early life. *Obsessive Becoming* returns to Reeves's early exploration of personal narrative forms, poetry, and his interest in creating a more spontaneous and direct fusion between language and video. Words and images of the expectations and disappointments of coming of age break down the boundaries of both mediums. Reeves draws from a wealth of images created since the 1940s in his family's enthusiasm for capturing time, featuring Polaroids and 16mm film. The essence of the work is insight, compassion, and healing. It suggests that we abandon memories that have created emotional barriers and deal with the past without letting it limit our passage through life. In Reeves's words, you "stand long enough and put off all that guards your heart."

Sabda
Daniel Reeves
1984, 15:00, U.S., color, sound
Reeves explores his personal journey to seek the center of existence through the teachings of Eastern religions. India is the source of images for his message about the eternal wheel of existence—life and its continuous process of change.
"Reeves uses a digital imaging technique ... in which images seem to be composed of a series of almost fragmented yet fluid stills, and all movement

becomes a procession of shadows. ... This gives a powerfully ethereal quality to the piece, one that underscores the theme of human existence."
—Marita Sturken, "What Is Grace in All This Madness: The Videotapes of Dan Reeves," *Afterimage* 13 (Summer 1985)

Smothering Dreams
Daniel Reeves
1981, 23:00, U.S., color, sound
Smothering Dreams is a tough, scathing condemnation of war and our country's fascination with violence. Reeves draws on his own experience as a U.S. Marine in Vietnam in the 1960s, juxtaposing actual combat footage, staged war games, and child's war play to make his message horrifyingly clear. This work is dedicated to the men of the 3rd Platoon Company A 1st AmTrac Battalion and the North Vietnamese soldiers who died on January 20, 1969 along the Cua Viet River.

Sombra y Sombra (Shadow to Shadow)
Daniel Reeves
1988, 26:00, U.S., color, sound
An example of what Reeves terms "video poetics," layered images of a deserted village in the Spanish countryside play counterpoint to poetry by Cesar Vallejo and Pablo Neruda. Using slick production techniques, Reeves marks the passing of time and human presence with a video transparency effect. What we see is a ghost of what was. Reeves's precise editing makes for an extraordinarily fluid tape, as images seem to fly through the landscape, through past, present, and future.

Thousands Watch
Daniel Reeves
1979, 7:00, U.S., color, sound
"A short image-processed work, *Thousands Watch* deals with the issue of nuclear suicide. The tape's central metaphor is derived from a 1936 Universal newsreel of a crowd looking on while a young man stands on the ledge of a tall building, threatening to—and eventually succeeding in—committing suicide. It begins with an image of time-lapsed colorized clouds racing across the sky at a frenzied pace while a low siren wail emerges on the soundtrack. This sound forms a pulsing heartbeat and builds into a tense crescendo as the tape progresses. Inter-cut with it are excerpts of familiar historical voices—Truman announcing the dropping of the bomb and Kennedy stating at the U.N. that, 'We all share this small planet.' Dense and tightly woven, the tape seems to accelerate stylistically and verge toward self-destruction."
—Marita Sturken, "What Is Grace in All This Madness: The Videotapes of Dan Reeves," *Afterimage* 13 (Summer 1985)

Smothering Dreams

Reinke, Steve

Steve Reinke's tapes typically have diaristic or collage formats, and his autobiographical voice-overs share his desires and pop culture appraisals with endearing wit. In the 1990s he produced the ambitious omnibus *The Hundred Videos* (1996). He has edited several books, including *By the Skin of Their Tongues: Artist Video Scripts* (co-edited with Nelson Henricks, 1997) and *LUX: A Decade of Artists' Film and Video* (co-edited with Tom Taylor, 2000).

Amsterdam Camera Vacation
Steve Reinke
2001, 12:00, U.S., color, sound
"I'm not going to go to the Anne Frank House. I don't think I could take it. Being a tourist is bad enough—though I'm not really a tourist. I'm here working. My camera's the one on vacation, taking holiday sounds and images. For me it's still the same old thing—talking and talking. I don't want to go inside the Anne Frank House. I don't even know why they call it that. She didn't own it. As far as I know she didn't have any real estate holdings—not in this neighborhood anyway—and I want to remember Shelly Winters as she was in *A Place in the Sun*. I don't care about the Oscar. I want to remember her tipping out of the boat—tippy canoe and beaver, too—falling into the lake and drowning. I don't want to remember her any other way—except possibly her other sea-faring role, *The Poseidon Adventure*."
—Steve Reinke

The Chocolate Factory

Reiss, Jonathan
(see Survival Research Laboratories in On
and Artists)

Rich, Kate
(see Bureau of Inverse Technology)

Riggs, Marlon

One of the most prominent media artists and
critics of the late '80s to early '90s, Marlon
Riggs made insightful, personal, and
controversial documentaries about black gay
identity. His works sparked debate over
government grants and of television censorship.

Rivera, Alex

While attending Hampshire College, Alex Rivera's
interests turned to media and politics,
particularly the politics of race in the

Anal Masturbation and Object Loss
Steve Reinke
2002, 6:00, U.S., color, sound
"Ever on the lookout for learning opportunities, Reinke envisions an art institute where you don't have to make anything and with a library full of books
glued together. All the information's there—you just don't have to bother
reading it!"
—New York Video Festival (2002)

The Chocolate Factory
Steve Reinke
2002, 26:00, U.S., color, sound
The Chocolate Factory is a suite of monologues in the voice of a fictionalized
serial killer—one monologue for each victim. The camera, with an almost structuralist rigor, pans up and down simple line drawings of each of the 17 victims. A Black Sabbath song, picked apart and extended, serves as
punctuation and soundtrack. Reinke has described the tape as, "My autobiography as Jeffrey Dahmer." But really, as the tape's narrator says, "It's all
about the victims."

J.-P. (Remix of "Tuesday and I" by Jean-Paul Kelly)
Steve Reinke
2003, 6:53, Canada, color, sound
A remix of the 20-minute performance "Tuesday and I" by young Canadian
artist Jean-Paul Kelly. Reinke leaves the one-take monologue intact, speeding
the tape up and slowing down to extract empathy for the subject and
squeeze sounds out of his body.

Sad Disco Fantasia
Steve Reinke
2001, 24:00, U.S., color, sound
"Living in Los Angeles is like being on vacation, or in a coma. I don't really
like it, but it's so pleasant I don't want to leave. I've only had one idea since
I've been here and that was to video a cake in the rain in MacArthur Park. But
it's only rained once, briefly in the night, and I was asleep, and dreaming of
snow."
—Steve Reinke
"*Sad Disco Fantasia* is Reinke's episodic tour through the void of L.A., slips
of pop culture, and Reinke's own astringent self-regard. Despite the blasts
of dry wit and the hopeful embrace of gay porn, this is a lament. What
grounds the tape like a bass line is Reinke's response to the death of his
mother. What stops it cold is his tossed-off remark that this is 'my last, my
final video.'"
—Cameron Bailey, "iMAGES: Reinke's Final Cut," *NOW Toronto* 20:32 (12-
18 April 2001)

Non, Je Ne Regrette Rien (No Regrets)
Marlon Riggs
1992, 38:00, U.S., color, sound
No Regrets features a series of interviews with HIV-positive black men.
Through music, poetry, and quiet—at times chilling—self-disclosure, five
seropositive black, gay men speak of their individual confrontations with
AIDS, illuminating the difficult journey African-American men make in coping
with the personal and social devastation of the epidemic.

Animaquiladora
Alex Rivera
1997, 10:00, U.S., color, sound
A significant amount of the hand-drawn animation seen on television today is
cartooned in sweatshop-like animation factories in Korea, China, and the

Rivera, Alex
(continued)

"information age." His work incorporates digital animation and addresses contemporary political issues with guts, personality, and humor. In addition to video, Rivera works in such varied formats as websites to docmentaries for television.

Why Cybraceros

Rose, Sheree
(see Flanagan, Bob)

Rosen, Bob
(see Monk, Meredith)

Rosenblatt, Jay

Since 1980, Jay Rosenblatt has been making films that explore our emotional and psychological cores with content that is personal yet universal in their appeal. His recent credits include *The Smell of Burning Ants* (1994), *Period Piece* (co-directed by Jennifer Frame, 1996), *Human Remains* (1998), and *King of the Jews* (2000).

Rosler, Martha

Since the early 1970s, Martha Rosler has used photography, performance, writing, and video to deconstruct cultural reality. Describing her work, Rosler says, "The subject is the commonplace—I am trying to use video to question the mythical explanations of everyday life. We accept the clash of public and private as natural, yet their separation is historical. The antagonism of the two spheres, which have in fact developed in

Philippines. The writers and animators who form Animaquiladora sharpened their skills in one such factory located in Tijuana, Mexico. After years of animating logos for the American talk show *Live with Regis and Kathie Lee*, Lalo Lopez and Alex Rivera escaped from the hellish sweatshop of Tijuana to seek better lives in Los Angeles and New York. The videos produced by Animaquiladora use a combination of the latest in digital imaging technology and cutting edge Latino political satire.

Papapapá
Alex Rivera
1995, 28:00, U.S., b&w and color, sound
An experimental video about immigration. Looking at the potato (which was first cultivated in Peru) *Papapapá* paints a picture of a vegetable that has traveled and been transformed—following the migrating potato North where it becomes the potato chip, the couch potato, and the French fry. *Papapapá* simultaneously follows another Peruvian in motion, the artist's father, Augusto Rivera. The stories of the two immigrants, the potato and Papa Rivera, converge, as Augusto becomes a Peruvian couch potato, sitting on an American sofa, eating potato chips, and watching Spanish language television.
Also available on the anthologies *The New McLennium, Program 2* and *Betraying Amnesia, Portraying Ourselves: Video Portraits by Latin American and Latino Artists.*

Why Cybraceros
Alex Rivera
1997, 4:30, U.S., color, sound
In the satirical short *Why Cybraceros* Alex Rivera imagines a future where anti-immigration sentiments and high technology combine to reach new xenophobic lows. The U.S. government creates a new telecommuting program that allows Mexican farm laborers to pick and sort produce via the internet, controlling robots through joysticks and key commands. Cheap, tedious labor is now available without the threat of illegal aliens stealing jobs or becoming cititzens!
Spanish subtitled version available.

Also available on the anthology *Frames of Reference: Reflections on Media, Volume 2, Program 1.*

Human Remains
Jay Rosenblatt
1998, 30:00, U.S., color/b&w, 16mm to video
In Jay Rosenblatt's film *Human Remains*, newsreels of Mao, Mussolini, Hitler, Stalin, and Franco are presented with mock confessionals by the dictators themselves: they detail their quotidian realities as we witness performances staged for the camera.
Spanish subtitled version available.

Only available on the anthology *Frames of Reference: Reflections on Media, Volume 4, Program 2.*

Born to Be Sold: Martha Rosler Reads the Strange Case of Baby M
Martha Rosler and Paper Tiger Television
1988, 35:00, U.S., color, sound
Martha Rosler tackles mainstream media's representation of the case of surrogate mother Mary Beth Whitehead. This tape uncovers the class and gender bias of the media's coverage and the courts, including the nefarious way in which Whitehead was discredited as the mother of the baby and portrayed as "psychologically unstable." Inventive graphics and kooky costumes illustrate Rosler's insightful analysis of the court battle, which cogently contrasts the financial rewards of the male professionals involved with those of the sur-

Rosler, Martha

(continued)

tandem, is an ideological fiction—a potent one. I want to explore the relationships between individual consciousness, family life, and culture under capitalism."

The East Is Red, West Is Bending

rogate mother—while placing surrogacy and parenthood within a larger political analysis of contemporary reproductive control in America.

Domination and the Everyday
Martha Rosler
1979, 32:00, U.S., color, sound
One of Rosler's more didactic videotapes, *Domination and the Everyday* delivers a pointed analysis of the instruments of domination in our society—the media and institutions of culture that spoon feed ideology while providing enough entertaining distractions to preempt recognition, on the viewer's part, of the content of mass media messages. In a text streaming across the bottom edge of the screen, Rosler identifies television news as an industrial product, and "information" as a carefully crafted commodity that reflects ruling ideologies, provided to ensure our acquiescence. Echoing a theme of Antonio Muntadas's work, Rosler explores how we are kept in our place not by warlords but by more subtle mechanisms.

The East Is Red, West Is Bending
Martha Rosler
1977, 20:00, U.S., color, sound
Rosler uses the format of a cooking demonstration (as in *Semiotics of the Kitchen*) to address cultural transaction—the meeting of Eastern and Western cultures. Reading directly from a West Bend Electric Wok instruction booklet, Rosler wryly comments upon the Oriental mystique conjured by the West Bend manufacturers, a mystique evoked and then "improved" upon through Western technology like non-stick surfaces and electric power. Drawing attention to the choice of the color red on the wok, Rosler, in typical deadpan fashion, raises the boogie man of Communist China, holding up a pamphlet of Chairman Mao Tse-Tung and saying, "Remember this guy?"

If It's Too Bad to Be True, It Could Be DISINFORMATION
Martha Rosler
1985, 17:00, U.S., color, sound
In a fusion of text and image, Rosler re-presents the *NBC Nightly News* and other broadcast reports to analyze their deceptive syntax and capture the confusion intentionally inserted into the news script. The artist addresses the fallibility of electronic transmission by emphasizing the distortion and absurdities that occur as a result of technical interference. Stressing the fact that there's never a straight story, Rosler asserts her presence in a character-generated text that rolls over the manipulated images, isolating excerpts from her sources. In Rosler's barrage of media information, the formal structure is inseparable from her political analysis.

Losing: A Conversation with the Parents
Martha Rosler
1977, 20:00, U.S., color, sound
Treating the problem of anorexia nervosa from the parents' perspective, Rosler presents a mother and father speaking about the tragedy of their daughter's death from dieting. The conversation turns toward the irony of self-starvation in a land of plenty and toward the international politics of food, where food is used as a negotiating tool. Confronting a serious issue, Rosler simultaneously plays with the confessional form and the staginess of talk show dramatics.

Seattle: Hidden Histories
Martha Rosler
1995, 13:00, U.S., color, sound
A series of one-minute interview-based spots Martha Rosler made with the American Indian community during her residence in Seattle from 1991 to 1995. Rosler reveals lost languages, unrecognized tribes, and the experiences of contemporary Native Americans living not on reservations but in the city. "Rosler shows that cultural history can emerge through a single letter as

in her videotape project *Seattle: Hidden Histories*. In the first of the series of short 'public service announcements,' the corruption of the indigenous name 'Se?ah,' pronounced approximately, 'si;ash,' into 'Seattle' reveals the corrupt underside of America's (colonial) history."
—Silvia Eiblmayr, "Martha Rosler's Characters," *Martha Rosler: Positions in the Life World*, ed. Catherine de Zegher (Cambridge, Mass: MIT Press, 1998)

Secrets from the Street: No Disclosure
Martha Rosler
1980, 11:00, U.S., color, sound, Super-8 to video
Reading the billboards, the trash, the cars, the people, and the graffiti of the street as cultural signs, Rosler extracts the network of social power and domination that determines whose culture gets represented where, asking, "Whose culture gets in the magazines and whose culture is required to exist in the street?" A collage of Super-8 footage shot while cruising the streets of a predominantly Latino neighborhood with a voiceover of Rosler's commentary, the tape successfully combines social analysis with everyday observation, drawing attention to the structure of society's fabric and reevaluating what the dominant culture calls "trash."

Semiotics of the Kitchen

Semiotics of the Kitchen
Martha Rosler
1975, 6:00, U.S., b&w, sound
From A to Z, Rosler shows and tells the ingredients of the housewife's day, giving us a tour that names and mimics the ordinary with movements more samurai than suburban. Rosler's slashing gestures as she forms the letters of the alphabet in the air with a knife and fork are rebellious, punching through the "system of harnessed subjectivity" from the inside out.
"I was concerned with something like the notion of 'language speaking the subject,' and with the transformation of the woman herself into a sign in a system of signs that represent a system of food production, a system of harnessed subjectivity."
—Martha Rosler
Also available on the anthology *I Say I Am: Program 1.*

A Simple Case for Torture
Martha Rosler
1983, 1:00:00, U.S., color, sound
Rosler identifies the totalitarian implications of an argument for torture—under certain circumstances—as it appears in the editorial pages of *Newsweek*. Her critique is presented as voiceover and an assemblage of print media–articles on subjects ranging from human rights to unemployment to global economics. Implicating the U.S. government and American businesses for supporting regimes that systematically use torture, she indicts the American press for its role as an agent of disinformation through selective coverage, its use of language, and for implicitly legitimizing points of view that support torture.

Vital Statistics of a Citizen, Simply Obtained

Vital Statistics of a Citizen, Simply Obtained
Martha Rosler
1977, 38:00, U.S., color, sound
Taking aim at the social standardization enforced on women's bodies, Rosler critiques the politics of "objective" or scientific evaluation that result in the depersonalization, objectification, and colonization of women. As Joseph Di Mattia has pointed out, "The title of the tape is ironic—just exactly to whom are these 'statistics' 'vital'? They are vital to a society which circumscribes the behavior and roles of women." Throughout this tape Rosler situates the female body as the site of an ideological struggle, a site of physically realized domination, which degrades, demeans, and subjugates women.
"[This] is the most pointedly feminist of Rosler's tapes. Every inch of the artist's nude body is measured and recorded by two doctors, while

voiceovers comment on standards, body ideals, and their relation to masochism."

—Mary Stofflett, "Art or television," *Studio International* 195 (June 1982)

Also available on the anthology *Surveying the First Decade, Program 4.*

Martha Rosler: An Interview (see On Art and Artists)

Rubnitz, Tom

A quintessential New York underground film/video artiste, the late Tom Rubnitz took a bite out of the Big Apple and spat it out in a wild kaleidoscope of unequivocal camp and hallucinogenic color. Ann Magnuson, the B-52s, The "Lady" Bunny, and the late John Sex are but a few of the stars that shine oh-so-brightly in Rubnitz's glittering oeuvre. A genre artist par excellence, Rubnitz treated the sexy-druggy-wiggy-luscious-desserty qualities of the '80s downtown club scene with the loving care only a true hedonist could show. Rubnitz died from an AIDS-related illness in 1992.

Drag Queen Marathon

The Fairies

"Bump and Grind It" (John Sex)
Tom Rubnitz

1986, 3:15, U.S., color, sound

A glittering, Las Vegas-inspired music video for John Sex's song "Bump and Grind It." With an outrageous fountain hairdo (by stylist Danilo), Sex sings his catchy pop lyrics, "You gotta put your love behind it/Bump, bump, bump and grind it."

Featuring the Bodacious Ta-Tas and inter-cut with Vegas showgirl footage.

Only available on the compilation *Sexy, Wiggy, Desserty: The Wild New York Underground Video World of Tom Rubnitz.*

Chicken Elaine
Tom Rubnitz

1983, 1:00, U.S., color, sound

Rubnitz's short cooking clip showcases a chicken casserole recipe from the kitchen of Elaine Clearfield. All you need is chicken, rice, a packet of Lipton onion soup mix, a can of cream of mushroom condensed soup, and water!

Only available on the compilation *Sexy, Wiggy, Desserty: The Wild New York Underground Video World of Tom Rubnitz.*

Drag Queen Marathon
Tom Rubnitz

1986, 5:00, U.S., color, sound

A dragumentary about a day in the life of a score of drag queens on the look-out for photo opportunities at Lincoln Center, the Guggenheim Museum, Tiffany's, and in SoHo. A tripped-out Hapi Phace shares her haiku, and The "Lady" Bunny pouts about the concept of unisex clothes.

Also featuring Sister Dimension and Dagmar Onassis.

Only available on the compilation *Sexy, Wiggy, Desserty: The Wild New York Underground Video World of Tom Rubnitz.*

The Fairies
Tom Rubnitz

1990, 10:00, U.S., color, sound

Based on a tale by Charles Perrault, *The Fairies* comes complete with frogs, princes, kind fairies, and evil stepsisters—all costumed à la Rubnitz. Featuring Sister Dimension as the fairy godmother, Michael Clark, and others, the tape playfully illustrates a familiar fairy tale moral as each person gets what they deserve. The evil girl spits up toads while flowers and jewels emerge from the mouth of Matilda the Good, and a dancing prince carries her away.

Only available on the compilation *Sexy, Wiggy, Desserty: The Wild New York Underground Video World of Tom Rubnitz.*

"Hustle with My Muscle" (John Sex)
Tom Rubnitz

1986, 4:00, U.S., color, sound

This rapid-montage music video for John Sex's song "Hustle with My Muscle" portrays the singer as a ladies' man with ample endowment to share. "Can you handle all the man below my belt?" he provocatively asks.

Only available on the compilation *Sexy, Wiggy, Desserty: The Wild New York Underground Video World of Tom Rubnitz.*

John Sex: The True Story
Tom Rubnitz
1983, 4:17, U.S., color, sound
A rockumentary about East Village club Pyramid star John Sex. The blonde, coifed performer exposes his penchant for padding his package with socks and explains that his last name is the result of his ancestors' "Americanization" of his native name Sexton.
Featuring Miss Maggie, Katy K, Tom Rubnitz, Kenny Scharf, and Kestutis Nakas.
Only available on the compilation *Sexy, Wiggy, Desserty: The Wild New York Underground Video World of Tom Rubnitz.*

Made for TV
Tom Rubnitz
1984, 15:00, U.S., color, sound
Combining Rubnitz's skillful manipulation of the familiar "look" of TV shows with an extraordinary range of characters, performer Ann Magnuson fabulously impersonates the array of female types seen on TV in a typical broadcast day. From glitzy to drab, from friendly housewife to desperate evangelist, Magnuson is a one-woman universe appearing on every channel—the star of every program giving her all as the chameleon woman who is always on display.
Also available on the compilation *Sexy, Wiggy, Desserty: The Wild New York Underground Video World of Tom Rubnitz.*

The Mother Show

The Mother Show
Tom Rubnitz
1991, 4:09, U.S., color, sound
Produced in collaboration with Tom Koken and Barbara Lipp, *The Mother Show* is a tribute to mothers everywhere, starring Frieda, the "living" doll. Frieda asks her mother a series of questions, such as "Mom, are there days when you feel not-so-fresh?" and spells out the meaning of the word "mother." The tape ends with her endearing pronouncement, "Mom, you're like a mother to me."
Only available on the compilation *Sexy, Wiggy, Desserty: The Wild New York Underground Video World of Tom Rubnitz.*

Pickle Surprise

Pickle Surprise
Tom Rubnitz
1990, 2:00, U.S., color, sound
A short, zany cooking mantra, featuring Sister Dimension, The "Lady" Bunny, RuPaul, David Dalrymple, Lahoma Van Zandt, and Maria Ayala. "Where's the pickle?" "That's the surprise!"
Only available on the compilation *Sexy, Wiggy, Desserty: The Wild New York Underground Video World of Tom Rubnitz.*

Sexy, Wiggy, Desserty: The Wild New York Underground Video World of Tom Rubnitz
Until his untimely death from AIDS in 1992, Tom Rubnitz produced short, humorous videotapes featuring some of New York's most outrageously talented musicians, artists, and drag queens. Influenced by mass media entertainment, Rubnitz crafted hilarious videos that simultaneously celebrated and parodied pop culture's bountiful energy and inventiveness. As Tom said, "I wanted to make things beautiful, funny, and positive—escapes that you could just get into and laugh through. That was really important to me. I felt like good could triumph over evil." We hope that this compilation will extend Tom's critically important, uplifting, and groundbreaking work to new audiences who have never had the privilege or pure pleasure of witnessing these exhilarating videos.
Total running time 1:13:11.
Contents:
The Mother Show, Tom Rubnitz, 1991, 4:09, U.S., color, sound

John Sex: The True Story, Tom Rubnitz, 1983, 4:17, U.S., color, sound
Chicken Elaine, Tom Rubnitz, 1983, 1:00, U.S., color, sound
Made for TV, Tom Rubnitz, 1984, 15:00, U.S., color, sound
Hustle with My Muscle, Tom Rubnitz, 1986, 4:00, U.S., color, sound
Bump and Grind It, Tom Rubnitz, 1986, 3:15, U.S., color, sound
Drag Queen Marathon, Tom Rubnitz, 1986, 5:00, U.S., color, sound
Wigstock: The Movie, Tom Rubnitz, 1987, 20:00, U.S., color, sound
Undercover Me!, Tom Rubnitz, 1988, 2:00, U.S., color, sound
Strawberry Shortcut, Tom Rubnitz, 1989, 2:00, U.S., color, sound
Pickle Surprise, Tom Rubnitz, 1990, 2:00, U.S., color, sound
The Fairies, Tom Rubnitz, 1990, 10:00, U.S., color, sound
Summer of Love PSA, Tom Rubnitz and MICA-TV, 1989, 0:30, U.S., color, sound

Strawberry Shortcut
Tom Rubnitz
1989, 2:00, U.S., color, sound
Having a party and in a fix for a dessert? The "Lady" Bunny has just the recipe: combine a doughnut, Cherry 7-Up, jelly, strawberries, and whipped topping.
Only available on the compilation *Sexy, Wiggy, Desserty: The Wild New York Underground Video World of Tom Rubnitz*.

Summer of Love PSA
Tom Rubnitz and MICA-TV
1989, 0:30, U.S., color, sound
Produced in collaboration with MICA-TV, *Summer of Love* is a public service announcement produced for the American Foundation for AIDS Research. Featuring The B-52's, David Byrne, Allen Ginsburg, Quentin Crisp, John Kelly, and others.
Only available on the compilation *Sexy, Wiggy, Desserty: The Wild New York Underground Video World of Tom Rubnitz*.

Undercover Me!
Tom Rubnitz
1988, 2:00, U.S., b&w, sound
A movie trailer for a non-existent Bond-style spy thriller "coming soon to a mini-mall cineplex near you!"
Featuring John Sex, Hapi Phace, Laura Levine, Dany Johnson, and The French Twist.
Only available on the compilation *Sexy, Wiggy, Desserty: The Wild New York Underground Video World of Tom Rubnitz*.

Wigstock: The Movie
Tom Rubnitz
1987, 20:00, U.S., color, sound
Rubnitz's tape celebrates and documents an early installment of the "story-wig-in," shot nearly a decade before the feature-length documentary. Presenting the festival during its Tompkins Square Park era, when the 1960s themes were still played up, the tape combines live performance footage with off-stage interviews and music video reverie.
Featuring The "Lady" Bunny, Lypsinka, Frieda, John Sex, John Kelly, Baby Gregor, Hapi Phace, Taboo, and many others.

Only available on the compilation *Sexy, Wiggy, Desserty: The Wild New York Underground Video World of Tom Rubnitz*.

Strawberry Shortcut

Wigstock: The Movie

Ruby, Sterling
Sterling Ruby says, "My work is an interpretation of the innate and an exploration of the perplexities surrounding the shifting borders of behavior, psychology, and biology. ... This

Agoraphobic
Sterling Ruby
2001, 11:06, U.S., color, sound
Agoraphobic is a portrayal of a specific case of New-Age impotence. The agoraphobic's pathology manifests itself as a need to drink his victim's blood in order to move from place to place. Set in an office interior, *Agoraphobic*

Ruby, Sterling

(continued)

epistemological inquiry suggests a body destroyed through a contact with the sublime. ... In order to route a path through these simulated, or uncanny, subjects, I often base my projects on the elements of introspection, emotional attachment, transference, environment, and symbolic consumption. Influences such as Mannerist art and the horror genre are incorporated within my artwork, merging the ornate and the visceral to suggest new corporeal boundaries."

Hole

becomes a play on the patient/therapist relationship, suggesting an imbalance in the transfer of baggage.

Forced Inanimate Connection: Climax Modeling 2002
Sterling Ruby
2002, 6:42, U.S., color, sound
In a meditation on the sexuality of the readymade, an off-camera artist forces one object into another.
"The best evidence yet that obscenity is easier recognized than defined."
–Anne Reecer, Cinematexas (Austin, 2003)
Also available on the compilation *Sterling Ruby: Interventionist Works 2001-2002.*

Hole
Sterling Ruby
2002, 1:46, U.S., color, sound
A portrayal of retail workers engaged in a repetitive act of hiding merchandise in a hole in the wall.
Also available on the compilation *Sterling Ruby: Interventionist Works 2001-2002.*

Human Touch
Sterling Ruby
2001, 2:11, U.S., color, sound
Human Touch documents an intimate gesture between hunter and prey.
Also available on the compilation *Sterling Ruby: Interventionist Works 2001-2002.*

Landscape Annihilates Consciousness
Sterling Ruby
2002, 11:40, U.S., color, sound
A celebrated landscape painter hypnotizes through brush stroke and voice.
Also available on the compilation *Sterling Ruby: Interventionist Works 2001-2002.*

Sterling Ruby: Interventionist Works 2001-2002
Four videos from Chicago-based artist Sterling Ruby that deal with quiet moments, capturing an atmospheric intimacy, both voyeuristic and perverse.
Total running time 22:19.
Contents:
Forced Inanimate Connection: Climax Modeling 2002, Sterling Ruby, 2002, 6:42, U.S., color, sound
Hole, Sterling Ruby, 2002, 1:46, U.S., color, sound
Human Touch, Sterling Ruby, 2001, 2:11, U.S., color, sound
Landscape Annihilates Consciousness, Sterling Ruby, 2002, 11:40, U.S., color, sound

Thoreauian
Sterling Ruby
2002, 13:30, U.S., color, sound
Thoreauian is a fictional representation of Henry David Thoreau, shot entirely in South Hadley, Massachusetts where the naturalist did his post-*Walden* studies. A transcendental figure navigates through the woods, while the proximity of Mount Holyoke women's college distracts him into fantasizing about a warmer season and companionship. Exterior shots of Skinner Mountain are juxtaposed with the interior of Mount Holyoke College, merging historical reference with ideas of identity and gender. *Thoreauian* reads as a slowed-down nature program fused with the early 1970s figurative performance work of Mount Holyoke's former student Joan Jonas.

Rulfo, Juan Carlos

Juan Carlos Rulfo has worked as a cinematographer, assistant director, editor, and sound recorder for film and as a photography curator. For his first feature, Rulfo, son of renowned Mexican poet Juan Rulfo, returned to his hometown to interview friends, family, and residents who recalled stories of his father.

Ryan, Paul

Paul Ryan's early work evolved from free-form collaborations with members of Raindance Corporation to studies of urban and natural ecological systems. He has also published *Birth and Death and Cybernation: Cybernetics of the Sacred* (1973), an anthology, and *Video Mind, Earth Mind* (1993). Raindance Corporation was a "countercultural thinktank" that embraced video as an alternative form of cultural communication. The collective produced tapes and writings and published the seminal video journal *Radical Software* (1970-74).

Salloum, Jayce

Jayce Salloum has been working in installation, photography, mixed media, and video since 1975, as well as curating exhibitions, conducting workshops, and coordinating cultural events. His work takes place in a variety of contexts, critically engaging itself in the representation of cultural manifestations and other cultures. A media arts philosopher and cultural worker, Salloum has lectured internationally and had numerous exhibitions throughout North and South America, Europe, Japan, and the Middle East.

Del olvido al no me acuerdo (I Forgot, I Don't Remember)

Juan Carlos Rulfo
1999, 1:10:00, Mexico, color, sound, 35mm to video, in Spanish with English subtitles

Ostensibly a documentary on the life of renowned Mexican author (and the filmmaker's father) Juan Rulfo, the stunningly photographed *Del olvido al no me acuerdo (I Forgot, I Don't Remember)* examines the constructions of narrative and memory themselves.

Only available on the anthology *Frames of Reference: Reflections on Media, Volume 3, Program 1.*

Proto Media Primer

Paul Ryan and Raindance Corporation
1970, 14:00, U.S., b&w, sound

As one of the early media collectives, Raindance Corporation celebrated an eclectic use of the Portapak by taping everything from man-on-the-street interviews to concerts and demonstrations. Intended to serve as a cultural data bank, their media primers provide an impressionistic smorgasbord of late '60s and early '70s American society. In this primer edited by Paul Ryan, Abbie Hoffman is interviewed shortly before the verdict of the Chicago 7 trial is delivered. Hoffman describes some of the politicized media theater that punctuated the trial for conspiracy to incite a riot of the demonstrators at the 1968 Democratic Presidential Nominating Convention. The tape concludes with a duel between Raindance's Portapak and a surveillance camera in a Safeway supermarket.

Only available on the anthology *Surveying the First Decade, Program 7.*

Kan Ya Ma Kan (This Is Not Beirut)/There Was and There Was Not

Jayce Salloum
1994, 49:00, Canada, color, sound

This Is Not Beirut is a personal project that examines the use and production of images and representations of Lebanon and Beirut, both in the West and in Lebanon itself. It also records Salloum's interactions and experiences while working in Lebanon, focusing on this representational process by a Westernized, foreign-born Lebanese mediator with cultural connections to and baggage from both the West and Lebanon. Salloum situates the tape between genres, looking from the inside out at each and critically engaging the assumptions involved, and thus broken, as sites for the construction and discovery of identity. Salloum collected more than 200 hours of Hi-8, VHS, and found film material in Lebanon during 1992. The project tries to make sense of the material and its acquisition—sometimes directly and at other times addressing the attempt itself—to produce works that frame relationships, sites, subjects, and practical and conceptual issues.

French subtitled version available.

Muqaddimah Li-Nihayat Jidal (Introduction to the End of an Argument): Speaking for Oneself, Speaking for Others)

Jayce Salloum and Elia Suleiman
1990, 45:00, Canada/U.S., b&w and color, sound, in English and Hebrew with English subtitles

With a combination of Hollywood, European, and Israeli film; documentary; news coverage; and excerpts of 'live' footage shot in the West Bank and Gaza strip, *Introduction to the End of an Argument* critiques representations of the Middle East, Arab culture, and the Palestinian people produced by the West. The tape mimics the dominant media's forms of representation, subverting its methodology and construction. A process of displacement and deconstruction is enacted attempting to arrest the imagery and ideology, decolonizing and recontextualizing it to provide a space for a marginalized voice consistently denied expression in the media.

Talaeen a Junuub (Up to the South)

Talaeen a Junuub (Up to the South)

Jayce Salloum and Walid Raad

1993, 1:00:00, Canada, color, sound

An oblique, albeit powerful documentary that examines the current conditions, politics, and economics of South Lebanon. The tape focuses on the social, intellectual, and popular resistance to the Israeli occupation as well as conceptions of "the land," culture, and imperiled identities of the Lebanese people. Simultaneously, the tape self-consciously engages in a critique of the documentary genre and its traditions.

"This documentary represents a new trend in artistic creativity in the Arab World. It sets new standards for political documentaries covering political turmoil in the region. Not ones to use cliches and ideological dogmas, these young artists approach the subject of South Lebanon with sensitivity and political maturity."

—As'ad Abu Khalil, Assistant Professor Political Science, California State University, Stanislaus

French subtitled version available.

untitled part 1: everything and nothing

Jayce Salloum

2001, 40:40, Canada, color, sound

An intimate dialogue with Soha Bechara, an ex-Lebanese National Resistance fighter, in her Paris dorm room. The interview was taped during the last year of the Israeli occupation, one year after her release from captivity in El-Khiam torture and interrogation center (South Lebanon) where she had been detained for ten years—six in isolation. Revising notions of resistance, survival, and will, the overexposed image of the survivor speaks quietly and directly to the camera—not speaking of the torture but of separation amid loss of what is left behind and what remains.

"I didn't ask her anything specifically about the torture she underwent or the trauma of detention; she was being interviewed to death by the European and Arab press over the details of her captivity and the minutiae of her surviving it and the conditions in El-Khiam and the detainees and the resistance. I went to her small dorm room, not much bigger than her cell (she is presently studying international law at the Sorbonne); she sat on her bed, and I asked her about the distance lived between Khiam and Paris, and Beirut and Paris. And what she left in Khiam, and what she brought with her."

—Jayce Salloum

French subtitled version available.

untitled part 2: beauty and the east

untitled part 2: beauty and the east

Jayce Salloum

2003, 50:15, Bosnia-Herzegovina/Croatia/Macedonia/Serbia/Montenegro/Slovenia/Austria/U.S./Canada, color, sound

Part 2 in a series of attempts at concretizing the notion of interstitiality, this videotape addresses issues of nationalism and the nation state, polarities of time, alienation, the refusal and construction of political identities, ethno-fascism, the body as object and metaphor, agents, monsters and abjectness, subjective affinities, and objective trusts. Material was taped while leaving home, arriving in New York and Vienna, then moving through the former Yugoslavia (stopping in Ljubljana, Zagreb, Sarajevo, Belgrade, and Skopje) shortly after the NATO bombing. The subjects conversing come from a range of constituencies; migrants, refugees, asylum seekers, residents (permanent and transient), students, workers, and cultural producers recounting experience, locating sites, shifts, events, and the theorizing and accounting of the issues at stake, and associated ambient imagery forming specific histories of locations, and locations of histories at the intersection of cultures in this/these particular place(s) and time(s). The speakers are framed closely, creating a complicity with and acknowledgement of the ongoing framing/mediation. Moving landscapes and cityscapes are used to materialize the verbal and localize the discourse through levels of physicality, materiality and immateriality.

With Boris Buden, Marina Grzinic, Eda Cufer, Renata Salecl, Dunja Blazevic, Zarana Papic, Slavica Indzevska, Mihajlo Acimovic, Ella Shohat, Ammiel Alcalay, and Carmen Aguirre, among others.

Sandin, Dan

Inventor and practitioner of the Image Processor (IP), Dan Sandin is a seminal figure in the technological development of the video medium. Trained in nuclear physics, Sandin first became interested in video in 1967 while helping organize student demonstrations on the University of Illinois campus. He considers his career has having three main thrusts: "the design of electronic instruments for visual performance and personal growth; the development of educational facilities and programs related to the use of electronic screens (electronic visualization); and the production and exhibition of visual works for personal expressive reasons."

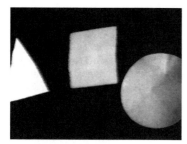

Triangle in Front of Square in Front of Circle

Schoolman, Carlotta Fay
(see Serra, Richard)

Scheurwater, Hester

Since 1996, Hester Scheurwater has made video installations and experimental films and videos that have been shown all over the world. In many of her short works, the camera explores relationships between human beings and space, relationships that rarely flourish. The modern individual appears isolated from reality, unable to connect with self or surroundings. In

Five-minute Romp through the IP
Dan Sandin
1973, 6:30, U.S., b&w, sound
In 1973, Dan Sandin designed and built a comprehensive video instrument for artists, the Image Processor (IP), a modular, patch programmable, analog computer optimized for the manipulation of grey level information of multiple video inputs. Sandin decided that the best distribution strategy for his instrument "was to give away the plans for the IP and encourage artists to build their own copies. This gave rise to a community of artists with their own advanced video production capabilities and many shared goals and experiences." In this segment, Sandin demonstrates the routing of the camera signal through several basic modules of the IP, producing a "primitive" vocabulary of the effects specific to video.
Also available on the anthology *Surveying the First Decade, Program 5*.

Spiral PTL
Dan Sandin, Tom DeFanti, and Mimi Shevets
1980, 7:00, U.S., color, sound
Short for "Probably The Last" (of the series), *Spiral PTL* uses the image processor like a musical instrument to create variations on a spiral, transforming its basic form into an ever-moving gyro. The movement is synchronous with an audio track that varies from electronic buzzes and space age voices to the quiet sounds of running water.

Triangle in Front of Square in Front of Circle
Dan Sandin
1973, 2:00, U.S., b&w, sound
In this elegant demonstration, Sandin explains the mistake of using common language concepts and spatial relations to describe what actually can happen on the video screen. The images generated in the tape act according to specific parameters set by the artist. Sandin has stated "The analog Image Processor was programmed to implement the logic equations; if square, if triangle, and circle, show circle." In this tape, Sandin is in effect arguing for a distinct video vocabulary that replaces the classical concept of perspective.
Only available on the anthology *Surveying the First Decade, Program 5*.

Wanda Wega Waters
Dan Sandin
1980, 14:00, U.S., color, sound
A rural sunset at the edge of the water in *Wanda Wega Waters*. The natural rhythmic movement of the water's surface becomes a highly colored abstraction in motion, a meditation on the intersection of nature and technology.

Dan Sandin: An Interview (see On Art and Artists)

Ground Floor
Hester Scheurwater
2001, 7:00, The Netherlands, color, sound
A woman is lying on her back on the floor. She seems to be tied down on the ground, but she is holding her own ankles with her own hands. She wears only tights and a pair of high-heeled red shoes. Her hair-covered face makes her an anonymous victim of the camera, which makes converging circles around her body.
Also available on the compilation *Hester Scheurwater Videoworks: Volume 1*.

Scheurwater, Hester

(continued)

Scheurwater's universe there is very little room for human warmth; the only hope that remains is the camera itself, feverishly searching for compassion in the remnants of decay.

I Must Be Beautiful Too

Heal Me
Hester Scheurwater
2000, 3:00, The Netherlands, color, sound
A woman is standing barefoot on a tile floor. In slow motion, the investigative camera circles around her. Her breasts are bared and liquid runs down her legs. Bit by bit, every part of her body is shown, except her face, which remains hidden behind her hair. The camera besets the woman, who remains silent.
Also available on the compilation *Hester Scheurwater Videoworks: Volume 1.*

Hester Scheurwater Videoworks: Volume 1
These five short videos examine the relationship between the female body and the camera's gaze.
"In Scheurwater's universe, there is hardly any room left for human warmth. The only living being that evokes a sense of pity is a dog. And the only hope that remains is the camera itself, feverishly searching for compassion in the remnants of decay."
–Stan van Herpen
Total running time 19:00.
Contents:
Heal Me, Hester Scheurwater, 2000, 3:00, The Netherlands, color, sound
I Must Be Beautiful Too, Hester Scheurwater, 2000, 3:00, The Netherlands, color, sound
Lisa, Hester Scheurwater, 2001, 3:00, The Netherlands, color, sound
I Wanted You, Hester Scheurwater, 2001, 3:00, The Netherlands, color, sound
Ground Floor, Hester Scheurwater, 2001, 7:00, The Netherlands, color, sound

I Must Be Beautiful Too
Hester Scheurwater
2000, 3:00, The Netherlands, color, sound
The title gives a bitter meaning to the uneasy image of a woman who is brushing her hair over her face with fierce movements. Mostly the face remains impersonally hidden under her hair; when it is uncovered, we see how the rough scratches of the brush against the skin have smeared her lipstick.
Also available on the compilation *Hester Scheurwater Videoworks: Volume 1.*

I Wanted You
Hester Scheurwater
2001, 3:00, The Netherlands, color, sound
I Wanted You shows a woman crawling over the floor. She is wearing only tights and a pair of red shoes with high heels. Her hair-covered face makes her an anonymous victim of the camera, which is making converging circles around her body.
Also available on the compilation *Hester Scheurwater Videoworks: Volume 1.*

Lisa
Hester Scheurwater
2001, 3:00, The Netherlands, color, sound
A video which explores the gaze on the female body, and the desires and violence overwhelming it.
Also available on the compilation *Hester Scheurwater Videoworks: Volume 1.*

Poster Girl
Hester Scheurwater
2003, 5:00, The Netherlands, color, sound
As if trapped inside a nightmare, the main protagonist of *Poster Girl* is haunted by disturbing visions, thoughts and fantasies, to which the viewer is privy. She is joined at various points in the video by another woman whose role in the narrative remains unclear. Is she meant to function as a guardian or a

demon? The video further complicates the matter by representing both women as simultaneously wounded and wounding, inviting and threatening, vulnerable and menacing. What results is a compelling, albeit disconcerting, glimpse into the tumultuous inner life of an adult woman.

Schneeman, Carolee

Schneemann's use of her nude body inspired a dialogue on the female body as a site of action, not objectification. This spirit was exemplified in Schneemann's infamous *Meat Joy* performances of the early '60s as nude and partially nude men and women writhed around the stage, in a sort of orgiastic Busby Berkeley choreography.

Up to and Including Her Limits
Carolee Schneemann
1973, 10:00 excerpt (of 29:00), U.S., color, sound
A direct result of Pollock's physicalized painting, Schneemann is suspended from a tree surgeon's harness on a 3/4-inch manila rope. Manually raising and lowering the rope, she sustains an entranced period of drawing in which she strokes the surrounding walls with crayons, accumulating a web of colored marks. The body becomes the agency of visual traces, vestige of the body's energy in motion.

Only available as an excerpt on the anthology *Endurance, Reel 2.*

Segalove, Ilene

A self-described "child of Beverly Hills," Ilene Segalove began pointing the camera at "familiar things," producing quasi-documentaries about her family (*The Mom Tapes*, 1973-75) and American TV culture (*TV is OK*, 1976). Segalove was also a member of the group Telethon, which designed installations using commercial TV collages and guest edited an issue of *Radical Software*, "The TV Environment" (2:2, 1971).

Five True Stories
Ilene Segalove
1980, 6:00, U.S., color, sound
Segalove relates a tale from her childhood of a man's exposure with text ("the painter wagged it at me right here"), while an arrow blinks over a shot of the house where she grew up. Segalove narrates: "I looked down and expected to see a can of green paint. I saw a pink penis instead, peeking out of the fly of his pants… I wondered how it had got so pink; had he painted it too?" This and four other memorable stories are humorously presented in a series of video one-liners.

I Remember Beverly Hills
Ilene Segalove
1980, 28:00, U.S., color, sound
Segalove comes out as the child of a movie star haven where messy lawns are reported to the police and designer labels are removed from hand-me-downs for the maids. She reveals some of the dirt among the manicured yards, including a local custom of girls jumping from a terraced lawn at Beverly Hills High to induce miscarriages and her friend Yasmin Hayworth's wish that Rita was a "natural mother."

The Mom Tapes

The Mom Tapes
Ilene Segalove
1974, 28:00, U.S., color, sound
Segalove takes her mom as subject in these short pieces, recording her stories, her advice, and her daily routine. What results is a portrait of a contemporary mother-daughter relationship, touchingly devoid of drama and full of whimsical humor. For example, in one piece Ilene's mother laments over a pair of shoes her daughter has chosen to hang on the wall instead of wear, saying, "With you, everything is art." In another segment the camera focuses on a pair of unoccupied, overstuffed chairs. The voice of a teenage girl whines, "Mom, I'm bored," then proceeds to reject each of her mother's suggestions by throwing objects across the room: books, food, sports equipment, the telephone, and so forth.

Excerpt (4:00) also available on the anthology *Surveying the First Decade, Program 4.*

More TV Stories
Ilene Segalove
1985, 14:00, U.S., color, sound
Segalove gives us another series of true incidents involving the powerful influence of television on life, relationships, and attitudes. Among them is the tale of a family in serious dialogue about their decision to censor the tube. After purchasing the "hard-core porno" channel with their cable service, the parents discuss possible rules for their daughter's television viewing.

My Puberty
Ilene Segalove
1987, 11:00, U.S., color, sound
Segalove re-enacts the trials and travails of her desperate, hormonal, pubescent years with actors dancing their way through what looks like a Technicolor version of the Cleaver's backyard. She plays herself, getting questionable advice from girlfriends, begging her mother for a bra and falling in love for the first time—with Moondoggie in *Gidget Goes Hawaiian.*

The Riot Tapes
Ilene Segalove
1984, 30:00, U.S., color, sound
"The Riot Tapes is a video biography of Segalove's political involvement in college, of her boyfriend (who became anorexic while dieting to evade the draft), and of her discovery that art could give her a voice and a forum for her political views. It is her first real political work. Segalove says, 'I'm trying to comment on the state of things. A lot of my peers spend a lot of time in a state of disbelief, but I'm tired of disengaging myself from the world by doing that.'"
—Gloria Ohland, "Segalove's Latest Is a Riot," *L.A. Weekly* 6:22 (27 April 1984)

The Riot Tapes

What Is Business?
Ilene Segalove
1982, 29:00, U.S., color, sound
Pursuing an answer to the title question, Segalove interviews kids, executives, consultants, and others in order to educate her as to the ins and outs of the financial world. Keen observations about wealth and success from experts are matched against Mr. Science demos and animated graphics in this somewhat mocking look at the culture of business. Segalove says, "*What Is Business?* is about growing up. The first building I would have blown up in '68 was the business building. Now, students are just going to college to get an MBA. That's all you hear about. MBA is what LSD used to be."

Whatever Happened to the Future
Ilene Segalove
1987, 17:00, U.S., color, sound
In this wistful tape, Segalove looks at how her childhood vision of the future holds up (or doesn't) in adulthood.
Commissioned by the Los Angeles County Museum of Art.

Why I Got into TV and Other Stories
Ilene Segalove
1983, 10:00, U.S., color, sound
"[Segalove] pursues her self-analysis via the popular culture and TV addiction of her youth: seeing JFK shot on TV, falling in love with the TV repairman, being glued to the tube while suffering from the requisite bout of mononucleosis, and associating the memory of watching her parents kiss with the soundtrack of *Dragnet.*"
—Marita Sturken, "Revising Romance: New Feminist Video," *Art Journal* 45 (Fall 1985)

Serra, Richard

Associated with the emergence of post-minimalism and process art, Richard Serra's lead-splashing sculptures were included in *The Warehouse Show* at the Leo Castelli Gallery and *Anti-Illusion: Procedures/Materials* at the Whitney Museum—both pivotal exhibitions that established a new discourse in the field of sculpture. His metal structures were the product of his experience working in a steel mill, his

Boomerang
Richard Serra and Nancy Holt
1974, 10:00, U.S., color, sound
This is a tape that analyzes its own discourse and processes as it is being formulated. The language of *Boomerang*, and the relation between the description and what is being described, is not arbitrary. Language and image are being formed and revealed as they are organized.
Only available on the anthology *Surveying the First Decade, Program 2.*

Serra, Richard

(continued)

theoretical training, and the influence of the New York school of art. Serra produced several films before making videotapes in the early '70s—including *Television Delivers People* (1973), *Prisoner's Dilemma* (1974), and *Boomerang* (1974)—that examine the medium as a structure for communication. He remains one of the most influential and revered contemporary sculptors.

Television Delivers People
Richard Serra and Carlotta Fay Schoolman
1973, 6:00, U.S., color, sound

Television Delivers People is a seminal work in the now well-established critique of popular media as an instrument of social control that asserts itself subtly on the populace through "entertainments" for the benefit of those in power: the corporations that mantain and profit from the status quo. While canned Muzak plays, a scrolling text denounces the corporate masquerade of commercial television to reveal the structure of profit that greases the wheels of the media industry. Television emerges as little more than a insidious sponsor for the corporate engines of the world. By appropriating the medium he is criticizing—using television, in effect, against itself—Serra employs a characteristic strategy of early, counter-corporate video collectives—a strategy that remains integral to video artists committed to a critical dismantling of the media's political and ideological stranglehold.

Only available on the anthology *Surveying the First Decade, Program 7.*

The Trial of Tilted Arc (see Serra, Richard in On Art and Artists)

Seymour, Erin

Erin Seymour is a New York-based video installation artist whose work seeks to transpose her subjects though the filters of technology, cinematic methodology, and the time-based visual medium. Her installations and single-channel videos have been exhibited nationally and internationally.

code switching
Erin Seymour
1999, 5:52, U.S., color, silent

"*code switching* began as a contemporary reaction to Adrian Piper's *Cornered* (1988). It goes on to explore the fracturing of contemporary identity within modern culture and the mechanisms by which individuals assign and create the cultural, racial, personal, and social identities around us. … The piece consists of videotape documenting a computerized sketch of my face. By placing three dollars into a mall photo booth, I was interpreted, drawn and given a representation of myself to carry home. …The text addresses the viewer directly, causing a flux in the interlocution from monitor screen to artist and then to the viewer directly. Sound is established when conscientiously acknowledged as thought. The individual in *code switching* exists in a purely technologically mediated world and has placement and development entirely within the viewer's interpretation and the assumptions he or she make on them."
—Erin Seymour

Only available on the anthology *e-[d]entity, Tape 2.*

Sherk, Bonnie

Since the 1960s, Bonnie Sherk has investigated the relationship between her body and the natural environment. Her work often points to the tensions between human life and nature by situating her body as a mediator between the natural and the man-made.

Excerpts from Selected Works by Bonnie Sherk, 1970-73
Bonnie Sherk
1970-73, 14:00, U.S., b&w and color, sound

This compilation presents excerpts of documentation of three works by installation and performance artist Bonnie Sherk. In *Portable Parks I-III*, Sherk created temporary parks, complete with palm trees, sod, benches, and animals in "dead" spaces in the city of San Francisco—including an unfinished shoulder of an expressway, a freeway on-ramp, and the Union Square neighborhood. *Sitting Still and Pacing* finds the artist seated in a garbage dump, on street corners and the Golden Gate Bridge, and in zoo cages; alternately, she also paces furiously on a pedestrian ramp adjacent to a busy street. For *Public Lunch*, she performed the work on a busy Saturday at the San Francisco Zoo. Locked in a cage in the lion house and situated between two live tiger exhibits, Sherk dined upon a catered meal at feeding time. Like the animal on display that she was, she ate a public lunch, paced around her cage, and napped.

Only available as an excerpt on the anthology *Endurance, Reel 2.*

Shevets, Mimi
(see Sandin, Dan)

Shulman, David

David Shulman's work explores new ways of seeing and understanding the power and influence of media. His videotapes are vital contributions to establishing the history of video

Everyone's Channel
David Shulman
1990, 58:00, U.S., b&w and color, sound

This tape documents the history of U.S. community television and public access TV, using rare video clips from across the nation. Combining unique archival footage from the early days of cable, rediscovered footage from the

Shulman, David

(continued)

art and alternative media in the United States. As a continuing investigator of the tactics of the news media, Shulman has exposed racist undercurrents in TV news reporting and investigated the insidious role of public relations in shaping opinion during the Persian Gulf crisis. He is currently a producer for the BBC in London.

Siegel, Eric

Eric Siegel designed and built the Siegel Colorizer in 1968 and a video synthesizer in 1970. His *Psychedelavision in Color* was included in the groundbreaking *Television as a Creative Medium* exhibition at the Howard Wise Gallery in 1969. In addition to producing his own work, Siegel collaborated with other video pioneers, including the Vasulkas and the Videofreex. He also contributed to the early issues of *Radical Software*. In 1972 Siegel traveled to India and produced *The Hindustan Tapes* (1973-75), a series on Indian culture.

Silver, Shelly

Quoting from the established genres of experimental, documentary, and fiction film and television, Shelly Silver's work is funny, poetic and formally beautiful, seducing the viewer into pondering such difficult issues as the cracks in our most common assumptions, the impossibility of a shared language, and the ambivalent and yet overwhelming need to belong—to a family, a nation, a gender, an ideology. Exploring the psychology of public and private space, the ambivalence inherent in familial and societal relations and the seduction and repulsion of voyeurism, Silver's work elicits equal amounts of pleasure and discomfort.

1/2-inch Portapak era, and interviews with access pioneers, *Everyone's Channel* provides an illuminating overview of the people, ideas, and technological developments that helped make cable access a reality and stresses the continuing need to see it as a vital necessity and right. From the birth of the video revolution, inspired by the marketing of portable TV equipment to the first access channels in New York City and beyond, *Everyone's Channel* portrays the evolution of an idea that refuses to die.

Turn It On, Tune It In, Take It Over!
David Shulman
1992, 52:00, U.S., b&w and color, sound
Turn It On, Tune It In, Take It Over! is a portrait of freedom of expression at the dawn of the Electronic Age. The video was distilled from hundreds of hours of footage shot mostly in the early 1970s, using the first portable video format—the 1/2-inch open-reel, black-and-white, battery-operated, video Portapak. The piece recovers an almost lost and forgotten era of television history, when participation set out to conquer passivity and when process was more important than product. Placing local needs above ratings and commercial interests, this era saw the birth of a dream: to produce a real alternative to network TV—a "people's television."

Einstine
Eric Siegel
1978, 5:00, U.S., color, sound
Eric Siegel, a child prodigy in electronics, built his first TV set out of scrap parts at the age of 14. He developed his first video synthesizer, the Processing Chrominance Synthesizer, in 1968-69; it was used to generate the installation *Psychedelevision in Color* for the seminal *TV as a Creative Medium* exhibition held at the Howard Wise Gallery in 1969. Because the early version of the machine was unable to record the images it generated, *Einstine* was re-created by Siegel after the exhibition. The tape uses colorized video feedback to generate its psychedelic effects as a picture of Albert Einstein dissolves into a shimmering play of light. Besides the reflection of a counter cultural sensibility, the tape romanticizes science through its coupling of Albert Einstein's image with the heraldic strains of Rimsky-Korsakov.

Only available on the anthology *Surveying the First Decade, Program 5.*

1
Shelly Silver
2002, 3:15, U.S., color, sound
The world will devour you. ... A group of cops laugh and talk while scanning the street for suspicious activity. An extreme close-up of a sensuously exposed neck; a soft pink fleshy ear turns to reveal an inquisitive hostile eye. ... 1 is a short tape about longing, threat, power, and seduction with the camera functioning in turn as aggressor, mediator, and confessor. The split-screen image as well as the eerie sound track, made up of two versions of the same Miles Davis song run simultaneously, underline Silver's ambivalent take on the controversial subject matter, as well as calling the work's title into question.

37 Stories about Leaving Home
Shelly Silver
1996, 51:30, U.S., color, sound
37 Stories about Leaving Home provides a rare and personal view into the lives of a group of Japanese women living in the Tokyo area. This beautifully constructed and complex video weaves stories told by grandmothers, mothers, and daughters, ranging in age from 15 to 83. The stories recount each woman's personal journey from childhood to adulthood—their experiences of leaving home. It points to the enormous societal changes that have occurred in Japan over the last few generations, showing how these women are both influencing and coping with these changes in their own different, individual, and creative ways.

Former East/Former West

Former East/Former West
Shelly Silver
1994, 1:02:00, U.S., color, sound
Former East/Former West was shot in Berlin three years after the German reunification. Comprised largely of street interviews conducted in various parts of the city, the video documents Berliners' feelings about their national identity. For 40 years, people in this divided city lived radically different lives—ideologically, economically, socially, and politically. These differences were also reflected in their everyday routines, relationships, and experiences, leading Silver to ponder what the two Germanys have in common, aside from language. Questions such as "Why did these two countries decide to become one again?" begin to undermine more basic and unchallenged concepts such as capitalism, socialism, freedom, history, patriotism, and the foundations of nations in general.

Getting In
Shelly Silver
1989, 3:00, U.S., color, sound
This very funny tape plays with the identification of the camera as phallus, as an instrument of power and domination intruding upon reality; never an innocent bystander, it is always the organizing locus of events. Over sequences in which the camera/viewer approaches entrances to houses, shops, and other buildings, the soundtrack carries the moans of a man and woman reaching orgasm. The pitch and urgency of their moaning increases as the camera nears and finally penetrates its target.

The Houses That Are Left
Shelly Silver
1991, 51:00, U.S., b&w and color, sound
With an amusing sense of drama, *The Houses That Are Left* illustrates Silver's technique of building an obscure narrative into a complex net of miscellaneous texts and images. Unfolding throughout the tape is the story of two friends who come together to try to figure out how to live in the modern world while being besieged by militant messages from the dead. Juxtaposing black-and-white film with color video and fusing narrative elements of drama, comedy, and documentary, Silver provides a structure that allows a plurality of voices to speak: two women who were childhood friends, people on the street interviewed for "market research," and the observations of dead people who watch the living on television monitors. *The Houses That Are Left* combines sitcom, documentary, and melodrama in a complex story of the living and the dead. While the living are rendered passive by their fear that something bad could happen to them, the dead, who no longer can have anything happen to them at all, strive to regain their ability to act through the only tool available to them: their televisions.

The Houses That Are Left

Meet the People
Shelly Silver
1986, 17:00, U.S., color, sound
Functioning as both a fake documentary and a fake advertisement, *Meet the People* deals with issues of desire, complicity, and identity in the age of mass media, as 14 "characters" talk about their lives, desires, and dreams.
"The fictions of the self overtly concern Shelly Silver in her tour-de-force *Meet the People*. In video verité style, she swiftly inter-cuts what appear to be her interviews of 14 individuals representing contemporary New York types: a cabby, a waitress, a housewife, a stripper, an Italian construction worker, a black army officer. At the end the credits reveal that all 14 are actors and all were apparently reading Silver's script. Silver wittily questions the very idea of the authentic—ultimately, she implies, 'personal truth' is a momentary and collaborative invention, a triborough bridge between actor, author-director, and audience—on TV and on the street."
—Anne Hoy, *Speechless* (New York: International Center of Photography, 1989)

small lies, Big Truth

small lies, Big Truth
Shelly Silver
1999, 18:48, U.S., color, sound
In turns funny, disturbing, and glisteningly sensual, *small lies, Big Truth* is a tape about love, relationships, and the joy and banality of sex in the late 20th century. It also touches on such issues as morality, voyeurism, nature vs. culture, and power, as eight people read fragments from the testimonies of President Bill Clinton and Monica Lewinsky, as published in the Starr report.

Things I Forget to Tell Myself
Shelly Silver
1989, 4:00, U.S., color, sound
A fragmented view of a city provides this poetic examination of disclosing and withholding—what is and isn't seen, and once it is seen, how is it read?
"In New York artist Shelly Silver's *Things I Forget to Tell Myself*, a fragmented textual statement. … is interspersed with imagery culled from NYC, much of it cropped by the camera operator's outstretched hand. Buildings, windows, signs, pedestrians, cops, and doors constitute a continuum of access and obstruction. The sometimes alternating, sometimes simultaneous patterns of disclosure and withholding, recognition and inobservance, are scrutinized to reveal the imprints of psychological processes and cultural codes, while testing boundaries between seeing and reading."
—Michael Nash, *Channels for A Changing TV* (Long Beach Museum of Art, 1991)

We
Shelly Silver
1990, 4:00, U.S., b&w and color, sound
In a visually difficult construction, Silver plays with the viewer's ability to focus and take in an entire image. This puzzling tape is composed of three basic elements: a scrolling text, an image of street traffic that occupies one half of the split screen, and on the other side the image of a man masturbating, focusing on the hand and penis. The viewer's attention is suspended and divided between these two disparate images, unable to make sense of their correlation. This confusion demonstrates the meaning of the text that reads, "If we keep attaching meanings to everything we perceive … we are bound to go crazy someday."

Silver, Suzie

Suzie Silver is a videomaker and sometime performance artist. She has worked collaboratively on videotapes, performances, and curatorial projects with Lawrence Steger—*La Vida Loca* (1987), *Peccatum Mutum* (1988), *In Through the Out Door*—and Iris Moore—*Bait & Switch: At Night Every Girl Is a Boy, Dangerous Pleasures*. Her tapes merge her interests in performance and video to play with her fascinations, which include "queer sexuality, pop culture, visual pleasure, gender disarray, and many other things that probably shouldn't be mentioned in polite company." Suzie Silver is currently on Faculty at Carnegie Mellon University.

Freebird
Suzie Silver
1993, 11:00, U.S., b&w and color, sound
Silver directs and performs all the roles in this raucous and hilarious music video rendition of Lynyrd Skynyrd's "Freebird," the infamous Southern rock anthem for an entire generation of 1970s male youth. In this spoof of straight mass culture, Silver flips ironically between roles: from a lesbian proudly proclaiming her sexuality at the Academy Awards to an in-concert Coors-drinking Ronnie Van Zant to a black-lace lesbian lounge swinger celebrating the wild, colorful world of "out" visibility. Silver uses an amazing array of found footage and special effects to bend genders and genres.

The Look of Love: A Gothic Romance
Suzie Silver
1998, 19:00, U.S., color, sound
The Look of Love: A Gothic Romance is an experimental video/audio collage in four acts. Performing in various guises, Suzie Silver embarks on a quest for the magnificence—and horror—of desire and pleasure. Her female characters are caught up in a cascade of subtle and spectacular cinematic images of sexual desire between women.

A Spy (Hester Reeve Does the Doors)
Suzie Silver
1992, 4:15, U.S., color, sound

Continuing Silver's interest in using performance in video, *A Spy* is a gender-bending and thought-provoking mixture of pure visual pleasure with disturbing undercurrents. As Reeve lip-syncs to a Doors' song ("I am a spy in the house of love/I know the dream that you're dreaming of/I know your deepest secret fear…"), we see a new manifestation of Jesus walking in a video field of pulsing rainbows, amoebic forms, and B-movie girls in black panties—suggesting the desires we try to hide from ourselves and others.

Simon, Jason

Jason Simon's work combines documentary with conceptual approaches to representation. *Production Notes* came out of a year of working for a high-end commercial television production company on jobs for Pepsi, McDonald's, Procter and Gamble, and other giants of consumer culture.

Production Notes: Fast Food for Thought
Jason Simon
1986, 28:00, U.S., color, sound
Production Notes allows us to eavesdrop on the business decisions behind the creation of our daily diet of television commercials. This tape undertakes to explode the address of seven TV ads by means of repetition, slow motion, and "production notes"—memos sent from the advertising agency to the production company prior to filming the spots to describe the intentions, desires, strategies, and ideology of the commercials and their creators. Stripping the commercial sequences of their glitz and fast pacing is a powerful technique that allows the viewer to examine the jingles with which they may have happily hummed along.

Sistach, Maryse and José Buil

Maryse Sistach and José Buil are Rockefeller Media Arts Fellows from Mexico.

La Línea Paterna (The Paternal Line)
Maryse Sistach and José Buil
1993, 1:00:00, U.S., color, sound, in Spanish with English subtitles.
Maryse Sistach and José Buil trace the Buil family's 20th century saga from Spain to Mexico, largely through dozens of home movies recorded by Buil's grandfather with his "Baby Pathé" camera.

Only available on the anthology *Frames of Reference: Reflections on Media, Volume 6, Program 1.*

Smid, Aina
(see Grzinik, Marina)

Smith, Barbara

Barbara Smith's work concentrates on human relationships, pushing the boundaries of art and life. Smith was among the first female performance artists to emerge during the late 1960s who directly confronted issues of the mind, the body, and the spirit.

Becoming Bald; Full Jar, Empty Jar; Perpetual Napkin
Barbara Smith
1974, 4:00, U.S., color, sound
This collection of performace tapes by Barbara Smith begins with *Becoming Bald*, a process video during which Smith's head is shaved in preparation for her meditation performance *Full Jar, Empty Jar*, shown in a still image. In *The Perpetual Napkin*, Smith uses the metaphor of running until exhausted so that she can "explore how life causes shifts in consciousness and growth to new understanding and development." Seeking to achieve higher powers related to "The Magician" or "transformer," the piece becomes a lesson on the levels of how art functions, i.e. direct seeing, play, exploration, discovery, skill, and technique, and finally shows art and especially the artist as a transmitter of energy as a living icon or tangka.

Only available on the anthology *Endurance, Reel 3.*

Smith, Cauleen

Los Angeles-based filmmaker Cauleen Smith made her feature film debut with *Drylongso* (1998). She has also made experimental videos, installations, and several film shorts, including *Daily Rains* (1990), *Chronicles of a Lying Spirit* by Kelly Gabron (1992), and *The Changing Same* (2001).

Drylongso
Cauleen Smith
1998, 87:00, U.S., color, sound, 16mm to video
In Cauleen Smith's coming-of-age drama *Drylongso*, a young Oakland woman begins photographing what she deems "America's most endangered species," African-American males.

Spanish subtitled version available.

Only available on the anthology *Frames of Reference: Reflections on Media, Volume 2, Program 2.*

Smith, John

John Smith has made more than 30 film, video, and installation works since 1972. His films blur the distinctions between experimental, narrative, and documentary film while at the same time creating a tension between the image and the soundtrack—a feat he accomplishes with a wit that makes his work accessible to non-avant garde audiences. Smith's films have been shown internationally in cinemas, art galleries, and on television and have been awarded major prizes at film festivals. Based in London, Smith teaches art at the University of East London and Central Saint Martins School of Art.

Blight

Associations
John Smith
1975, 7:00, U.K., color, sound

Images from magazines and color supplements accompany a spoken text taken from Herbert H. Clark's "Word Associations and Linguistic Theory" (in *New Horizons in Linguistics*, ed. John Lyons, 1970). By using the ambiguities inherent in the English language, *Associations* sets language against itself. Image and word work together and against each other to destroy and create meaning.

"*Associations* is a straightforward rebus—a game in which words are replaced by pictures. But the text is so dense with contemporary linguistic theory, and the combination of visual puns so extensive, that a simple, unique reading of the film is impossible."
–A.L. Rees, *Unpacking 7 Films* (1980)
Also available on the compilation *John Smith: Program 1.*

The Black Tower
John Smith
1987, 24:00, U.K., color, sound

"John Smith uses humour to repeatedly subvert and frustrate potentially threatening content in an economically constructed tale of the narrator's descent into paranoia and, ultimately, oblivion, as he is pursued, haunted, and finally destroyed by a mysterious peripatetic black tower. Throughout, both verbal and visual imagery are low key to the point of banality; shots of familiar inner-city landscapes—terraces, tower blocks, and scruffy wastelands—are set against a narrative that is laconic and bathetic in the best traditions of English suburban comedy. There is a (frequently hilarious) reflexive relationship between sound and image, and while the early sections appear to pursue a conventional storyline, these are gradually undermined by an increased emphasis on and deliberate misuse or overplaying of filmic conventions. The tower becomes a 'trick of the imagination' as the disappearing cars are shown to be a trick in the editing."
–Catherine Lacey, *The Elusive Sign* (London: Arts Council/British Council exhibition catalog, 1987)
Also available on the compilation *John Smith: Program 1.*

Blight
John Smith
1996, 14:00, U.K., color, sound

"*Blight* was made in collaboration with composer Jocelyn Pook. It revolves around the building of the M11 Link Road in East London, which provoked a long and bitter campaign by local residents to protect their homes from demolition. Until 1994, when our houses were destroyed, both the composer and I lived on the route of this road. The images in the film are a selective record of some of the changes, which occurred in the area over a two-year period, from the demolition of houses through to the start of motorway building work. ... Like much of my earlier work, *Blight* exploits the ambiguities of its material to produce new meanings and metaphors, fictionalizing reality through framing and editing strategies. The emotive power of music is used in the film to overtly aid this invention, investing mundane images with artificial importance. A specific 'real' context for the depicted events only becomes apparent at the end of the film. What is presented is simultaneously fact and fiction."
–John Smith
Also available on the compilation *John Smith: Program 2.*

Frozen War
John Smith
2002, 11:00, U.K., color, sound

A spontaneous response to the bombing of Afghanistan triggered by a disorientating experience in an Irish hotel room.

"Shot early in the morning, just after the U.S. and Britain started bombing Afghanistan, it's narrated by Smith, who describes how he worried about a

blown-up transmitter when he found only a static face on TV. The slow pace and rambling form become apt correlatives for Smith's own confusion."
–Fred Camper, "Pushed to the Limit," *Chicago Reader* (7 September 2002)

Gargantuan

Gargantuan
John Smith
1992, 1:00, U.K., color, sound
"To master the one-minute time span requires considerable discipline, and few pieces, if any, had been shaped as genuine miniatures—most having the appearance of being extracts from larger works. The notable exception was John Smith's 'Gargantuan,' which was not only the right length for the idea, but actually incorporated a triple pun on the word 'minute.'"
–Nicky Hamlyn, "One Minute TV 1992," *Vertigo* (Spring 1993)
Also available on the compilation *John Smith: Program 1.*

The Girl Chewing Gum
John Smith
1976, 12:00, U.K., b&w, sound
"In *The Girl Chewing Gum* a commanding voiceover appears to direct the action in a busy London street. As the instructions become more absurd and fantasized, we realize that the supposed director (not the shot) is fictional; he only describes—not prescribes—the events that take place before him. Smith embraced the 'spectre of narrative' (suppressed by structural film) to play word against picture and chance against order. Sharp and direct, the film anticipates the more elaborate scenarios to come: witty, many-layered, punning, but also seriously and poetically haunted by drama's ineradicable ghost."
–A.L. Rees, *A Directory of British Film and Video Artists* (Luton, UK: Arts Council of England/University of Luton Press, 1996)
Also available on the compilation *John Smith: Program 1.*

John Smith: Program 1
"The films of John Smith conduct a serious investigation into the combination of sound and image but with a sense of humour that reaches out beyond the traditional avant-garde audience. His films and videos move between narrative and absurdity, constantly undermining the traditional relationship between the visual and the aural. By blurring the perceived boundaries of experimental film, fiction, and documentary, Smith never delivers what he has led the spectator to expect."
–Mark Webber, Leeds International Film Festival (2000)
Total running time 48:00.
Contents:
Associations, John Smith, 1975, 7:00, U.K., color, sound
The Black Tower, John Smith, 1987, 24:00, U.K., color, sound
Gargantuan, John Smith, 1992, 1:00, U.K., color, sound
The Girl Chewing Gum, John Smith, 1976, 12:00, U.K., b&w, sound
Om, John Smith, 1986, 4:00, U.K., color, sound

John Smith: Program 2
These diverse works, at once humorous and melancholic, share a preoccupation with memory, change, and the impermanence of the world.
Total running time 1:21:00.
Contents:
Blight, John Smith, 1996, 14:00, U.K., color, sound
The Kiss, John Smith and Ian Bourn, 1999, 5:00, U.K., color, sound
Regression, John Smith, 1999, 17:00, U.K., color, sound
Slow Glass, John Smith, 1991, 40:00, U.K., color, sound
The Waste Land, John Smith, 1999, 5:00, U.K., color, sound

The Kiss

The Kiss
John Smith and Ian Bourn
1999, 5:00, U.K., color, sound
A depiction of the forced development of a hothouse flower. A more sinister mechanical process progressively overtakes organic growth.
"The makers manage very convincingly to wrong-foot the viewer in just five minutes in this minimalist, lyrical film about a blossoming flower."
—International Film Festival Rotterdam (2000)
Also available on the compilation *John Smith: Program 2.*

Lost Sound
John Smith and Graeme Miller
2001, 28:00, U.K., color, sound
Lost Sound documents fragments of discarded audio tape found by the artists within a small area of East London, combining the sound retrieved from each piece of tape with images of the place where it was found. The work explores the potential of chance, creating portraits of particular places by building formal, narrative, and musical connections between images and sounds linked by the random discoveries of the tape samples.
"Hanging from trees like mistletoe, from lampposts and awnings like flotsam from an impossible high tide, blown by a breeze saturated with radio waves and mobile phone signals, Smith and Miller make a modern tangleweed of magnetic tape sing its discarded memories. Yet far from nostalgically organising this material, the tape becomes a formal cue to render time and space according to an ulterior rhythm."
—Pandaemonium Festival (London, 2001)

Om

Om
John Smith
1986, 4:00, U.K., color, sound
A film about haircuts, clothes, and image/sound relationships.
"This four-minute film explores our response to stereotypes—aural, visual, and ideological. Smith signals these stereotypes to the viewer through a chiefly associational system, which deftly manipulates the path of our expectations. The structure is stunningly simple and deceptively subtle. We are taken on a journey from one concrete stereotype to its diametric opposite, as images transform and juxtapose to, ultimately, invert our interpretation of what we see and hear."
—Gary Davis
Also available on the compilation *John Smith: Program 1.*

Regression
John Smith
1999, 17:00, U.K., color, sound
A portrait of the artist as a not-so-young man. The filmmaker attempts to enter the digital age by making a new video version of one of his old films.
"The award of the Short Film Festival goes to a video in which the reflection of artistic work becomes a form itself. John Smith manages to give us a self-ironic humorous experiment about art and time."
—International Short Film Festival (Oberhausen, 2000)
Also available on the compilation *John Smith: Program 2.*

Slow Glass
John Smith
1991, 40:00, U.K., color, sound
A nostalgic glazier shows off his knowledge and expounds his theories. Taking glassmaking processes and history as its central theme, *Slow Glass* explores ideas about memory, perception, and change.
"The rich visual surface and engaging voiceover of *Slow Glass* convey an extended metaphor, which links light, glass, and lens. An 'opening' shot (a smashed windowpane) and a 'closing' one (the window bricked up) frame the film. As it slowly reveals its own artifice, the realist surface is interrupted, as

when a car mirror shows reflections of a different journey than the one visible through the windscreen. These constructed 'mistakes,' which break the flow, are so crafted as to invade the image and unsettle the word. Direct evocation of the past—a 1950s childhood—allows the film to question its depiction of the present... Smith brings formidable skill to bear in a film which scrutinizes the very 'speculations' it incites."
—A.L. Rees, *A History of Experimental Film and Video* (London: British Film Institute, 1999)
Also available on the compilation *John Smith: Program 2*.

The Waste Land
John Smith
1999, 5:00, U.K., color, sound
A personal interpretation of the poetry and letters of T.S. Eliot that explores the ambiguities of language and space in a scenario built around an anagram.
"A brilliant, absurd staging of Eliot's *The Waste Land* in the local pub by the master of irony himself, John Smith. Smith's use of the subjective camera tradition of independent film takes the viewer on a shaky journey from bar to bog and back again."
—UK/Canadian Video Exchange (touring program, 2002)
Also available on the compilation *John Smith: Program 2*.

Worst Case Scenario
John Smith
2003, 18:00, U.K., color, sound
"This new work by John Smith looks down onto a busy Viennese intersection and a corner bakery. Constructed from hundreds of still images, it presents situations in a stilted motion, often with sinister undertones. Through this technique we're made aware of our intrinsic capacity for creating continuity, and fragments of narrative, from potentially (no doubt actually) unconnected events."
—Mark Webber, London Film Festival (2003)

Smith, Michael

Michael Smith is a video and performance artist who uses humor to comment on the impact of television on everyday life, drawing attention to the bland consistency maintained and celebrated by the medium. Smith follows the television tradition of entertainment, appropriating its language and formats—commercial, music video, and talk show—to create a satire of present-day America. Smith's tapes and performances revolve around the adventures and insight of a central persona, a paradoxical and ridiculous being named "Mike"—a modern-day, less-than-super hero, overly influenced by what he sees on television.

Down in the Rec Room
Michael Smith
1979-81, 14:00, U.S., color, sound
Like all of Smith's videotapes, *Down in the Rec Room* is based on a performance that finds Mike once again all dressed up with nowhere to go. Smith mimes along with a children's "let's play make believe" record and then repeats the action—this time disco dancing along with Donny and Marie on the TV set. *Down in the Rec Room* continues Smith's critique of American fantasy culture by depicting the sorry life of the average guy.

Go for It, Mike
Michael Smith
1984, 5:00, U.S., color, sound
Smith's gentle, recusant comedy is a critique of masculine domination, focusing on the myth of manifest destiny. Believing the moral of the Old West that "everything is there for the taking," mild-mannered Mike is inspired to "go for it!" and to conquer wide-open spaces in the modern way: as a real estate developer of suburban sub-divisions. Dressed as a cowboy and mime riding a horse in front of images of mobile homes, Smith updates the notion of "rugged individualism" to include personal theme music and a chorus. Mike is an unassuming television anti-hero, the figure thousands of television viewers rely upon to "go for it!" for them.

It Starts at Home
Michael Smith
1982, 25:00, U.S., color, sound
Tapping into cable because of his lousy reception, Mike gets more than he bargained for as he unwittingly becomes trapped in the medium—the "star" of his own cable TV show. Due to an incomprehensible mishap, Mike's rewired

TV now transmits his image to the world; the observer has become the observed. Turning the tables on viewership in a way that reflects the banality of television, Smith touches on identification with television and the manner in which television re-presents our world back to us.

Mike Builds a Shelter
Michael Smith
1985, 25:00, U.S., color, sound

Mike Builds a Shelter is a performance comedy with apocalyptic overtones, a narrative extension of Smith's installation *Government Approved Home Fallout Shelter/Snack Bar*. In this darkly humorous morality play, Smith contrasts Mike's rural adventures in a pastoral landscape with his home fallout shelter. Throughout, the dual narratives are inter-cut with episodes of *Mike's Show* on cable, in which Mike's banal domestic activities are eagerly if passively received by living-room TV viewers. The government-approved provisions for nuclear fallout that Mike so readily accepts, typical of the naivete of 1950s' public safety policies, are seen in stark contrast to the reality of the contemporary crisis of a radioactive environment.

Mike Builds a Shelter

Secret Horror
Michael Smith
1980, 14:00, U.S., color, sound

This social satire on total, faceless authority begins with Smith bewildered by forces he doesn't understand. Like Chicken Little, Mike is threatened by the falling ceiling, while spooks dressed in conventional white sheets invite him to a party in his own house. In Smith's characteristic parody, *Secret Horror* is an allegory for the fate of individuals lost in the social sauce, hopelessly out of touch with the glamorous. Trapped in his pathetic lifestyle, Mike, in the end, consoles himself with Neil Diamond's anthem "Forever in Blue Jeans," forever mediocre.

The World of Photography
Michael Smith and William Wegman
1986, 24:00, U.S., color, sound

A day in the life of a professional photographer (Wegman) and his eager student (Smith), this tape offers a humorous, at times surreal, how-to instructional course in photography. Filled with practical advice, the tape sardonically centers itself more on the need to cultivate an effective artistic persona than actually taking any photographs. Wegman asks, "Before you carve out your own niche, it's important to ask yourself one tough question: Do you have the aptitude?"

Snyder, Bob

Bob Snyder is a Chicago-based composer and video artist who has been experimenting with sound and video synthesis since the '60s. As a musician, his interest has always been in the relationship between music and imagery. In Snyder's work music is the central generative source of meaning, although he also considers the dialogue between nature and architecture. Snyder is a professor in the sound department at the School of the Art Institute of Chicago.

Hard and Flexible Music
Bob Snyder
1988, 6:00, U.S., color, sound

In this video diptych, Snyder uses image and music to depict opposing forces in semi-abstract terms. Exploring processes of fracture and permutation, *Hard and Flexible Music* contrasts two groups of images, gridded architectural structures and fluid natural imagery, on opposite sides of the screen. The experimental music soundtrack carries two synthesized tracks with differing musical qualities.

Also available on the compilation *Bob Snyder: Sound and Video 1975-1990*.

Icron
Bob Synder
1978, 11:00, U.S., color, sound

Using the image processor as it was intended as a performance instrument, *Icron* exploits the processor's real-time capabilities: the image and soundtrack were generated through simultaneous improvisation, although the color was added later. The title of the piece is a neologism created by fusing "icon" with "chron" as a reference to the effect of temporal changes on images. Snyder combines iconographic elements of broadcast television with the structural features of music by deconstructing the face of a newscaster into scan lines. The newscaster's speech is also re-modulated to produce a cartoonish effect that is equally humorous and sinister. Because the content of his discourse is obscured, only the rhetorical tics of authoritarian pronouncement remain.

Also available on the compilation *Bob Snyder: Sound and Video 1975-1990*.

Lines of Force

Lines of Force
Bob Snyder
1979, 10:00, U.S., color, sound
Lines of Force opens with footage of a dramatic explosion. For most of the piece, the screen is divided: into a triptych at first and slowly into horizontal and vertical bars. Electronically manipulated footage shows a man walking, a marching band, ferns, cartoons, a window, and a train arriving on a set of tracks. The naturally occurring lines in the array of images presented mirror the electronically created bars and lines that divide the screen. Natural scenes provide a respite from the frantic pace of the images.

Also available on the compilation *Bob Snyder: Sound and Video 1975-1990*.

Bob Snyder: Sound and Video 1975-1990
A compilation of all of Snyder's works, remarkable for their formal elegance, conceptual scope and sensual lusciousness.
Total running time 54:00.
Contents:
Hard and Flexible Music, Bob Snyder, 1988, 6:00, U.S., color, sound
Icron, Bob Synder, 1978, 11:00, U.S., color, sound
Lines of Force, Bob Synder, 1979, 10:00, U.S., color, sound
Spectral Brands, Bob Synder, 1984, 15:00, U.S., color, sound
Trim Subdivisions, Bob Snyder, 1981, 6:00, U.S., color, sound
Winter Notebook, Bob Snyder, 1975, 6:00, U.S., color, sound
Available on video or laserdisc.

Spectral Brands

Spectral Brands
Bob Synder
1984, 15:00, U.S., color, sound
"[This] is my first attempt to construct a video piece using one set of generative intervals for both sound and color. All of the color in the piece is orchestrated in brightness 'octaves' corresponding to the registration of the pitches in the soundtrack. Each hue from a circle of 12 corresponds to one of the pitches of a tempered scale. The articulation of the piece consists of a series of loudness and brightness ripples which move across the piece in speed relationships derived from the hue and pitch proportions. The image content, or the 'instruments' through which the colors resonate, are an alphabetical set of identifying symbols for 32 of the largest corporations in the world."
–Bob Snyder

Also available on the compilation *Bob Snyder: Sound and Video 1975-1990*.

Trim Subdivisions
Bob Snyder
1981, 6:00, U.S., color, sound
Snyder manipulates images of tract houses in a small Indiana town to create Cubist reconstructions of the monotonous facades. Elaborate pans ripple the image plane into accordion folds.

Also available on the compilation *Bob Snyder: Sound and Video 1975-1990*.

Winter Notebook
Bob Snyder
1975, 6:00, U.S., color, sound
This tape exemplifies Snyder's early experiments with the image processor. Articulated patterns of alternating wavelength and amplitude of both sound and light are arranged to produce abstract compositions. Voltages processed by an Emu sound synthesizer are systematized through characteristic interval

structures that affect the image processor's functions.

Also available on the compilation *Bob Snyder: Sound and Video 1975-1990*.

Bob Snyder: An Interview (see On Art and Artists)

Sobell, Nina

Nina Sobell is a New York-based artist who has produced a broad body of work embracing various themes through video, performance, installation, sculpture, and live TV. A participant in the feminist movement of the 1970s, her conceptually based work ranges from taboo performances and museum installations to interactive video matrixes for public participation. Exploring video-sculpture, Sobell was intrigued with creating psycho-sociological transformations via video technology, making environments and mobile structures to physically engage the viewer.

Hey! Baby Chickey

Chicken on Foot
Nina Sobell
1979, 8:00, U.S., b&w, sound
"Tersely but accurately titled, Sobell's *Chicken on Foot* opens to reveal a naked leg diagonally traversing the screen. A hand attempts to balance an egg upon the knee, and no sooner is this accomplished than the egg is smashed. As the goo runs down the leg, the foot attached kicks high in the air. A knee-jerk response, you say, but more follows. A pan-ready chicken, leaving the foot, is treated to trips up and down the slime-covered leg, dangled on the knee and engaged in some sophisticated baby talk. Finally, as its off-screen mother decides to take it to some egg laying, it says bye-bye to the camera and to us. The tape is funky in a way Rufus Thomas would never have imagined, and neo-humanist readings aside, what I liked best about it is that it's so entirely off the wall, so entirely incompatible with my mundane reality, that I get a glimpse of a profoundly original frame of consciousness. By investigating thoroughly idiosyncratic territory, Sobell has circumvented the disadvantages most video artists stumble over and made a tape in which comparisons with commercial video are neither possible nor relevant."
–David James, "Laughing at TV," *Artweek* 14:23 (18 June 1983)
Also available on the anthology *I Say I Am: Program 1*.

Hey! Baby Chickey
Nina Sobell
1978, 10:00, U.S., b&w, sound
"In her performance art video *Hey! Baby Chickey* Nina Sobell appears nude 'playing' with a raw cooking chicken. With a few simple manipulations, she eradicates the cultural distance between mother and woman as sexual being. … Playing on the symbolic connection between food and sex, cooking is transformed into sexuality, but the involvement of the dead chicken pushes that sexuality towards bestiality and necrophilia. The scene is further complicated when the same chicken is given the role of baby. Sobell plays with the chicken, rocking it, holding it up by its arms as if teaching it to walk, and swinging it from breast to breast in what can only be described as a milking dance. This collapsing of the baby role with the chicken's already established roles of dead animal, food material, and sexual object violates other taboos, including infanticide, cannibalism, and pedophilia."
–Chris Straayer, *Deviant Eyes, Deviant Bodies: Sexual Re-orientations in Film and Video* (New York: Columbia University Press, 1996)
Also available on the anthology *I Say I Am: Program 1*.

Soe, Valerie

Valerie Soe is a fourth-generation Chinese-American from the Bay Area. Her video pieces are personal expressions of her experience as a Chinese-American woman and treat intersecting issues of race, social prejudice, and the politics of difference in mainstream American culture and marginalized Chinese-American culture.

"ALL ORIENTALS LOOK THE SAME"
Valerie Soe
1986, 1:30, U.S., b&w, sound
Snapshots of individuals from all parts of Asia and the Pacific Islands form a stream of images that blankly proves the fallacy of the title phrase. Soe challenges viewers to recognize the failure of vision that underlies this common misperception, and the failure of understanding that creates and propagates such generalizations.

Spanish subtitled version available.

Also available on the anthology *Frames of Reference: Reflections on Media, Volume 2, Program 2*.

Sollfrank, Cornelia

German digital media artist Cornelia Sollfrank explores the changing role of the artist in the Information Age, the gender-specific handling of

have script, will destroy
Cornelia Sollfrank
2000, Germany, 15:00, color, sound
"For quite some time the Hamburg artist Cornelia Sollfrank has been researching female hackers and found that hacking is a field completely under

Sollfrank, Cornelia

(continued)

technology, communication, and networking as art. For *Female Extension* (1997) she hacked into the first net.art competition initiated by a museum and flooded the network with submissions by 300 virtual female net artists. She also edited *First* and *Next Cyberfeminist International.*

Sonnier, Keith

Having worked extensively in neon sculpture, Keith Sonnier introduced video to his work in the 1970s as a representation of a medium working with and against itself. Sonnier began experimenting with the formal properties of computer-generated video by using a Scanimate computer, and his work exploits feedback, amplification, and transmitted light's tactile quality. As an artist embracing technology, Sonnier's work challenges artistic conventions and opens new channels of communication at the cutting edge of technology.

male domination. Nonetheless she was able to produce a series of several videos in which she interviewed female hackers. In December 1999 she came to know a U.S. hacker who attended the annual hackers' convention held by the Chaos Computer Club (CCC). She did the video interview *have script, will destroy* with her on condition that the woman, code-named Clara G. Sopht, remained anonymous and did not provide specific information about her work. The result is a highly theoretical interview about current forms of political resistance, undermined by seductively beautiful and enigmatically diffuse pictures of a woman wearing sunglasses and a cap, moving around in a low-tech scenario."
−Yvonne Volkart, "Tamed Girls Running Wild, Figurations of Unruliness in Contemporary Video Art" in *<hers>: Video as a Female Terrain*, ed. Stella Rollig (Graz: Catalogue Styrian Automn, 2000)

Only available on the anthology *e-[d]entity, Tape 2.*

Animation 1
Keith Sonnier
1973, 14:00, U.S., color, sound
With the Watergate hearings as a backdrop, quotes from various newspapers and magazines−including the story of Robert Smithson's death in a plane crash−build a picture of the confusing and tragic events of July 1973. Sonnier uses appropriated footage and reproduced newspaper clippings to create a richly layered video that attempts to sort out the truth from the available information. Sonnier's instructions to the computer operator reference the making of the tape and thereby create a self-conscious, limiting frame. This title was in the original Castelli-Sonnabend video art collection.

Animation 2
Keith Sonnier
1974, 17:00, U.S., color, sound
Concentrating on abstract shapes and color value, *Animation 2* is a record of images manipulated through computer animation. By recording the data screens of the animators and the voices of the controllers, Sonnier discloses the process of making the tape. "This tape is about media, and it seems totally unedited, because we hear him talking over the intercom with the engineer … The engineer interjects, 'Do you want to save any of this stuff?' Yes, indeed; Sonnier saves and shows it all, the whole process."
− Jonathan Price, "Video Art: a Medium Discovering Itself," *Art News* 76 (January 1977)
This title was in the original Castelli-Sonnabend video art collection.

Send/Receive I and Send/Receive II (see Béar, Liza)

TV In and TV Out
Keith Sonnier
1972, 10:00, U.S., color, sound
"In Sonnier's video tape *TV In and TV Out,* two images are superimposed, one shot off network television and the other shot from a studio performance situation involving some of the materials and visual qualities of his sculptures. This live image is colorized by a device which adds color to a black and white image and in turn manipulates the color. Colorized color is more opaque and less three-dimensionally tactile than synthesized color, but it is tactile in its video scan-line texture. …
"The measure of Sonnier's color video tapes is not the extent to which he extends painterly values, though there is some continuity there, but the extent to which he defines the surface, space, and color of the material of video."
−Bruce Kurtz, "Video Is Being Invented," *Arts Magazine* (Dec./Jan. 1973)

Sorrondeguy, Martin

Martin Sorrondeguy was the lead singer of the Latino punk band Los Crudos, which toured the U.S., Mexico, Europe, Japan, and South America.

Beyond the Screams: A U.S. Latino Hardcore Punk Documentary
Martin Sorrondeguy
1999, 29:00, U.S., color, sound
Former Los Crudos vocalist Martin Sorrondeguy produced this powerful and

uplifting documentary about the U.S. Latino punk scene and the DIY movement. The video features live performances by bands, including Huasipungo, Los Crudos, Subsistencia, Sbitch, and many more. "The Latino punk scene in the early '90s really exploded because all of a sudden we had a hell of a lot to sing about. What started happening politically in the U.S. pissed us off so much, and we were feeling targeted and we were feeling so cornered as a community that we began writing songs about it."
—Martin Sorrondeguy

Spiro, Ellen

Ellen Spiro's unconventional approach to documentary is fueled by a history of working in experimental film, art, and activist video; she produces, directs, shoots and edits her own work. Known as a pioneer in small format video technology, Spiro made her first documentary for $564; dubbed "the little video that could," *DiAna's Hair Ego* was the first documentary shot on 8mm consumer video equipment to be shown on television in the U.S. Her subsequent work has focused on atypical Americana, such as queer life in the South and a nuclear waste junk collector in New Mexico.

Greetings from Out Here

Atomic Ed & the Black Hole
Ellen Spiro
2002, 39:40, U.S., color, sound
Atomic Ed & the Black Hole tells the story of a scientist-turned-atomic junk collector known as Atomic Ed. More than 30 years ago, Ed quit his job making "better" atomic bombs and he began collecting what he calls "nuclear waste," non-radioactive high-tech discards from the Los Alamos National Laboratory. As the self-appointed curator of an unofficial museum of the nuclear age called "The Black Hole," Atomic Ed reveals and preserves a history of government waste that was literally thrown in a trash heap.
Spanish subtitled version available.
Also available on the anthology *Frames of Reference: Reflections on Media, Volume 3, Program 2*.

DiAna's Hair Ego: AIDS Info Upfront
Ellen Spiro
1989, 28:00, U.S., color, sound
Recognizing the extreme inadequacy of information on AIDS prevention, cosmetologist DiAna DiAna and her partner Dr. Bambi Sumpter took on the task of educating the black community in Columbia, South Carolina. This video documents the growth of the South Carolina AIDS Education Network, which originated and operates in DiAna's Hair Ego, DiAna's beauty salon. Working in repressive times to teach a sex-positive and compassionate response to the AIDS crisis in the "buckle of the Bible belt," the work of the South Carolina AIDS Education Network has met with harsh criticism. Despite political pressure, DiAna and Sumpter refuse to compromise their teachings in order to get state funding. Since 1986 they have been operating solely on the beauty shop's tips. Their creative strategies and non-judgmental concern offer a model for making a difference.

Greetings from Out Here
Ellen Spiro
1993, 58:00, U.S., color, sound
Spiro traveled for one year on the back roads of the southern United States gathering footage for this mobile video project capturing the richness, vitality, and courage of "out" gay Southern life. Accompanied by her dog Sam and a video camera, she travels from Virginia to Texas and back. Her van (which breaks down frequently) serves as office, apartment, editing suite, and runabout. Spiro's witty eye and spectacular footage create many insightful portraits of small town gay and lesbian Southerners at such celebratory events as the Texas Gay Rodeo, Rhythm Fest, a gay Mardi Gras ball, and the Rural Fairy Gathering. Through her adventures she not only discovers strength in the many diverse gay and lesbian people she gets to know but also allows spontaneous encounters with local eccentrics and mechanics to highlight her road documentary.
Major funding for this program was provided by the Independent Television Service.

(In)Visible Women
Ellen Spiro
1991, 26:00, U.S., color, sound
(In)Visible Women shows the heroic responses of three women with AIDS in the context of their respective communities. In the face of adversity, these

women confront all aspects of the AIDS crisis in their lives. Through poetry, art, activism, and dance, they explode notions of female invisibility and complacency in the face of AIDS. We hear each woman describe how she came to terms with being HIV+ and joined others in speaking out about the neglected needs of women.

(In)Visible Women is the second video in the *Fear of Disclosure Project*, initiated by the late Phil Zwickler and produced by Zwickler and Jonathan Lee. Available with Spanish subtitles.

Roam Sweet Home
Ellen Spiro
1996, 58:00, U.S., color, sound
Inventing freedom as they roam, videomaker Ellen Spiro and her dog Sam go west in a vintage Airstream trailer in search of elderly dropouts and their dogs who have pulled out of society and into by-the-side-of-the-road trailer communities. Our mutt narrator tells his tale, sharing his thoughts on America's smells, the foibles of humans, and his view that aging is just another journey. In unplanned meetings with gray nomads, psychic misfits, and free spirits, *Roam Sweet Home* takes the myths of growing older and turns them on their head. The director and her dog join an adventurous and spirited community of roamers and loners on wheels that live by the road full-time. Major funding for this program was provided by the Corporation for Public Broadcasting through the Independent Television Service and Channel 4, London.

Spin
Brian Springer
1995, 57:30, U.S., color, sound
Pirated satellite feeds revealing U.S. media personalities' contempt for their viewers come full circle in *Spin*. TV outtakes appropriated from network satellite feeds unravel the tightly-spun fabric of television—a system that silences public debate and enforces the exclusion of anyone outside the pack of journalists, politicians, spin doctors, and televangelists who manufacture the news. *Spin* moves through the L.A. riots and the floating TV talk show called the 1992 U.S. presidential election.

Bad
Steina
1979, 2:00, U.S., color, sound
BAD is the mnemonic command for the B-Address register of the Buffer Oriented Digital Device, a tool for stretching or squeezing images. Starting with the register at zero and adding one level of distortion at a pre-programmed speed, the tape moves to an increasing complexity of images that escalates in density of color, composition, and texture.

Calligrams
Steina
1970, 4:00, U.S., b&w, sound
Calligrams is one of Steina's earliest experiments with altering the analog video image. An image is rescanned from the monitor "to capture and preserve the violated state of the standard television signal." The "violations" include deliberately re-adjusting the horizontal hold of the monitor, and then slowly advancing the reel-to-reel tape manually. The repetition of the horizontally drifting video image not only functions as visual rhythm but is also key to the conceptualization of the video image as unrestricted by the concrete frame, as in film. Steina's commitment to foregrounding a new electronic image vocabulary and working with other artists/engineers to develop new video instrumentation led to work that reveals the process of its making. Only available on the anthology *Surveying the First Decade, Program 5.*

Roam Sweet Home

Springer, Brian

Brian Springer installed two satellites on his rooftop in Buffalo to capture the unpackaged satellite feeds used in the 1992 presidential campaign. This footage was used in the documentary *Feed*, which in effect was his own creative take on media coverage of the 1992 Presidential election.

Steina
(see also The Vasulkas and Vasulka, Woody)

Steina was born in Reykjavik and studied violin and music theory in Prague. There she met and married Woody Vasulka in 1964; a year later the two moved to New York, where she worked as a musician. She began experimenting with video in 1969, and through her solo work and collaborations with her husband, Steina emerged as one of the formalist pioneers of video art. Although her main focus is creating videotapes and installations, Steina has become involved in interactive performance in public places, playing a digitally adapted violin to move video images displayed on large video projectors.

In Search of the Castle
Steina
1981, 9:00, U.S., color, sound
In Search of the Castle is an optical journey that combines Steina's abstraction of real images and Woody's digital effects. Taped from a car passing through the flat landscape of New Mexico, computer effects create an interesting play of movement and lines, adding a degree of tension as the rhythm of the electronic distortion intensifies.
"Encapsulated in a computer globe, the Vasulkas' imagery of America is revealed to us as an electronic journey."
—Marita Sturken, *Steina and Woody Vasulka: Machine Media* (San Francisco: San Francisco Museum of Modern Art, 1996)

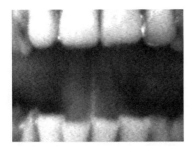

Let It Be

Let It Be
Steina
1972, 4:00, U.S., b&w, sound
"The 1972 Women's Video Festival [at the Kitchen] opened with an award-winning short by Steina Vasulka. Featuring close-ups of her mouth twitching and grimacing in accompaniment to the Beatles's 'Let It Be.' Somewhere behind its humor and satire I feel a certain 'tristesse' which Steina might not like to reveal, but which penetrates into my socks like spring snow."
—Shigeko Kubota
Also available on the anthology *I Say I Am: Program 2.*

Selected Tree Cuts
Steina
1980, 9:00, U.S., color, sound
Building a shimmering effect through a rhythmic collage, images of trees are spun, frozen, colorized, and digitized by means of an imaging computer. The soundtrack shifts back and forth between mechanical and natural sounds as the jumping shifts of color and orientation, made possible by the computer, oddly simulate the effects of natural chaotic phenomena. The cumulative effect of the alterations is a dizzying sense of disorientation as nature is transformed and re-constructed through technology.

Summer Salt
Steina
1982, 18:00, U.S., color, sound
This tape is part of a larger work entitled *Southwestern Landscapes*, a series exploring the landscape surrounding the Vasulkas' New Mexico home, manipulating space and time through various recording methods. Experimenting with a video camera, microphone, and mirrored ball, this dizzying tape demonstrates Steina's use of video as a direct experience, the camera acting not only as a surrogate eye but an independent body (and mind) occupying space in the world.

Switch! Monitor! Drift!

Switch! Monitor! Drift!
Steina
1976, 4:00, U.S., b&w, sound
Switch! Monitor! Drift! is one of a series of "machine visions" constructed by Steina in the '70s. In this documentation of a studio landscape, two cameras' signals are combined through a luminance keyer. One camera is mounted on a turntable; the second camera is pointed at the first. The image from the stationary camera is time-base adjusted so that it appears to drift horizontally across the monitor, exposing the horizontal framing interval, a black (low voltage) area that is normally hidden from view. The signal of the revolving camera is keyed into this area. The revolving second camera continuously pans the studio, occasionally revealing Steina walking around and flipping a directional switch at the turntable. As the tape progresses the luminance key is adjusted to include a broader tonal range through which the signal from the revolving camera is increasingly visible.
Only available on the anthology *Surveying the First Decade, Program 5.*

Urban Episodes
Steina
1980, 9:00, U.S., color, sound
Shot in downtown Minneapolis in 1980, *Urban Episodes* is part of the Machine Vision Series, Steina's ongoing investigation of the intersection of mechanical systems and the electronic image. Ordinarily, the camera view is associated with the human viewpoint, paying attention to the human condition that surrounds it. In this series, by constructing rotating devices with cameras, prisms, and mirrors, Steina redefines that idea of space, situating the camera as part of a larger machine, controlled by the mechanized decision-making of instruments. The movements and gaze of the camera are directed toward its own non-human, mechanical viewpoints.

Stoeltje, Gretchen
(see Finley, Jeanne C.)

Stoney, George
(and Austin Community TV)

An early advocate of video as a tool for social change, George Stoney was the Executive Producer of the National Film Board of Canada's *Challenge for Change/Societe Nouvelle* from 1966-70. In 1972, he co-founded (with Red Burns) the Alternate Media Center at New York University, and in 1976 he founded the National Federation of Local Cable Programmers.

First Transmission of ACTV
George Stoney and Austin Community Television
1972, 4:00, U.S., b&w, sound
This tape documents the first cablecast of Austin Community Television (ACTV) in which George Stoney and a group of University of Texas students assembled playback equipment on a hilltop at the cable system's head-end. The head-end is the site of the cable company's antenna where broadcast signals are pulled down, amplified, and distributed through the cable network. George Stoney, shown here telling of his experience with cable access in Mexico, was a community access pioneer.

Only available on the anthology *Surveying the First Decade, Program 6.*

Stracke, Caspar

Caspar Stracke is a media and installation artist from Hamburg, Germany who has been living and working in New York City since 1993. He worked in the realm of experimental cinema until 1997 and then switched focus and medium to digital media and media archaeology. *Circle's Short Circuit* (1999) is his first feature-length project.

Circle's Short Circuit
Caspar Stracke
1999, 1:16:00, U.S., color, sound
Circle's Short Circuit is an experimental feature-length work with neither a beginning nor end—the film can be viewed from any random point. It moves through a circle of five interlocking episodes that describe the phenomenon of interruption in contemporary communication through various forms and modes, investigating causes, consequences, and side-effects. Genres shift along the episodic path of this circle, moving from documentary to essay, through collage, simulated live coverage, and silent film. At the center of the film is a documentary segment on the origin of the biggest upheaval in communication history: the invention of the telephone, initiated by the "man who contracted space," Alexander Graham Bell. The episode features an interview with Avital Ronell, a theorist, philosopher, and author of *The Telephone Book*, who thematically ties up the wires of telephonic circuits and their transcendental counterparts. The film includes homages to the deconstructive toolmaker Jacques Derrida, the French writer Boris Vian, and the ghost of Japanese experimental theater and cinema, Shuji Terayama.

Stratton, Margaret

Margaret Stratton works in photography and video, shooting black-and-white landscapes and autobiographical tapes. Her videotapes have been screened in venues internationally, and her photography has been published in *Reframings: New Feminist Photographies* (1995) and *Lesbian Art in America* (2000). Stratton is a professor at the University of Iowa.

Kiss the Boys and Make Them Die
Margaret Stratton
1994, 30:00, U.S., sound, color
Kiss the Boys and Make Them Die explores how memory, sexuality, and the self are created and enforced through the family story. The video chronicles how the social act of loving women becomes channeled into narratives of incest, desire for the mother, loss of the father, separation from the family, death and self-destruction. In this work, sexuality, difference, and language are paralleled with haunting memories of a childhood ghost that both desires and hates women. Finally, *Kiss the Boys and Make Them Die* is a story of childhood trauma and the adult need to exorcise the past and create an independent self.

Miracle
Margaret Stratton
2001, 33:00, U.S., sound, color
A video odyssey documenting one woman's search for the miracle of the Virgin Mary. A must-see for recovering Catholics, their families, and friends worldwide. From Italy to Portugal, from France to Georgia, from Iowa to Peru, *Miracle* recovers a newly minted set of the Seven Deadly Sins on the way to immortalizing the latest modern religious trend: "Spiritual Tourism." Rated S for satirical.

Subrin, Elisabeth

Elisabeth Subrin's films and videos examine the intersections of history and subjectivity within female biography. In addition, she has curated numerous film and video programs for festivals and galleries. She has taught in the Department of Visual and Environmental Studies at Harvard University and currently lives in Brooklyn.

Elisabeth Subrin: Trilogy
These award-winning works from Elisabeth Subrin are available as a comprehensive collection. Engaging conventions of documentary and personal narrative, the works strategically undermine their own forms, shifting historical periods, genres, and identifications to explore the residual impact of feminism and the hazy boundaries between fiction and non-fiction.
Total running time 1:40:30.
Contents:
Swallow, Elisabeth Subrin, 1995, 28:00, U.S., color, sound
Shulie, Elisabeth Subrin, 1997, 36:30, U.S., b&w and color, sound
The Fancy, Elisabeth Subrin, 2000, 36:00, U.S., color, sound

The Fancy
Elisabeth Subrin
2000, 36:00, U.S., color, sound
The Fancy is a speculative, experimental work that explores the life of Francesca Woodman (1958-1981), evoked by the published catalogues of and about her photographs. Structural in form, the video radically reorganizes information from the catalogues in order to pose questions about biographical form, history and fantasy, female subjectivity, and issues of authorship and intellectual property.
"Continuing her exploration of experimental biographical forms, the maker of *Swallow* and *Shulie* turns her critical gaze to the life and art of a renowned young female photographer whose early death left behind a controversial body of work rife with psychosexual implication. Rigorously structural in form, this speculative bringing-to-light meticulously sifts physical evidence and sketchy facts in an attempt to uncover the traces of a seemingly suppressed history embedded behind the photographer's pictures."
—Nicole Armour, "Disappearing Acts," *Film Comment* 36:6 (November/December 2000)
Also available on the compilation *Elisabeth Subrin: Trilogy*.

Shulie

Shulie
Elisabeth Subrin
1997, 36:30, U.S., b&w and color, sound
"A cinematic doppelgänger without precedent, Elisabeth Subrin's *Shulie* uncannily and systemically bends time and cinematic code alike, projecting the viewer 30 years into the past to rediscover a woman out of time and a time out of joint—and in Subrin's words, 'to investigate the mythos and residue of the late '60s.' Staging an extended act of homage, as well as a playful, provocative confounding of filmic propriety, Subrin and her creative collaborator Kim Soss resurrect a little-known 1967 documentary portrait of a young Chicago art student, who a few years later would become a notable figure in Second Wave feminism, and author of the radical 1970 manifesto, *The Dialectic of Sex: The Case for Feminist Revolution*. Reflecting on her life and times, *Shulie* functions as a prism for refracting questions of gender, race, and class that resonate in our era as in hers, while through painstaking mediation Subrin makes manifest the eternal return of film."
—Views from the Avant-Garde (New York Film Festival, 1997)
Also available on the compilation *Elisabeth Subrin: Trilogy*.

Swallow

Elisabeth Subrin

1995, 28:00, U.S., color, sound

Based on accounts of girlhood anorexia, *Swallow* unravels the masked and shifting symptoms that define clinical depression. With a densely layered soundtrack, humorous and painful scenes of potential psychological break-down reveal a critical loss of meaning, and the failure to diagnose mental illness. Weaving narrative, documentary, and experimental strategies, *Swallow* intimately traces the awkward steps from unacknowledged depression to self-recognition.

Also available on the compilation *Elisabeth Subrin: Trilogy.*

"Well, Well, Well" (Le Tigre)

Elisabeth Subrin

2002, 3:45, U.S., color, sound

An experimental video for electro-feminist performance artists Le Tigre, the early '80s MTV aesthetic unpacks a thoroughly current obsession: the hidden erotics of office supplies.

Survival Research Labs
(see On Art and Artists)

Sweeney, Skip

In 1968 Skip Sweeney was a founder of Electric Eye, an early media collective concerned with video performances and experiments that changed its name to Video Free America in 1970. Sweeney's work in video includes abstract image-processing and synthesis, autobiographical documentaries and portraits, and video installations for theater. Tuning and tinkering for hours to produce shimmering, interweaving video mandalas, Sweeney was one of the few people who mastered video feedback. Sweeney later collaborated with Joanna Kelly on video dance tapes, video art, and documentaries.

Illuminatin' Sweeney

Skip Sweeney

1975, 5:00 excerpt (of 28:38), U.S., color, sound

Skip Sweeney was an early and proficient experimenter with video feedback. A feedback loop is produced by pointing a camera at the monitor to which it is cabled. Infinite patterns and variations of feedback can be derived from manipulating the relative positions of camera and monitor, adjusting the monitor control, becoming a swirling vortex. Sweeney and others were intrigued with feedback's ability to generate pulsing images like a living organism. He claimed he would "just as soon be a video rock-and-roll musician" and produce feedback as a performance instrument (Anthology Film Archives, 1981). Sweeney produced many variations of feedback and processed imagery and is especially noted for his works incorporating dance and movement. *Illuminatin' Sweeney* was produced for WNET-New York's Video and Television Review. This sampling of Sweeney's work shows feedback processed through a combination of a Moog audio synthesizer and the Vidium colorizing synthesizer invented by Bill Hearn in 1969. Recorded off the monitor with a black and white camera, the images were later colorized. Sweeney produced this feedback during a "video jam session" at Video Free America.

Only available as an excerpt on the anthology *Surveying the First Decade, Program 5.*

Tajiri, Rea

Rea Tajiri's work plays with viewer expectations by employing strategies of media deconstruction to highlight the way images obtain meaning and how a viewer or reader supplies an image when one is lacking. Educated at CalArts and currently living in New York, Tajiri's work draws on both American and Japanese images to explore issues of cultural representation, including material that is systematically obscured from these representations.

History and Memory: For Akiko and Takashige

Rea Tajiri

1991, 32:00, U.S., b&w and color, sound

"A search for a non-existent image, a desire to create an image where there is none," leads to Rea Tajiri's composition on recorded history and non-recorded memory. Framed by the haunting facts of the post-Pearl Harbor Japanese internment camps (which dislocated 120,000 Japanese Americans during World War II), Tajiri creates a version of her family's story through interviews and historical detail, remembering a time that many people would rather forget. This video surveys the impact of images (real images, desired images made real, and unrealized dreams) on our lives, drawing from sources such as Hollywood, U.S. Department of Defense films, newsreels, memories of the living, and spirits of the dead. Relics of the camps, contrasted with human efforts to forget their existence, create a sense of taxonomic insistence that these camps were indeed real.

Hitchcock Trilogy
Rea Tajiri
1987, 15:00, U.S., color, sound
"On the surface, Rea Tajiri's work reads like the standard deconstruction of appropriated popular media via text to which we have grown accustomed in the '80s. But this is a work of remarkable evocation and resonance that counterpoints and complements the scores of Hitchcock films with 'meta-narrative' possibilities. These possibilities occur by doubling the inherent distance from the appropriated subject, standing twice removed in the realm of parallels rather than parodies. *Vertigo* offers obliquely drawn character studies, *Psycho* dwells ominously on the portraiture of two women, and *Torn Curtain* offers a procession of endless beginnings. In each, Tajiri 'mirrors the mirror'–she departs from her own subjective perception rather than the original, and creates a new scenario."
–Michael Nash, *Reconstructed Realms* (Long Beach Museum of Art, 1989)

Little Murders
Rea Tajiri
1998, 19:44, U.S., color, sound
Rea Tajiri incorporates film noir, Hong Kong action, and crooner standards into this ultracontemporary detective story. The characters cruise around nocturnal Los Angeles–a city of fallen angels–in this tape that portrays the disparate pop culture styles and referents that comprise post-modern genres and identities.

Spanish subtitled version available.

Only available on the anthology *Frames of Reference: Reflections on Media, Volume 4, Program 1.*

Little Murders

Off Limits
Rea Tajiri
1988, 7:30, U.S., color, sound
Juxtaposing the text of *Off Limits*, a film made in 1987 about Saigon circa 1968, with the soundtrack and image of the last five minutes of the 1968 film *Easy Rider*, Tajiri parallel edits these representations to play with the evocation and emptiness of the image. Tajiri blacks out the screen image of *Easy Rider* while the words of a Vietnamese assassin crawl up the screen, building a structure of selective memory. Tajiri's *Off Limits* points to the similarities and contradictions between 1960s hippie iconography and memories of the Vietnam war.

Tam, Ho

Ho Tam was born in Hong Kong and educated in Toronto. He worked in advertising firms and community psychiatric facilities before turning to art. His first video, *The Yellow Pages*, was commissioned by the arts group Public Access for an installation/projection at Toronto's Union Station in 1994.

The Books of James
Ho Tam
2002, 16:30, U.S., color, sound
Through a stack of personal journals, this video reconstructs a biography of the South Dakota-born, New York City-enlightened artist James Wentzy. Tracing his days starting out as a struggling artist and later involved as an AIDS activist, the video provides an intimate portrait of a neglected hero. Wentzy reads from journals and shares old family snapshots and notebook sketches. "I hope I don't die of sainthood," Wentzy jokes in an entry from 1990–the pivotal time when he was becoming involved with ACT-UP and beginning to live healthier after the revelation of his HIV-positive status.

Tamblyn, Christine

Cultural critic, educator, and video and performance artist Christine Tamblyn began making electronic art in 1974. Her writings were published in many art magazines and academic journals including *Art News*, *Afterimage*, *Leonardo*, and *High Performance*. Her articles on feminist performance and video have been anthologized in *Illuminating Video* (1990) and *Resolutions* (1996). Tamblyn died in 1998.

Archival Quality
Christine Tamblyn
1998, U.S., color, sound, CD-ROM
Archival Quality is comprised of four segments. In the first, "Memorativa," powerful childhood experiences of secrets are evoked. In "Olfatus," documentation of the artist's performances are revealed by clicking on symbols in landscape. The third segment, "Gustus," is co-named "Slices of Life, My Videotapes (1976-89)" and takes the form of a giant pizza, slices of which, when clicked, advance towards the reader. "Vermio," the fourth segment, con-

sists of four text-and-image collages, sections of which can be "peeled off" to reveal loops of sound and image. Christine Tamblyn devoted the last year or so of her life to producing an overview, or compendium, of more than three decades of her life and art in the form of an archive on CD-ROM. "I think of it as a vindication of my aesthetic project. It proves that it isn't just my own fantasy, somehow. It gives my work veracity."

Note: only available on CD-ROM.

Mistaken Identities
Christine Tamblyn
1995, U.S., color, sound, CD-ROM
An interactive CD-ROM inspired by the lives and work of ten famous women: Josephine Baker, Simone de Beauvoir, Catherine the Great, Colette, Marie Curie, Marlene Dietrich, Isadora Duncan, Frida Kahlo, Margaret Mead, and Gertrude Stein. The CD-ROM is an investigation into the intersecting economies of sexuality, authorship, eroticism, and gender that inform the lives of women. Their identities are configured in the negotiated space between self and other, a negotiation that continues in Tamblyn's relationship to them as narrator.

Note: only available on CD-ROM.

She Loves It, She Loves It Not
Christine Tamblyn
1993, U.S., color, sound, CD-ROM
From cyborg feminism to erotic robotic fantasies, this CD-ROM maps the visual and textual landscape of technology, science fiction, and virtual reality and their relationship to representations of gender and sexuality, women's work, desire, and "real" or virtual fantasies. An exhaustive, riotous catalogue of our collective cyborg unconscious.

Note: only available on CD-ROM.

Tanaka, Janice

California-based Janice Tanaka is considered a pioneer in the use of processed images within experimental narrative form. She brings a painter's sensibility to her intricately textured video collages that blend social and political observations, philosophical inquiries, and personal introspection. Her work uses original footage, appropriated media images, and densely layered electronic processing to address Asian-American history and identity, from the enduring trauma of internment camps during World War II to the blending of cultural values from the Old to New World.

Beaver Valley
Janice Tanaka
1981, 7:00, U.S., b&w and color, sound
In this angry answer to the expectations that advertising culture places on women and their bodies, Tanaka deftly edits commercial images and sound-bite slogans to underscore the message such images carry: that women exist to please men as wives, mothers, and lovers. Tanaka balances such mainstream images with black-and-white footage of herself lying naked next to her own doubled image, rejecting the mainstream model of female sexuality that regularly consists of seductive glances and suggestive poses arranged and pre-ordained for the male gaze of the spectator. The tape reveals the commodification of women and their desire.

Also available on the anthology *I Say I Am: Program 1*.

Duality Duplicity
Janice Tanaka
1980, 7:00, U.S., color, sound
This arresting early work conveys a tension that emanates from what Tanaka posits as life's basic dualities: male/female, past/present, known/unknown. By focusing issues of identity, doubt, wonder, and awareness through the body—and the bodies of her ancestors—Tanaka succeeds in creating a work with both personal and political power. Tanaka creates a unique voice that speaks of her experience of maturing into womanhood, repeating the refrain, "I, my mother." An experimental tape, this work contains one of the first examples of flicker editing.

Memories from the Department of Amnesia
Janice Tanaka
1990, 13:00, U.S., color, sound
Tanaka passionately evokes the loss of her mother by visually recreating the ominous and disempowering feeling of isolation that accompanies mourning.

The tape enunciates the painful phases of grieving: the claustrophobic results of dealing with the inevitability of death, the transitional void where one is lost between the comfortable orientation of one's world and nothing, and the new sense of clarity where images from the past resurface from the abyss of forgetfulness. The piece is an elegy to Tanaka's mother, whose attempts at balance and security were constantly disrupted by social, cultural, political, and personal forces beyond her control.

No Hop Sing, No Bruce Lee
Janice Tanaka
1998, 31:51, U.S., b&w and color, sound
The popular images of Asian-American males historically propagated in the mass media range from "silent, sex-less, obedient houseboy" to "mystic martial arts master." Invisibility has been a core element in the public's perceptions and is reflected in the one-dimensional representation of Asian men. This is a program by and about Asian-American men. Through their experiences and voices we become privy to the peculiar and insidious ways in which racism affects their evolving self-identities.

Who's Gonna Pay for These Donuts Anyway?
Janice Tanaka
1992, 58:00, U.S., color, sound
This experimental documentary chronicles Janice Tanaka's search for a father she has not seen since she was three years old. Tanaka searched for her missing father for three and a half years, possessing only sketchy information: that he had protested the internment of Japanese-American citizens after the bombing of Pearl Harbor by writing letters to the President and that he had been arrested by the FBI and subsequently diagnosed as a schizophrenic with paranoid tendencies and institutionalized. Tanaka blends social and personal memory into an evocative portrait of identity and loss, addressing issues of culture from the perspective of someone who feels pulled in two directions. Blending documentary, diary, narrative, and experimental genres, *Who's Gonna Pay* is emotionally powerful and beautifully made.

Who's Gonna Pay for These Donuts Anyway?

Thomas, Jennet

"The forms that my films and videos take come from an eclectic and multiply discursive history: underground, live film/performances that read dislocated narratives alongside film and slide projections, experiments with animation and film trick effects, and impulses stemming from my years as a painter—a curiosity about animating matter and images through time. I always strive for clarity and accessibility, and—with challenging human content often in the foreground, my work generally contains a good amount of dark humour. A consistent theme is the drive to play with narrative—an ongoing experiment with ways of imploding storytelling."—Jennet Thomas

4 Ways he tried to tell you
Jennet Thomas
1999, 7:00, U.K., color, sound, digital video and Super-8 to video
A fragmented puzzle of a sinister narrative turned inside out and comprised of digital video, digital video animation, and Super-8 with model animation and human pixelation.
"This is a video about the thing that won't go away. It has been trying to contact me by altering bits of my reality for several years now, and this 7 minutes is a clear demonstration of that. My 8-year old nephew got drawn into the whole thing, and that's why his voice is on this tape. I'm not sure if it's dead now. We'll just have to see."
—Jennet Thomas
Also available on the compilation *Jennet Thomas: 6 pieces from my head.*

Gorgeous Operation
Jennet Thomas
1996, 8:00, U.K., color, sound, Super-8 and 8mm to video
A meditation on the nature of "Nature" and the uncertainty of "Cause and Effect." Super-8 and 8mm, film mattes, painting directly onto film, and model/object animation.
"Originally (like most of my earlier film work) this was a performance piece: text performed alongside the projected image. A complex and absurd 'story' about a man who thought there was something wrong with his eye. He goes to the doctor, who can't help him much, but he finds a way he can operate on himself with uplifting yet troubling results."
—Jennet Thomas
Also available on the compilation *Jennet Thomas: 6 pieces from my head.*

Heady
Jennet Thomas
1996, 8:00, U.K., color, sound, Super-8 to video
"Starring an inflatable wig holder that I got at a car boot sale in Bremen, Germany, this film began as a demonstration of different film animation techniques but evolved into a bizarre improvised narrative in which the head escapes from the violent clutches of a mixed-up model girl, is sent to Poland in a wicker basket where it has a nice holiday (I took it on holiday to Poland with me and animated it in the countryside), and finally returns on the ferry."
—Jennet Thomas
Also available on the compilation *Jennet Thomas: 6 pieces from my head.*

Important Toy
Jennet Thomas
1997, 8:20, U.K., color, sound
A young girl buys a weird toy from a charity shop. She forms such an intense relationship with it that it develops special ways of communicating and a strange connection to her that seems to defy the laws of physics. As the situation escalates, it seems that repression is the only way forward. First conceived of as a kind of fairy tale that goes wrong, this is a piece about learning the "rules" of grown-up reality and an extrapolation of the consequences of "over-identifying" with toys. A digital video with digital video effects, live-action, and model/object animation.
Also available on the compilation *Jennet Thomas: 6 pieces from my head.*

Important Toy

4 Ways he tried to tell you

Jennet Thomas: 6 pieces from my head
"This compilation is a selection of six short films and videos, made in London over the period 1994 to 1999. These pieces develop my own fusion of experimental writing/monologues with underground film forms, playing with fractured forms of storytelling and film trick conceits. The compilation encompasses the period before I started editing digitally, using Super-8 animated film and monologue, as on *Heady* and *Gorgeous Operation*. My first videos experimented with frame-by-frame digital 'hand crafted' animation, using 'fairy tale'-like narrative devices—*Important Toy*, *'What are you doing with your fingers?'* and a combination of both (with an imploding narrative) in *4 Ways he tried to tell you*. In *The Spectacular Murder of Mervyn*, the challenge was to take an impossible-to-film, bizarre 'given' literary text, and make it into a film using Super-8 alone."
—Jennet Thomas
Total running time 43:20.
Contents:
4 Ways he tried to tell you, Jennet Thomas, 1999, 7:00, U.K., color, sound, digital video and Super-8 to video
Gorgeous Operation, Jennet Thomas, 1996, 8:00, U.K., color, sound, Super-8 and 8mm to video
Heady, Jennet Thomas, 1996, 8:00, U.K., color, sound, Super-8 to video
Important Toy, Jennet Thomas, 1997, 8:20, U.K., color, sound
The Spectacular Murder of Mervyn, Jennet Thomas, 1999, 6:00, U.K., color, sound, Super-8 to video
"What are you doing with your fingers?" Jennet Thomas, 1996, 6:00, U.K., color, sound

The Local Sky Enlarger
Jennet Thomas
2002, 28:30, U.K., color, sound
In this surreal experimental narrative there's something wrong with a patch of sky. As it travels over Southern England, objects cast up into it come down hugely enlarged and bloated. Meanwhile in London, the patch is in fact a troubling scab on a crippled old man's head. As the scab develops, all he can do is wait, going through the changes, led on gently by the idiot-savant son with his childlike multiple identities. Behind the curtains, the lady controlling everything is making sure that the giant twin in the sky is heading straight

for him, ready to meet him in the back garden and implant him—when he's ripe—with God's dark sperm. There are two musical numbers, featuring an instructive folk song, to help everyone understand exactly what is going on. Part one of a three-part trilogy-in-progress.

Perfect Spot
Jennet Thomas
2003, 14:30, U.K., color, sound
A daughter leads her mother on a rope while they take a walk, looking for a place where the mother can bid her final farewell. Before she leaves, they have a picnic, she sings a song, and they chat about the family. An absurd domestic drama played out against the background of a summer's day by the seaside.

SHARONY!
Jennet Thomas
1996, 10:30, U.K., color, sound
This is the story of two young girls who dig up a tiny woman from the back garden. They incubate her in their mouths and in their bed, and then they lock her in a doll's house wallpapered with pornography to make her grow up faster, feeding her through a tube in the door. When she is life-sized and ready to play, they take her to the disco. A dark, comic, experimental fantasy on the implications of little girls' toys—with the existential melancholy of Frankenstein's monster.

SHARONY!

The Spectacular Murder of Mervyn
Jennet Thomas
1999, 6:00, U.K., color, sound, Super-8 to video
An adaptation of the gruesome and fantastical ending chapter of the notorious experimental anti-novel *Maldoror*, first published in 1868 and written by a young man (who died soon after writing it) who called himself Comte de Lautréamont. A joyful return to the necessity of Super-8 film tricks, this is part of a larger Anglo-German collaborative feature film *Maldoror*, shot entirely on Super-8 in sections by 15 underground filmmakers working independently. Includes Super 8, model animation, photo animation, and live action.
Also available on the compilation *Jennet Thomas: 6 pieces from my head.*

"What are you doing with your fingers?"
Jennet Thomas
1996, 6:00, U.K., color, sound, digital video, live action, digital video effects, human pixelation, and model animation.
"Featuring myself as a woman who is lured into the garden by the cries of foliage, given a dinner she doesn't want by a mysterious organic being, and then turned into something else or maybe not. A piece about self-consciousness and the fearful noise of wind in the trees. My first foray into digital editing and special hand-crafted frame-by-frame effects."
—Jennet Thomas

Also available on the compilation *Jennet Thomas: 6 pieces from my head.*

Thorne, David
(see Meltzer, Julia)

Thornton, Leslie
Leslie Thornton's lush, complex works explore the mechanisms of desire and meaning, while probing past the boundaries of language and narrative conventions. Difficult to categorize or describe, Thornton's works are steeped in theoretical interest and filled with rich and intuitive imagery in experimental narratives crossing science fiction, ethnographic, and documentary forms. She teaches in the Modern Culture and Media Program at Brown University.

[Dung Smoke Enters the Palace]
Leslie Thornton
1989, 16:00, U.S., b&w, sound, 16mm to video
An anti-narrative adventure traveling through a phantasmagoric environment void of stability. The tape presents a bizarre compendium of archival and industrial footage accompanied by a noisy soundtrack of music and voices from the past, as if echoing the ether of the viewer's mind. Thornton's distinctive visual style of collaging random elements elicits an eerie sense of being lost amidst past and present, breeding a confusion that complicates any clear reading of the image.

The Last Time I Saw Ron

The Last Time I Saw Ron
Leslie Thornton
1994, 12:11, U.S., b&w, sound, 16mm to video
During the winter of 1994, actor Ron Vawter was in Brussels working on a theater production about the mythical Greek warrior Philoktetes. Odysseus abandoned Philoktetes on the island of Lemnos after a snake had bitten him while on route to Troy. Odysseus betrayed him because his wound would not heal, provoking mournful cries and a stench that distressed the other soldiers. When Ron was diagnosed with AIDS, this story of anguish and isolation took on added poignancy, and he arranged to collaborate with Dutch director Jan Ritsema on a theatrical production inspired by the myth. An international group of artists came together to develop *Philoktetes Variations* under the auspices of the Kaaitheater in Belgium. Ron passed away just as the production reached fruition. *The Last Time I Saw Ron* is made from footage shot for the play and includes stunning material of Ron's figure flying through the cosmic and destructive events. A pregnant woman drifts alongside him as his body merges with the time and space of the universe. The tape is a moving meditation on the power of art as a life-giving force and one man's extraordinary belief in that power.

Old Worldy
Leslie Thornton
1998, 25:00, U.S., b&w, sound, 16mm to video
"*Old Worldy* re-contextualizes three 'found' media artifacts: 1) a series of cabaret dancers, probably filmed in the 1940s to show to army audiences…; 2) archival ethnographic footage of indigenous dance forms and religious rituals, shot in the Far East in the 1920s and '30s; and 3) a tongue-in-cheek rendition of 1990s techno-ambient disco rock as the dominant sound track. … *Old Worldy* might best be described as an anti-musical, since it disarticulates and subverts the forms conventionally used in musicals to naturalize and convey pleasure. In a similar vein, it is anti-ethnography, since it neither speaks for nor recuperates any people or group to a pre-established order. And finally, *Old Worldy* may be considered a kind of acinema, an artifact that constantly and unexpectedly problematizes the relation between spectator and spectacle, whether of an intimate, scopophilic nature, or at an official and scientific scale. It is a work that causes us to rethink, again and again, what cinema might be."
—Thomas Zummer, *Views from the Avant-Garde* (New York, 1999)

Peggy and Fred and Pete
Leslie Thornton
1988, 17:00, U.S., sepia, sound, 16mm to video
Peggy and Fred meet up with Peter the Penguin to make their way through the fragmentary remains of 20th-century American culture. They fashion a tumultuous, arbitrary world that teeters dangerously on the edge of nonsense and oblivion. The makings are familiar: technologies, accoutrements, and stories of our culture, leveled against an endless and disorderly horizon. As a commentary on the state of cultural messages and meaning, Thornton's work outlines a "poetics of dystopia" that has all the ambient charm of a bomb shelter, preserving random cultural elements for future generations.

Peggy and Fred in Hell: The Prologue
Leslie Thornton
1985, 19:40, U.S., b&w, sound, 16mm to video
Peggy and Fred In Hell is one of the strangest cinematic artifacts of the last 20 years, revealing the abuses of history and innocence in the face of catastrophe as it chronicles two small children journeying through a post-apocalyptic landscape to create their own world. Breaking genre restrictions, Thornton uses improvisation, planted quotes, archival footage, and formless time frames to confront the viewer's preconceptions of cause and effect.

Peggy and Fred in Hell: The Prologue

Peggy and Fred in Kansas
Leslie Thornton
1989, 11:00, U.S., b&w, sound, 16mm to video
Peggy and Fred, sole inhabitants of post-apocalyptic Earth, weather a prairie twister and scavenge for sense and sustenance amid the ruined devices of a ghosted culture. The improvised and playful dialogue of the children provides a key to understanding the tape; their distracted sense of make-believe floats between realities, between acting their parts and doing what they want—patching together identities that, like fidgeting children, refuse to stand still.

Strange Space
Leslie Thornton
1994, 5:00, U.S., color, sound, 16mm to video
Thornton asks viewers to question how one sees "space"—whether literally or figuratively—and what is being revealed. Images of a sonogram session grant viewers access to what is typically reserved for medical analysis—"inner space." The body, probed and revealed through technology, is collaged with imagery from lunar probes, drawing parallels with how technology also allows us to see where we were previously unable—"outer space." A poem by Rilke about the interior quality of thought is contrasted with the clinical voice accompanying the images.

There was an unseen cloud moving
Leslie Thornton
1988, 58:00, U.S., b&w and color, sound
A fragmented, experimental biography of the 19th-century poet and writer Isabelle Eberhardt, whose brief, unusual life ended abruptly in a flash flood in the desert. The tape makes no claims to telling the "truth" about Isabelle, choosing rumors about her tyrannical, nihilistic father and her flight to Armenia, where she dressed as a man and "wrote one of the strangest documents a woman has ever given to the world." Following Eberhardt's travels and the strangely syncretic vision of her father, Thornton creates a portrait of cultural cross-breeding in which "neither this world nor the other remains." In all, *There was an unseen cloud moving* is an arresting mixture of rare and iconic images that undermines its authenticity through re-enacted "historical" scenes and deliberate anachronisms that place Neil Armstrong in 19th-century Geneva.

There was an unseen cloud moving

T.R. Uthco
(see Ant Farm)

TV Escola
(see Video in the Villages)

TVTV
(Top Value Television)

TVTV was formed in 1972 by Michael Shamberg, Megan Williams, Tom Weinberg, and Allen Rucker and enlisted the support of media collectives including Raindance Corporation, Ant Farm, and the Videofreex to provide alternative coverage of the 1972 Presidential nominating conventions. The Democratic tape, *The World's Largest TV Studio* (1972), and its Republican companion piece, *Four More Years* (1972), were among the first video documentaries to be broadcast. Influenced by New Journalism and the versatility and novelty of portable video equipment, TVTV created a critically acclaimed, graphically inventive, intimate style of documentary satire. Frustrated by public television's failure to support independent documentaries, the group created projects for cable and network TV, ultimately producing an unsuccessful comedy pilot, *The TVTV Show,* for NBC in 1978. The group disbanded in 1979.

Four More Years
TVTV
1972, 1:00:00, U.S., b&w, sound
TVTV's inside view of the 1972 Republican National Convention made broadcast history. While network cameras focused on the orchestrated re-nomination of Richard Nixon, TVTV's rag-tag army of guerrilla television activists turned their cameras on to the cocktail parties, anti-war demonstrations, hype, and hoopla that accompanied the show.
Also available on the anthology *Surveying the First Decade, Program 8.*

Lord of the Universe
TVTV
1974, 1:00:00, U.S., b&w and color, sound
Sixteen-year-old guru Maharaj Ji attempts to levitate the Houston Astrodome in this 1973 DuPont award-winning documentary. Follow the guru from his New York mansion to limousines in Houston and listen to his followers—celebrities and non-celebrities alike—extol his virtues. TVTV's creative use of graphics, live music, and wide-angle conveys the desperate efforts of these lost children to find a leader.
"If this guy is God, then this is the God the United States of America deserves."
—Abbie Hoffman

TVTV Goes to the Super Bowl
TVTV
1976, 45:00, U.S., color, sound
Bill Murray and Christopher Guest lead a behind-the-scenes tour of the 1976 showdown between the Dallas Cowboys and the Pittsburgh Steelers. This irreverent view of football and America's most popular sports event examines the "Woodstock of corporate America" from the viewpoint of the players, the wives, the fans, and the media. The big business of sports, the high stakes, the pressures, the cost in health and happiness are all covered in this kaleidoscopic view of another American ritual.

TVTV Looks at the Academy Awards
TVTV
1976, 1:00:00, U.S., color, sound
Mixing documentary reality with clever comic invention, TVTV decked itself out in tuxedos and ankle-length gowns to cover Hollywood's annual celebration. Following several nominees on the day of the event, TVTV takes the viewer behind the scenes, exposing the hazards and exhilaration of being a "star." Throughout, Lily Tomlin appears as a middle-American housewife watching the awards at home on TV, and her deadpan humor about the ephemeral nature of fame serves as a delightful counterpoint to all the serious ego-stroking going on.

Umen, Alix

Early on Alix Umen discovered the differences between boys and girls. With a dislike for the conventional, she often cut her hair short and made G.I. Joe wear dresses. She made her directorial debut with *Mad About the Boy* (1994).

Mad about the Boy
Alix Umen and Lisel Banker
1994, 7:00, U.S., b&w, sound
This experimental Pixelvision piece explores the tenuous boundaries of gender through a series of mini-sequences, among them a group of anecdotes told by women who have been mistaken for men and a must-see synchronized barbershop scene.

University Community Video

In 1973, student and community activists in Minneapolis joined forces to create University Community Video. Founders Miles Mogelescu, Ron McCoy, and Stephen Kulczycki, among others, offered courses in portable video production, supported by student fees from the University of Minnesota. UCV developed *Changing Channels*, a weekly alternative video magazine. In early 1975, UCV produced a companion program, *Everybody's TV Time*, an open-access program. UCV changed its name twice, eventually becoming Intermedia Arts, now a regional media arts center.

The Business of Local News
University Community Video
1974, 15:00 excerpt (of 25:00), U.S., b&w, sound
Showcasing local documentaries made on 1/2-inch equipment, *Changing Channels* was a weekly alternative video magazine produced by University Community Video (UCV) and aired on public television station KTCA-St. Paul. In *The Business of Television News,* which aired as part of the *Changing Channels* series, several area television news operations were asked to examine their objectives and their markets. The candid comments of news directors and station managers outline the conflicting forces of entertainment (market share) and information that continue to shape the nature of television news across the country.

Only available as an excerpt on the anthology *Surveying the First Decade, Program 7.*

Valadão, Virginia
(see Video in the Villages)

Valdovino, Luis

Luis Valdovino is part of a wave of Latino videomakers creating works that testify to the experiences of Latino Americans in confronting categorical discrimination on the basis of language and culture. With the viewpoint of an insider, Valdovino raises difficult issues of racism and exclusion in our supposedly "democratic" society.

Work in Progress
Luis Valdovino
1990, 14:00, U.S., color, sound
An experimental video about cultural and political disputes surrounding immigration and naturalization processes, *Work in Progress* explores the effects of the 1986 U.S. Immigration Reform Law on individuals who did not qualify for amnesty under this reform, therefore remaining undocumented. Interweaving government policies, media exposure, xenophobia, Latin folklore, and cultural conditioning—as revealed through interviews and stock footage—

Valdovino interrelates the complex forces that shape illegal alien identity and experience for Mexicans who cross the border and take on the "terminal disease of discrimination and hatred of foreigners" that often characterizes our society.

Vamos, Igor

Igor Vamos is a media artist and culturejammer living and working in New York. Vamos is well-known for his collaborative public art projects such as the Barbie Liberation Organization and the Center for Land Use Interpretation, a non-profit organization dedicated to the increase and dissemination of knowledge about the nature of human interaction with the Earth. Currently, Vamos is teaching at Rensselaer Polytechnic Institute.

Suggested Photo Spots
Igor Vamos
1997, 10:00, U.S., color, sound
Strap on your seat belts and get comfortable for a 7,000-mile drive. This documentary invites you to travel along with the Center for Land Use Interpretation as they find suggested photo spots across North America. Journey from coast to coast, stopping long enough to take snap shots of unusual or exemplary land-use sites across North America. You will even get to take a picture of Kodak's own wastewater treatment plant in Rochester, NY.

Undeniable Evidence
Igor Vamos
1995, 30:00, U.S., color, sound
A provocative half-hour of guerrilla artists caught in the act on videotape, *Undeniable Evidence* is a public art extravaganza assembled by Igor Vamos and anonymous culturejammers.

Vasquez, Gustavo
(see Gómez-Peña, Guillermo and Lord, Chip)

Vasulka, Woody
(see also Steina and The Vasulkas)

Born in Brno, Czechoslovakia, Woody Vasulka studied metal technology and hydraulic mechanics before moving to Prague to learn filmmaking. There he also met his wife and collaborator Steina. In 1965, he emigrated to New York City, where he worked as a multi-screen film editor and designer and began experimenting with electronic sound, stroboscopic light, and video. In 1974, he taught at the Center for Media Study at SUNY-Buffalo and continued his investigation of the machinery behind the electronic signal. After working with the Rutt/Etra Scan Processor, Vasulka collaborated with Don MacArthur and Jeffrey Schier in 1976 to build a computer controlled personal imaging facility called the Digital Image Articulator. In the 1980s he made two major tapes, *The Commission* (1983) and *Art of Memory* (1987). Vasulka has also curated electronic art exhibitions and published essays on the medium.

Art of Memory
Woody Vasulka
1987, 36:00, U.S., b&w and color, sound
Manipulating a variety of sources, Vasulka uses creative imaging tools to situate historical images against southwestern landscapes of incredible beauty. Contorting the images into a variety of isomorphic forms, Vasulka creates a literal shape for these memories, developing these shapes as metaphors for the processes of fragmentation, condensation, and inversion that inevitably contort fact into memory. While much of the raw material for the tape is drawn from World War II and its rehearsals—the Spanish Civil War and the Russian Revolution—*Art of Memory* is really an extended meditation seeking to reconcile the blurry, banal photographs of historic figures with the mass destruction they helped engineer.

Artifacts
Woody Vasulka
1980, 23:00, U.S., color, sound
This tape is an important record of Woody's process of experimentation and play: a collection of images initiated by basic algorithmical procedures to verify the functional operation of a newly created tool—the "Digital Image Articulator"—designed and constructed by Woody and Jeffrey Schier. Saying at the beginning of the tape, "The images come to me as they come to you, in a spirit of experimentation." Vasulka presents a series of manipulations in which the image shifts and moves, dissolving through two- into three-dimensionality. As images are replicated, stretched and shifted, the tape hypnotizes the viewer for a climactic assault of pulsating light and sound.

C-Trend
Woody Vasulka
1974, 7:00 excerpt (of 9:00), U.S., color, sound
In *C-Trend*, one of Woody Vasulka's "dialogues with tools," the Rutt-Etra Scan Processor (a scan deflection tool designed by Steve Rutt and Bill Etra in 1973) controls the video raster or monitor screen. Vasulka modifies the camera image of urban traffic while the synchronous audio remains clearly recognizable. Two basic modifications of the electronic image are evident: each horizontal line scanned by the electron beam is translated into a live graphic display of voltage, radically reconfiguring the luminance information and the

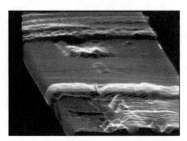

C-Trend

video image and functioning as a wave form monitor. The shape of the video frame itself, the raster, is also skewed. The deflection coils, which electromagnetically control the electron gun and thus the raster, receive mathematically re-coded analog information and reconfigure the normally rectilinear video frame. The "empty spaces" between the altered frames, which appear to drift or roll throughout *C-Trend*, are the horizontal and vertical blanking intervals between electronic frames.

Only available as an excerpt on the anthology *Surveying the First Decade, Program 5.*

The Commission
Woody Vasulka
1983, 44:55, U.S., color, sound
"*The Commision* is an ambitious narrative in operatic form that blends video effects and electronically manipulated sound with stylized docu-drama. Based on the real-life drama of Niccolo Pagnini, the 19th century violinist and composer (Ernest Gusella), and his contemporary, Hector Berlioz (Robert Ashley); the work addresses the exploitation of genius, the artist as tragic hero, and the historical exploration of inspiration in the Romantic tradition."
–Bob Riley, *FOCUS: Steina and Woody Vasulka* (Boston: Institute of Contemporary Art, 1986)

Cantaloup
The Vasulkas
1981, 28:00, U.S., color, sound
Following the Vasulkas' effort to build their own computer imager, Steina explains how the video processor works, digitizing the image, inserting color, reassigning value, density, and texture to specific areas of the video image. The constant experimentation and development of technological tools yields an incredible range of possible image manipulations. Emerging as a subtext of the tape is the Vasulkas' struggle to identify and define the programming languages necessary to creatively engage and alter existing technology.

Participation
The Vasulkas
1969, 6:00 excerpt (of 30:00), U.S., b&w, sound
Shortly after they arrived in the United States from Prague in 1965, Steina and Woody Vasulka began documenting New York City's underground theater and music scenes with a Portapak. Steina has remarked that she learned the craft of camerawork as documentarian of these celebratory, countercultural scenes of the "sexual avant-garde." These excerpts from *Participation* feature a performance by an anonymous rhythm & blues group led by a young, charismatic singer, a pulsing light show projection at the Fillmore East, and a scene from an Off-Broadway drag theater.

Only available as an excerpt on the anthology *Surveying the First Decade, Program 6.*

Progeny
The Vasulkas
1981, 18:00, U.S., color, sound
After seeing an installation of Steina's *Machine Vision* involving mechanized cameras moving to pre-programmed patterns, sculptor Bradford Smith suggested that his work be used as the subject of a video investigation. Slowly panning over the encrusted surfaces of the sculptures, Steina's camera records a fantastic landscape of twisted figures and gruesome armor. The varying speed, orientation, and distortion of the images transform the three-dimensional sculptures into a visceral four-dimensional experience.

Binary Lives: Steina and Woody Vasulka (see On Art and Artists)

The Vasulkas
(see also Steina and Vasulka, Woody)

Steina and Woody Vasulka, collaboratively known as The Vasulkas, met and married in Prague before moving to New York City in 1965. In their early collaborative work, the Vasulkas examined the electronic nature of video and sound, developing specialized imaging tools and strategies while also using the medium to document the city's expanding underground culture. The Vasulkas and Andreas Mannik founded The Kitchen as a media arts theater in 1971, and that year they also organized *A Special Videotape Show* at the Whitney Museum of American Art. Working with innovative engineers, The Vasulkas invented and modified video production instruments. They have lived in Santa Fe since 1980 and have maintained their decades-long presence on the international media art scene, formulating and articulating aesthetic strategies of the new media.

Progeny

Velez, Edín

Edín Velez approaches documentary through an explicitly subjective lens more poetic and personal than standard forms permit, generating video essays and experimental narratives. His videotapes have exhibited at museums and galleries internationally. Velez lives and works in New York City.

Videofreex
(see Cort, David)

Video Free America
(see Ginsberg, Arthur)

Video in the Villages

Brazil-based Video in the Villages works to bring an understanding of the power of TV technology to indigenous peoples as an empowering tool in their fight to preserve their lands and ways of life. The Video in the Villages project is an ongoing series that grew out of the frustrating experiences the native Brazilian Waiãpi had with ethnographic film and video shoots in their villages. Initiated in 1985 by husband and wife Vincent Carelli and Virginia Valadão through the Centro de Trabalho Indigenista in São Paulo (the project has been independent since 2000), the project has had a profound effect on native image and self-image, inter-tribal relations, and relations with white institutions. Through the project, members of several native groups learn about video technology and participate in the production and editing of the videotapes to represent themselves and their cultures. Carelli continues to collaborate with indigenous media makers; Valadão died in 1998.

Indians in Brazil, Part One: Good Trip Ibantu!

This and That (and other minor misunderstandings)
Edín Velez
2001, 13:00, U.S./Puerto Rico, color, sound, in English, Spanish, and French
Edín Velez's *This and That (and other minor misunderstandings)*, is a layered exploration of shifting memories, rapidly changing geographic and psychic climates, and family ties made and unmade as the artist reflects on his father's Alzheimer's Disease.
Available in Spanish language.
Only available on the anthology *Frames of Reference: Reflections on Media, Volume 6, Program 1.*

Free for All in Sararé
Video in the Villages
1992, 27:00, Brazil, color, sound, in Portuguese with English subtitles
More than 6,000 gold prospectors invaded the reserve of the Nambiquara of Sararé, and loggers raid the mahogany-rich forests, which are threatened by extinction. Pressure on the World Bank (with whom the government of Mato Grosso is negotiating a loan) could end prospecting, but the pillage of the forest continues.
Directed by Vincent Carelli, Maurizio Longobardi, and Virginia Valadão; edited by Tutu Nunes.

From the Ikpeng Children to the World
Video in the Villages
2002, 35:00, Brazil, color, sound, in Ikpeng with English subtitles
Four Ikpeng children reply to a video-letter from the children of Sierra Maestra in Cuba, introducing their village, families, toys, celebrations, and ways of life with grace and lightheartedness. Curious to know about children from other cultures, they ask to continue the correspondence.
Direction and camera by Karané, Kumaré, and Natuyu Yuwipo Txicão; edited by Mari Corrêa

Girl's Celebration
Video in the Villages
1987, 18:00, Brazil, color, sound, in Portuguese with English subtitles
Chief Pedro Mãmãindê (who directed the proceedings and the shoot itself) describes the necessity of strengthening the girls of his village by secluding them after their first menses. After several months, the village throws a party with singing, feasting, and the ritual abduction of the girl by an allied village. When the Nambiquara of Mato Grosso see videotape of themselves performing this ritual, the excess of Western clothing makes them uncomfortable. The ritual is then re-enacted with traditional body painting and adornment. Euphoric, they resolve to take up the lip and nose piercing of boys again in front of the camera, re-establishing a tradition abandoned for more than 20 years.
Directed and recorded by Vincent Carelli; edited by Cleiton Capelossi.

Indians in Brazil, Part One: Good Trip Ibantu!
Video in the Villages and TV Escola
2000, 18:00, Brazil, color, sound, in Portuguese with English subtitles
Indians in Brazil is an educational series for Brazilian public schools that invites students to experience cultural diversity. Four teenagers are invited to discover a new world and participate in Indian daily life in two different communities. They show their emotions, curiosity, and fears and are surprised by their new friends. *Good Trip Ibantu!* is a highly emotional account of a meeting of the four teenagers with the Krahô Indians. The Krahô receive them warmly and the integration is immediate. The youth take part in the daily life and ceremonies of the village. They are painted and receive Indian names. Their departure is pure emotion.
Directed by Vincent Carelli.

*Indians in Brazil, Part Two: When God
Visits the Village*

Indians in Brazil, Part Two: When God Visits the Village
Video in the Villages and TV Escola
2000, 18:00, Brazil, color, sound, in Portuguese with English subtitles
Part Two of the series sees the teenagers invited to visit the Kaiowá people
in South Mato Grosso. Expecting something similar to the Krahô village they
had previously visited, they are, at first, shocked. The houses in the village are
dispersed, and everyone is dressed in rags. But as they penetrate beneath
the appearances, the youths discover the intense religious life of the villagers
and the oppression they suffer from the ranchers that have taken most of
their lands.
Directed by Vincent Carelli.

Jane Moraita (Our Celebrations)
Video in the Villages
1995, 32:00, Brazil, color, sound, in Waiãpi with English subtitles
The Waiãpi videomaker Kasiripinã decides to show white people the documentation he did on his people in Amapo. He presents and comments on
three celebrations that represent episodes of the myth-cycle of the creation
of the universe. The theme of the Tamoko celebration is war, and it presents
the death of a cannibal monster. In the second celebration, Pikyry, the
dancers act out the spawning of fish. The last is the Turé, the dance of the
flutes, in which the Waiãpi reenact the death of the tapir in honor of the creator, Janejar.
Directed by Kasiripinã Waiãpi.

Jungle Secrets
Video in the Villages
1998, 37:00, Brazil, color, sound, in Waiãpi with English subtitles
Four tales about cannibal monsters narrated and performed by the Waiãpi
Indians. "We have made the video," say the Waiãpi, "to teach people to be
more careful with monsters they never heard about. Even a white man can be
eaten as he goes into the forest."
Directed by Vincent Carelli and Dominique Gallois; edited by Tutu Nunes.

Kinja Iakaha, A day in the village
Video in the Villages
2003, 40:00, Brazil, color, sound, in Waimiri and Atroari with English subtitles
Six Indians of different Waimiri and Atroari villages, located in the Amazon,
document the day-to-day life of their relatives in the Cacau village. These
images transport us to intimate scenes of their lifestyle and their intense rela-
tionship with nature.
Directed and photographed by Araduwá Waimiri, Iawusu Waimiri, Kabaha
Waimiri, Sanapyty Atroari, Sawá Waimiri, and Wamé Atroari; edited by
Leonardo Sette.

Meeting Ancestors
Video in the Villages
1993, 22:00, Brazil, color, sound, in Waiãpi with English subtitles
Chief Waiwai recounts for his village the story of a trip he and a small
entourage made to meet the Zo'é, a recently contacted group whom the
Waiãpi "know" through video. Both groups speak Tupi dialects and share
many cultural traditions, but the Zo'é are currently experiencing the phenomena of contact that the Waiãpi underwent 20 years ago. Waiãpi cameraman
Kasiripinã illustrates the Waiwai's account of the trip with video. The Zo'é
afford their visitors the chance to re-encounter the way of life and wisdom of
their ancestors. The Waiãpi bring information on the dangers of the white
world that the Zo'é are eager to understand.
Directed by Vincent Carelli.

Spanish subtitled version available.

Also available on the anthology *Frames of Reference: Reflections on Media,
Volume 1, Program 2.*

Morayngava

Morayngava

Video in the Villages

1997, 16:00, Brazil, color, sound, in Assurini with English subtitles

Morayngava: the "design of things." Yngiru: the box of the spirits, the films, just like xaman dreams. This is how the Asurini define video, which has just arrived in their village. After discovering that it is possible to store their images, the old men lament that they never stored images of their ancestors and decided to register the initiation of a xaman, a tradition threatened by new times.

Directed by Virginia Valadão and Regina Müller.

Moyngo: The Dream of Maragareum

Video in the Villages

2003, 44:00, Brazil, color, sound, in Ikpeng with English subtitles

During a video workshop, the Ikpeng community decides to act out the myth of the origin of the tattooing ceremony. The mythical hero, Maragareum, dreams about the collective death of the villagers of his friend's Eptxum's village. Arriving in this village, he finds, in fact, that everyone is dead. As night falls, he hides in the hut, and observes and learns the Moyngo ceremony from the spirits of the dead.

Directed and photographed by Karané, Kumaré, and Natuyu Ikpeng; edited by Leonardo Sette.

Pemp

Video in the Villages

1988, 27:00, Brazil, b&w and color, sound, in Portuguese with English subtitles

Pemp traces the 25-year struggle of the Parakatêjê (Gavião) to maintain autonomy in the face of huge development projects in the south of Pará. From the initial recovery of their lands in 1957 through dealings with FUNAI in the 1970s and the appropriation of Brazil nut monopolies to their current negotiations with the government, *Pemp* shows the Parakatêjê's most precious project; the preservation of their ceremonies and songs. The Kokrenum, chief and keeper of the group's traditions, uses video to transmit them to future generations.

Directed and photographed by Vincent Carelli.

The Rainy Season

Video in the Villages

1999, 38:00, Brazil, color, sound, in Ashaninka with English subtitles

A daily chronicle of the Ashaninka community during the rainy season, recorded on video during a workshop in a village on the Amônia River in the state of Acre. The involvement of the filmmakers with the Ashaninka community makes the film go beyond a mere description of activities, reflecting the rhythm of the village and the humor of its inhabitants.

Direction and photography by Valdete, Isaac, and Tsirotsi Ashaninka, Llullu Manchineri, Maru Kaxinawá, Nelson Kulina, Fernando Katuquina, and André Kanamari; edited by Mari Corrêa.

Shomõtsi

Video in the Villages

2001, 42:00, Brazil, color, sound, in Ashaninka with English subtitles

A picture of the day-to-day life of Shomõtsi, an Ashaninka Indian living on the border of Brazil and Peru. Valdete, a teacher and one of the village video makers, highlights his hardheaded and witty uncle.

Directed by Valdete Pinhanta Ashaninka; edited by Mari Corrêa.

Signs Don't Speak

Video in the Villages

1996, 27:00, Brazil, color, sound, in Waiãpi with English subtitles

A remarkable work about the struggle of the Waiãpi tribe, an indigenous people of Brazil, to combat the encroachment of prospectors on their land. Using

performative storytelling as well as documentary footage, the tape builds a history of the many negotiations and public performances that the Waiãpi engaged in with the Brazilian government to demarcate and preserve some of their land, and to regain control of their resources.
Directed by Vincent Carelli and Dominique Gallois.

The Spirit of TV
Video in the Villages
1990, 18:00, Brazil, color, sound, in Waiãpi with English subtitles
Beginning with the arrival by canoe of a TV and VCR in their village, *The Spirit of TV* documents the Waiãpi people's first encounter with TV images of themselves and others. They view a tape from their chief's first trip to Brasilia to speak to the government, news broadcasts, and videos of other Brazilian native peoples and record a session directed by Chief Waiwai for villages in his territory. The tape translates the reactions of individual Waiãpi to the power of images, the diversity of native peoples, and their common struggles with federal agents, gold miners, trappers, and loggers.
Directed by Vincent Carelli.

The Spirit of TV

Thank You Brother
Video in the Villages
1998, 17:00, Brazil, color, sound, in Portuguese with English subtitles
Divino explains how he got introduced to video. "Filming is my profession; that's what I was born to do ... not for the work with the axe. I wasn't born to plant. I already said this to my wife." Today, Divino dominates the language of video and its filming and editing techniques. He also talks about working in partnership with his community.
Directed by Divino Tserewahu; edited by Tutu Nunes.

Video Cannibalism
Video in the Villages
1995, 17:00, Brazil, color, sound, in Enauenê-Nauê with English subtitles
Video is introduced to the Enauênê Nauê Indians, a group still isolated in the North of Mato Grosso. An outgoing group, they respond with a surprising high-spirited performance that includes a good measure of clowning around and a re-enactment of an attack they suffered at the hands of their neighbors, the Cinta-Larga, not long ago. After growing accustomed to watching movies on video, they decide to produce their own.
Directed and photographed by Vincent Carelli.

Video Cannibalism

Video in the Villages
1989, 10:00, Brazil, color, sound, in Nambiquara, Gavião, Tikuna, and Kaiapó with English subtitles
An overview of the *Video in the Villages Project*, this documentary shows how four different Amazonian native groups (Nambiquara, Gavião, Tikina, and Kaiapó) have embraced video and incorporated it in the service of their projects for political and ethnic affirmation.
Directed and photographed by Vincent Carelli.

Video in the Villages Presents Itself
Video in the Villages
2002, 33:00, Brazil, color, sound, in Portuguese with English subtitles
Video in the Villages presents its recent progress, its indigenous workshops for training and production. Founded in 1987, the project began with the introduction of video to indigenous communities that produced documentaries for their own purposes. In 1995, the opening of a space on educational TV in Cuiabá led to "Indigenous Program." Since 1997, Video in the Villages has invested in the formation of the first generation of indigenous documentary filmmakers through national and regional workshops.
Directed by Mari Corrêa and Vincent Carelli; edited by Corrêa.

Wai'a Rini: The Power of the Dream

Video in the Villages

2001, 1:05:00, Brazil, color, sound, in Xavante with English subtitles

Within the long cycle of initiation ceremonies of the Xavante People, the Wai'a celebration introduces young men to spiritual life and puts them in contact with supernatural forces. Filmmaker Divino Tserewahu speaks with his father (one of the leaders of this ritual) about what can be disclosed of this secret celebration of men, where the initiated go through many trials and tribulations.

Directed by Divino Tserewahú.

Wai'a: The Secret of Men

Video in the Villages

1988, 15:00, Brazil, color, sound, in Xavante with English subtitles

Among the Xavante of Mato Grosso, the Wai'a is an important stage in a male initiation ritual that happens once every 15 years. *Wai'a: The Secret of Men* documents the ceremonies that prepare young men for contact with supernatural forces. The young people of the village directed the filming and assisted with the editing to make a record for the next generation.

Directed by Virginia Valadão.

Wapté Mnhõnõ: The Initiation of a Young Xavante

Video in the Villages

1999, 1:15:00, Brazil, color, sound, in Xavante with English subtitles

A documentary about the initiation ritual for young Xavante Indians, created during a training workshop for the Video in the Villages project. Invited by Divino from the Sangradouro village, one Suyú and four Xavantes Indians film together for the first time. While filming the ritual, various members of the village explain the significance of the complex ceremony's elements.

Directed and photographed by Bartolomeu Patira, Caimi Waiassé, Divino Tserewahú, Jorge Protodi, Whinti Suyá; edited by Tutu Nunes.

We Gather as Family

We Gather as Family

Video in the Villages

1993, 32:00, Brazil, color, sound, in Portuguese with English subtitles

This tape documents a cultural exchange between the Parakatêjê (Gavião) of Pará and their "relatives," the Krahô of Tocantins. Kokrenum, the charismatic chief of the Parakatêjê, organizes a visit to the Krahô, who speak the same language and maintain their traditions. The 50 young Parakatêjê he brings along participate in a ceremony consisting of singing, body painting, and preparations for the long, strenuous relay race through the savannah. The following year, the Parakatêjê return the invitation and the Krahô travel to Kokrenum's village. The two chiefs discuss cultural issues and seal a pact of friendship between their groups.

Directed and photographed by Vincent Carelli.

Yãkwá

Video in the Villages

1996, 54:00, Brazil, color, sound, in Enawenê-Nauê with English subtitles

A four-part documentary, *Yãkwá* shows the most important ritual of the Enauênê-Nauê Indians (Brazil). For seven months every year, the spirits are venerated with offerings of food, song, and dance so that they will protect the community. In "The World Outside the Rock" the Yaõkwá festivities open with the Enauênê-Nauê preparing for the big fish-catch by making salt, canoes, and fish traps. In "Dataware's Revenge" groups of men leave the villages for two months and build dams on forest waterways to catch fish as they return from spawning. In "Harikare, the Spirit's Host" everyone returns after the fish-catch with smoked fish that will be offered to the spirits and eaten by the villagers until the end of the ritual. In the most spectacular phase of the ceremony, the spirits make their stormy entrance into the village. In "The Little Cassava Girl" the Indians cut down and plant cassava root on the collective fields, the field of the Yãkwá spirit. The Indians relive the myth of the girl who was buried by her mother and who transformed herself into the first cassava root.

Directed by Virginia Valadão; edited by Tutu Nunes.

Viola, Bill

Bill Viola describes his early single-channel tapes both as "songs" and as "visual poems-allegories in the language of subjective perception." His early single channel pieces employ formal strategies associated with structural film that also operate as metaphors for transcendent vision, creativity, and symbolic transformation/illumination. One of the most prominent video artists of the past three decades, he currently produces large scale installations.

Sweet Light
Bill Viola
1977, 9:08, U.S., color, sound

Viola has referred to *Sweet Light* and other tapes from this period as "songs"–personal, lyrical statements. Articulated through precise editing, *Sweet Light* incorporates symbolic imagery, changes of scale, and a radically mobile camera suggesting shifting points of view. The tape is grounded in common references to illumination–incandescent lamplight, daylight, flashlight, and firelight–that serve as metaphors for artistic inspiration. Viola's access to sound facilities at the ZBS studio in Fort Edward, New York and to video post-production at the TV Lab at WNET-New York allowed him to exercise precise and rhythmic flexibility in editing this tape.

Only available on the anthology *Surveying the First Decade, Program 2.*

Wallace, Linda

Linda Wallace is an artist and curator. She has curated new media exhibitions in China, the UK, New Zealand, the Netherlands, India, Thailand, Singapore, and Malaysia. She is director of the Machine Hunger Company.

lovehotel
Linda Wallace
2000, 6:45, Australia, color, sound

lovehotel uses excerpts from the book *Fleshmeat* by Australian Internet artist Francesca da Rimini, detailing her life online from 1994 to 1997.

"Linda Wallace's video *lovehotel* is about the emergence of new spaces of interaction, of new technologies and of new formations of desire; it is about the meandering of an 'Aberrant Intelligence' which hovers above and insinuates itself into our familiar habitats (physical and cyber) like a kind of inscrutable and formless spectre of the future."
–Chris Rose, "Formula for the Emergence of the New," *Life 3.0* (Madrid: Fundación Telefónica, 2000)

Only available on the anthology *e-[d]entity, Tape 2.*

Wegman, William

William Wegman began producing short, performance-oriented videotapes in the early 1970s, which are considered classics. Many featured his canine companion, a Weimaraner named Man Ray. These tapes are deadpan parodies of "high art" using sight gags, minimalist performance, and understated humor. Recorded as single takes in real time, Wegman used portable video's intimacy and low-tech immediacy to create idiosyncratic narrative comedy. Wegman was among a group of artists to produce work through WGBH's Television Lab. In recent years, Wegman has become famous for his hilarious and touching photographs of other Weimeraners who are Man Ray's successors.

Selected Works, Reel 1
William Wegman
1970-72, 35:00, U.S., b&w, sound
Contents:
Microphone, Pocketbook Man, Anet and Abtu, The Ring, Randy's Sick, Milk/Floor, Stomach Song, Happy Song, The Door, William Wegman in Chinese, Elbows, Dress Curtain, Hot Sake, Caspar, Handy, Out and In, Plunger Series, Nosy, Firechief, Come In, Hidden Utensil, Contract, Puppet, Shadows, Ventriloquism, Light Trails, and *Cape On.*
This title was in the original *Castelli-Sonnabend* video art collection.

Selected Works, Reel 2
William Wegman
1972, 14:00, U.S., b&w, sound
Contents:
Sanforized, Coin Toss, Monkey Business, Same Shirt, Diving Board, Straw and String, Product, In the Cup, The Kiss, and *Treat and Bottle.*
This title was in the original Castelli-Sonnabend video art collection.

Selected Works, Reel 3
William Wegman
1972-73, 20:00, U.S., b&w, sound
Contents:
Stick and Tooth, Emperor and Dish, Lucky T-Shirt, Rage and Depression, Speed Reading, Born with No Mouth, Dual Function, Massage Chair, Raise Treat, Man Ray, Do You Want To?, Crooked Finger, Crooked Stick, Deodorant, Bubble Up, and *47 Seconds.*
This title was in the original Castelli-Sonnabend video art collection.

Car Salesman

Selected Works, Reel 4
William Wegman
1973-74, 20:57, U.S., b&w, sound
A collection of 21 comedic performances to camera, both with and without the droll participation of Man Ray.
Contents:
Man Ray's Alarm Clock, Cross Country Road Trip, Waiting for an Ambulance, Wegman Signing a Visit to the Laundromat, Wegman Signing Three Movies Seen Yesterday, Cocktail Waiter, Wegman in the Nail Business, Calling Man Ray, Car Salesman, Man Ray Poses with Bowling Ball, Man Ray and Crouching Wegman, Radar Screen Wegman, Wegman and Luggage—"Airplane Crash," "You've Got a Word Spelled Wrong,"Trip to Egypt, Wegman Showing Cities Located on a Ball, Shaky Handwriting on the Bus, Man Ray on the Sofa with Falling Pieces of Paper, Wegman Growls, and *Wegman Consults with Man Ray Over His Spelling Test.*
This title was in the original Castelli-Sonnabend video art collection.

Selected Works, Reel 5
William Wegman
1975, 29:00, U.S., b&w, sound
Contents:
Stalking, Nocturne, Audio Tape and Video Tape, Dancing Tape, Hobo on Train, Drinking Milk, Copyright, Buying a House, Lerch Hairpieces, Tammy and Can of Plums, Loves Water, Average Guy, Over for Drink, Marbles, Ball Drop, and *Treat Table.*
This title was in the original Castelli-Sonnabend video art collection.

Wegman's Selected Works
William Wegman
1972, 8:00, U.S., b&w, sound
Wegman uses the area framed by the camera as his performance space, employing a single, fixed camera to record the scenes as he and Man Ray, his Weimaraner, act them out. It has been suggested that Wegman's performances with Man Ray are uncanny invocations of broadcast television's manipulations of its viewers. Man Ray and his companion are collectively mesmerized by a tennis ball. The misrepresentations and lewd stroking of Man Ray as Wegman delivers a used car salesman's monologue apes television's crass marketing. Man Ray's pursuit of a dog biscuit inside a glass bottle creates the type of narrative suspense that draws us into the action on the screen. These tapes are a selection from the hours of short performances Wegman recorded in his studio from 1970-78. *Selected Works* includes *Two Dogs and Ball* (silent), *Used Car Salesman,* and *Dog Biscuit in Glass Jar.* Only available on the anthology *Surveying First Decade, Program 1.*

The World of Photography (see Smith, Michael)

Weiner, Lawrence

Working in a wide variety of media, including video, film, books, audio tapes, sculpture, performance, installation, and graphic art, Lawrence Weiner consistently invokes social situations that elicit responses to issues of language, philosophy, theater, and art. Identified with conceptual art, Weiner is notable for his fervent desire to invent new forms and transformations. Unlike some conceptualists, Weiner does not shy away from materializing the art object; instead he tries to work across artistic conventions. He is committed to democratic art, an art that adapts and changes form in response to cultural and social changes.

Affected and/or Effected
Lawrence Weiner
1974, 20:37, U.S./The Netherlands, b&w, sound
Affected and/or Effected begins with a close-up of a girl resting her head on her hand, reading. On the overlapping tracks a male voice states "affected," followed by a female voice that responds "and/or effected...." This pattern of dividing words in half and presenting them in alternating male and female voices continues throughout the tape. While what is seen is separated from what is heard, the boundaries between the audio and video portions of the tape are complicated by other sounds. The statement of intent is spoken: "An artist may construct an art. An art may be fabricated. ..."

Altered to Suit
Lawrence Weiner
1979, 23:00, U.S./The Netherlands, b&w, sound, 16mm to video
The whole story takes place in the mise-en-scène of the artist's studio. The

delicate psychological allegory of "a day in the life of ..." anchors the displacement of (filmic) reality and the alienation of the (player's) self. Devices such as incongruity between the image and the soundtrack, odd camera angles, and plays on objective focus are integral and explicit components of the narrative. *Altered to Suit* diverges from preceding films in that the dialogue is not solely related to the work; rather, the work serves as a central frame of reference from which the story unfolds. This is also the first time that the narrative dominates the structure of the film. Shot in black-and-white, the photography is sensual and seductive.

Beached

Beached
Lawrence Weiner
1970, 2:30, U.S./The Netherlands, b&w, sound
The soundtrack begins with the artist stating the conditions: "An artist may construct a work and/or a work may be fabricated and/or a work need not be built. I elected five possibilities for videotape." These possibilities are the actions executed in *Beached*. They are shot in five sequences and consist of throwing, pulling, lifting, dragging, and using leverage. This tape has been remastered, though traces of the historical picture loss remain.

A Bit of Matter and a Little Bit More
Lawrence Weiner
1976, 23:00, U.S./The Netherlands, color, sound
The male/female, subject/object investigation in *A Bit of Matter and a Little Bit More* has no titillating introduction; the appetite is not whetted beforehand. The opening hardcore shot shows male and female bodies engaged in coitus. At the end of the tape a male voice says, "Some questions and five answers relative to moved pictures, five questions and some answers relative to moved pictures"—a reference to the artist's book *100 Rocks on a Wall.*

Broken Off
Lawrence Weiner
1971, 1:30, U.S./The Netherlands, b&w, sound
In this video the artist states that a public work demonstrates what qualifies as art within his conception. Like *Beached*, it was also shot in a marshy area near the sea and in sequences separated by dissolves. One sees five different actions related to *Broken Off*. The artist breaks a tree branch, scrapes and kicks the ground with his foot, snaps a stick in two on a fence, scrapes a stone with his fingernail. At the end he pulls the line plug from the video, drawing attention to the mechanics of the medium.

Do You Believe in Water?
Lawrence Weiner
1976, 39:00, U.S./The Netherlands, color, sound
The performers are seated around a pink octagonal table on pink, violet, and silver cinder blocks. One performer (Robert Stearns) stands up, recites the credits for the tape, and then says, "Do you believe in water? Robert Stearns." He claps and turns to the next performer who asks the same question and gives his name. Next the players split into pairs and attempt to relate to each other—playing tug-of-war, making love, arguing over who has the most integrity, and fighting for possession of the props. As the different relationships evolve, the triple-layered soundtrack interfaces with the players. We hear puzzling rhetorical questions such as: "Is tongue kissing like ass kissing?" "Heads or tails?" "Can you make that kind of quality judgement about colors?" "Do you think there is an emotional response to color?"

Done To
Lawrence Weiner
1974, 20:00, U.S./The Netherlands, color, sound, 16mm to video
Done To (alternately titled *It Is, Done To*) consists of simple still frames accompanied by a complex, incongruous soundtrack or silence. There are instances where image and sound coalesce; however, the majority of the

images are overwhelmed by the at-times symphonic, at-times cacophonous soundtrack, displacing the normal film viewing experience. The standard film format of going from frame to frame—and then and then and then—is what this film is concerned with.

Eyes on the Prize: Part One of Hearts and Helicopters
Lawrence Weiner
1999, 19:25, U.S./The Netherlands, color, sound
There are times when concurrent multiple realities demand an attempt to determine who has this "place in the sun" and where, exactly, it is located. *Hearts and Helicopters* occurs at that moment in the lives of four people. Also available on the compilation *Hearts and Helicopters: A Trilogy.*

A First Quarter
Lawrence Weiner
1973, 1:25:00, U.S./The Netherlands, b&w, sound
Using the structure of a feature film as its basic format, *A First Quarter* adopts the principles of *nouvelle vague* cinema. Simultaneous realities, altered flashbacks, and plays on time and space are all components of the form and content of this film. Because it was originally shot on video, then kinescoped to 16mm film, *A First Quarter* has acquired a softened, poetic look. The dialogue derives entirely from the creation of the work as it is spoken and read, built, enacted, written, and painted by the players. As scenarios build, they appear as tropes, one after another.

For Example Decorated
Lawrence Weiner
1977, 23:00, U.S./The Netherlands, color, sound
For Example Decorated is a talk show featuring art world personalities Britte Le Va, Peter Gordon, and James Sarkis. The show begins with Le Va reciting the credits; then she introduces herself, Soviet style—as in *Do You Believe in Water?*—by saying her name, then clapping. The other guests follow, and as the three converse about the role of art in life, they build little structures with the Lego blocks that cover the coffee table. The soundtrack is composed of three different audio channels: Le Va and Weiner reading artist "conditions" ("The artist may construct the work; the work may be fabricated; the work need not be built..."), Le Va speaking generally about how to make friends with transvestites (their likes and dislikes, etc.), and Le Va singing a version of Marlene Dietrich's "Falling in Love Again."

Green As Well As Blue As Well As Red

Green As Well As Blue As Well As Red
Lawrence Weiner
1976, 18:00, U.S./The Netherlands, color, sound
A table is set with two red books placed at diagonal corners and a stack of three poker chips placed in the center. Two women enter, sit, and begin to play with the books and poker chips. Different soundtracks converge; the dialogue begins to sound like an interrogation as one character asks, "What is the structural definition of logical positivism? Lawrence Weiner, what is the structural form as in the manner and use of your language? Does it not have a direct relation to logical positivism?"

Hearts and Helicopters: A Trilogy
A three-part series featuring important new works by internationally renowned conceptual artist Lawrence Weiner, these works continue the themes of role- and game-playing and the use of language. There are times when concurrent multiple realities of place demand at least a simple attempt to determine who in fact has, and where is, this "place in the sun." *Hearts and Helicopters* occurs at that moment in the lives of four people.
Total running time 52:25.
Contents:
Eyes on the Prize, Lawrence Weiner, 1999, 19:25, U.S./The Netherlands, color, sound

How Far Is There, Lawrence Weiner, 1999, 17:00, U.S./The Netherlands, color, sound

With a Grain of Salt, Lawrence Weiner, 2000, 16:00, U.S./The Netherlands, color, sound

How Far Is There: Part Two of Hearts and Helicopters

How Far Is There: Part Two of Hearts and Helicopters
Lawrence Weiner
1999, 17:00, U.S./The Netherlands, color, sound
There are times when concurrent multiple realities of place demand at least an attempt to determine who in fact has, and where is, this place in the sun. *Hearts and Helicopters* occurs at that moment in the lives of four people. Also available on the compilation *Hearts and Helicopters: A Trilogy*.

Nothing to Lose
Lawrence Weiner
1984, 22:00, U.S./The Netherlands, color, sound
Footage from a performance produced at Forum en Scene in Middleburg, Holland of the players continually enacting the same tasks. *Nothing to Lose* opens with a young, androgynous sailor standing between two buildings, while the song "Nothing to Lose" plays off a record. The camera pans to two people in the national costume of Zeeland: one is peeling cucumbers and the other is washing sheets, shouting, "Good manners ruin good food." A woman sits in her window and shouting to the sailor. Finally, the young sailor kisses this woman on the cheek and walks off the set smiling.

Nothing to Lose (The Book)
Lawrence Weiner
2000, 3:30, The Netherlands, color, sound, CD-ROM
A structure of Lawrence Weiner.
Based upon the LP *Niets Aan Verloren* (1976) and the performance tape *Niets Aan Verloren* (1984).
Players: Alice Zimmerman, Sophie Calle, Peter Gordon, Kim Gordon, and Kirsten Vibeke Thueson
Still photography: Alice Zimmerman
Photography: Moved Pictures
Computer editing: K. Hassett
Voices: Coosje Van Bruggen and Lawrence Weiner
Only available on the compilation *There Are Things That Move Outside of Motion*.

Passage to the North

Passage to the North
Lawrence Weiner
1981, 16:00, U.S./The Netherlands, color, sound, 16mm to video
Passage to the North is a companion film to *Plowman's Lunch*. It is set in the same location as *Altered To Suit*, and some of the players appear for a second or third time—Coosje van Bruggen and Kirsten Vibeke Thueson were in *A Second Quarter;* Thueson and Michael Shamberg were in *Altered To Suit*. Although there does not seem to be a relationship between the roles each has played from movie to movie, there are some similarities in the situations these characters find themselves in. They are a group; they are under some sort of duress that comes from the outside; they also have access to the media. They are a motley, disheveled bunch, but they are obviously not "nobodies."

Plowman's Lunch
Lawrence Weiner
1982, 28:00, U.S./The Netherlands, color, sound, 16mm to video
Plowman's Lunch is called a documentary because its intent was to explore actual occurrences—be these the building of the work or what befalls the players. It still uses an open form, but the characters are more developed; they have "names," and some of the scenes were truly dangerous for them to produce. As in the other films (with the exception of *Done To*) there is a

nucleus of three characters–Boris, Jamiee, and Steentje, a transvestite. The music, composed expressly for the piece, is harmonious with its developments. Cartoon-like framing and intense colors give the film a composed, painterly quality.

Reading Lips
Lawrence Weiner and Steen Møller Rasmussen
1996, 10:00, The Netherlands, color, sound
"There has to be a way to win" is the refrain. Three women fold clothes, stroll and shop as they discuss jealousy, murder, and dead bodies. An enquiry into the generosity of women.
Players: Trina Vester, Karin Westerlund, and Lise Kellemann
Shot on location in Kobenhavn.

A Second Quarter

A Second Quarter
Lawrence Weiner
1975, 1:25:00, U.S./Germany, color, sound, 16mm to video
The second feature film–there were to be four quarters–retains the cinematic structure of *A First Quarter* and builds upon it. *A Second Quarter* is decidedly European; the "place" (Berlin) is the catalyst for the "action" (the work). The works recited in the film are concerned with barriers and borders, physical and geophysical phenomena. The characters also translate, count, and recite the alphabet. They build a narrative that is not a story to be followed dogmatically but rather a pattern from which to extract one's version of what is seen. The scenes are set in an old bourgeois apartment, in an office near the West Berlin train station, and at the ruins of the Anhalter Bahnhof and its vicinity, with the Berlin Wall in the background.

Shifted from the Side
Lawrence Weiner
1972, 1:00, U.S., b&w, sound
Shifted From the Side is conceptually identical to *To And Fro...* and was probably made the same afternoon. The object used to demonstrate five possibilities of what could–but not necessarily should–be the artwork is a pack of Lucky Strike cigarettes. As in *To And Fro...*, the camera is static. The pack is on the right side of the screen; as the text is read, the pack is shifted back and forth. The hand retreats from the object each time an act is completed before sliding it from side to side across the table.
This title was in the original Castelli-Sonnabend video art collection.

Some Things History Don't Support
Lawrence Weiner
2000, 3:30, U.S./The Netherlands, color, sound
A structure of Lawrence Weiner.
Photography: Moved Pictures
Computer Graphics: K. Hassett
"A New Pair of Shoes", "Ships at Sea", "Sailors and Shoes"
Music: Ned Sublette, ASCAP
Lyrics: Lawrence Weiner, BMI
Only available on the compilation *There Are Things That Move Outside of Motion.*

There Are Things That Move Outside of Motion
A structure of Lawrence Weiner.
Originally a compilation of 4 CD-ROMs.
Each functioning apart (akin to a 45 RPM record). Each functioning as a part of a whole. Attempting to ascertain what in fact is motion.
Total running time 14:00.
Contents:
Nothing to Lose (The Book), Lawrence Weiner, 2000, 3:30, U.S./The Netherlands, color, sound
Some Things History Don't Support, Lawrence Weiner, 2000, 3:30, U.S./The

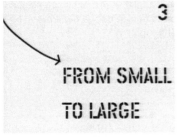

There Are Things That Move Outside of Motion

Netherlands, color, sound
Trailer for Mortal Sin (The Book), Lawrence Weiner, 2000, 3:30, U.S./The
Netherlands, color, sound
Wind and the Willows, Lawrence Weiner, 2000, 3:30, U.S./The Netherlands,
color, sound

There But For
Lawrence Weiner
1980, 20:00, U.S./The Netherlands, color, sound
There But For resembles a soap opera; its characters—a couple whose relationship has seen better days, a ball-and-jack playing adult/child, and a couple that comes to visit the family—are in the midst of their day-to-day lives (an
imitation of life). The music was composed and performed live on the set as
the play unfolded. *There But For* is a free-form chance operation within the
defined boundaries of place (an apartment) and the assigned roles of the
players: the mother (bitch), the father (jerk), their kid (retard), and their visitors. The players continually argue as they feel their way through this structure, where ambiguity is the form. The kid asks, "Is mediocrity its own
reward?" Perhaps the clue for the viewer is in the tape's title: *There But For*
(the grace of God go I).

To and Fro. Fro and To. And To and Fro. And Fro and To.
Lawrence Weiner
1972, 1:00, U.S./The Netherlands, b&w, sound
Reportedly shot in the back office at Leo Castelli's New York gallery, an ashtray is used to demonstrate five different actions related to artistic work. With
the camera static, the video opens with the ashtray in the center of the
screen. A hand approaches from above and slides the object up and down,
then back up and back down. Each time an act is completed, the hand
retreats from the object, marking a separation from the next "possibility." The
actions (or movements) mimic language (e.g. "to and fro") as it is spoken.
This title was in the original *Castelli-Sonnabend* video art collection.

Trailer for Mortal Sin (The Book)
Lawrence Weiner
2000, 3:30, U.S./The Netherlands, color, sound
A structure of Lawrence Weiner.
Player: Alice Zimmerman
Computer Graphics: K. Hassett
Sound clips from "Postcards from Heaven," "Ships at Sea," "Sailors and
Shoes"
Music: Ned Sublette, ASCAP
Lyrics: Lawrence Weiner, BMI
Only available on the compilation *There Are Things That Move Outside of
Motion.*

Trailer for Plowman's Lunch

Trailer for Plowman's Lunch
Lawrence Weiner
1982, 6:00, U.S./The Netherlands, color, sound
Zachte Berm (from Weiner's film *Plowman's Lunch*) sits with her back to the
camera in front of a large mirror—her face, covered with shaving cream, is
seen in its reflection. As the soundtrack begins, she tries to lip-sync to the
spoken words, "Art is not a metaphor upon the relationship of human beings
to objects and objects to objects in relation to human beings but a representation of an empirical existing fact," while shaving.

Wind and the Willows
Lawrence Weiner
2000, 3:30, U.S./The Netherlands, color, sound
A structure of Lawrence Weiner.
Graphics and Computer Editing: K. Hassett
The Song: "Wind and the Willows"

Music: Ned Sublette, ASCAP
Lyrics: Lawrence Weiner BMI
Cover Photo: Alice Weiner
Only available on the compilation *There Are Things That Move Outside of Motion.*

With a Grain of Salt: Part Three of Hearts and Helicopters
Lawrence Weiner
2000, 16:00, U.S./The Netherlands, color, sound
There are times when concurrent multiple realities of place demand at least a simple attempt to determine who in fact has and where is this place in the sun. *Hearts and Helicopters* occur at that moment in the lives of four people.

Also available on the compilation *Hearts and Helicopters: A Trilogy.*

Wilcha, Christopher

In 1993, Christopher Wilcha got a job at Columbia House, the largest mail-order CD and tape club in America. He brought a camcorder to the office and *The Target Shoots First* was culled from more than 200 hours of Hi-8 footage Wilcha collected while employed by the Sony-owned company.

The Target Shoots First
Christopher Wilcha
1999, 1:10:00, U.S., color, sound
"Christopher Wilcha's fascinating feature-length video reminds us how seldom we're allowed to see certain businesses operating from the inside. Wilcha, a 22-year-old college graduate and alternative-rock enthusiast, was hired by the Columbia Record and Tape Club—apparently as a fluke—to help launch a whole new niche-marketing division, which brought him face-to-face with the contradictory meanings of the term 'alternative' once it's been embraced by the mass market. He brought his video camera to work every day, and what emerge are selective glimpses of—and thoughtful reflections on—his extended stint with the company."
—Jonathan Rosenbaum, "Chicago Underground Film Festival," *Chicago Reader* (13 August 1999)
"Guerrilla infiltration? Or a sly spin on corporate marketing? Subversives aside, *The Target Shoots First* is a hilarious, hyper peek inside that mail-order music monster, Columbia House."
—Steve Seid (Berkeley: Pacific Film Archive, 1999)

Woolery, Reginald

Reginald Woolery is an artist working in film, video, CD-ROM, websites, and other digital media forms. Woolery's work deals with issues of race, democracy, community, and the public cybersphere. He teaches at Cornell University.

World Wide Web/Million Man March
Reginald Woolery
1998, U.S., color, sound, CD-ROM
The question is asked: "What is the difference between a community based on identity and identity based on community?" Broken down into four central areas: desire, spirit, identity, and pleasure, *World Wide Web/Million Man March* suggests the fluidity of "race and place" denied in contemporary dialogues centering on technology and emergent social bodies. One area of misplaced cultural rhetoric is the paranoia and utopia attributed to both the internet and black masculine activist practices. Moving beyond dualistic binarisms, *World Wide Web/Million Man March* resigns itself to a babble of humour, paradox, urban rhythm, and endless impressions of transitional color.

Only available on CD-ROM.

Wrobel, Kate

Wrobel spent the summer of 1992 shooting video at demonstrations at abortion clinics; the anti-abortion protesters caught her attention because she was raised Catholic and considered herself "pro-life" as a child.

How I Spent My Summer Vacation
Kate Wrobel
1994, 10:00, U.S., color, sound
An eloquent personal narrative about the meaning of childhood and the use of children as political tools—specifically by "Right-to-Lifers" participating in the blockades of abortion clinics. Rather than merely constructing a video document of the daily drama surrounding the protests, Wrobel slows down the event and extracts the children's stories. She interlaces this with personal memories of her playful and carefree childhood and exposes how she, too, was susceptible when young. Neither preachy nor accusatory, Wrobel's combination of street images with personal experience allows viewers to reach their own conclusions in an extremely powerful manner.

Yin, Chi-Jang

Chi-Jang Yin is a video, photography, and performance artist. She was born in China, grew up in Hong Kong and Taiwan, and immigrated to Canada; her family moved 21 times. Her works are mainly focused on autobiography as an essential subject of the struggle in political instability and social conflict. Yin teaches at the School of Art Institute of Chicago and DePaul University.

Yonemoto, Bruce and Norman

Bruce and Norman Yonemoto are brothers who have been an effective collaborative team since 1975. The Yonemoto brothers base their videotapes on familiar narrative forms and then circumvent convention through direct, over-eager adoption of heavily cliched dialogue, music, gestures, and scenes that register recognition in the viewer's memory without being identifiable. Their tapes effectively illustrate how the televised representation of the world becomes the model for living, with individuals not only copying the fashions, gestures, and dialogue of TV characters but also using the situational patterns of TV as the way to understand their life. Their work also addresses the intersections of traditional Japanese and contemporary American cultures.

Another Clapping
Chi-Jang Yin
2000, 24:00, U.S., color, sound
Another Clapping explores the relationship triangle between a daughter, her mother, and the Chinese Cultural Revolution. It is an experimental documentary based on the mother's violent past with its traumatic political history and an unsuccessful marriage. Through their subsequent experiences as immigrants in Canada and the complex process of remembering and reviewing the past, history comes to signify the characteristic of the individual. The tracing of memory illuminates the difficulties of identifying mother and daughter as different people. *Another Clapping* is about the intimate and sublime relationship between a mother and daughter and the struggle between their actual history and the collective memory of family issues and public trauma. It is about the personal, political, and conceptual implications of a traced and displaced identity.

Kappa
Bruce Yonemoto and Norman Yonemoto
1986, 25:00, U.S., color, sound, in English and Japanese
In this satirical tape the Yonemotos deconstruct the myth of Oedipus within the framework of the myth of Kappa: a malevolent and hedonistic Shinto god of fresh water whose prankish harassment of young maidens includes hiding beneath outhouses to pinch their behinds. The Kappa figure (Mike Kelley) encounters an Oedipal scene—updated Southern California style—and acts as the conscience and proxy of Eddie and Jocasta, supplying an ambiguous poetic resolution to their desires. All three characters are associated in the quest for insight beyond apparent reality, illustrating "the essence of the Oedipal complex as the project of becoming God, replacing the father in order to become the father of oneself." This tape comments on the position of both legends in their respective societies.

Made in Hollywood
Bruce Yonemoto and Norman Yonemoto
1990, 53:00, U.S., color, sound
Revolving around a movie mogul's familial intrigues, *Made in Hollywood* tells the story of two artists selling out to make movies, and a simple country girl's angelic rise to fame despite it all. As a copy of a copy, this tape parodies what it mimics, and, by reveling in the glitz and glamour of image-obsessed stars, exploits the love/hate relationship viewers have with their media icons: simultaneously viewing them as perfect models and ridiculous trumped-up figures existing only in the fantasyland that is Hollywood.
Principal cast includes Patricia Arquette, Michael Lerner, Ron Vawter, and Mary Woronov.

Vault
Bruce Yonemoto and Norman Yonemoto
1984, 12:00, U.S., color, sound
"We are hoping that in presenting this story in such a minimal way it would become evident that this Freudian logic is a conceptual and visual cliché. We want our audience to have an emotional response to the work, but at the same time realize that they're being manipulated."
—Bruce and Norman Yonemoto
"In *Vault*, the Yonemotos reconstruct a traditional narrative of desire—boy meets girl, boy loses girl—that knowingly employs the melodramatic syntax of Hollywood movies and commercial television. They illustrate the psychoanalytic subtext of advertising, film, and TV language through the recurrent use of Freudian symbols and flashbacks to the characters' childhood traumas, humourously underscoring the power of these devices in creating personal fiction."
—Bruce and Norman Yonemoto, "Made in Hollywood: A Treatment for a Video Feature and Discussion of Aesthetic Strategies," in *Resolution: A Critique of Video Art*, ed. Patti Podesta (Los Angeles: Los Angeles Contemporary Exhibitions, 1986)

Zando, Julie

Julie Zando is a videomaker and former director of Squeaky Wheel Film and Video Coalition in Buffalo, New York. Her work exploits the raw and edgy properties of Hi-8 video with potent results while investigating the intermingling issues of power, sexual identity, and desire. Her work has shown nationally and internationally.

The Bus Stops Here

The Aha Experience!
Julie Zando
1988, 5:00, U.S., color, sound

The "a-ha experience" is the moment when a child first recognizes its own image in a mirror; it is critical to the development of intelligence and identity. It is also the moment when the "self" is surrendered to the control of an external influence. The child accepts the power of the mother to confer or withhold love; it is the mother's power to fulfill desire that shapes a child's sense of identity. Similarly, a camera controls love by directing or not directing its attention to the desiring subject. The narration in this fascinating video describes a scene in which a young woman, on the brink of sexual awakening, is shocked by the presence of her mother in her bed. This image haunts her, and the imagined presence of the mother's body provides the backdrop for all further sexual encounters, and all desire is subsequently understood as a derivative of this experience. It is the mother's desire (her presence in the bed) that directs and controls the scene of passion—she is the ultimate subject whose love confers sexual and psychic identity.

The Apparent Trap
Julie Zando
1999, 24:00, U.S., b&w, sound

This work attempts to further the critical dialogue surrounding the strategies of repetition and re-enactment. *The Apparent Trap* is a work that reminds the audience of the psychoanalytic implications of these strategies. It examines Walt Disney's *The Parent Trap* (1961), a story in which twins decide to switch identities. The conceit of identity, the violence that erupts when one is confronted with one's mirror image, and the "trap" of identification with the Other are all themes explored by re-enacting selected video art that speaks to these issues. Vito Acconci's *Pryings,* for example, is reinterpreted as a search for recognition rather than simply as a rape scenario. The subject seeks recognition by forcing open the eyes of the other. Ultimately, *The Apparent Trap* contributes to the art historical dialogue exploring the dual nature of re-enactment, as both radically emancipatory (Benjamin) and tragically limiting (Lacan).

The Bus Stops Here
Julie Zando
1990, 30:00, U.S., color and b&w, sound

The Bus Stops Here is an experimental narrative about two sisters, Judith and Anna, plunged into depression by their struggle to gain control over their lives. Narrated by Judith's counselor, *The Bus Stops Here* traps these women in a narrative in which their unmediated voices are rarely heard; instead, the viewer learns about them only through the interceding power structures of narrative, family, and psychiatric establishment. Zando chose black-and-white film and a drifting camera style, inter-cut with home movie footage, to capture the grim struggle these sisters endure as they march toward the question of "what do I need to feel satisfied?"—a question these women must ultimately answer for themselves.

Hey Bud
Julie Zando
1987, 11:00, U.S., color, sound

Hey Bud revolves around the suicide of Bud Dwyer, a government official who killed himself in front of a television audience. Zando compares the suicide to a kind of pornographic sex act that plays upon the tension created between exhibitionist and voyeur. It forces viewers to take either an empathetic position vis-à-vis the exhibitionist or to act as voyeur through release of the repressed desire to see the forbidden face of death. The piece attempts to understand the power gained through exhibitionism and how that power is lost through death. Zando compares the suicide to the position of women who seek power through exhibitionism and exploitation, the price being death of the self.

I Like Girls for Friends

Julie Zando

1987, 3:00, U.S., b&w, sound

This tape is about seduction. The female narrator seduces the audience, while at the same time repelled by the seductress' desperate need for love and approval. The title is ironic: although the narrator "likes girls for friends better than boys," the attraction is masochistic and destructive.

Let's Play Prisoners

Julie Zando

1988, 22:00, U.S., b&w, sound

A haunting look at the hidden issues of erotic power relationships between women, told through the reconstructed story of two girlhood friends. In Zando's tape, the origins of desire and domination are traced to the early stages of the childhood relation between mother and daughter, as revealed in the often fearful and cruel framework of childhood play. In the paradigm of need and dependency versus power and control, the submissive impulse is linked to the transcendent yearning to reunite with the pre-natal mother.

Let's Play Prisoners

Uh Oh!

Julie Zando

1993, 39:00, U.S., color, sound

Uh Oh! is a love story that revolves around the classic text *The Story of O.* Not an adaptation, it is rather a critical analysis of masochism that investigates the relationship between love, risk-taking, spirituality, power, and sex. An all-female cast plays cowboys who stage sado-masochistic rituals in the basement of a diner. A waitress named Oh (Emanuela Villorini) falls in love with a cowboy (New York poet Eileen Myles). Through complex interweaving of metaphor and suggestion, their ensuing love story is told against the backdrop of sexual and spiritual submission, which (like the novel) suggests that submission is the ultimate expression of romantic love—a love that precludes a dangerous loss of ego but promises deep psycho-sexual fulfillment.

Anthologies

American Psycho(drama): Sigmund Freud vs. Henry Ford

This humorous selection of performance-oriented videos maps a trajectory between consumer society and psychoanalytic confession. HalfLifers perform two rescue missions using colored snack food and everyday objects as means towards transcendence. In *The Horror*, Emily Breer and Joe Gibbons recuperate Coppola's *Apocalypse Now* as a day at the beach. Gibbons's solo work *Multiple Barbie* features the artist as a smooth-talking psychoanalyst, gently attempting to fuse the mute doll's shattered plastic psyche. Three works by Anne McGuire all employ genre conventions derived from popular culture (the variety show, the talk show, and the rock video); McGuire's presence as a performer amplifies the sense of strangeness that lies at the heart of the familiar, creating a vertigo between form and content. Animal Charm's interventions in this program are homemade commercials and infomercials, sampled from a reservoir of neglected or useless images.
Curated by Nelson Henricks.
Total running time 1:17:00.

Actions in Action

Contents:
Stuffing, Animal Charm, 1998, 4:00, U.S., color, sound
Control Corridor, HalfLifers, 1997, 11:00, U.S., color, sound
Caddy, Emily Breer, 1997, 1:00, U.S., color, sound
The Horror, Emily Breer, 1997, 2:00, U.S., color, sound
Pool Boy, Emily Breer, 1997, 1:00, U.S., color, sound
I Am Crazy and You're Not Wrong, Anne McGuire, 1997, 11:00, U.S., b&w, sound
Ashley, Animal Charm, 1997, 9:00, U.S., color, sound
Actions in Action, HalfLifers, 1997, 10:30, U.S., color, sound
The Telling, Anne McGuire, 1998, 3:30, U.S., color, sound
Multiple Barbie, Joe Gibbons, 1998, 9:00, U.S., b&w, sound
Cardoso Flea Circus, Maria Fernanda Cardoso and Ross Rudesch Harley, 1997, 8:00, Australia, color, sound
When I Was a Monster, Anne McGuire, 1996, 6:00, U.S., color, sound
Lightfoot Fever, Animal Charm, 1996, 1:30, U.S., color, sound

Betraying Amnesia, Portraying Ourselves: Video Portraits by Latin American and Latino Artists

By remembering and repositioning, the artists involved in *Betraying Amnesia* use video to traverse the cultural and political landscape of imperialism. These portraits also reinforce how an intimate portrait of a relatively unknown individual is as significant as that of a recognized celebrity.
Guest curated by Liz Miller and Dara Greenwald.
Total running time 1:16:50.

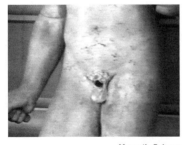

Magnetic Balance

Contents:
A pessoa é para o que nasce (You Are What You Are Born For), Roberto Berliner, 1999, 6:00, Brazil, color, sound, in Portuguese with English subtitles
Calle Chula, Veronica Majano, 1998, 12:00, U.S., color, sound
Papapapá, Alex Rivera, 1995, 28:00, U.S., b&w and color, sound
Magnetic Balance, Magaly Ponce, 1998, 7:20, U.S., color, sound, in English and Spanish
Hombres Muertos de Amor y la Jauria de Mujeres, German Bobe, 1991, 8:00, Chile, color, sound
Carlos Nader, Carlos Nader, 1998, 15:30, Brazil, color, sound, in Portuguese with English subtitles

e-[d]entity: Female Perspectives on Identity in Digital Environments

e-[d]entity: Female Perspectives on Identity in Digital Environments is a two-part collection of videoworks created over the last two decades that explores the cyber environment and how it affects, expands, confuses, and involves female identity.
Curated by Kathy Rae Huffman.
Total running time 1:55:37.

Etant donné le bleu

Tape 1: *e-[d]entity: More about Games*
Total running time 1:02:42.
Contents:
Etant donné le bleu (Given the Blue), Arghyro Paouri, 1992, 2:00, France, color, sound
Hiatus, Ericka Beckman, 1999, 30:00, U.S., color, sound
On the Flies of the Market Place, Marina Grzinic and Aina Smid, 1999, 7:00, Slovenia, color, sound
Watch Out for Invisible Ghosts, Kristin Lucas, 1996, 5:00, U.S., b&w, sound
U & I dOt cOm, Branda Miller, 1999, 18:42, U.S., color, sound

Tape 2: *e-[d]entity: Even More about Identity*
Total running time 52:55.
Contents:
Leaving the 20th Century, Max Almy, 1982, 11:00, U.S., color, sound
Alphabetically Sorted, Rebeca Bollinger, 1994, 5:18, U.S., b&w, sound
Seduction of a Cyborg, Lynn Hershman Leeson, 1994, 6:00, U.S., color, sound
<chatlandia>, Julia Meltzer and Amanda Ramos, 2000, 3:00, U.S., color, sound
code switching, Erin Seymour, 1999, 5:52, U.S., color, silent
have script, will destroy, Cornelia Sollfrank, 2000, Germany, 15:00, color, sound
lovehotel, Linda Wallace, 2000, 6:45, Australia, color, sound

Endurance: The Video Program

Originally presented at Exit Art in New York City, *Endurance* is an international survey of contemporary video and performance artists whose individual and collective works test the physical, mental, and spiritual endurance of the body. The works included derive from performance, body art action, and conceptual art works from the 1960s to the present. *Endurance* presents emphatic work about extreme forms of presence, existence, real time, and the limitations of the body and will.
Total running time 3:54:50.

Revolving Upside Down

Endurance, Reel 1
Total running time: 1:11.25
Contents:
Revolving Upside Down, Bruce Nauman, 1968, 10:00 excerpt (of 1:00:00), U.S., b&w, sound
Waterways: 4 Saliva Studies, Vito Acconci, 1971, 22:25, U.S., b&w, sound
Gilbert & George: The Singing Sculpture, Gilbert and George and Philip Haas, 1992, 23:00, U.S., color, sound
Nail Sharpening and Material Interchange, Dennis Oppenheim, 1970, 6:00, U.S., color, silent
Body/Hair, Geoffrey Hendricks, 1971, 10:00 excerpt (of 8:00:00), U.S., color, sound

Endurance, Reel 2
Total running time 57:00.
Contents:
Excerpts from Selected Works by Bonnie Sherk, 1970-73, Bonnie Sherk, 1970-73, 14:00, U.S., b&w and color, sound
Up to and Including Her Limits, Carolee Schneemann, 1973, 10:00 excerpt (of 29:00), U.S., color, sound
Black and White Tapes, Paul McCarthy, 1975, 33:00, U.S., b&w, sound

Up to and Including Her Limits

Endurance, Reel 3
Total running time 59:32.
Contents:
Mitchell's Death, Linda M. Montano, 1978, 22:00, U.S., b&w, sound
San Francisco Walk, Kim Jones, 1979, 6:00, U.S., color, sound

Opération Réussie (Successful Operation)

Becoming Bald; Full Jar, Empty Jar; Perpetual Napkin, Barbara Smith, 1974, 4:00, U.S., color, sound
Clock Shower, Gordon Matta-Clark, 1976, 13:50, U.S., color, silent, 16mm to video
Marks, Skip Arnold, 1984, 13:23, U.S., color, sound
Punch, Skip Arnold, 1992, 00:10, U.S., color, sound

Endurance, Reel 4
Total running time 46:53.
Contents:
AxVapor, Sherman Fleming, 1989, 10:00, U.S., color, sound
Autopsy, Bob Flanagan, Sheree Rose, and Kirby Dick, 1994, 15:40, U.S., color, sound
Linda M. Montano's Seven Years of Living Art, Maida Barbour, 1994, 13:13, U.S., color, sound
Opération Réussie (Successful Operation), Orlan, 1994, 8:00, France, color, sound, in French and English

Frames of Reference: Reflections on Media

"*Frames of Reference* features recent work by film- and videomakers who examine the roles that television, photography, film, video, and technology play in constructing private and public identities. Many of the artists included in this exhibition critique the pervasive influence of the mass media in order to examine how the camera shapes perceptions of reality, while others turn to more personal forms, such as home movies and diaristic videos. Exhibiting a wide range of styles and subjects, this series offers new strategies for critical engagement with the media of film and video."
—Maria-Christina Villaseñor
The *Frames of Reference: Reflections on Media* project is a selected version of a program originally curated by Maria-Christina Villaseñor, Associate Curator of Film and Media Arts for the Solomon R. Guggenheim Museum in New York City. All works in this anthology have been made by Rockefeller Media Arts Fellows. Special thanks to Tania Blanich, Rockefeller Media Arts Fellowships Program Coordinator, and John G. Hanhardt, Senior Curator of Film and Media Arts, Guggenheim Museum.
Spanish subtitled version available.
Total running time 18:55:44

Corpus (A Home Movie for Selena)

Volume 1, Program 1: Idle Worship
These works examine the media's power to fashion political and popular icons, at times offering wry commentary on the cult of personality and its adherents.
Total running time 1:09:37.
Contents:
No Sell Out, Tony Cokes and X-Prez (Doug Anderson, Kenseth Armstead, and Mark Pierson), 1995, 5:37, U.S., color, sound
Girl Power, Sadie Benning, 1992, 15:00, U.S., b&w, sound
Corpus (A Home Movie for Selena), Lourdes Portillo, 1998, 49:00, U.S., color, sound, in English and Spanish with English subtitles

Volume 1, Program 2: Alternate Voices
Alternate Voices includes works created by ethnic groups overlooked by the mass media and posits media as a potential tool of collective empowerment and personal exploration.
Total running time 2:08:00.
Contents:
Meeting Ancestors, Video in the Villages, 1993, 22:00, Brazil, color, sound, in Waiãpi with English subtitles
Comrades, Mitko Panov, 2000, 1:46:00, Macedonia/U.S., color, sound

Volume 2, Program 1: Border Allegories
The works in this program examine U.S./Mexico relations, Latino identity, and representation as seen from both sides of the border.

Total running time 1:48:30.
Contents:
Why Cybraceros, Alex Rivera, 1997, 4:30, U.S., color, sound
El Jardín del Edén (The Garden of Eden), María Novaro, 1994, 1:44:00,
  Mexico, color, sound, in English and Spanish with English subtitles, 35mm
  film to video

Volume 2, Program 2: In Plain View
The invisibility or limited representation of ethnic minorities in the arts and
mass media is challenged in these works.
Total running time 1:32:00.
Contents:
I Turn My Head, Melanie Printup Hope, 1993, 3:00, U.S., color, sound
"ALL ORIENTALS LOOK THE SAME", Valerie Soe, 1986, 2:00, U.S., b&w,
  sound
Drylongso, Cauleen Smith, 1998, 1:27:00, U.S., color, sound, 16mm to video

"ALL ORIENTALS LOOK THE SAME"

Volume 3, Program 1: Fragmented Memory, Part 1
Collective versus individual memory and historic specificities versus romanti-
cized recollections are the focuses of this program, which features works in
which the power of the cinematic image indelibly captures both the epic and
the intimate dramas of life.
Total running time 1:32:00.
Contents:
B-52—Excerpts from a Work in Progress, Harmut Bitomsky, 2002, 22:00,
  U.S., color, sound
Del olvido al no me acuerdo (I Forgot, I Don't Remember), Juan Carlos
  Rulfo, 1999, 1:10:00, Mexico, color, sound, 35mm to video, in Spanish with
  English subtitles

Volume 3, Program 2: Fragmented Memory, Part 2
Atomic Ed & the Black Hole, Ellen Spiro, 2002, 39:40, U.S., color, sound

Volume 3, Program 3: Geographies
In *Geographies* the camera is used to navigate and chart geographic, social,
and psychological spaces.
Total running time 1:26:00.
Contents:
Medias Mentiras (Half-Lies), Ximena Cuevas, 1995, 37:00, Mexico, color,
  sound, in Spanish with English subtitles
Tierra Sagrada en Zona de Conflicto (Sacred Land in a Conflict Zone),
  Carlos Martínez Suarez, 1999, 49:00, Mexico, color, sound

Volume 4, Program 1: Genre Studies
Traditional film genres are examined, updated, and reinvented in these works
to present contemporary social issues in innovative new styles.
Total running time 59:54.
Contents:
Don't Run, Johnny, Tom E. Brown, 1996, 7:10, U.S., b&w, sound, 16mm
  to video
Little Murders, Rea Tajiri, 1998, 19:44, U.S., color, sound
Pretty Vacant, Jimmy Mendiola, 1996, 33:00, U.S., b&w, sound

Pretty Vacant

Volume 4, Program 2: Authenticating Features
The notion of authenticity is put to the test in these works, which re-contextu-
alize purportedly historical footage to question the assumptions and interpre-
tations latent in the filmic text.
Total running time 1:56:58.
Contents:
Human Remains, Jay Rosenblatt, 1998, 29:27, U.S., color/b&w, 16mm
  to video
Ruins, Jesse Lerner, 1999, 87:31, U.S., b&w, sound, in Spanish and English
  with English and Spanish subtitles

Suicide Box

*This and That (and other
minor misunderstandings)*

Volume 5, Program 1: Cybernoia
Technology takes a sinister turn in these works, which alternately satirize and darkly comment on the omnipresence of electronic telecommunications, surveillance video, and broadcast propaganda in contemporary life.
Total running time 1:31:41.
Contents:
Suicide Box, Bureau of Inverse Technology, 1996, 13:00, U.S., color, sound
Fresh Kill, Shu Lea Cheang, 1994, 1:08:41, U.S., color, sound

Volume 5, Program 2: Investigations
This program examines the use of video as an investigative tool, incorporating archival film, testimonial footage, and evidentiary video to construct complex works that call into question black-and-white representations of cause and effect, fact and fiction.
Total running time 2:00:04.
Contents:
Stranger with a Camera, Elizabeth Barret, 2000, 1:01:00, U.S., color, sound
Animal Attraction, Kathy High, 2001, 59:04, U.S., color, sound

Volume 6, Program 1: Family as History, Part 1
These constructions and deconstructions of family history, as depicted in home movies and personal video, foreground issues of photographic "truth," oral versus visual history, and the staging of family dramas.
Total running time 1:12:00.
Contents:
La Línea Paterna (The Paternal Line), Maryse Sistach and José Buíl, 1993, 60:00, U.S., color, sound
This and That (and other minor misunderstandings), Edín Velez, 2001, 12:00, U.S./Puerto Rico, color, sound, in English, Spanish, and French

Volume 6, Program 2: Family as History, Part 2
Nobody's Business, Alan Berliner, 1996, 1:00:00, U.S., color, sound

I Say I Am: Women's Performance Video From the 1970s
A collection of early feminist tapes, these video performances by 11 women artists, made between 1972 and 1980, sketch a time when feminism was a new and powerful liberatory movement, when video was a relatively new invention, and when social institutions, including the art world, were undergoing radical re-evaluation. The subject matter of '70s feminist performance video was personal, often articulated in the direct address of an artist performing alone. Autobiography, identity, relation of self to others, questioning of female stereotypes, and the expansion of self through personae were recurrent themes.
Curated by Maria C. Troy.
Total running time 2:14:00.

Program 1
Total running time 1:01:12.
Contents:
Learn Where the Meat Comes From, Suzanne Lacy, 1976, 14:00, U.S., b&w, sound
Hey! Baby Chickey, Nina Sobell, 1978, 10:00, U.S., b&w, sound
Chicken on Foot, Nina Sobell, 1979, 8:00, U.S., b&w, sound
Semiotics of the Kitchen, Martha Rosler, 1975, 6:00, U.S., b&w, sound
Feathers: An Introduction, Barbara Latham, 1978, 28:00, U.S., b&w, sound
Beaver Valley, Janice Tanaka, 1981, 7:00, U.S., b&w and color, sound

Program 2
Total running time 1:12:48.
Contents:
Two Faces, Hermine Freed, 1972, 8:00, U.S., b&w, sound
Now, Lynda Benglis, 1973, 10:00, U.S., color, sound
Let It Be, Steina, 1972, 4:00, U.S., b&w, sound

Mitchell's Death, Linda M. Montano, 1978, 22:00, U.S., b&w, sound
Take Off, Susan Mogul, 1974, 10:00, U.S., b&w, sound
The Adventures of a Nurse, Eleanor Antin, 1976, 15:00 excerpt (of 1:04:00), U.S., color, sound

The New McLennium

As the expansiveness of video and its accompanying new technologies continue to transform our culture and our world, another historical tension is developing, not unlike the technological revolution seen at the last turn of the century. That tension is felt, analyzed, and articulated in all of these mid- to late-'90s experimental videos—a tension oscillating between the expansive promise of global communications that inspire new freedoms and social patterns on one hand and the use of new media forms to simply reinforce existing hierarchies and capitalistic power structures on the other. The spectre of a "brave new world" looms on the horizon—one that is sanitized, homogenized, commodified, and Americanized—the new McLennium.
Curated by Mindy Faber.
Total running time 2:02:50.

It Is a Crime

Program 1
Total running time 1:01:00.
Contents:
Suicide Box, Bureau of Inverse Technology, 1996, 13:00, U.S., color, sound
Ocularis: Eye Surrogates, Tran T. Kim-Trang, 1997, 21:00, U.S., color, sound
Rumour of True Things, Paul Bush, 1996, 26:00, U.K., color, sound

Program 2
Total running time 1:01:50.
Contents:
Manifestoon, Jesse Drew, 1995, 8:20, U.S., color, sound
Papapapá, Alex Rivera, 1995, 28:00, U.S., b&w and color, sound
It Is a Crime, Meena Nanji, 1996, 5:30, U.S., color, sound
Shanghaied Text, Ken Kobland, 1996, 20:00, U.S., color, sound

Surveying the First Decade: Video Art and Alternative Media

This comprehensive package on the history of experimental and independent video includes nearly 17 hours of historic video on 9 VHS tapes.
Curated by Christine Hill, produced by Kate Horsfield, and coordinated by Maria C. Troy.
Total running time 16:23:19.

Performer/Audience/Mirror

Program 1: *Exploration of Presence, Performance, and Audience*
Total running time 1:55:30.
Contents:
Performer/Audience/Mirror, Dan Graham, 1975, 23:00, U.S., b&w, sound
Wegman's Selected Works, William Wegman, 1972, 8:00, U.S., b&w, sound
Baldessari Sings LeWitt, John Baldessari, 1972, 4:00 excerpt (of 12:35), U.S., b&w, sound
Undertone, Vito Acconci, 1972, 10:00 excerpt (of 37:20), U.S., b&w, sound
Vertical Roll, Joan Jonas, 1972, 19:30, U.S., b&w, sound
My Father, Shigeko Kubota, 1975, 15:00, U.S., b&w, sound
Exchange, Robert Morris, 1973, 36:00, U.S., b&w, sound

Program 2: *Investigations of the Phenomenal World—Space, Sound and Light*
Total running time 1:55:54.
Contents:
Black and White Tapes, Paul McCarthy, 7:00 excerpt (of 33:00), U.S., 1972, U.S., b&w, sound
Stamping in the Studio, Bruce Nauman, 1968, 5:00 excerpt (of 1:01:35), U.S., b&w, sound
Double Vision, Peter Campus, 1971, 15:00, U.S., b&w, sound
Boomerang, Richard Serra and Nancy Holt, 1974, 11:00, U.S., color, sound

Island Song, Charlemagne Palestine, 1976, 16:29, U.S., b&w, sound
Cycles of 3s and 7s, Tony Conrad, 1976, 3:00 excerpt (of 30:54), U.S., b&w, sound
Children's Tapes, Terry Fox, 1974, 30:00, U.S., b&w, sound
Soundings, Gary Hill, 1979, 18:00, U.S., color, sound
Lightning, Paul and Marlene Kos, 1976, 1:17, U.S., b&w, sound
Sweet Light, Bill Viola, 1977, 9:08, U.S., color, sound

Program 3: *Approaching Narrative-"There are Problems to be Solved"*
Total running time 2:05:00.
Contents:
The Red Tapes, Tape 2, Vito Acconci, 1976, 58:00, U.S., b&w, sound
Out of Body Travel, Richard Foreman, 1976, 24:00 excerpt (of 42:00), U.S., b&w, sound
The Continuing Story of Carel and Ferd, Arthur Ginsberg and Video Free America, 1972, 33:00 excerpt (of 1:00:00), U.S., b&w, sound

The Continuing Story of Carel and Ferd

Program 4: *Gendered Confrontations*
Total running time 1:54:00.
Contents:
Art Herstory, Hermine Freed, 1974, 15:00 excerpt (of 22:00), U.S., color, sound
Female Sensibility, Lynda Benglis, 1973, 14:00, U.S., color, sound
Ama L'Uomo Tuo (Always Love Your Man), Cara DeVito, 1975, 19:00, U.S., b&w, sound
The Mom Tapes, Ilene Segalove, 1974, 4:00 excerpt (of 28:00), U.S., color, sound
Primal Scenes, Linda M. Montano, 1980, 11:00, U.S., b&w, sound
Nun and Deviant, Nancy Angelo and Candace Compton, 1976, 13:00 excerpt (of 20:00), U.S., b&w, sound
Vital Statistics of a Citizen, Simply Obtained, Martha Rosler, 1977, 38:00, U.S., color, sound

Program 5: *Performance of Video Imaging Tools*
Total running time 1:50:30.
Contents:
Calligrams, Steina, 1970, 4:00, U.S., b&w, sound
Illuminatin' Sweeney, Skip Sweeney, 1975, 5:00 excerpt (of 28:38), U.S., color, sound
Video Weavings, Stephen Beck, 1976, 4:00 excerpt (of 28:00), U.S., color, sound
Five-minute Romp through the IP, Dan Sandin, 1973, 6:30, U.S., b&w, sound
Triangle in Front of Square in Front of Circle, Dan Sandin, 1973, 2:00, U.S., b&w, sound
Video-Taping, Ernest Gusella, 1974, 3:00, U.S., b&w, silent
Exquisite Corpse, Ernest Gusella, 1978, 8:00, U.S., color, silent
Einstine, Eric Siegel, 1978, 5:00, U.S., color, sound
General Motors, Phil Morton, 1976, 10:00 excerpt (of 1:00:00), U.S., color, sound
Merce by Merce by Paik, Nam June Paik, Shigeko Kubota, and Charles Atlas, 1975, 28:00, U.S., color, sound
Crossings and Meetings, Ed Emshwiller, 1974, 4:00 excerpt (of 27:33), U.S., color, sound
Complex Wave Forms, Ralph Hocking, 1977, 4:00 excerpt (of 5:00), U.S., color, sound
Pictures of the Lost, Barbara Buckner, 1978, 8:00 excerpt (of 23:00), U.S., color, silent
Video Locomotion, Peer Bode, 1978, 5:00, U.S., b&w, silent
Music on Triggering Surfaces, Peer Bode, 1978, 3:00, U.S., b&w, sound
C-Trend, Woody Vasulka, 1974, 7:00 excerpt (of 9:00), U.S., color, sound
Switch! Monitor! Drift!, Steina, 1976, 4:00, U.S., b&w, sound

Five-minute Romp through the IP

Participation

vision. Commercial
Television. is the
Audience.

Television delivers
people to an
advertiser.

Television Delivers People

Program 6: *Decentralized Communication Projects*
Total running time 1:54:00.
Contents:
Mayday Realtime, David Cort and Mary Curtis Ratcliff, 1971, 10:00 excerpt
(of 1:00:00), U.S., b&w, sound
*Women's Liberation March NYC, Gay Pride March NYC, Young Lords
Occupy Manhattan Church, Native American Action at Plymouth Rock*,
Peoples Video Theater (Elliot Glass and Ken Marsh), 1971-72, 28:00, U.S.,
b&w, sound
Participation, The Vasulkas, 1969, 6:00 excerpt (of 30:00), U.S., b&w, sound
First Transmission of ACTV, George Stoney and Austin Community TV, 1972,
4:00, U.S., b&w, sound
*Jonesboro Storytelling Festival: Kathryn Windham Telling Ghost Stories (The
Jumbo Light)*, Broadside TV, 1974, 6:00, U.S., b&w, sound
The Politics of Intimacy, Julie Gustafson, 1974, 10:00 excerpt (of 52:20),
U.S., b&w, sound
Attica Interviews, Portable Channel, 1971, 8:00 excerpt (of 30:00), U.S.,
b&w, sound
Queen Mother Moore Speech at Greenhaven Prison, People's
Communication Network, 1973, 17:00, U.S., b&w, sound
The Laughing Alligator, Juan Downey, 1979, 27:00, U.S., color, sound

Program 7: *Critiques of Art and Media as Commodity and Spectacle*
Total running time 1:50:00.
Contents:
The Eternal Frame, Ant Farm, 1976, 23:00, U.S., color, sound
Television Delivers People, Richard Serra and Carlotta Fay Schoolman,
1973, 6:00, U.S., color, sound
The Business of Local News, University Community Video, 1974, 15:00
excerpt (of 25:00), U.S., b&w, sound
Proto Media Primer, Paul Ryan and Raindance Corporation, 1970, 14:00,
1984, U.S., b&w, sound
About Media, Anthony Ramos, 1977, 17:00 excerpt (of 26:00), U.S., color,
sound
Fifty Wonderful Years, Optic Nerve, 1973, 28:00, U.S., b&w, sound
Technology/Transformation: Wonder Woman, Dara Birnbaum, 1978, 7:00,
U.S., color, sound

Program 8: *Independents Address Television Audiences*
Total running time 2:58:25.
Contents:
Healthcare: Your Money or Your Life, Downtown Community Television,
1978, 1:00:00, U.S., color, sound
The Ruling Classroom, Peter Bull and Alex Gibney, 1979-80, 58:25, U.S.,
color, sound
Four More Years, TVTV, 1972, 1:00:00, U.S., b&w, sound

ON ART AND ARTISTS

The On Art and Artists Collection: An Introduction

Kate Horsfield

The On Art and Artists collection of 255 titles represents 27 years of producing and collecting information on contemporary artists and their work. Our project began during the height of feminism in 1974 at Artemisia Gallery in Chicago when Lyn Blumenthal and I recorded a short interview with Marcia Tucker, a former curator at the Whitney Museum of American Art. Tucker was in Chicago to present slides of emerging women artists' work to a group of (largely) feminist artists. Blumenthal and I had recently purchased a porta-pak (portable record and playback deck) solely for the purpose of documenting women artists talking about the development of their work. The early 70s was a period of tremendous research for feminist scholars, educators and activists. As graduate students during this era, our original motive in making the interviews was purely feminist—and designed to focus on questions of current interest to feminists, particularly "Is there a female creativity that is separate from that of the male"? How has the critical apparatus of the male art world prevented talented women from succeeding? We chose well-known artists such as Joan Mitchell, Lee Krasner and Louise Nevelson to be interviewed for this inquiry. While these older women artists mostly rejected feminist concepts, all agreed that it was very difficult for a female artist to be taken seriously or get as many opportunities as a male artist. Even without a direct feminist approach to art-making it turned out each of these artists was very eloquent and generous in describing their intentions and the driving forces behind their work.

We chose the new meduim of video as a recording medium because it was cheap and provided a desirable intimacy in the interview process (often recorded in the artists' studios) as artists quietly expressed the intentions, influences, accidents, and changes in direction that formed the path to noted accomplishments in their work. Even the first tapes we made had the characteristics we still use to this day: single camera fixed on the artist with interviewer off camera as voice. This style was appropriate for keeping the viewer focused on the artist and the detailed, often emotional description of the work and its development. Since editing equipment was rarely available in the 70s, slides of the artists work was shown on a screen above the taped image on the screen. In spite of these visual restrictions, these tapes became broadly used in colleges and universities for the education of young artists. The project was quickly expanded to include male artists as well as artists working outside the visual arts in film, video, and performance.

Lee Krasner: An Interview
Lyn Blumenthal and Kate Horsfield, 1980

In 1976 Lyn Blumenthal and I were hired to catalog a very small collection of in-house student-produced videotapes in the video department at the School of the Art Institute of Chicago. This collection was called the Video Data Bank, named after a column in the newly published *Radical Software*. Our interviews were added to the existing collection of video art tapes and taped lectures in the collection and we began to concentrate on building a larger collection of tapes for the school. We continued to produce interviews with artists in their studios in Chicago, California and New York City and were also responsible for documenting visiting artists brought in through the Visiting Artists' Program at the school as they came in to give lectures for the student body.

Many interviews are of artists who were already very influential in the art world, however we were also very interested in taping artists of promise in a period when the artist was still emerging or had not fully developed the concepts and working styles for which they have become known. Historically we selected artists to be interviewed for a variety of complex reasons, not the least of which was accessibility. We are very grateful to each of the artists for opening their studios and minds to the interview process, particularly to those artists who have never given filmed or taped interviews before or since the ones listed here. The reader should notice the date the tapes were made and keep in mind that the descriptive text for each interview reflects the time in which the interview was made. The age of the tapes can also be seen in the technical resolution of each interview. While recent interviews are made on digital format, the early tapes were made on 1/2- inch open reel tape. Some tapes have poor image quality and/or poor sound due to the limitations of the technology used at the time.

John Cage: Artist Reading
Artists TV Network, 1978

Many interviews are still unedited due to the fact that the Video Data Bank did not have access to editing equipment until almost 10 years into the project. However, a major effort is currently in progress to get all the tapes listed in this catalog preserved, edited and/or re-edited before 2009. This editing project is funded by a generous grant from the Lyn Blumenthal Memorial Fund for Independent Media and is ongoing at the rate of approximately 25 tapes per year. As each tape is edited a new preservation master is created. While it is our intention to leave the tapes as they were recorded with little change, several tapes have had to be modified in the editing process. Change is made on a case by case basis and is purely a result of technical flaws found in the original footage. An example is that all tapes recorded in the 1980s with a very cheap color camera have been remastered in black and white to improve the viewing experience. Sound problems have been fixed whenever possible. Some tapes of prominent artists have extensive technological problems. Almost all of these tapes are not listed in this catalog but are available for on-site screening in the VDB Screening Room for research only. The VDB website offers an up-to-date listing of newly edited interviews as they are completed.

Buckminster Fuller: An Interview
Lyn Blumenthal and Kate Horsfield, 1984

The growth of the collection was designed to present a very broad range of ideas and working processes used by contemporary artists. The target audience was educators and younger artists and art students who were seeking to develop their own ideas and creative processes. The Video Data Bank began to distribute the On Art and Artists interviews in the late 1970s. As the interviews became more widely used in curricula in other college and university art programs, interviews produced by other individuals and organizations were added to the list of titles in distribution. Some of these titles were produced for broadcast on access channels on television and others for closed-circuit venues in museums or other cultural spaces. Like all the descriptive text, the biographical information on each individual or organization who made the interview(s) reflects the same period in which the interview was made. Several of these programs and organizations were prominent in a previous decade but no longer exist now.

Here are brief descriptions of most of these producers and programs.

D.J. Spooky: An Interview
Visiting Artist Program and
Video Data Bank, 2001

The Artists TV Network was formed to further the development of television as a medium for art and artists, with a view toward bringing a broad range of contemporary arts and programming to the television-viewing audience on a regular basis. Through *Soho Television* and *The Live Show*, the Artists TV Network presented regular weekly telecasts of programs on Manhattan cable from 1978 to 1983. These programs featured original works by visual and performing artists, and each program was specifically related to the television structure through rigid time scales and cooperative working procedures. Soho Television's founder and executive director, Jaime Davidovich, awarded the organization's significant archive of programming to the University of Iowa Art Department in 1988, and the Video Data Bank is extremely pleased to offer their programs for distribution.

Maida Barbour made the tape *Linda M. Montano's Seven Years of Living Art* while working on her MFA in film at the University of Texas-Austin.

Maria Beatty is a film- and videomaker living and working in New York City. Her early work documented historical downtown New York art scenes; more recently she has produced an extensive body of work exploring female sexuality, lesbian desire and fetish erotica.

Shu Lea Cheang is a film/videomaker who has recently become involved with producing art on the internet.

Patricia Erens is a well-known author and editor of books on feminist film criticism.

Fellows of Contemporary Art is a southern California independent organization established in 1975 to sponsor exhibitions, catalogues and videotapes in the field of contemporary art.

During the late '60s Hermine Freed taught at New York University, working as program editor for a NYU-sponsored series on art books for WNYC. Assisted by colleague Andy Mann, she began using video to produce a series of contemporary artist portraits, beginning with painter James Rosenquist. Although the program did not meet WNYC's broadcast standards, Freed continued to produce the series, showing the tapes to her students and at other venues.

The High Museum of Art is the leading art museum in the southeastern United States. The High's collections include African art, American art, decorative arts, European art, folk art, modern and contemporary art and photography.

Nancy Holt is an internationally known artist who makes videotapes as well as environmental sculpture and installations.

Olafur Eliasson: An Interview
Visiting Artist Program and Video
Data Bank, 1998

Since 1985 Peter Kirby has produced and directed more than 60 works, including a series of profiles of contemporary artists and architects and multi-screen touring media exhibitions for the Museum of Contemporary Art-Los Angeles. In addition to these works, he has produced and directed films and installations for a variety of clients, both in the art world and the corporate sphere.

MICA-TV was the collaborative effort between Carole Ann Klonarides and Michael Owen, which began making video portraits of contemporary artists in 1980. Unlike most film or video programs about art and artists, MICA-TV developed a unique video equivalent of the artist's work—an approach stemming from the belief that a viewer can learn more about the artist's work by seeing his ideas directly visualized in another medium. Klonarides is also an artist and curator; Owen owns and operates a film and television production company.

Branda Miller makes experimental videotapes and works in collaboration with community and youth groups.

Lars Movin is a Danish writer, director, and video producer who has been creating artists' documentaries for more than ten years. His books include two volumes of interviews with American and European artists, *Videologier* (2001 and 2003) and *Danish Video Art: A Survey* (1992). Movin is also a journalist for the Danish cultural TV-magazine *Kultur-Kompaniet* and organizer of the Lyrik and Billeder Festival in Odense. Movin is currently working on a book based upon his extensive world travels.

Antonio Muntadas' internationally recognized videotapes and media installations investigate the contradictory messages projected by print and broadcast media, architecture and language. His tape series *Between the Frames* is a four-hour compilation of interviews that presents a look at the composition of the art world featuring influential "players" from several countries.

The Museum of Contemporary Art is one of the leading cultural institutions in Chicago. During the late 1970s they were involved in producing numerous video interviews with artists.

Bill Page began making video tapes about artists in 1988 after being on the New York art scene for a number of years and meeting many of the interesting and historical figures that had helped shape art history. Much of his work has been on artists over the age of 65.

Tom Rubnitz was a videomaker best known for his savvy and witty videotapes, which are collected in the compilation *Sexy, Wiggy, Desserty: The Wild New York Underground Video World of Tom Rubnitz.*

Irene Sosa is a New York-based independent film/videomaker whose work includes tapes on domestic violence, women artists, and adult literacy.

Survival Research Laboratories was conceived and founded by Mark Pauline in 1978.

Since its inception, SRL has operated as an organization of creative technicians dedicated to re-directing the techniques, tools and tenets of industry, science, and the military away from their typical manifestations in practicality, product or warfare. SRL stages performances consisting of unique sets of ritualized interactions between machines, robots and special effects devices, employed in developing themes of socio-political satire. Jonathan Reiss got his start in filmmaking at the San Francisco alternative media company Target Video, where he covered much of the west coast punk explosion. Reiss' first credits as director and producer came through the documentaries of Survival Research Laboratories. More recently, he has directed two critically acclaimed feature films, *Cleopatra's Second Husband* (1998) and *Better Living through Circuitry* (1999).

Bela Ugrin is a photographer.

What Follows… is an ongoing series of videotaped interviews with artists, critics and curators who have participated in the Visiting Artists Program of the Department of Fine Arts at the University of Colorado-Boulder.

The Visiting Artists Program of the School of the Art Institute of Chicago sponsors ongoing dialogues on contemporary art through lecture and performance presentations by art practitioners, scholars, historians and individuals working in art related fields. The Program maintains a long-standing commitment to ethnic and gender diversity and has been at the forefront of the movement towards a more socially engaged and historically informed aesthetic dialogue. The Visiting Artists Program is an internationally recognized center for higher education in the visual arts designed for the public.

The On Art and Artists collection of interviews and other forms of documentation on art and artists forms the largest single collection of video works on art. Many of the interviewers are noted for their contributions to the art field. Some of these are: David Ross, former director of the San Francisco Museum of Modern Art; Robert Storr, former Senior curator at the Museum of Modern Art; James Rondeau, Curator of Contemporary Art at the Art Institute of Chicago; Carol Becker, Dean of Faculty at the School of the Art Institute of Chicago; Philip Yenawine, former Director of Education at the MCA-Chicago and the Museum of Modern Art in New York City; and Mary Jane Jacob, a Chicago-based independent curator. Seen as a whole, this collection provides an unprecedented public record of the depth and range of ideas and creativity in photography and the visual and media arts during the past 30 years.

Acconci, Vito

Vito Acconci: An Interview
Lyn Blumenthal and Kate Horsfield
1983/re-edited 2003, 1:03:00, color to b&w, sound
A poet of the New York School in the early and mid-'60s, Vito Acconci moved toward performance, sound, and video work at the end of the decade. His work moved in a different direction in order to "define my body in space, find a ground for myself, an alternate ground for the page ground I had as a poet." Acconci's early performances, including *Claim* (1971) and *Seedbed* (1972), were extremely controversial—transgressing assumed boundaries between public and private space and between audience and performer. Positioning his own body as the simultaneous subject and object of his work, Acconci's early videotapes took advantage of the medium's self-reflexive potential in mediating his own and the viewer's attention. Consistently exploring the dynamics of intimacy, trust, and power, the focus of Acconci's projects gradually moved from his physical body (*Conversions*, 1971) toward the psychology of interpersonal transactions (*Pryings*, 1971) and, later, to the cultural and political implications of the performative space he set up for the camera (*The Red Tapes*, 1976). Since the late '70s, Acconci has designed architectural and installation works for public spaces.

Vito Acconci: Conversations
Artists TV Network
1980, 28:00, U.S., color, sound
Confrontation is the element that defines Acconci's work, from explorations of the body and self to his performances, videos, and installations to the more recent "transporting and self-erecting architecture." Throughout his work Acconci has aggressively challenged the status quo: he has violated sexual/cultural roles and has pointed out social/political ambivalence—and in doing so, his notorious activities have stretched the boundaries of what we accept as art. This tape was produced for the Artists TV Network series *Conversations*.

Adams, Dennis

Dennis Adams: An Interview
Video Data Bank
1990, 30:00, U.S., color, sound
Dennis Adams began as a painter, but by 18 he had become decidedly interested in relief space and then architectural space. By the time he was 20, Adams had become fascinated with family photographs and films. Adams was interested in the societal implications of images in general. Adams is a conceptual artist whose work includes photography, text, and installation. He is best known for his projects involving structures placed in urban bus shelters, uncompromisingly inserted into the public sphere. These politically charged photographs and their accompanying texts are not used to make overtly ideological statements but are open-ended in ways that challenge viewers to test their own convictions.

Ahwesh, Peggy

Peggy Ahwesh: An Interview
Video Data Bank
2002, unedited, U.S., color, sound
Peggy Ahwesh has made mesmerizing, experimental films for two decades. Her eclectic works explore gender and cultural identities through deeply textured visuals and fascinating narratives. She has taught at Brown University, the San Francisco Art Institute, University of Wisconsin-Milwaukee, the School of Visual Arts, and Bard College.

Akerman, Chantal

Chantal Akerman: An Interview
Lyn Blumenthal and Kate Horsfield, 1976, 28:00, U.S., b&w, sound
Chantal Akerman gained international recognition with her three and a half hour masterpiece, *Jeanne Dielman, 23 Quai du Commerce, 1080 Bruxelles* (1975), which portrays a housewife's dull existence and eventual violent action. She has continued to be one of Europe's most innovative filmmakers with more than 40 films and television projects to her credit. Akerman's work is minimalist, structuralist, and feminist. Major themes in her films include women at work and at home; women's relationships to men, other women, and children; food, love, sex, romance, art, and storytelling. In this interview from 1976, Akerman discusses her early films and the development of her particular vision. Interview by B. Ruby Rich.

Anderson, Laurie

Laurie Anderson: An Interview
Lyn Blumenthal and Kate Horsfield
1977/re-edited 2004, 43:30, U.S., b&w, sound
Laurie Anderson began as a downtown gallery artist, specializing in photography. She soon moved from creative to critical work as a writer for *Art News* and *Art in America*. She returned to the art world, making groundbreaking multimedia performance art. Her most famous work dates back to the early-to-mid-'80s and is marked by innovative use of technology in blending media-based and stage performance. The range of her subject matter—from politically charged critiques of American society to more personal subjects—has inspired many artists and secured her position as an icon of American performance art. This early interview of Anderson is a rare view of the artist from 1977.

Laurie Anderson: Conversations
Artists TV Network
1980, 28:00, U.S., color, sound
Laurie Anderson is perhaps best known as a performance artist who works in both the art and commercial worlds. Anderson talks to Steven Poser through a voice manipulator, commenting on how performing abroad has informed her work and her perspective on American culture, especially regarding issues of language and voice in communication. This tape was produced for the Artists TV Network series *Conversations*.

Animal Charm

Animal Charm: An Interview
Video Data Bank
1999, unedited, U.S., color, sound
Animal Charm is the collaborative project of Rich Bott and Jim Fetterley, sound and media artists and graduates of the School of the Art Institute of Chicago. Assuming a deconstructive take on propriety, Animal Charm began creating videos as an act of Electronic Civil Disobedience. Diving the dumpsters of video production companies and scrounging through countless hours of industrial, documentary, and corporate video footage, Animal Charm often edited the tapes in a live mix session before an audience. By re-editing images derived from a wide variety of sources, they scramble media codes, creating a kind of tic-ridden, convulsive babble that often invests conventional forms with subversive meanings.

Antin, Eleanor

Eleanor Antin: An Interview
Lyn Blumenthal and Kate Horsfield
1979/re-edited 2005, 44:00, U.S., b&w, sound
Through her performances and videotapes, Antin creates characters (King, Ballerina, Black Movie Star, and Nurse) while spinning tales that blur fiction and history. She avoids good taste and flaunts concealed intentions, forcing one to stretch all possible associations to the breaking point. "I believe interesting art has always been conceptual ... that it appeals to the mind. That does not mean that it cannot seduce and attract through the eye," Antin says in this interview with Nancy Bowen.

Asher, Betty

Betty Asher
David Ross/LBMA Video
1975-77, 18:00, U.S., b&w, sound
Part of the Long Beach Museum of Art's Institute for Art and Urban Resources' *Collectors of the Seventies* series, this tape focuses on the Betty Asher's acquisitions. "I started collecting in 1939. I didn't really start collecting per se," Asher says in this interview with David Ross, Virginia Dwan, and Alanna Heiss. "I bought things, and one morning I woke up and—all of a sudden—people were calling me a collector."

Ashley, Robert

Robert Ashley: An Interview
Video Data Bank
1988, 34:00, U.S., color, sound
Contemporary American composer and performance artist Robert Ashley has been a pioneer in the development of large-scale, collaborative performance works and new uses of language in operas and recordings. His landmark project, *Perfect Lives*, was opera produced for television in seven half-hour episodes. As explored in this interview with Peter Gena, his interests include an exploration of visual media such as video to express musical ideas.

Ault, Julie

Julie Ault: What Follows...
University of Colorado Visiting Artists Program
1991, 29:20, U.S., color, sound
Julie Ault is an artist, curator, and founding member of the artist collective Group Material, which has organized exhibitions on themes such as the US's involvement in Central America, AIDS, education, and mass consumerism. Her exhibitions question traditional gallery and museum systems by asking "how is culture made and for whom?" Interview by Michael Crane.

Aycock, Alice

Alice Aycock: An Interview
Lyn Blumenthal and Kate Horsfield
1977, 37:00, U.S., b&w, sound
During her graduate studies at Hunter College, Alice Aycock began to forge links between personal and more inclusive subject matter and form. In her quest for contemporary monuments, Aycock wrote her Master's thesis on U.S. highway systems. Aycock's large environmental sculpture creates intense psychological atmospheres. Although she uses primitive rites and architecture as sources, her implementation of contemporary materials removes those specific connotations. More recently, Aycock has begun collaborating with architects, installing site-specific works upon pre-existing or newly planned structures. Interview by Kate Horsfield.

Azaceta, Luis Cruz

Luis Cruz Azaceta: An Interview
Video Data Bank
1990, 35:00, U.S., color, sound
Luis Cruz Azaceta's paintings and mixed media works use the recurring theme of the displaced individual. Marked by his own exile from Cuba—he was born there in 1942 and emigrated to the U.S. in 1960, in the wake of Castro's take-over—the artist realized that home is something he carries with him from place to place. Through his piercing expressionism, Azaceta depicts the frailty of human existence in a world full of social anarchy, historically mandated violence, and natural chaos.

Baca, Judy and Olivia Gude

Judy Baca & Olivia Gude: An Interview
Video Data Bank
1991, 1:00:00, U.S., color, sound
Judy Baca is a visual artist, arts activist, and community leader best known for her large-scale mural projects—most famously the *Great Wall of Los Angeles*, a mural in the Tujunga Wash Flood Control Channel that spans one-half mile and illustrates the ethnic history of California. Olivia Gude is a Chicago-based muralist and mosaic artist who has made more than 30 community-based art projects. Gude interviews Baca about her experiences, organizing community projects, and her art works.

Baldessari, John

John Baldessari: An Interview
Lyn Blumenthal and Kate Horsfield
1979/re-edited 2003, 33:00, U.S., color to b&w, sound
From his photo-text canvases in the 1960s to his video works in the 1970s to his installations in the 1980s, John Baldessari's varied work has been seminal in the field of conceptual art. Integrating semiology and mass media imagery, he employed such strategies as appropriation, deconstruction, decontextualization, sequentiality, and text/image juxtaposition. With an ironic wit, Baldessari's work considers the gathering, sorting, and reorganizing of information. "Something that is part of my personality is seeing the world slightly askew. It's a perceptual stance. The real world is absurd sometimes, so I don't make a conscious attempt, but because I come at it in a certain way, it seems really strange," Baldessari says in this interview with Nancy Bowen.

John Baldessari: Some Stories
Peter Kirby
1990, 29:00, U.S., color, sound
This tape reveals Baldessari's thoughts and intentions for his work over the course of his career, providing clues to the understanding of his paintings, books, and photos. What emerges is a portrait of a rebellious artist who attempts to undermine the categories and dogmas of the art world—with the full realization that in the long run, some category or other will be named to label his work.

Bartlett, Jennifer

Jennifer Bartlett: An Interview
Lyn Blumenthal and Kate Horsfield
1976, 52:00, U.S., b&w, sound
Jennifer Bartlett is a writer and painter who makes large paintings with enamels on fabricated panels. She uses an overall grid structure on which she repeats images in a variety of styles ranging from lyric abstraction to childlike representation. Near the end of this interview with Kate Horsfield, she reads the chapter "Dreaming" from her book *The History of the Universe* (1985). "I decided: 1) I didn't want to stretch a canvas again, 2) I wanted to be able to work on a lot of things at once. I didn't want to exercise my own taste, which seemed boring and hideous. I wanted something modular, a constant surface".

Bearden, Romare

Romare Bearden: An Interview
Lyn Blumenthal and Kate Horsfield
1984/re-edited 2003, 28:00, U.S., color to b&w, sound
Romare Howard Bearden's collages combine the formal vocabulary of Cubism with a Byzantine stylization in compositions of improvisatory rhythms that echo jazz music. His images, which use symbols of his own devising, are visions of rural and urban black life. "Artists can't talk about the future because art is an adventure and a search. It would be like a hunter saying he was going out to shoot a stag, two rabbits, and a pheasant. You have to take what you find," Bearden says in this interview with Kate Horsfield. This tape is for research only.

Benglis, Lynda

Lynda Benglis: Dual Natures
Susan Elmiger/High Museum of Art
1990, 11:00, U.S., color, sound
Feminist artist Lynda Benglis is known for her sculptures, video performances, paintings, and photography. Her work in the 1970s was controversial, delving into issues of gender roles within and outside the art world. Produced in conjunction with her retrospective at the High Museum of Art in Atlanta, *Dual Natures* provides an introduction to Benglis's work and includes excerpts from her videos of the mid-'70s and footage of the artist at work. Super-8 footage documents the fabrication of an expansive poured polyurethane installation in 1971, and other footage shows her later metallic pieces in process. Benglis discusses her unusual working process, the sources of her abstract imagery, and her investigation of gender roles and sensory experience.

Beuys, Joseph

Joseph Beuys: An Interview
Lyn Blumenthal and Kate Horsfield
1980/re-edited 2003, 1:01:00, color to b&w, sound
Joseph Beuys was born in Kleve, Germany in 1921. After serving as a volunteer in the German military, Beuys attended the Dusseldorf Academy of Art to study sculpture, where in 1959 he became a professor. Much of his artwork reflects his attempt to come to terms with his involvement in the war. During the '60s, Beuys became acquainted with the group Fluxus and artists such as Nam June Paik. The Fluxus movement inspired Beuys, and he staged "actions" to promote the idea that the artistic process was more important than a final product; for example, Beuys felt that all people were artists because they shape the content of their particular environment. Beuys's political activism, his broad concept of creativity, and his commitment to both art and education challenged the traditional role of an artist. While he considered activism, discussion, and teaching essential to his expanded definition of art, Beuys also engaged in traditional artistic practice, creating objects and installations and performing. Interview by Kate Horsfield.

Blake, Jeremy

Jeremy Blake: An Interview
SAIC Visiting Artist Program and Video Data Bank
2004, unedited, U.S., color, sound
Jeremy Blake uses digital media to create works that function on a flexible spectrum between being more painting-like or more film-like. He creates continually looping digital animations with sound to be projected or presented on plasma screens. Blake often begins by making the digital C-prints, which he conceives to be somewhat like paintings. If he thinks the imagery and idea of one of these works lend itself as such, he might then extrapolate from and expand on it to begin creating a digital animation. These have ranged in time from 3 to 20 minute repeating loops. He does not rely on overt displays of technological complexity. Rather, through his talented and insightful use of relatively basic applications, he creates compelling visual narratives that oper-

ate on a variety of levels. Blake's works typically have a color field as well as an architectonic foundation, with a sense of neo-modernist design and film noir-like attitude combining the representational and the abstract. Interview by Romi Crawford.

Botha, Andries

Andries Botha: An Interview
Video Data Bank
1998, unedited, U.S., color, sound
Andries Botha's sculptural forms made of found objects and natural materials serve to interrogate the natural and social order. In his questioning of natural order, Botha serves to interpret histories. His work has been exhibited extensively throughout Africa and Europe; he lives in Durban, South Africa. Interview by Carol Becker.

Bourgeois, Louise

Louise Bourgeois: An Interview
Lyn Blumenthal and Kate Horsfield
1975/re-edited 2002, 30:40, U.S., b&w, sound
Louise Bourgeois has utilized wood, metal, plaster, and bronze in creating her sculptures. Among the many themes in her work are the house (or lair) and the so-called "toi-et-moi" or "you and me." Both of these subjects derive from a self-defined problem in Bourgeois's life, the desire to find and express a means of getting along with other people. For Bourgeois, the relationship of one person to another is all-important, and life has little meaning without it. Louise Bourgeois's remarkable career spans both the modern and postmodern eras. Her early sculptures are pioneering examples of American surrealism; her later explorations of the body and of feminine identity ushered in a new sensibility, one that has profoundly shaped contemporary art. Interview by Kate Horsfield.

Brakhage, Stan

Stan Brakhage: An Interview
Lyn Blumenthal
1976, 38:00, U.S., b&w, sound
A major figure among underground filmmakers, Stan Brakhage's career spanned more than 50 years and 300 films, making him the most prolific American filmmaker at the time of his death in 2003. His personal, independent films range in length from nine seconds to several hours and contemplate such fundamental issues as form, life, and death—most famously in *Window Water Baby Moving* (1959), *Dog Star Man* (1961-65), and *The Act of Seeing with One's Own Eyes* (1971). His early writings and journals about filmmaking are collected in *Metaphors on Vision* (1976). His work incorporated a wide variety of innovative and uniquely expressive forms and techniques, explored in-camera, in the editing room, and on the surface of the celluloid itself. "I've had many definitions of art, and it's like building a ship in a bottle. It's a very marvelous and engaging activity, and you end up with something absolutely useless or simply decorative, which astonishes little children," Brakhage says in this interview with B. Ruby Rich.

Bramson, Phyllis

Phyllis Bramson: An Interview
Lyn Blumenthal and Kate Horsfield,
1979, 42:00, U.S., color, sound
Phyllis Bramson is a Chicago painter whose post-imagist style emphasizes content and the deeply personal. Bramson's paintings are private scenarios that include figures (or performers) who carry out highly charged activities with strong psychological meaning. They perform in highly theatrical, Oriental settings of almost cubist space and acid greens, yellows, and reds.

Bristol, Horace

Horace Bristol: Photojournalist
Fellows of Contemporary Art
1988, 11:35, U.S., color, sound
Horace Bristol discusses his long career in photography, which began with shooting for *Life* and *Fortune* magazines in the 1930s. His photojournalism took him to the Dutch East Indies and post-war Japan. His documents of Depression-era workers famously inspired John Steinbeck to write the classic *The Grapes of Wrath*. "I felt I was not an artist but a worker, so as a photojournalist, I had a job to do," Bristol says.

Only available on the Fellows of Contemporary Art compilation.

Brooke, Kaucyila

Kaucyila Brooke: An Interview
Video Data Bank
1990, 36:30, U.S., color, sound
"Kaucyila Brooke makes what she describes as 'wall size photographic sequences in comic-strip format that consider lesbian relationships within American popular culture.' Produced over the past five years, Brooke's large-scale photo-text installations look at aspects of lesbian culture and alternative communities. Wry and often quite critical, they probe some of the ways lesbian relationships both challenge and reproduce the power relations and narratives of the wider culture."
–Liz Kotz, *S.F. Camerawork Quarterly* (Summer 1990)

Brown, Joan

Joan Brown: An Interview
Lyn Blumenthal and Kate Horsfield
1979/re-edited 2004, 34:34, U.S., color to b&w, sound
Joan Brown has long been recognized as one of the most important artists to emerge from the creative milieu of the San Francisco Bay Area of the late 1950s. Brown's style incorporated abstract expressionism and figurative painting. "How do I know when I've finished a painting? It's when that element of surprise is there. I can feel the flow start to happen just in terms of working, which is actually an altered state of consciousness," Brown says in this interview with Kate Horsfield. She died in October 1990, at the age of 52, in India.

Brown, Roger

Roger Brown: An Interview
Lyn Blumenthal and Kate Horsfield
1979, 25:00, U.S., color, sound

Roger Brown's quirky, stylized paintings were influenced by such disparate sources as comic strips, hypnotic wallpaper patterns, medieval panel paintings, and early works of Magritte. His work is epitomized by a series of claustrophobic urban scenes with their drop-curtain-like gray clouds and cardboard-box apartment buildings, suggesting an amalgamation of boyish enthusiasm for model making and adult despondency.

Brown died in 1997 and he donated his apartment, complete with all of his belongings, artworks, and writings to the School of the Art Institute of Chicago, where it is on public display at the Roger Brown Study Center.

Buchanan, Nancy

Nancy Buchanan: Video Viewpoints
LBMA Video
1983, 21:00, U.S., color, sound
In this interview video and performance artist Nancy Buchanan discusses her feminist and political work. Buchanan comments upon the advantages of video over performance in terms of accessibility—the ability for her tapes to circulate and reach audiences she physically cannot, and their brevity and completed form—and her strategies to create an atmosphere for change. This *Video Portrait* features two of Buchanan's tapes in their entireties: the anti-nuclear weapons work *An End to All Our Dreams* (1982) and the more straightforwardly feminist *Webs* (1983). The videos are framed by interview segments with Kathy Rae Huffman, curator at the Long Beach Museum of Art. This tape was produced in connection with the exhibition *Shared Realities: Media, Arts & Issues*, a survey of a decade of feminist art works.

Buchloh, Benjamin

Benjamin Buchloh
Antonio Muntadas
1986, 52:00, U.S., color, sound
Benjamin Buchloh is an influential art critic and historian; he has written extensively on contemporary art for journals and exhibition catalogs, as well as his monograph *Neo-Avantgarde and Culture Industry* (2002). This interview with Buchloh is one of several collected by Antonio Muntadas for his series *Between the Frames*. In this video Buchloh discusses the relationship between people and institutions.

Burckhardt, Rudy

Rudy Burckhardt: An Interview
Lyn Blumenthal and Kate Horsfield
1981/re-edited 2003, 35:43, U.S., color to b&w, sound
Rudy Burckhardt—best known as a photographer and filmmaker—moved to New York from his native Basel in 1935 at age 21. Burckhardt shot portraits of many artists for *Art News* during the 1950s and early '60s, capturing their work methods in candid and intimate photos. His films, frequently portraying cityscapes and urban life, include *The Pursuit of Happiness* (1940), *Under the Brooklyn Bridge* (1953), *What Mozart Saw on Mulberry Street* (1956), *Square Times* (1967), and *Inside Dope* (1971). "Life consists of two states," Burckhardt says in this interview with Robert Storr. "The ordinary waking life where things make sense, where

you think you're in control of something … and then there's the other state—which is at least as real, if not more so—where all those things that people make up—history, achievement, development—just fall apart." Burckhardt died in 1999.

Burden, Chris

Chris Burden
Peter Kirby
1989, 28:00, U.S., color, sound
Chris Burden came into prominence in the late 1960s, but unlike many of the performance artists of his generation, Burden was interested in empirical and scientific investigations. His goal was to return the control of art making to the artist and to question the relevancy of more established art practices. In this documentary Burden talks about his hard-hitting performances in the '70s that took a jaded art world by surprise and continues on to discuss the sculptural and installation works of the '80s. Where his early performance work created a single, minimalist image—a frozen moment that captured the essence of a pure action—later work moved away from the body toward objects and environmentally ordered installations.

Burgin, Victor

Victor Burgin: What Follows…
University of Colorado Visiting Artists Program
1987, 53:33, U.S., color, sound
Photographer, theorist, and lecturer Victor Burgin lives and works in London. A Professor of Fine Art at Goldsmiths College and Professor Emeritus of the History of Consciousness at University of California-Santa Cruz, Burgin's work explores the semiotics of meaning in visual art. His books include *The End of Art Theory: Criticism and Postmodernity* (1986), *In/Different Spaces: Place and Memory in Visual Culture* (1996) and, as editor, *Thinking Photography* (1986), *Between* (1986) and *Formations of Fantasy* (1986). Interview by Barbara Jo Revelle.

Victor Burgin: An Interview
Kate Horsfield in collaboration with Cornerhouse
2002, 45:48, U.S., color, sound
Burgin's work has established him as both a highly influential artist and a renowned theorist of still and moving images. After 13 years in the United States, Burgin recently returned to live and work in Britain. This interview offers a critical overview of a body of work that combines conceptual rigour with poetic elegance, and remains an essential reference for succeeding generations of artists. Burgin returned to London to take up the prestigious post of Millard Professor of Fine Art at Goldsmiths College. Interview by Catsou Roberts.

Cage, John

John Cage: Artist Reading
Artists TV Network
1978, 28:00, U.S., color, sound
John Cage's work has had an immeasurable influence on 20th century music and art, and his formal and technological innovations were tied to his desire to push the

boundaries of the art world. In 1951 he initiated the first recording on magnetic tape, and in 1952 he staged a theatrical event that is considered the first Happening. His invention of the prepared piano and his work with percussion instruments led him to imagine and explore many unique and fascinating ways of structuring the temporal dimension of music. Cage was involved in the Fluxus movement, asserting that that the importance of the artistic process outweighed the finished product. He is universally recognized as the originator and principal figure in the field of indeterminate composition by means of random operations. In this tape he reads 36 of his mesostics.

John Cage: Conversations
Artists TV Network
1978, 27:00, U.S., color, sound
John Cage's compositions and performances have had a profound influence on generations of musicians and artists. In this tape, he initiates *For the Third Time* as author Richard Kostelanetz interviews him. "I've left the punctuation out, but I've distributed it by chance operations on the page, like an explosion," Cage says. "You can replace the punctuation where you wish."

Cai Guo-Qiang

Cai Guo-Qiang: An Interview
SAIC Visiting Artist Program and Video Data Bank
2000, unedited, U.S., color, sound
Cai Guo-Qiang is a sculptor and installation artist who was born in China and trained in stage design at the Shanghai Drama Institute. He continued his training in Tokyo, where he lived from 1986 to 1995. His conceptual and installation work blend cultures and materials (including tea and gunpowder) to address political, spiritual, and social issues. He draws heavily on his native culture by incorporating herbal medicine, serpents, dragons, and Genghis Khan into his "fleeting" and site-specific works. His works *Cultural Melting Bath: Projects for the 20th Century* and *Cry Dragon/Cry Wolf: The Ark of Genghis Khan* comment on the religious, philosophical, and aesthetic differences between the East and the West. He has lived in New York since 1995. Interview by Christina Carlson, translated by Jennifer Ma.

Camera, Ery

Ery Camera: An Interview
Video Data Bank
1999, unedited, U.S., color, sound
Ery Camera is originally from Daker, Senegal and now lives in Mexico City. He exhibits his paintings while also working as a museum professional, independant curator, and critic. His critical work analyzes the relation between audience and cultural institution, noting that institutions are hierarchical structures organized in order to reach objectives, aims, or power, the impact of which can be measured. These are used by the ruling classes, to increase knowledge and affect cultural behavior within communities. Interview by Mary Jane Jacob.

Chambers, Eddie

Eddie Chambers: An Interview
SAIC Visiting Artist Program and Video Data Bank
2000, unedited, U.S., color, sound
One of the most uncompromising voices of the art establishment, Eddie Chambers is a curator and a regular contributor to *Art Monthly* and two European journals on contemporary art. His writings were collected in *Run Through the Jungle* (1999). He lives and works in Bristol, U.K. Interview by Andrea Barnwell and Audrey Colby.

Cheang, Shu Lea

Shu Lea Cheang: An Interview
SAIC Visiting Artist Program and Video Data Bank
1998, unedited, U.S., color, sound
Shu Lea Cheang tackles conceptions of racial assimilation in American culture, examining the political underbelly of everyday situations that affect the relationship between individuals and society. Using video in formally innovative installations, her works include the *Airwaves Project*, which focused on the one-way flow of global information and industrial waste, and *Those Fluttering Objects of Desire*, an installation presenting the work of women artists negotiating interracial sexual politics. Cheang's single-channel work, distributed by VDB, focuses on lesbian desire and Asian identity. Interview by Gregg Bordowitz.

Chicago, Judy

Judy Chicago: An Interview
Lyn Blumenthal and Kate Horsfield
1974, 17:00, U.S., b&w, sound
Judy Chicago outlines her feminist theoretical perspectives and how they inform her work. Interview by Lyn Blumenthal.

Judy Chicago: The Dinner Party
Lyn Blumenthal and Kate Horsfield
1976, 28:00, U.S., b&w, sound
Judy Chicago is an artist, author, feminist, educator, and intellectual whose career now spans four decades. In 1974, Chicago turned her attention to the subject of women's history to create her best known work, *The Dinner Party*, which was executed between 1974 and 1979 with the participation of hundreds of volunteers. This monumental multimedia project, a symbolic history of women in western civilization, has been seen by more than one million viewers during its 16 exhibitions held at venues spanning six countries. Chicago and collaborator Diane Gelon discuss *The Dinner Party* with Lyn Blumenthal.

Chin, Mel

Mel Chin: An Interview
Video Data Bank
1991, 43:00, U.S., color, sound
Mel Chin received national attention when he had to defend the artistic merits of his work *Revival Field* to the NEA in 1990. The work is a public sculpture aimed at cleansing toxically polluted areas of land through the

introduction of hyperaccumulators, plants that absorb heavy metals through their vascular systems. In this interview with Craig Adcock, Chin discusses the research and development that went into *Revival Field*, which combines such disciplines as alchemy, botany, and ecology, and the subsequent controversy that resulted from the piece. Through his creative-scientific collaborations, Chin hopes to break the prevailing isolation of artists and restore their roles as active and vital forces in society.

Chong, Ping

Ping Chong: An Interview
SAIC Visiting Artist Program and Video Data Bank
1998, unedited, U.S., color, sound
Ping Chong is choreographer, theater director, and installation artist. Considered a pioneer of avant-garde performance, Chong's work incorporates many stylistic innovations including projections, sound scores, and ritualized movement. He created a trilogy constructed around historical narratives of the colonization of Asian society: *Deshima* investigated the history of an island near Nagasaki where early Dutch traders were confined, *Chinoiserie* explored Chong's own Chinese heritage, and *After Sorrow* considered Vietnam's relationships with Asian countries and the West. Interview by Peter Taub.

Clark, John

John Clark: An Interview
Video Data Bank
1988, 37:00, U.S., color, sound
British painter John Clark describes his youth experiences in Northern England, finding escape in the library stacks in art books and at the milk bars where he could hear American rock'n'roll. Clark not only discusses the evolution of his work but also his geographical history, living and painting away from the urban art scenes in London, Toronto, and New York. Interview by Kate Horsfield.

Close, Chuck

Chuck Close: An Interview
Lyn Blumenthal and Kate Horsfield
1980/re-edited 2004, 46:30, U.S., color to b&w, sound
Chuck Close has been a leading figure in contemporary art since the early 1970s. As a young artist in the mid-'60s, Close turned away from the model of Abstract Expressionism to develop a simple but labor-intensive working method based upon repetition and small color elements. Denying himself expressive gesture, Close builds shapes and tonal variations within a working grid that provides the structure for large-scale, close-up portraits. Close's formal analysis and methodological reconfiguration of the human face have radically changed the definition of modern portraiture. This 1980 interview with Kate Horsfield was conducted before Close's debilitating illness, which limited his mobility and confined him to a wheelchair has not prevented him from painting.

Cobo, Chema

Chema Cobo: An Interview
Video Data Bank
1994, 1:00:00 unedited, U.S., color, sound
Spanish painter Chema Cobo discusses his early years of studying and creating art in Southern Spain. His career began in the mid-1970s, exhibiting at the Buades and Vandrés galleries, along with a generation of now-established artists. His work began showing outside of Spain in the '80s. Cobo also talks about the ways that his Spanish background and identity has informed his work.

Cohen, Jem

Jem Cohen: An Interview
SAIC Visiting Artist Program and Video Data Bank
2001-06, unedited, U.S., color, sound
Jem Cohen is a New York-based film- and videomaker. Often shooting in hundreds of locations with little or no additional crew, Cohen collects street footage, portraits, and sounds. The projects built from these archives thrive on the collision between documentary, narrative, and experimental approaches. Some of the projects are personal/political city portraits made on travels around the globe. Many center on daily life and ephemeral moments: things seen out of the corner of the eye and pulled into the center. Interview by Abina Manning and Kate Horsfield.

Coleman, A.D

A. D. Coleman: An Interview
Lyn Blumenthal and Kate Horsfield
1977, 44:00, U.S., b&w, sound
A.D. Coleman is a freelance critic who has written for *The Village Voice*, *Artforum*, *The New York Times*, and *Camera 35*. In this tape Coleman talks about photography and photo criticism in historical context. "I would hope that the emphasis in photographic education would be to teach everybody to at least make those images in their own lives more effectively, so that they might be able to communicate more articulately, more powerfully some of the poignancy of being human and passing through time as we do," Coleman says.

Colescott, Robert

Robert Colescott: What Follows…
University of Colorado Visiting Artists Program
1991, 30:00, U.S., color, sound
Robert Colescott paints expressive parodies of Western masterpieces. His work—which has transformed Leutze's *George Washington Crossing the Delaware* (1851) into *George Washington Carver Crossing the Delaware* (1975), Van Gogh's *The Potato Eaters* (1885) into *Eat Dem Taters*, (1975), and Picasso's *Les Demoiselles d'Avignon* (1907) as *Les Demoiselles d'Alabama* (1985)—deals with stereotypes and the role of blacks in American culture. Interview by Jim Johnson.

Cumming, Robert

Robert Cumming: An Interview
Video Data Bank
1976, 22:00, U.S., b&w, sound
Robert Cumming is a photographer/sculptor/bookmaker who borrows from the artifice of theatrical sets to construct his elaborate and often absurd images. He has also published several books of photography and narration. "I started to go against the avant-garde 'less is more' and began to work on more varied levels—sculpture, photography, and writing that has a number of layers. Illusion worked in under that guise," Cumming says in this interview with Alex Sweetman.

Dine, Jim

Jim Dine: An Interview
Lyn Blumenthal and Kate Horsfield
1978/re-edited 2004, 38:00, U.S., color to b&w, sound
Jim Dine first emerged as an avant-garde artist creating Happenings and performances with Allan Kaprow, Claes Oldenburg, and others in the early 1960s. Ultimately, he rejected the performances that led to his early success in favor of an introspective search for identity. Using banal objects as subjects for his paintings and prints, Dine displayed a growing sense of self-awareness. "I felt that art was the thing that would save me. I'm aware that things you think are going to save you don't hold your interest once they've saved you. But this has. It's what I'm here for," Dine says in this interview with Kate Horsfield.

DJ Spooky (Miller, Paul D.)

DJ Spooky: An Interview
SAIC Visiting Artist Program and Video Data Bank
2001, 24:43, U.S., color, sound
Paul D. Miller is a conceptual artist, writer, and musician better known as DJ Spooky. A popular and prolific recording artist, he has collaborated with Ryuichi Sakamoto, Butch Morris, Yoko Ono, Thurston Moore (of Sonic Youth), Kool Keith, and Killa Priest (of Wu Tang Clan). Spooky's work uses a wide variety of digitally created music as a form of postmodern sculpture. He has written articles for *The Source, Artforum, Raygun, Rap Pages,* and *Paper,* and works as co-publisher of the magazine *A Gathering of the Tribes* and as editor-at-large of the digital media magazine *Artbyte: The Magazine of Digital Culture.* In addition, Miller made his foray into fiction with his novel *Flow My Blood the DJ Said.* Interviewed by Romi Crawford and Carol Becker.

Doherty, Willie

Willie Doherty: An Interview
SAIC Visiting Artist Program and Video Data Bank
1999, unedited, U.S., color, sound
Willie Doherty works in photography and video installations. Since the late 1980s, his work has responded to the urban setting and rural outskirts of his hometown of Derry, North Ireland. He considers the violence and media representations of the region as a danger zone.

Dorksy, Nathaniel

Nathaniel Dorsky: An Interview
SAIC Visiting Artist Program and Video Data Bank
2000, unedited, U.S., color, sound
Nathaniel Dorsky's films are precise articulations of cinematic qualities: the surprise of an edit, the composition of framing, and the flash of the image. Dubbed the "filmmaker's filmmaker," Dorsky's work captures the fleeting moments of everyday life in its poetic chaos in such films as *Pneuma* (1976-82), *Triste* (1974-96), *Alaya* (1976-87), and *Variations* (1992-98). Using a springwound Bolex and 16mm reversal stock film, Dorsky's films operate in the realm of the purely visual. Interview by Jeffrey Skoller.

Dos Santos, Jonas

Jonas Dos Santos: What Follows...
University of Colorado Visiting Artists Program
1991, 32:58, U.S., color, sound
Jonas Dos Santos is a performance and installation artist from Brazil who came to the U.S. in 1968. His early work consisted of sculptural pieces in atypical spaces—caves and parks. His work remains informed by Brazilian iconography and rituals such as Carnival while also integrating responses to American culture's tendency toward waste. His work, in particular his performance art, comes out of improvisation and intuition. This tape incorporates still images of Dos Santos's sculptures and footage of his performances. Interview by Toni Rosato.

Dougherty, Cecilia

Cecilia Dougherty: An Interview
Video Data Bank
2001, unedited, U.S., color, sound
In this interview Dougherty describes her work and her explorations into family interactions, outsider psychology, role-playing, lesbian sexuality, and popular culture. Her tapes *Grapefruit* (1989) and *Coal Miner's Granddaughter* (1991) work from within mass culture norms to create a lesbian dialogue within the "normal"— what Dougherty calls "the life of the ordinary lesbian and her working-class family." Her more recent tapes explore lesbian identity within a separate social sphere. Dougherty lives in Dublin, where she and her partner own the Anthology bookstore. Interview by Amy Sillman.

Downes, Rackstraw

Rackstraw Downes: An Interview
Lyn Blumenthal and Kate Horsfield
1980/re-edited 2004, 38:00, U.S., color to b&w, sound
Rackstraw Downes's "observation" paintings, executed on-site at ponds, intersections, and baseball parks, began as a mischievous response to the dogma of style and modernist criticism. "There was a tremendous intellectual back-up, essentially against a lot of the figurative painting being done in the '60s," Downes says in this interview with Robert Storr. "If I show my slides in an art school I'll get, 'Your paintings are very nice but how can you go backwards from Cézanne?'"

Dunlap, David

David Dunlap: What Follows...
University of Colorado Visiting Artists Program
1990, 30:00, U.S., color, sound
Painter/mixed media artist David Dunlap creates installations and performances that draw from the notebooks he has kept since the mid-'70s—giving three-dimensional, public form to his intimate thoughts and diaries. He lives and works in Iowa City, where he is a professor of art at the University of Iowa.

Durham, Jimmie

Jimmie Durham: What Follows...
University of Colorado Visiting Artists Program
1990, 43:00, U.S., color, sound
Cherokee-American artist Jimmie Durham has worked in performance since the mid-'60s. In the '70s, he immersed himself in activism, working for Native American rights as part of the American Indian Movement. In the '80s, his focus returned to producing art in multiple forms—performance, poetry, and mixed-media visual works—that consider Native American identity and critique American domestic colonialism. He has also published numerous critical essays.

Ehrenberg, Felipe

Felipe Ehrenberg: An Interview
Video Data Bank
40:00, 1988, U.S., color, sound
Felipe Ehrenberg is a prominent Mexican artist who has been actively producing interactive political art, installations, and murals for more than 30 years. Also a writer, Ehrenberg has run a small press in Mexico City and has published numerous articles for art journals in the United States. Interview by Carol Becker.

Eliasson, Olafur

Olafur Eliasson
SAIC Visiting Artist Program and Video Data Bank
1998, unedited, U.S., color, sound
Berlin-based Danish artist Olafur Eliasson complicates and simulates perception through his installations, sculptures, and photographs. He has created disorienting artificial illuminations and reproduced natural phenomena such as clouds, glaciers and the sun through large-scale, high-tech installations. Interview by James Rondeau.

Eshun, Kodwo

Kodwo Eshun: An Interview
SAIC Visiting Artist Program and Video Data Bank
2001, unedited, U.S., color, sound
London-based writer, DJ, and music critic Kodwo Eshun thinks of his science fiction work as "theory on fast forward." His debut book *More Brilliant than the Sun: Adventures in Sonic Fiction* (1999) is a manifesto that espouses alienation via technology and machine culture. For Eshun "the key thing to do now is to move into a new field. I've stopped calling myself a writer, for the book I'm just going to call myself a concept engineer. What we're doing is engineering, is grasping fictions, grasping concepts, grasping hallucinations from our own area, translating them into another one, mixing them, and seeing where we go with them." Interview by Romi Crawford.

Fine, Jud

Red Is Green: Jud Fine
Fellows of Contemporary Art
1988, 10:41, U.S., color, sound
Southern California visual artist Jud Fine seeks to promote democracy in art—the idea that anyone can be an artist. This tape presents the artist and his work in a style that reflects the multi-layered dimensions of his artwork.

Only available on the *Fellows of Contemporary Art* compilation.

Finley, Karen

Karen Finley: An Interview
Video Data Bank
1990, 47:00, U.S., color, sound
Karen Finley is well known for her confrontational monologues, often performed in clubs and bars, that exploit the stereotype of the hysterical woman to address the sexual and political taboos associated with femininity. Using a variety of unusual props, such as Jello, chocolate syrup, stuffed animals, and glitter, Finley provokes her audience into thinking about a range of repressions and contradictions in contemporary society. She gained mainstream attention when Congress questioned her NEA funding in the early 1990s. Interview by Tom Jaremba.

Finster, Reverend Howard

Reverend Howard Finster: Man of Vision
Tom Rubnitz
Date unknown, 27:25, U.S., color, sound
Reverend Howard Finster was a preacher-turned-folk artist. He created Paradise Gardens Park & Museum, a product of all his murals, drawings, sculptures, and mosaics—and Summerville, Georgia's largest tourist attraction. He began Paradise Gardens around 1961; in 1976 he responded to a vision to paint sacred art. As this tape begins, Finster is painting with his hands in his studio. Finster then embarks on his first visit to New York City and comments upon his work showing at Phyllis Kind Gallery. He spins rhythmic narratives that turn into miniature sermons. His impassioned manner and Southern drawl make him stand out as an unlikely art star, and the tape also treats the viewer to one of Finster's banjo performances. Finster died in 2001.

Fischer, R.M.

R.M. Fischer: An Industrial
MICA-TV
1983, 04:00, U.S., color, sound
R.M. Fischer's lamp sculptures, made from found industrial parts in a hybrid style of high-tech slickness and Baroque exaggeration suggested parodies of industrial commercials. The narration sounds like advertising hype but is actually composed from critical reviews of Fischer's work. The slick, serious look of the final tape

was accomplished in part by using a professional voiceover actor, a commercial photographer, and music composed for a brand-name commercial. Unlike most film or video programs about art and artists, MICA-TV does not attempt to look at their subjects from a detached or biographical standpoint. Rather, they develop a TV/video equivalent of the artist's work, an approach stemming from the belief that a viewer can learn more directly about the artist's work by seeing his ideas directly re-visualized in another medium.

Only available on the *Crossover Series* compilation.

Fischl, Eric

Eric Fischl: An Interview
Lyn Blumenthal and Kate Horsfield
1984/re-edited 2004, 48:19, color to b&w, sound
Eric Fischl's early works were large-scale abstract paintings. While teaching in Nova Scotia, Fischl began to shift from abstraction to smaller, image-oriented paintings, beginning with narrative works that investigated a fisherman's family. By the time Fischl left Halifax the narrative element was gone, but the middle-class melodrama centered on the family matrix remained. In the '80s Fischl's large figurative paintings, aggressive in their confrontation with the viewer, began to receive attention. His paintings are charged with repressed adolescent sexuality that implicates the viewer, as well as the artist, as voyeur. Along with painting, he produces photographs and monotypes. Interview by Robert Storr.

Fishman, Louise

Louise Fishman: An Interview
Lyn Blumenthal and Kate Horsfield
1977, 55:00, U.S., b&w, sound
Louise Fishman is a gestural abstractionist painter who uses knives and brushes to create subtle but forceful painting surfaces. Her complex layered compositions use shapes, lines, colors, strokes, light to express deeply internal emotion and exterior response to the sensations of the world. "Almost everything is covered in my paintings. I go through numerous changes in them. I used to think that I was losing a lot of images. More recently I discovered that I was travelling through a process where an image would come back not exactly as it had been before. My unconscious memory is alive," she says in this interview with Kate Horsfield.

Flack, Audrey

Audrey Flack: An Interview
Lyn Blumenthal and Kate Horsfield
1978, 38:00, U.S., b&w, sound
Audrey Flack works from slides and uses an airbrush to produce large photorealistic paintings. She selects subjects with great personal significance that also represent fragments of contemporary American life. The three paintings discussed in detail in this tape are from the *Vanitas* series. "Every still-life painter has her bag of tricks. You have your prop closet and just pull them out," Flack says in this interview with Kate Horsfield. "One of the beauties of being an artist is that no one can tell me what to paint."

Fluxus

The Misfits: 30 Years of Fluxus
Lars Movin
1993, 1:16:00, Denmark, color, sound
Lars Movin presents a video portrait of artists who have radically disrupted our conception of art since the 1960s. A large part of the video was made in Venice in 1990, when many of the original Fluxus artists met to hold a large exhibition in connection with the Biennale. The tape includes interviews with most of the leading Fluxus artists, documentation of their works, and clips from videos and films made during the 30 years of this ungovernable art form. With Eric Anderson, Philip Corner, Henry Flynt, Ken Friedman, Alison Knowles, Jonas Mekas, Yoko Ono, John Cage, Joseph Beuys, Geoffrey Hendricks, and many more.

Foster, Hal

Hal Foster: An Interview
SAIC Visiting Artist Program and Video Data Bank
2001, unedited, U.S., color, sound
Hal Foster is Professor of Modern Art at Princeton University and has written and edited numerous influential books on postmodernism, art, and culture. His books include *Recodings: Art, Spectacle, Cultural Politics* (1985); *The Return of the Real: The Avant-Garde at the End of the Century* (1996); and, as editor, *The Anti-Aesthetic: Essays on Postmodern Culture* (1983); *Vision and Visuality* (1988); and *Richard Serra* (2000). Interview by David Raskin.

Foucault, Michel

Michel Foucault: The Fifth Republic
Branda Miller
1981, 26:00, U.S., color, sound
Michel Foucault was one of the most influential philosophers and cultural historians of the 20th century, reconceiving power and identities as historically specific social relations and discourses. His studies challenged the works of Marx and Freud, offering new understandings of institutional practices and their effects on the human body and psyche in his studies of prisons, mental illness, medicine, and sexuality. His influential writings include *Discipline and Punish, The Order of Things, Madness and Civilization, The Birth of the Clinic*, and the three-part *History of Sexuality*. He died of an AIDS-related illness in 1984. This tape presents an informal conversation between Foucault and Branda Miller, Patti Podesta, and Jim Czarencki, taped in Foucault's hotel room during a conference visit to Los Angeles.

Frampton, Hollis

Hollis Frampton: An Interview
Video Data Bank
1978, 28:00, U.S., b&w, sound
In the 1960s and '70s, Hollis Frampton emerged as one of the most important experimental filmmakers, creating structuralist works such as *Zorns Lemma* (1970), *Poetic Justice* (1972), and *Nostalgia* (1973). In this tape he talks about the relationship between photography and filmmaking as well as the development of his own work from his early days as a poet in New York to filmmaking.

He also recalls the friendship and influence of Ezra Pound. Interview by Adele Friedman.

Fuller, Buckminster

Buckminster Fuller: An Interview
Lyn Blumenthal and Kate Horsfield
1981/re-edited 2003, 53:00, U.S., color to b&w, sound
Buckminster Fuller was both a pioneer architect of the modern era and a global theorist. Fuller developed a system of geometry that he called "Energetic-Synergetic geometry," the most famous example of which is the geodesic dome. His many designs for automobiles and living spaces were applications of a wider theory. "I tended to think that if we could solve problems with technology and not just hot air there would come a day when we would free humanity from the sewer lines and water lines and the real estate man; the wealth is the land and not in the ingenuity of wealth," Fuller says in this interview with Robert Storr.

Gibbons, Joe

Joe Gibbons: An Interview
Video Data Bank
2002, unedited, U.S., color, sound
Joe Gibbons conveys his dry humor through obsessive monologues that suggest a monomaniacal mind spilling forth with fantasies of power, destruction, and death. In his tapes, the hand-held camera allows Gibbons's alter ego to surface as he gives vent to tyrannical rants that comically invert social values. Interview by Kate Horsfield.

Ginsberg, Allen

Allen Ginsberg: An Interview
Video Data Bank
1988/re-edited 2004, 28:00, U.S., color, sound
Allen Ginsberg was a leading American poet who gained notoriety in the 1950s and '60s through his association with the Beat Generation and the San Francisco Renaissance. One of the most controversial poets of his time, his book *Howl and Other Poems* faced an obscenity trial in 1957 and became one of the most widely read poems of the 20th century. In the '60s and '70s, Ginsberg studied under gurus and Zen masters. He went on to co-found the Jack Kerouac School of Disembodied Poetics at the Naropa Institute in Colorado and later became a Distinguished Professor at Brooklyn College. He died in 1997 in New York City. Interview by Barry Silesky.

Goldstein, Jack

Jack Goldstein: What Follows...
University of Colorado Visiting Artists Program
1987, 30:00, U.S., color, sound
Painter and multi-media artist Jack Goldstein lived and worked in New York City. His airbrushed paintings of lightning and night skies are shown here accompanied by synthetic music, which the artist also composed. Goldstein committed suicide in 2003. Interviewed by Jim Johnson.

Gorchov, Ron

Ron Gorchov: An Interview
Lyn Blumenthal and Kate Horsfield
1979, 42:00, U.S., b&w, sound
Ron Gorchov paints on convex/concave saddle-shape canvases with recurring pairs of symmetrical, oar-like images. These unique frames have become the basis for a wide range of experimentation through the use of color, surface, form, and shape. "It wasn't until 1970, when the first real photographs of the planet Earth astounded everyone, ... [that] you could say objectively that never before was an object seen that was so beautiful. Then, I thought, 'That's what we have to compete with'," Gorchov says in this interview with Kate Horsfield.

Gormley, Antony

Antony Gormley: An Interview
Video Data Bank
1988, 46:00, U.S., color, sound
Antony Gormley is a British sculptor who casts his own body in organic materials and then wraps them in sheets of lead that are soldered together to create slightly larger-than-life figures. The figures, which are arrested in simple actions such as walking, crouching, or looking, dramatize interior and exterior space and generalize archetypes of the human form. Gormley's commitment to figurative work sets him apart from his contemporaries in recent British sculpture. Interview by Nancy Bowen.

Graves, Nancy

Nancy Graves: An Interview
Lyn Blumenthal and Kate Horsfield
1978/re-edited 2003, 24:44, U.S., b&w, sound
Nancy Graves was a sculptor, painter, and filmmaker who used natural history as a reference for dealing with the relationships between time, space, and form. In this tape she discusses her transition from a static form (sculpture) to a moving form (film), and finally, to painting. She lived in New York until her death in 1995. "The making of it and the viewing of it are the areas with which I'm most concerned, because I'm an artist, not a philosopher," Graves says in this interview with Kate Horsfield.

Grossman, Nancy

Nancy Grossman: An Interview
Lyn Blumenthal and Kate Horsfield
1975, 57:00, U.S., b&w, sound
Multi-disciplinary artist Nancy Grossman is best known for one aspect of her work: leather-covered sculptures of abstract heads. As a female artist in the early 1960s, she pioneered the use industrial materials to create three-dimensional mixed-media sculptures. The formal diversity of Grossman's art reflects her fundamental concerns about how the human condition is threatened by the alienation from machines. Juxtaposing the environment of the 20th century—what she calls "materials of civilization"—primitive, instinctual, or animalistic human nature pervades her work and is at the root of its dialectical nature. Interview by Kate Horsfield.

Guerrilla Girls

Guerrilla Girls: An Interview
Video Data Bank
1989, 35:00, U.S., color, sound
The Guerilla Girls are an anonymous activist group who refer to themselves as "the conscience of the art world" and whose stated goal is to combat racism and sexism. Through posters, magazine ads, exhibitions, and panels, they have educated and agitated the art world with statistics on the under-representation of women and minorities in galleries, museums, and the press. This interview is conducted with three Guerrilla Girls, who appear adorned in their trademark gorilla masks to ensure their anonymity. Interview by Carole Tormollan.

Guerrilla Girls: What Follows...
University of Colorado Visiting Artists Program
1989, 37:00, U.S., color, sound
Guerilla Girls are artist activists who have dedicated themselves to informing the public of the gender and racial inequalities that persists in the art world. Dressed in gorilla masks, they discuss their postering activities and their collaborative projects. Interview by Lucy Lippard.

Haacke, Hans

Hans Haacke: An Interview
Lyn Blumenthal and Kate Horsfield
1980, 28:00, U.S., color, sound
Conceptual artist Hans Haacke's two most notorious works took unsavory Manhattan real estate dealing as their subject, which triggered the cancellation of his exhibition *Real-Time Social System* at the Guggenheim Museum in 1971. With the conscientiousness of an investigative reporter, Haacke continues to scrutinize the rough edges between art and life. "I was pretty stifled for a number of years. I couldn't show in New York ... and still today—that is nine years after the event—not a single museum has shown a single work of mine since then, and I expect this is going to continue for quite a while," Haacke says in this interview by Kate Horsfield.

Halleck, DeeDee

DeeDee Halleck and Bob Hercules: An Interview
Video Data Bank
1991, 1:00:00 unedited, U.S., color, sound
DeeDee Halleck is a media activist, one of the founders of Paper Tiger Television and the Deep Dish Satellite Network, and was a professor in the Department of Communication at the University of California-San Diego. Her first film, *Children Make Movies* (1961), was about a filmmaking project at the Lillian Wald Settlement in Lower Manhattan. She has led media workshops with elementary school children, reform school youth, and migrant farmers. In this tape, Halleck shares experiences and ambitions with interviewer Bob Hercules, an independent documentarian whose work has been seen nationally at film festivals and through numerous PBS broadcasts. Hercules was a frequent contributor to the PBS series *The '90s* during its three-year run, and a cofounder and past producer for the award-winning cable series *Labor Beat*.

Harrison, Helen and Newton

Helen and Newton Harrison: Altering Discourse
Fellows of Contemporary Art
1989, 12:00, U.S., color, sound
Eco-artists Helen and Newton Harrison define truth as a series of interactions that anyone may join. The Harrisons choose survivalist subjects because "we have so encroached upon this environment, we must give it every advantage we can."
Only available on the Fellows of Contemporary Art compilation.

Helen and Newton Harrison: An Interview
Lyn Blumenthal and Kate Horsfield
1978, 28:00, U.S., b&w, sound
The Harrisons' collaborations reflect their growing dissatisfaction with the values of production and consumption, as well as their desires to raise public awareness through their art. Interview by Kate Horsfield.

Helen and Newton Harrison: What Follows...
University of Colorado Visiting Artists Program
1989, 29:00, U.S., color, sound
This husband and wife team has collaborated on numerous projects in the U.S.and abroad. Their approach to making art involves finding solutions to ecological problems. Both are emeritus professors in the department of visual arts at the University of California-San Diego. Interview by Michael Crane.

Heineken, Robert

Robert Heineken: An Interview
Video Data Bank
1976, 30:00, U.S., b&w, sound
Robert Heineken uses technically sophisticated photographic methods to mingle erotic images with visuals from TV and advertising. In this interview, Heineken is framed in front of playback monitors, and the camera alternately zooms in on Heineken and his video image. He discusses his influences, education, and his interest in the audiences' ability to respond to images without necessarily knowing how they are created.

Hercules, Bob (see Halleck, DeeDee)

Hess, Elizabeth

Elizabeth Hess: What Follows...
University of Colorado Visiting Artists Program
1991, 51:00, U.S., color, sound
Elizabeth Hess addresses issues of censorship, AIDS, war, feminism, and politics in general. She has written extensively on women's issues, contributes to *The Village Voice*, and is co-author of *Re-Making Love: The Feminization of Sex* (1986). Interview by Lucy Lippard.

Holt, Nancy

Art in the Public Eye: The Making of Dark Star Park
Nancy Holt
1988, 33:00, U.S., color, sound
A documentary about Holt's public installation work *Dark Star Park* in Arlington, Virginia, this tape is about

the process of developing and building the park. It includes commentary from the architects, contractors, foremen, and engineers who worked on the project, as well as with people who frequent the park. Holt transforms a site of urban blight into an aesthetically stimulating spot that addresses environmental issues.

Hope, Andy (see Knapp, Joe)

Hudlin, Warrington

Warrington Hudlin: An Interview
Video Data Bank
1984, 27:20, U.S., color, sound
Documentarian and independent film producer Warrington Hudlin co-founded the Black Filmmaker Foundation in the late-1970s to help develop and promote emerging artists. More recently, he has been involved in DV Republic, a web-based alternative media site that is "socially concerned, entertainment driven," and the screening series *World Cinema Showcase*, hosted by the American Museum of the Moving Image. Interview by Shelley Shepard.

Irwin, Robert

Robert Irwin: An Interview
Lyn Blumenthal and Kate Horsfield
1976/re-edited 2003, 40:32, U.S., b&w, sound
Robert Irwin's early art followed in the Abstract Expressionist tradition until he shifted his focus onto installation projects that play upon sight-specific uses of light. Since the 1980s, he has created large-scale public space designs that use natural light, plants, and garden architecture; his monumental garden at the Getty Center in Los Angeles, opened in 1997, ranks as perhaps his most famous public project to date. In this interview, he discusses the historical context of how his work moved from using paint to uses of light in space.

Ito, Miyoko

Miyoko Ito: An Interview
Lyn Blumenthal and Kate Horsfield
1978, 28:00, U.S., b&w, sound
Miyoko Ito was an "abstract surrealist" who worked in Chicago. Her paintings are landscape-based abstractions of very intense subtleties of structure and color. "People say my paintings are the act of creation, and they are. The paintings are very much a part of life, like breathing. It's very much do or die. I'm growing all the time. All those years of painting is the beginning all over again. It's so wonderful," Ito says in this interview with Kate Horsfield.

Jaar, Alfredo

Alfredo Jaar: An Interview
Video Data Bank
1990, 41:00, U.S., color, sound
Alfredo Jaar is a politically motivated artist whose work includes installation, photography, and film. Born in Chile and now living in the U.S., Jaar's socio-critical installations explore global political issues, frequently focusing on the Third World and the relationship between con-

sumption and power. A 1986 installation in a subway station in New York involved dramatic photographs of impoverished gold miners in Brazil interspersed with quotations of current gold prices, drawing an unexpected parallel between the material desires that motivate people in both poverty-stricken Brazil and affluent Manhattan. Interview by Joyce Fernandes.

Jacquette, Yvonne

Yvonne Jacquette: An Interview
Lyn Blumenthal and Kate Horsfield
1981, 33:00, U.S., color, sound
Yvonne Jacquette is a realist painter whose preoccupation has been with light-suffusing interiors and landscapes. Recently she has concentrated on aerial views of rural topology and the cityscape. Her works may seem nearly formalistic in treatment, but in fact they contain quite specific information about the land below and its human network. "I've always felt very involved with landscape, even as a child," Jacquette says in this interview with Kate Horsfield. "It started to seem like the only real subject matter for me with a kind of absolute finality."

Johnson, Ray

Connections: Ray Johnson On-Line
Lars Movin and Steen Møller Rasmussen
2001, 41:00, Denmark, color, sound
Connections presents a portrait of the American artist Ray Johnson (1927-95), the driving force behind the New York Correspondence School of the early 1960s. Johnson was known for his numerous mail art projects, which invited recipients to contribute to his work. In addition to mail art, Johnson worked on collages, assemblages, and performance throughout his life. This film is comprised of personal interpretations of Johnson's artistic strategies, using the telephone and the Internet to connect to sound and image sources. The film includes statements from William Anastasi, Mark S. Bloch, Dot Capuano, Christo, Jeanne-Claude, John Giorno, Coco Gordon, Helen Harrison, Jon Hendricks, Les Levine, Kalie Seiden, Lawrence Weiner, and John Willenbecher.

Jones, Art

Art Jones: An Interview
Video Data Bank
1993, unedited, U.S., color, sound
Art Jones is an image/sound manipulator working with film, digital video, and hybrid media. Feeling that the representations of African-Americans were insufficient, Jones began making videotapes that challenged the prevailing perspectives. His films, tapes, CD-ROMs, and live video-mixes combine audio/visual samples with original material to create time-based collages.

July, Miranda

Miranda July: An Interview
Video Data Bank
2001, unedited, U.S., color, sound
Miranda July makes performances, movies, and recordings—often in combination. Her videos (*The Amateurist, Nest of Tens, Getting Stronger Every Day*) present complicated parallel narratives with characters who experi-

ence loneliness, exploitation, unexpected phobias, and often inexplicable relationships. July has also recorded several performance albums released by Kill Rock Stars and K Records. In 1995 she founded Joanie 4 Jackie, an on-going movie distribution network for independent women movie makers. Interview by Dara Greenwald and Blithe Riley.

Kaprow, Allan

Allan Kaprow: An Interview
Lyn Blumenthal and Kate Horsfield
1979/re-edited 2002, 49:00, U.S., b&w, sound
In 1952, Allan Kaprow wrote an article on Abstract Expressionism entitled "The Legacy of Jackson Pollock" in which he suggested the separation of the art-making activity from the art itself. Kaprow's concept was most famously realized through Happenings, during which the traditional role of artist-creator was replaced by what he called "the social occasion." In these events divisions between artist and audience—and between the artwork and the perception of it—were dissolved. "I couldn't really handle the public exposure. It seemed to imply show biz, and in fact a lot of my crisis was attributable to exposure on television, *Life* magazine articles, being called by revolutionaries for help, and so on. So I pulled back—not into the past, but into a private world," Kaprow says in this interview with Arlene Raven.

Kattab, Daoud

Daoud Kattab: An Interview
SAIC Visiting Artist Program and Video Data Bank
2002, 51:53, U.S., color, sound
Daoud Kattab, one of the best-known Palestinian journalists, has fought for a free media in Palestine under both the Israeli occupation and the Palestinian Authority. Throughout his career, his creative initiatives have helped drive the development of an independent Palestinian press. Interview by Sharif Youssef.

Katz, Alex

Alex Katz: An Interview
Lyn Blumenthal and Kate Horsfield
1977/re-edited 2003, 38:30, U.S., b&w, sound
Alex Katz has produced a remarkable and impressive body of work but is best known for his large-scale, flat, yet realistic portraits of friends and family notable for their relaxed attitudes and uncomplicated bearing. In this interview from 1977, Katz talks about the development of his work and the decision to continue making figural work during the high-energy period of Abstract Expressionism. "I knew I had to paint what I saw," Katz says in this interview with Kate Horsfield. "I never really felt comfortable with generalizations."

Kelly, Mary

Mary Kelly: An Interview
Video Data Bank
1989, 40:00, U.S., color, sound
Since the 1970s Mary Kelly worked at the fore of feminist art and theory. She has continued to address issues and methods of activist politics, psychoanalysis, political science, literature, and the history of women and gender.

Kelly received recognition in the early '80s for her epic six-year project, *The Post-Partum Document*, a mixed-media work chronicling her and her son's development. Kelly says her work revolves "around the recurring themes of body, money, history, and power" in this interview with Judith Russi Kirschner.

Kertesz, Andre

Andre Kertesz: A Poet with a Camera
Video Data Bank
1985, 28:00, U.S., color, sound
A pioneer of the small-format camera, Andre Kertesz's photographic vision shaped the course of contemporary photojournalism. Self-taught and non-conformist, he began photographing in Hungary in 1912 and remained there until 1925, at which time he moved to Paris. In 1936 he moved to New York City, where he felt displaced and forgotten. It wasn't until 1964 that he was "rediscovered" and began showing in London, Paris, and New York. This videotape was shot five weeks before Kertesz's death in 1985 at the age of 91. More than 70 photographs are depicted from the three creative periods of his life—Hungary, France, and the United States. The tape centers on a meeting between Kertesz and Cornell Capa, director of the International Center of Photography in New York. Interview by Bela Ugrin.

Knapp, Ben and Andy Hope

Ben Knapp and Andy Hope: An Interview
SAIC Visiting Artist Program and Video Data Bank
2001, unedited, U.S., color, sound
Media artists Ben Knapp and Andy Hope develop "human-computer interface designs"—or interactive computer installations. Knapp is Director of Technology for Moto Development Group. Interview by Romi Crawford.

Kozloff, Joyce

Joyce Kozloff: Public Art Works
Hermine Freed, 1996, 56:00, U.S., color, sound
Joyce Kozloff was at the forefront of the 1970s pattern and decoration movement—a feminist effort to incorporate typically "feminine" and popular decorative arts into the fine arts. She has been involved with public art and murals for more than two decades. In this tape, Kozloff prepares and installs her mural *Around the World on the 44th Parallel*, which features sections of maps from 12 cities around the world on the same latitude. The work was constructed at the Tile Guild in Los Angeles and installed at the library at Minnesota State University-Mankato. The tape juxtaposes interview footage of the artist reflecting on her development with period footage of Freed speaking in the 1970s.

Krasner, Lee

Lee Krasner: An Interview
Lyn Blumenthal and Kate Horsfield
1980/re-edited 2004, 42:00, U.S., color to b&w, sound
Lee Krasner was one of the few women to play a major part in the transition from modernist painting in the 1930s to Abstract Expressionism in the 1950s. Married to Jackson Pollock, Krasner was largely overlooked by the art world for far too long. Pollock, with Krasner,

launched the New York School after World War II. Always challenging herself to take risks, her work is an ever-changing work in progress. "I have a horror of fixed images," Krasner says in this interview with Kate Horsfield. "It seems to me that as long as I'm alive there will be change. You put it up, hope for the best, and take your chances on what comes through."

Kruger, Barbara

Barbara Kruger: An Interview
Lyn Blumenthal and Kate Horsfield
1980/re-edited 2004, 31:30, U.S., color, sound
At 19 Kruger worked as a commercial artist designing for Conde Nast. This job taught her to use the powerful elements of advertising and commercial design. She used these strategies to combine contemporary graphics with social critique, the elements that run throughout all of Kruger's work – photography, readings, poetry, collages, and criticism. Language and image work together, referencing the manipulations of the advertising media. Kruger is internationally recognized for her signature black, white, and red photomurals, which have been displayed internationally on billboards and posters as well as in galleries and museums. She has edited books on cultural theory and has published articles in *The New York Times, Artforum,* and other periodicals. In this early interview, Kruger discusses her lesser-known, earlier works and the origins of the process she is most known for.

Kubota, Shigeko

Shigeko Kubota: An Interview
Video Data Bank
1983, 36:00, U.S., color, sound
For Shigeko Kubota the video image-making process is a cultural and personal experience. She has explored cross-cultural relationships in her video diaries, transient images captured by portable equipment while traveling– Kubota's "comparative videology." She has also combined fleeting video images with the "objecthood" of sculptural form in her series of video sculptures inspired by Duchamp. "I'm a sculptor," Kubota says in this interview with Jeanine Mellinger. "I want to make video, but I also want to make objects. The video part is my mirror for my memory, or my life, but the object is creating my creation."

Kurtz, Steve

Steve Kurtz: An Interview
Video Data Bank
1999, 35:31, U.S., color, sound
Steve Kurtz is a founding member of the Critical Art Ensemble and Associate Professor of Art at University of Buffalo. His areas of focus are contemporary art history and theory as well as post-studio practices. As a student Kurtz collaborated with Steve Barnes on low-tech videos, which they developed into a broad-based artist and activist collective known as the Critical Art Ensemble. Interview by Gregg Bordowitz.

Lawson, Thomas

Thomas Lawson: An Interview
Lyn Blumenthal and Kate Horsfield
1984, 56:00, U.S., color, sound
Thomas Lawson has played many roles in the art world– a painter, critic, and founding editor of *REAL LIFE* magazine and, more recently, Dean of of the school of art at CalArts. His paintings are tied to the particularities of the present, and he is especially critical of the current art world's infatuation with ego and creativity. His portraits, appropriated from the print media, represent an intervention in that vein. "In some long-term way, art is a moral force. I believe that pretty strongly, and that's why I get so upset with a lot of stuff that seems to me to be either taking that responsibility pretty lightly or disregarding it completely, because that degrades the entire discourse," Lawson says in this interview with Kate Horsfield.

Leaf, June

June Leaf: An Interview
Philip Yenawine and the Museum of Contemporary Art
1978, 20:00, U.S., color, sound
June Leaf's work is the embodiment of contradiction. It is expressionistic yet carefully structured, anecdotal yet not specifically narrative. Leaf looks at life with a sort of humor that reveals the absurdities we humans make of things, combining a painterly satire with a tinkerer's interest in constructing realities. "It was exhausting. It's always that way, but that's how I live. That's how I work. If I don't feel totally exhausted at the end of the day– totally, utterly spent–somehow when I wake up in the morning, I'm not as alive as I should be," Leaf says in this interview with Philip Yenawine.

LeCompte, Elizabeth

Elizabeth LeCompte: An Interview
Video Data Bank
1990, 43:00, U.S., color, sound
Elizabeth LeCompte is the director of the Wooster Group, an experimental theater company that operates out of its own theater, the Performing Garage, in New York City. The group's working process begins with "source" texts which are quoted, reworked, and juxtaposed with fragments of popular, cultural, and social history, as well as the personal and collective experiences of the group. The resulting productions reflect a continuing refinement of a non-linear, abstract aesthetic that at once subverts and pays homage to modern theatrical realism. Interview by Lin Hixon.

Levine, Les

Les Levine
Artists TV Network
1980, 28:00, U.S., color, sound
Les Levine has had a longstanding involvement with media. His works–video, installations, public posters, and other forms–have often dealt with the effect of images on our lives. "Media is in direct opposition to consciousness because it wants essentially to be your meta-consciousness; it wants you to respond to the world the way it has defined responses," Levine says in this interview with Steven Poser.

LeWitt, Sol

Sol LeWitt: An Interview
Lyn Blumenthal and Kate Horsfield
1977/re-edited 2003, 46:00, U.S., b&w, sound
Although Sol LeWitt began working primarily in painting, he has also worked in sculpture and photography. Best known for his cubes, he used the grid as a foundation for many artworks. Seeing himself in the role of architect or composer, LeWitt is most concerned with the concept behind the piece rather than the final product. He strips away extraneous information and presents the bare essentials, usually in a serial nature. In this interview from 1977, LeWitt talks about the art-making practice and the role of commodity within the art world. "The big problem today which many artists are concerned with is not if the art is made or not made, but what happens to it after it's made and the fact that it becomes an object and a piece of commerce and is traded. The artist is seen like a producer of commodities, like a factory that turns our refrigerators. I believe that the artist's involvement in the capitalist structure is disadvantageous to the artist and forces him to produce objects in order to live," LeWitt says in this interview with Kate Horsfield.

Lichtenstein, Roy

Roy Lichtenstein: Still Life Paintings
Hermine Freed
1972, 21:00, U.S., b&w, sound
Until 1957 Roy Lichtenstein worked as a commercial artist and designer before turning to Abstract Expressionism. In 1960, he began infusing his work with elements of commercial art and soon emerged as one of the leading painters of Pop Art. In this tape Lichtenstein is seen at work on several different stages of his paintings, from collage sketch to partial restoration. He discusses reasons for choosing the still life motifs, as well as themes that he has used in the past.

Lippard, Lucy

Lucy Lippard 1974: An Interview
Lyn Blumenthal and Kate Horsfield
1974, 28:00, U.S., b&w, sound
One of the most influential and up-to-the-moment art critics, Lucy Lippard was among the first writers to recognize the de-materialization at work in conceptual art and an early champion of feminist art. She has written numerous influential books of art history and criticism, including *Pop Art* (1966), *Changing: Essays in Art Criticism* (1971), and *Six Years, the Dematerialization of the Art Object from 1966 to 1972* (1973). Interview by Lyn Blumenthal.

Lucy Lippard 1979: An Interview
Lyn Blumenthal and Kate Horsfield
1979/re-edited 2003, 1:03:00, U.S., b&w, sound
In this interview with Kate Horsfield, Lippard, author of *From the Center: Feminist Essays on Womens' Art* (1976), discusses the journal *Heresies: A Feminist Publication on Art and Politics* and her novel, *I See/You Mean* (1979). Lippard published a second anthology of her essays on feminist art, *The Pink Glass Swan*, in 1995. Interview by Kate Horsfield.

Lucy Lippard: What Follows...
University of Colorado Visiting Artists Program
1987, 18:25, U.S., color, sound
Writer and activist Lucy Lippard divides her time between Boulder and New York City. She narrates a reading set to selected "politically motivated" art works. Interview by Jim Johnson.

Lockhart, Sharon

Sharon Lockhart: An interview
SAIC Visiting Artist Program and Video Data Bank
2000, unedited, U.S., color, sound
Sharon Lockhart is a photographer and filmmaker. Her photographic and filmic works interrogate the inversion of the static image as cinematic and the manipulation of the moving image into a static/stop-motion frame. Her work also contemplates how we perceive our own real-time realities. Her first film, *Khabil, A Woman Under the Influence,* was completed in 1994. In 1996 Lockhart was awarded a grant from the Asian Cultural Council to spend three months in Japan. While there, Lockhart made her first feature film, *Goshogaoka*, which features a suburban junior high school girls' basketball team. Lockhart has exhibited her photographs internationally and teaches at UCLA and the Art Center College of Design. Interview by Dominique Mahoney.

Lowe, Rick

Rick Lowe: An Interview
Video Data Bank
1997, unedited, U.S., color, sound
Rick Lowe is a Houston-based artist and activist. Trained as a painter, he integrates art into everyday social experience within the African-American community. In 1992, he founded Project Row Houses, an arts and cultural community located in a historically significant site in Houston. Integrating artists' studio spaces with transitional housing for single parents and children, Project Row Houses transformed a section of one of the city's poorest neighborhoods into a community cultural center. Lowe subsequently worked on the Watts House in conjunction with the exhibition *Uncommon Sense* at the Museum of Contemporary Arts in Los Angeles. Interview by Joyce Fernandes.

Lyons, Nathan

Nathan Lyons: An Interview
Lyn Blumenthal and Kate Horsfield
1978, 50:00, U.S., b&w, sound
Nathan Lyons has contributed to the field of photography as a critic, author, curator, educator, and photographer. He has published several books and catalogs, including *Photographers on Photography* (1966), *Photography in the 20th Century* (1967), *Towards a Social Landscape* (1967), *Persistence of Vision* (1968), and *Notations in Passing* (1974). Interview by Alex Sweetman.

Malpede, John

John Malpede: An Interview
Video Data Bank
1989, 44:00, U.S., color, sound

John Malpede is a performance artist and Director of the Los Angeles Poverty Department (LAPD), a performance art and theater group whose members include the city's homeless. Through LAPD, Malpede provides an opportunity for homeless people to articulate the reality of their lives for themselves and audiences. Malpede was well known for his collaboration with performer Gill Gordh as Dead Dog and Lonely Horse. In one performance he took on the role of a street person, contrasting the wealth and excess of the 1984 Olympics in Los Angeles with the city's struggle against homelessness. Interview by Lin Hixon.

Martin, Agnes

Agnes Martin 1974: An Interview
Lyn Blumenthal and Kate Horsfield
1974/re-edited 2003, 41:00, U.S., b&w, sound
Originally from Canada, Agnes Martin moved to the U.S. in 1931. Martin lived in Taos, New Mexico from 1954 to 1957 and then returned to New York, where she established herself as an important minimalist painter. Her work differed conceptually from the minimalists in that it was anti-intellectual and intensely spiritual, and her grids represented meditative reflections on Taoism. For years, Martin worked only in black, white, and (occasionally) brown. Shortly after Ad Reinhart died in 1967 she left New York and traveled around the United States for two years before settling in New Mexico. Her devotees consider her a visionary—an artist possessed of perceptive powers that have transformed her painting style and palette into a heightened visual experience. Interview by Kate Horsfield.

Agnes Martin 1976: An Interview
Lyn Blumenthal and Kate Horsfield
1976/re-edited 2003, 31:00, U.S., b&w, sound
Martin's art has been called classical, minimal, or romantic, depending on who's looking at it. There is no question that she has influenced a generation of younger artists. This tape was shot at Martin's adobe home, which she built herself in Cuba, New Mexico. Interview by Kate Horsfield.

Mekas, Jonas

Jonas Mekas
Video Data Bank
1985, 15:00, U.S., color, sound
An intimate interview with filmmaker, videomaker, film critic, poet, lecturer, and curator Jonas Mekas. Born into a farming family in Lithuania on December 24, 1922, Mekas was imprisoned in a forced labor camp in Nazi Germany from 1944 to 1945, studied philosophy at the University of Mainz from 1946 to 1948, and relocated to the U. S. in 1949. In 1954, Mekas became editor-in-chief of *Film Culture* magazine and wrote a film column in *The Village Voice* from 1958 to 1975. He was President of New American Cinema Group (Film-makers' Cooperative) from 1961 to 1980 and has been program director of Anthology Film Archives since 1970. In this tape Mekas discusses his background, the art of moving images, the history of avant-garde film, and *Film Culture* magazine. Interview with Jordi Torrent.

Mendieta, Ana

Ana Mendieta: Fuego De Tierra
Kate Horsfield, Nereida Garcia-Ferraz, and Branda Miller
1987, 49:00, U.S., color, sound
Performance artist/sculptor Ana Mendieta worked with natural materials such as water, mud, fire, rock, and grass. Her politics and poetics fill her work with an emotionally charged vision, which is also powerfully conveyed in this posthumous video profile. Drawing upon the spiritual power of Afro-Cuban religion, Mendieta used her art as a ritualistic and symbolic activity to celebrate the forces of life and the continuum of change. She used her own silhouette, inserted in the land, to emphasize the universal and primal relations between the two bodies: female and earth.

Also available with Spanish subtitles.

Michelson, Annette

Annette Michelson
Artists TV Network
1980, 28:00, U.S., color, sound
Annette Michelson is a founding editor of the journal *October* and former professor of cinema studies at New York University. Before starting *October*, Michelson was the film critic for *Artforum*. Michelson's influential work has focused on modernity, Russian and French avant-garde film, and American underground cinema. In this Soho TV interview with Steven Poser she acknowledges that advertising shapes the editorial content of art magazines (including *Artforum*) and discusses her objectives in starting *October*: creating a space where different art forms—dance, sculpture, film—could be written about together in a rigorous way and where artists' writings and documents could be published. "It was our hope that [*October*] could celebrate that conjunction of innovation in the arts and certain kinds of political consciousness and awareness … to be defined as undoubtedly oriented toward the left. For myself, the issues of Marxist methodology are still alive," Michelson says.

Miller, Paul D. (see DJ Spooky)

Minh-ha, Trinh T.

Trinh T. Minh-ha: An Interview
Video Data Bank
1989, 32:30, U.S., color, sound
Trinh T. Minh-ha is a world-renowned feminist filmmaker and theorist of avant-garde and post-colonial film. Minh-ha came to the United States from Vietnam at the age of 17 in 1970. She is the maker of *Reassemblage* (1982) and *Surname Viet Given Name Nam* (1989) and the author of *Woman Native Other* (1989) and *The Moon Waxes Red* (1991), among other films and books. Currently she is professor of women's studies and rhetoric at the University of California-Berkeley.

Miss, Mary

Mary Miss: An Interview
Lyn Blumenthal and Kate Horsfield
1979, 35:00, U.S., color, sound

From her earlier sculptural work, Mary Miss has moved into concerns with illusion, distance, and perception. The work has grown to environmental scale and frequently uses both ancient and modern architecture as references. "A lot of things I do are illusionistic or have been almost like painting, like flattening something out while trying at the same time to give the experience of space. I'm interested in that very thin line that happens between these two different things," Miss says in this interview with Kate Horsfield.

Mitchell, Joan

Joan Mitchell: An Interview
Lyn Blumenthal and Kate Horsfield
1974/re-edited 2004, U.S., b&w, sound
Joan Mitchell was the daughter of physician James Herbert Mitchell and poet Marion Strobel. Mitchell spent much of the '50s in New York, living on St. Mark's Place on the Lower East Side, and was deeply involved with the second generation of the New York School. While other members of the second generation moved painting toward cool, formalist images, Mitchell persisted in maintaining the basis of her style in action painting and achieved paintings of great emotional and intellectual intensity. During the 1960s Mitchell moved to France, where she lived until her death in 1992. Interview by Kate Horsfield.

Monk, Meredith

Meredith Monk: An Interview
Kate Horsfield
1977, 48:00, U.S., b&w, sound
Meredith Monk has been composing, choreographing, and performing since the mid-1960s. Her voice has a unique timbre, which she explores through a capella singing and speech. As a dancer and choreographer, she creates hybrid, theatrical productions that incorporate ritualistic movements, lighting effects, and small props. "I alternate between doing pieces in which all my cards are on the table—white lights, no illusions at all—or pieces like *Quarry*, which deals with dense layers of theatricality—dense layers of light, illusion, and mystery," Monk says in this interview with Ellen Fisher.

Montano, Linda M.

Linda M. Montano: An Interview
Lyn Blumenthal and Kate Horsfield
1984, 26:00, U.S., color, sound
At the source of Linda M. Montano's work is her search for a personal harmony and balance. She seeks to synthesize the intuitive processes that transform the private self with the rationality and pragmatism of the public persona, extending this synthesis to both art and life. In this tape, Montano discusses her childhood, the influence of the Catholic church, its rituals, and the sources that lead to her subsequent performances, such as her year-long performance *Art/Life* (1983-84) in which Montano and Sam Hsieh remained attached by an eight-foot rope. Interview by Lyn Blumenthal.

Linda M. Montano's Seven Years of Living Art

Maida Barbour
1994, 13:13, U.S., color, sound
This video collage chronicles Linda M. Montano's seven-year performance piece in which she devoted a year to each of the seven chakras. Beginning as a piece devoted to themes of commitment and limitation, the work becomes a fascinating hybrid of art and life, as Montano experiences the onset of menopause, her mother's death, her choice to enter and then leave a convent, the suffering of a stroke, and thoughts of her own death—all within the structural confines of an intense work of art. Contributors to the work include Ellen Fullman, Gisela Gamper, and Annie Sprinkle.
Also available on the anthology *Endurance, Reel 4*.

Morton, Ree

Ree Morton: An Interview
Video Data Bank
1974, 30:00, U.S., b&w, sound
Ree Morton (1936-77) was an American artist working with large-scale mixed media installations. Her mature career was brief—from 1971 to 1977, however, her output and growth during these years was unusually original. "You can see how I collect just junk—over there. I have things around, and then as I work, it's almost a kind of drawing process. It involves picking something up, placing it over there, looking at it, putting something else with it, seeing how they relate to one another, bringing a third thing in, taking it out. It's really physical manipulation," Morton says in this interview with Horsfield.

Mulvey, Laura

Laura Mulvey: An Interview
Video Data Bank
1993, 30:00, U.S., color, sound
Laura Mulvey published her seminal essay "Visual Pleasure and Narrative Cinema" in 1975; it has subsequently become the most influential work in film theory. Using a psychoanalytic methodology to discuss spectatorship, it was groundbreaking in its feminist critique of the sadistic, misogynistic mode of classical Hollywood cinema in which women were objects of fetishistic display for male viewers' pleasure. She has also written extensively on melodrama, published three books, and co-directed six films, including *Riddles of the Sphinx* with Peter Wollen (1974).

Antonio Muntadas

Antonio Muntadas: Video Portrait
LBMA Video
1983, 28:00, U.S., color, sound
Originally from Barcelona and trained there and in New York, Antonio Muntadas is a media artist interested in the investigation of the social and educational aspects of media. His internationally recognized videotapes and media installations investigate the contradictory messages projected by print and broadcast media, architecture, and language. Throughout his work, Muntadas recontextualizes available imagery in order to provoke the viewer into re-thinking their meanings. This videotape produced for the Long Beach Museum of Art includes interview segments with Muntadas and curator Kathy

Rae Huffman, as well as examples of his works.

Murray, Elizabeth

Elizabeth Murray 1977: An Interview
Lyn Blumenthal and Kate Horsfield
1977, 38:00, U.S., b&w, sound
Elizabeth Murray's paintings have been referred to as "dandyish abstraction." Although her work has gone through a number of stylistic changes, it has always been characterized by a personal alteration of the conventions of painting. Her work is distinctive in her use of color, shape, and surface. This is the first of two interviews between Murray and Kate Horsfield.

Elizabeth Murray 1982: An Interview
Lyn Blumenthal and Kate Horsfield
1982/re-edited 2003, 48:00, color to b&w, sound
"I think that there's been so much repression in the name of issues. And there always have been in terms of art. ... But I felt at that moment that I wasn't involved with issues very, very strongly—that the issues were being taken care of by other people. ... I was much more interested in taking all the stuff that I knew and all the kinds of beautiful potentials of abstraction and making it into something very personal," Murray says in this interview with Kate Horsfield.

Neel, Alice

Alice Neel: An Interview
Lyn Blumenthal and Kate Horsfield
1975/re-edited 2003, 30:00, U.S., b&w, sound
Alice Neel is known for portrait paintings of well-known persons and eccentric New York street types. Neel worked as a figurative painter throughout the decades of WPA realism, postwar abstract expressionism, 1960s Pop, and 1970s minimalism. She persevered in her work despite a turbulent personal life and critical neglect that continued until the 1960s. Neel lived and worked in New York City from 1932 until her death in 1984. Interview by Kate Horsfield.

Nestle, Joan

Joan Nestle: An Interview
Video Data Bank
1998, unedited, U.S., color, sound
In 1973 Joan Nestle co-founded the Lesbian Herstory Archives, an essential collection of documents, writings, and artifacts of lesbian cultural history. In 1979 she began writing erotic stories and has published two collections of writings: *A Restricted Country* (1987) and *A Fragile Union* (1998). She took a controversial stance in opposition to the 1980s feminist anti-pornography movement, thus becoming a fervent pro-sex activist in the "Sex Wars." Interview by Nina Levitt.

Newkirk, Kori

Kori Newkirk: An Interview
SAIC Visiting Artist Program and Video Data Bank
2004, unedited, U.S., color, sound
Kori Newkirk is currently gaining recognition for his mixed-media paintings and sculpture installations. Many of his paintings are urban landscapes in the form of beaded curtains made with plastic pony beads (typically used as hair ornaments) strung on stands of artificial braid. Newkirk also uses hair pomade to create wall paintings. Evocative in both texture and smell, this sensual material embodies cultural references that are both personal and political. His installations resonate with underlying social implications that speak to issues of self, identity, race, and urbanity. Interview by Dominic Molon.

Oppenheim, Dennis

Dennis Oppenheim
Artists TV Network
1980, 28:00, U.S., color, sound
Dennis Oppenheim was a prominent figure in various art developments throughout the '70s. Oppenheim moved through body/performance art and related video work to earthworks to his current large-scale "factories." In all of his work, the transference of energy is an underlying concern. "Reading a commercial factory as a mental metaphor might be correct. Maybe what's out there is hallucinated thought structures. Maybe Con Edison [the New York City utilities company] has a lot more to do with mental facsimile than one cares to believe," Oppenheim says in this interview with Steven Poser produced for Soho TV.

Orlan

Orlan: An Interview
SAIC Visiting Artist Program and Video Data Bank
1998, unedited, U.S., color, sound, in French and English
French performance artist Orlan uses her own body as a sculptural medium. Since 1990, she has worked on *La Reincarnation de Sainte-Orlan*, a process of plastic surgeries that she "performs," making elaborate spectacles with surgeons dressed in sci-fi costumes and broadcasting the operations live via satellite to galleries worldwide. By exploring a total transformation of self, Orlan delves into issues of identity and the malleability of the flesh. She lives and works in Paris, exhibiting and performing internationally. Interview by Shadie Grandis, via translator.

Ottinger, Ulrike

Ulrike Ottinger: An Interview
Video Data Bank
1991, 34:00, U.S., color, sound
Ulrike Ottinger is a prolific German filmmaker whose work includes *Madame X* (1977), *Ticket of No Return* (1979), *Freak Orlando* (1981), *Johanna d'Arc of Mongolia* (1989), *Countdown* (1989), and *Exile Shanghai* (1997). Starting her visual arts career in Munich and Paris in painting, photography, and performance, Ottinger's commitment to film took off with her move to Berlin. In this tape, Ottinger speaks about her use of collage to layer different historical moments, her interest in flaneur lifestyles, and her technical and aesthetic methods of non-sync sound and long takes.

Owens, Craig

Craig Owens: An Interview
Lyn Blumenthal and Kate Horsfield
1985, 35:00, U.S., color, sound
Craig Owens was a critic who wrote and lectured extensively on contemporary art. He showed particular interest in the issues of photography, postmodernism, feminism, and Marxist thought. A former associate editor for *October* and senior editor for *Art in America,* as well as professor of art history at Yale University and Barnard College, his writings were collected in *Beyond Recognition: Representation, Power, and Culture* (1994). Owens died of an AIDS-related illness in 1990. "I'm arguing for an art that is culturally relevant. I'm arguing for an art that does not remain content to address the problems of the 19th century society. I expect art to mediate my cultural experience," Owens says in this interview with Martha Rosler.

Paschke, Ed

Ed Paschke: An Interview
Lyn Blumenthal and Kate Horsfield
1983, 40:00, U.S., color, sound
Ed Paschke exhibited with other Chicago artists—known collectively as the Imagists—whose work shared references to surrealist art and images from popular culture—employed brilliant color throughout a busy and carefully worked surface. Paschke's paintings depict well-known as well as fringe characters overlaid with references to television scan lines in his vibrantly electronic paintings. Paschke's concern was the manner in which reality is transformed, stylized, perceived, and accepted. "I think film and television have had a lot to do with forming our ideas of a sense of self," Paschke says in this interview with Kate Horsfield. "They're about relationships, they're about isolation.... they're about reaching out beyond isolation."

Pearlstein, Philip

Philip Pearlstein: An Interview
Lyn Blumenthal and Kate Horsfield
1977, 1:00:00, U.S., b&w, sound
Philip Pearlstein began painting figures in the 1960s and is known as a leading figure in American Realism. His paintings evolved from an expressionistic style to a meticulously analytical vision. He attempts to present the model as a documentation of the painting session, and his paintings are closely rendered under the existing studio lighting. "I made up my mind that I was not a good existentialist. I'm not concerned with what's going on in other people's minds. I'm happiest when I can just paint what I see," he says in this interview with Kate Horsfield.

Peyton, Elizabeth

Elizabeth Peyton: An Interview
Video Data Bank
Date unknown, unedited, U.S., color, sound
Elizabeth Peyton paints and draws portraits of people from magazines, books, and her own snapshots. Her subjects are often personal friends, but many are historical figures or celebrities, blurring the lines of intimacy and personal acquaintance. Interview by Jennifer Reeder.

Phipps, Cyrille

Cyrille Phipps: An Interview
Video Data Bank
1993, 21:00, U.S., color, sound
Media artist Cyrille Phipps has been involved with numerous alternative media and lesbian activist projects, including Dyke TV and the Gay and Lesbian Emergency Media Campaign. Her video projects include *Respect Is Due* (1991), *Black Women, Sexual Politics and the Revolution* (with Not Channel Zero, 1992), *Our House: Gays and Lesbians in the Hood* (with Not Channel Zero, 1992), *Sacred Lives, Civil Truths* (with Catherine Saalfield, 1993), *Dreaming Ourselves... Healing Darkness* (1995), and *Mumia Abu-Jamal: Facing the Death Penalty* (with Paper Tiger TV, 1995).

Pindell, Howardena

Howardena Pindell
Hermine Freed
1972, 25:00, U.S., b&w, sound
Taped shortly after the creation of the Air Gallery, this conversation between painter Howardena Pindell and Hermine Freed concerns the women's independent gallery and its role in the feminist movement. Pindell also discusses the development of her work and the relation between black artists and the art world.

Piper, Adrian

Adrian Piper: What Follows...
University of Colorado Visiting Artists Program
1989, 28:00, U.S., color, sound
A philosopher and inter-media artist, Adrian Piper focuses on xenophobia, racism, and racial stereotyping. "As a black woman who can 'pass' and a Professor of Philosophy who leads a double life as an avant-garde artist, Piper has understandably focused on self-analysis and social boundaries. Over the years her work in performance, texts, newspaper, unannounced street events, tapes, and photographs has developed an increasingly politicized and universalized image of what the self can mean."
—Lucy Lippard, *Issue: Social Strategies for Women Artists* (London: ICA, 1980) Interview by Dale Jamieson.

Pollard, Ingrid

Ingrid Pollard: An Interview
SAIC Visiting Artist Program and Video Data Bank
1999, unedited, U.S., color, sound
Ingrid Pollard is a photographer living in London. Her photographic works, generally of people and landscape, serve to provide a human context for issues of transmigration and "fleeting" identity. Combining personal photographs with traditional views of the English countryside, Pollard questions as well as reconstructs the concept of "Britishness." In doing so, Pollard also scrutinizes the location of the "other," and contrasts actual physical similarity or material likeness of people and places with perceived or socially constructed difference. Through text, Pollard further elaborates on this comparison, exposing the fictional uniformity of travel brochures and postcards.

Poole, Tom

Tom Poole: An Interview
SAIC Visiting Artist Program and Video Data Bank
2002, unedited, U.S., color, sound
Tom Poole is executive director of Pittsburgh Community Television, a cable access network committed to alternative media. His has a history of working as a media activist and has produced work with Free Speech TV and Deep Dish TV. Interview by Romi Crawford.

Poons, Larry

Larry Poons - His Endless Creativity
Bill Page
2001, 29:00, U.S., color, sound
This tape includes an interview with Larry Poons in his "barn" studio, combined with at a talk he gave at the New School. Poons is highly charged, articulate, and doesn't give a damn about the New York art world that made him famous in the 1960s for his dot paintings. Shown speaking and in creative action, Poons addresses his own history in this video and tells anecdotes along the way, revealing himself as a notoriously feisty, creative person. Poons is simple but distinguished, forceful, blunt, streetwise, and intelligent.

Prince, Richard

Richard Prince: Crossover Series
MICA-TV
1982, 7:00, U.S., color, sound
Richard Prince appropriates images from commercial advertising and travelogues for his photographs. Choosing these images for their melodramatic, super-real power, he then isolates their stylistic realism to accentuate its rhetoric. In this portrait/performance, Prince narrates experiences that demonstrate his extreme sensitivity to appearances and context. He relates the event of buying his first car as the imprinting of a certain aesthetic impression.

Only available on the MICA-TV *Crossover Series* compilation.

Rainer, Yvonne

Yvonne Rainer: An Interview
Lyn Blumenthal and Kate Horsfield
1984, 56:00, U.S., color, sound
Yvonne Rainer trained as a modern dancer in New York and began to choreograph her own work in 1960. When Rainer made her first feature-length film in 1972, she had already influenced the world of dance and choreography for nearly a decade. From the beginning of her film career she inspired audiences to think about what they saw—interweaving the real and fictional, the personal and political, the concrete and abstract in imaginative, unpredictable ways. By 1968, Rainer began to mix short films into live performances. By 1975 she had made a complete transition to film. Her films include *A Film About A Woman Who...* (1974), *Kristina Talking Pictures* (1976), *Journeys From Berlin/1971* (1980), *The Man Who Envied Women* (1985) and *MURDER and murder* (1996)—all have been shown extensively in festivals and alternative venues throughout the world. Interview by Lyn Blumenthal.

Raven, Arlene

Arlene Raven: An Interview
Lyn Blumenthal and Kate Horsfield
1979, 40:39, U.S., b&w, sound
Arlene Raven is a feminist historian, theoretician, poet, and art historian who has published numerous books on contemporary art and written criticism for *The Village Voice* and a variety of other newspapers, art magazines, exhibition catalogues, and scholarly journals since 1969. She is a pioneer in progressive education and was an architect of the educational programs of the Feminist Studio Workshop, an independent school. She is also the founder of the Women's Caucus for Art, the Los Angeles Woman's Building, and *Chrysalis* magazine. She became interested in art at an early age, believing that it separated all the boring facts of life into something magical and special. "At the Woman's Building, we developed a theory of feminist education which was a transition from the way that women relate to one another through competition, isolation, and silence, to a situation of support. Women have the supreme ability, through acculturation, not to criticize, and I strongly believe that we shape one another through our criticism," she says in this interview with Lyn Blumenthal.

Resnick, Milton

Milton Resnick: An Interview
Video Data Bank
1988/re-edited 2003, 1:02:00, color, sound
Milton Resnick was born in Bratslav, Russia in 1917, and immigrated to the United States in 1922. Resnick was one of the few survivors of the second generation Abstract Expressionists and is known for his large, thickly painted abstract canvases. Like other painters of the time, Resnick was striving for an overall quality to his paintings, a way to unite the foreground and background. While others moved toward throwing or dragging quantities of paint across the face of the canvas, Resnick retained a particularly personal and impassioned relation to brush painting. "The activity of paint is such that you cannot keep your eye still, and yet it's contained," Resnick died in 2004. Interview with Kate Horsfield.

Rosenthal, Rachel

Rachel Rosenthal: An Interview
SAIC Visiting Artist Program and Video Data Bank
1999, unedited, U.S., color, sound
Rachel Rosenthal is a performance artist and director of the Rachel Rosenthal Company. Her ensemble produces text, voice, and movement-based work rooted in the spectacle of theater. Her work addresses subversion of the natural order through vocal experimentation and varying the performer's relation to objects in space. In this performative interview, Matthew Goulish plays word association with Rosenthal, offering 39 names, concepts, and phrases for Rosenthal to address.

Rosler, Martha

Martha Rosler: An Interview
Lyn Blumenthal and Kate Horsfield

1984, 56:00, U.S., color, sound
Martha Rosler has produced seminal works in the fields of photography, performance, video, installation, criticism, and theory. Committed to an art that engages a public beyond the confines of the art world, Rosler investigates how socioeconomic realities and political ideologies dominate everyday life. Rosler's work has entered the canon of contemporary art through a process of steady, stealthy infiltration. Lacking commercial gallery representation until 1993, her endeavors as a prolific essayist, lecturer, and political agitator enabled her agenda to trickle down through critical channels.

Ross, Richard

Frame and Context: Richard Ross
Fellows of Contemporary Art
1989, 12:00, U.S., color, sound
Richard Ross discusses his interest in photographing museums—their display of objects, frames, the entire context—in order to question our definitions of the museum. The tape also covers his ongoing series of triptychs made using a child's plastic camera, which Ross turns into "art historical soap operas" by playing off the interactions of the groupings.

Only available on the Fellows of Contemporary Art compilation.

Rothenberg, Susan

Susan Rothenberg: An Interview
Lyn Blumenthal and Kate Horsfield
1984/re-edited 2003, 48:27, U.S., color to b&w, sound
Susan Rothenberg's poetic images—from her well-known early horse paintings to her more recent paintings of athletes and dancers—have always been subservient to the flatness and objectivity of her gesturally dense surfaces. Ultimately, though, image and surface combine in a private symbolism and restrained drama that resonates physically and emotionally. Rothenberg currently lives and works in New Mexico.

Ryman, Robert

Robert Ryman 1979: An Interview
Lyn Blumenthal and Kate Horsfield
1979/reedited 2003, 27:00, U.S., b&w, sound
Robert Ryman first moved to New York City with the intention of becoming a jazz musician. Working for several years as a gallery attendant at the Museum of Modern Art and a brief assignment in the Art Division of the Public Library comprised his "art education." From the outset, Ryman was not interested in realistic representation. In his first paintings and collages from the mid-1950s, he experimented with material, color, and brushwork, eventually reducing the painting to its barest elements. Eventually, he settled on a square with white paint as the basis of his investigation. "I don't really know what it will look like when its finished—sometimes it's a big surprise, which is good, when some discovery has been made that I didn't consider at the beginning," Ryman says in this interview with Kate Horsfield.

Robert Ryman 1993: An Interview
Kate Horsfield and Robert Storr

1993/ re-edited 2004, 30:00, U.S., color, sound
Interviewed in concert with a retrospective at the Museum of Modern Art, Ryman discusses seeing his work displayed chronologically for the first time.

Saar, Betye and Alison

Similar Differences: Betye and Alison Saar
Fellows of Contemporary Art
1990, 9:30, U.S., color, sound
This tape profiles mother and daughter artists Betye and Alison Saar. Both artists work with sculpture and installation, frequently using found objects, wood, and sheet metal to evoke sacred African-American rituals and images. *Similar Differences* was produced in concert with their first collaborative exhibition in a decade, *Secrets, Dialogues, Revelations*, which opened at UCLA's Wight Gallery in January 1990 and toured nationally in 1992.

Sacco, Joe

Joe Sacco: An Interview
SAIC Visiting Artist Program and Video Data Bank
2001, unedited, U.S., color, sound
Joe Sacco is a cartoonist who has contributed to a wide range of comic magazines including *Drawn and Quarterly, Prime Cuts, Real Stuff, Buzzard,* and *R. Crumb's Weirdo*; he continues to illustrate the semi-regular *Painfully Portland* cartoon strip for the *Willamette Week.* He was a recipient of the prestigious American Book Award in 1996 for his work *Palestine* (1996), which combines techniques of eyewitness reportage with comic strip storytelling. More recently Socco completed a 240-page exploration of a small Muslim enclave in Serbia, entitled *SAFE AREA GORAZDE: The War in Eastern Bosnia* (1992-1995) (2002), based on his travels to the war-torn region. Interview by Mark Pascal.

Sanchez, Juan

Juan Sanchez: An Interview
Video Data Bank
1990, 45:00, U.S., color, sound
Juan Sanchez explores his Puerto Rican heritage and the issue of Puerto Rican independence through his work as an artist and writer. Combining painting, photography, collage, and printmaking techniques, Sanchez's art joins images of contemporary barrio life with memories of Puerto Rico and addresses a fragmented Latino community fraught with political resistance and cultural alienation. Interview by Bibiana Suarez.

Sandin, Dan

Dan Sandin
Christine de Lignieres
1980, 18:00, U.S., color, sound
Dan Sandin designed the Image Processor that, partly because of his decision to give away his plans, has effected an energetic and aesthetic investigation of the technological structures of electronic media. He sees the Image Processor as both an event and an environment for artists to explore and experience. During the interview, Sandin spontaneously synthesizes his own image. Interview by John Manning.

Saul, Peter

Peter Saul: What Follows...
University of Colorado Visiting Artists Program
1988, 29:00, U.S., color, sound
Painter Peter Saul's iconoclastic paintings parody various aspects of contemporary American life, from politics to sex to violence. He has been an inspiration to several generations of American painters and is retired from the Department of Fine Arts at University of Texas-Austin. Interview by Jim Johnson.

Schapiro, Miriam

Miriam Schapiro: An Interview
Lyn Blumenthal and Kate Horsfield
1977, 38:00, U.S., b&w, sound
Miriam Schapiro was one of the great energies behind the feminist movement in art. Originally painting in an Abstract Expressionist manner, she developed a new, more personal style of assemblage she called "femmage" as she became more politically involved. She was also one of the first to create a curriculum on Feminist Art at CalArts. Interview by Lyn Blumenthal.

Schechner, Richard

Richard Schechner: An Interview
Video Data Bank
1989, 38:00, U.S., color, sound
Richard Schechner is Professor of Performance Studies at New York University, author of numerous books including *Performance Theory* (1988) and *The Future of Ritual* (1993), and editor of *The Drama Review*. This interview with Nancy Forest Brown was conducted during an event at the School of the Art Institute of Chicago. "Performers are very shrewd. ... The closer you get to them, the more you realize that as soon as you have a spectator situation artifice is involved. Because, if you're skilled at it, you become aware that there's a manipulative struggle going on between the eye looking and the creative self trying to control the eye that's trying to contain you."

Schjeldahl, Peter

Peter Schjeldahl: An Interview
Lyn Blumenthal and Kate Horsfield
1982/re-edited 2003, 46:00, color to b&w, sound
Peter Schjeldahl began writing his "poetical criticism" for Tom Hess at *ArtNews* in the mid 1960s. He has since written for both popular and specialized publications including *The New York Times*, *Art in America*, and *The Village Voice*, among others. In this interview from 1982, Schjeldahl discusses the critic's relationship to the artist, the audience, artwork, and the professional community of art critics. He also reads some of his own poetry. "Maybe at the root of the critical impulse is a kind of adolescent outrage of growing up and discovering that the world is not nearly what you'd hoped or thought it might be ... and that the art critic has invented a career of trying to ... move it over ... and make it more habitable for one's sensibility," he says in this interview with Robert Storr. Currently, Schjeldahl writes for the *New Yorker* and various art journals.

Serra, Richard

The Trial of Tilted Arc
Shu Lea Cheang
1986, 52:00, U.S., color, sound
The artwork on trial is Richard Serra's public sculpture *Tilted Arc*, commissioned and installed by the U.S. government in 1981. Four years later, a public hearing was held to consider the removal of the sculpture from its site in Federal Plaza in New York City. In documenting the climactic General Services Administration hearing, *The Trial of Tilted Arc* is a thought-provoking indictment of the state of the arts. At issue is the validity of a contract between an artist and the government, the freedom of artistic expression, and the "public's" involvement in designing the visual environment. In this dialogue/debate between the art community and the bureaucrats *Tilted Arc* has variously been described with terms ranging from "masterpiece" to "mouse trap."

Serrano, Andres

Andres Serrano: What Follows...
University of Colorado Visiting Artists Program
1991, 31:00, U.S., color, sound
Andres Serrano's work came to the attention of the general public as part of the controversy surrounding censorship and the NEA. His photograph, *Piss Christ*, was singled out by conservative forces as an example of the immorality and decadence of our society. Serrano's work incorporates bodily fluids and staged props to provoke questions on the nature of art, religion, and culture. This interview, from 1991, took place at the height of the controversy and features the artist discussing his work from the early stages of his career up to his Ku Klux Klan portrait series.

Sherman, Cindy

Cindy Sherman: Crossover Series
MICA-TV
1980, 10:00, U.S., color, sound
Cindy Sherman is best known for her black-and-white *Untitled Film Stills*, which she made in the late '70s and early '80s. In carefully designed settings and wearing a variety of costumes, wigs, and make-up, Sherman shot herself in various scenarios suggestive of B-movies from the 1950s. These tableaux touch on feminist theories of representation and body politics, though their mysterious quality allows for differing interpretations based on the perceived irony in the work. The shifting, changeable self that Sherman presents is closely allied with performance art and influenced much of postmodern art production to come. Sherman's later photographic series—generally in large, color formats—took on subjects such as pornography, Old Masters, and fairy-tales. In this tape, produced by MICA-TV, Sherman has assumed both roles as artist and interviewer.

Only available on the MICA-TV *Crossover Series* compilation.

Sigler, Hollis

Hollis Sigler 1983: An Interview
Lyn Blumenthal and Kate Horsfield
1983, 35:00, U.S., color, sound
Chicago-based painter Hollis Sigler discusses the influ-

ences and development of her work, from her early huge paintings of underwater swimmers to the wild, explosive, scratchy, dramatic autobiographical paintings of interiors for which she is known. "The sexuality that exists in the drawings isn't meant as a focus, except for the feeling part of it. How it's read by other people I never intended to be important. Some people look at them and wonder 'if it is a man and a woman or a woman and a woman—what's the sexuality of these people?' I can only say that sexuality enters into every relationship... whether it is with our parents, our siblings, or our friends. They are all like love affairs," Sigler says in this interview with Kate Horsfield.

Hollis Sigler 1996: An Interview
Kate Horsfield and B. Ruby Rich
1996, unedited, U.S., color, sound
In 1985, Hollis Sigler, a leading feminist artist in Chicago, was diagnosed with breast cancer, a disease that had also stricken her mother and great-grandmother. This interview with Hollis Sigler focuses on the period of her life beginning with the work entitled *Breast Cancer Journals*, a series of paintings, drawings, and collages expressing a wide range of emotional responses to the various stages of her struggle with cancer encompassing more than 100 works. *Art in America* called Sigler's *Breast Cancer Journal* "one of contemporary art's richest and most poignant treatments of sickness and health. Taking on a kind of religious conviction, her jewel-colored symbols imbue a death-haunted situation with miraculous, celebratory life." These works—and the commentaries that the artist inscribed on many of them—combine personal experience with family history, medical statistics, and political consciousness raising. Sigler had a 15-year struggle with breast cancer prior to her death in 2001. Interview by B. Ruby Rich.

Simmons, Laurie

Laurie Simmons: Crossover Series
MICA-TV
1982, 5:00, U.S., color, sound
Laurie Simmons's photographs are brought to life in *Laurie Simmons: A Teaser*, MICA-TV's portrait of the acclaimed photographer. In the early 1980s, Simmons focused on underwater photographs of women, which suggested the stylized tableaux of Esther Williams's water ballets. Taping through a glass window in the bottom of a swimming pool, Michael Owen and Carole Ann Klonarides recorded Simmons while she was shooting her models. The viewer observes Simmons's "bathing beauties" swimming in unchoreographed abandon, as Owen and Klonarides transform the video screen into an evocative, blue-filtered aquarium.
Only available on the MICA-TV *Crossover Series* compilation.

Simonds, Charles

Charles Simonds: An Interview
Lyn Blumenthal and Kate Horsfield
1979, 43:00, U.S., b&w, sound
Charles Simonds's sculptures are enchanting architectural miniatures. Most are landforms with small chambers and towers; some are abstract organic shapes. Carefully built brick by tiny brick, Simonds's sculptures engage the child in everyone. He began to build the small dwellings in the streets of New York City in the early 1970s. The dwellings were places along curbs or within the masonry of buildings—the homes of an imaginary group of migrating people whom Simonds called the "little people." Interview by Kate Horsfield.

Sischy, Ingrid

Ingrid Sischy
Artists TV Network
1980, 28:00, U.S., color, sound
Ingrid Sischy was editor of *Artforum* in the 1980s and has been editor-in-chief of *Interview* magazine since the 1990s. In this interview with Robin White, Sischy discusses *Artforum's* priorities, purpose, and goals. "It's an intricate history where painting, sculpture, performance, video, and photography are extremely connected to each other. As the editor of *Artforum*, I would feel at great fault to not include the best and the most interesting questions of each because they affect each other, and artists' choices are not made in a vacuum."

Smith, Alexis

Alexis Smith: "Life in America"
Peter Kirby
1991, 26:21, U.S., color, sound
For the past 20 years Alexis Smith's work has explored primal American myths: the open road, the bad/good guy/gal, the quest for romance, and the search for paradise. This portrait of the artist explores the roots of her thought and work and was produced in conjunction with her exhibition at the Whitney Museum of American Art in November 1991.

Snowden, Sylvia

Sylvia Snowden: What Follows...
University of Colorado Visiting Artists Program
1990, 29:00, U.S., color, sound
Washington, D.C.-based African-American artist Sylvia Snowden paints what she calls "figural or structural abstract expressionist" works. Three years after this tape was produced, her son was shot to death, and she spent the next three years producing 87 works in a variety of media.

Snyder, Bob

Bob Snyder: An Interview
Video Data Bank
1985, 40:00, U.S., color, sound
Bob Snyder is a Chicago-based composer, video artist, and author who has been experimenting with sound and video synthesis since the '60s. As a musician, his interest has always been in the relationship between music and visual imagery. In Snyder's work music is the central generative source of meaning, although he also creates a dialogue between sound and images of nature and architecture. Interview by Rafael Franca.

Spero, Nancy

Nancy Spero: An Interview
Lyn Blumenthal and Kate Horsfield
1982/re-edited 2003, 35:00, color to b&w, sound
Best known for her graphic imagery, Nancy Spero has worked as an oil painter on both paper and canvas and with prints. She has been active in many radical groups including WAR (Women Artists and Revolution) and AIR (Artists in Residence), the first women's cooperative gallery in New York.

Woman as Protagonist: The Art of Nancy Spero
Irene Sosa
1993, 45:00, U.S., color, sound
Woman as Protagonist: The Art of Nancy Spero is an invigorating look at the 40-year career of acclaimed feminist artist Nancy Spero, who, in her own works, is concerned with "rewriting the imaging of women through historical time." With Spero's own voice as narration, this documentary tracks her development as she matured against the grain of Abstract Expressionism, Minimalism, and Pop Art when "there wasn't room in the art world to make way for political or activist art." This tape includes footage of the artist at work on installations in the United States, Northern Ireland, and Spain that no longer exist.

Spiegelman, Art

Art Spiegelman: An Interview
Video Data Bank
1990, 29:00, U.S., color, sound
Art Spiegelman has long been acknowledged as one of our era's foremost comic book artists. However, it was *Maus*, published by Pantheon in two volumes in 1986 and 1991, which first brought his work to a mass audience. *Maus* tells the true family stories of a Jewish survivor of Nazi Germany and his cartoonist son. Portraying the Jews as mice and the Nazis as cats, the cartoon approaches the "unspeakable through diminutive." *Maus* won a Pulitzer Prize—the first, and only, graphic novel to do so. Spiegelman is co-founder/editor of *Raw*, the acclaimed magazine of avant-garde comics and graphics. Interview by Mark Pascale.

Steir, Pat

Pat Steir 1975: An Interview
Lyn Blumenthal and Kate Horsfield
1975, 60:00, U.S., b&w, sound
In the 1970s Pat Steir's work thought through signs and symbols and was close to Minimal and Conceptual art, though she didn't quite fit into either category. She developed an iconography that included isolated brushstrokes, color charts, words, and crossed-out images. Interview by Kate Horsfield.

Pat Steir 1980: An Interview
Lyn Blumenthal and Kate Horsfield
1980, 45:00, U.S., color, sound
In this interview, Pat Steir discusses the influences and development of her work, which is characterized by pencil scrawls, words, and squiggled notations that echo, repeat, punctuate, and change. In this tape, as in her

work, Pat Steir persistently moves in and out of the frame, yet her restlessness stands for freedom rather than discontent. "Thinking about what the next idea will be or where it will go is a very narrow consideration," Steir says in this interview with Kate Horsfield. "Art is really about a curiosity and a romance with being alive and … very silent, personal insight about the way that things fit together."

Pat Steir 1993: An Interview
Video Data Bank
1993, 60:00, U.S., color, sound
This interview was made around the time of the *Elective Affinities* exhibition in which Steir continues to develop the abstract waterfall images. She discusses the threads in all her previous styles that lead up to the waterfall imagery. Interview by Kate Horsfield.

Stuart, Michelle

Michelle Stuart: An Interview
Lyn Blumenthal and Kate Horsfield
1978, 36:00, U.S., color, sound
Michelle Stuart works with natural materials, rubbing and pounding rock fragments into hand-made paper. Her work begins with the selection of a site and then collects fragments to use as tools on paper. She has recently begun to compile small objects (a bone, a feather) and layers of rubbed paper into book format. The volumes collect artifacts found on the site, recording its geographical history and passage through time. Interview by Kate Horsfield.

Survival Research Laboratories

A Bitter Message of Hopeless Grief
Jonathan Reiss and Survival Research Laboratories
1988, 13:00, U.S., color, sound, 16mm to video
Performance engineers Survival Research Laboratories (SRL) construct machines that live in their own fictional world, acting out scenarios of perpetual torment, exasperated consumption, and tragic recognition. This film presents a fractured narrative featuring these large anthropomorphic robots and represents Jonathan Reiss and SRL's collaborative desire to go beyond the restraints of event documentation.

Pleasures of Uninhibited Excess
Jonathan Reiss and Survival Research Laboratories
1990, 45:00, U.S., color, sound
Pleasures of Uninhibited Excess documents three shows by Survival Research Laboratories: *Illusions of Shameless Abundance Degenerating into an Uninterrupted Sequence of Hostile Encounters* (San Francisco, 28 May 1989), *Computer Generated Installation at ArtsSpace* (San Francisco, 11 July-19 August 1989), and *A Carnival of Misplaced Devotion Calculated to Arouse Resentment for the Principles of Order* (Seattle, 23 June 1990). This tape combines footage of SRL's destructive, noisy, and flame-throwing machines in action with audience reactions to SRL's simulations of hazardous experiences. The engineers and programmers of SRL delight in the machinery's anarchic danger, commenting on an electrical tower's

20-30-foot "kill radius" and the physiological dangers of high-volume frequencies. Interviews with SRL director Mark Pauline illuminate the group's processes and intentions. Pauline comments, "Anything that powerful seems like it should be illegal." But, as one observer states, "Art can affect you, and art should affect you."

A Scenic Harvest from the Kingdom of Pain
Jonathan Reiss, Joe Rees, and Survival Research Laboratories
1984, 42:00, U.S., color, sound
Flesh meets robotics in this early video documentation of SRL's spectacular exhibitions of collective invention, anti-corporate technology, and satirical mass destruction. In the performances documented here, various animal corpses are integrated into the action as the clawed and spiked machines attack dummies, each other, and, occasionally, the audience. The tape begins with the song "Stairwell to Hell," an appropriate prologue.

The Will to Provoke
Jonathan Reiss and Survival Research Laboratories
1988, 43:00, U.S., color, sound
Director Jonathan Reiss and cinematographer/editor Leslie Asako Gladsjo traveled to Europe with SRL to produce this entertaining and challenging portrait of the innovative group of artist technicians. The tape shows their machines in action and provides insight to their inspirations, political objectives, and budgetary constraints. The tape also reveals SRL's efforts to confound and confront their foreign audiences with an artform that is, perhaps, uniquely American.

Tagg, John

John Tagg: An Interview
Video Data Bank
1990, 40:00, U.S., color, sound
John Tagg is a writer, educator, and a leading contributor to the development of art-historical and photographic theory, focusing on political analysis of institutionalized culture and interventions within it. He is a professor of art history at State University of New York-Binghamton and author of *Grounds of Dispute: Art History, Cultural Politics and the Discursive Field* (1992) and *The Burden of Representation: Essays on Photographies and Histories* (1988). Interview by James Hugunin.

Teasdale, Parry

Parry Teasdale: An Interview
Video Data Bank
2000, unedited, U.S., color, sound
Parry Teasdale is a founding member of the early alternative media group Videofreex and its off-shoot Media Bus. More recently, he published a historical memoir, *Videofreex: America's First Pirate TV Station and the Catskills Collective That Turned It On* (1999). Interview by Kate Horsfield

Tisdale, Danny

Danny Tisdale: An Interview
Video Data Bank
1992, 40:00 unedited, U.S., color, sound

Danny Tisdale's performance installations critique and challenge the prevailing notions of race and assimilation by allowing passers-by the opportunity to explore different racial identities. He has also produced projects that examine policies of museum archiving and display and that expose the chameleon-like nature of politics promoting a political platform.

Tomaselli, Fred

Fred Tomaselli: An Interview
SAIC Visiting Artist Program and Video Data Bank
1998, unedited, U.S., color, sound
Fred Tomaselli's mosaics and collages compose patterns and images that suggest ancient global influences. His materials, however, are products of modern consumption, addiction, bodily abuse, and pleasure: pills, nicotine patches, bandages, and the like. The surfaces are coated with a lacquered veneer, making these mundane sources of highs or healing gleam. Interview by James Rondeau.

Torreano, John

John Torreano's Art World Wizard
MICA-TV
1986, 28:00, U.S., b&w and color, sound
Modeled after NBC's long-running science program *Watch Mr. Wizard*, this tape features painter John Torreano as Mr. Wizard, instructing a skeptical boy on how to build a diamond out of pieces of wood. The boy remains unimpressed until Torreano uses a "video paintbox" to create flashy special effects. Torreano's use of galaxy clusters as a reference for his fake jewel-studded canvases and diamond-shaped sculptures suggested the nostalgic format of this video profile by MICA-TV.

Tucker, Marcia

Marcia Tucker: An Interview
Lyn Blumenthal and Kate Horsfield
1974, 30:00 (unedited), U.S., b&w, sound
Tucker had just left her post as curator at the Whitney Museum of American Art. She was in Chicago presenting slides of paintings by emerging women artists such as Pat Steir, Louise Fishman, Joan Snyder, and many others. This short interview was the first made by Lyn Blumenthal and Kate Horsfield.

Marcia Tucker: An Interview
Lyn Blumenthal and Kate Horsfield
1977, 49:00, U.S., color, sound
Marcia Tucker founded and was the first director of the New Museum of Contemporary Art. This interview was taped in 1977, a few months prior to the New Museum's opening, offering rare insight into an arts institution and its administration during its development. "What artists don't like about the museums is that the museums don't like artists. They don't like artists because they can't be controlled, preserved, categorized or tucked away. Also, museum people say that artists are egocentric. Of course they are, think of the nature of the enterprise! They have to both make it and support it themselves," Tucker says in this interview with Kate Horsfield.

Tworkov, Jack

Jack Tworkov: An Interview
Lyn Blumenthal and Kate Horsfield
1981/re-edited 2003, 48:00, color to b&w, sound
Jack Tworkov was an important member of the first generation of Abstract Expressionist painters and was, for a number of years, head of the Yale University art program. Late in his career, his work became more geometric, as the mark and gesture was increasingly determined by isometric grid structures. This tape was shot a year before Tworkov's death in 1982. "I came to the conclusion that the subconscious was banal. I began looking for some kind of form for constants that you could hold on to," Tworkov says in this interview with Kate Horsfield. "Given a grid, the possibility of forms becomes infinite. What you choose is still spontaneous."

Ukeles, Mierle Laderman

Mierle Laderman Ukeles: An Interview
Video Data Bank
1991, 50:00, U.S., color, sound
Since 1977 Mierle Laderman Ukeles has been a volunteer artist-in-residence at the New York City Department of Sanitation, allowing her to introduce radical art into a public system. Since she wrote the *Manifesto for Maintenance Art* (1969), virtually all of Ukeles's work has been public. Recent permanent commissions include *Percent for Art Fresh Kills Landfill Project*, New York City, the world's largest landfill; *Schuylkill River Park*, Philadelphia; *Creative Time*, New York City; and *Ayalon Park*, Israel. Her temporary exhibitions include installations about Israel's landfill at the Tel Aviv Museum and *Unburning Freedom Hall* at the Los Angeles Museum of Contemporary Art. Interview by Craig Adcock.

Vance, Carole S.

Carole S. Vance: An Interview
Video Data Bank
1990, 42:00, U.S., color, sound
Carole S. Vance is an anthropologist and writer and Associate Research Scientist of Public Health and Director of the Program for the Study of Sexuality, Gender, Health and Human Rights at Columbia University. She has written extensively on sexuality and public policy, as well as issues of gender, health, and medical anthropology. Her books include *Pleasure and Danger: Exploring Female Sexuality* (1984 and 1993) and *Caught Looking: Feminism, Pornography, and Censorship* (1988). Interview by Carole Tormollan.

Vasulkas, The

Binary Lives: Steina and Woody Vasulka
Peter Kirby
1997, 46:00, U.S., color, sound
In 1964, Steina Vasulka (then Steinunn Bjarnadottir) married Woody Vasulka, a Czech engineer with a background in film. They later moved to New York where, with Andreas Mannik, they founded The Kitchen, a performance space dedicated to new media. The Vasulkas collaborated on a series of video works whose imagery arose primarily through the manipulation of the video signal at the level of the electron beam itself. This master-fully constructed documentary by Peter Kirby gives insight into the pioneering impact of their lives and work. A must-see for any follower of electronic media.

Vitiello, Stephen

Stephen Vitiello: An Interview
Video Data Bank
2001, unedited, U.S., color, sound
Electronic musician and sound artist Stephen Vitiello creates sonic installations that function to give a physical form or space to audio. He has also composed soundtracks for film and media artists such as Nam June Paik, Tony Oursler, and Dara Birnbaum. Interview by Kate Horsfield.

Vogel, Dorothy and Herbert

Dorothy and Herbert Vogel
David Ross/LBMA Video
1975-79, 13:00, U.S., color, sound
Part of the Long Beach Museum of Art's *Collectors of the Seventies* series, this tape enters the home and art collection of Dorothy and Herbert Vogel. The Vogels live in a nondescript high-rise in the Yorkville section of New York City's East Side. Their three and a half rooms serve as their museum for Larry Poons, Robert Morris, Philip Pearlstein, Robert Mangold, Sylvia Mangold, Dennis Oppenheim, Richard Nonas, Richard Tuttle, Sol Lewitt, Dan Graham, John Chamberlain, Christo, Donald Judd, Carl Andre, and Robert Ryman. Interview by Douglas Davis.

Wall, Jeff

Jeff Wall: An Interview
SAIC Visiting Artist Program and Video Data Bank
1999, unedited, U.S., color, sound
Although trained as an art historian, Jeff Wall has been working on his expansive light boxes of staged scenes for more than 25 years. Using back-lit, photographic transparencies typically used for advertising display, Wall subverts their commercial association by filling them with quotidian objects.

Wallace, Michele

Michele Wallace: An Interview
Kate Horsfield and Ellen Spiro
1991, 43:00, U.S., color, sound
Michele Wallace's attention to the invisibility and/or fetishization of black women in the gallery and museum worlds has made possible new critical thinking around the intersection of race and gender in African-American visual and popular culture, particularly in what she has called "the gap around the psychoanalytic" in contemporary African-American critical discourse. Wallace has taught creative writing at several universities, as well as women's studies at the City College of New York. She is author of *Black Macho and the Myth of the Superwoman* (1979 and 1990), *Invisibility Blues: From Pop to Theory* (1990) and the organizer of *Black Popular Culture*, edited by Gina Dent (1992). Wallace has written widely on feminism, gender, art, and culture for such publications as *The Village Voice, The New York Times, Ms. Magazine, Artforum, The Nation, Art in*

America, Transition, Renaissance, Noire, Aperture, and *Essence*, as well as a range of other journals.

Wiley, William T.

William T. Wiley: An Interview
Lyn Blumenthal and Kate Horsfield
1979, 39:00, U.S., b&w, sound
William T. Wiley combines a variety of materials (found objects, wood, animal hides, rope, paint) with poetry, puns, hearsay, and legends to present a very complex and enigmatic personal vision. Besides making sculpture, he also does prints, drawings, and paintings. His witty and often ironic work emphasizes both the commonality and impenetrability of everyday life and its contents. Wiley continues to live and work in the San Francisco Bay area. "Walking down the road, something will catch your eye, and you pick it up. An object, forked stick, piece of glass, that object has the power to stimulate 'I know right where this will go' and gives me an idea," Wiley says in this interview with Kate Horsfield.

Williams, Linda

Linda Williams: An Interview
Video Data Bank
1993, 30:00, color, sound
Linda Williams writes on what she calls "body genres": melodrama, horror, and, most famously, pornography. One of the most influential feminist film scholars to emerge in the 1980s, she wrote important essays on women's film (melodrama) before publishing her most influential work, *Hard Core: Power, Pleasure, and the Frenzy of the Visible* (1989 and 1999). *Hard Core* studies the visual modes and political meanings of pornography–that enormously popular but ill-reputed strain of cinema that had largely been neglected by academia–in a rigorous study without getting bogged down in the divisive anti-pornography versus sex-positive feminist debates. Williams's most recent monograph is *Playing the Race Card: Melodramas of Black and White, from Uncle Tom to O.J. Simpson* (2001). She is a professor in the rhetoric department and director of film studies at University of California-Berkeley.

Williams, Pat Ward

Pat Ward Williams: An Interview
Video Data Bank
1990, 40:00, U.S., color, sound
Pat Ward Williams's socially charged works confront issues of race, often dealing specifically with African-American history and identity. Using a variety of photographic processes, video, audio tapes, assemblage and text, Williams layers meanings and images. Her subjects range from the autobiographical to the public, often combining documentary techniques with personal responses. "When I make photos about my family, I think my family is not a lot different than other peoples' families, so that is a way people can access my work … and have it move them also," Williams says in this interview with Angela Kelly.

Wilson, David

David Wilson: An Interview
SAIC Visiting Artist Program and Video Data Bank
1998, unedited, U.S., color, sound
David Wilson is the founder and curator of the Museum of Jurassic Technology in Los Angeles. His collection of found and contributed objects provides an astonishing array of materials derived from craft and nature. Interview by Rachel Weiss.

Wilson, Millie

Millie Wilson: An Interview
SAIC Visiting Artist Program and Video Data Bank
1998, unedited, U.S., color, sound
Millie Wilson is an installation artist whose work proposes a relationship between modernist art practices and modernity's production of deviance, particularly regarding lesbian stereotypes. She uses humor, parody, and beauty as disruptive strategies to insist on a dyke presence in postmodern revisionism. Wilson has exhibited her work internationally and is on faculty at CalArts. Interview by Robert Blanchon.

Winsor, Jackie

Jackie Winsor: What Follows…
University of Colorado Visiting Artists Program
1988, 27:10, U.S., color, sound
Sculptor Jackie Winsor creates large-scale constructions in wood, fiber, twine, and wire. Recent works are subjected to explosions and fire. Winsor lives and works in New York City. Interview by Kay Miller and Albert Alhadeff.

Jackie Winsor: Works in Progress
Liza Béar
1975-78, 56:00, U.S., b&w and color, sound
This is a three-part tape shot in 1975, '76, and '78 as Winsor was working on three pieces: *50/50, Copper Piece,* and *Burnt Piece.* The rhythms and rituals of her working process as well as her comments on the work are documented. Part 3 is the only filmic record of the final stage of construction of *Burnt Piece.*

Zeisler, Claire

Claire Zeisler: An Interview
Patricia Erens
1979, 34:00, U.S., color, sound
Fiber artist Claire Ziesler discusses her techniques, ideas on art, and training; the conversation is inter-cut with images from her 1979 retrospective at the Art Institute of Chicago. "I … realized I cannot change my techniques too often. I would rather use techniques that I know and keep on perfecting them because I feel that in keeping on and perfecting them, I'm going to find something else to say," Zeisler says in this interview with Rhona Hoffman. "I thought at the time that an artist had to change techniques, change ideas, keep current with what's going on, and that's very superficial."

A Tribute to Claire Zeisler
Scott Rankin and Dennis Adrian

1991, 14:00, U.S., color, sound
In this tape made shortly after fiber and sculpture artist Claire Zeisler's death, art critic Dennis Adrian discusses her influence and aesthetic strategies. Adrian's commentary is inter-cut with images of her work and archival footage of an interview with the artist.

Multiple Artists and Movements (listed alphabetically by maker)

Artists TV Network

Alternatives in Retrospect
Artists TV Network
1981, 56:00, U.S., color, sound
This tape presents a history of alternative spaces in New York City during the late 1960s and early 1970s, focusing on two galleries that no longer exist. The work produced in these two spaces forms the basis of the New Museum of Contemporary Art's 1981 exhibition *Alternatives in Retrospect: An Overview 1969-1975.* Curator Jacki Apple, who produced the tape, assembled documentation from the galleries and reconstructed artworks for the exhibition. "I remember people saying that galleries had certain kinds of disadvantages. I saw these disadvantages ... and thought there should be some kind of free space where there wasn't any jurisdiction of criteria, so that art could grow in a very natural way," Jeffrey Lew, Founder of 112 Greene Street, says.

Performance Work (The Live! Show)
Artists TV Network
1982, 28:00, U.S., color, sound
In this episode of *The Live! Show*, hosted by Jaime Davidovich, Eric Bogosian brings seven characters to life in seven minutes, Michael Smith plays the best driver in the world, Mitchell Kriegman offers a helping hand during the show's popular call-in segment, and Louis Grenier demonstrates the organic face lift viewers can do at home.

Perspectives on the Avant Garde
Artists TV Network
1981, 58:00, U.S., color, sound
This tape examines the meaning, impact, and future of the early-1980s avant-garde through interviews with artists (Scott B., Robert Longo, Walter Robinson, Michael Smith), an art dealer (Helene Winer, Metro Pictures), a museum director (Marcia Tucker, The New Museum of Contemporary Art), and an art historian (Roselee Goldberg). "Whenever you feel confident that you know what's happening at the outside edge, something's always happening that you don't know about. The avant-garde, if it exists at all... is determined by the artist, not the peripheral people like myself," Tucker says.

Time and Space Concepts
Artists TV Network
1978, 1:21:00, U.S., color, sound
This tape was produced by Artists TV Network, documenting a symposium that included composer John Cage, choreographer Merce Cunningham, writer Richard Kostelanetz, and video artist Nam June Paik with art critic Dore Ashton serving as moderator. This free-wheeling symposium taped before a live audience ranges from individual reminiscences to discussion of then-current art community concerns about music, literature, theater, art, dance, video, and technology.

Beatty, Maria

Sphinxes without Secrets
Maria Beatty
1990, 58:00, U.S., color, sound
Sphinxes without Secrets is an energetic and transgressive account of outstanding female performance artists and an invaluable document of feminist avant-garde work of the 1970s and '80s. No Mona Lisa smiles here, as performance artists reveal what outrages and delights them. Performers, curators, and critics unravel the mysteries of a new art form and ponder the world women confront today. This tape establishes that it was feminist artists who first exploited performance for purposes of self-empowerment, cultural criticism, and the presentation of revisionist histories. *Sphinxes without Secrets* is an invaluable teaching tool: insightful, thorough, and engaging. Featuring Diamanda Galas, Holly Hughes, Robbie McCauley, and Rachel Rosenthal with brief clips of Lenora Champagne, Ellie Covan, Ron Ehmke, Adrian Piper, Arlene Raven, Mark Russell, Carolee Schneemann, Dianne Torr, and Martha Wilson; plus Laurie Anderson, Laurie Carlos, Ann Carlson, Dancenoise, Jessica Hagadorn, Jennie Hutchins, Judith Jackson, Joan Jonas, Lisa Kron, Suzanne Lacy, Carol Leigh, Pat Oleszko, Marty Pottenger, Liz Prince, Nancy Reilly, Reno, Beatrice Roth, Louise Smith, Annie Sprinkle, and Johanna Went.

Blumenthal, Lyn

Women with a Past
Lyn Blumenthal
1988, 1:20:00, U.S., b&w and color, sound
Women with a Past brings together four 20th century artists—Yvonne Rainer, Christine Choy, Martha Rosler, and Nancy Spero—in videotaped interviews, shaped and edited by Lyn Blumenthal to examine the art of documentary. In a skillfully woven series of scenes in which the interviewer's voice is not heard, the interviewees appear to be talking directly, intimately to the viewer. Blumenthal used short segments of each woman's work to demonstrate how her philosophical and political stances are articulated.

Fellows of Contemporary Art

Experience: Perception, Interpretation, Illusion
Joe Leonardi/Fellows of Contemporary Art
1989, 14:00, U.S., color, sound
Consisting of 13 brief spots, *Experience: Perception, Interpretation, Illusion* features works by artists showing in a Pasadena Armory exhibition. Curator Noel Korten says the artists in the show have all reached mid-career and are now less concerned with expanding the boundaries of contemporary art than on reflecting back on culture through their own perspectives. Artists include Karen Carsen, John Outterbridge, Michael C. McMillen, Margit Omar, Scott Geiger, Jerry McMillan, James Doolin, Carol Caroompas, John Valadez, Michael Davis,

William Leavitt, Ann Page, and Raul Guerrero.
Only available on the *Fellows of Contemporary Art* compilation.

Fellows of Contemporary Art compilation
A compilation tape that includes profiles of artists produced by the independent contemporary arts support organization.
Contents:
Experience: Perception, Interpretation, Illusion, Joe Leonardi/Fellows of Contemporary Art, 1989, 14:00, U.S., color, sound
Frame and Context: Richard Ross, Fellows of Contemporary Art, 1989, 12:00, U.S., color, sound
Helen and Newton Harrison: Altering Discourse, Fellows of Contemporary Art, 1989, 12:00, U.S., color, sound
Horace Bristol: Photojournalist, Fellows of Contemporary Art, 1988, 11:35, U.S., color, sound
Red Is Green: Jud Fine, Fellows of Contemporary Art, 1988, 10:41, U.S., color, sound

LMBA Video (Long Beach Museum of Art)

Artist Profile Series (Hill, Harding, Birnbaum, Em, Viola, and Almy
Joseph Leonardi/LBMA Video
1981-3, 47:41, U.S., color, sound
This collection includes profiles of six artists, most of them working in video: Gary Hill (08:30), Noel Harding (06:48), Dara Birnbaum (10:00), David Em (05:55), Bill Viola (10:00), and Max Almy (03:30). Hill speaks about his introduction into the video work and his use of mechanical—rather than computer—technology to produce his sonic images. Installation artist Harding states, "In art we get confused with what the issue is, really. … My ideas are more important than the medium." Documentation reveals that his media for the exhibition *Enclosure for Conventional Habit* include chickens in a glassed-in runway and mobile plants on a track. Birnbaum speaks about working in between the art world and commercial television. "Video cannot define itself solely in term of art but also has to define itself in terms of television," she states. "For me that was very important and carried with it the kind of social responsibility that I very much believe in." Painter, video artist, and sometime sculptor Em addresses the ways medium specificity fixes an artist's identity and raises the question of whether electronic or mechanically produced works really are art. He says he would be most content leaving technology behind and working with natural media such as plants and rocks in the desert. Video artist Viola speaks about his efforts to problematize the video medium through technical experiments and to reconfigure time through expansion and compression. Viola also argues for the importance of sound in video work, suggesting that ambient noise is a constant in lived experience. Almy expresses her pre-millennial anxiety and wonder at technology; in this brief tape she also admits that stylishness is a primary concern in her work.

The Artists: Part 1 (Belinoff, Krusoe, Holmes, and Clark)
LBMA Video
1988, 26:00, U.S., color, sound
This tape features California artists: drawer and painter Deanne Belinoff, sculptor and poet Sana Krusoe, wood relief carver and painter Palema Holmes, and New York-based video artist Shirley Clark. *The Artists: Part 1* was produced in concert with the exhibition *Four Solo Exhibitions* at the Long Beach Museum of Art in 1988. The artists are introduced by LBMA's senior curator Josine Ianco-Starrels. The tape presents and contrasts the diverse styles, media, and personalities of these four women artists.

The Artists: Part 2 (Dill, Walding, and Delap)
LBMA Video
1988, 16:00, U.S., color, sound
This tape profiles the work and insight of California artists: sculptor, painter, and installation artist Laddie John Dill and painter and sculptor Clark Walding. It also includes a mini-documentary on Tony Delap's *The Big Wave*, a public art sculpture that crosses Wilshire Boulevard in Santa Monica.

The Artists: Part 3 (Baron, Nadius, and Robinson)
LBMA Video
1987-88, 26:00, U.S., color, sound
Part 3 profiles three California women artists: sculptor and lint and installation artist Slater Baron, mixed media installation artist Beverly Nadius, and book artist Sue Ann Robinson.

The Artists: Performance Art (Coates, Rosenthal, and Paul Drecher Ensemble)
LBMA Video
1988, 35:00, U.S., color, sound
This tape compiles three profiles of performance artists: *A Creative Synthesis: George Coates Performance Works* (10:00), *The Performance World of Rachel Rosenthal* (16:00), and *Paul Dresher Ensemble* (08:00). The two LBMA-produced tapes use interviews with the artists to illuminate documentation of performances that combine singing, movement, costume, music, projection; the *Paul Drecher Ensemble* originated when performers working with Coates decided to branch off and explore different strategies. Both groups, however, stress the centrality of collaboration to their processes. Rachel Rosenthal directed her self-portrait, with post-production at LBMA. She autobiographically recounts her transient experiences of emigrating from France to Portugal to Brazil to the U.S., and offers evidence of her power and singular wit as a performer. "The oscillating tension between being an artist and an asshole is killing me," she quips. Her performances explore themes of identity and masquerade, aging, and mortality.

The Artists: Photography (Knowlton, Burchfield, and Giles)
LBMA Video
1987 and 1989, 38:00, U.S., color, sound
This tape contains two programs on contemporary photography produced by LBMA Video, which combine

artist interviews, documentation of the artists' processes, and still images of their finished works. The first program, made in 1989, profiles two photographers who expand the boundaries of photography: Charlene Knowlton, who merges painting with photography by shooting models who have been hand-painted, and Jerry Burchfield, who creates photograms (cameraless images on photo-sensitive paper) using human subjects who leave light-reliefs on the surface of the work. The second program is a 1987 episode of *Art Off the Wall*, hosted by Stephen Garrett, featuring an interview with William Giles by Garrett and Senior Curator Josine Ianco-Starrels during an exhibition at Long Beach Museum of Art. Giles creates textural photographs, informed by a period of childhood blindness when his sense of touch had to "see" for his failing eyes. Through his camera, he transforms landscapes and found objects so that a piece of metal resembles a cow's eye and tar drippings on a roof suggest hieroglyphics. The artists on this tape offer contrasting approaches to the photographic medium: Burchfield resists the mediation of a camera, whereas Giles says, "I don't really see things until I see through my camera." The first segment was directed by Joe Leonardi and Cathleen Kane; the second by Leonardi.

Thank You You're So Beautiful
Joe Leonardi and Cathleen Kane/LBMA Video
1988, 10:43, U.S., color, sound
This tape is a media arts collaboration between Joe Leonardi, Cathleen Kane, and radio artist Joe Frank. It is a synthesis of three "dark humored" radio pieces adapted for video.

Viewpoints on Video: Envisioning the Black Aesthetic
Long Beach Museum of Art
1989, 54:03, U.S., color, sound
This tape was produced in connection with *Icono Negro*, a three-artist show at Long Beach Museum of Art exploring the dynamics and distinctions of black video art. Three works featured in the show—including Tony Cokes's *Black Celebration*, Philip Mallory Jones's *What Goes Around*, and Lawrence Andrews's *An I for an I*— are shown in their entireties and commented upon by curator Claire Aguilar and video artists Ulysses Jenkins and O. Funmilayo Makarah. This tape presents an all-too-rare case of art presented in full and in dialogue with critical response.

Viewpoints on Video: Open Channels
Long Beach Museum of Art
1990, 56:00, U.S., color, sound
This tape surveys the works supported during the first five years of Open Channels, a grant program sponsored by Long Beach Museum of Art that gives artists production facilities at local cable stations, critical feedback from staff, and exhibition at the museum and on cable. Although essentially a promotional video, this tape offers insight into the important but rarely portrayed issues of artist funding and residencies. This retrospective offers excerpts from and context for 24 tapes, including *Open Channels I*: Mary Daval's *5 Dances for Small Spaces*, Scott Rankin's *Fugue*, Aron Ranen and Kevin Bender's *Television Believers*, Sherry Millner's *Scenes from the Micro War*, and Ezra Litwaks' *Stranded*; *Open Channels II*: David Stout's *Prisoner of Light*, Ed Jones's *Bemused in Babylon*, Jeanne Finley's *Common Mistakes*, John Arvanites's *Blues for Piggy*, and Tony Labat's *Mayami: Between Cut and Action*; *Open Channels III*: David Bunn's *The Torrid Zone*, Jim Shaw's *Billy Goes to a Party #4*, Paul McCarthy's *Family Tyranny*, Donna Matorin's *Quickening*, and Paul Kos's *Tower of Babel*; *Open Channels IV*: Lynn Kirby and Erika Suderburg's *Memory Inversion (Los Angeles)*, Bruce and Norman Yonemoto with Jeffrey Vallance's *Blinky*, Jayce Salloum's *Once You've Shot the Gun You Can't Stop the Bullet*, Victoria Bearden's *There Is No History in Heaven*, and Hilja Keading's *Let Me (Entertain You)*; and *Open Channels V*: Lawrence Andrews's *Strategies for the Development of/Redesigning the Purpose Served, Art in the Age of ... aka, The Making of the Towering Inferno*, Nancy Buchanan's *Mouth(Piece)*, Fu-Ding Cheng's *The Winged Cage*, and Paul Tassie's *Remember Flavor*.

MICA-TV

Crossover Series (Sherman, Prince, Simmons)
MICA-TV
1981-82, 26:00, U.S., color, sound
In ten-minute segments devoted to three photographers (Cindy Sherman, Richard Prince, Laurie Simmons), MICA-TV uses video to mirror the photographic techniques of each artist. For example, Sherman tells a faux interviewer about her work, while morphing into the different "B-movie" characters represented in her photos.

New Urban Landscapes Exhibition
MICA-TV
1988, 23:00, U.S., color, sound
In 1988 the World Financial Center asked artists and architects to produce installations that centered on "the rapid development of the modern city and its enormous impact on how people live and work" for the *New Urban Landscapes* exhibition. MICA-TV produced profiles of the artists whose work was featured in the show, including Vito Acconci, Dennis Adams and Andrea Blum, Joel Otterson, Kawamata, Mierle Laderman Ukeles, Jon Kessler, Jean Nouvel, Stephen Willats, Martha Schwartz, and Haim Steinbach.

Muntadas, Antonio

Between the Frames
Antonio Muntadas
1992, 6:00:00, U.S., color, sound
"Begun in 1983 and completed in 1992, *Between the Frames* offers a glimpse into contemporary history that is already past, a portrait of personalities and opinions shaping what and how art reaches a public forum. Initiated in response to the radical shift of values apparent in the 1980s, when 'product' and 'performance' were measurable and desirable, and [when] painting styles and supply-and-demand forces emerged as the main topics of discussion in contemporary art. Muntadas's four-hour compilation of interviews with

'players' from several countries was completed just as the bottom had fallen out of the buy-and-sell game. Issues other than prestige and financial gain were again in effect."
–Barbara London, *Muntadas: Between the Frames* program notes (New York: Museum of Modern Art, 1994)
Contents:

The Dealers: Between the Frames, Chapter 1 and *The Galleries: Between the Frames, Chapter 3*, Antonio Muntadas, 1991, 37:26, U.S., color, sound, in English, French, Spanish, Catalan, Portuguese, and Italian
The Collectors: Between the Frames, Chapter 2, Antonio Muntadas, 1991, 20:40, U.S., color, sound
The Museum: Between the Frames, Chapter 4, Antonio Muntadas, 1991, 53:17, U.S., color, sound, in English, French, Spanish, and Catalan
The Docents: Between the Frames, Chapter 5, Antonio Muntadas, 1991, 13:00, U.S., color, sound
The Critics: Between the Frames, Chapter 6, Antonio Muntadas, 1991, 53:50, U.S., color, sound, in English, French, and Italian
The Media: Between the Frames, Chapter 7, Antonio Muntadas, 1991, 49:09, U.S., color, sound, in English, French, and Catalan
Epilogue: Between the Frames, Chapter 8, Antonio Muntadas, 1991, 38:32, U.S., color, sound in English, Italian, French, and Portuguese

The Dealers: Between the Frames, Chapter 1 and *The Galleries: Between the Frames, Chapter 3*
Antonio Muntadas
1991, 37:26, U.S., color, sound, in English, French, Spanish, Catalan, Portuguese, and Italian
Between the Frames begins when art goes to market. Chapters 1 and 3, which focus on major U.S. and European dealers and galleries, are integrated into a single tape. The dealers and gallerists appear in talking-head format, discussing their roles, values, markets, networks, fashions, and audiences. The speakers—including Lucio Amelio, Daniel Templon, Ronald Feldman, Leo Castelli, Richard Kuhlenschmidt, Ivan Karp, and Holly Solomon, Ileana Sonnabend, Mario Diacono, Rodolphe Stadler, Michel Durand-Dessert, Joan de Muga, Marisa Díez, Glenn Lewis, Marian Goodman, Richard Bellamy, Rosamund Felsen, Joy Silverman, Mary Boone, Helen Winer, and Al Nodal—are not identified until the end of the tape, and their voices are recorded in native languages without subtitles. The interviews are connected with images shot from the Vancouver Skytrain, an automated transit system that was newly finished when Muntadas shot the footage.

The Collectors: Between the Frames, Chapter 2
Antonio Muntadas
1991, 20:40, U.S., color, sound
Art collectors offer various explanations of why and what they acquire. With Herman Daled, Robert Rowan, Eric and Sylvie Boissonas, Giuseppe Panza di Biumo, Marcia Weisman, Fernando Vijande, Bob Calle, Acey and Bill Wolgin, Gianni Rampa, Isabel de Pedro, Rafael Tous, and Toshio Ohara.

The Museum: Between the Frames, Chapter 4
Antonio Muntadas
1991, 53:17, U.S., color, sound, in English, French, Spanish, and Catalan
Curators and museum directors discuss the role of the museum in presenting, preserving, and contexualizing works of art for their visitors. Interview subjects represents such museums as the Centre Pompidou, Van Abbe Museum, Neue Gallery, Basler Kunstverein, Mönchengladbach Museum, W.R. Museum, Kunstmuseum Luzern, Palazzo dei Diamanti, Muse d'Art de Catalunya, Philadelphia Museum, Institute of Contemporary Art-Boston, Hayden Gallery-MIT, Whitney Museum of American Art, Museum of Modern Art, Tel Aviv Museum of Art, Israel Museum, Museum of Contemporary Art-Los Angeles, Santa Barbara Museum, Solomon R. Guggenheim Museum, New Museum of Contemporary Art, DIA Art Foundation, Centro de Arte Reina Sofia, Porticus, and Musée d'art contemporain. The subjects' comments are inter-cut with the perpetual motion of escalators in close-up.

The Docents: Between the Frames, Chapter 5
Antonio Muntadas
1991, 13:00, U.S., color, sound
Although it appears sequentially as Chapter 5 in the series, *The Docents* was the first episode completed for this project. In this installment, museum tour guides share their views on contemporary art as well as gallery goers who may not "get" the art on exhibit. While the docents' comments play on the soundtrack, Mundatas alternates between images of Los Angeles expressways and still frames of interactions between visitors and guides.

The Critics: Between the Frames, Chapter 6
Antonio Muntadas
1991, 53:50, U.S., color, sound, in English, French, and Italian
In this chapter of *Between the Frames*, Muntadas interviews an array of theorists, historians, and writers who have been influential in their studies of contemporary art, including Benjamin Buchloh, Bernard Marcade, Pierre Restany, Filiberto Menna, Achille Bonito-Oliva, Nina Dimitrijevic, Guy Brett, Thomas Wulffen, Yves Michaud, Tommaso Trini, Lorenzo Mango, Lucy Lippard, Peter Frank, Catherine Strasser, Bernard Lamarche-Vadel, Catherine Millet, Maria Luisa Borras, Daniel Giralt-Miracle, Victoria Combalía, Christopher Knight, Donald Kuspit, Craig Owens, Dore Ashton, and Jeanne Randolph. Offering a variety of viewpoints on their positions in relation to art, the critics' comments are unified by their serious passion for art and images of ocean tides.

The Media: Between the Frames, Chapter 7
Antonio Muntadas
1991, 49:09, U.S., color, sound, in English, French, and Catalan
Representatives of television, radio, and print media—as well as academia—comment upon the functions formats, fashions, networks, and audiences of the media's cover-

age of fine art. Interviewees include Robert Atkins, Shelly Rice, Heidi Grundman, Mary-Anne Staniszeski, Paul Taylor, Roman Gubern, Rene Berger, David Antin, and writers, journalists, and editors for *Flash Art*, *L'Art Vivant*, *Le Monde*, *RFT-Paris*, *Art Aktuell*, *La Vanguardia*, *Radio 4-Barcelona*, *R.T.B.-Brussels*, *Umbrella*, *The New York Times*, *Art in America*, and *Mizue*. Interview clips are inter-cut with slow vertical pans of urban spaces shot from exterior elevators.

Epilogue: Between the Frames, Chapter 8
Antonio Muntadas
1991, 38:32, U.S., color, sound in English, Italian, French, and Portuguese
The concluding section of *Between the Frames* returns the final word to the artists. Images of factory machines play against the commentary from Joseph Beuys, Daniel Buren, Luciano Fabro, John Baldessari, Regina Silveira, Fernando de Fillipi, Adrian Piper, Jaume Xifra, Dan Graham, Hans Haacke, Allan Kaprow, Braco Dimitrijevich, and Krzystof Wodiczko.

Stedelijk Museum

The Luminous Image
Rene Coelho/Openbaar Kunstbezit
1984, 56:00, The Netherlands, color, sound
The Luminous Image was an international exhibition of video installations held in fall 1984 at the Stedelijk Museum in Amsterdam. This videotape of the same name is an exceptional document that serves as an audiovisual catalog for the show, combining tours of the installations and short interviews with the artists, including: Marina Abramovic and Ulay, Vito Acconci, Max Almy, Dara Birnbaum, Michel Cardena, Brian Eno, Marie-Jo LaFontaine, Kees de Groot, Nan Hoover, Michael Klier, Shigeko Kubota, Thierry Kuntzel, Mary Lucier, Marcel Odenbach, Tony Oursler, Nam June Paik, Al Robbins, Lydia Schouten, Elsa Stansfield and Madelon Hooykaas, Francesc Torres, Bill Viola, and Robert Wilson.

University of Colorado Visiting Artists Program

Mixing It Up II (Rickard, McCauley, Baca, and Sun)
University of Colorado Visiting Artists Program
1989, 35:25, U.S., color, sound
The second in a series of cross-cultural symposia organized by Lucy Lippard, the four artists interviewed here—Jolene Rickard, Robbie McCauley, Judy Baca, and May Sun—discuss their work and its cultural contexts. Moderated by Lucy Lippard.

Mixing It Up III (Lamar, Liu, Simpson, and Vargas)
University of Colorado Visiting Artists Program
1990, 54:00, U.S., color, sound
The third in a series of cross-cultural symposia organized by Lucy Lippard, the four artists interviewed here—Jean Lamar, Hung Liu, Lorna Simpson, and Kathy Vargas—discuss their work and its cultural contexts. Moderated by Lucy Lippard.

Mixing It Up IV (Kano, O'Grady, Sakiestewa, and Alvarez Munoz)
University of Colorado Visiting Artists Program
1991, 34:35, U.S., color, sound
The fourth in a series of cross-cultural symposia organized by Lucy Lippard, the five artists interviewed here—Japanese-American painter and political activist Betty Kano, conceptual and performance artist Lorraine O'Grady, Hopi weaver Ramona Sakiestewa, and Chicana narrative and installation artist Celia Alvarez Munoz—discuss their work and its cultural contexts. Interviewed by Lucy Lippard.

Mixing It Up V (Barranza, Cheang, Scott, and Tsinhnahjinnie)
University of Colorado Visiting Artists Program
1992, 40:50, U.S., color, sound
The fifth in a series of cross-cultural symposia organized by Lucy Lippard, the four artists interviewed here—Tejana tableaux artist Santa Barranza, Taiwanese video and interactive installation artist Shu Lea Cheang, African American sculptor and installation artist Joyce Scott, Native-American photographer Hulleah Tsinhnahjinnie—discuss their work and its cultural contexts. Moderated by Lucy Lippard.

Mixing It Up VI: Image Wars (Harris, Buitron, Green, Lord, and Soe)
University of Colorado Visiting Artists Program
1993, 49:17, U.S., color, sound
The sixth in a series of cross-cultural symposia organized by Lucy Lippard, the four artists interviewed here—gay activist and self portrait artist Lyle Ashton Harris, Chicano photographer and tourist Robert Buitron, Cherokee writer, curator, and video creator Rayna Green, photography critic and professor at University of California-Irvine Catherine Lord, and Chinese-American video artist Valerie Soe—discuss the role of photography and creation of culture. Moderated by Lucy Lippard.

Mixing It Up VII: Mixed-Blood Issue: (Starr-Brown, Fulbeck, Imagire, and López)
University of Colorado Visiting Artists Program
1994, 46:00, U.S., color, sound
The seventh in a series of cross-cultural symposia organized by Lucy Lippard, the four artists interviewed here—visual anthropologist Wendi Starr-Brown, Hapa video and performance artist Kip Fulbeck, Japanese-American artist Dorothy Imagire, Chicana mixed-media artist Yolanda López—address the role of mixed-race identity in their work. Moderated by Corissa Schweitz Gold.

Ordering Information

Formats

All titles listed in this catalog are available for rent or purchase in the following formats: Digital Betacam, Betacam, Umatic, SVHS, VHS, mini-DV and DVD. Tapes in PAL format are available at an additional cost. We can also provide laser disc copies for museum exhibitions. If you are purchasing for a museum, library or other long-term or archival collection, we recommend that you purchase on Betacam or Digital Betacam format.

When you purchase a tape in any of the above formats, you will receive VDB's Standard License Agreement, which outlines the terms and conditions of your purchase. You are required to sign and return the Agreement prior to our shipment of the tapes. While most of our titles are only available for institutional purchase, some titles are also available for individual purchase. Please contact us for more information on individual prices. PLEASE NOTE: Purchase means for the "life of the tape".

Previews

The VDB provides "preview only" copies of new work for curators, broadcast programmers, educators, libraries and critics on NTSC VHS format only. We charge $10.00 for preview reels plus shipping charges. Preview charges must be prepaid before shipping, and preview tapes must be returned within seven days of receipt unless otherwise noted.

PLEASE NOTE: All customers are required to ship preview and rental tapes back at their own expense. Client will be held responsible for the full replacement cost of the tape if it is damaged while in the clients' possession, during shipment, or if the tapes are not returned at all.

Custom Programs

The VDB will compile tapes into programs for exhibition for an additional fee. Contact us for a quote. We will be happy to provide estimates for extended exhibitions, broadcasts, and large volume discounts. Please fax or email a description of your programming needs. Tapes can also be purchased with limited duplication rights via written purchase agreement.

Broadcast/Cablecast

Many of VDB's tapes are available for broadcast and cablecast. All broadcast and cablecast rights are reserved. Contact VDB for terms, fees and licensing information.

Stills

The VDB can provide stills for promotional purposes. We do not provide production stills. We can email video stills at 72 dpi. We can also ship stills – a fee may apply. The photo credit line must read "Courtesy of the Video Data Bank" in all publications.

Prices

Send email requests for details and specific prices of tapes or check the Video Data Bank website at www.vdb.org.

Copyright

Liability and Copyright Rental of all VDB titles include public performance rights; basic purchase also includes public performance rights for screenings within museums, galleries, libraries, community-based centers, or educational institutions. Tapes may not be used at fundraising events or at auctions without the written permission of the artist. No tapes may be duplicated in whole or in part while in the possession of anyone who does not own the rights to the footage. All titles are solely owned by the copyright holder as listed in the credits of the tape and all tapes are protected by international copyright law. Purchase or rental does not include the rights to alter the tape, offer it for sub-distribution, lend it to others, broadcast or transmit by any electronic means including video streaming on the internet without the written permission of the Video Data Bank and the copyright holder of the tape.

Payment for Domestic Orders

Once we have given you a quote and you have confirmed the order, proof of payment is required (institutional purchase order [domestic clients only], credit card, wire transfer, or pre-payment by check). Most domestic orders can be processed and shipped within two weeks of receiving proof of payment. International orders may take longer. Please confirm and pay for your order at least two weeks in advance, or rush fees will apply. In case of cancellation, notice must be received by us at least ten days prior to the screening date or you will be billed for the full order.

Payment for International Orders

All International orders must be pre-paid in US dollars. We prefer payment by credit card, however you may pay by wire transfer. We can only ship after we have received confirmation that the transfer of the payment has been received at our bank in Chicago, Illinois. Confirming the transfer of international funds can take up to 4 weeks, so you should place your order six to eight weeks in advance of the screening to guarantee that we have ample time to ship the order before the screening date. All international orders carry a $25.00 administrative fee If you pay by wire transfer and this transaction has been completed by your bank, please fax a copy of the bank wire transfer to VDB at 312-541-8073.

Shipping

International shipping rates are determined by weight and the shipping service used. Packages being shipped via Federal Express are priced according to Federal Express's current rates. International shipping arrangements must be determined upon confirmation of your order. Client is responsible for all additional shipping costs, such as airfreight, VAT, and customs charges for international orders, and rush-shipping charges for orders placed late. If the screening location is in the United States, tapes will be sent out to arrive at least two days before the screening date. Arrivals for Canada and other international orders will be sent out to arrive at least four days prior to the screening date. Tapes must be checked before screening date. If you have NOT received tapes according to this schedule, please call us immediately so we have enough time to trace and/or replace the shipment.

Returns

All tapes must be returned promptly after the end of the rental period (one week in most cases). Previews must be returned within one week and if not returned promptly, the customer will be charged a rental fee. Tapes can be returned via first class airmail or via UPS or a courier service such as Federal Express or Airborne. Client must pay all fees for returning tapes.

PLEASE NOTE: Tapes should NEVER be shipped in fiber filled bags or envelopes. Any tape returned in a fiber bag will have to be destroyed and the user will be charged at least $25.00 in damages. Bubble envelopes are the preferred shipping material.

We encourage you to send us copies of any promotional materials, program notes, reviews or audience feedback that result from the screening of VDB programs. Where possible, please credit VDB as the distributor on your print materials.

Video Data Bank
c/o School of the Art Institute of Chicago
112 South Michigan Ave, 3rd Floor
Chicago, IL 60603
Tel: 312-345-3550 Fax: 312-541-8073
Email: info@vdb.org

INDEXES

Artist Index

Title Index